SUPERMAN IN THE SEVENTIES

SUPERMAN CREATED BY
JERRY SIEGEL AND JOE SHUSTER

SUPERMAN IN THE SEVENTIES
Published by DC Comics. Cover, introduction and compilation copyright © 2000 DC Comics.
All Rights Reserved. Originally published in single magazine form as ACTION COMICS 484;
DC COMICS PRESENTS 14; SUPERMAN 233, 247, 248, 249, 270, 271, 276, 286, 287; SUPERMAN'S
GIRL FRIEND LOIS LANE 106; SUPERMAN'S PAL JIMMY OLSEN 133. Copyright © 1970, 1972,
1973, 1974, 1975, 1978 DC Comics. All Rights Reserved. All characters, their distinctive likenesses
and related elements featured in this publication are trademarks of DC Comics. The stories,
characters and incidents featured in this publication are entirely fictional. DC Comics does not
read or accept unsolicited submissions of ideas, stories or artwork.
DC Comics, 1700 Broadway, New York, NY 10019
A Warner Bros. Entertainment Company
Printed in Canada. Second Printing.
ISBN: 1-56389-638-9
ISBN 13: 978-1-56389-638-5
Cover illustration by Neal Adams.
Cover color by Digital Chameleon.
Publication design by Louis Prandi.
Interior text by Mark Waid.

CURT SWAN
(1920-1996)

Under his hand, a legend soared to unprecedented heights.

TABLE OF CONTENTS

INTRODUCTION

For thousands of years humanity has been both blessed and cursed by the ability to perceive and to imagine. We are only too keenly aware of our fallibility and mortality, but at the same time we can conjure up an opposite image of ourselves. Fiction and mythology throughout the ages tell the stories of gods, warriors, explorers, and heroes who demonstrate superhuman powers and fulfill our longing to be like them.

Since 1938 Superman has been an American icon, a direct descendant of ancient mythology. For more than 60 years he has reflected the needs of successive generations. In the late '30s he was a distraction from the grim reality of the Depression. During World War II he inspired American soldiers in combat. In the '50s he provided a vivid contrast to a relatively bland decade of normalcy. In the '60s he was "hip" and in the '70s he was the last line of defense against evil forces bent on world domination.

It was my privilege to play Superman — or perhaps more accurately, to be the custodian of the character — in the 1970s. For the first time audiences could enjoy sophisticated film technology that made Superman more spectacular than ever before. In fact the poster advertising the film simply stated, "You'll believe a man can fly." Now Superman flew across 70 mm screens accompanied by the London Symphony Orchestra and sound effects in Dolby stereo.

These advances in filmmaking gave me a real advantage. They made it possible for me to underplay the character. Clark Kent owed much to early Cary Grant movies, and director Dick Donner and I grounded Superman in his response to Lois Lane's question "Who are you?" Answer: "A friend?"

I hope you will enjoy this book about Superman in the '70s. I'm always grateful when kids and even grownups who have just seen the film for the first time on video still respond as audiences did 23 years ago. Many heroes come and go, but thanks to creators Siegel and Shuster, Superman endures.

Christopher Reeve

ALL NEW COLLECTORS' EDITION $2.00

DC SUPERMAN VS. Wonder Woman

THE BATTLE YOU NEVER
THOUGHT YOU'D SEE!

ALL NEW COLLECTORS' EDITION

DC SUPERMAN VS. SHAZAM!

THE MAN OF STEEL AGAINST
THE WORLDS MIGHTIEST
MORTAL!

A 72-
PAGE
SUPER-ACTION
NOVEL!
"WHEN EARTHS
COLLIDE!"

WORLD'S FINEST

DC WORLD'S FINEST
PRESENTS
SUPERMAN and the FLASH

NOV.

THEY'RE
OFF!

THE THIRD RACE BETWEEN THE WORLD'S
FASTEST SUPER-HEROES! AND THIS TIME
THERE MUST BE A WINNER!

THE BIG BATTLES

The problem with being number one is
that there are always challengers for
the title. In the 1970s, opponents flew at
Superman from all sides, sometimes
surprising us with their prowess. The Flash
actually outraced the Man of Steel in
a marathon across the galaxy (though
by barely a length). In SUPERMAN VS.
MUHAMMAD ALI (a.k.a. ALL NEW COLLEC-
TORS' EDITION C-56), the once and future
champ made headlines — again — by kay-
oing a depowered Metropolis Kid while the
galaxy looked on (though all as part of an
elaborate ruse to thwart alien warlords).

But when it came to all-out throwdowns,
Superman quickly turned enemies into
allies — including Wonder Woman, Marvel
Comics' Spider-Man, and himself (!) time-
traveling as a teenager. Just because a guy
is a strange visitor from another planet
doesn't keep him from championing the
Brotherhood of Man, and besides — when
you're number one, you don't have to prove
anything.

In the 1940s, Superman's greatest rival
had been Fawcett Comics' Captain Marvel,
whose own comic had outsold even
Superman's for a brief period before folding
in the early 1950s. In the early 1970s, DC
itself revived the Big Red Cheese, in doing
so renewing the decades-old schoolyard
argument over who was the better super-
hero. Eventually the two Men of Might
would meet in battle, but not before writer
Elliot Maggin arranged a mock bout with a
doppelganger named "Captain Thunder."
The tale was clearly staged to fan the
Controversy — and it worked, providing a
memorable super-adventure in the process.

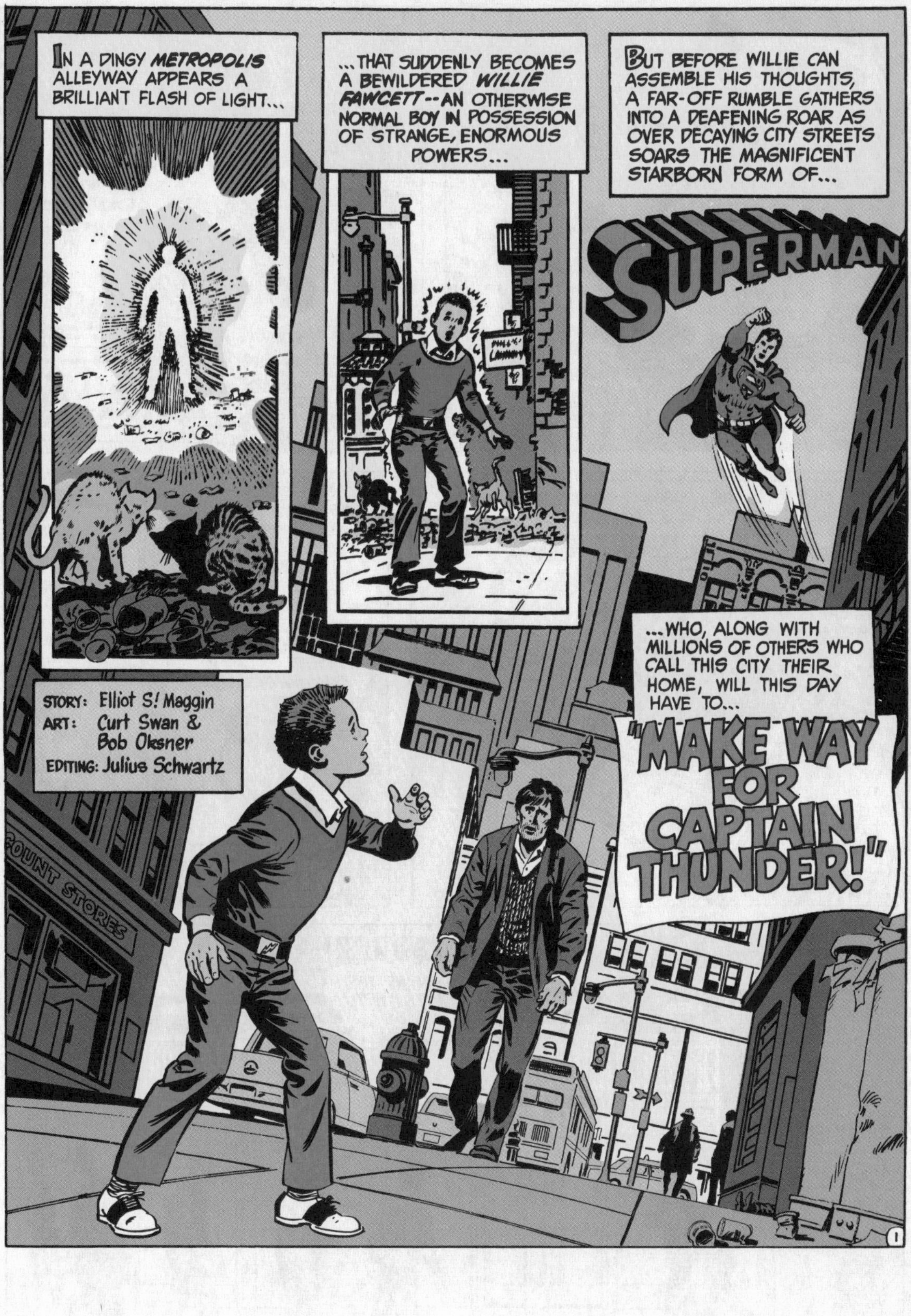
IN A DINGY METROPOLIS ALLEYWAY APPEARS A BRILLIANT FLASH OF LIGHT...
...THAT SUDDENLY BECOMES A BEWILDERED WILLIE FAWCETT--AN OTHERWISE NORMAL BOY IN POSSESSION OF STRANGE, ENORMOUS POWERS...
BUT BEFORE WILLIE CAN ASSEMBLE HIS THOUGHTS, A FAR-OFF RUMBLE GATHERS INTO A DEAFENING ROAR AS OVER DECAYING CITY STREETS SOARS THE MAGNIFICENT STARBORN FORM OF...
SUPERMAN
...WHO, ALONG WITH MILLIONS OF OTHERS WHO CALL THIS CITY THEIR HOME, WILL THIS DAY HAVE TO...
"MAKE WAY FOR CAPTAIN THUNDER!"
STORY: Elliot S! Maggin
ART: Curt Swan & Bob Oksner
EDITING: Julius Schwartz
COUNT STORES
1

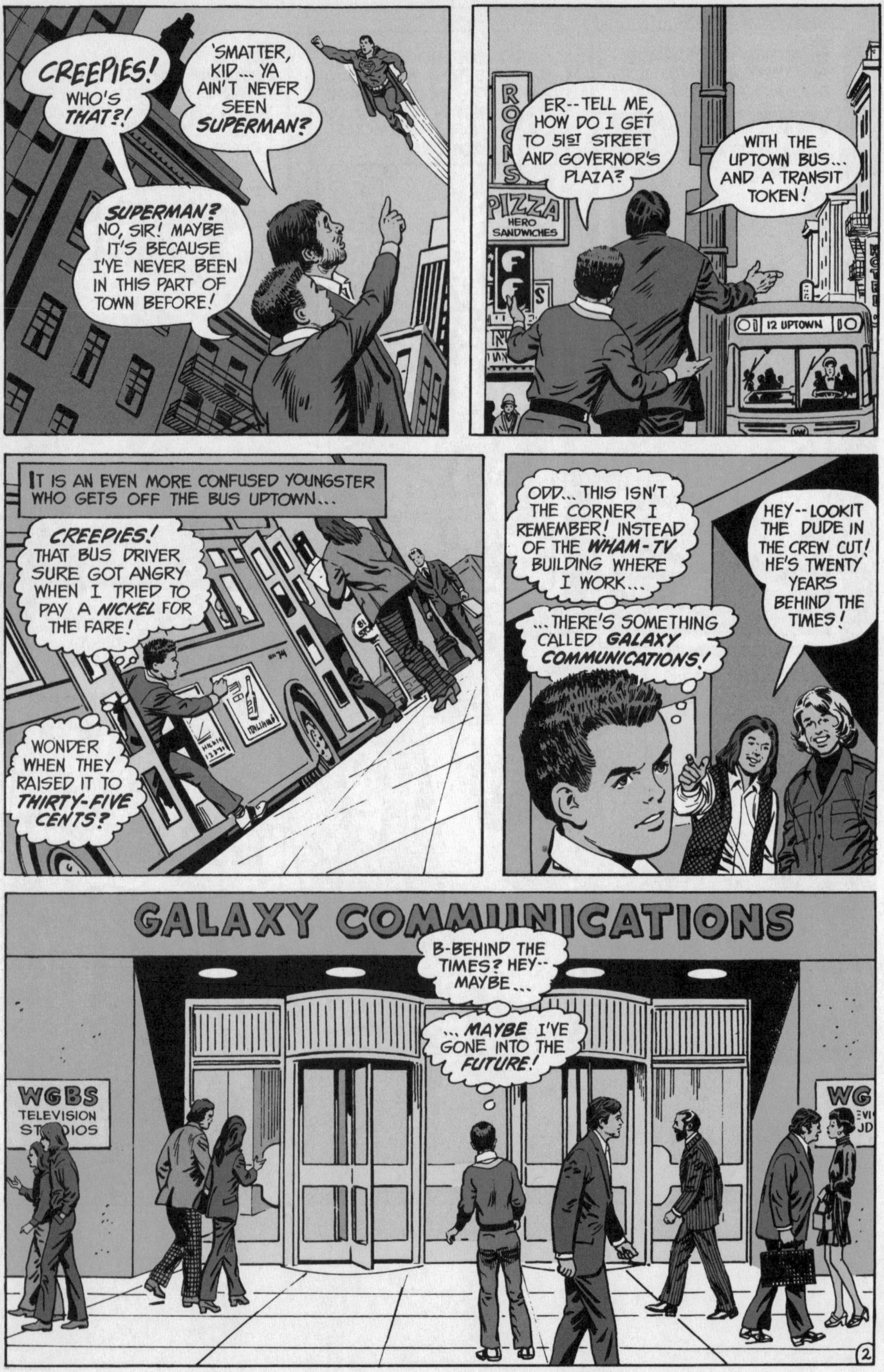
CREEPIES! WHO'S THAT?!
'SMATTER, KID... YA AIN'T NEVER SEEN SUPERMAN?
SUPERMAN? NO, SIR! MAYBE IT'S BECAUSE I'VE NEVER BEEN IN THIS PART OF TOWN BEFORE!
ROOMS
PIZZA HERO SANDWICHES
ER--TELL ME, HOW DO I GET TO 51ST STREET AND GOVERNOR'S PLAZA?
WITH THE UPTOWN BUS... AND A TRANSIT TOKEN!
12 UPTOWN
IT IS AN EVEN MORE CONFUSED YOUNGSTER WHO GETS OFF THE BUS UPTOWN...
CREEPIES! THAT BUS DRIVER SURE GOT ANGRY WHEN I TRIED TO PAY A NICKEL FOR THE FARE!
WONDER WHEN THEY RAISED IT TO THIRTY-FIVE CENTS?
ODD... THIS ISN'T THE CORNER I REMEMBER! INSTEAD OF THE WHAM-TV BUILDING WHERE I WORK...
...THERE'S SOMETHING CALLED GALAXY COMMUNICATIONS!
HEY--LOOKIT THE DUDE IN THE CREW CUT! HE'S TWENTY YEARS BEHIND THE TIMES!
GALAXY COMMUNICATIONS
B-BEHIND THE TIMES? HEY--MAYBE...
...MAYBE I'VE GONE INTO THE FUTURE!
WGBS TELEVISION STUDIOS
2

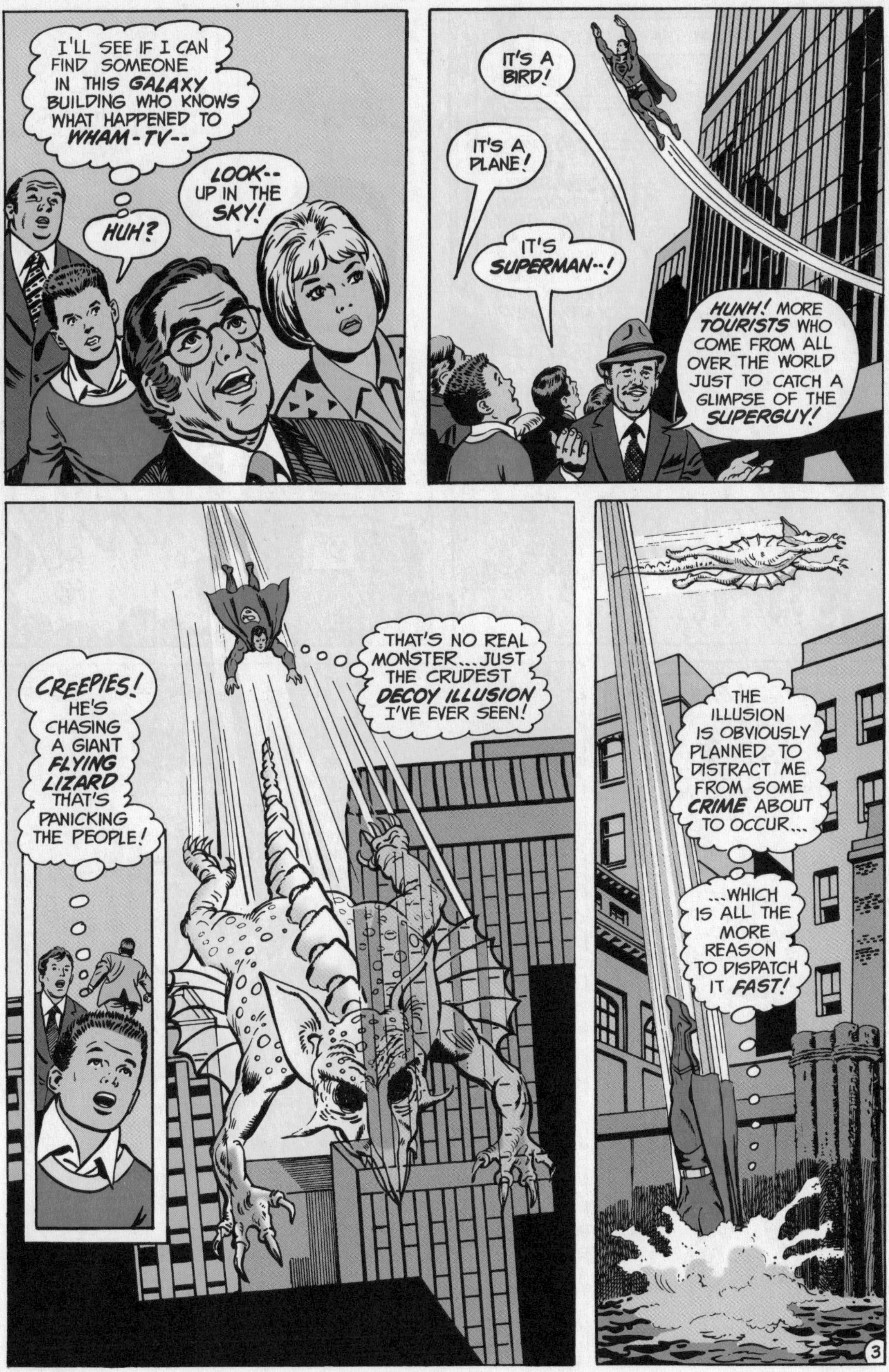

I'LL SEE IF I CAN FIND SOMEONE IN THIS GALAXY BUILDING WHO KNOWS WHAT HAPPENED TO WHAM-TV--
HUH?
LOOK-- UP IN THE SKY!
IT'S A BIRD!
IT'S A PLANE!
IT'S SUPERMAN--!
HUNH! MORE TOURISTS WHO COME FROM ALL OVER THE WORLD JUST TO CATCH A GLIMPSE OF THE SUPERGUY!
CREEPIES! HE'S CHASING A GIANT FLYING LIZARD THAT'S PANICKING THE PEOPLE!
THAT'S NO REAL MONSTER... JUST THE CRUDEST DECOY ILLUSION I'VE EVER SEEN!
THE ILLUSION IS OBVIOUSLY PLANNED TO DISTRACT ME FROM SOME CRIME ABOUT TO OCCUR...
...WHICH IS ALL THE MORE REASON TO DISPATCH IT FAST!
3

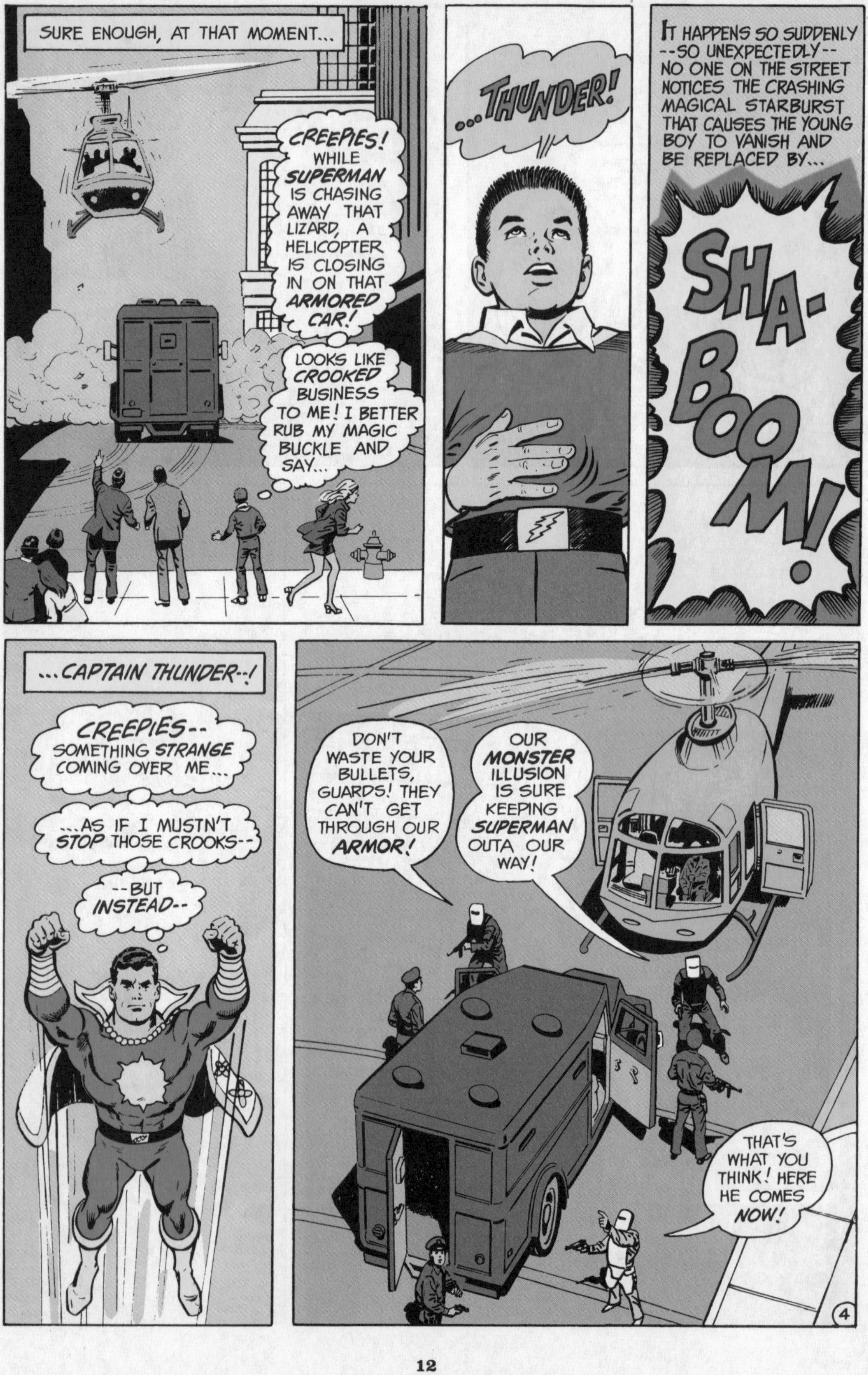
SURE ENOUGH, AT THAT MOMENT...
CREEPIES! WHILE SUPERMAN IS CHASING AWAY THAT LIZARD, A HELICOPTER IS CLOSING IN ON THAT ARMORED CAR!
LOOKS LIKE CROOKED BUSINESS TO ME! I BETTER RUB MY MAGIC BUCKLE AND SAY...
...THUNDER!
IT HAPPENS SO SUDDENLY --SO UNEXPECTEDLY-- NO ONE ON THE STREET NOTICES THE CRASHING MAGICAL STARBURST THAT CAUSES THE YOUNG BOY TO VANISH AND BE REPLACED BY...
SHA-BOOM!
...CAPTAIN THUNDER--!
CREEPIES-- SOMETHING STRANGE COMING OVER ME...
...AS IF I MUSTN'T STOP THOSE CROOKS--
--BUT INSTEAD--
DON'T WASTE YOUR BULLETS, GUARDS! THEY CAN'T GET THROUGH OUR ARMOR!
OUR MONSTER ILLUSION IS SURE KEEPING SUPERMAN OUTA OUR WAY!
THAT'S WHAT YOU THINK! HERE HE COMES NOW!
4

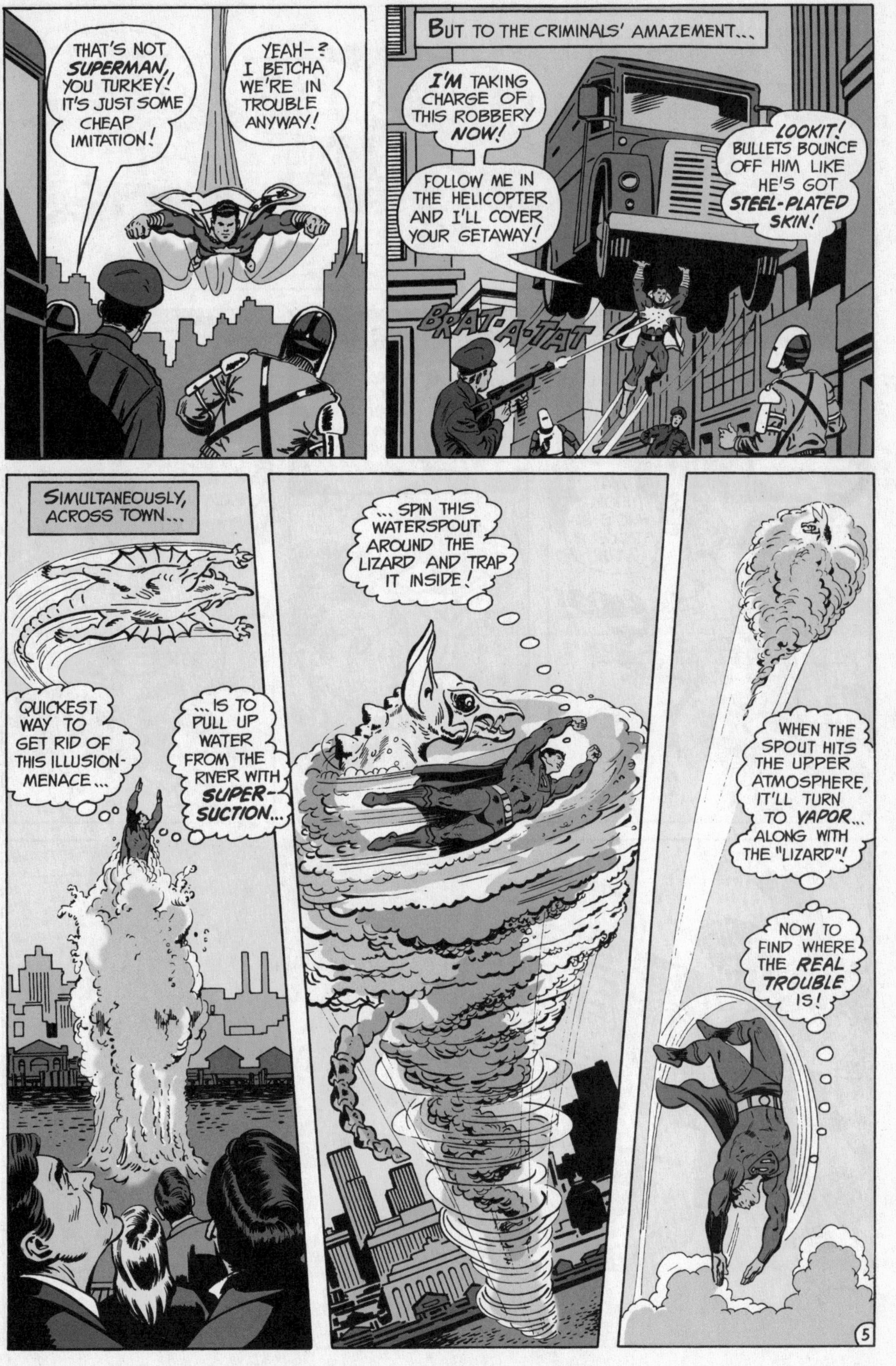
THAT'S NOT SUPERMAN, YOU TURKEY! IT'S JUST SOME CHEAP IMITATION!
YEAH-? I BETCHA WE'RE IN TROUBLE ANYWAY!
BUT TO THE CRIMINALS' AMAZEMENT...
I'M TAKING CHARGE OF THIS ROBBERY NOW!
FOLLOW ME IN THE HELICOPTER AND I'LL COVER YOUR GETAWAY!
LOOKIT! BULLETS BOUNCE OFF HIM LIKE HE'S GOT STEEL-PLATED SKIN!
BRAT-A-TAT
SIMULTANEOUSLY, ACROSS TOWN...
QUICKEST WAY TO GET RID OF THIS ILLUSION-MENACE...
...IS TO PULL UP WATER FROM THE RIVER WITH SUPER-SUCTION...
...SPIN THIS WATERSPOUT AROUND THE LIZARD AND TRAP IT INSIDE!
WHEN THE SPOUT HITS THE UPPER ATMOSPHERE, IT'LL TURN TO VAPOR... ALONG WITH THE "LIZARD"!
NOW TO FIND WHERE THE REAL TROUBLE IS!
5

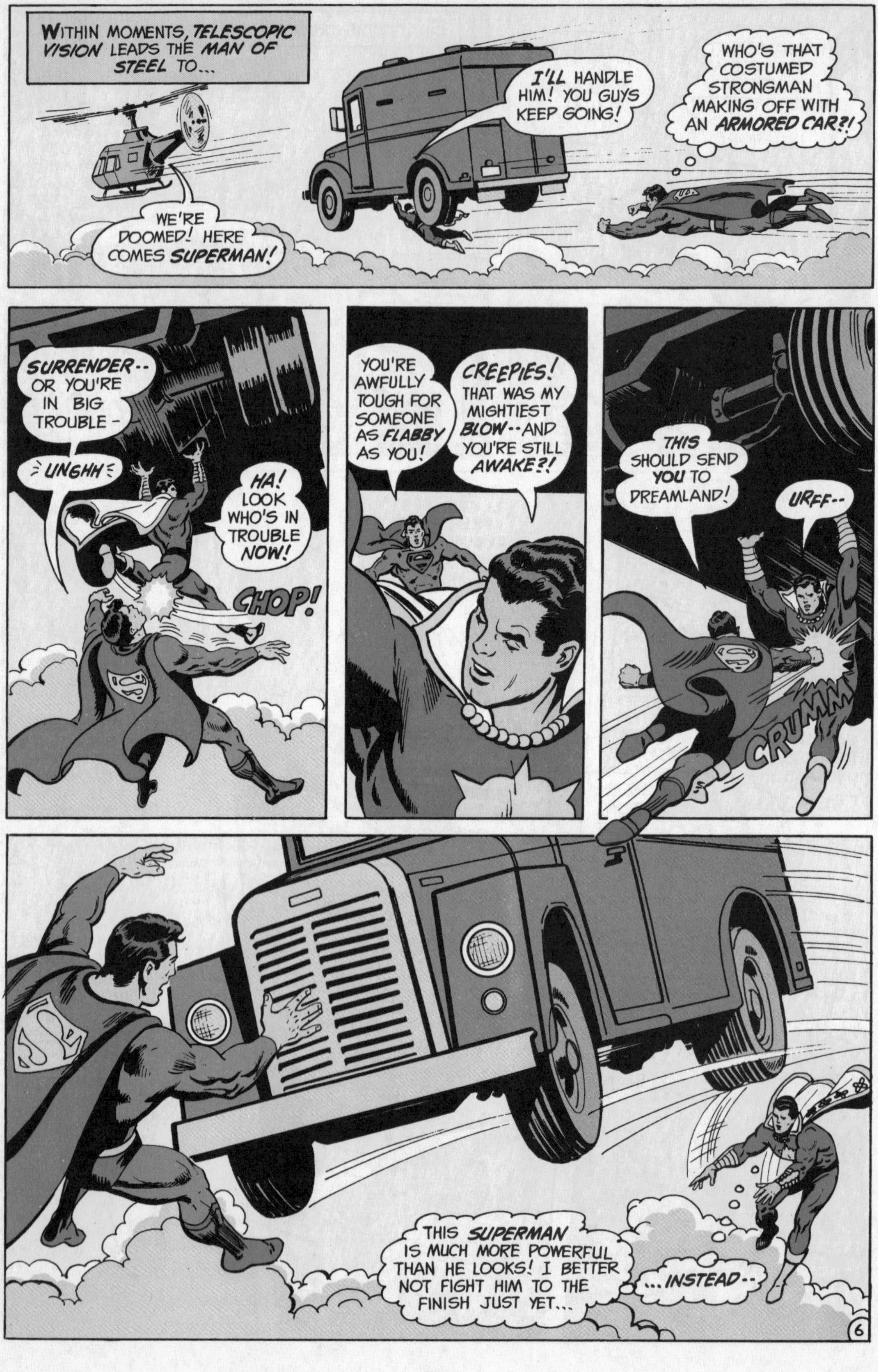
WITHIN MOMENTS, TELESCOPIC VISION LEADS THE MAN OF STEEL TO...
I'LL HANDLE HIM! YOU GUYS KEEP GOING!
WHO'S THAT COSTUMED STRONGMAN MAKING OFF WITH AN ARMORED CAR?!
WE'RE DOOMED! HERE COMES SUPERMAN!
SURRENDER-- OR YOU'RE IN BIG TROUBLE -
UNGHH
HA! LOOK WHO'S IN TROUBLE NOW!
CHOP!
YOU'RE AWFULLY TOUGH FOR SOMEONE AS FLABBY AS YOU!
CREEPIES! THAT WAS MY MIGHTIEST BLOW--AND YOU'RE STILL AWAKE?!
THIS SHOULD SEND YOU TO DREAMLAND!
URFF--
CRUMM
THIS SUPERMAN IS MUCH MORE POWERFUL THAN HE LOOKS! I BETTER NOT FIGHT HIM TO THE FINISH JUST YET...
...INSTEAD--
6

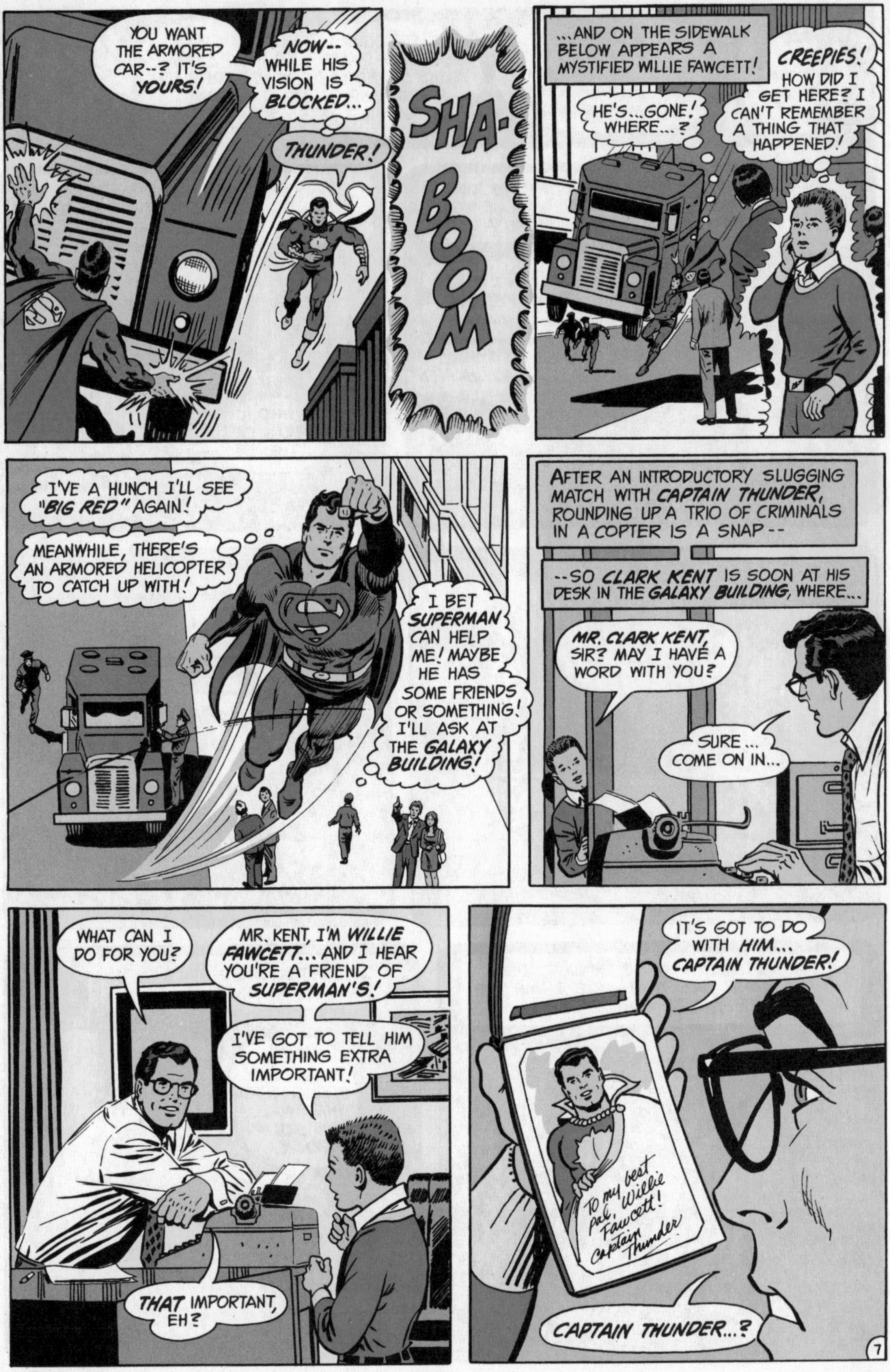
YOU WANT THE ARMORED CAR--? IT'S YOURS!
NOW-- WHILE HIS VISION IS BLOCKED...
THUNDER!
SHA-BOOM
...AND ON THE SIDEWALK BELOW APPEARS A MYSTIFIED WILLIE FAWCETT!
HE'S...GONE! WHERE...?
CREEPIES! HOW DID I GET HERE? I CAN'T REMEMBER A THING THAT HAPPENED!
I'VE A HUNCH I'LL SEE "BIG RED" AGAIN!
MEANWHILE, THERE'S AN ARMORED HELICOPTER TO CATCH UP WITH!
I BET SUPERMAN CAN HELP ME! MAYBE HE HAS SOME FRIENDS OR SOMETHING! I'LL ASK AT THE GALAXY BUILDING!
AFTER AN INTRODUCTORY SLUGGING MATCH WITH CAPTAIN THUNDER, ROUNDING UP A TRIO OF CRIMINALS IN A COPTER IS A SNAP--
--SO CLARK KENT IS SOON AT HIS DESK IN THE GALAXY BUILDING, WHERE...
MR. CLARK KENT, SIR? MAY I HAVE A WORD WITH YOU?
SURE... COME ON IN...
WHAT CAN I DO FOR YOU?
MR. KENT, I'M WILLIE FAWCETT... AND I HEAR YOU'RE A FRIEND OF SUPERMAN'S!
I'VE GOT TO TELL HIM SOMETHING EXTRA IMPORTANT!
THAT IMPORTANT, EH?
IT'S GOT TO DO WITH HIM... CAPTAIN THUNDER!
To my best pal, Willie Fawcett! Captain Thunder
CAPTAIN THUNDER...?
7

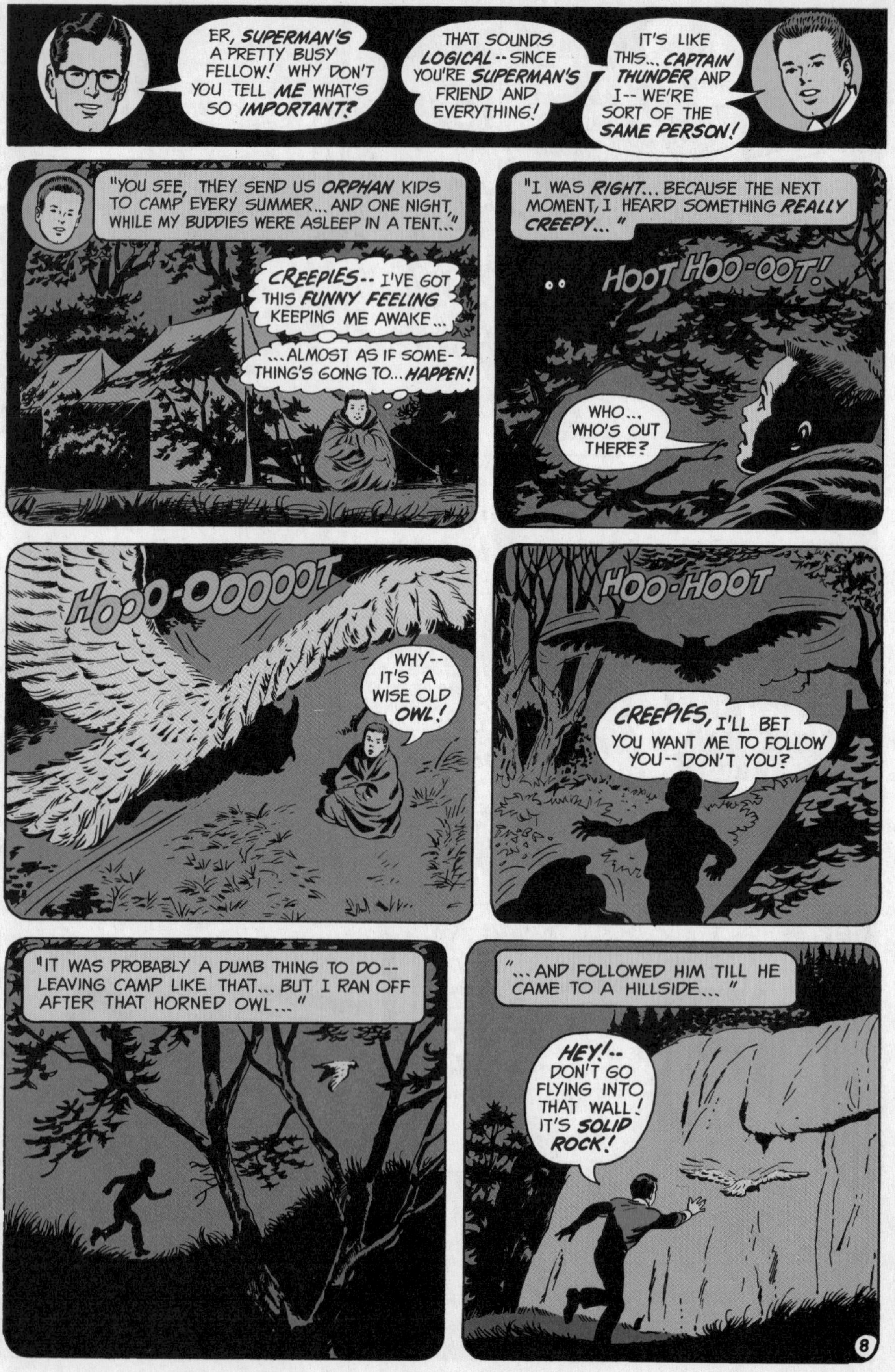
ER, SUPERMAN'S A PRETTY BUSY FELLOW! WHY DON'T YOU TELL ME WHAT'S SO IMPORTANT?
THAT SOUNDS LOGICAL -- SINCE YOU'RE SUPERMAN'S FRIEND AND EVERYTHING!
IT'S LIKE THIS... CAPTAIN THUNDER AND I-- WE'RE SORT OF THE SAME PERSON!
"YOU SEE, THEY SEND US ORPHAN KIDS TO CAMP EVERY SUMMER... AND ONE NIGHT, WHILE MY BUDDIES WERE ASLEEP IN A TENT..."
CREEPIES-- I'VE GOT THIS FUNNY FEELING KEEPING ME AWAKE...
...ALMOST AS IF SOMETHING'S GOING TO... HAPPEN!
"I WAS RIGHT... BECAUSE THE NEXT MOMENT, I HEARD SOMETHING REALLY CREEPY..."
HOOT HOO-OOT!
WHO... WHO'S OUT THERE?
HOOO-OOOOOT
WHY-- IT'S A WISE OLD OWL!
HOO-HOOT
CREEPIES, I'LL BET YOU WANT ME TO FOLLOW YOU-- DON'T YOU?
"IT WAS PROBABLY A DUMB THING TO DO-- LEAVING CAMP LIKE THAT... BUT I RAN OFF AFTER THAT HORNED OWL..."
"...AND FOLLOWED HIM TILL HE CAME TO A HILLSIDE..."
HEY!-- DON'T GO FLYING INTO THAT WALL! IT'S SOLID ROCK!
8

"BUT BEFORE I KNEW IT..."

CREEPIES! THE *HILL!*-- IT'S OPENING UP!

"I GUESS I SHOULD'VE BEEN SCARED TO FOLLOW HIM...BUT SOMEHOW I WASN'T..."

"...AND WHAT I FOUND INSIDE WAS *FAN-TASTIC*..."

C-C-CREEPIES!

LONG HAS *MEROKEE,* LAST OF THE GREAT *MEDICINE MEN* OF THE *MOHEGAN* TRIBE, AWAITED YOUR COMING, *WILLIE FAWCETT!*

COME FORWARD!

TRIBAL LEGENDS FORETOLD THAT ONE DAY A BOY WOULD COME FORTH WHO WAS *NOBLE OF SPIRIT!*

HE WOULD BE INVESTED WITH GREAT POWERS BY THE LAST OF THE GREAT *MOHEGAN SHAMANS*--

--WILLIE FAWCETT, YOU ARE THAT BOY!

WHEN YOU WEAR THIS MAGIC BELT-BUCKLE YOU WILL HAVE THESE *SEVEN SPIRITUAL POWERS!*

TORNADO... POWER
HARE... SPEED
UNCAS... BRAVERY
NATURE...WISDOM
DIAMOND...TOUGHNESS
EAGLE... FLIGHT
RAM... TENACITY

UNCAS -- AN OUTSTANDING WARRIOR CHIEF OF THE *MOHEGAN* TRIBE -- *Editor.*

⑨

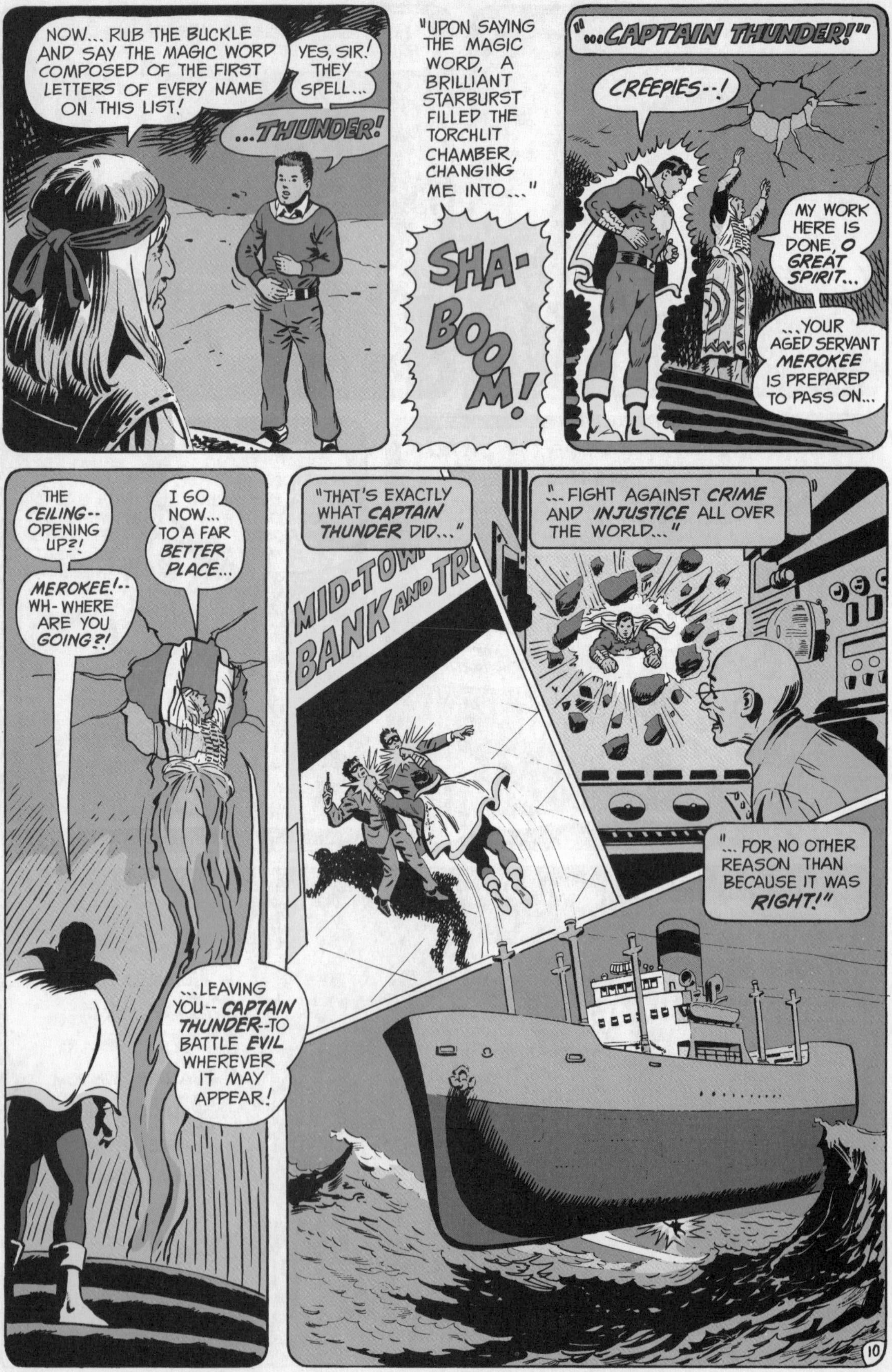
NOW... RUB THE BUCKLE AND SAY THE MAGIC WORD COMPOSED OF THE FIRST LETTERS OF EVERY NAME ON THIS LIST!
YES, SIR! THEY SPELL...
...THUNDER!
"UPON SAYING THE MAGIC WORD, A BRILLIANT STARBURST FILLED THE TORCHLIT CHAMBER, CHANGING ME INTO..."
SHA-BOOM!
"...CAPTAIN THUNDER!"
CREEPIES--!
MY WORK HERE IS DONE, O GREAT SPIRIT...
...YOUR AGED SERVANT MEROKEE IS PREPARED TO PASS ON...
THE CEILING--OPENING UP?!
I GO NOW... TO A FAR BETTER PLACE...
MEROKEE!--WH-WHERE ARE YOU GOING?!
...LEAVING YOU--CAPTAIN THUNDER--TO BATTLE EVIL WHEREVER IT MAY APPEAR!
"THAT'S EXACTLY WHAT CAPTAIN THUNDER DID..."
MID-TOWN BANK AND TRU
"...FIGHT AGAINST CRIME AND INJUSTICE ALL OVER THE WORLD..."
"...FOR NO OTHER REASON THAN BECAUSE IT WAS RIGHT!"
10

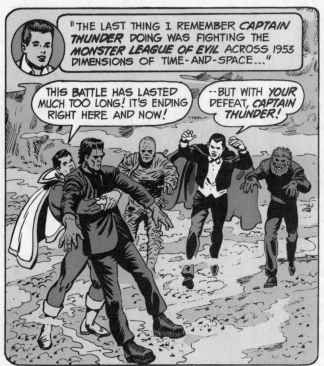

"THE LAST THING I REMEMBER *CAPTAIN THUNDER* DOING WAS FIGHTING THE *MONSTER LEAGUE OF EVIL* ACROSS 1953 DIMENSIONS OF TIME-AND-SPACE..."

THIS BATTLE HAS LASTED MUCH TOO LONG! IT'S ENDING RIGHT HERE AND NOW!

--BUT WITH *YOUR* DEFEAT, *CAPTAIN THUNDER!*

LET'S CHANGE THAT TO *YOUR* DEFEAT, *MONSTER LEAGUE!*

IMPRISONED IN THIS DIMENSION, YOU FIENDS WILL NEVER MENACE EARTH AGAIN!

THAT MAY BE SO, *CAPTAIN THUNDER,* BUT AFTER WHAT WE'VE SECRETLY DONE TO *YOU*... YOU'LL NEVER BE THE SAME!

I CROSSED THE TIME-AND-SPACE BARRIER ON MY WAY HOME... BUT LANDED IN AN ALLEY ON SOME STREET I'D NEVER SEEN BEFORE!

I FIGURE I MUST'VE RETURNED TO *EARTH* IN THE *FUTURE!*

I DON'T THINK THAT'S THE ANSWER, WILLY!

YOU SEE, THERE'S NO RECORD ON *EARTH* OF THERE *EVER* HAVING BEEN A *CAPTAIN THUNDER!*

YET... STRANGELY ENOUGH...THERE'S BEEN A REPORT *TODAY* OF A *SUPER-CRIMINAL* OF *CAPTAIN THUNDER'S* DESCRIPTION BEING INVOLVED IN AN ARMORED CAR ROBBERY!

CREEPIES! NOW I KNOW WHY I CAN'T REMEMBER ANYTHING AS *CAPTAIN THUNDER!*

11

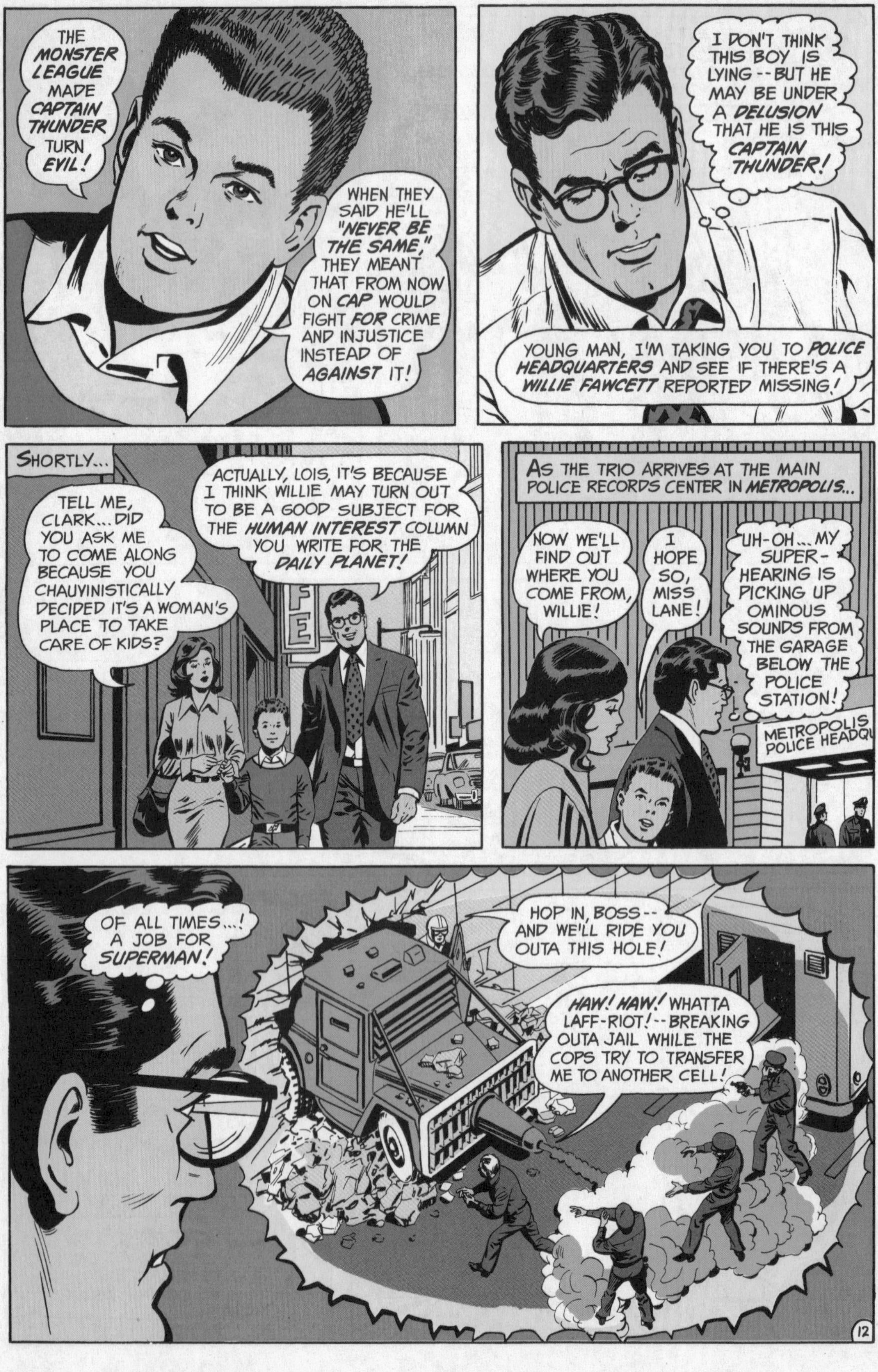
THE MONSTER LEAGUE MADE CAPTAIN THUNDER TURN EVIL!
WHEN THEY SAID HE'LL "NEVER BE THE SAME," THEY MEANT THAT FROM NOW ON CAP WOULD FIGHT FOR CRIME AND INJUSTICE INSTEAD OF AGAINST IT!
I DON'T THINK THIS BOY IS LYING -- BUT HE MAY BE UNDER A DELUSION THAT HE IS THIS CAPTAIN THUNDER!
YOUNG MAN, I'M TAKING YOU TO POLICE HEADQUARTERS AND SEE IF THERE'S A WILLIE FAWCETT REPORTED MISSING!
SHORTLY...
TELL ME, CLARK... DID YOU ASK ME TO COME ALONG BECAUSE YOU CHAUVINISTICALLY DECIDED IT'S A WOMAN'S PLACE TO TAKE CARE OF KIDS?
ACTUALLY, LOIS, IT'S BECAUSE I THINK WILLIE MAY TURN OUT TO BE A GOOD SUBJECT FOR THE HUMAN INTEREST COLUMN YOU WRITE FOR THE DAILY PLANET!
AS THE TRIO ARRIVES AT THE MAIN POLICE RECORDS CENTER IN METROPOLIS...
NOW WE'LL FIND OUT WHERE YOU COME FROM, WILLIE!
I HOPE SO, MISS LANE!
UH-OH... MY SUPER-HEARING IS PICKING UP OMINOUS SOUNDS FROM THE GARAGE BELOW THE POLICE STATION!
METROPOLIS POLICE HEADQU
OF ALL TIMES...! A JOB FOR SUPERMAN!
HOP IN, BOSS -- AND WE'LL RIDE YOU OUTA THIS HOLE!
HAW! HAW! WHATTA LAFF-RIOT! -- BREAKING OUTA JAIL WHILE THE COPS TRY TO TRANSFER ME TO ANOTHER CELL!
12

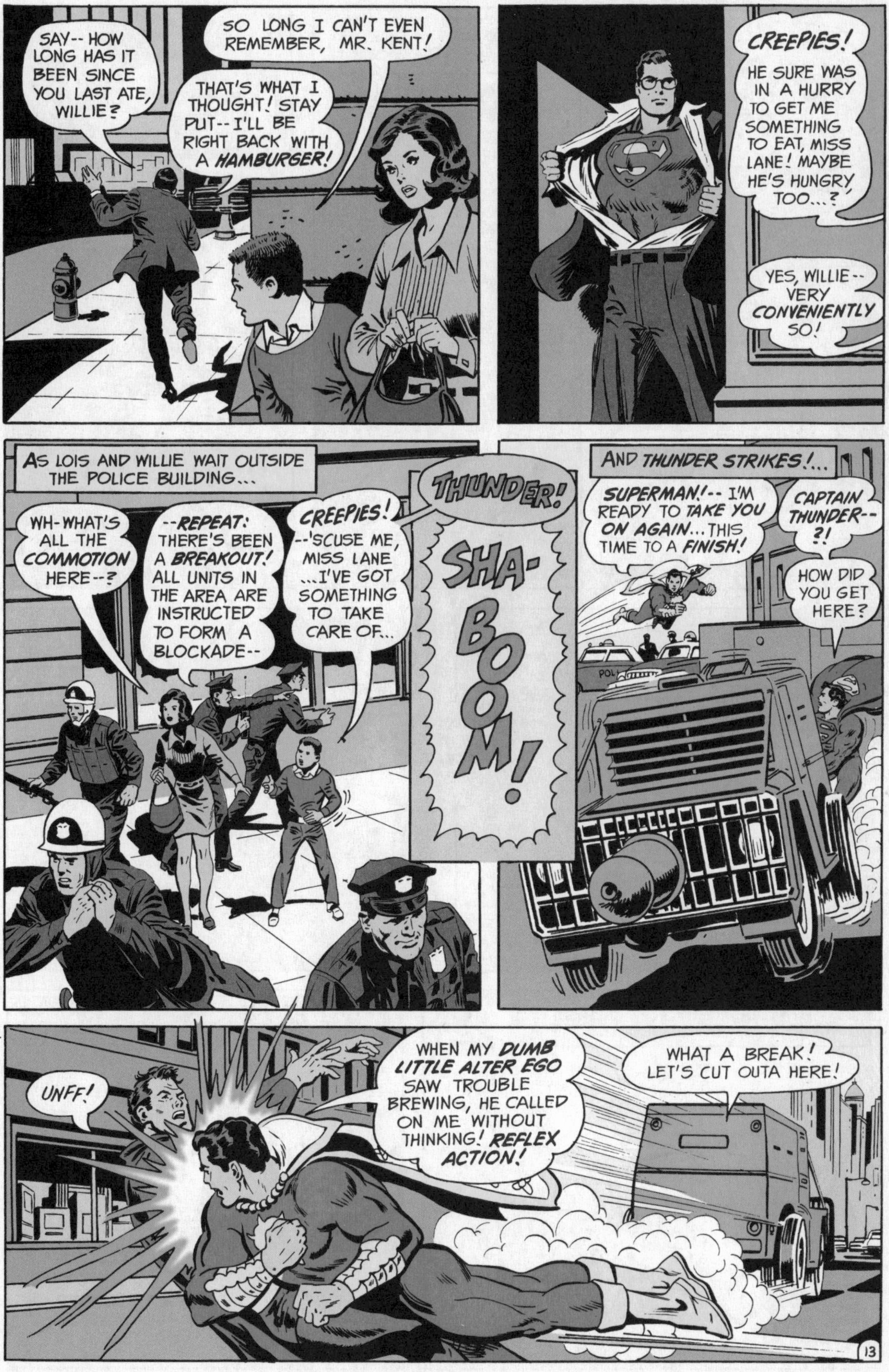
SAY-- HOW LONG HAS IT BEEN SINCE YOU LAST ATE, WILLIE?
SO LONG I CAN'T EVEN REMEMBER, MR. KENT!
THAT'S WHAT I THOUGHT! STAY PUT--I'LL BE RIGHT BACK WITH A HAMBURGER!
CREEPIES! HE SURE WAS IN A HURRY TO GET ME SOMETHING TO EAT, MISS LANE! MAYBE HE'S HUNGRY TOO...?
YES, WILLIE-- VERY CONVENIENTLY SO!
AS LOIS AND WILLIE WAIT OUTSIDE THE POLICE BUILDING...
WH-WHAT'S ALL THE COMMOTION HERE--?
--REPEAT: THERE'S BEEN A BREAKOUT! ALL UNITS IN THE AREA ARE INSTRUCTED TO FORM A BLOCKADE--
CREEPIES! --'SCUSE ME, MISS LANE ...I'VE GOT SOMETHING TO TAKE CARE OF...
THUNDER!
SHA-BOOM!
AND THUNDER STRIKES!...
SUPERMAN!-- I'M READY TO TAKE YOU ON AGAIN... THIS TIME TO A FINISH!
CAPTAIN THUNDER--?!
HOW DID YOU GET HERE?
UNFF!
WHEN MY DUMB LITTLE ALTER EGO SAW TROUBLE BREWING, HE CALLED ON ME WITHOUT THINKING! REFLEX ACTION!
WHAT A BREAK! LET'S CUT OUTA HERE!
13

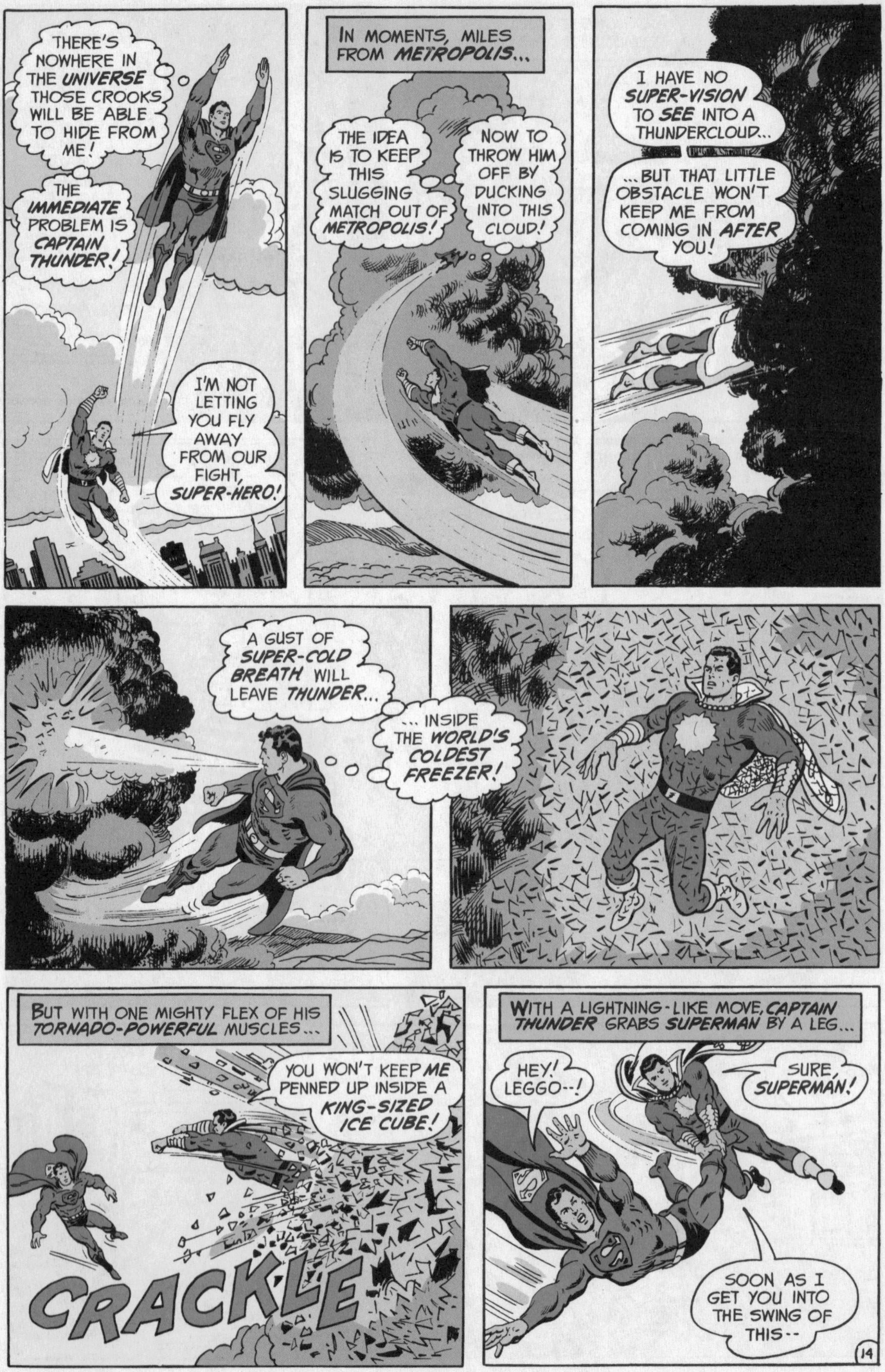
THERE'S NOWHERE IN THE UNIVERSE THOSE CROOKS WILL BE ABLE TO HIDE FROM ME!
THE IMMEDIATE PROBLEM IS CAPTAIN THUNDER!
I'M NOT LETTING YOU FLY AWAY FROM OUR FIGHT, SUPER-HERO!
IN MOMENTS, MILES FROM METROPOLIS...
THE IDEA IS TO KEEP THIS SLUGGING MATCH OUT OF METROPOLIS!
NOW TO THROW HIM OFF BY DUCKING INTO THIS CLOUD!
I HAVE NO SUPER-VISION TO SEE INTO A THUNDERCLOUD...
...BUT THAT LITTLE OBSTACLE WON'T KEEP ME FROM COMING IN AFTER YOU!
A GUST OF SUPER-COLD BREATH WILL LEAVE THUNDER...
...INSIDE THE WORLD'S COLDEST FREEZER!
BUT WITH ONE MIGHTY FLEX OF HIS TORNADO-POWERFUL MUSCLES...
YOU WON'T KEEP ME PENNED UP INSIDE A KING-SIZED ICE CUBE!
CRACKLE
WITH A LIGHTNING-LIKE MOVE, CAPTAIN THUNDER GRABS SUPERMAN BY A LEG...
HEY! LEGGO--!
SURE, SUPERMAN!
SOON AS I GET YOU INTO THE SWING OF THIS--
14

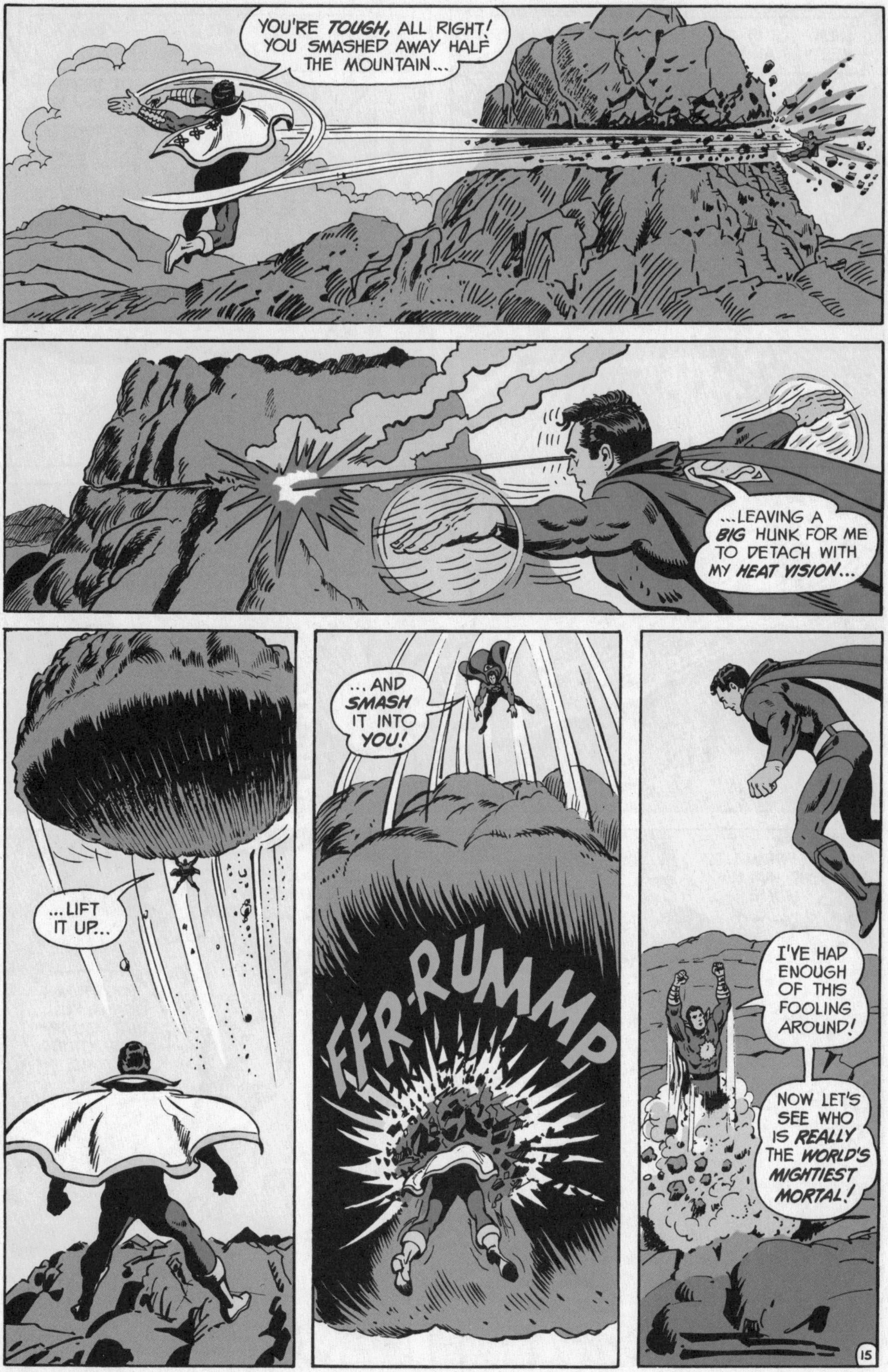
YOU'RE TOUGH, ALL RIGHT! YOU SMASHED AWAY HALF THE MOUNTAIN...
...LEAVING A BIG HUNK FOR ME TO DETACH WITH MY HEAT VISION...
...LIFT IT UP...
...AND SMASH IT INTO YOU!
FFR-RUMMP
I'VE HAD ENOUGH OF THIS FOOLING AROUND!
NOW LET'S SEE WHO IS REALLY THE WORLD'S MIGHTIEST MORTAL!
15

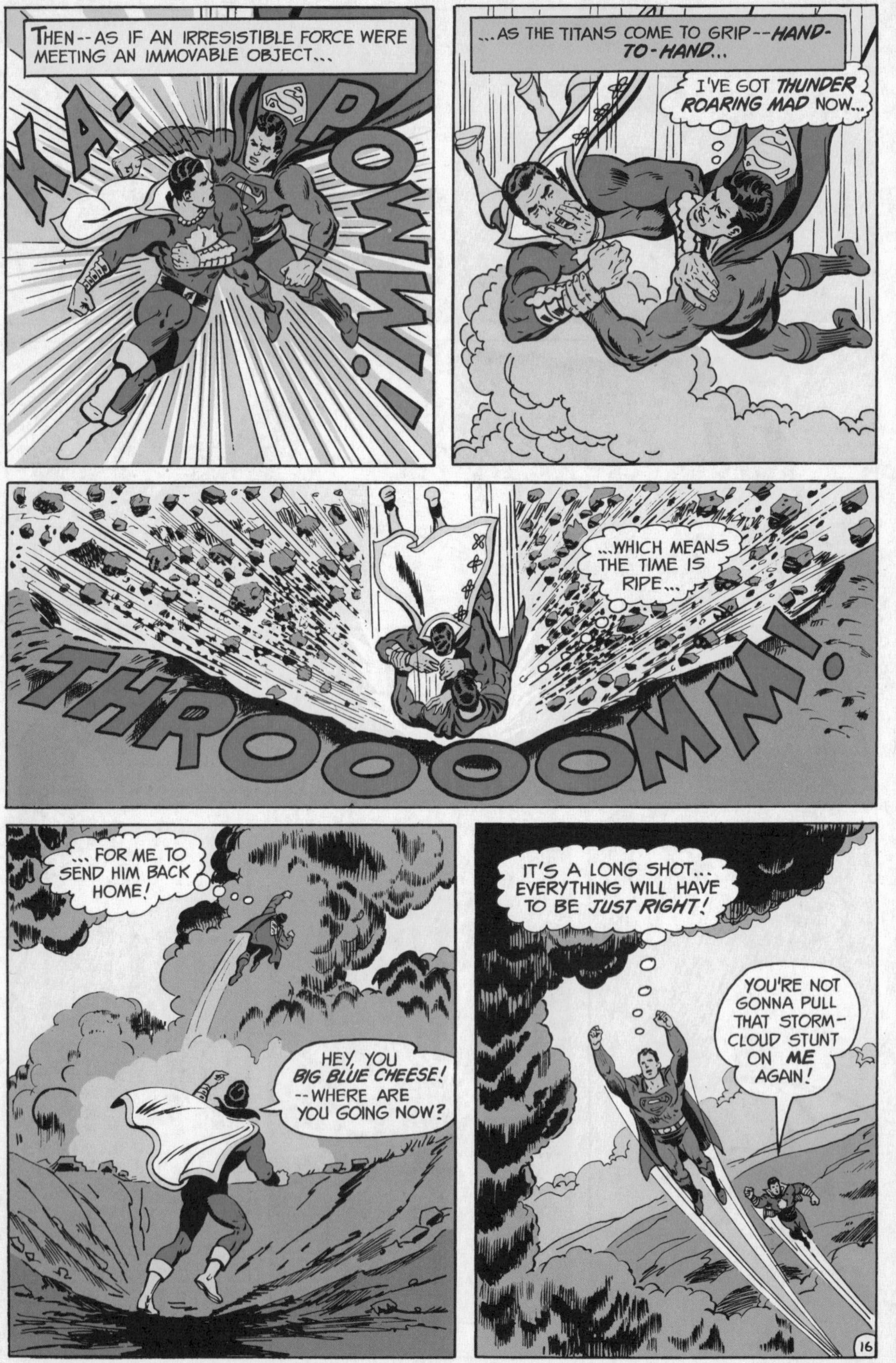
THEN--AS IF AN IRRESISTIBLE FORCE WERE MEETING AN IMMOVABLE OBJECT...
KA-POWW!
...AS THE TITANS COME TO GRIP--HAND-TO-HAND...
I'VE GOT THUNDER ROARING MAD NOW...
...WHICH MEANS THE TIME IS RIPE...
THROOOOMM!
...FOR ME TO SEND HIM BACK HOME!
HEY, YOU BIG BLUE CHEESE! --WHERE ARE YOU GOING NOW?
IT'S A LONG SHOT... EVERYTHING WILL HAVE TO BE JUST RIGHT!
YOU'RE NOT GONNA PULL THAT STORM-CLOUD STUNT ON ME AGAIN!
16

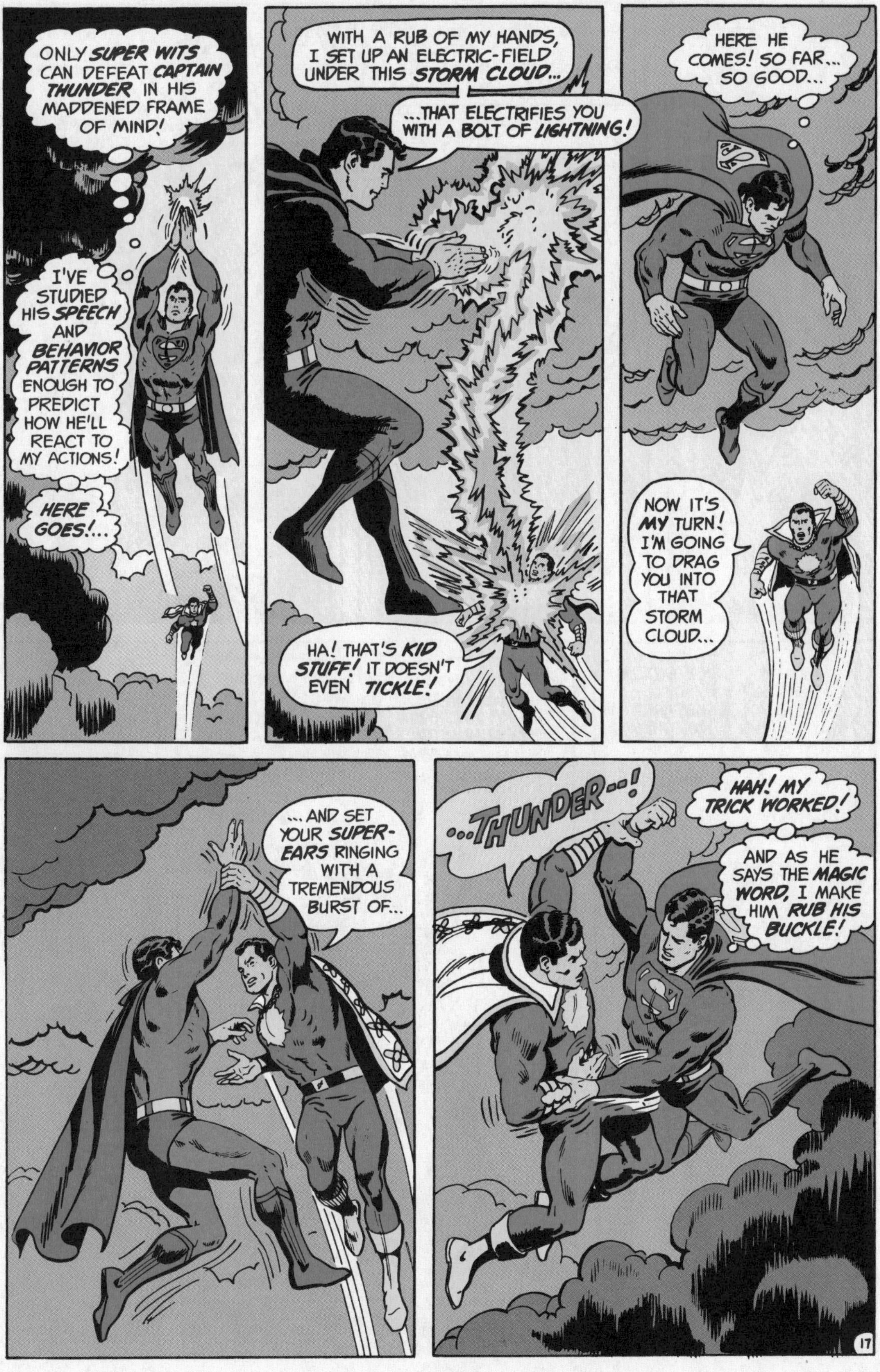
ONLY SUPER WITS CAN DEFEAT CAPTAIN THUNDER IN HIS MADDENED FRAME OF MIND!
I'VE STUDIED HIS SPEECH AND BEHAVIOR PATTERNS ENOUGH TO PREDICT HOW HE'LL REACT TO MY ACTIONS!
HERE GOES!...
WITH A RUB OF MY HANDS, I SET UP AN ELECTRIC-FIELD UNDER THIS STORM CLOUD...
...THAT ELECTRIFIES YOU WITH A BOLT OF LIGHTNING!
HA! THAT'S KID STUFF! IT DOESN'T EVEN TICKLE!
HERE HE COMES! SO FAR... SO GOOD...
NOW IT'S MY TURN! I'M GOING TO DRAG YOU INTO THAT STORM CLOUD...
...AND SET YOUR SUPER-EARS RINGING WITH A TREMENDOUS BURST OF...
...THUNDER--!
HAH! MY TRICK WORKED!
AND AS HE SAYS THE MAGIC WORD, I MAKE HIM RUB HIS BUCKLE!
17

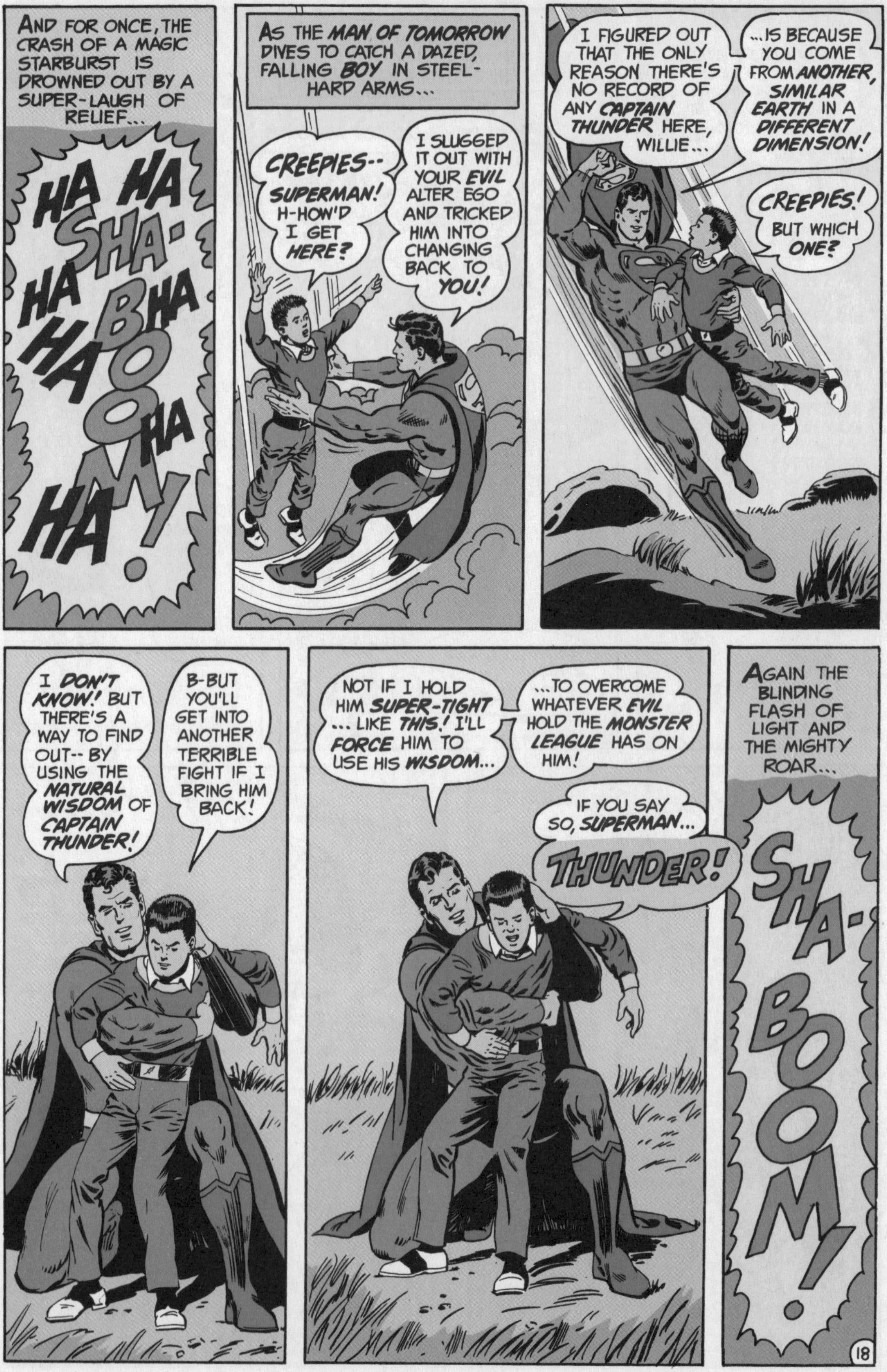
AND FOR ONCE, THE CRASH OF A MAGIC STARBURST IS DROWNED OUT BY A SUPER-LAUGH OF RELIEF...
HA HA HA HA HA HA HA HA
SHA-BOOM!
AS THE MAN OF TOMORROW DIVES TO CATCH A DAZED, FALLING BOY IN STEEL-HARD ARMS...
CREEPIES-- SUPERMAN! H-HOW'D I GET HERE?
I SLUGGED IT OUT WITH YOUR EVIL ALTER EGO AND TRICKED HIM INTO CHANGING BACK TO YOU!
I FIGURED OUT THAT THE ONLY REASON THERE'S NO RECORD OF ANY CAPTAIN THUNDER HERE, WILLIE...
...IS BECAUSE YOU COME FROM ANOTHER, SIMILAR EARTH IN A DIFFERENT DIMENSION!
CREEPIES! BUT WHICH ONE?
I DON'T KNOW! BUT THERE'S A WAY TO FIND OUT-- BY USING THE NATURAL WISDOM OF CAPTAIN THUNDER!
B-BUT YOU'LL GET INTO ANOTHER TERRIBLE FIGHT IF I BRING HIM BACK!
NOT IF I HOLD HIM SUPER-TIGHT ... LIKE THIS! I'LL FORCE HIM TO USE HIS WISDOM...
...TO OVERCOME WHATEVER EVIL HOLD THE MONSTER LEAGUE HAS ON HIM!
IF YOU SAY SO, SUPERMAN...
THUNDER!
AGAIN THE BLINDING FLASH OF LIGHT AND THE MIGHTY ROAR...
SHA-BOOM!
18

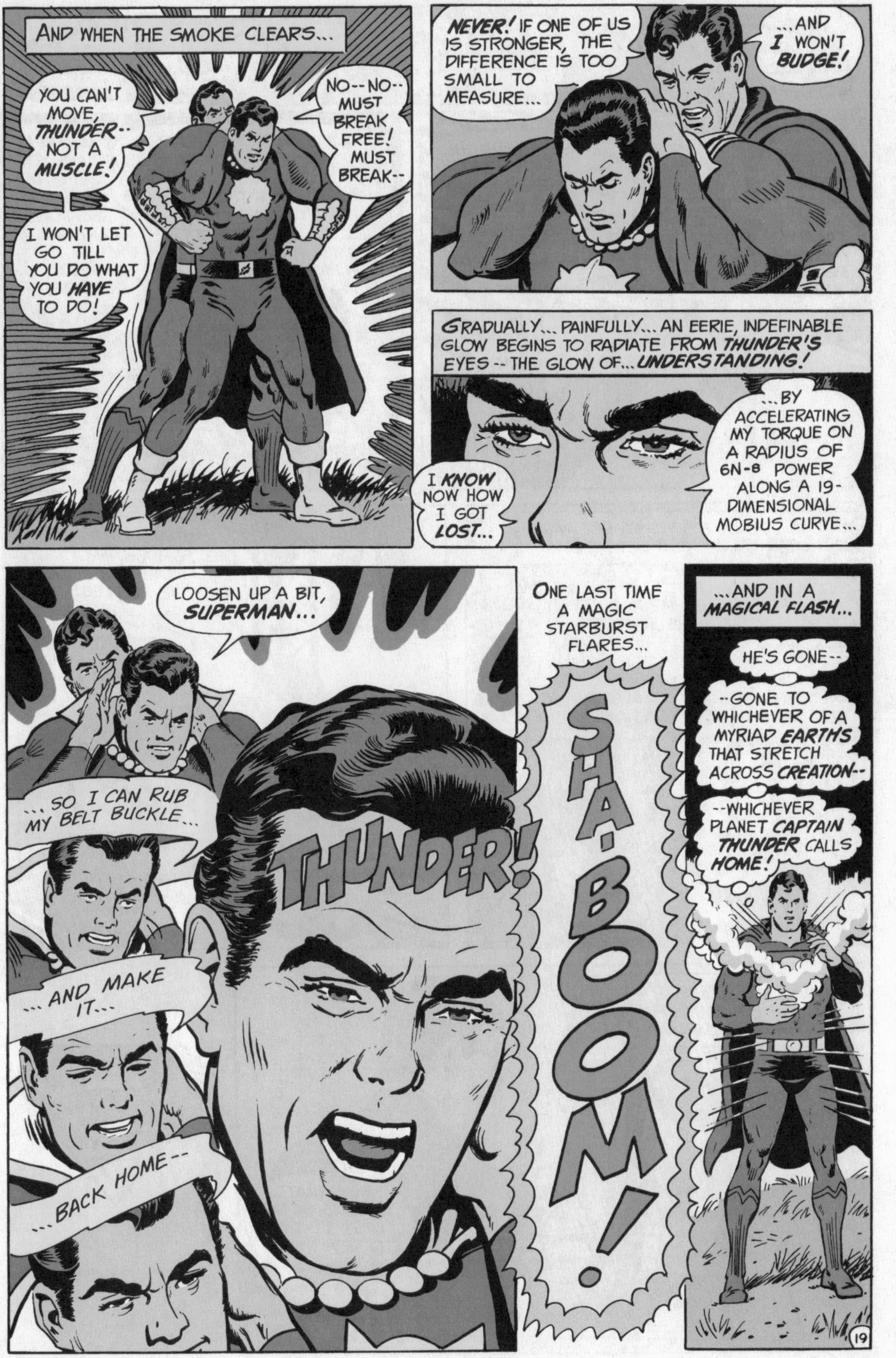

AND WHEN THE SMOKE CLEARS...
YOU CAN'T MOVE, THUNDER-- NOT A MUSCLE!
NO--NO-- MUST BREAK FREE! MUST BREAK--
I WON'T LET GO TILL YOU DO WHAT YOU HAVE TO DO!
NEVER! IF ONE OF US IS STRONGER, THE DIFFERENCE IS TOO SMALL TO MEASURE...
...AND I WON'T BUDGE!
GRADUALLY... PAINFULLY... AN EERIE, INDEFINABLE GLOW BEGINS TO RADIATE FROM THUNDER'S EYES -- THE GLOW OF... UNDERSTANDING!
...BY ACCELERATING MY TORQUE ON A RADIUS OF 6N-8 POWER ALONG A 19-DIMENSIONAL MOBIUS CURVE...
I KNOW NOW HOW I GOT LOST...
LOOSEN UP A BIT, SUPERMAN...
...SO I CAN RUB MY BELT BUCKLE...
...AND MAKE IT...
...BACK HOME--
THUNDER!
ONE LAST TIME A MAGIC STARBURST FLARES...
SHA-BOOM!
...AND IN A MAGICAL FLASH...
HE'S GONE--
--GONE TO WHICHEVER OF A MYRIAD EARTHS THAT STRETCH ACROSS CREATION--
--WHICHEVER PLANET CAPTAIN THUNDER CALLS HOME!
19

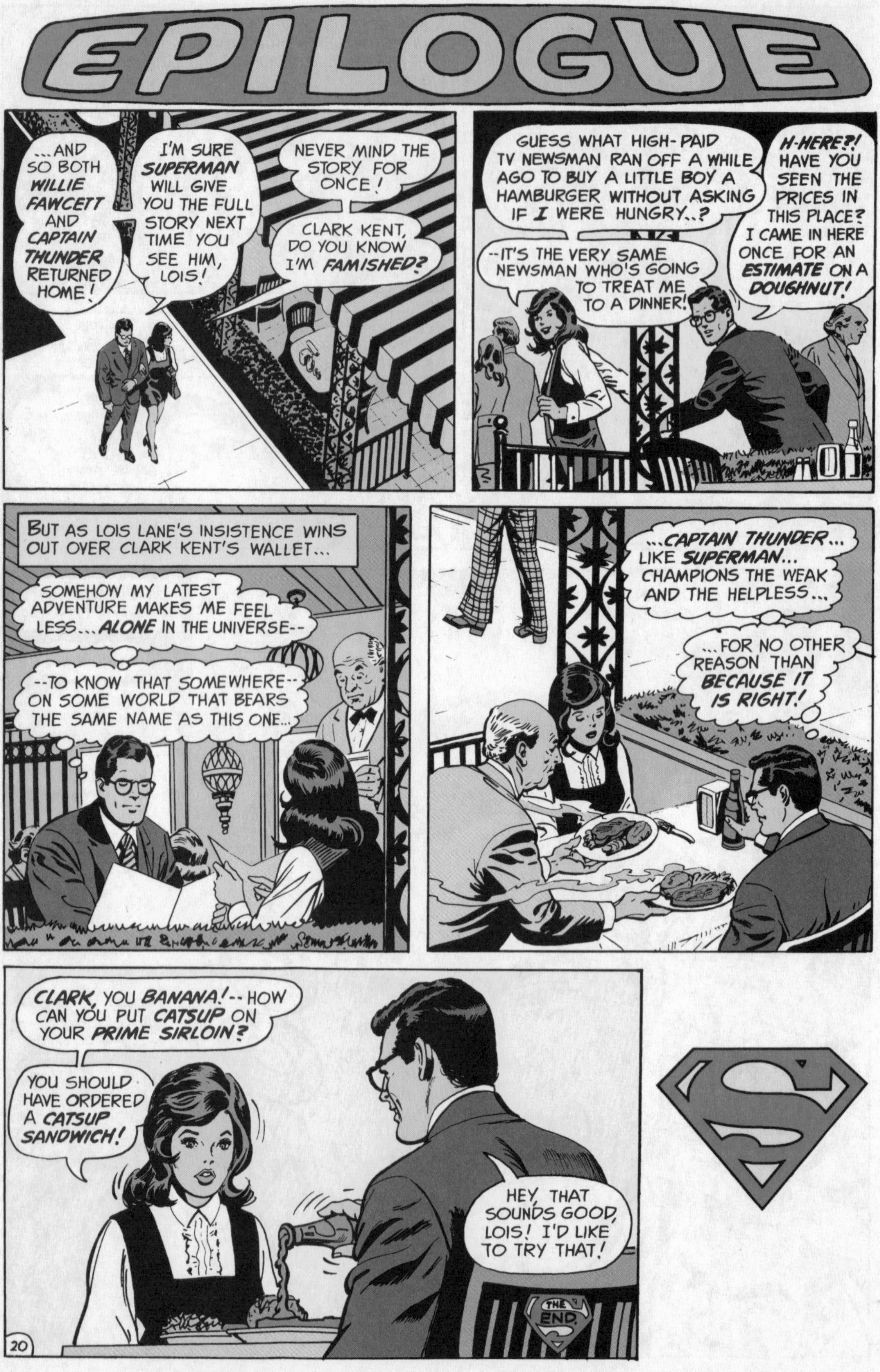
EPILOGUE
...AND SO BOTH WILLIE FAWCETT AND CAPTAIN THUNDER RETURNED HOME!
I'M SURE SUPERMAN WILL GIVE YOU THE FULL STORY NEXT TIME YOU SEE HIM, LOIS!
NEVER MIND THE STORY FOR ONCE!
CLARK KENT, DO YOU KNOW I'M FAMISHED?
GUESS WHAT HIGH-PAID TV NEWSMAN RAN OFF A WHILE AGO TO BUY A LITTLE BOY A HAMBURGER WITHOUT ASKING IF I WERE HUNGRY..?
--IT'S THE VERY SAME NEWSMAN WHO'S GOING TO TREAT ME TO A DINNER!
H-HERE?! HAVE YOU SEEN THE PRICES IN THIS PLACE? I CAME IN HERE ONCE FOR AN ESTIMATE ON A DOUGHNUT!
BUT AS LOIS LANE'S INSISTENCE WINS OUT OVER CLARK KENT'S WALLET...
SOMEHOW MY LATEST ADVENTURE MAKES ME FEEL LESS... ALONE IN THE UNIVERSE--
--TO KNOW THAT SOMEWHERE--ON SOME WORLD THAT BEARS THE SAME NAME AS THIS ONE...
...CAPTAIN THUNDER... LIKE SUPERMAN... CHAMPIONS THE WEAK AND THE HELPLESS...
...FOR NO OTHER REASON THAN BECAUSE IT IS RIGHT!
CLARK, YOU BANANA!--HOW CAN YOU PUT CATSUP ON YOUR PRIME SIRLOIN?
YOU SHOULD HAVE ORDERED A CATSUP SANDWICH!
HEY, THAT SOUNDS GOOD, LOIS! I'D LIKE TO TRY THAT!
THE END
20

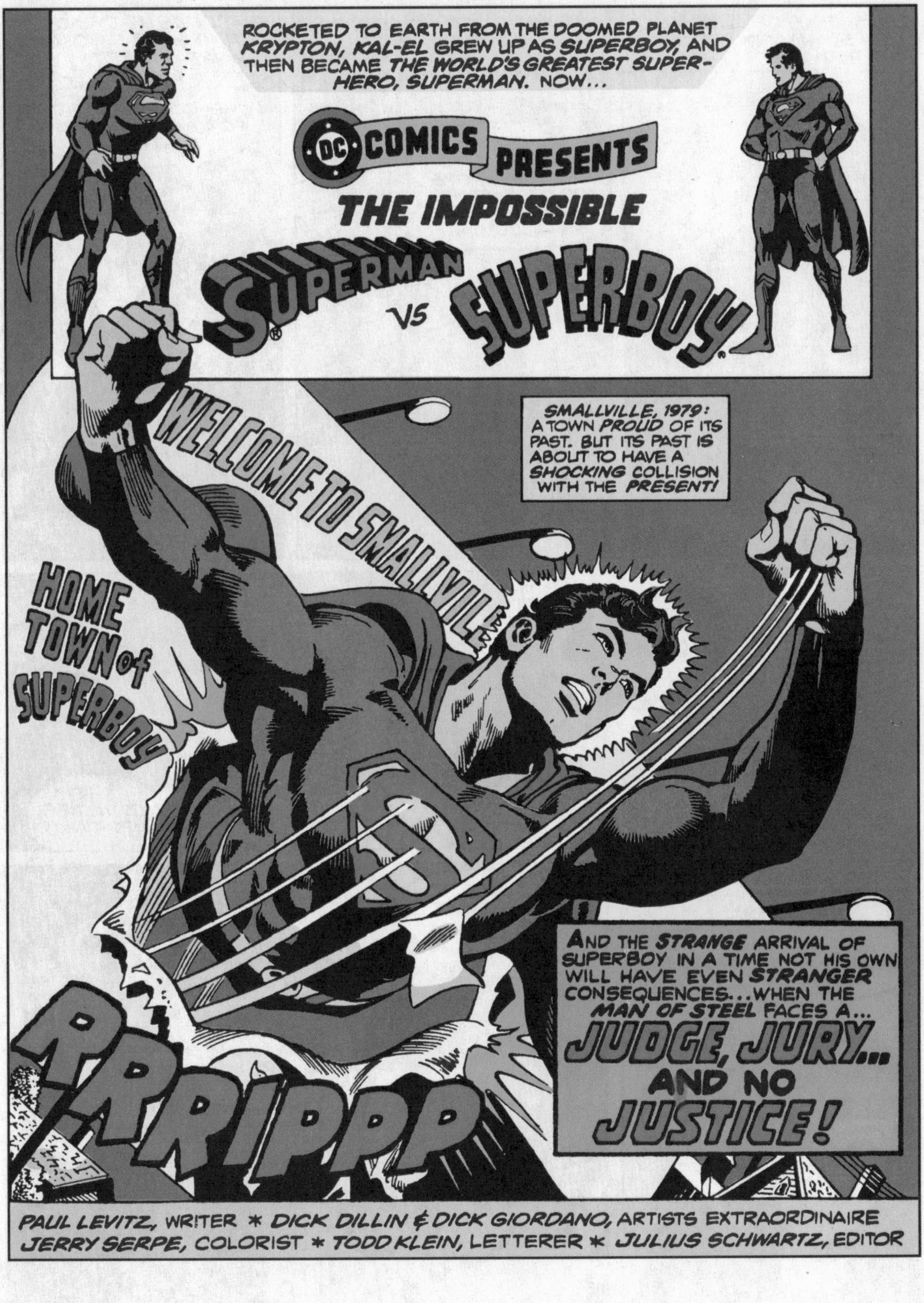
ROCKETED TO EARTH FROM THE DOOMED PLANET KRYPTON, KAL-EL GREW UP AS SUPERBOY, AND THEN BECAME THE WORLD'S GREATEST SUPER-HERO, SUPERMAN. NOW...
DC COMICS PRESENTS
THE IMPOSSIBLE
SUPERMAN VS SUPERBOY
WELCOME TO SMALLVILLE
HOME TOWN of SUPERBOY
SMALLVILLE, 1979: A TOWN PROUD OF ITS PAST. BUT ITS PAST IS ABOUT TO HAVE A SHOCKING COLLISION WITH THE PRESENT!
AND THE STRANGE ARRIVAL OF SUPERBOY IN A TIME NOT HIS OWN WILL HAVE EVEN STRANGER CONSEQUENCES...WHEN THE MAN OF STEEL FACES A...
JUDGE, JURY... AND NO JUSTICE!
RRRIPPP
PAUL LEVITZ, WRITER * DICK DILLIN & DICK GIORDANO, ARTISTS EXTRAORDINAIRE
JERRY SERPE, COLORIST * TODD KLEIN, LETTERER * JULIUS SCHWARTZ, EDITOR

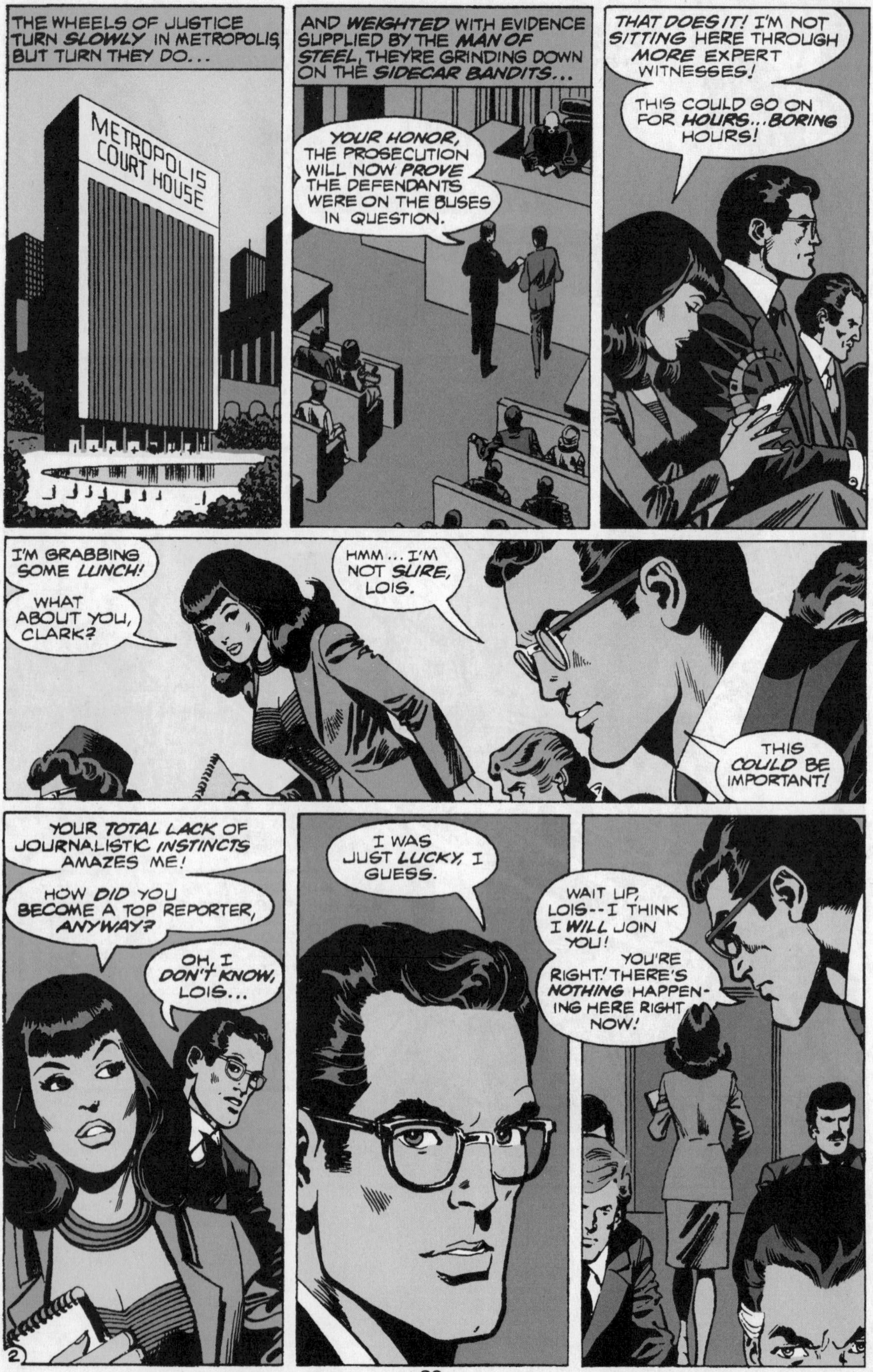

THE WHEELS OF JUSTICE TURN SLOWLY IN METROPOLIS, BUT TURN THEY DO...
METROPOLIS COURT HOUSE
AND WEIGHTED WITH EVIDENCE SUPPLIED BY THE MAN OF STEEL, THEY'RE GRINDING DOWN ON THE SIDECAR BANDITS...
YOUR HONOR, THE PROSECUTION WILL NOW PROVE THE DEFENDANTS WERE ON THE BUSES IN QUESTION.
THAT DOES IT! I'M NOT SITTING HERE THROUGH MORE EXPERT WITNESSES!
THIS COULD GO ON FOR HOURS... BORING HOURS!
I'M GRABBING SOME LUNCH!
WHAT ABOUT YOU, CLARK?
HMM... I'M NOT SURE, LOIS.
THIS COULD BE IMPORTANT!
YOUR TOTAL LACK OF JOURNALISTIC INSTINCTS AMAZES ME!
HOW DID YOU BECOME A TOP REPORTER, ANYWAY?
OH, I DON'T KNOW, LOIS...
I WAS JUST LUCKY, I GUESS.
WAIT UP, LOIS--I THINK I WILL JOIN YOU!
YOU'RE RIGHT! THERE'S NOTHING HAPPENING HERE RIGHT NOW!
2

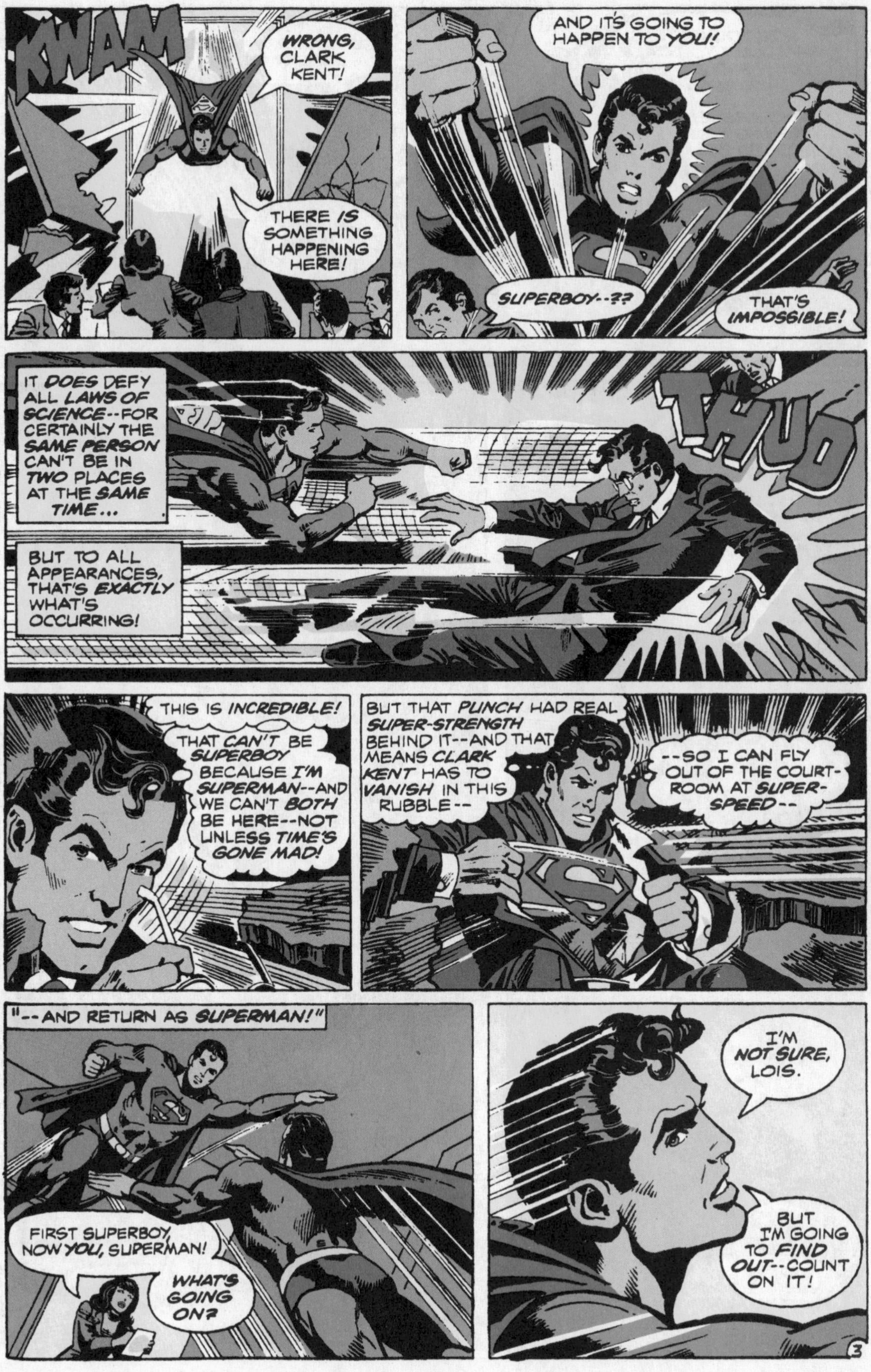
KWAM
WRONG, CLARK KENT!
THERE IS SOMETHING HAPPENING HERE!
AND IT'S GOING TO HAPPEN TO YOU!
SUPERBOY--??
THAT'S IMPOSSIBLE!
IT DOES DEFY ALL LAWS OF SCIENCE--FOR CERTAINLY THE SAME PERSON CAN'T BE IN TWO PLACES AT THE SAME TIME...
THUD
BUT TO ALL APPEARANCES, THAT'S EXACTLY WHAT'S OCCURRING!
THIS IS INCREDIBLE!
THAT CAN'T BE SUPERBOY BECAUSE I'M SUPERMAN--AND WE CAN'T BOTH BE HERE--NOT UNLESS TIME'S GONE MAD!
BUT THAT PUNCH HAD REAL SUPER-STRENGTH BEHIND IT--AND THAT MEANS CLARK KENT HAS TO VANISH IN THIS RUBBLE--
--SO I CAN FLY OUT OF THE COURT-ROOM AT SUPER-SPEED--
"--AND RETURN AS SUPERMAN!"
FIRST SUPERBOY, NOW YOU, SUPERMAN!
WHAT'S GOING ON?
I'M NOT SURE, LOIS.
BUT I'M GOING TO FIND OUT--COUNT ON IT!
3

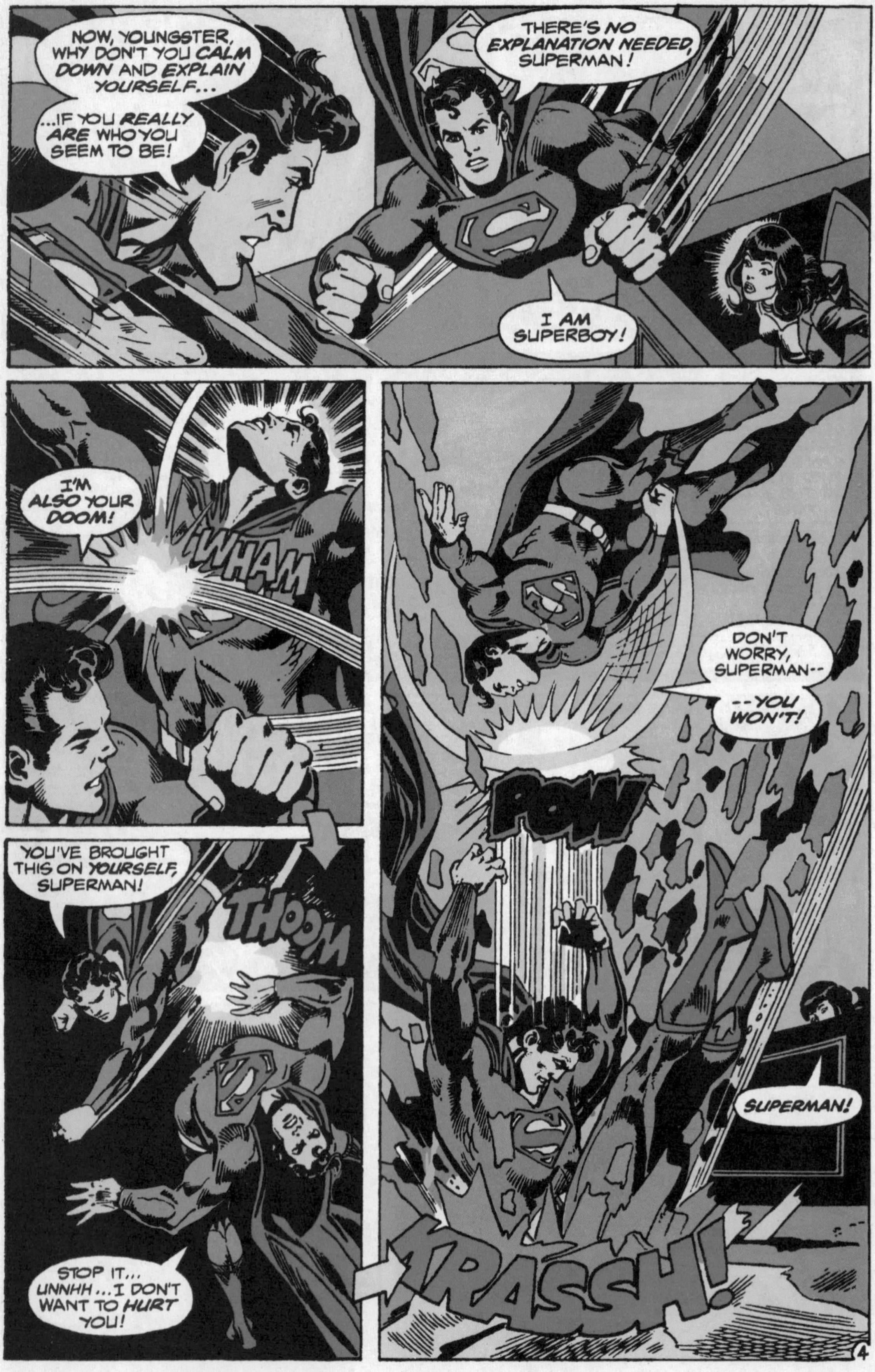
NOW, YOUNGSTER, WHY DON'T YOU CALM DOWN AND EXPLAIN YOURSELF...
...IF YOU REALLY ARE WHO YOU SEEM TO BE!
THERE'S NO EXPLANATION NEEDED, SUPERMAN!
I AM SUPERBOY!
I'M ALSO YOUR DOOM!
WHAM
YOU'VE BROUGHT THIS ON YOURSELF, SUPERMAN!
THOOM
STOP IT... UNNHH ...I DON'T WANT TO HURT YOU!
DON'T WORRY, SUPERMAN--
--YOU WON'T!
POW
SUPERMAN!
KRASSH!
4

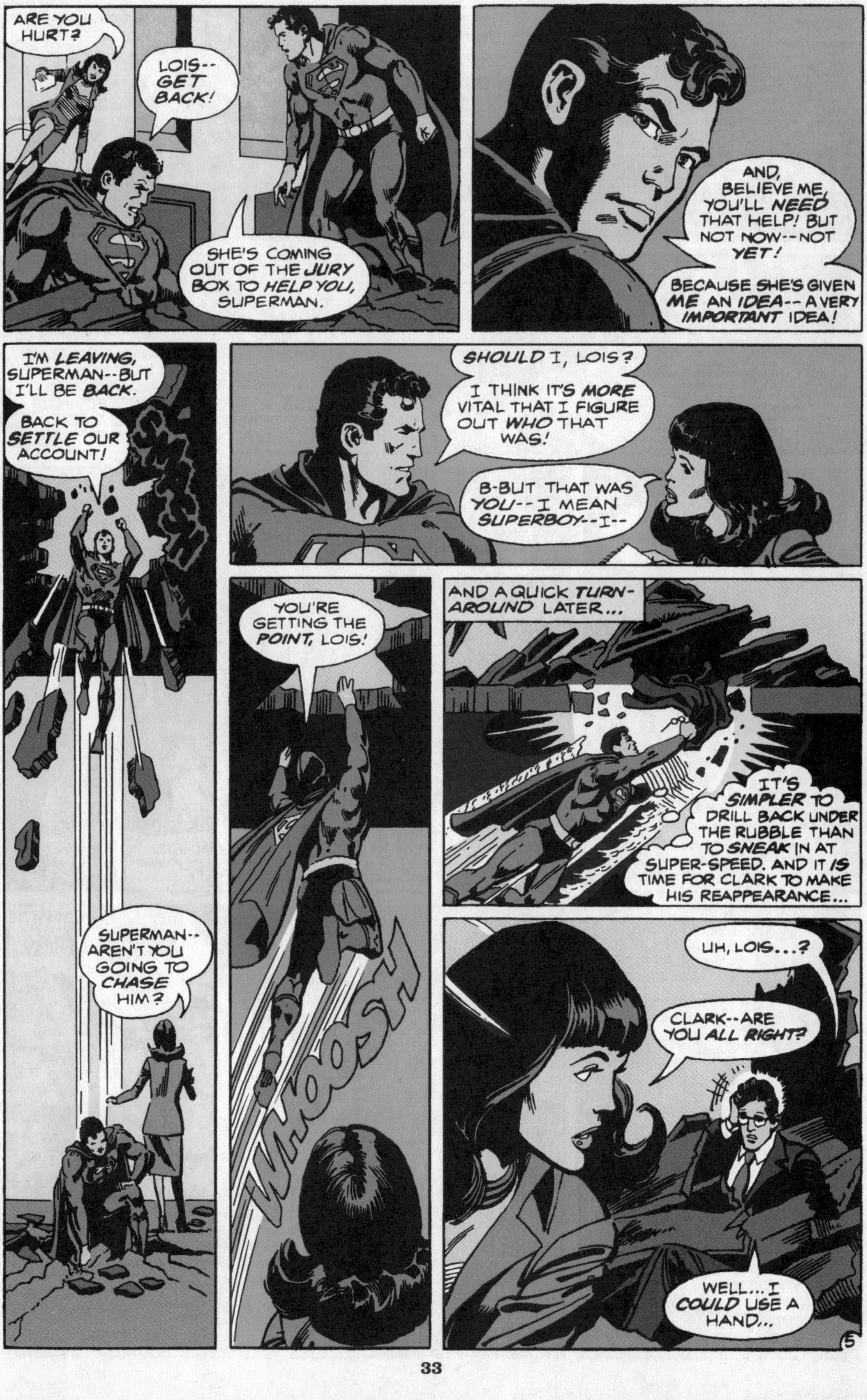
ARE YOU HURT?
LOIS-- GET BACK!
SHE'S COMING OUT OF THE JURY BOX TO HELP YOU, SUPERMAN.
AND, BELIEVE ME, YOU'LL NEED THAT HELP! BUT NOT NOW--NOT YET!
BECAUSE SHE'S GIVEN ME AN IDEA-- A VERY IMPORTANT IDEA!
I'M LEAVING, SUPERMAN--BUT I'LL BE BACK.
BACK TO SETTLE OUR ACCOUNT!
SUPERMAN-- AREN'T YOU GOING TO CHASE HIM?
SHOULD I, LOIS?
I THINK IT'S MORE VITAL THAT I FIGURE OUT WHO THAT WAS!
B-BUT THAT WAS YOU--I MEAN SUPERBOY--I--
YOU'RE GETTING THE POINT, LOIS!
WHOOSH
AND A QUICK TURN-AROUND LATER...
IT'S SIMPLER TO DRILL BACK UNDER THE RUBBLE THAN TO SNEAK IN AT SUPER-SPEED. AND IT IS TIME FOR CLARK TO MAKE HIS REAPPEARANCE...
UH, LOIS...?
CLARK--ARE YOU ALL RIGHT?
WELL... I COULD USE A HAND...
5

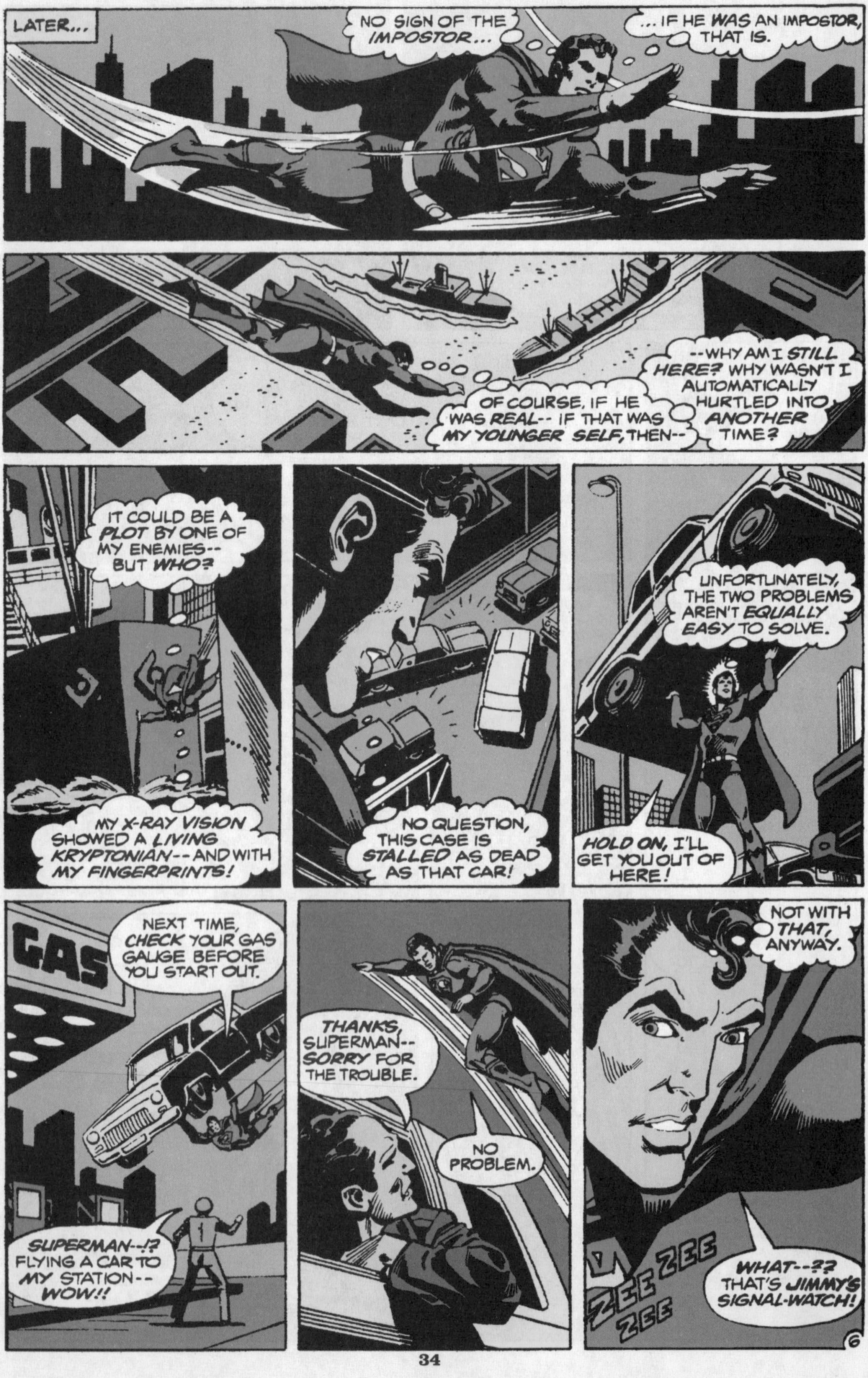
LATER...
NO SIGN OF THE IMPOSTOR...
...IF HE WAS AN IMPOSTOR, THAT IS.
OF COURSE, IF HE WAS REAL-- IF THAT WAS MY YOUNGER SELF, THEN--
--WHY AM I STILL HERE? WHY WASN'T I AUTOMATICALLY HURTLED INTO ANOTHER TIME?
IT COULD BE A PLOT BY ONE OF MY ENEMIES-- BUT WHO?
MY X-RAY VISION SHOWED A LIVING KRYPTONIAN-- AND WITH MY FINGERPRINTS!
NO QUESTION, THIS CASE IS STALLED AS DEAD AS THAT CAR!
UNFORTUNATELY, THE TWO PROBLEMS AREN'T EQUALLY EASY TO SOLVE.
HOLD ON, I'LL GET YOU OUT OF HERE!
GAS
NEXT TIME, CHECK YOUR GAS GAUGE BEFORE YOU START OUT.
SUPERMAN--!? FLYING A CAR TO MY STATION-- WOW!!
THANKS, SUPERMAN-- SORRY FOR THE TROUBLE.
NO PROBLEM.
NOT WITH THAT, ANYWAY.
ZEE ZEE ZEE
WHAT--?? THAT'S JIMMY'S SIGNAL-WATCH!
6

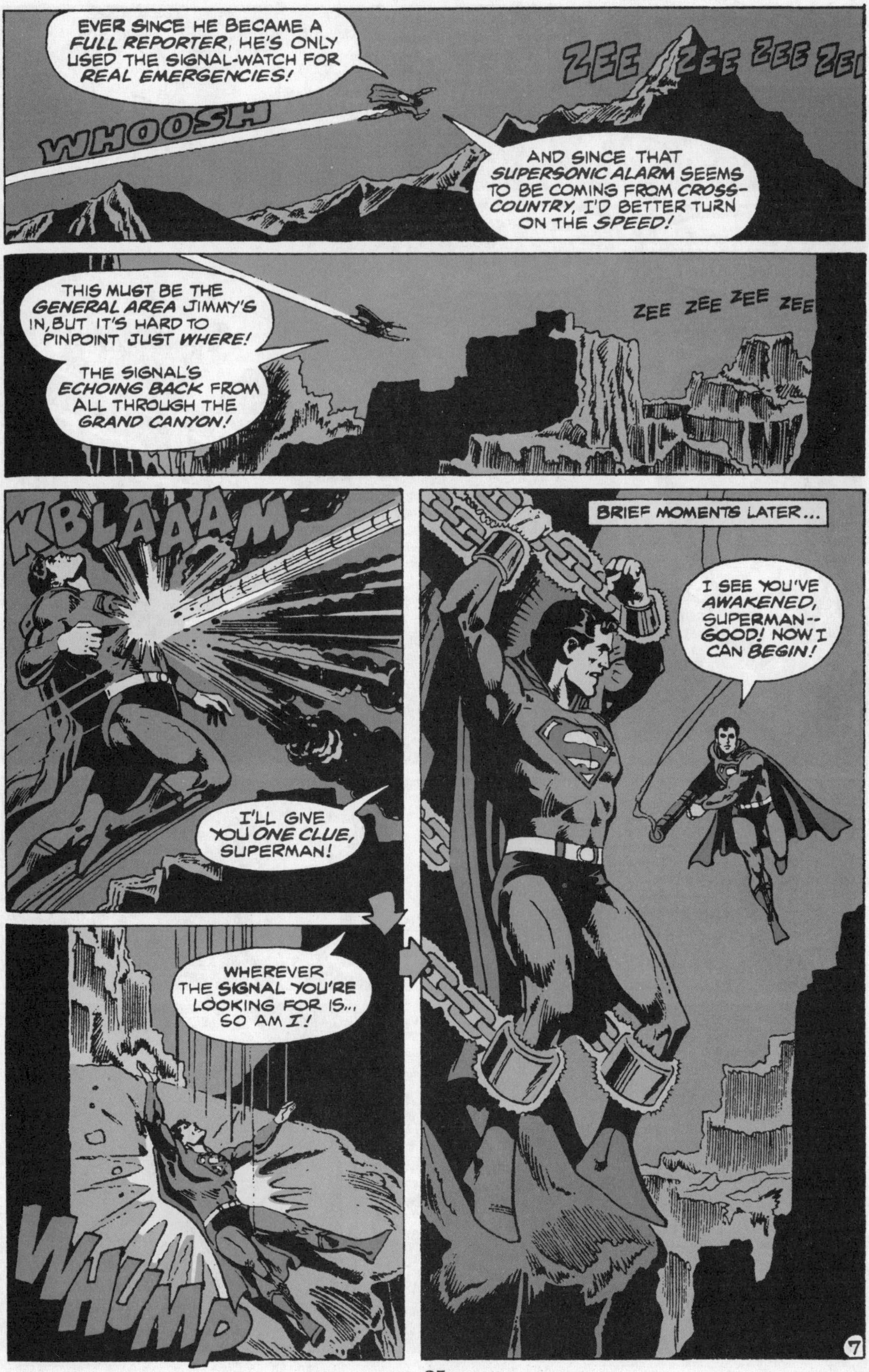
EVER SINCE HE BECAME A FULL REPORTER, HE'S ONLY USED THE SIGNAL-WATCH FOR REAL EMERGENCIES!
ZEE ZEE ZEE ZEE
WHOOSH
AND SINCE THAT SUPERSONIC ALARM SEEMS TO BE COMING FROM CROSS-COUNTRY, I'D BETTER TURN ON THE SPEED!
THIS MUST BE THE GENERAL AREA JIMMY'S IN, BUT IT'S HARD TO PINPOINT JUST WHERE!
THE SIGNAL'S ECHOING BACK FROM ALL THROUGH THE GRAND CANYON!
ZEE ZEE ZEE ZEE
KBLAAAM
I'LL GIVE YOU ONE CLUE, SUPERMAN!
WHEREVER THE SIGNAL YOU'RE LOOKING FOR IS... SO AM I!
WHUMP
BRIEF MOMENTS LATER...
I SEE YOU'VE AWAKENED, SUPERMAN-- GOOD! NOW I CAN BEGIN!
7

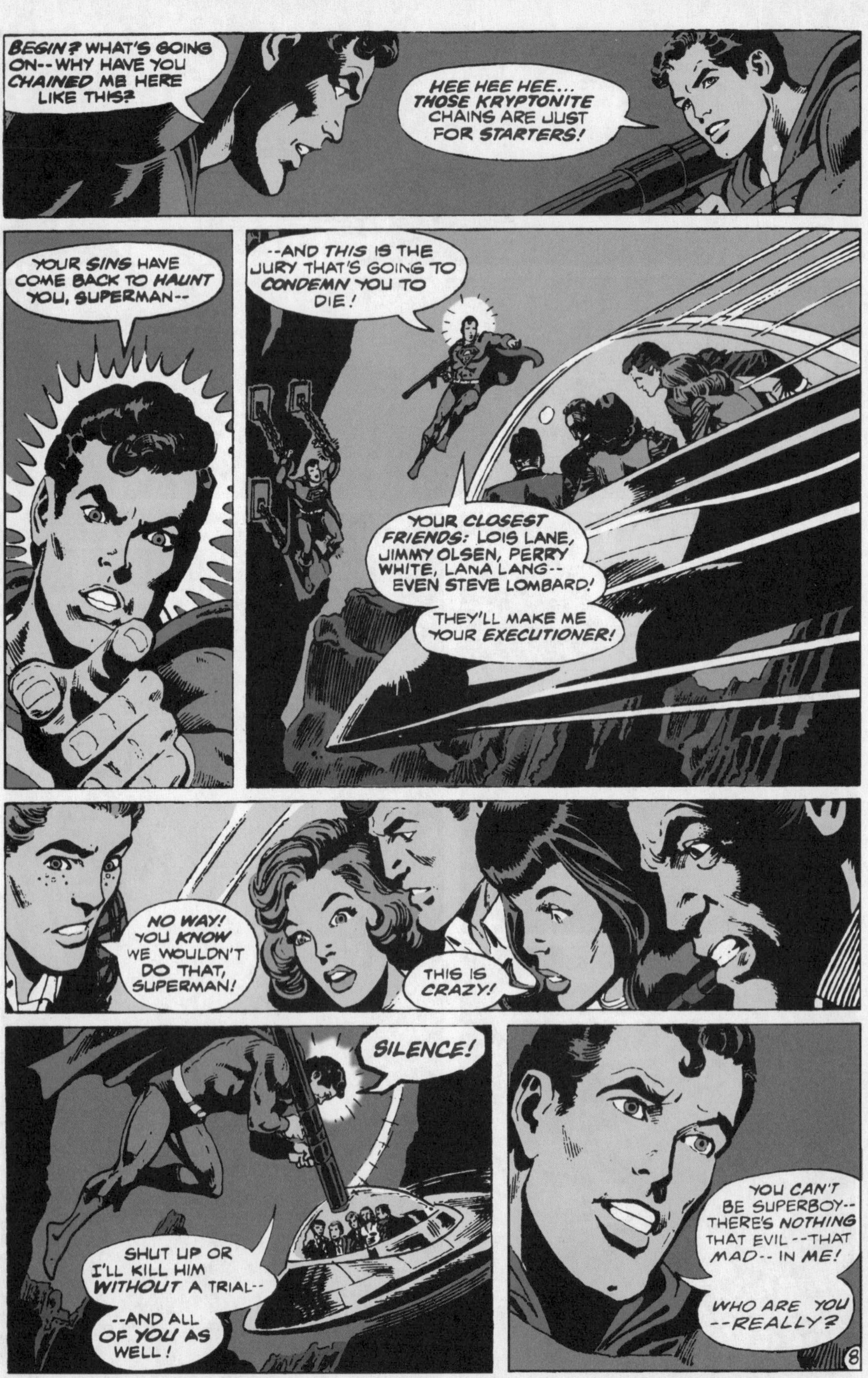

BEGIN? WHAT'S GOING ON--WHY HAVE YOU CHAINED ME HERE LIKE THIS?
HEE HEE HEE... THOSE KRYPTONITE CHAINS ARE JUST FOR STARTERS!
YOUR SINS HAVE COME BACK TO HAUNT YOU, SUPERMAN--
--AND THIS IS THE JURY THAT'S GOING TO CONDEMN YOU TO DIE!
YOUR CLOSEST FRIENDS: LOIS LANE, JIMMY OLSEN, PERRY WHITE, LANA LANG--EVEN STEVE LOMBARD!
THEY'LL MAKE ME YOUR EXECUTIONER!
NO WAY! YOU KNOW WE WOULDN'T DO THAT, SUPERMAN!
THIS IS CRAZY!
SILENCE!
SHUT UP OR I'LL KILL HIM WITHOUT A TRIAL--
--AND ALL OF YOU AS WELL!
YOU CAN'T BE SUPERBOY--THERE'S NOTHING THAT EVIL--THAT MAD--IN ME!
WHO ARE YOU --REALLY?
8

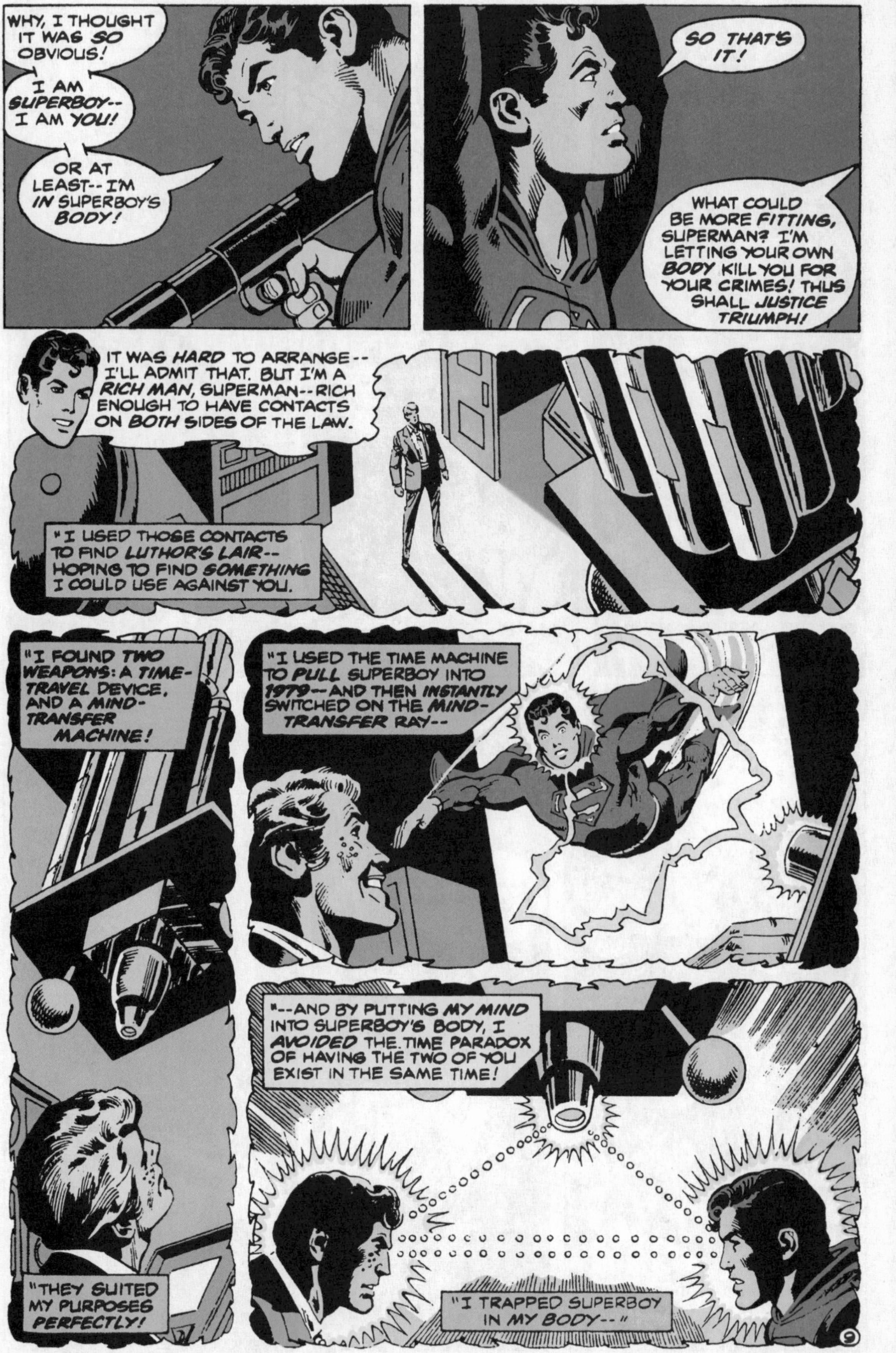
WHY, I THOUGHT IT WAS SO OBVIOUS!
I AM SUPERBOY-- I AM YOU!
OR AT LEAST-- I'M IN SUPERBOY'S BODY!
SO THAT'S IT!
WHAT COULD BE MORE FITTING, SUPERMAN? I'M LETTING YOUR OWN BODY KILL YOU FOR YOUR CRIMES! THUS SHALL JUSTICE TRIUMPH!
IT WAS HARD TO ARRANGE-- I'LL ADMIT THAT. BUT I'M A RICH MAN, SUPERMAN--RICH ENOUGH TO HAVE CONTACTS ON BOTH SIDES OF THE LAW.
"I USED THOSE CONTACTS TO FIND LUTHOR'S LAIR-- HOPING TO FIND SOMETHING I COULD USE AGAINST YOU.
"I FOUND TWO WEAPONS: A TIME-TRAVEL DEVICE, AND A MIND-TRANSFER MACHINE!
"I USED THE TIME MACHINE TO PULL SUPERBOY INTO 1979--AND THEN INSTANTLY SWITCHED ON THE MIND-TRANSFER RAY--
"THEY SUITED MY PURPOSES PERFECTLY!
"--AND BY PUTTING MY MIND INTO SUPERBOY'S BODY, I AVOIDED THE TIME PARADOX OF HAVING THE TWO OF YOU EXIST IN THE SAME TIME!
"I TRAPPED SUPERBOY IN MY BODY--"
9

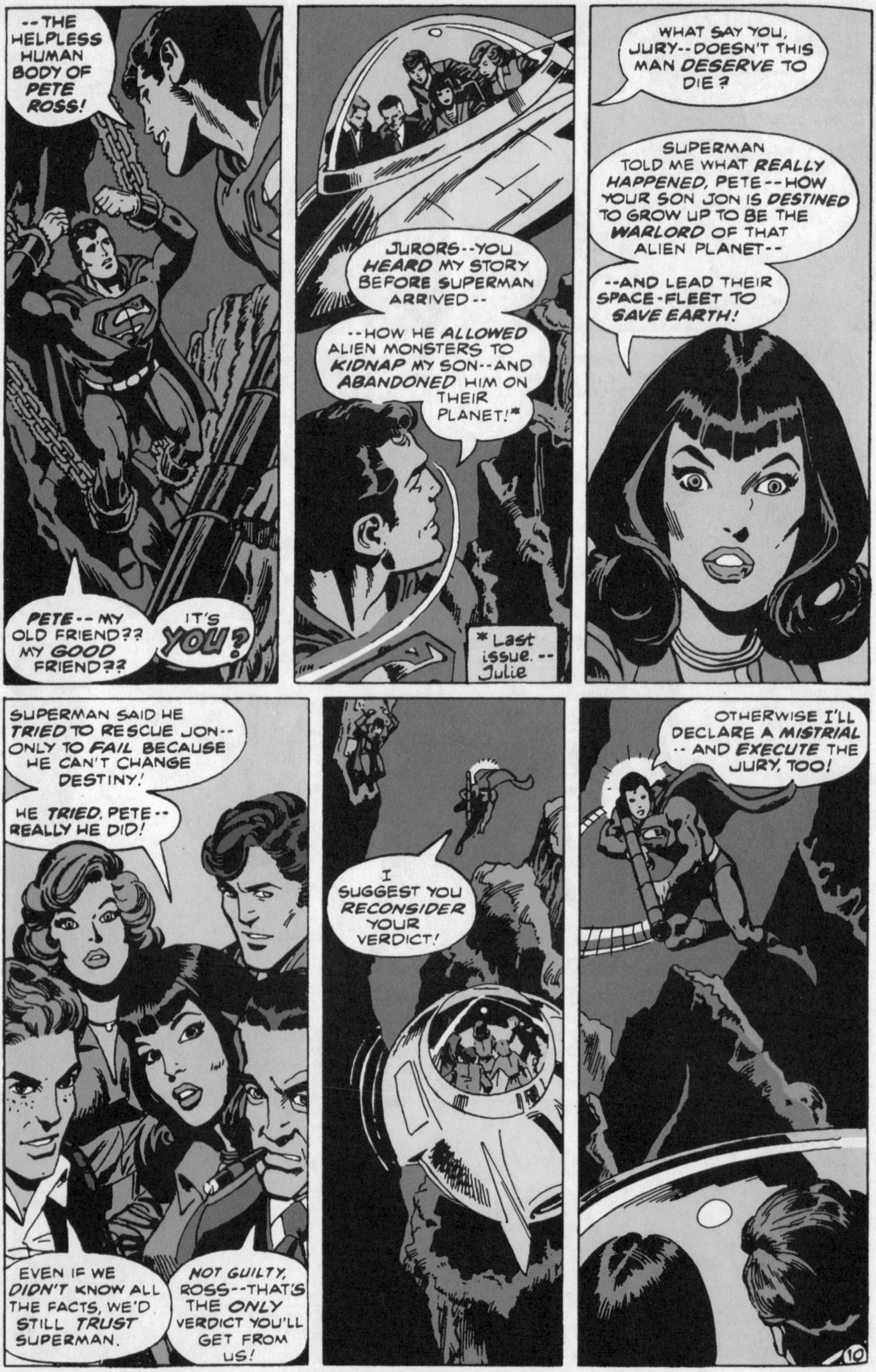
--THE HELPLESS HUMAN BODY OF PETE ROSS!
PETE--MY OLD FRIEND?? MY GOOD FRIEND??
IT'S YOU?
JURORS--YOU HEARD MY STORY BEFORE SUPERMAN ARRIVED--
--HOW HE ALLOWED ALIEN MONSTERS TO KIDNAP MY SON--AND ABANDONED HIM ON THEIR PLANET!*
* Last issue. --Julie
WHAT SAY YOU, JURY--DOESN'T THIS MAN DESERVE TO DIE?
SUPERMAN TOLD ME WHAT REALLY HAPPENED, PETE--HOW YOUR SON JON IS DESTINED TO GROW UP TO BE THE WARLORD OF THAT ALIEN PLANET--
--AND LEAD THEIR SPACE-FLEET TO SAVE EARTH!
SUPERMAN SAID HE TRIED TO RESCUE JON--ONLY TO FAIL BECAUSE HE CAN'T CHANGE DESTINY!
HE TRIED, PETE--REALLY HE DID!
EVEN IF WE DIDN'T KNOW ALL THE FACTS, WE'D STILL TRUST SUPERMAN.
NOT GUILTY, ROSS--THAT'S THE ONLY VERDICT YOU'LL GET FROM US!
I SUGGEST YOU RECONSIDER YOUR VERDICT!
OTHERWISE I'LL DECLARE A MISTRIAL--AND EXECUTE THE JURY, TOO!
10

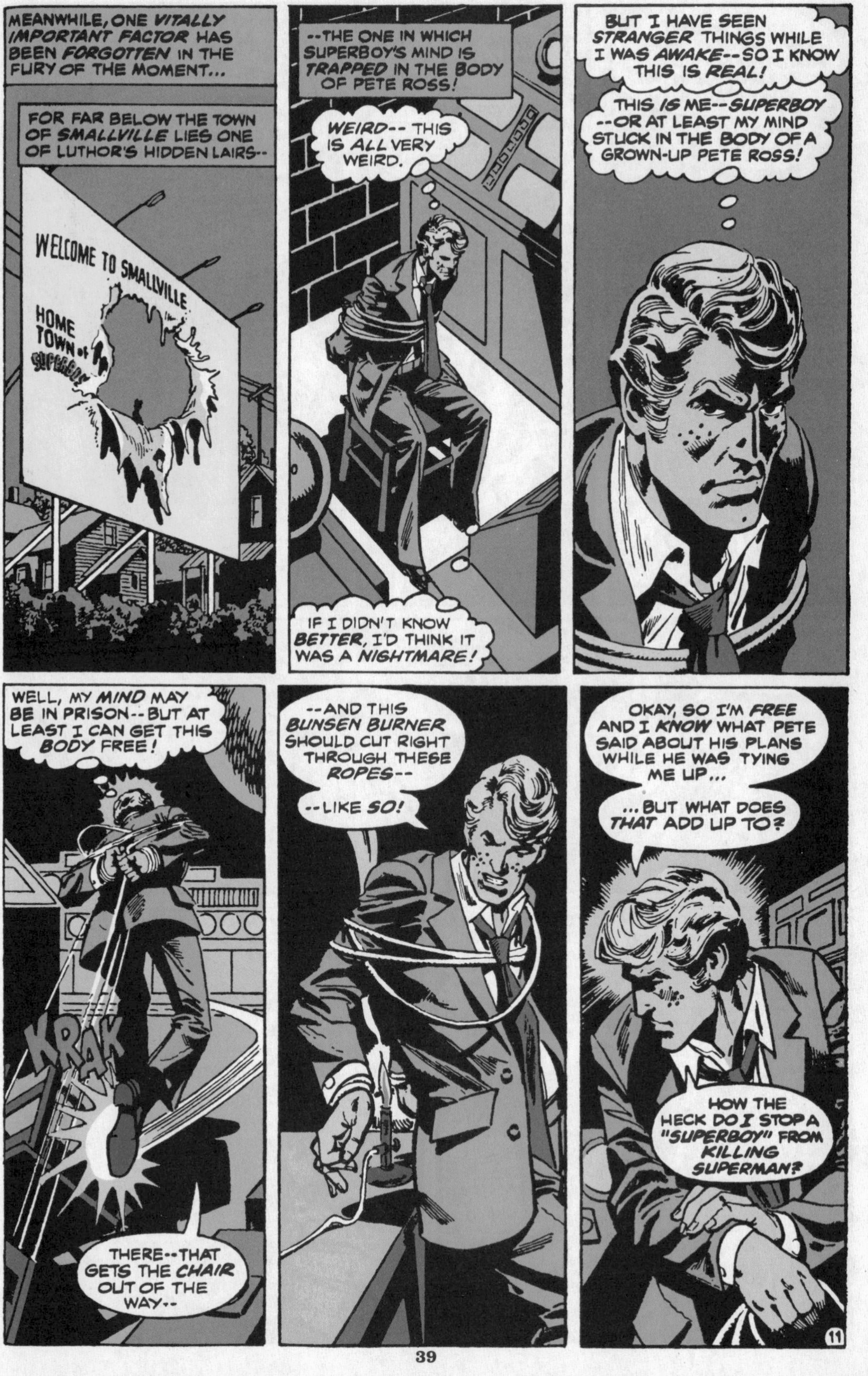
MEANWHILE, ONE VITALLY IMPORTANT FACTOR HAS BEEN FORGOTTEN IN THE FURY OF THE MOMENT...
FOR FAR BELOW THE TOWN OF SMALLVILLE LIES ONE OF LUTHOR'S HIDDEN LAIRS--
WELCOME TO SMALLVILLE
HOME TOWN of
--THE ONE IN WHICH SUPERBOY'S MIND IS TRAPPED IN THE BODY OF PETE ROSS!
WEIRD-- THIS IS ALL VERY WEIRD.
IF I DIDN'T KNOW BETTER, I'D THINK IT WAS A NIGHTMARE!
BUT I HAVE SEEN STRANGER THINGS WHILE I WAS AWAKE--SO I KNOW THIS IS REAL!
THIS IS ME--SUPERBOY --OR AT LEAST MY MIND STUCK IN THE BODY OF A GROWN-UP PETE ROSS!
WELL, MY MIND MAY BE IN PRISON--BUT AT LEAST I CAN GET THIS BODY FREE!
KRAK
THERE--THAT GETS THE CHAIR OUT OF THE WAY--
--AND THIS BUNSEN BURNER SHOULD CUT RIGHT THROUGH THESE ROPES--
--LIKE SO!
OKAY, SO I'M FREE AND I KNOW WHAT PETE SAID ABOUT HIS PLANS WHILE HE WAS TYING ME UP...
...BUT WHAT DOES THAT ADD UP TO?
HOW THE HECK DO I STOP A "SUPERBOY" FROM KILLING SUPERMAN?
11

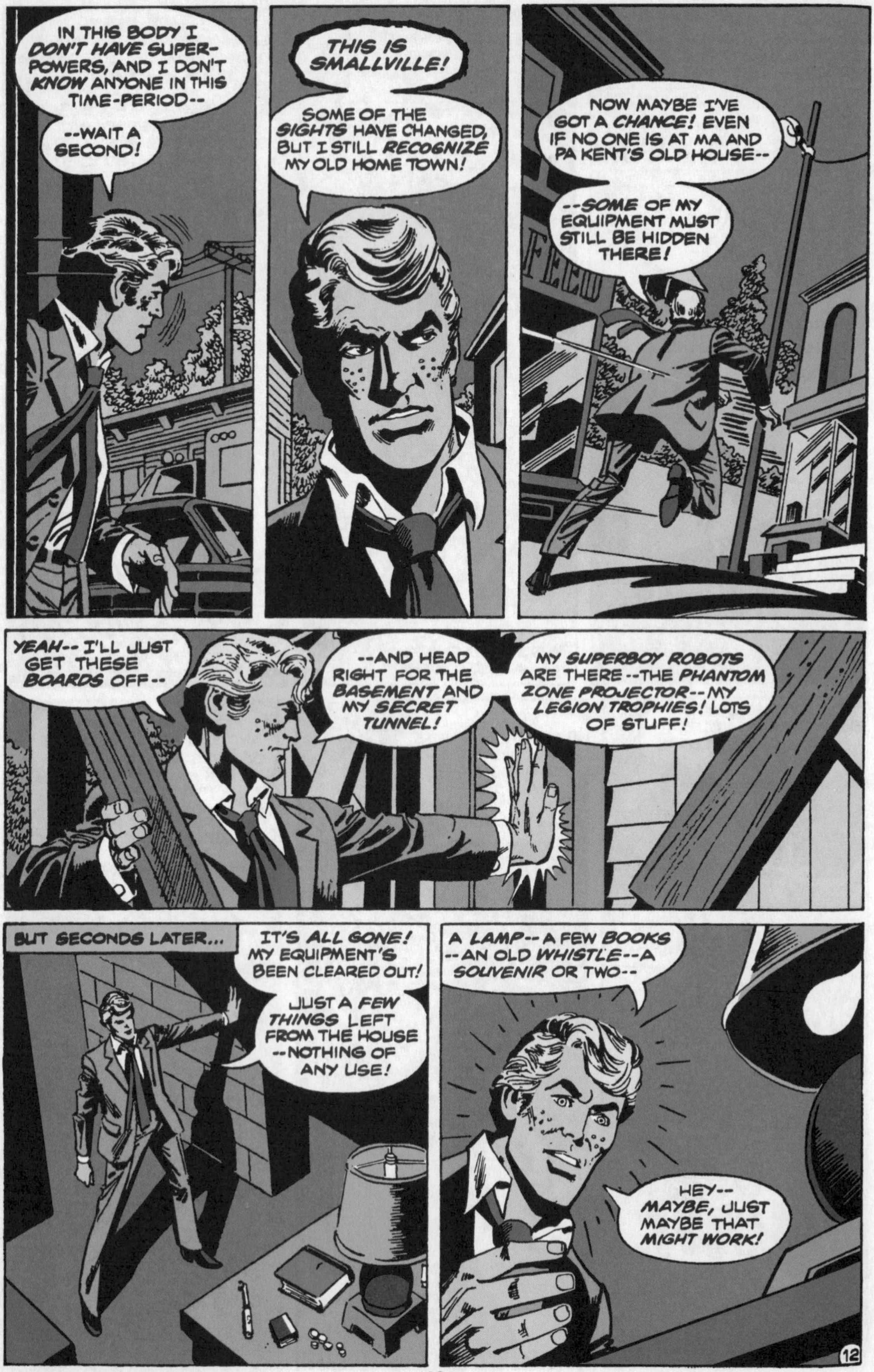
IN THIS BODY I DON'T HAVE SUPER-POWERS, AND I DON'T KNOW ANYONE IN THIS TIME-PERIOD--
--WAIT A SECOND!
THIS IS SMALLVILLE!
SOME OF THE SIGHTS HAVE CHANGED, BUT I STILL RECOGNIZE MY OLD HOME TOWN!
NOW MAYBE I'VE GOT A CHANCE! EVEN IF NO ONE IS AT MA AND PA KENT'S OLD HOUSE--
--SOME OF MY EQUIPMENT MUST STILL BE HIDDEN THERE!
FEED
YEAH-- I'LL JUST GET THESE BOARDS OFF--
--AND HEAD RIGHT FOR THE BASEMENT AND MY SECRET TUNNEL!
MY SUPERBOY ROBOTS ARE THERE--THE PHANTOM ZONE PROJECTOR--MY LEGION TROPHIES! LOTS OF STUFF!
BUT SECONDS LATER...
IT'S ALL GONE! MY EQUIPMENT'S BEEN CLEARED OUT!
JUST A FEW THINGS LEFT FROM THE HOUSE --NOTHING OF ANY USE!
A LAMP-- A FEW BOOKS --AN OLD WHISTLE--A SOUVENIR OR TWO--
HEY-- MAYBE, JUST MAYBE THAT MIGHT WORK!
12

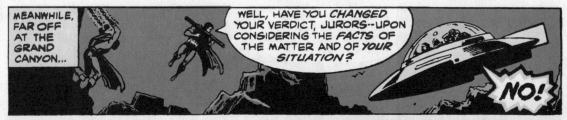

MEANWHILE, FAR OFF AT THE GRAND CANYON...

WELL, HAVE YOU *CHANGED* YOUR *VERDICT*, JURORS--UPON *CONSIDERING* THE *FACTS* OF THE MATTER AND OF *YOUR SITUATION?*

NO!

I *TOLD* YOU, ROSS--SUPERMAN'S *NOT GUILTY!*

NOW GET US *OUT* OF THIS FLYING SAUCER, YOU *LUNATIC!*

NO, MISTER WHITE--YOU'RE NOT GOING ANYWHERE!

YOU'RE MY *WITNESSES*--

--TO SUPERMAN'S *EXECUTION!*

BLAM

THE *GREEN KRYPTONITE SHELL* BURSTS FROM THE *LEADEN* BAZOOKA-- ITS *RADIATION* SPELLING CERTAIN DOOM FOR THE MAN OF STEEL!...

BUT AS THE SHELL SPEEDS *CLOSER*, THE STRAINING SUPERMAN GIVES ONE LAST HEROIC *BURST* OF STRENGTH--

SNAP

KRAK

--AND IT IS THE *MAN* IN HIM-- *NOT* THE SUPERMAN --THAT FINDS THE STRENGTH TO *BREAK FREE*--

KABLAM

NO! I *DON'T BELIEVE* IT--HE SNAPPED THE CHAINS!

IT *DOESN'T MATTER*, THOUGH --HE'S LYING ON THE GROUND *UNCONSCIOUS* AND *HELPLESS*--

--EVEN IF IT TAKES *EVERY* LAST ERG OF STRENGTH LEFT IN HIS BODY!

13

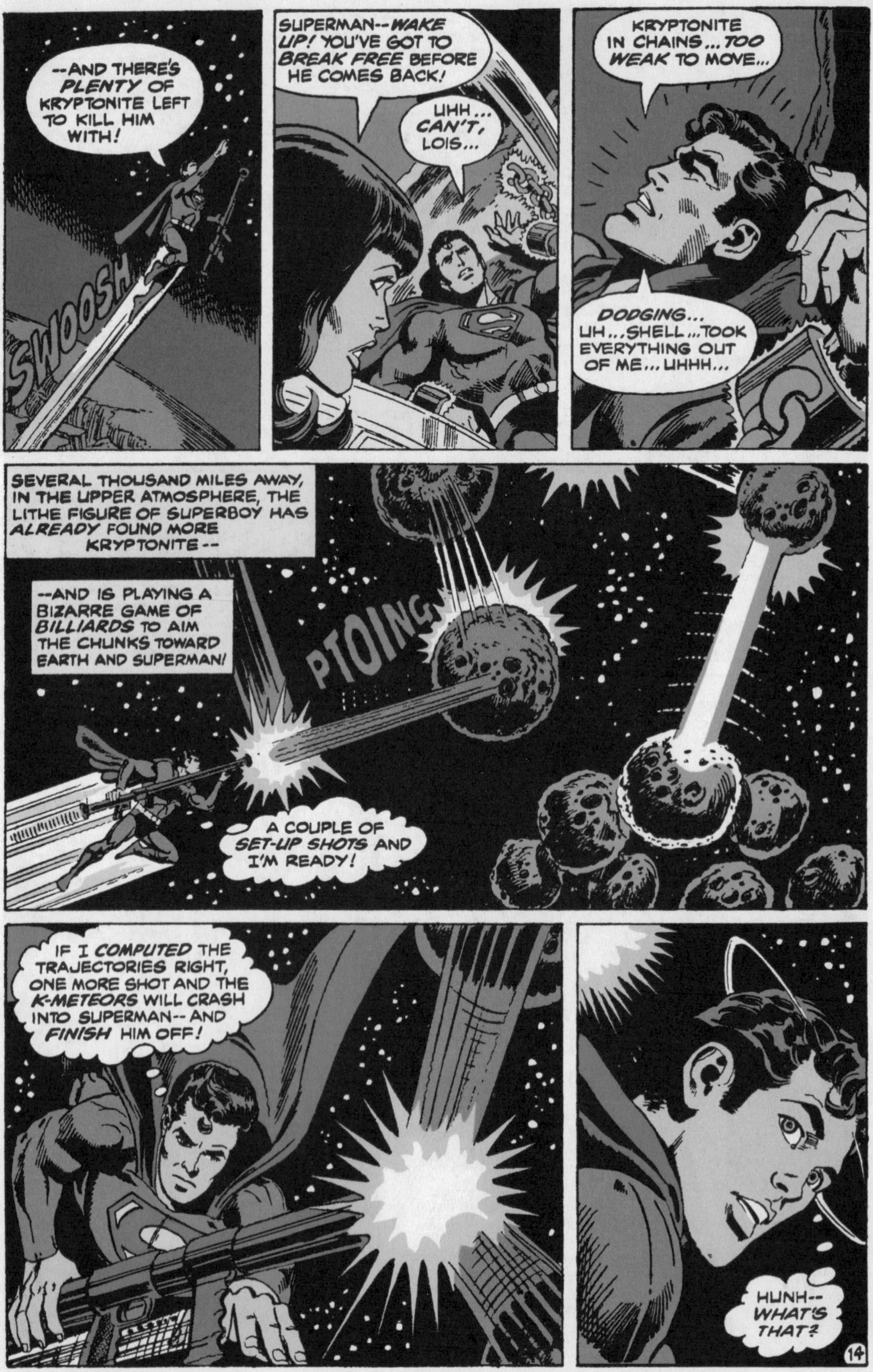
--AND THERE'S PLENTY OF KRYPTONITE LEFT TO KILL HIM WITH!
SWOOSH
SUPERMAN--WAKE UP! YOU'VE GOT TO BREAK FREE BEFORE HE COMES BACK!
UHH... CAN'T, LOIS...
KRYPTONITE IN CHAINS... TOO WEAK TO MOVE...
DODGING... UH... SHELL... TOOK EVERYTHING OUT OF ME... UHHH...
SEVERAL THOUSAND MILES AWAY, IN THE UPPER ATMOSPHERE, THE LITHE FIGURE OF SUPERBOY HAS ALREADY FOUND MORE KRYPTONITE--
--AND IS PLAYING A BIZARRE GAME OF BILLIARDS TO AIM THE CHUNKS TOWARD EARTH AND SUPERMAN!
PTOING
A COUPLE OF SET-UP SHOTS AND I'M READY!
IF I COMPUTED THE TRAJECTORIES RIGHT, ONE MORE SHOT AND THE K-METEORS WILL CRASH INTO SUPERMAN-- AND FINISH HIM OFF!
HUNH-- WHAT'S THAT?
14

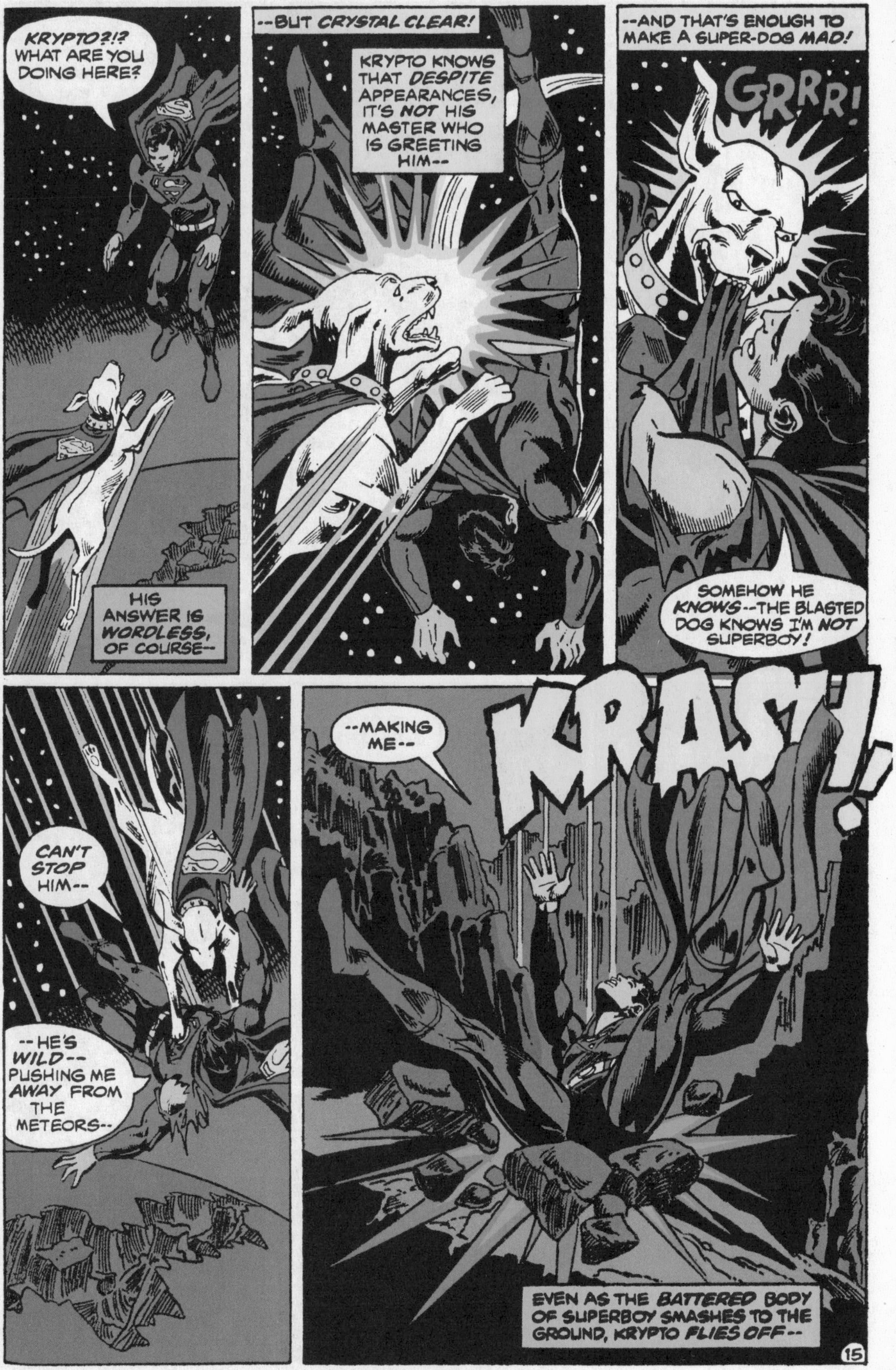
KRYPTO?!? WHAT ARE YOU DOING HERE?
HIS ANSWER IS WORDLESS, OF COURSE--
--BUT CRYSTAL CLEAR!
KRYPTO KNOWS THAT DESPITE APPEARANCES, IT'S NOT HIS MASTER WHO IS GREETING HIM--
--AND THAT'S ENOUGH TO MAKE A SUPER-DOG MAD!
GRRR!
SOMEHOW HE KNOWS--THE BLASTED DOG KNOWS I'M NOT SUPERBOY!
CAN'T STOP HIM--
--HE'S WILD--PUSHING ME AWAY FROM THE METEORS--
--MAKING ME--
KRASH!!
EVEN AS THE BATTERED BODY OF SUPERBOY SMASHES TO THE GROUND, KRYPTO FLIES OFF--
15

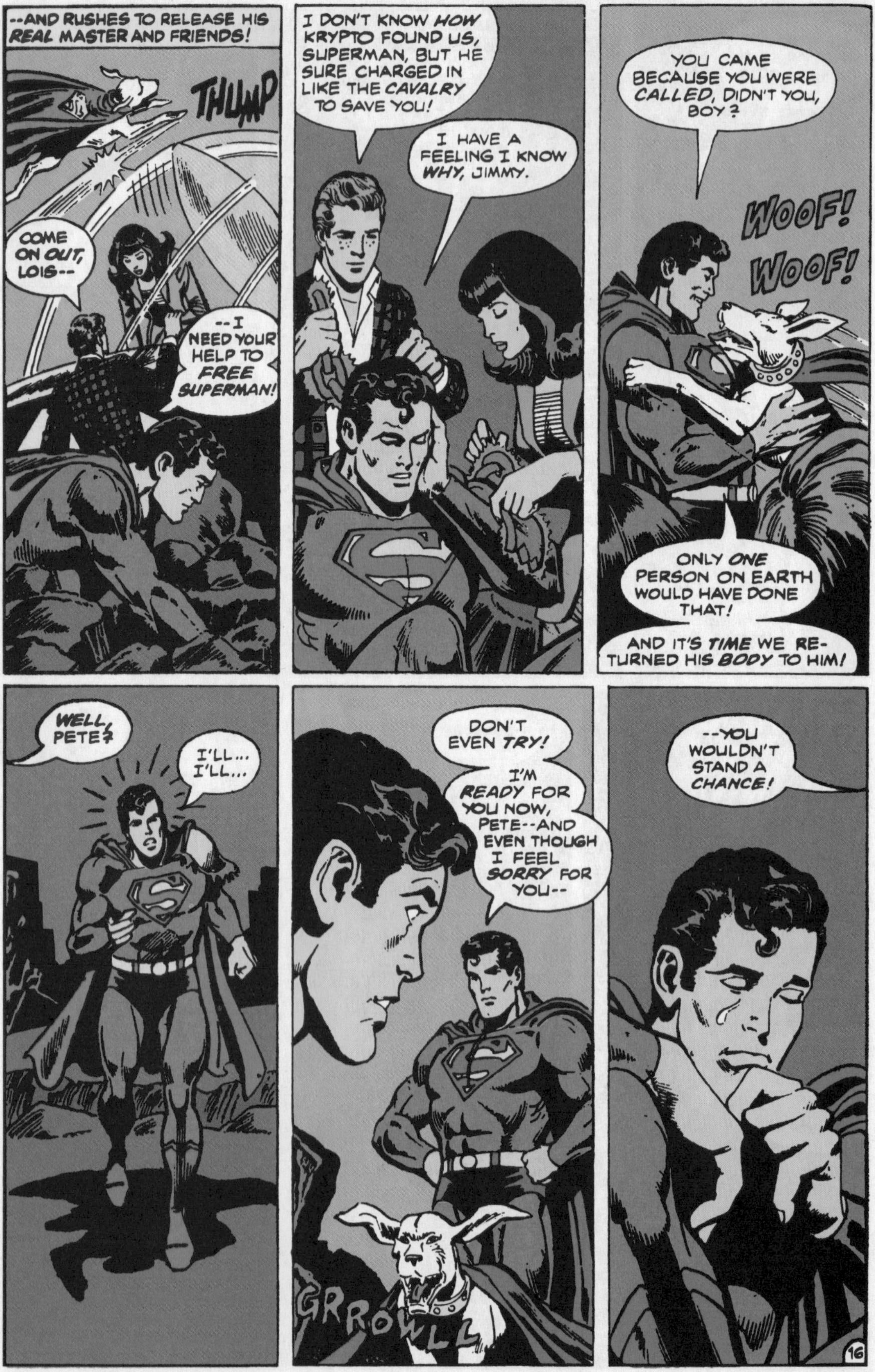
--AND RUSHES TO RELEASE HIS *REAL* MASTER AND FRIENDS!
THUMP
COME ON *OUT*, LOIS--
--I NEED YOUR HELP TO *FREE SUPERMAN*!
I DON'T KNOW *HOW* KRYPTO FOUND US, SUPERMAN, BUT HE SURE CHARGED IN LIKE THE *CAVALRY* TO SAVE YOU!
I HAVE A FEELING I KNOW *WHY*, JIMMY.
YOU CAME BECAUSE YOU WERE *CALLED*, DIDN'T YOU, BOY?
WOOF! WOOF!
ONLY *ONE* PERSON ON EARTH WOULD HAVE DONE THAT!
AND IT'S *TIME* WE RE-TURNED HIS *BODY* TO HIM!
WELL, PETE?
I'LL... I'LL...
DON'T EVEN *TRY*!
I'M *READY* FOR YOU NOW, PETE--AND EVEN THOUGH I FEEL *SORRY* FOR YOU--
GRROWLL
--YOU WOULDN'T STAND A *CHANCE*!
16

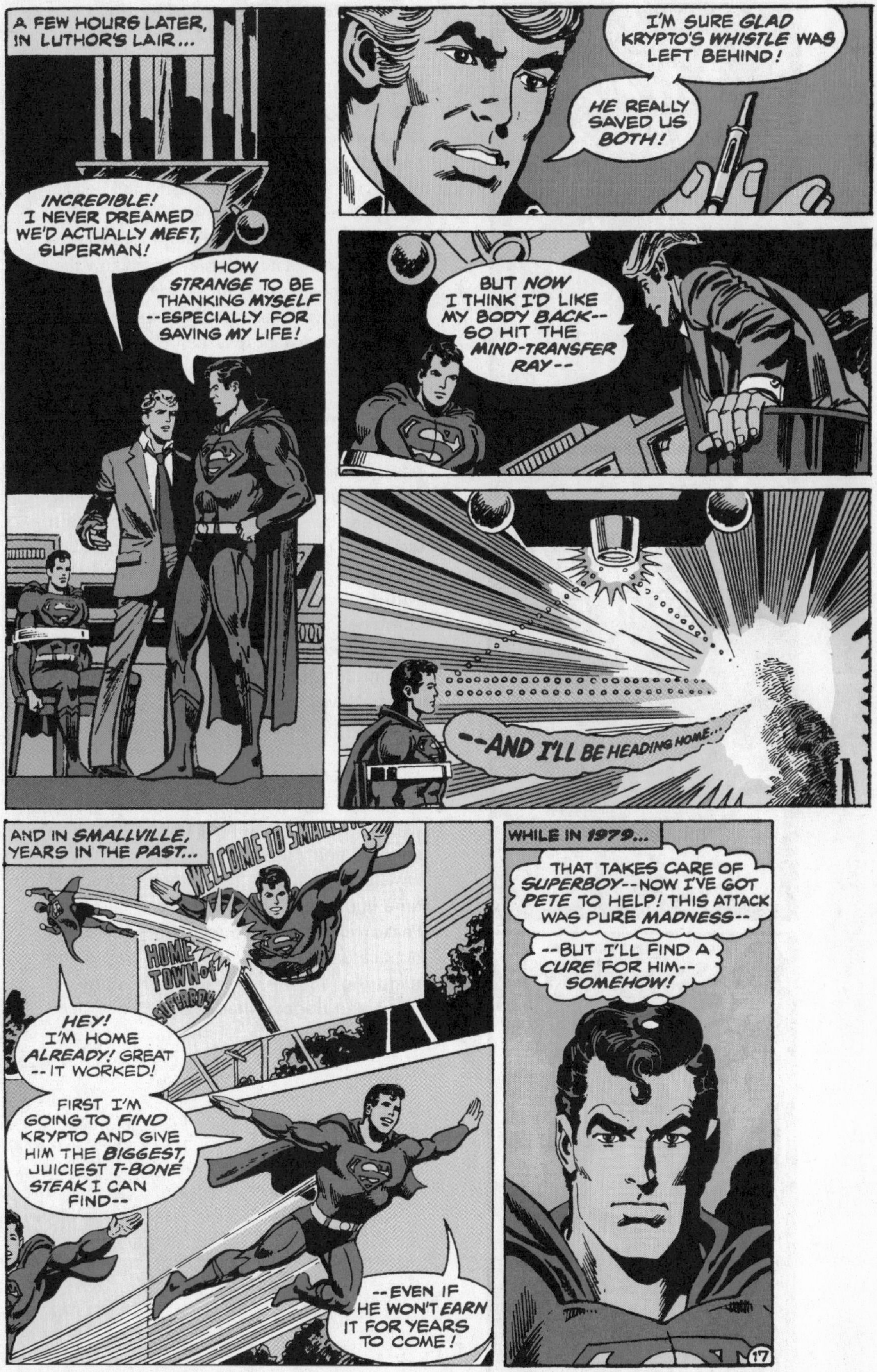
A FEW HOURS LATER, IN LUTHOR'S LAIR...
INCREDIBLE! I NEVER DREAMED WE'D ACTUALLY MEET, SUPERMAN!
HOW STRANGE TO BE THANKING MYSELF --ESPECIALLY FOR SAVING MY LIFE!
I'M SURE GLAD KRYPTO'S WHISTLE WAS LEFT BEHIND!
HE REALLY SAVED US BOTH!
BUT NOW I THINK I'D LIKE MY BODY BACK-- SO HIT THE MIND-TRANSFER RAY--
--AND I'LL BE HEADING HOME...
AND IN SMALLVILLE, YEARS IN THE PAST...
WELCOME TO SMALLV
HOME TOWN of SUPERBOY
HEY! I'M HOME ALREADY! GREAT --IT WORKED!
FIRST I'M GOING TO FIND KRYPTO AND GIVE HIM THE BIGGEST, JUICIEST T-BONE STEAK I CAN FIND--
--EVEN IF HE WON'T EARN IT FOR YEARS TO COME!
WHILE IN 1979...
THAT TAKES CARE OF SUPERBOY--NOW I'VE GOT PETE TO HELP! THIS ATTACK WAS PURE MADNESS--
--BUT I'LL FIND A CURE FOR HIM-- SOMEHOW!
17

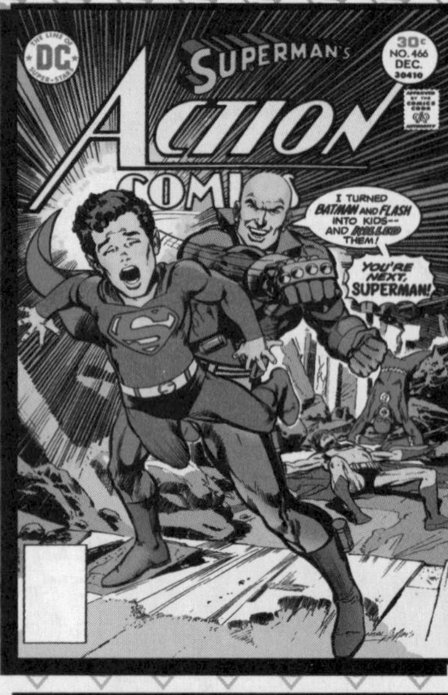
SUPERMAN'S
ACTION COMICS
30¢ NO. 466 DEC.
I TURNED BATMAN AND FLASH INTO KIDS--
YOU'RE NEXT, SUPERMAN!

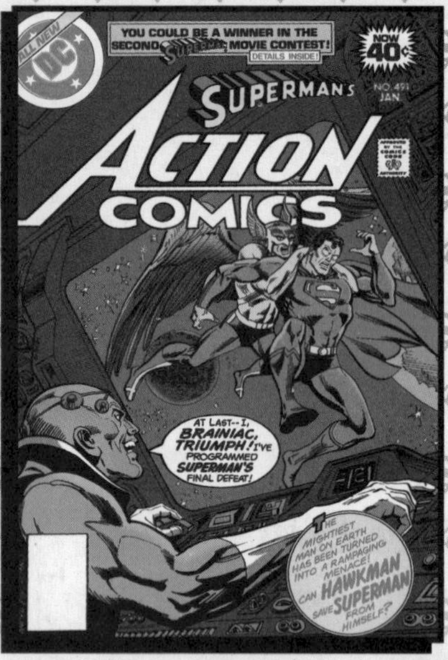
YOU COULD BE A WINNER IN THE SECOND SUPERMAN MOVIE CONTEST! DETAILS INSIDE!
NOW 40¢
SUPERMAN'S
ACTION COMICS
AT LAST--I, BRAINIAC, TRIUMPH! I'VE PROGRAMMED SUPERMAN'S FINAL DEFEAT!
THE MIGHTIEST MAN ON EARTH HAS BEEN TURNED INTO A RAMPAGING MENACE! CAN HAWKMAN SAVE SUPERMAN FROM HIMSELF?

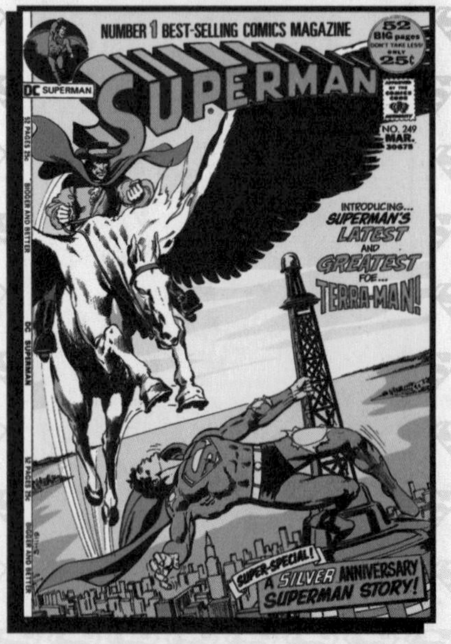
NUMBER 1 BEST-SELLING COMICS MAGAZINE
52 BIG pages 25¢
SUPERMAN
NO. 249 MAR.
INTRODUCING... SUPERMAN'S LATEST AND GREATEST FOE... TERRA-MAN!
SUPER-SPECIAL! A SILVER ANNIVERSARY SUPERMAN STORY!

THE VILLAINS

For Superman's Rogues Gallery, the seventies was a decade of redefinition and resurgence. Lex Luthor received the biggest makeover; formerly a paunchy, physically unimpressive man clad exclusively in prison grays, he adopted an action suit which at last allowed him to go toe-to-toe with his hated nemesis. Meanwhile, super-scribes Len Wein, Cary Bates and Elliot Maggin took turns delving into the evil genius's dark psyche, exploring his hatred for the Man of Steel and giving it a depth that would make readers shudder.

Longtime foes Brainiac and Parasite, on the other hand, spent increasingly less time bedeviling the Man of Steel, edged out by the new gunslinger in town — Terra-Man, inspired by the then-popular spaghetti westerns of Clint Eastwood. Created by Bates, Terra-Man (or "Earth-Man," an ironic wink at Superman's alien heritage) combined the past of the Old West with the science-fiction world of tomorrow to commit fantastic crimes astride his winged horse, Nova.

Shortly thereafter, writer Marty Pasko "adopted" two more long-ignored super-enemies as his own. First, Pasko recast the laughable Toyman as a homicidal maniac with a penchant for deadly mechanical soldiers and razor-edged Frisbees, making him seem genuinely dangerous for the first time in... well, ever. Immediately thereafter, Pasko reintroduced Superman's imperfect duplicate, Bizarro, tweaking his powers and restoring to the character an edge of fright and tragedy that has not since been forgotten.

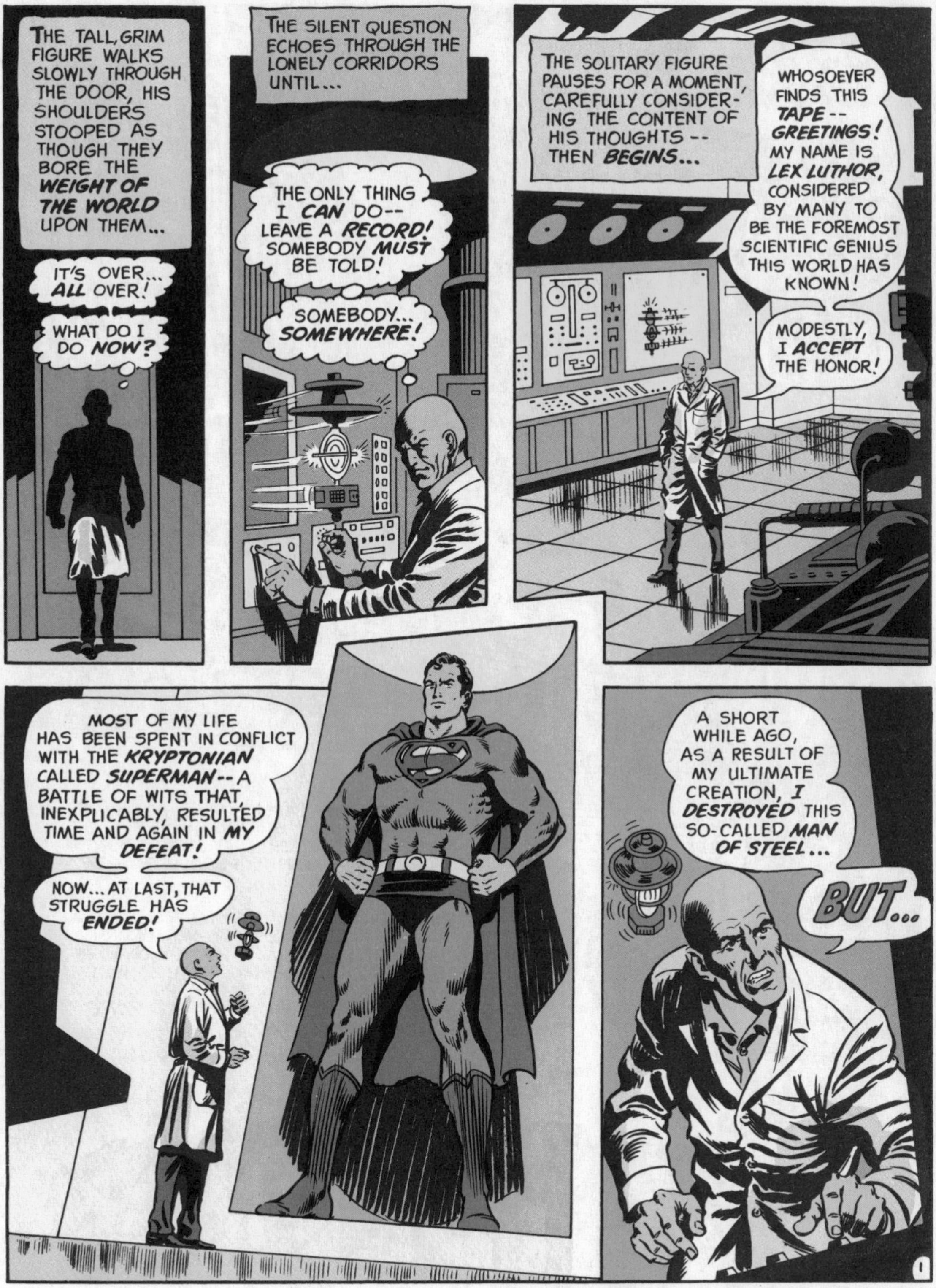
THE TALL, GRIM FIGURE WALKS SLOWLY THROUGH THE DOOR, HIS SHOULDERS STOOPED AS THOUGH THEY BORE THE WEIGHT OF THE WORLD UPON THEM...
IT'S OVER... ALL OVER!
WHAT DO I DO NOW?
THE SILENT QUESTION ECHOES THROUGH THE LONELY CORRIDORS UNTIL...
THE ONLY THING I CAN DO-- LEAVE A RECORD! SOMEBODY MUST BE TOLD!
SOMEBODY... SOMEWHERE!
THE SOLITARY FIGURE PAUSES FOR A MOMENT, CAREFULLY CONSIDERING THE CONTENT OF HIS THOUGHTS -- THEN BEGINS...
WHOSOEVER FINDS THIS TAPE -- GREETINGS! MY NAME IS LEX LUTHOR, CONSIDERED BY MANY TO BE THE FOREMOST SCIENTIFIC GENIUS THIS WORLD HAS KNOWN!
MODESTLY, I ACCEPT THE HONOR!
MOST OF MY LIFE HAS BEEN SPENT IN CONFLICT WITH THE KRYPTONIAN CALLED SUPERMAN-- A BATTLE OF WITS THAT, INEXPLICABLY, RESULTED TIME AND AGAIN IN MY DEFEAT!
NOW... AT LAST, THAT STRUGGLE HAS ENDED!
A SHORT WHILE AGO, AS A RESULT OF MY ULTIMATE CREATION, I DESTROYED THIS SO-CALLED MAN OF STEEL...
BUT...

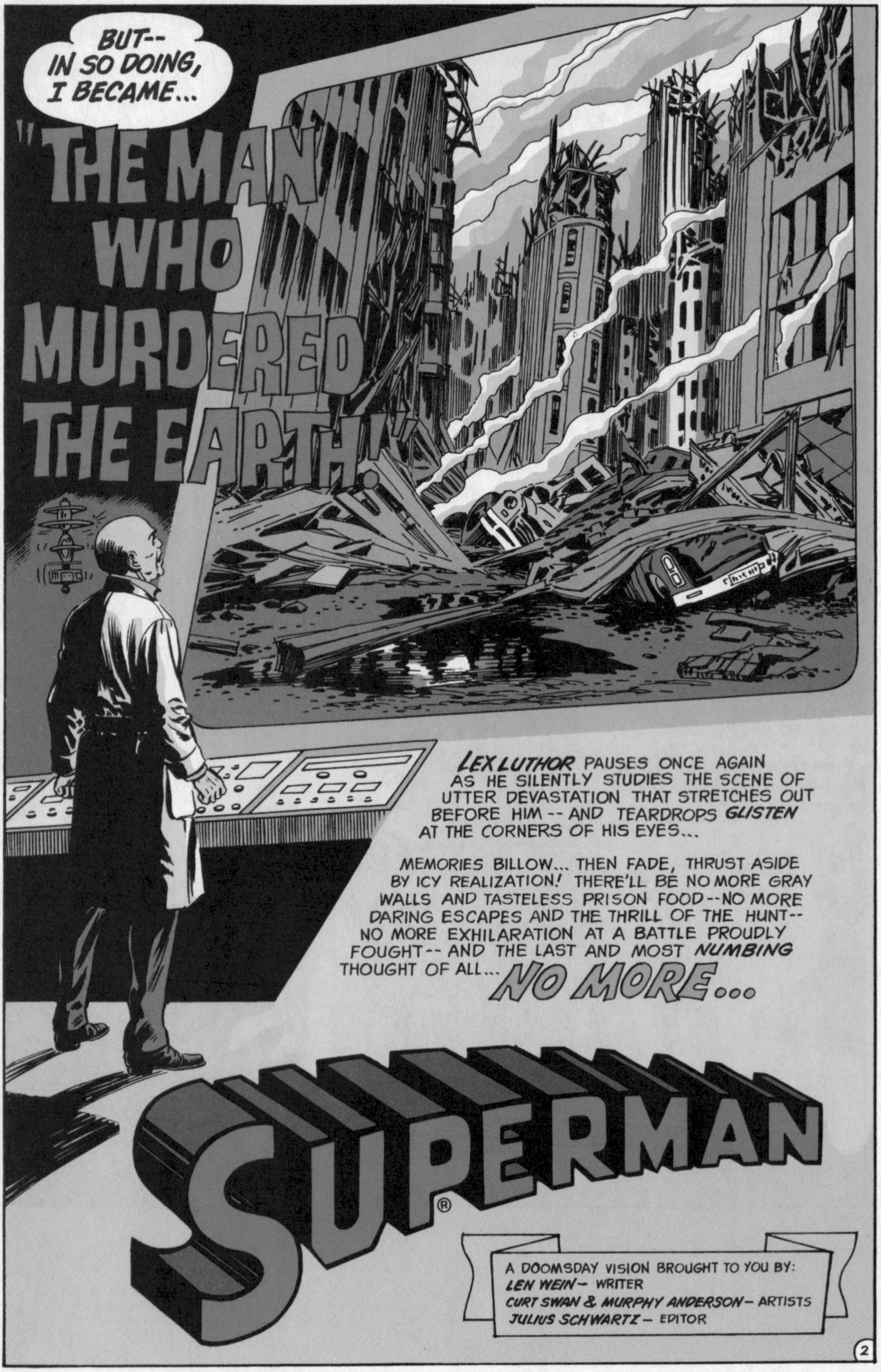
BUT-- IN SO DOING, I BECAME...
"THE MAN WHO MURDERED THE EARTH!"
LEX LUTHOR PAUSES ONCE AGAIN AS HE SILENTLY STUDIES THE SCENE OF UTTER DEVASTATION THAT STRETCHES OUT BEFORE HIM -- AND TEARDROPS GLISTEN AT THE CORNERS OF HIS EYES...
MEMORIES BILLOW... THEN FADE, THRUST ASIDE BY ICY REALIZATION! THERE'LL BE NO MORE GRAY WALLS AND TASTELESS PRISON FOOD--NO MORE DARING ESCAPES AND THE THRILL OF THE HUNT-- NO MORE EXHILARATION AT A BATTLE PROUDLY FOUGHT-- AND THE LAST AND MOST NUMBING THOUGHT OF ALL... NO MORE...
SUPERMAN®
A DOOMSDAY VISION BROUGHT TO YOU BY:
LEN WEIN- WRITER
CURT SWAN & MURPHY ANDERSON- ARTISTS
JULIUS SCHWARTZ- EDITOR
2

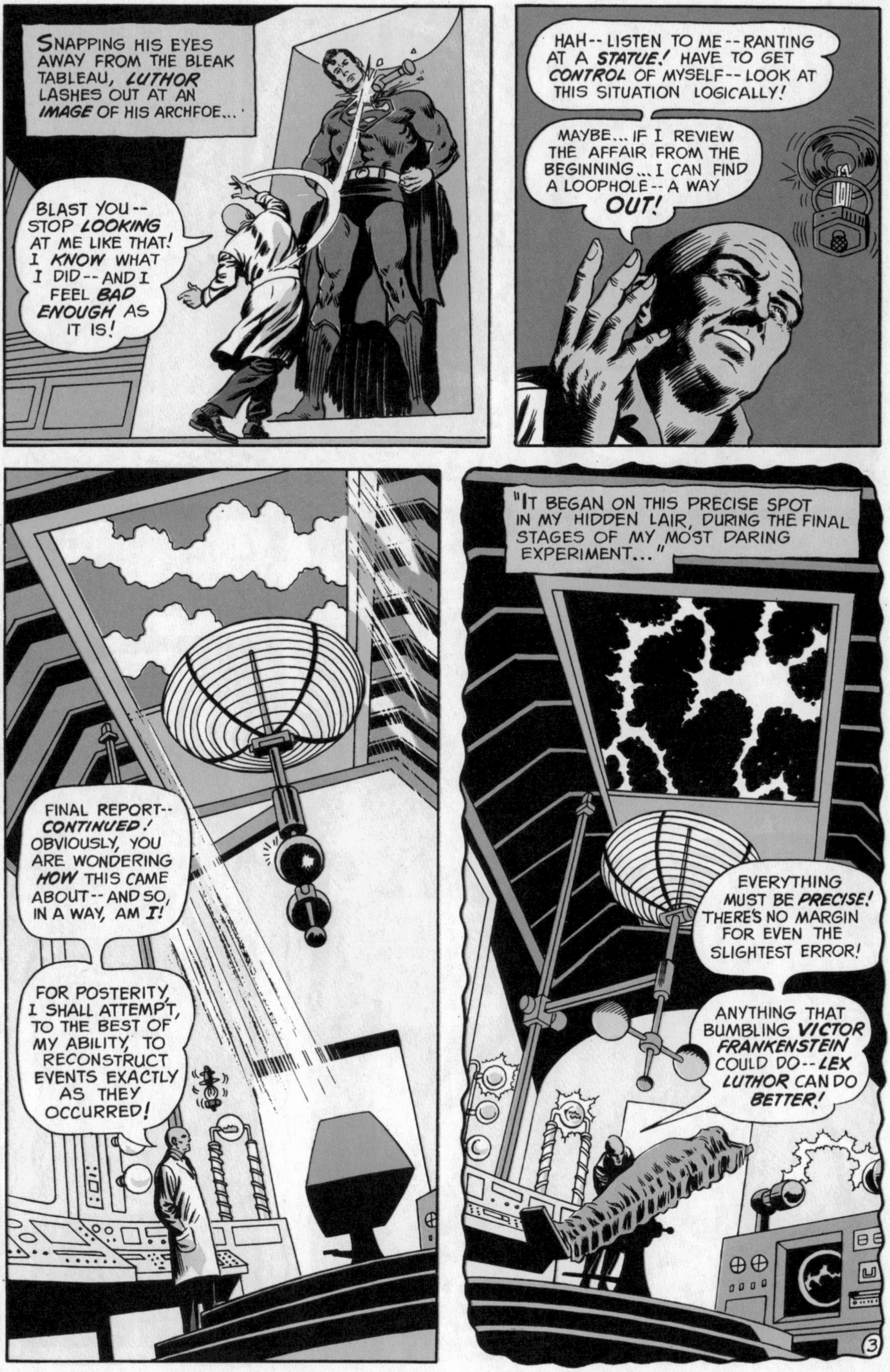
SNAPPING HIS EYES AWAY FROM THE BLEAK TABLEAU, LUTHOR LASHES OUT AT AN IMAGE OF HIS ARCHFOE...
BLAST YOU-- STOP LOOKING AT ME LIKE THAT! I KNOW WHAT I DID--AND I FEEL BAD ENOUGH AS IT IS!
HAH--LISTEN TO ME--RANTING AT A STATUE! HAVE TO GET CONTROL OF MYSELF--LOOK AT THIS SITUATION LOGICALLY!
MAYBE...IF I REVIEW THE AFFAIR FROM THE BEGINNING...I CAN FIND A LOOPHOLE--A WAY OUT!
FINAL REPORT-- CONTINUED! OBVIOUSLY, YOU ARE WONDERING HOW THIS CAME ABOUT--AND SO, IN A WAY, AM I!
FOR POSTERITY, I SHALL ATTEMPT, TO THE BEST OF MY ABILITY, TO RECONSTRUCT EVENTS EXACTLY AS THEY OCCURRED!
"IT BEGAN ON THIS PRECISE SPOT IN MY HIDDEN LAIR, DURING THE FINAL STAGES OF MY MOST DARING EXPERIMENT..."
EVERYTHING MUST BE PRECISE! THERE'S NO MARGIN FOR EVEN THE SLIGHTEST ERROR!
ANYTHING THAT BUMBLING VICTOR FRANKENSTEIN COULD DO--LEX LUTHOR CAN DO BETTER!
3

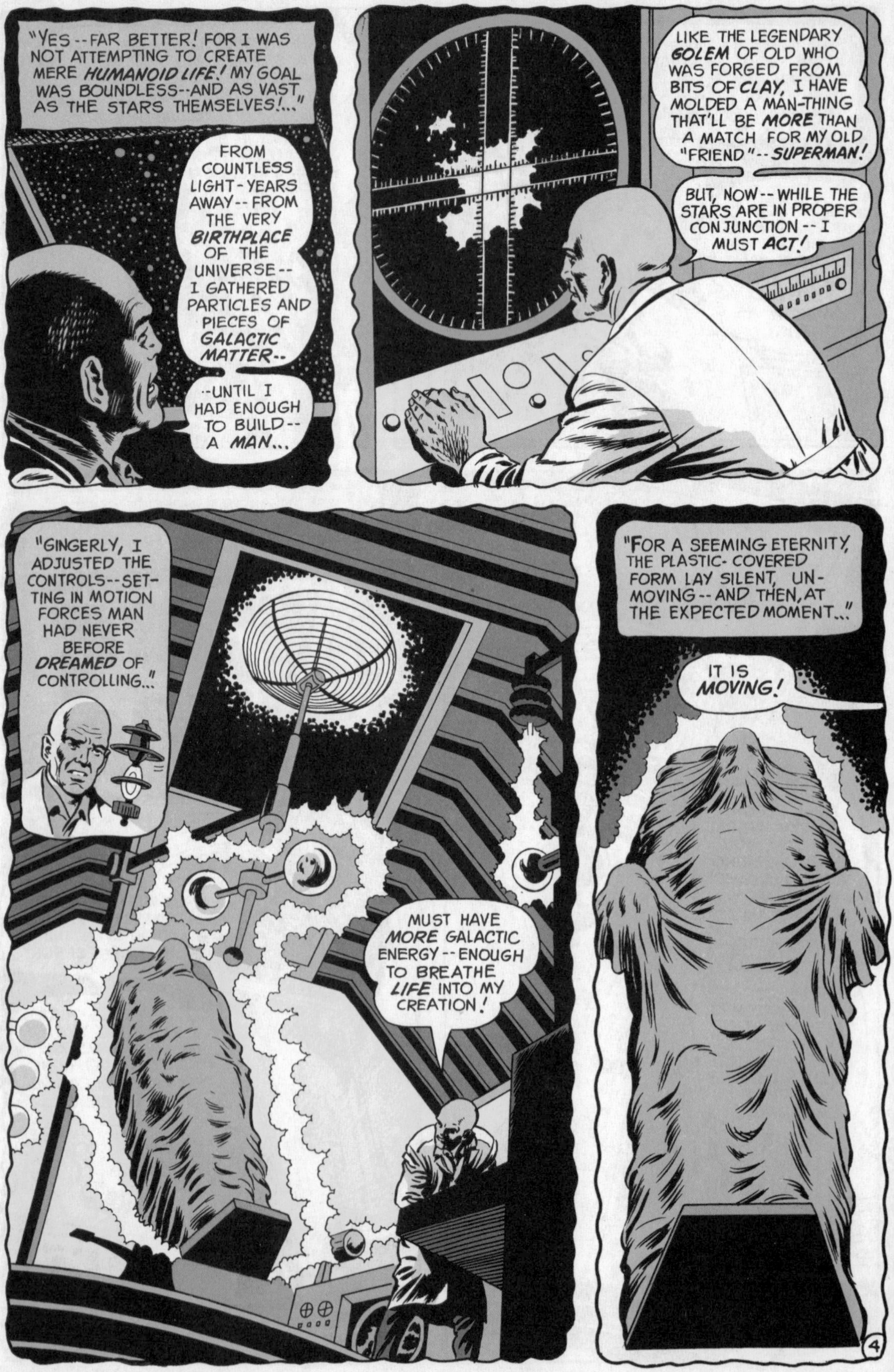
"YES -- FAR BETTER! FOR I WAS NOT ATTEMPTING TO CREATE MERE HUMANOID LIFE! MY GOAL WAS BOUNDLESS--AND AS VAST AS THE STARS THEMSELVES!..."
FROM COUNTLESS LIGHT-YEARS AWAY -- FROM THE VERY BIRTHPLACE OF THE UNIVERSE -- I GATHERED PARTICLES AND PIECES OF GALACTIC MATTER --
--UNTIL I HAD ENOUGH TO BUILD -- A MAN...
LIKE THE LEGENDARY GOLEM OF OLD WHO WAS FORGED FROM BITS OF CLAY, I HAVE MOLDED A MAN-THING THAT'LL BE MORE THAN A MATCH FOR MY OLD "FRIEND" -- SUPERMAN!
BUT, NOW -- WHILE THE STARS ARE IN PROPER CONJUNCTION -- I MUST ACT!
"GINGERLY, I ADJUSTED THE CONTROLS--SETTING IN MOTION FORCES MAN HAD NEVER BEFORE DREAMED OF CONTROLLING..."
MUST HAVE MORE GALACTIC ENERGY -- ENOUGH TO BREATHE LIFE INTO MY CREATION!
"FOR A SEEMING ETERNITY, THE PLASTIC-COVERED FORM LAY SILENT, UNMOVING -- AND THEN, AT THE EXPECTED MOMENT..."
IT IS MOVING!
4

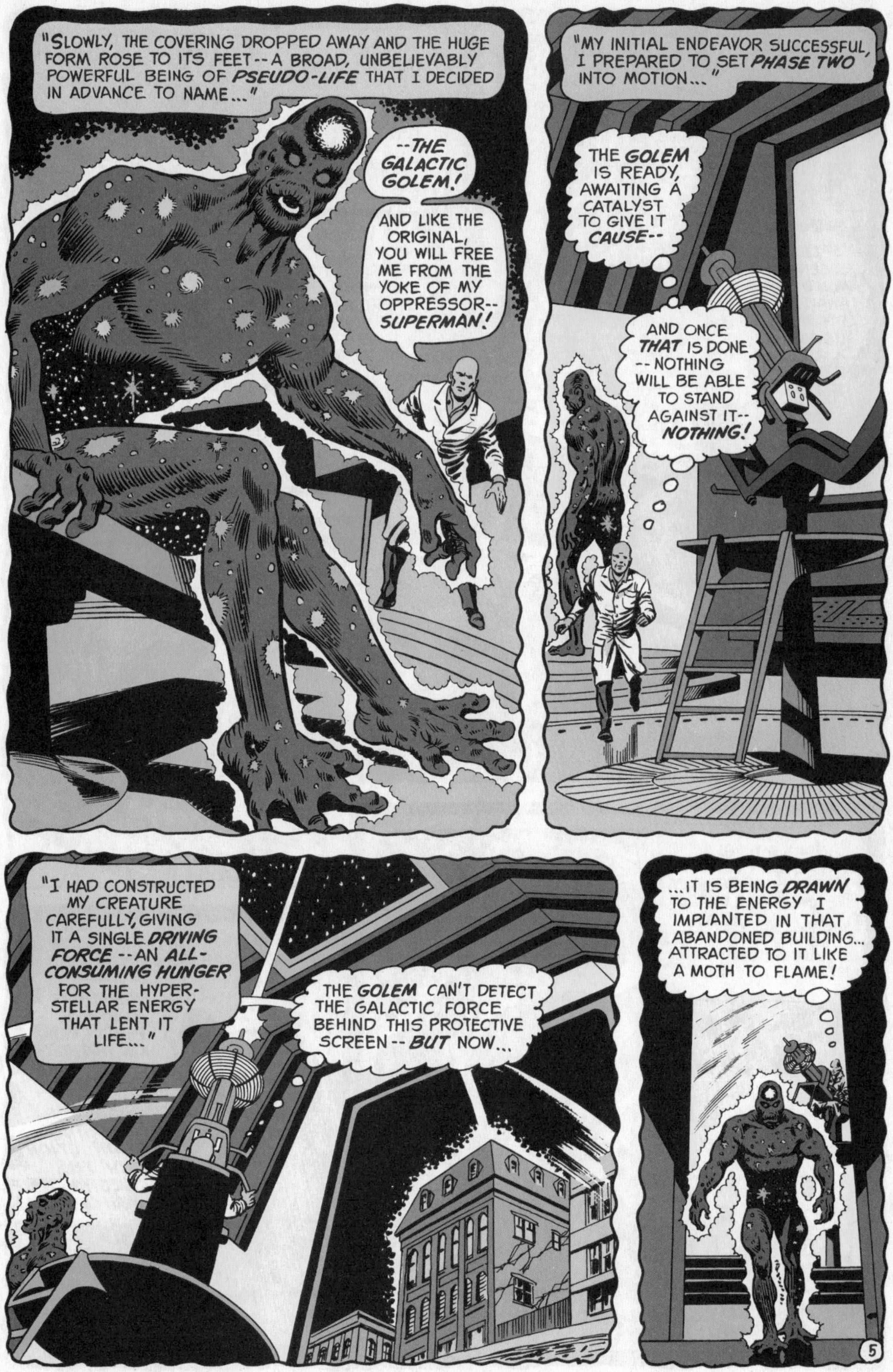
"SLOWLY, THE COVERING DROPPED AWAY AND THE HUGE FORM ROSE TO ITS FEET -- A BROAD, UNBELIEVABLY POWERFUL BEING OF PSEUDO-LIFE THAT I DECIDED IN ADVANCE TO NAME..."
--THE GALACTIC GOLEM!
AND LIKE THE ORIGINAL, YOU WILL FREE ME FROM THE YOKE OF MY OPPRESSOR-- SUPERMAN!
"MY INITIAL ENDEAVOR SUCCESSFUL, I PREPARED TO SET PHASE TWO INTO MOTION..."
THE GOLEM IS READY, AWAITING A CATALYST TO GIVE IT CAUSE--
AND ONCE THAT IS DONE -- NOTHING WILL BE ABLE TO STAND AGAINST IT-- NOTHING!
"I HAD CONSTRUCTED MY CREATURE CAREFULLY, GIVING IT A SINGLE DRIVING FORCE --AN ALL-CONSUMING HUNGER FOR THE HYPER-STELLAR ENERGY THAT LENT IT LIFE..."
THE GOLEM CAN'T DETECT THE GALACTIC FORCE BEHIND THIS PROTECTIVE SCREEN -- BUT NOW...
...IT IS BEING DRAWN TO THE ENERGY I IMPLANTED IN THAT ABANDONED BUILDING... ATTRACTED TO IT LIKE A MOTH TO FLAME!
5

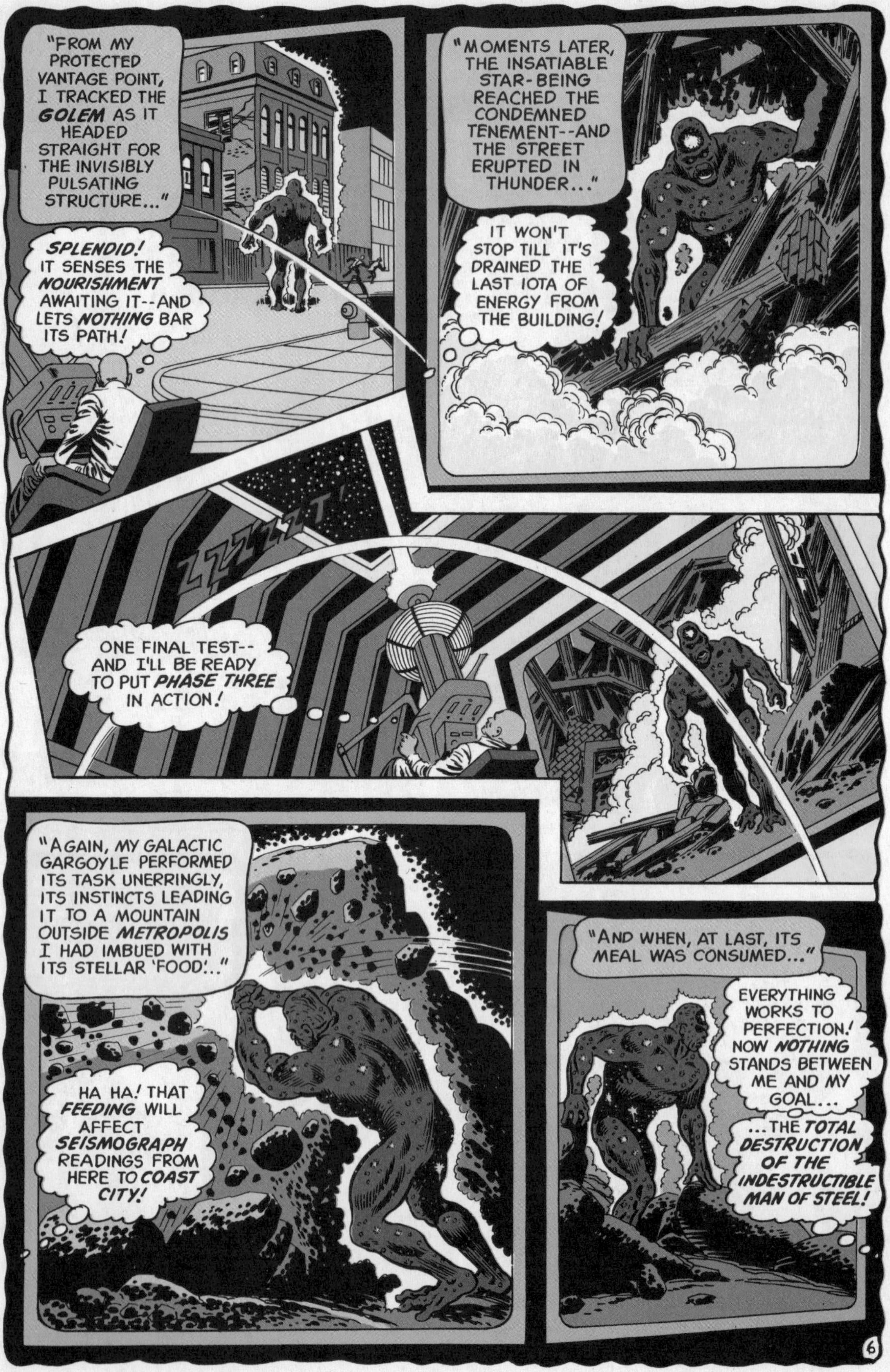
"FROM MY PROTECTED VANTAGE POINT, I TRACKED THE GOLEM AS IT HEADED STRAIGHT FOR THE INVISIBLY PULSATING STRUCTURE..."
SPLENDID! IT SENSES THE NOURISHMENT AWAITING IT--AND LETS NOTHING BAR ITS PATH!
"MOMENTS LATER, THE INSATIABLE STAR-BEING REACHED THE CONDEMNED TENEMENT--AND THE STREET ERUPTED IN THUNDER..."
IT WON'T STOP TILL IT'S DRAINED THE LAST IOTA OF ENERGY FROM THE BUILDING!
ZZZZZT!
ONE FINAL TEST--AND I'LL BE READY TO PUT PHASE THREE IN ACTION!
"AGAIN, MY GALACTIC GARGOYLE PERFORMED ITS TASK UNERRINGLY, ITS INSTINCTS LEADING IT TO A MOUNTAIN OUTSIDE METROPOLIS I HAD IMBUED WITH ITS STELLAR 'FOOD'..."
HA HA! THAT FEEDING WILL AFFECT SEISMOGRAPH READINGS FROM HERE TO COAST CITY!
"AND WHEN, AT LAST, ITS MEAL WAS CONSUMED..."
EVERYTHING WORKS TO PERFECTION! NOW NOTHING STANDS BETWEEN ME AND MY GOAL...
...THE TOTAL DESTRUCTION OF THE INDESTRUCTIBLE MAN OF STEEL!
6

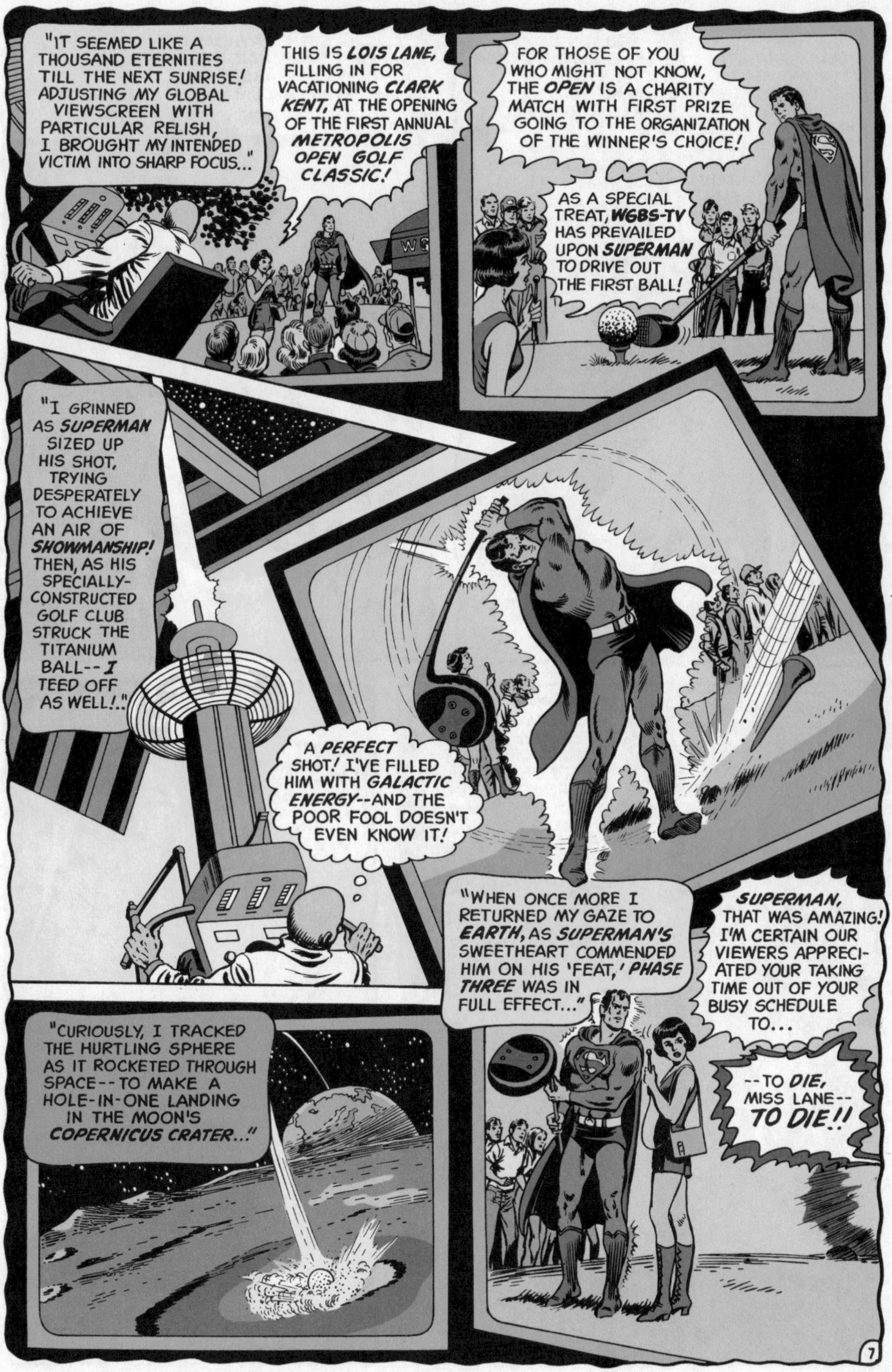
"IT SEEMED LIKE A THOUSAND ETERNITIES TILL THE NEXT SUNRISE! ADJUSTING MY GLOBAL VIEWSCREEN WITH PARTICULAR RELISH, I BROUGHT MY INTENDED VICTIM INTO SHARP FOCUS..."
THIS IS LOIS LANE, FILLING IN FOR VACATIONING CLARK KENT, AT THE OPENING OF THE FIRST ANNUAL METROPOLIS OPEN GOLF CLASSIC!
FOR THOSE OF YOU WHO MIGHT NOT KNOW, THE OPEN IS A CHARITY MATCH WITH FIRST PRIZE GOING TO THE ORGANIZATION OF THE WINNER'S CHOICE!
AS A SPECIAL TREAT, WGBS-TV HAS PREVAILED UPON SUPERMAN TO DRIVE OUT THE FIRST BALL!
"I GRINNED AS SUPERMAN SIZED UP HIS SHOT, TRYING DESPERATELY TO ACHIEVE AN AIR OF SHOWMANSHIP! THEN, AS HIS SPECIALLY-CONSTRUCTED GOLF CLUB STRUCK THE TITANIUM BALL--I TEED OFF AS WELL!."
A PERFECT SHOT! I'VE FILLED HIM WITH GALACTIC ENERGY--AND THE POOR FOOL DOESN'T EVEN KNOW IT!
"CURIOUSLY, I TRACKED THE HURTLING SPHERE AS IT ROCKETED THROUGH SPACE--TO MAKE A HOLE-IN-ONE LANDING IN THE MOON'S COPERNICUS CRATER..."
"WHEN ONCE MORE I RETURNED MY GAZE TO EARTH, AS SUPERMAN'S SWEETHEART COMMENDED HIM ON HIS 'FEAT,' PHASE THREE WAS IN FULL EFFECT..."
SUPERMAN, THAT WAS AMAZING! I'M CERTAIN OUR VIEWERS APPRECIATED YOUR TAKING TIME OUT OF YOUR BUSY SCHEDULE TO...
--TO DIE, MISS LANE--TO DIE!!
7

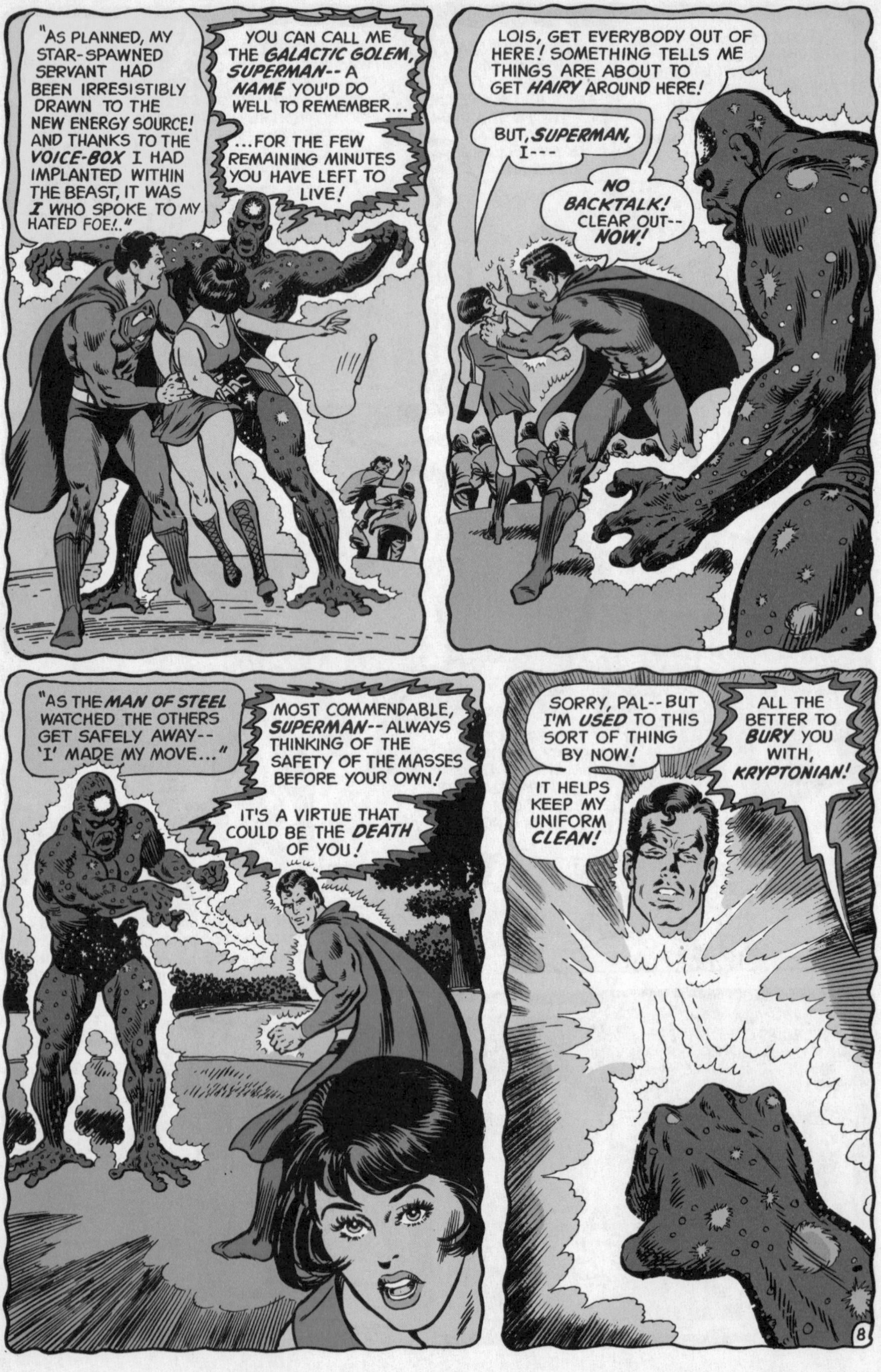
"AS PLANNED, MY STAR-SPAWNED SERVANT HAD BEEN IRRESISTIBLY DRAWN TO THE NEW ENERGY SOURCE! AND THANKS TO THE VOICE-BOX I HAD IMPLANTED WITHIN THE BEAST, IT WAS I WHO SPOKE TO MY HATED FOE!.."
YOU CAN CALL ME THE GALACTIC GOLEM, SUPERMAN-- A NAME YOU'D DO WELL TO REMEMBER...
...FOR THE FEW REMAINING MINUTES YOU HAVE LEFT TO LIVE!
LOIS, GET EVERYBODY OUT OF HERE! SOMETHING TELLS ME THINGS ARE ABOUT TO GET HAIRY AROUND HERE!
BUT, SUPERMAN, I---
NO BACKTALK! CLEAR OUT-- NOW!
"AS THE MAN OF STEEL WATCHED THE OTHERS GET SAFELY AWAY-- 'I' MADE MY MOVE..."
MOST COMMENDABLE, SUPERMAN-- ALWAYS THINKING OF THE SAFETY OF THE MASSES BEFORE YOUR OWN!
IT'S A VIRTUE THAT COULD BE THE DEATH OF YOU!
SORRY, PAL--BUT I'M USED TO THIS SORT OF THING BY NOW!
IT HELPS KEEP MY UNIFORM CLEAN!
ALL THE BETTER TO BURY YOU WITH, KRYPTONIAN!
8

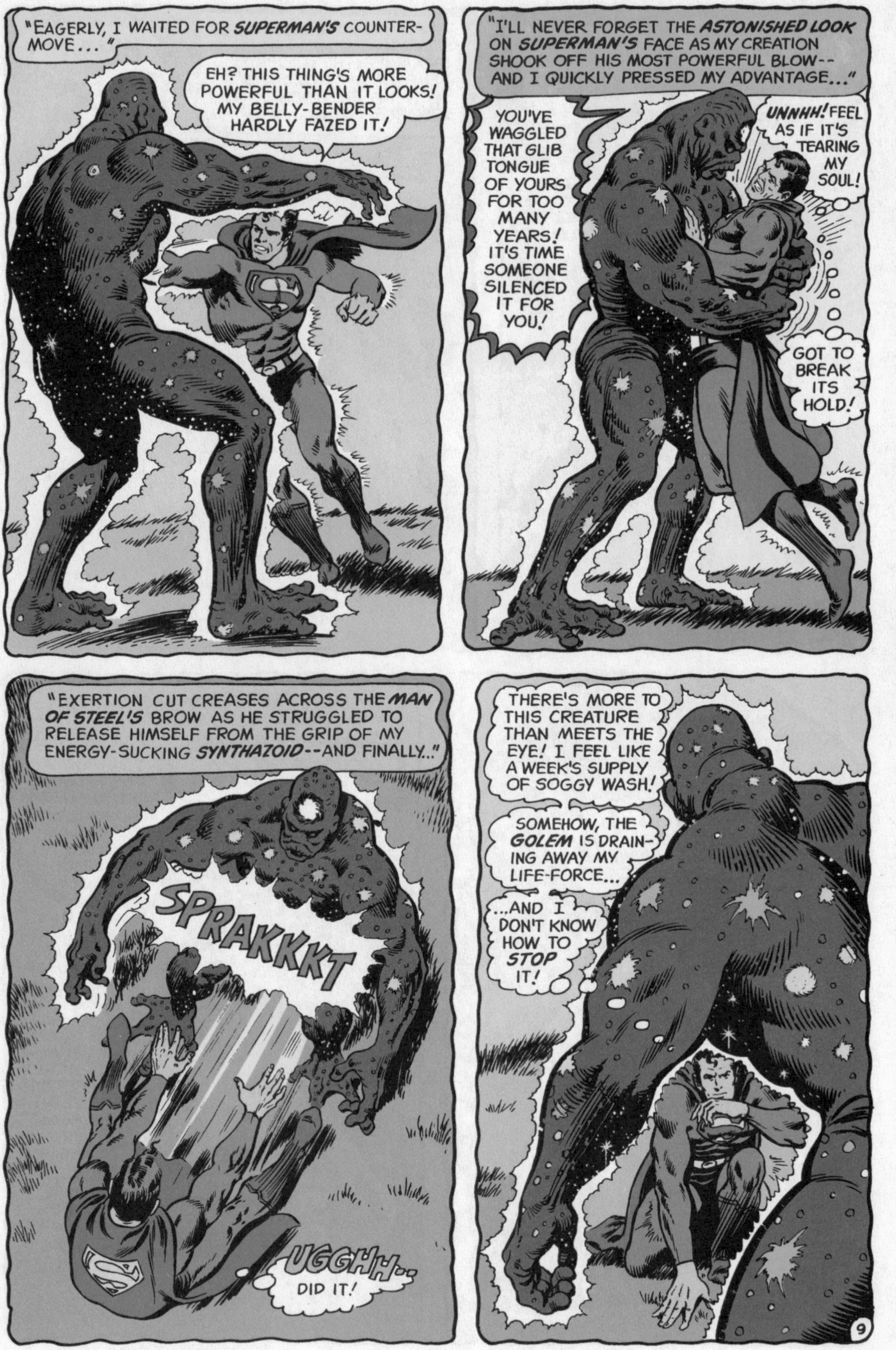
"EAGERLY, I WAITED FOR SUPERMAN'S COUNTER-MOVE..."
EH? THIS THING'S MORE POWERFUL THAN IT LOOKS! MY BELLY-BENDER HARDLY FAZED IT!
"I'LL NEVER FORGET THE ASTONISHED LOOK ON SUPERMAN'S FACE AS MY CREATION SHOOK OFF HIS MOST POWERFUL BLOW-- AND I QUICKLY PRESSED MY ADVANTAGE..."
YOU'VE WAGGLED THAT GLIB TONGUE OF YOURS FOR TOO MANY YEARS! IT'S TIME SOMEONE SILENCED IT FOR YOU!
UNNHH! FEEL AS IF IT'S TEARING MY SOUL!
GOT TO BREAK ITS HOLD!
"EXERTION CUT CREASES ACROSS THE MAN OF STEEL'S BROW AS HE STRUGGLED TO RELEASE HIMSELF FROM THE GRIP OF MY ENERGY-SUCKING SYNTHAZOID--AND FINALLY..."
SPRAKKKT
UGGHH.. DID IT!
THERE'S MORE TO THIS CREATURE THAN MEETS THE EYE! I FEEL LIKE A WEEK'S SUPPLY OF SOGGY WASH!
SOMEHOW, THE GOLEM IS DRAINING AWAY MY LIFE-FORCE...
...AND I DON'T KNOW HOW TO STOP IT!
9

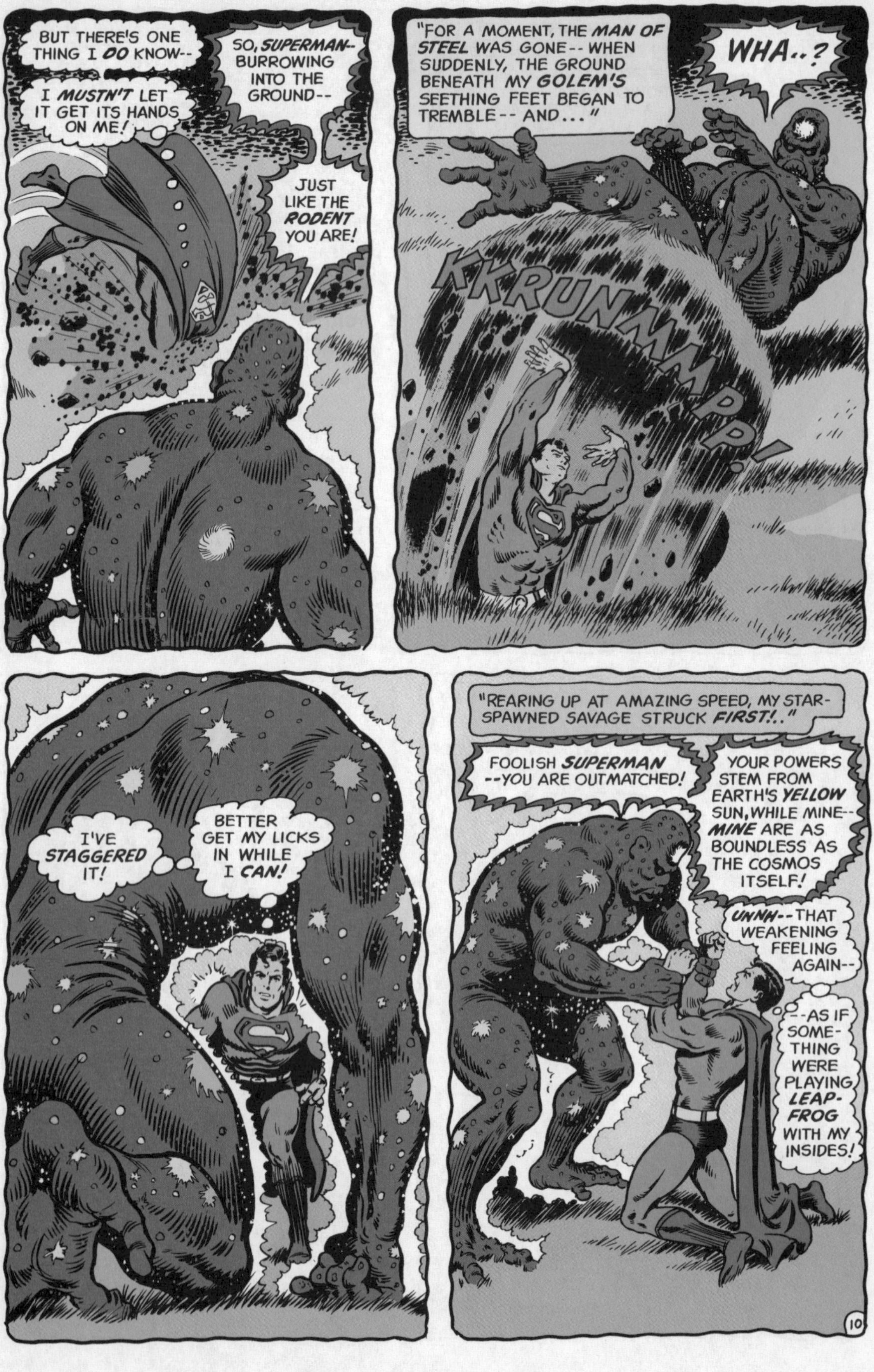

BUT THERE'S ONE THING I DO KNOW--
I MUSTN'T LET IT GET ITS HANDS ON ME!
SO, SUPERMAN-- BURROWING INTO THE GROUND--
JUST LIKE THE RODENT YOU ARE!
"FOR A MOMENT, THE MAN OF STEEL WAS GONE-- WHEN SUDDENLY, THE GROUND BENEATH MY GOLEM'S SEETHING FEET BEGAN TO TREMBLE-- AND..."
WHA..?
KKRUNMMMP!
I'VE STAGGERED IT!
BETTER GET MY LICKS IN WHILE I CAN!
"REARING UP AT AMAZING SPEED, MY STAR-SPAWNED SAVAGE STRUCK FIRST!."
FOOLISH SUPERMAN --YOU ARE OUTMATCHED!
YOUR POWERS STEM FROM EARTH'S YELLOW SUN, WHILE MINE-- MINE ARE AS BOUNDLESS AS THE COSMOS ITSELF!
UNNH--THAT WEAKENING FEELING AGAIN--
--AS IF SOMETHING WERE PLAYING LEAP-FROG WITH MY INSIDES!
10

"THE *KRYPTONIAN* SEEMED TO CRUMPLE BENEATH THE *GOLEM'S* AWESOME ONSLAUGHT --WHEN..."

SORRY TO USE YOU FOR *LEVERAGE*-- BUT I JUST COULDN'T RESIST SUCH A TEMPTING TARGET!

THUMPK!

"THEN I WITNESSED SOMETHING I THOUGHT *I* WOULD *NEVER* SEE! THE MIGHTY *SUPERMAN* TURNED--AND *FLED!*..."

IF I KEEP TRYING TO PLAY *HERO,* THAT MONSTROSITY'S GOING TO DRAIN ME DRIER THAN A FIG!

GOTTA GATHER MY THOUGHTS-- FIGURE OUT A WAY TO HANDLE THIS MESS!

"LIKE A SCARED SPARROW, MY ARCH-FOE SOARED OVER THE CITY--BUT 'I' WAS NOT ABOUT TO LET HIM GET AWAY UNSCATHED..."

ARGGHH-- BLASTED THING *HIT* ME--WITH ANOTHER ENERGY BLAST!

FALLING..!

"AND THE SOUND OF HIS IMPACT WAS ENOUGH TO *SHOCK* THE CITY..."

KWA

RAMMM

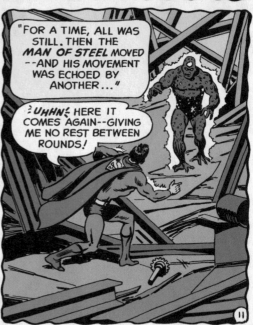

"FOR A TIME, ALL WAS STILL. THEN THE *MAN OF STEEL* MOVED --AND HIS MOVEMENT WAS ECHOED BY ANOTHER..."

¿*UHHN*¿ HERE IT COMES AGAIN--GIVING ME NO REST BETWEEN ROUNDS!

11

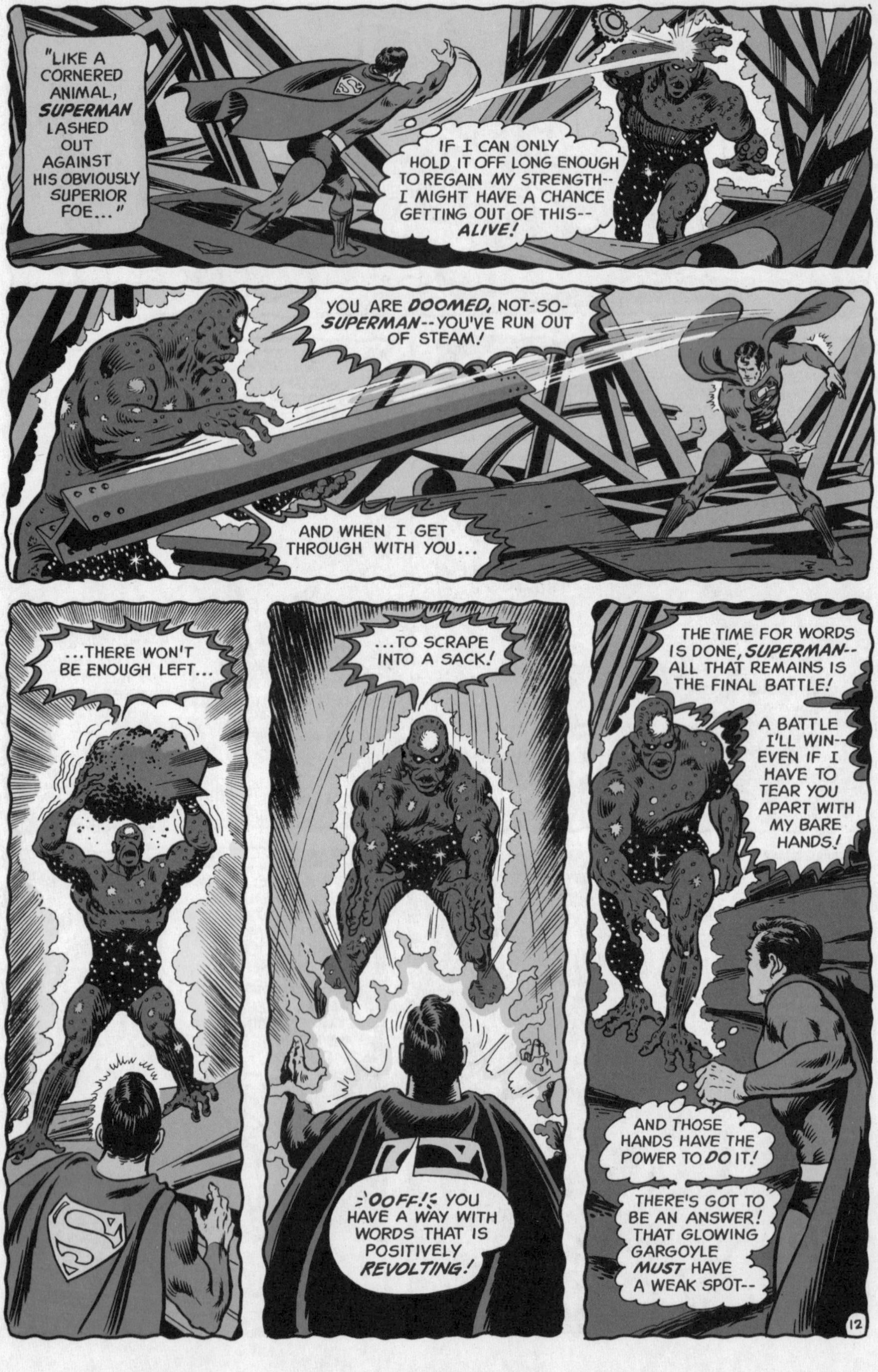
"LIKE A CORNERED ANIMAL, SUPERMAN LASHED OUT AGAINST HIS OBVIOUSLY SUPERIOR FOE..."
IF I CAN ONLY HOLD IT OFF LONG ENOUGH TO REGAIN MY STRENGTH-- I MIGHT HAVE A CHANCE GETTING OUT OF THIS-- ALIVE!
YOU ARE DOOMED, NOT-SO-SUPERMAN--YOU'VE RUN OUT OF STEAM!
AND WHEN I GET THROUGH WITH YOU...
...THERE WON'T BE ENOUGH LEFT...
...TO SCRAPE INTO A SACK!
OOFF! YOU HAVE A WAY WITH WORDS THAT IS POSITIVELY REVOLTING!
THE TIME FOR WORDS IS DONE, SUPERMAN-- ALL THAT REMAINS IS THE FINAL BATTLE!
A BATTLE I'LL WIN-- EVEN IF I HAVE TO TEAR YOU APART WITH MY BARE HANDS!
AND THOSE HANDS HAVE THE POWER TO DO IT!
THERE'S GOT TO BE AN ANSWER! THAT GLOWING GARGOYLE MUST HAVE A WEAK SPOT--
12

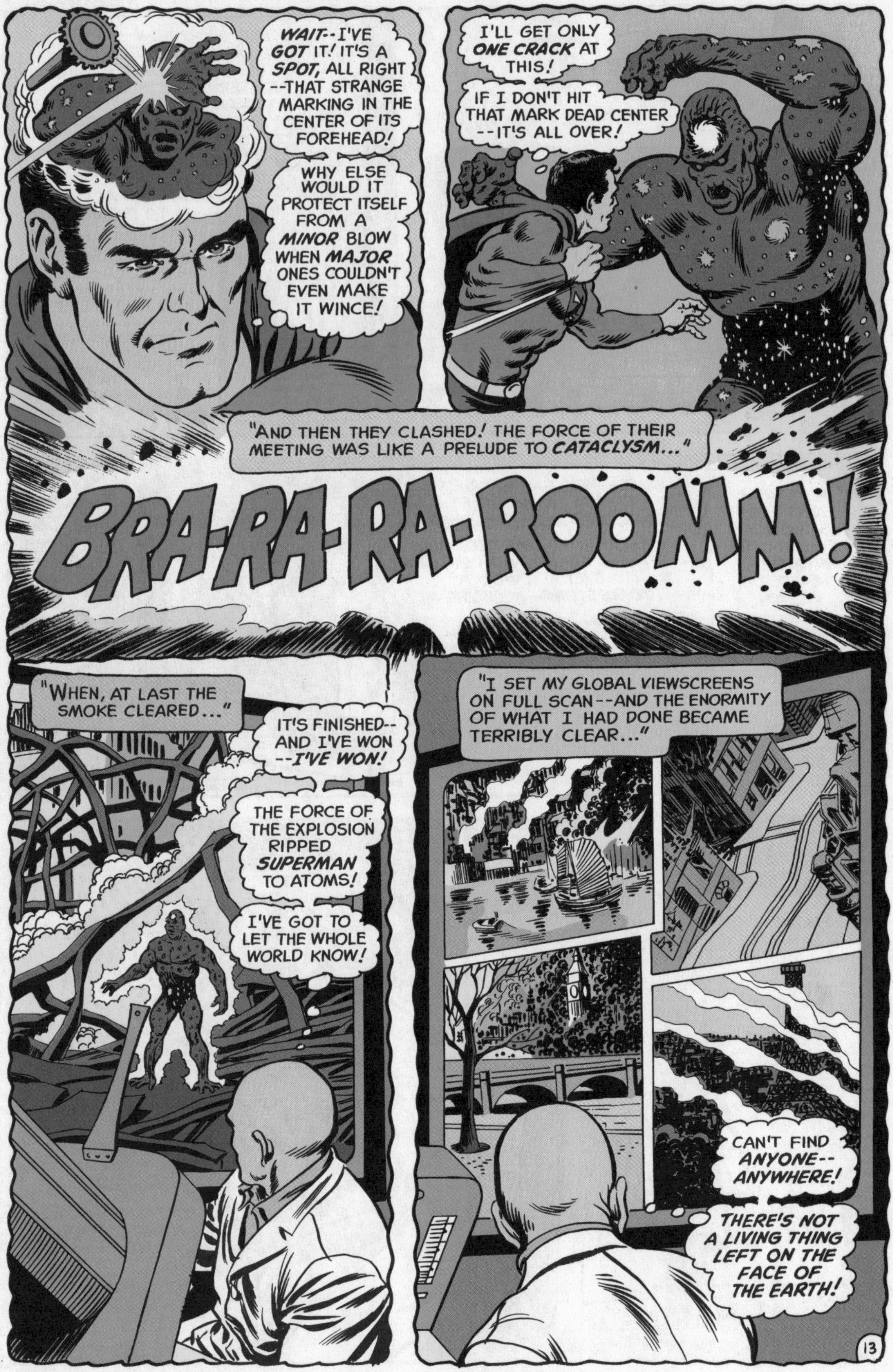
WAIT--I'VE GOT IT! IT'S A SPOT, ALL RIGHT --THAT STRANGE MARKING IN THE CENTER OF ITS FOREHEAD!
WHY ELSE WOULD IT PROTECT ITSELF FROM A MINOR BLOW WHEN MAJOR ONES COULDN'T EVEN MAKE IT WINCE!
I'LL GET ONLY ONE CRACK AT THIS!
IF I DON'T HIT THAT MARK DEAD CENTER --IT'S ALL OVER!
"AND THEN THEY CLASHED! THE FORCE OF THEIR MEETING WAS LIKE A PRELUDE TO CATACLYSM..."
BRA-RA-RA-ROOMM!
"WHEN, AT LAST THE SMOKE CLEARED..."
IT'S FINISHED-- AND I'VE WON --I'VE WON!
THE FORCE OF THE EXPLOSION RIPPED SUPERMAN TO ATOMS!
I'VE GOT TO LET THE WHOLE WORLD KNOW!
"I SET MY GLOBAL VIEWSCREENS ON FULL SCAN--AND THE ENORMITY OF WHAT I HAD DONE BECAME TERRIBLY CLEAR..."
CAN'T FIND ANYONE-- ANYWHERE!
THERE'S NOT A LIVING THING LEFT ON THE FACE OF THE EARTH!
13

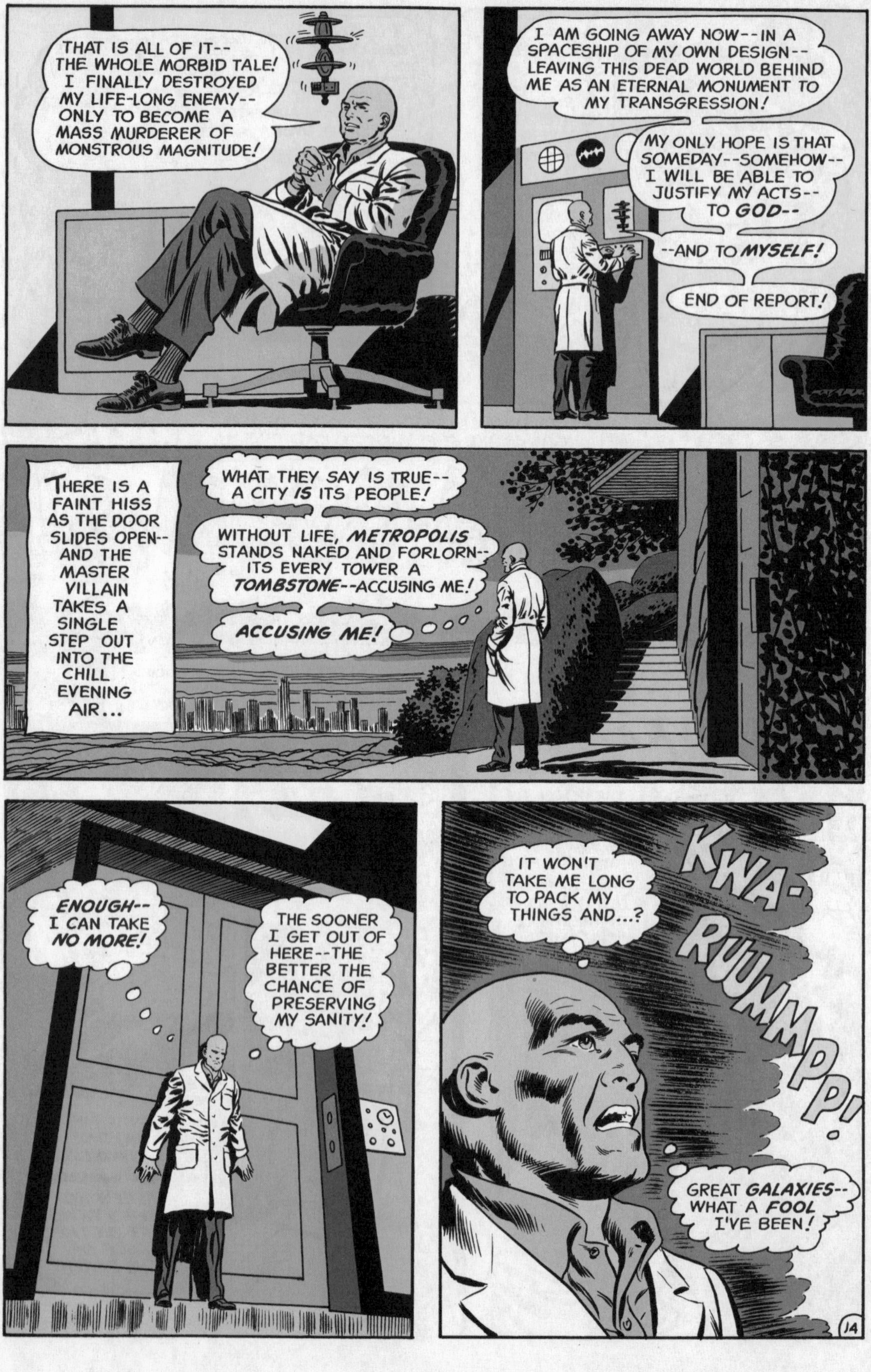
THAT IS ALL OF IT-- THE WHOLE MORBID TALE! I FINALLY DESTROYED MY LIFE-LONG ENEMY-- ONLY TO BECOME A MASS MURDERER OF MONSTROUS MAGNITUDE!
I AM GOING AWAY NOW--IN A SPACESHIP OF MY OWN DESIGN-- LEAVING THIS DEAD WORLD BEHIND ME AS AN ETERNAL MONUMENT TO MY TRANSGRESSION!
MY ONLY HOPE IS THAT SOMEDAY--SOMEHOW-- I WILL BE ABLE TO JUSTIFY MY ACTS-- TO GOD--
--AND TO MYSELF!
END OF REPORT!
THERE IS A FAINT HISS AS THE DOOR SLIDES OPEN-- AND THE MASTER VILLAIN TAKES A SINGLE STEP OUT INTO THE CHILL EVENING AIR...
WHAT THEY SAY IS TRUE-- A CITY IS ITS PEOPLE!
WITHOUT LIFE, METROPOLIS STANDS NAKED AND FORLORN-- ITS EVERY TOWER A TOMBSTONE--ACCUSING ME!
ACCUSING ME!
ENOUGH-- I CAN TAKE NO MORE!
THE SOONER I GET OUT OF HERE--THE BETTER THE CHANCE OF PRESERVING MY SANITY!
IT WON'T TAKE ME LONG TO PACK MY THINGS AND...?
KWA-RUUMMPP!
GREAT GALAXIES-- WHAT A FOOL I'VE BEEN!
14

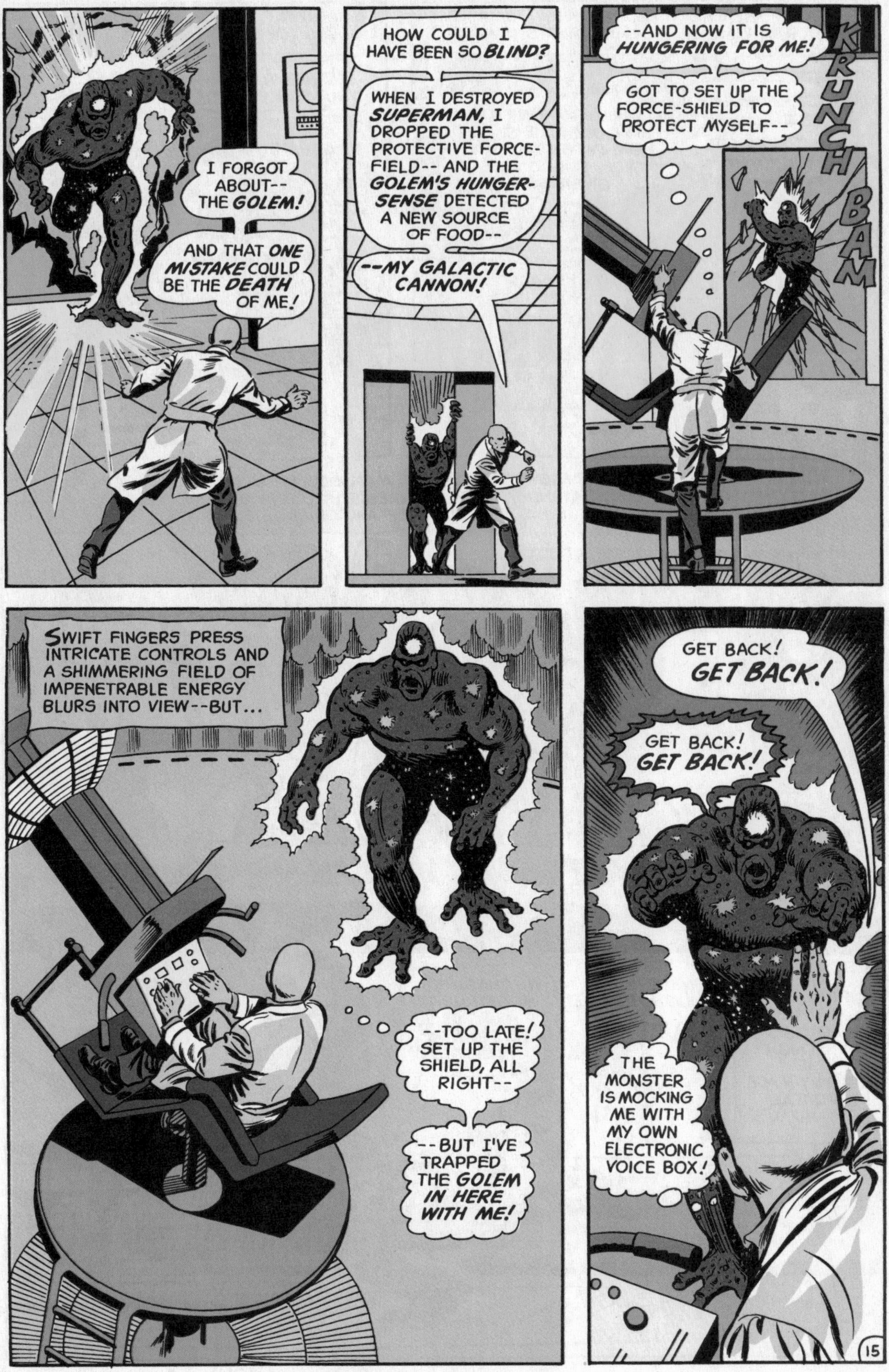
I FORGOT ABOUT-- THE GOLEM!
AND THAT ONE MISTAKE COULD BE THE DEATH OF ME!
HOW COULD I HAVE BEEN SO BLIND?
WHEN I DESTROYED SUPERMAN, I DROPPED THE PROTECTIVE FORCE-FIELD-- AND THE GOLEM'S HUNGER-SENSE DETECTED A NEW SOURCE OF FOOD--
--MY GALACTIC CANNON!
--AND NOW IT IS HUNGERING FOR ME!
GOT TO SET UP THE FORCE-SHIELD TO PROTECT MYSELF--
KRUNCH
BAM
SWIFT FINGERS PRESS INTRICATE CONTROLS AND A SHIMMERING FIELD OF IMPENETRABLE ENERGY BLURS INTO VIEW--BUT...
--TOO LATE! SET UP THE SHIELD, ALL RIGHT--
--BUT I'VE TRAPPED THE GOLEM IN HERE WITH ME!
GET BACK! GET BACK!
GET BACK! GET BACK!
THE MONSTER IS MOCKING ME WITH MY OWN ELECTRONIC VOICE BOX!
15

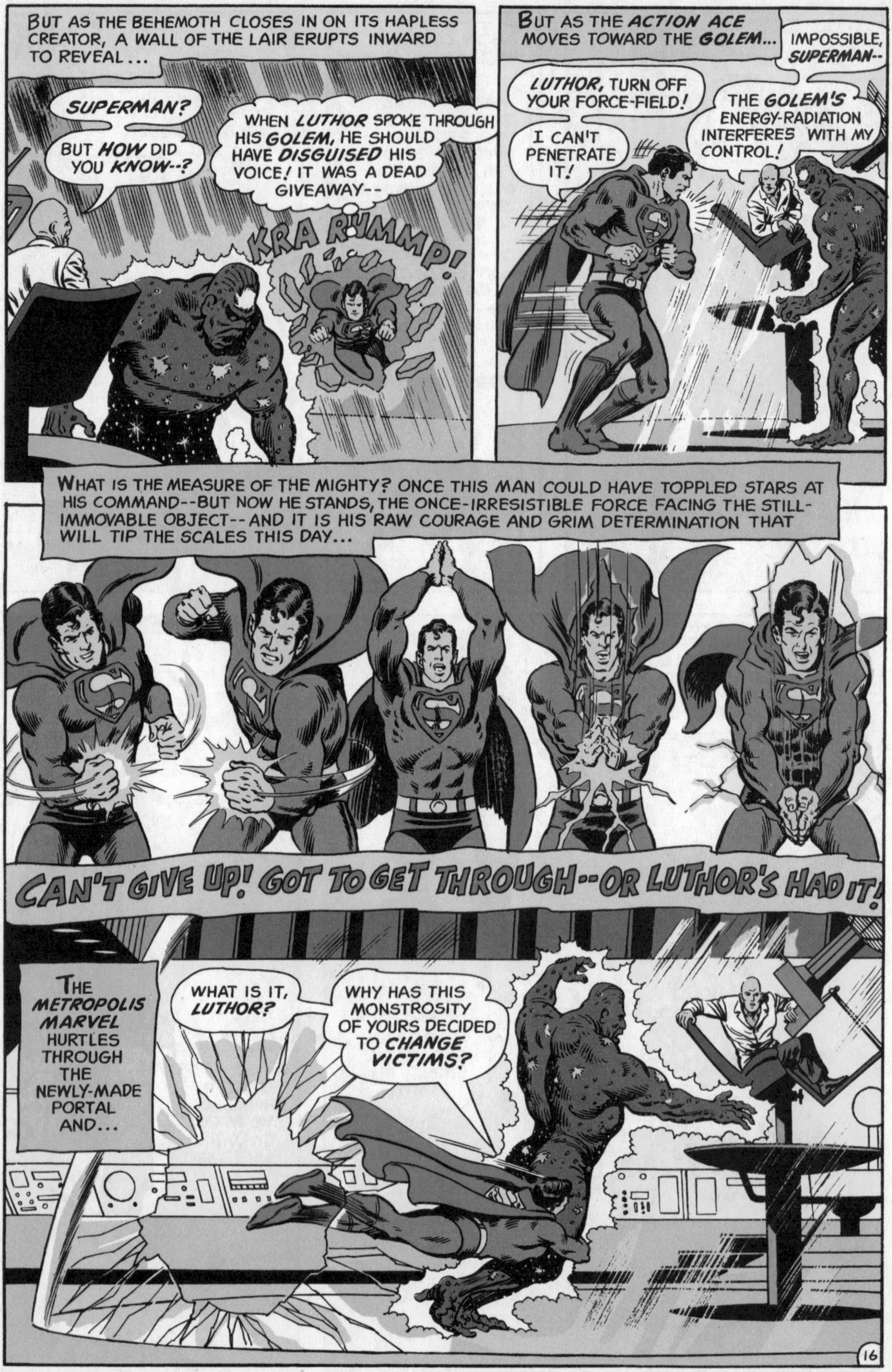

BUT AS THE BEHEMOTH CLOSES IN ON ITS HAPLESS CREATOR, A WALL OF THE LAIR ERUPTS INWARD TO REVEAL...
SUPERMAN?
BUT HOW DID YOU KNOW--?
WHEN LUTHOR SPOKE THROUGH HIS GOLEM, HE SHOULD HAVE DISGUISED HIS VOICE! IT WAS A DEAD GIVEAWAY--
KRA RUMMP!
BUT AS THE ACTION ACE MOVES TOWARD THE GOLEM...
LUTHOR, TURN OFF YOUR FORCE-FIELD!
I CAN'T PENETRATE IT!
IMPOSSIBLE, SUPERMAN--
THE GOLEM'S ENERGY-RADIATION INTERFERES WITH MY CONTROL!
WHAT IS THE MEASURE OF THE MIGHTY? ONCE THIS MAN COULD HAVE TOPPLED STARS AT HIS COMMAND--BUT NOW HE STANDS, THE ONCE-IRRESISTIBLE FORCE FACING THE STILL-IMMOVABLE OBJECT--AND IT IS HIS RAW COURAGE AND GRIM DETERMINATION THAT WILL TIP THE SCALES THIS DAY...
CAN'T GIVE UP! GOT TO GET THROUGH--OR LUTHOR'S HAD IT!
THE METROPOLIS MARVEL HURTLES THROUGH THE NEWLY-MADE PORTAL AND...
WHAT IS IT, LUTHOR?
WHY HAS THIS MONSTROSITY OF YOURS DECIDED TO CHANGE VICTIMS?
16

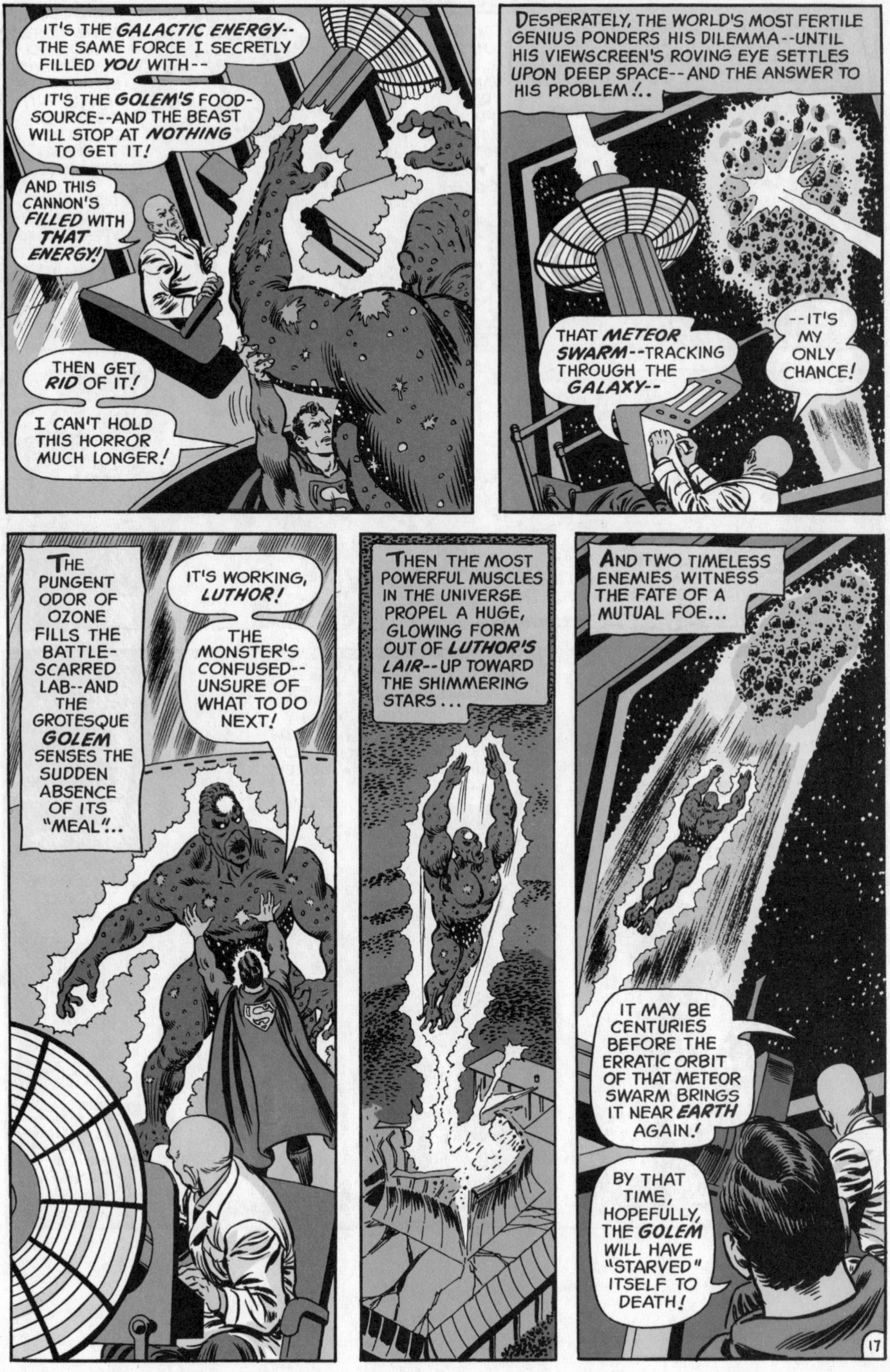
IT'S THE GALACTIC ENERGY-- THE SAME FORCE I SECRETLY FILLED YOU WITH--
IT'S THE GOLEM'S FOOD-SOURCE--AND THE BEAST WILL STOP AT NOTHING TO GET IT!
AND THIS CANNON'S FILLED WITH THAT ENERGY!
THEN GET RID OF IT!
I CAN'T HOLD THIS HORROR MUCH LONGER!
DESPERATELY, THE WORLD'S MOST FERTILE GENIUS PONDERS HIS DILEMMA--UNTIL HIS VIEWSCREEN'S ROVING EYE SETTLES UPON DEEP SPACE--AND THE ANSWER TO HIS PROBLEM!..
THAT METEOR SWARM--TRACKING THROUGH THE GALAXY--
--IT'S MY ONLY CHANCE!
THE PUNGENT ODOR OF OZONE FILLS THE BATTLE-SCARRED LAB--AND THE GROTESQUE GOLEM SENSES THE SUDDEN ABSENCE OF ITS "MEAL"!..
IT'S WORKING, LUTHOR!
THE MONSTER'S CONFUSED-- UNSURE OF WHAT TO DO NEXT!
THEN THE MOST POWERFUL MUSCLES IN THE UNIVERSE PROPEL A HUGE, GLOWING FORM OUT OF LUTHOR'S LAIR--UP TOWARD THE SHIMMERING STARS...
AND TWO TIMELESS ENEMIES WITNESS THE FATE OF A MUTUAL FOE...
IT MAY BE CENTURIES BEFORE THE ERRATIC ORBIT OF THAT METEOR SWARM BRINGS IT NEAR EARTH AGAIN!
BY THAT TIME, HOPEFULLY, THE GOLEM WILL HAVE "STARVED" ITSELF TO DEATH!
17

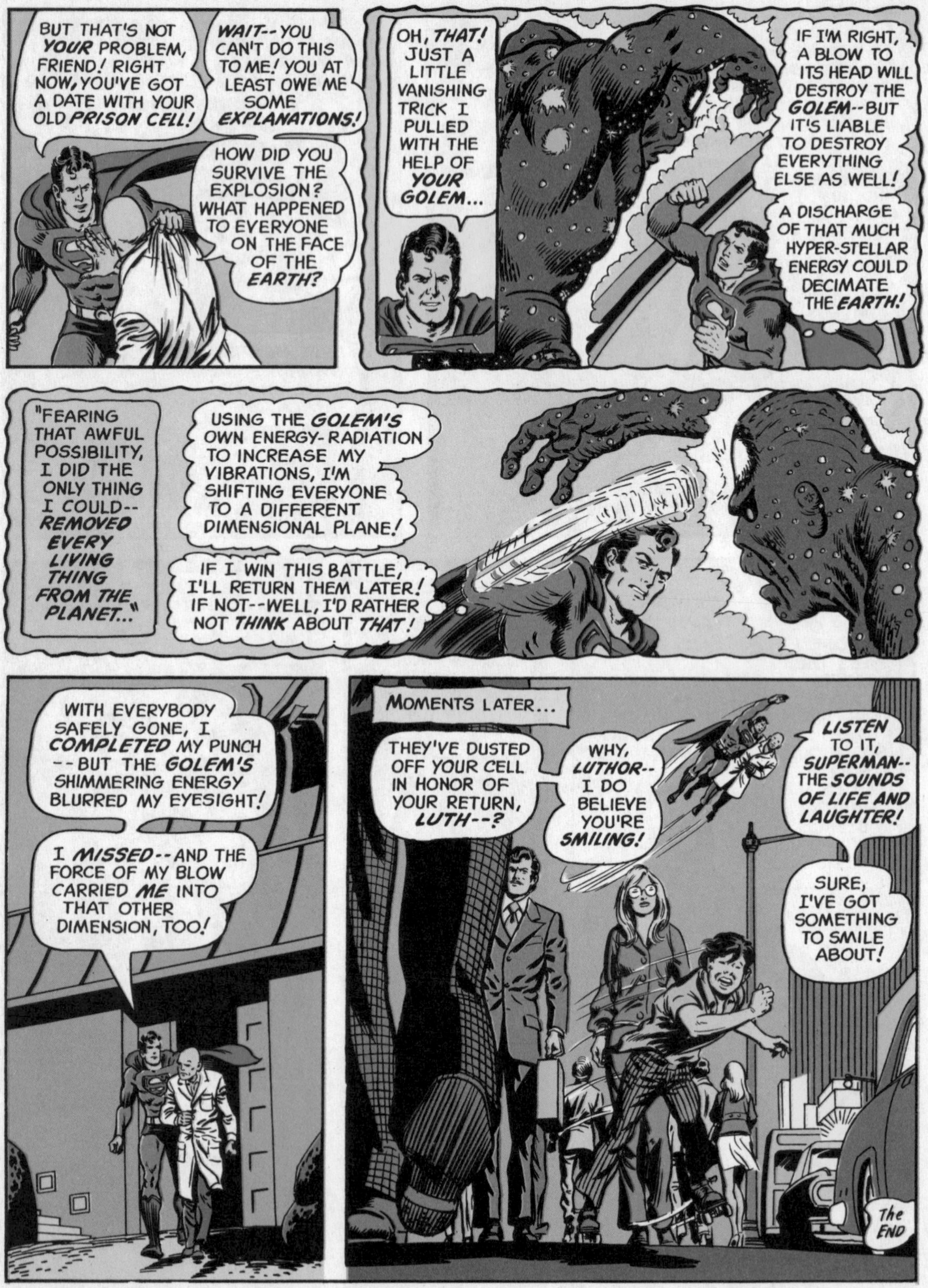

BUT THAT'S NOT *YOUR* PROBLEM, FRIEND! RIGHT NOW, YOU'VE GOT A DATE WITH YOUR OLD *PRISON CELL!*
WAIT-- YOU CAN'T DO THIS TO ME! YOU AT LEAST OWE ME SOME *EXPLANATIONS!*
HOW DID YOU SURVIVE THE EXPLOSION? WHAT HAPPENED TO EVERYONE ON THE FACE OF THE *EARTH?*
OH, *THAT!* JUST A LITTLE VANISHING TRICK I PULLED WITH THE HELP OF *YOUR GOLEM...*
IF I'M RIGHT, A BLOW TO ITS HEAD WILL DESTROY THE *GOLEM*--BUT IT'S LIABLE TO DESTROY EVERYTHING ELSE AS WELL!
A DISCHARGE OF THAT MUCH HYPER-STELLAR ENERGY COULD DECIMATE THE *EARTH!*
"FEARING THAT AWFUL POSSIBILITY, I DID THE ONLY THING I COULD-- *REMOVED EVERY LIVING THING FROM THE PLANET...*"
USING THE *GOLEM'S* OWN ENERGY-RADIATION TO INCREASE MY VIBRATIONS, I'M SHIFTING EVERYONE TO A DIFFERENT DIMENSIONAL PLANE!
IF I WIN THIS BATTLE, I'LL RETURN THEM LATER! IF NOT--WELL, I'D RATHER NOT *THINK* ABOUT *THAT!*
WITH EVERYBODY SAFELY GONE, I *COMPLETED* MY PUNCH --BUT THE *GOLEM'S* SHIMMERING ENERGY BLURRED MY EYESIGHT!
I *MISSED*--AND THE FORCE OF MY BLOW CARRIED *ME* INTO THAT OTHER DIMENSION, TOO!
MOMENTS LATER...
THEY'VE DUSTED OFF YOUR CELL IN HONOR OF YOUR RETURN, *LUTH--?*
WHY, *LUTHOR*-- I DO BELIEVE YOU'RE *SMILING!*
LISTEN TO IT, *SUPERMAN*-- THE *SOUNDS OF LIFE AND LAUGHTER!*
SURE, I'VE GOT SOMETHING TO SMILE ABOUT!
The End

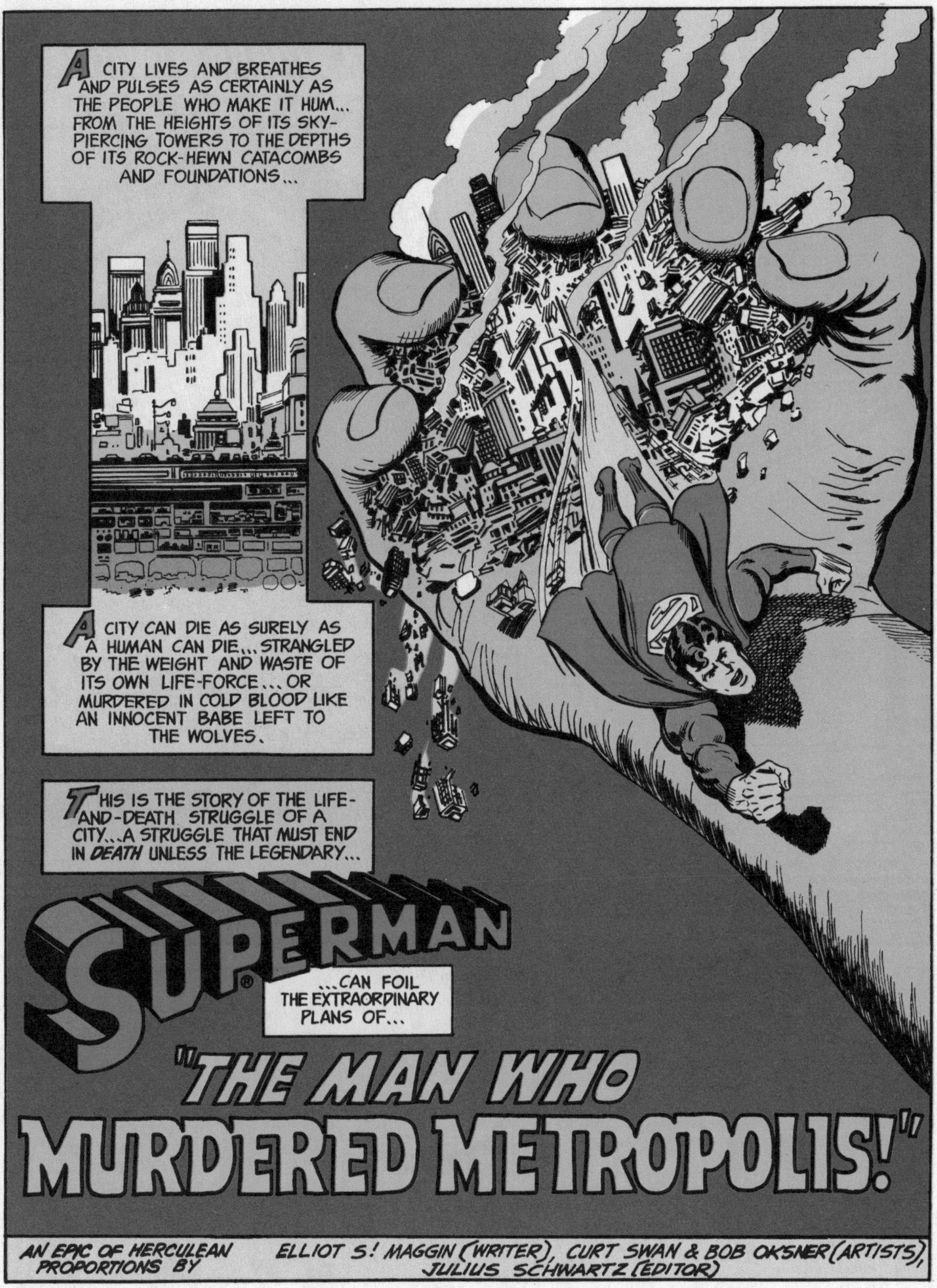
A CITY LIVES AND BREATHES AND PULSES AS CERTAINLY AS THE PEOPLE WHO MAKE IT HUM... FROM THE HEIGHTS OF ITS SKY-PIERCING TOWERS TO THE DEPTHS OF ITS ROCK-HEWN CATACOMBS AND FOUNDATIONS...
A CITY CAN DIE AS SURELY AS A HUMAN CAN DIE... STRANGLED BY THE WEIGHT AND WASTE OF ITS OWN LIFE-FORCE... OR MURDERED IN COLD BLOOD LIKE AN INNOCENT BABE LEFT TO THE WOLVES.
THIS IS THE STORY OF THE LIFE-AND-DEATH STRUGGLE OF A CITY... A STRUGGLE THAT MUST END IN DEATH UNLESS THE LEGENDARY...
SUPERMAN®
...CAN FOIL THE EXTRAORDINARY PLANS OF...
"THE MAN WHO MURDERED METROPOLIS!"
AN EPIC OF HERCULEAN PROPORTIONS BY
ELLIOT S! MAGGIN (WRITER), CURT SWAN & BOB OKSNER (ARTISTS), JULIUS SCHWARTZ (EDITOR)

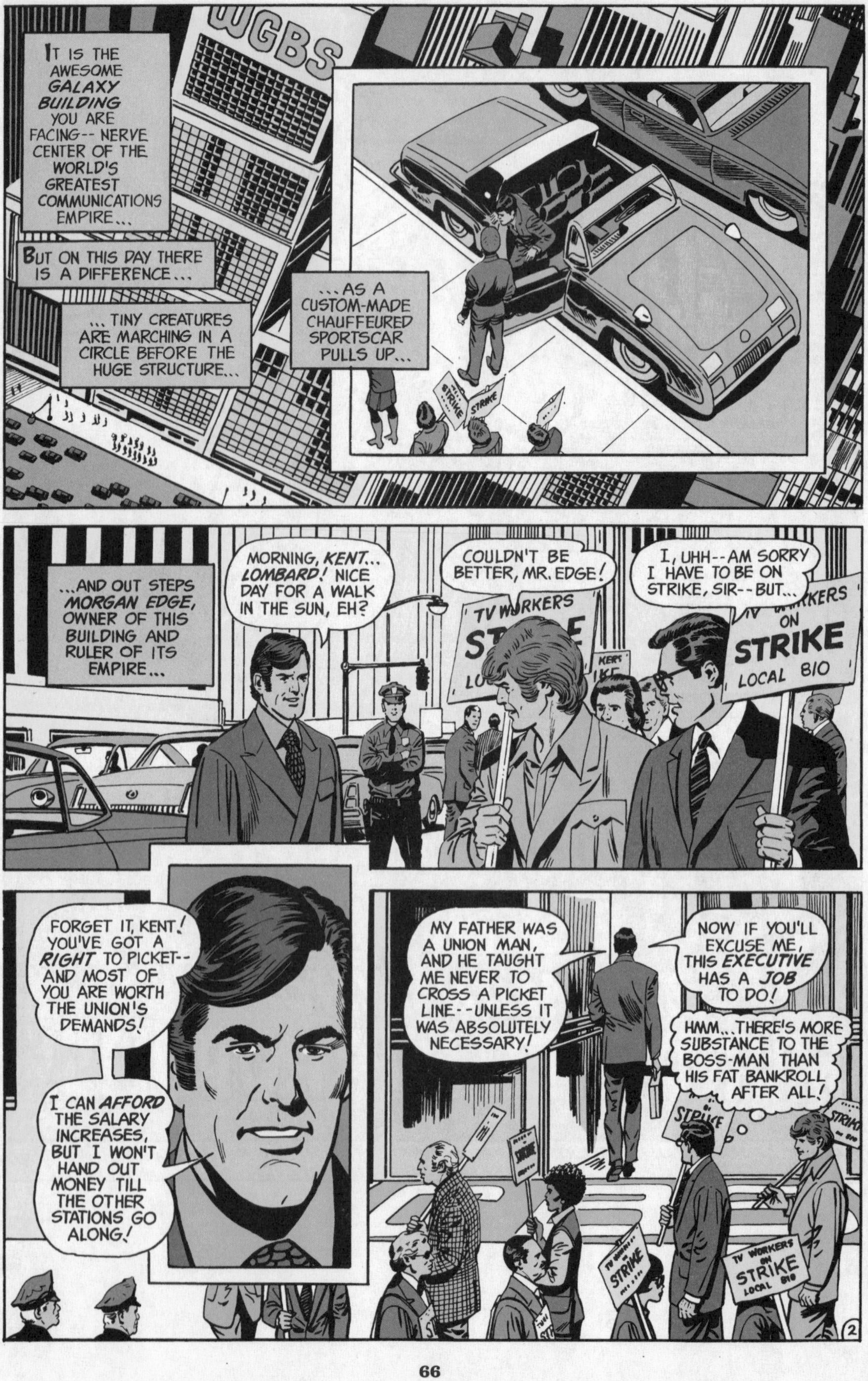
WGBS
IT IS THE AWESOME GALAXY BUILDING YOU ARE FACING-- NERVE CENTER OF THE WORLD'S GREATEST COMMUNICATIONS EMPIRE...
BUT ON THIS DAY THERE IS A DIFFERENCE...
...TINY CREATURES ARE MARCHING IN A CIRCLE BEFORE THE HUGE STRUCTURE...
...AS A CUSTOM-MADE CHAUFFEURED SPORTSCAR PULLS UP...
STRIKE
STRIKE
...AND OUT STEPS MORGAN EDGE, OWNER OF THIS BUILDING AND RULER OF ITS EMPIRE...
MORNING, KENT... LOMBARD! NICE DAY FOR A WALK IN THE SUN, EH?
COULDN'T BE BETTER, MR. EDGE!
I, UHH--AM SORRY I HAVE TO BE ON STRIKE, SIR--BUT...
STRIKE LOCAL 810
FORGET IT, KENT! YOU'VE GOT A RIGHT TO PICKET--AND MOST OF YOU ARE WORTH THE UNION'S DEMANDS!
I CAN AFFORD THE SALARY INCREASES, BUT I WON'T HAND OUT MONEY TILL THE OTHER STATIONS GO ALONG!
MY FATHER WAS A UNION MAN, AND HE TAUGHT ME NEVER TO CROSS A PICKET LINE--UNLESS IT WAS ABSOLUTELY NECESSARY!
NOW IF YOU'LL EXCUSE ME, THIS EXECUTIVE HAS A JOB TO DO!
HMM...THERE'S MORE SUBSTANCE TO THE BOSS-MAN THAN HIS FAT BANKROLL AFTER ALL!
TV WORKERS ON STRIKE LOCAL 810
2

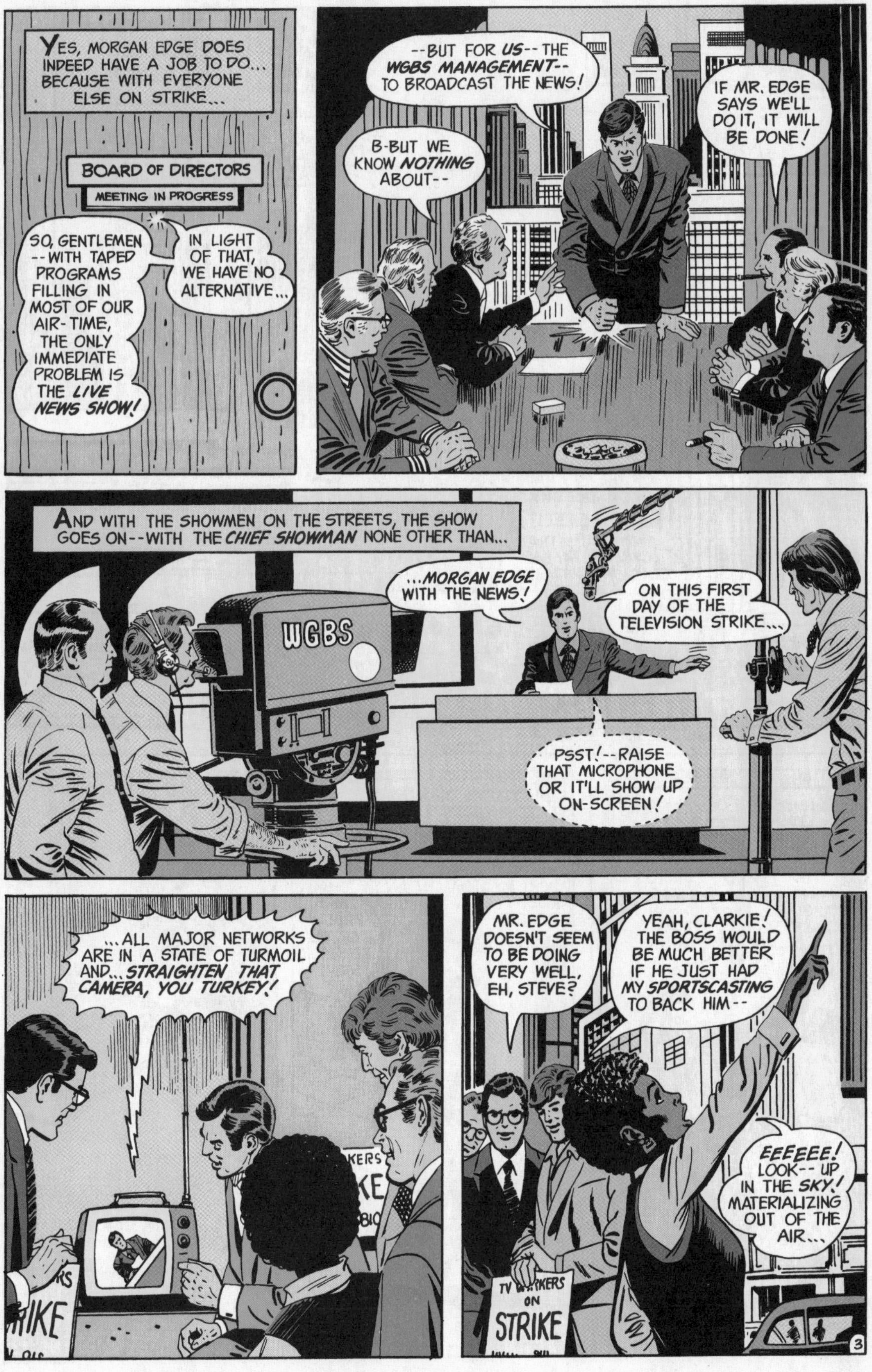
YES, MORGAN EDGE DOES INDEED HAVE A JOB TO DO... BECAUSE WITH EVERYONE ELSE ON STRIKE...
BOARD OF DIRECTORS
MEETING IN PROGRESS
SO, GENTLEMEN --WITH TAPED PROGRAMS FILLING IN MOST OF OUR AIR-TIME, THE ONLY IMMEDIATE PROBLEM IS THE LIVE NEWS SHOW!
IN LIGHT OF THAT, WE HAVE NO ALTERNATIVE...
--BUT FOR US-- THE WGBS MANAGEMENT-- TO BROADCAST THE NEWS!
B-BUT WE KNOW NOTHING ABOUT--
IF MR. EDGE SAYS WE'LL DO IT, IT WILL BE DONE!
AND WITH THE SHOWMEN ON THE STREETS, THE SHOW GOES ON--WITH THE CHIEF SHOWMAN NONE OTHER THAN...
...MORGAN EDGE WITH THE NEWS!
WGBS
ON THIS FIRST DAY OF THE TELEVISION STRIKE...
PSST!--RAISE THAT MICROPHONE OR IT'LL SHOW UP ON-SCREEN!
...ALL MAJOR NETWORKS ARE IN A STATE OF TURMOIL AND... STRAIGHTEN THAT CAMERA, YOU TURKEY!
MR. EDGE DOESN'T SEEM TO BE DOING VERY WELL, EH, STEVE?
YEAH, CLARKIE! THE BOSS WOULD BE MUCH BETTER IF HE JUST HAD MY SPORTSCASTING TO BACK HIM--
EEEEEE! LOOK-- UP IN THE SKY! MATERIALIZING OUT OF THE AIR...
TV WORKERS ON STRIKE
3

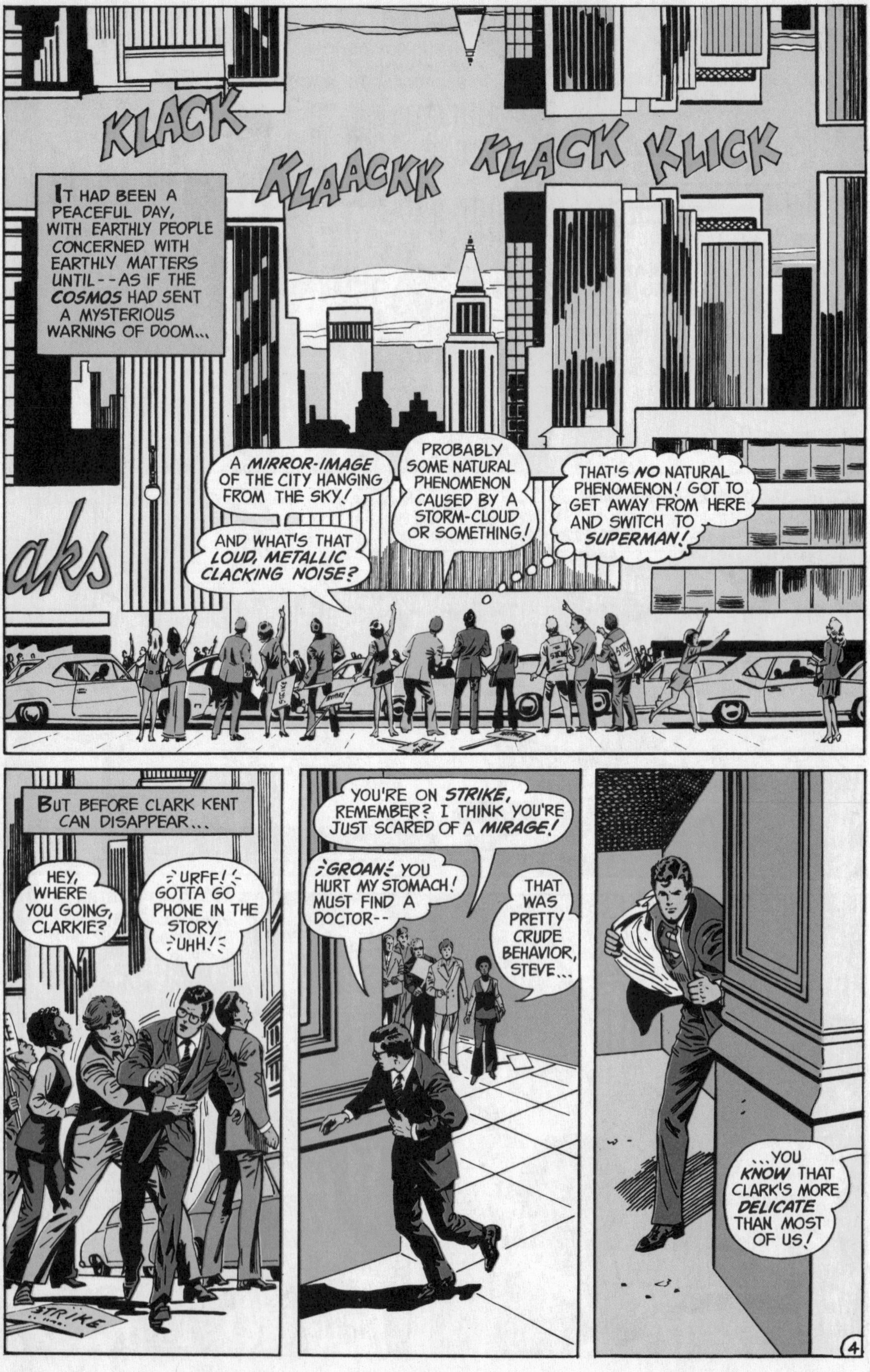
KLACK
KLAACKK
KLACK
KLICK
IT HAD BEEN A PEACEFUL DAY, WITH EARTHLY PEOPLE CONCERNED WITH EARTHLY MATTERS UNTIL--AS IF THE COSMOS HAD SENT A MYSTERIOUS WARNING OF DOOM...
A MIRROR-IMAGE OF THE CITY HANGING FROM THE SKY!
AND WHAT'S THAT LOUD, METALLIC CLACKING NOISE?
PROBABLY SOME NATURAL PHENOMENON CAUSED BY A STORM-CLOUD OR SOMETHING!
THAT'S NO NATURAL PHENOMENON! GOT TO GET AWAY FROM HERE AND SWITCH TO SUPERMAN!
BUT BEFORE CLARK KENT CAN DISAPPEAR...
HEY, WHERE YOU GOING, CLARKIE?
URFF! GOTTA GO PHONE IN THE STORY UHH!
STRIKE
YOU'RE ON STRIKE, REMEMBER? I THINK YOU'RE JUST SCARED OF A MIRAGE!
GROAN! YOU HURT MY STOMACH! MUST FIND A DOCTOR--
THAT WAS PRETTY CRUDE BEHAVIOR, STEVE...
...YOU KNOW THAT CLARK'S MORE DELICATE THAN MOST OF US!
4

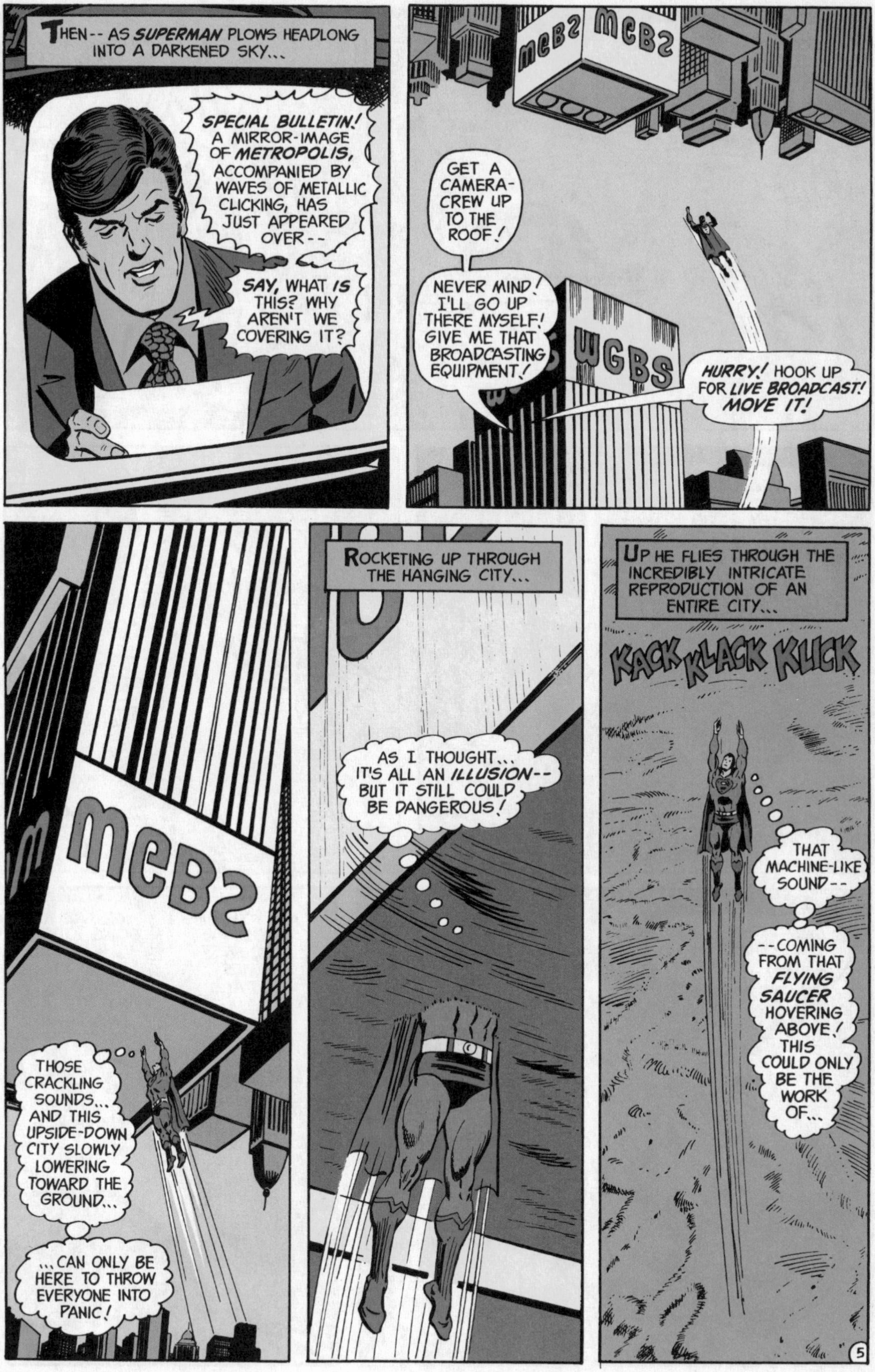
THEN-- AS SUPERMAN PLOWS HEADLONG INTO A DARKENED SKY...
SPECIAL BULLETIN! A MIRROR-IMAGE OF METROPOLIS, ACCOMPANIED BY WAVES OF METALLIC CLICKING, HAS JUST APPEARED OVER--
SAY, WHAT IS THIS? WHY AREN'T WE COVERING IT?
GET A CAMERA-CREW UP TO THE ROOF!
NEVER MIND! I'LL GO UP THERE MYSELF! GIVE ME THAT BROADCASTING EQUIPMENT!
HURRY! HOOK UP FOR LIVE BROADCAST! MOVE IT!
WGBS
THOSE CRACKLING SOUNDS... AND THIS UPSIDE-DOWN CITY SLOWLY LOWERING TOWARD THE GROUND...
...CAN ONLY BE HERE TO THROW EVERYONE INTO PANIC!
ROCKETING UP THROUGH THE HANGING CITY...
AS I THOUGHT... IT'S ALL AN ILLUSION-- BUT IT STILL COULD BE DANGEROUS!
UP HE FLIES THROUGH THE INCREDIBLY INTRICATE REPRODUCTION OF AN ENTIRE CITY...
KACK KLACK KLICK
THAT MACHINE-LIKE SOUND--
--COMING FROM THAT FLYING SAUCER HOVERING ABOVE! THIS COULD ONLY BE THE WORK OF...
5

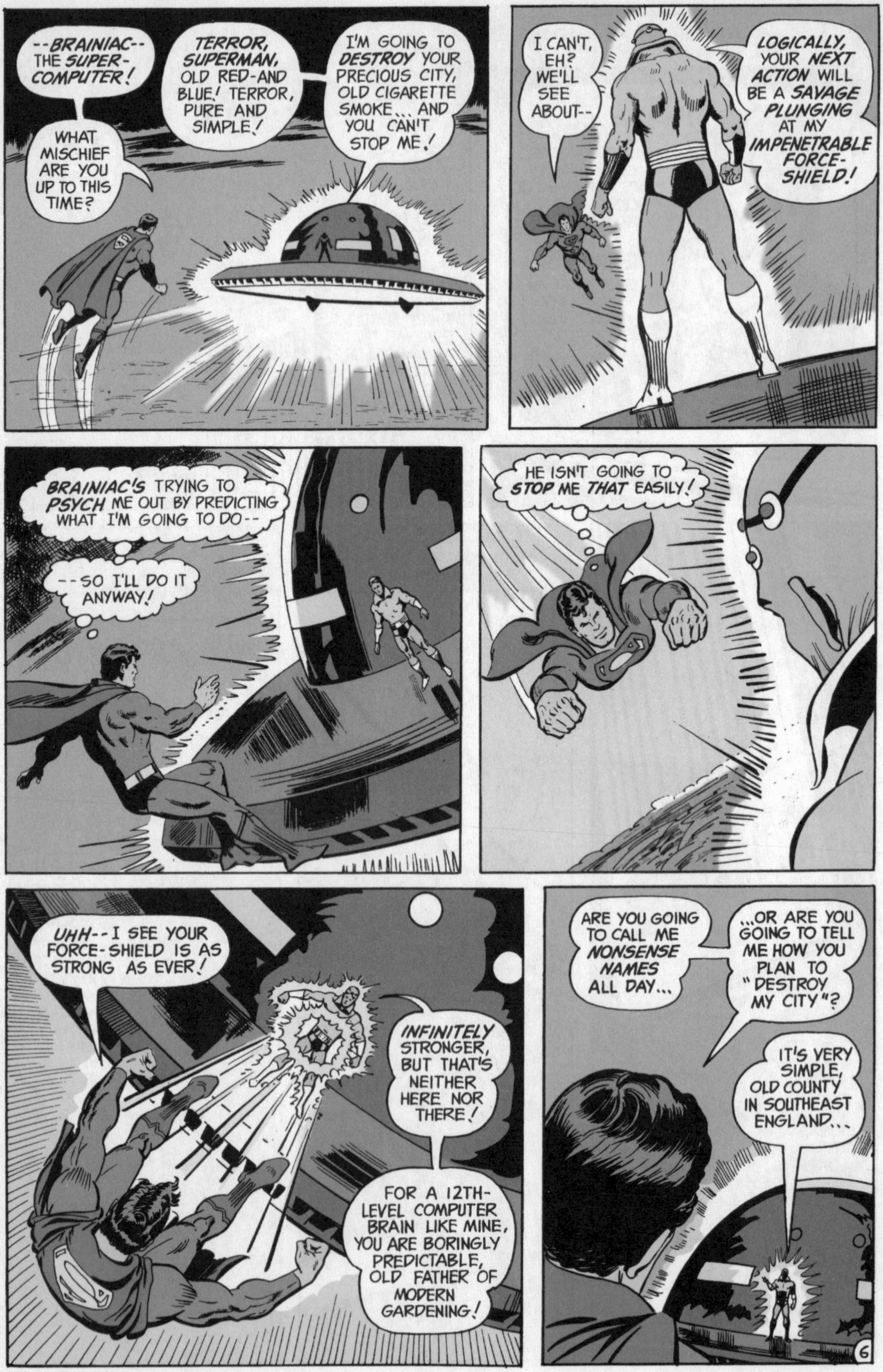
--BRAINIAC-- THE SUPER-COMPUTER!
WHAT MISCHIEF ARE YOU UP TO THIS TIME?
TERROR, SUPERMAN, OLD RED-AND BLUE! TERROR, PURE AND SIMPLE!
I'M GOING TO DESTROY YOUR PRECIOUS CITY, OLD CIGARETTE SMOKE... AND YOU CAN'T STOP ME!
I CAN'T, EH? WE'LL SEE ABOUT--
LOGICALLY, YOUR NEXT ACTION WILL BE A SAVAGE PLUNGING AT MY IMPENETRABLE FORCE-SHIELD!
BRAINIAC'S TRYING TO PSYCH ME OUT BY PREDICTING WHAT I'M GOING TO DO--
--SO I'LL DO IT ANYWAY!
HE ISN'T GOING TO STOP ME THAT EASILY!
UHH--I SEE YOUR FORCE-SHIELD IS AS STRONG AS EVER!
INFINITELY STRONGER, BUT THAT'S NEITHER HERE NOR THERE!
FOR A 12TH-LEVEL COMPUTER BRAIN LIKE MINE, YOU ARE BORINGLY PREDICTABLE, OLD FATHER OF MODERN GARDENING!
ARE YOU GOING TO CALL ME NONSENSE NAMES ALL DAY...
...OR ARE YOU GOING TO TELL ME HOW YOU PLAN TO "DESTROY MY CITY"?
IT'S VERY SIMPLE, OLD COUNTY IN SOUTHEAST ENGLAND...
6

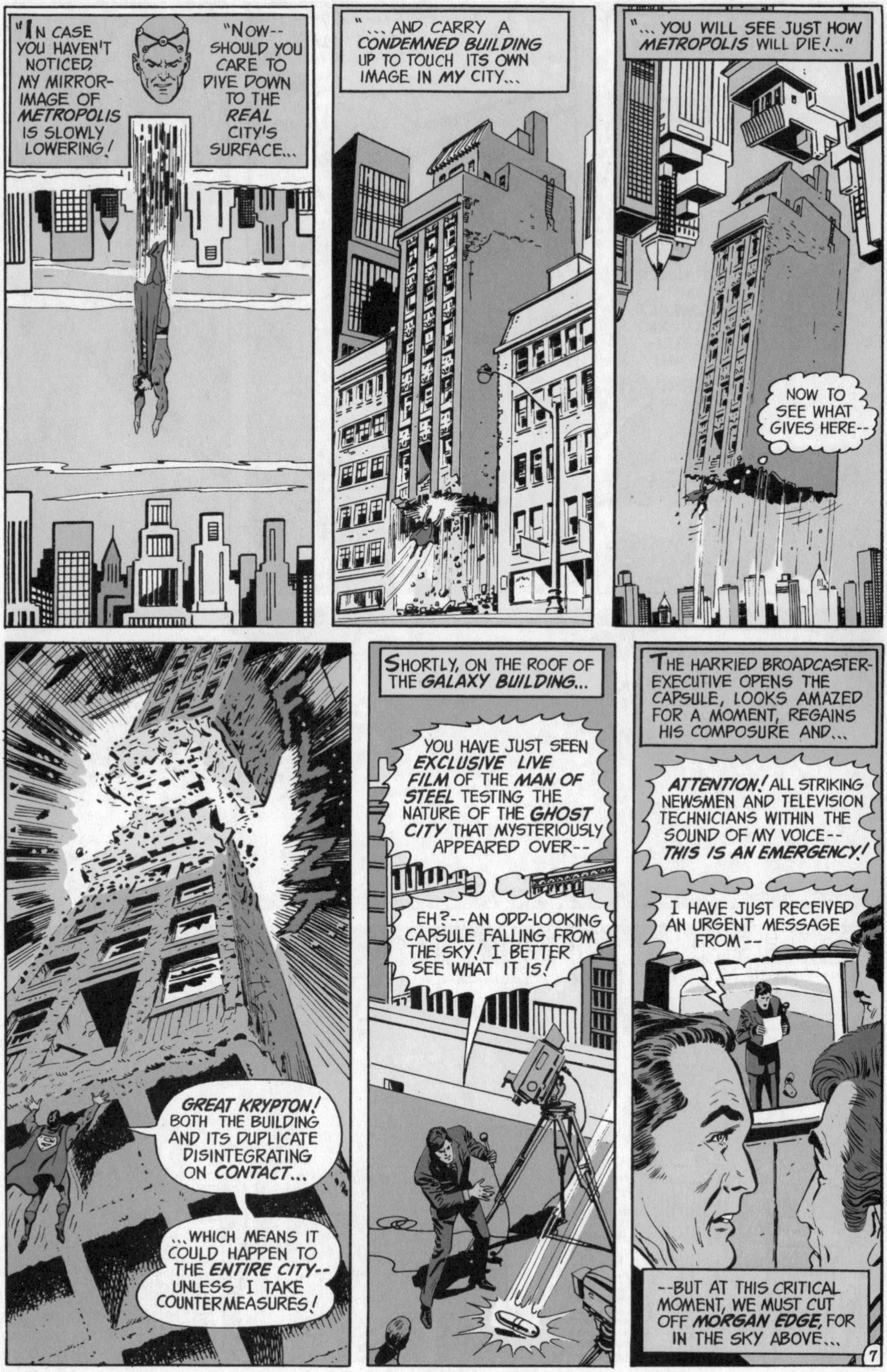
"IN CASE YOU HAVEN'T NOTICED, MY MIRROR-IMAGE OF METROPOLIS IS SLOWLY LOWERING!
"NOW-- SHOULD YOU CARE TO DIVE DOWN TO THE REAL CITY'S SURFACE...
"... AND CARRY A CONDEMNED BUILDING UP TO TOUCH ITS OWN IMAGE IN MY CITY...
"... YOU WILL SEE JUST HOW METROPOLIS WILL DIE!..."
NOW TO SEE WHAT GIVES HERE--
GREAT KRYPTON! BOTH THE BUILDING AND ITS DUPLICATE DISINTEGRATING ON CONTACT...
... WHICH MEANS IT COULD HAPPEN TO THE ENTIRE CITY-- UNLESS I TAKE COUNTERMEASURES!
SHORTLY, ON THE ROOF OF THE GALAXY BUILDING...
YOU HAVE JUST SEEN EXCLUSIVE LIVE FILM OF THE MAN OF STEEL TESTING THE NATURE OF THE GHOST CITY THAT MYSTERIOUSLY APPEARED OVER--
EH?-- AN ODD-LOOKING CAPSULE FALLING FROM THE SKY! I BETTER SEE WHAT IT IS!
THE HARRIED BROADCASTER-EXECUTIVE OPENS THE CAPSULE, LOOKS AMAZED FOR A MOMENT, REGAINS HIS COMPOSURE AND...
ATTENTION! ALL STRIKING NEWSMEN AND TELEVISION TECHNICIANS WITHIN THE SOUND OF MY VOICE-- THIS IS AN EMERGENCY!
I HAVE JUST RECEIVED AN URGENT MESSAGE FROM --
--BUT AT THIS CRITICAL MOMENT, WE MUST CUT OFF MORGAN EDGE, FOR IN THE SKY ABOVE...
7

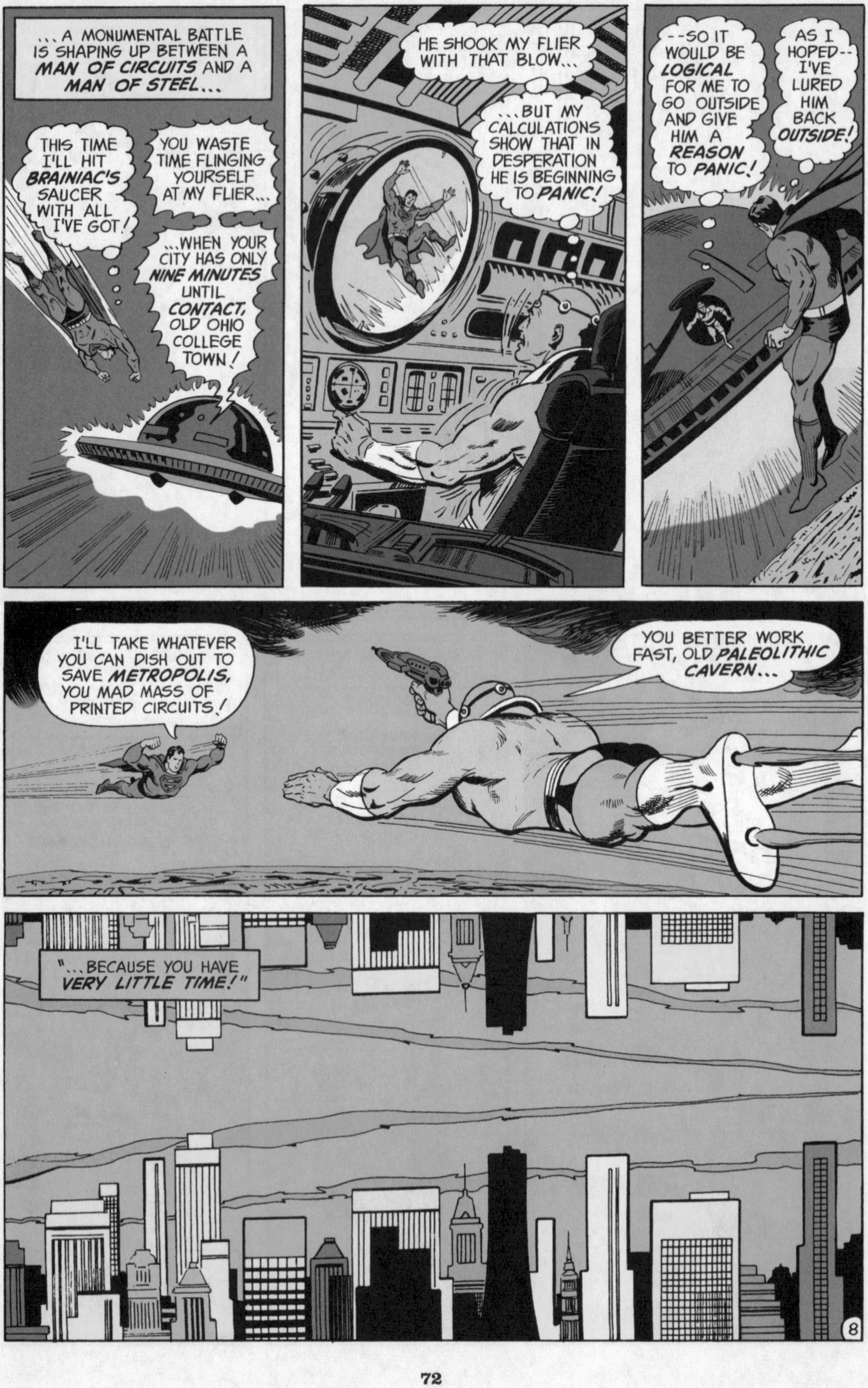

...A MONUMENTAL BATTLE IS SHAPING UP BETWEEN A MAN OF CIRCUITS AND A MAN OF STEEL...
THIS TIME I'LL HIT BRAINIAC'S SAUCER WITH ALL I'VE GOT!
YOU WASTE TIME FLINGING YOURSELF AT MY FLIER...
...WHEN YOUR CITY HAS ONLY NINE MINUTES UNTIL CONTACT, OLD OHIO COLLEGE TOWN!
HE SHOOK MY FLIER WITH THAT BLOW...
...BUT MY CALCULATIONS SHOW THAT IN DESPERATION HE IS BEGINNING TO PANIC!
--SO IT WOULD BE LOGICAL FOR ME TO GO OUTSIDE AND GIVE HIM A REASON TO PANIC!
AS I HOPED-- I'VE LURED HIM BACK OUTSIDE!
I'LL TAKE WHATEVER YOU CAN DISH OUT TO SAVE METROPOLIS, YOU MAD MASS OF PRINTED CIRCUITS!
YOU BETTER WORK FAST, OLD PALEOLITHIC CAVERN...
"...BECAUSE YOU HAVE VERY LITTLE TIME!"
8

AND ON THE *GALAXY BUILDING* ROOF...

LOMBARD! SET UP THOSE TWO MICROPHONES EXACTLY THE RIGHT DISTANCE APART!

GET THOSE CAMERAS IN PLACE--WE'VE GOT ONLY A FEW MINUTES!--HERE COMES THE 'COPTER!

YOU TWO--HURRY AND HELP THE HELICOPTER CREW!

REMEMBER-- THIS IS AN EMERGENCY!

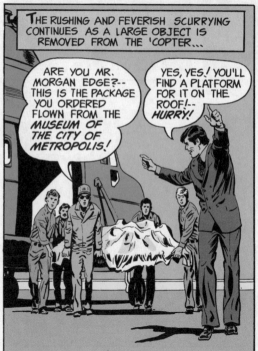

THE RUSHING AND FEVERISH SCURRYING CONTINUES AS A LARGE OBJECT IS REMOVED FROM THE 'COPTER...

ARE YOU MR. MORGAN EDGE?-- THIS IS THE PACKAGE YOU ORDERED FLOWN FROM THE *MUSEUM OF THE CITY OF METROPOLIS!*

YES, YES! YOU'LL FIND A PLATFORM FOR IT ON THE ROOF!-- *HURRY!*

WHILE *SUPERMAN* GRAPPLES WITH HIS FOE MILES ABOVE THE CITY...

...THE *GHOST IMAGE* OF *METROPOLIS* DROPS PERILOUSLY CLOSER...

9

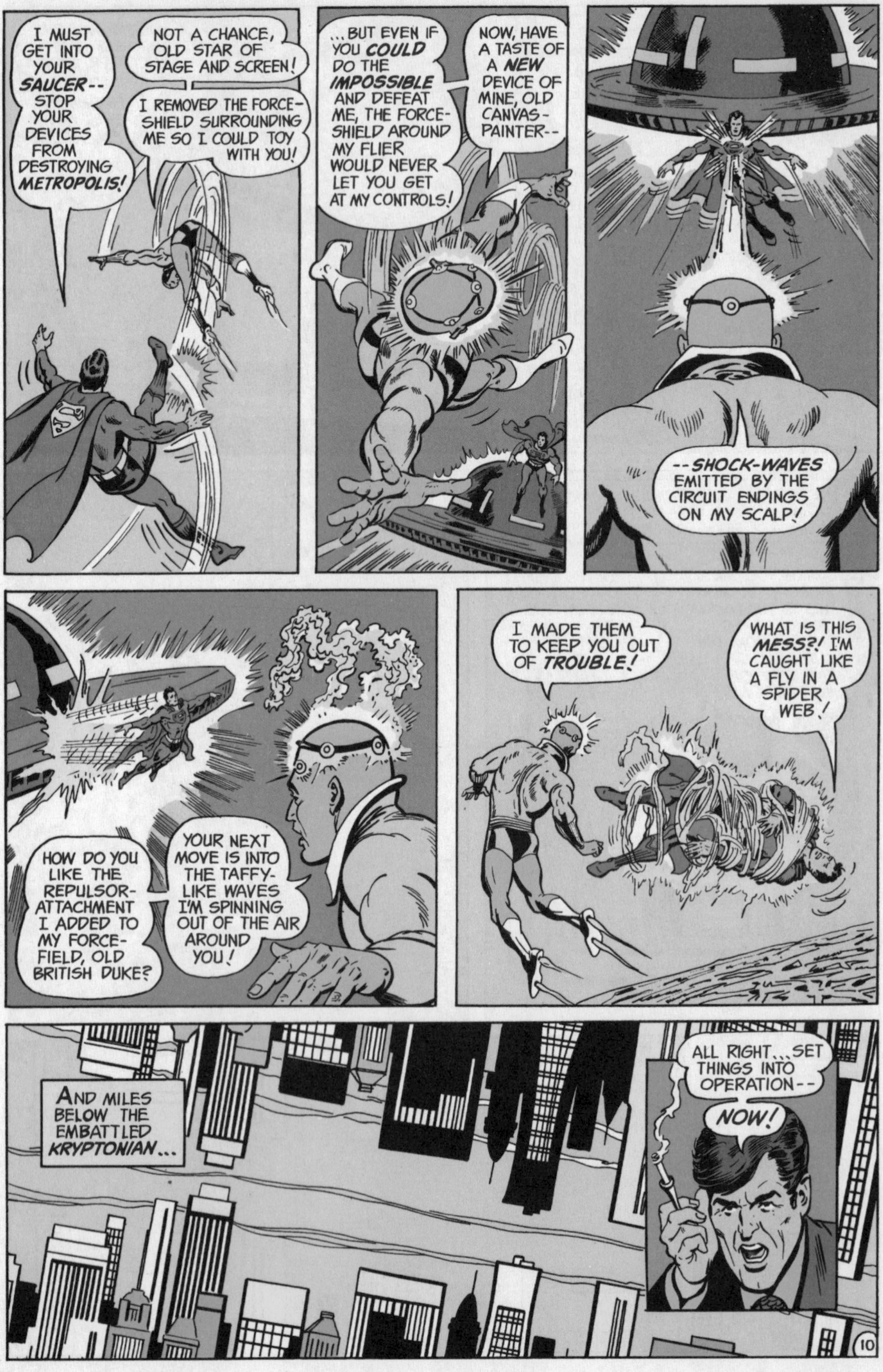

I MUST GET INTO YOUR SAUCER-- STOP YOUR DEVICES FROM DESTROYING METROPOLIS!
NOT A CHANCE, OLD STAR OF STAGE AND SCREEN!
I REMOVED THE FORCE-SHIELD SURROUNDING ME SO I COULD TOY WITH YOU!
...BUT EVEN IF YOU COULD DO THE IMPOSSIBLE AND DEFEAT ME, THE FORCE-SHIELD AROUND MY FLIER WOULD NEVER LET YOU GET AT MY CONTROLS!
NOW, HAVE A TASTE OF A NEW DEVICE OF MINE, OLD CANVAS-PAINTER--
--SHOCK-WAVES EMITTED BY THE CIRCUIT ENDINGS ON MY SCALP!
HOW DO YOU LIKE THE REPULSOR-ATTACHMENT I ADDED TO MY FORCE-FIELD, OLD BRITISH DUKE?
YOUR NEXT MOVE IS INTO THE TAFFY-LIKE WAVES I'M SPINNING OUT OF THE AIR AROUND YOU!
I MADE THEM TO KEEP YOU OUT OF TROUBLE!
WHAT IS THIS MESS?! I'M CAUGHT LIKE A FLY IN A SPIDER WEB!
AND MILES BELOW THE EMBATTLED KRYPTONIAN...
ALL RIGHT... SET THINGS INTO OPERATION-- NOW!
10

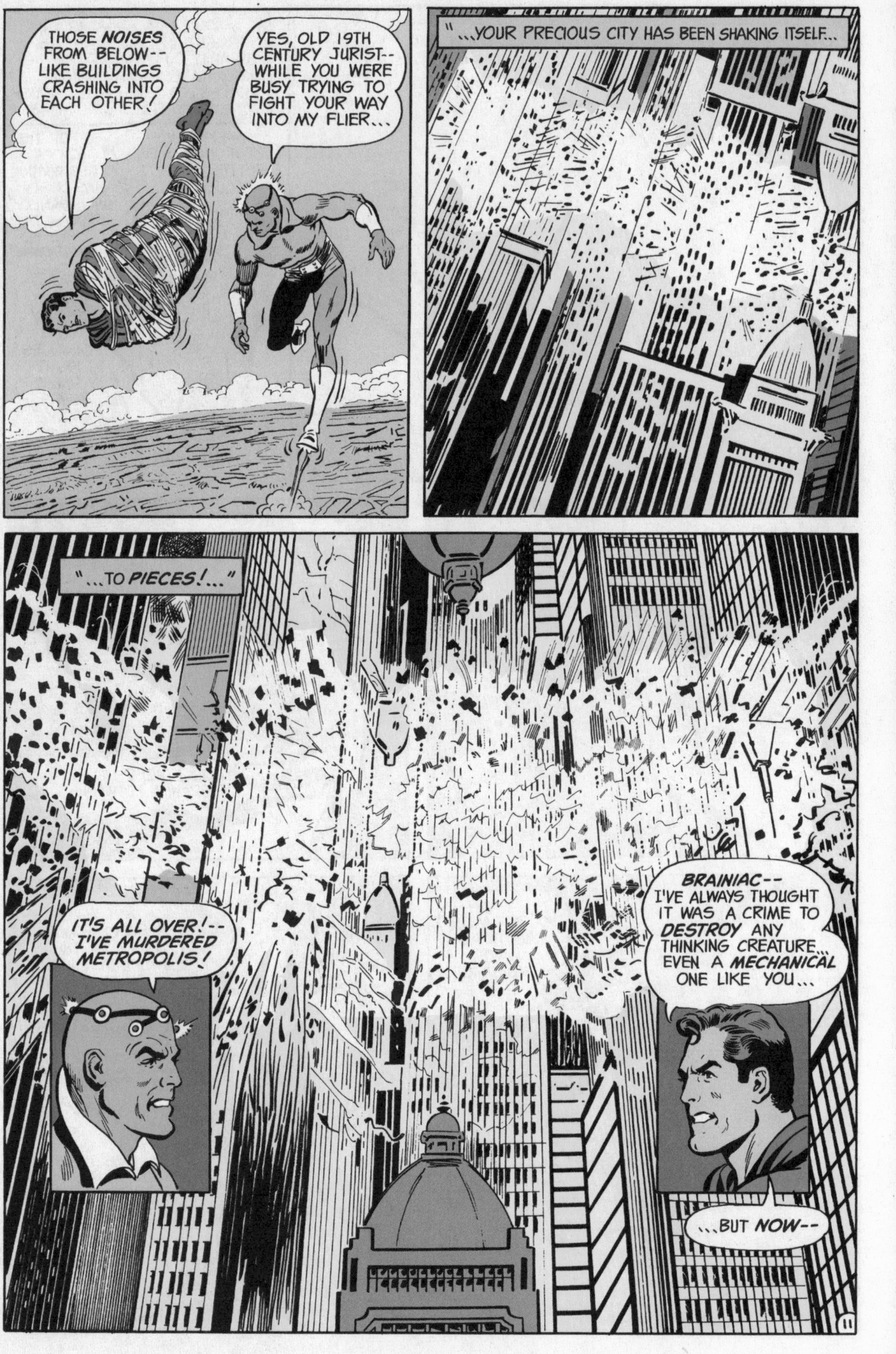

THOSE NOISES FROM BELOW-- LIKE BUILDINGS CRASHING INTO EACH OTHER!
YES, OLD 19TH CENTURY JURIST-- WHILE YOU WERE BUSY TRYING TO FIGHT YOUR WAY INTO MY FLIER...
"...YOUR PRECIOUS CITY HAS BEEN SHAKING ITSELF...
"...TO PIECES!..."
IT'S ALL OVER!-- I'VE MURDERED METROPOLIS!
BRAINIAC-- I'VE ALWAYS THOUGHT IT WAS A CRIME TO DESTROY ANY THINKING CREATURE... EVEN A MECHANICAL ONE LIKE YOU...
...BUT NOW--
11

SOMEHOW--SOME WAY--THE *MIGHTIEST MAN WHO EVER LIVED* BURSTS FREE AND...

LOOK OUT, MURDERER!

BUT HOLD IT RIGHT HERE...

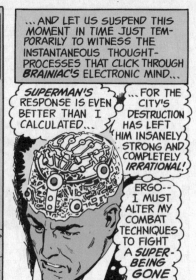

...AND LET US SUSPEND THIS MOMENT IN TIME JUST TEMPORARILY TO WITNESS THE INSTANTANEOUS THOUGHT-PROCESSES THAT CLICK THROUGH *BRAINIAC'S* ELECTRONIC MIND...

SUPERMAN'S RESPONSE IS EVEN *BETTER* THAN I CALCULATED...

...FOR THE *CITY'S DESTRUCTION* HAS LEFT HIM *INSANELY STRONG* AND COMPLETELY *IRRATIONAL!*

ERGO-- I MUST ALTER MY COMBAT TECHNIQUES TO FIGHT A *SUPER-BEING GONE MAD!*

BUT FIRST, OF COURSE...

MY *SENSORS* TELL ME METROPOLIS LIES IN *RUINS!*

SUPERMAN'S *SANITY* HAS ALREADY BEEN *SNAPPED!*

HIS *WILL TO FIGHT* MUST BREAK SOON AS WELL!

ALL I NEED DO IS KEEP HIM FIGHTING...

...UNTIL HE GIVES UP *FOREVER!* MY CALCULATIONS SHOW I AM ON A PATH TOWARD *INEVITABLE TOTAL VICTORY!*

I'LL WASH YOU OUT WITH THIS TIDAL WAVE, MURDERER!

NOT WHILE THE SHOCK-WAVES FROM THE CIRCUIT ENDINGS ON MY *SCALP* STILL WORK, OLD WRITER OF SCIENCE-FICTION!

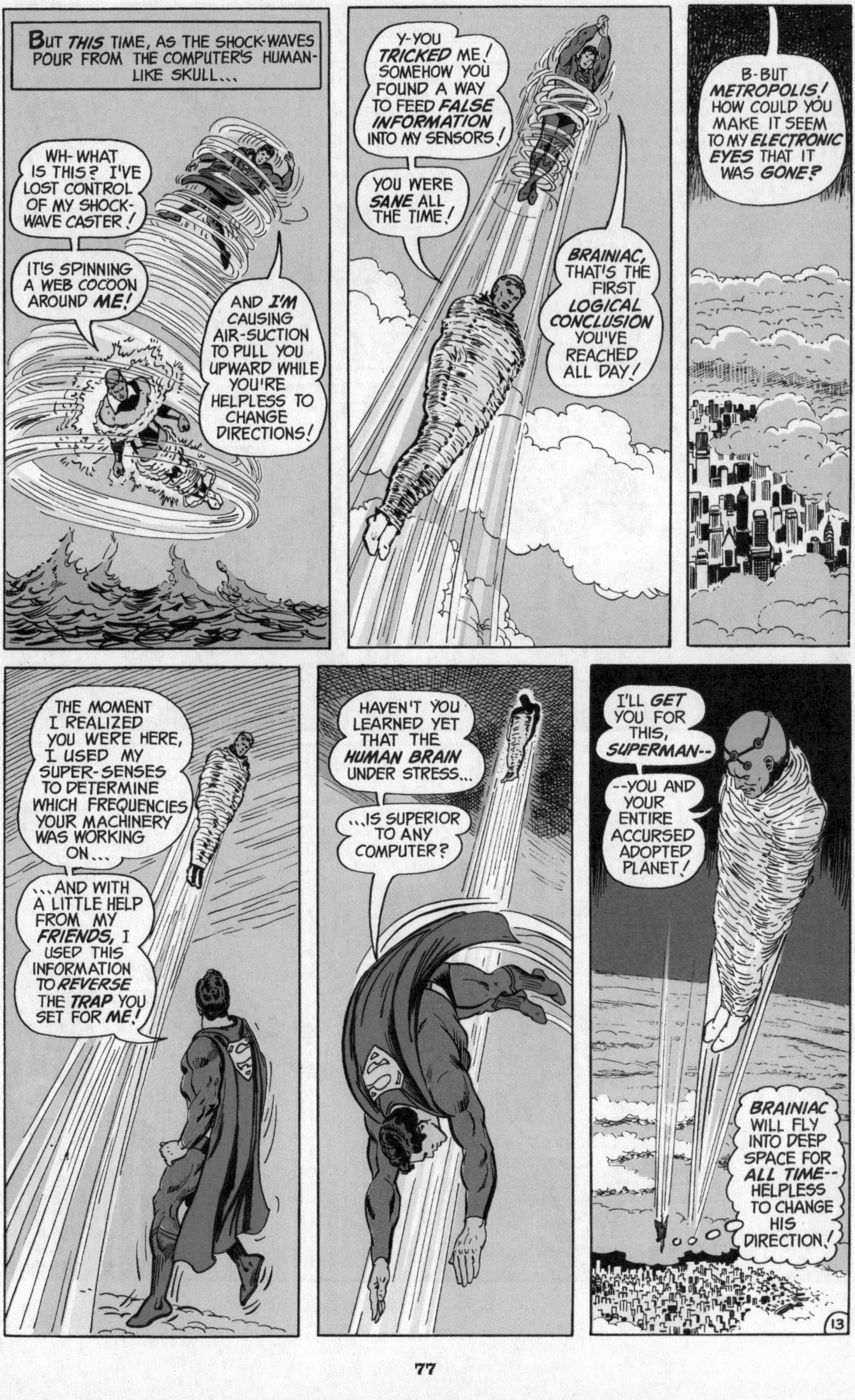

BUT THIS TIME, AS THE SHOCK-WAVES POUR FROM THE COMPUTER'S HUMAN-LIKE SKULL...
WH-WHAT IS THIS? I'VE LOST CONTROL OF MY SHOCK-WAVE CASTER!
IT'S SPINNING A WEB COCOON AROUND ME!
AND I'M CAUSING AIR-SUCTION TO PULL YOU UPWARD WHILE YOU'RE HELPLESS TO CHANGE DIRECTIONS!
Y-YOU TRICKED ME! SOMEHOW YOU FOUND A WAY TO FEED FALSE INFORMATION INTO MY SENSORS!
YOU WERE SANE ALL THE TIME!
BRAINIAC, THAT'S THE FIRST LOGICAL CONCLUSION YOU'VE REACHED ALL DAY!
B-BUT METROPOLIS! HOW COULD YOU MAKE IT SEEM TO MY ELECTRONIC EYES THAT IT WAS GONE?
THE MOMENT I REALIZED YOU WERE HERE, I USED MY SUPER-SENSES TO DETERMINE WHICH FREQUENCIES YOUR MACHINERY WAS WORKING ON...
...AND WITH A LITTLE HELP FROM MY FRIENDS, I USED THIS INFORMATION TO REVERSE THE TRAP YOU SET FOR ME!
HAVEN'T YOU LEARNED YET THAT THE HUMAN BRAIN UNDER STRESS...
...IS SUPERIOR TO ANY COMPUTER?
I'LL GET YOU FOR THIS, SUPERMAN--
--YOU AND YOUR ENTIRE ACCURSED ADOPTED PLANET!
BRAINIAC WILL FLY INTO DEEP SPACE FOR ALL TIME--HELPLESS TO CHANGE HIS DIRECTION!
13

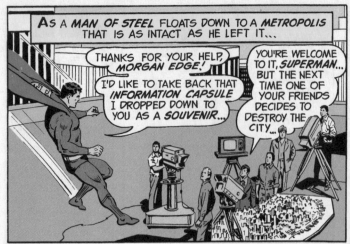

AS A *MAN OF STEEL* FLOATS DOWN TO A *METROPOLIS* THAT IS AS INTACT AS HE LEFT IT...

THANKS FOR YOUR HELP, *MORGAN EDGE!*

I'D LIKE TO TAKE BACK THAT *INFORMATION CAPSULE* I DROPPED DOWN TO YOU AS A *SOUVENIR...*

YOU'RE WELCOME TO IT, *SUPERMAN...* BUT THE NEXT TIME ONE OF YOUR FRIENDS DECIDES TO DESTROY THE CITY...

...PLEASE LET MY NEWS DEPARTMENT KNOW IN *ADVANCE* SO IT CAN SCHEDULE A STRIKE FOR SOME OTHER TIME!

YOU FOLLOWED INSTRUCTIONS VERY WELL, MORGAN!

I SENT THE CAPSULE TO *YOU* BECAUSE YOU'RE THE MOST *SKILLED MAN* AT ORGANIZING FORCES AND GIVING ORDERS I KNOW!

YOUR TECHNICIANS FOLLOWED MY INSTRUCTIONS TO REVERSE THE POLES OF *BRAINIAC'S* EQUIPMENT WHILE I DISTRACTED HIM...

...CAUSING HIM TO BELIEVE THAT THIS *PROJECTED IMAGE* OF A *SCALE MODEL* OF METROPOLIS FROM THE MUSEUM...

...WAS THE *REAL THING* AND HAD BEEN *DESTROYED!*

YOU DID ALL RIGHT AS A NEWSMAN, MR. EDGE...

...BUT I'LL BET YOU'RE GLAD THE STRIKE WAS SETTLED AFTER ONLY ONE DAY!

I'M JUST GLAD WE HAVE SOMEONE LIKE *SUPERMAN* TO PROTECT OUR CITY!

BUT TALKING ABOUT THE STRIKE, WHERE IS *CLARK KENT?* I HAVEN'T SEEN HIM SINCE I RAN INTO HIM *PICKETING* THIS MORNING!

MR. EDGE, I WOULDN'T BE SURPRISED IF *CLARKIE* IS STILL HIDING UNDER HIS PICKET SIGN SOMEWHERE!

THE END

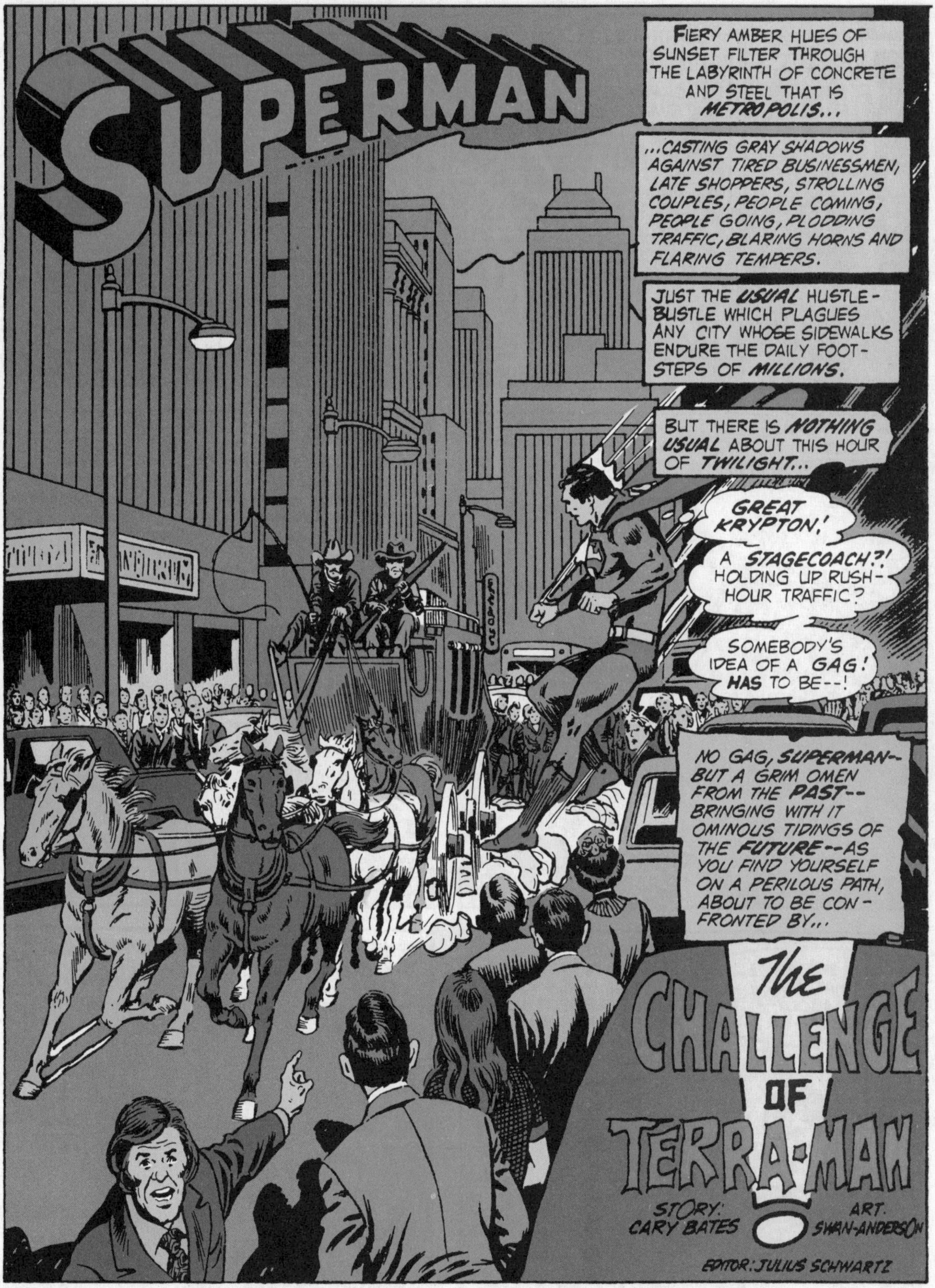
SUPERMAN
FIERY AMBER HUES OF SUNSET FILTER THROUGH THE LABYRINTH OF CONCRETE AND STEEL THAT IS METROPOLIS...
...CASTING GRAY SHADOWS AGAINST TIRED BUSINESSMEN, LATE SHOPPERS, STROLLING COUPLES, PEOPLE COMING, PEOPLE GOING, PLODDING TRAFFIC, BLARING HORNS AND FLARING TEMPERS.
JUST THE USUAL HUSTLE-BUSTLE WHICH PLAGUES ANY CITY WHOSE SIDEWALKS ENDURE THE DAILY FOOT-STEPS OF MILLIONS.
BUT THERE IS NOTHING USUAL ABOUT THIS HOUR OF TWILIGHT...
GREAT KRYPTON!
A STAGECOACH?! HOLDING UP RUSH-HOUR TRAFFIC?
SOMEBODY'S IDEA OF A GAG! HAS TO BE--!
NO GAG, SUPERMAN-- BUT A GRIM OMEN FROM THE PAST-- BRINGING WITH IT OMINOUS TIDINGS OF THE FUTURE--AS YOU FIND YOURSELF ON A PERILOUS PATH, ABOUT TO BE CON-FRONTED BY...
THE CHALLENGE OF TERRA-MAN!
STORY: CARY BATES
ART. SWAN-ANDERSON
EDITOR: JULIUS SCHWARTZ

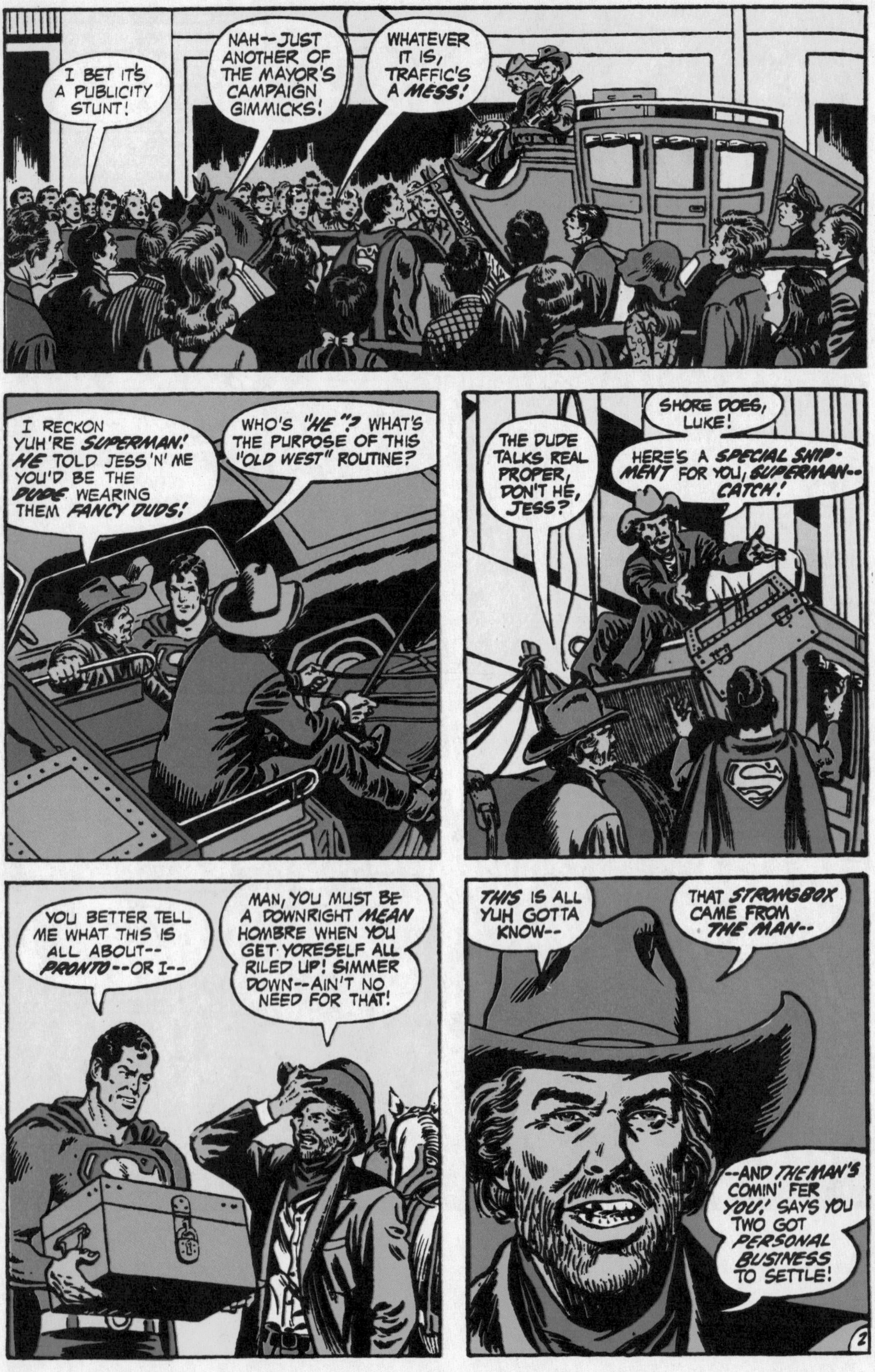

I BET IT'S A PUBLICITY STUNT!
NAH--JUST ANOTHER OF THE MAYOR'S CAMPAIGN GIMMICKS!
WHATEVER IT IS, TRAFFIC'S A MESS!
I RECKON YUH'RE SUPERMAN! HE TOLD JESS 'N' ME YOU'D BE THE DUDE WEARING THEM FANCY DUDS!
WHO'S "HE"? WHAT'S THE PURPOSE OF THIS "OLD WEST" ROUTINE?
THE DUDE TALKS REAL PROPER, DON'T HE, JESS?
SHORE DOES, LUKE!
HERE'S A SPECIAL SHIPMENT FOR YOU, SUPERMAN--CATCH!
YOU BETTER TELL ME WHAT THIS IS ALL ABOUT--PRONTO--OR I--
MAN, YOU MUST BE A DOWNRIGHT MEAN HOMBRE WHEN YOU GET YORESELF ALL RILED UP! SIMMER DOWN--AIN'T NO NEED FOR THAT!
THIS IS ALL YUH GOTTA KNOW--
THAT STRONGBOX CAME FROM THE MAN--
--AND THE MAN'S COMIN' FER YOU! SAYS YOU TWO GOT PERSONAL BUSINESS TO SETTLE!
2

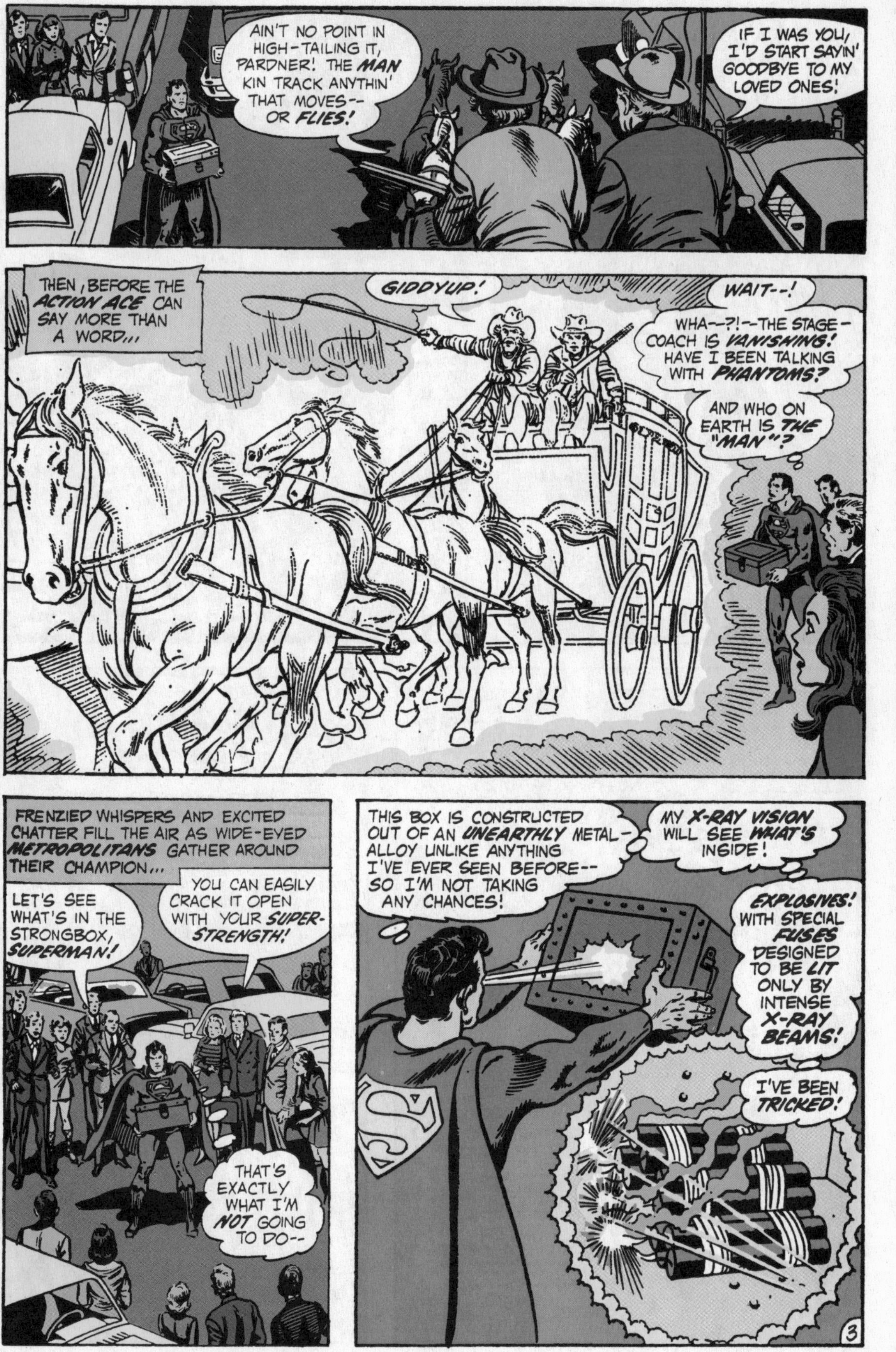
AIN'T NO POINT IN HIGH-TAILING IT, PARDNER! THE MAN KIN TRACK ANYTHIN' THAT MOVES-- OR FLIES!
IF I WAS YOU, I'D START SAYIN' GOODBYE TO MY LOVED ONES!
THEN, BEFORE THE ACTION ACE CAN SAY MORE THAN A WORD...
GIDDYUP!
WAIT--!
WHA--?!--THE STAGE-COACH IS VANISHING! HAVE I BEEN TALKING WITH PHANTOMS?
AND WHO ON EARTH IS THE "MAN"?
FRENZIED WHISPERS AND EXCITED CHATTER FILL THE AIR AS WIDE-EYED METROPOLITANS GATHER AROUND THEIR CHAMPION...
LET'S SEE WHAT'S IN THE STRONGBOX, SUPERMAN!
YOU CAN EASILY CRACK IT OPEN WITH YOUR SUPER-STRENGTH!
THAT'S EXACTLY WHAT I'M NOT GOING TO DO--
THIS BOX IS CONSTRUCTED OUT OF AN UNEARTHLY METAL-ALLOY UNLIKE ANYTHING I'VE EVER SEEN BEFORE-- SO I'M NOT TAKING ANY CHANCES!
MY X-RAY VISION WILL SEE WHAT'S INSIDE!
EXPLOSIVES! WITH SPECIAL FUSES DESIGNED TO BE LIT ONLY BY INTENSE X-RAY BEAMS!
I'VE BEEN TRICKED!
3

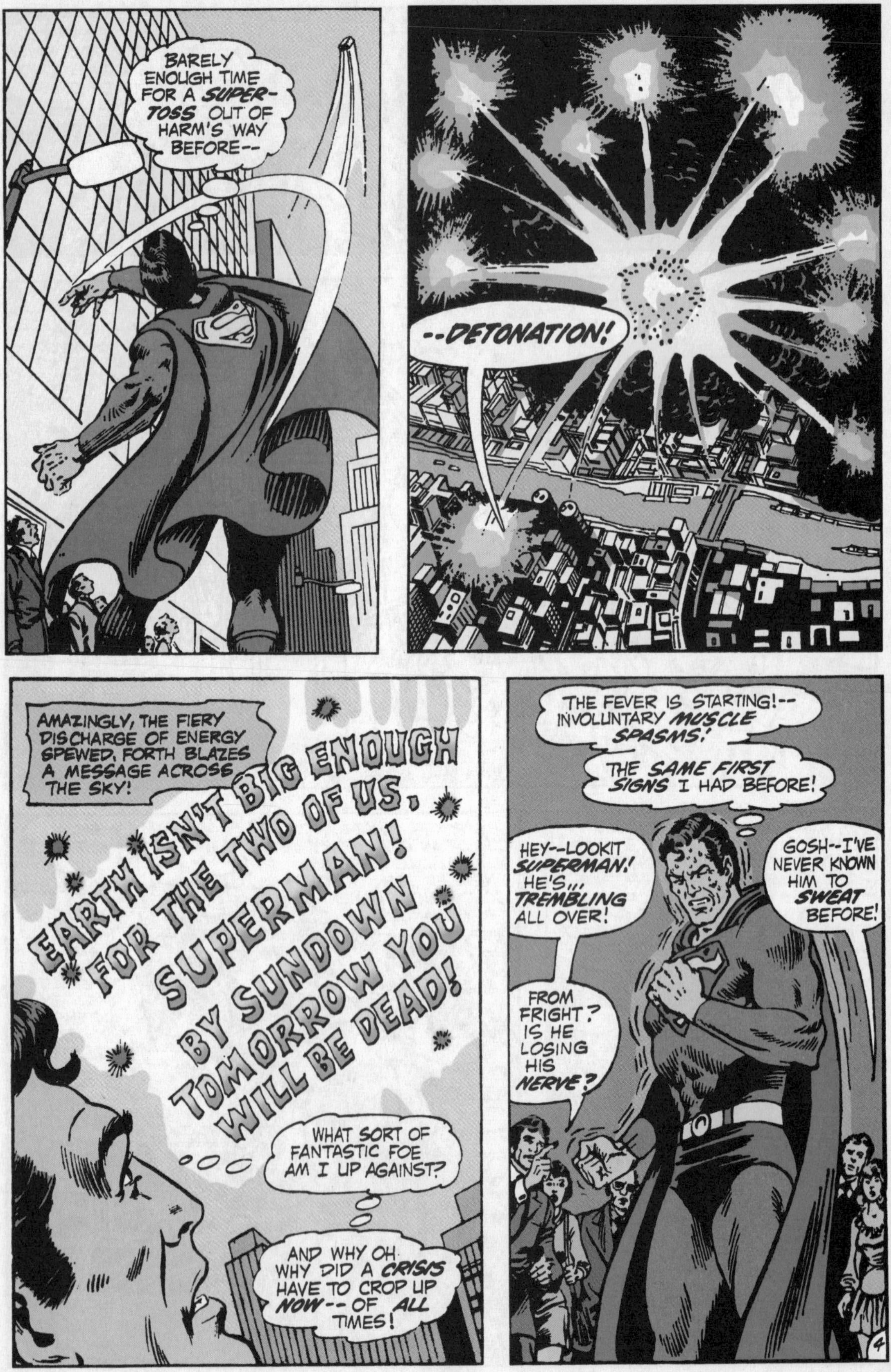
BARELY ENOUGH TIME FOR A SUPER-TOSS OUT OF HARM'S WAY BEFORE--
--DETONATION!
AMAZINGLY, THE FIERY DISCHARGE OF ENERGY SPEWED FORTH BLAZES A MESSAGE ACROSS THE SKY!
EARTH ISN'T BIG ENOUGH FOR THE TWO OF US, SUPERMAN! BY SUNDOWN TOMORROW YOU WILL BE DEAD!
WHAT SORT OF FANTASTIC FOE AM I UP AGAINST?
AND WHY OH WHY DID A CRISIS HAVE TO CROP UP NOW--OF ALL TIMES!
THE FEVER IS STARTING!--INVOLUNTARY MUSCLE SPASMS!
THE SAME FIRST SIGNS I HAD BEFORE!
HEY--LOOKIT SUPERMAN! HE'S... TREMBLING ALL OVER!
GOSH--I'VE NEVER KNOWN HIM TO SWEAT BEFORE!
FROM FRIGHT? IS HE LOSING HIS NERVE?
4

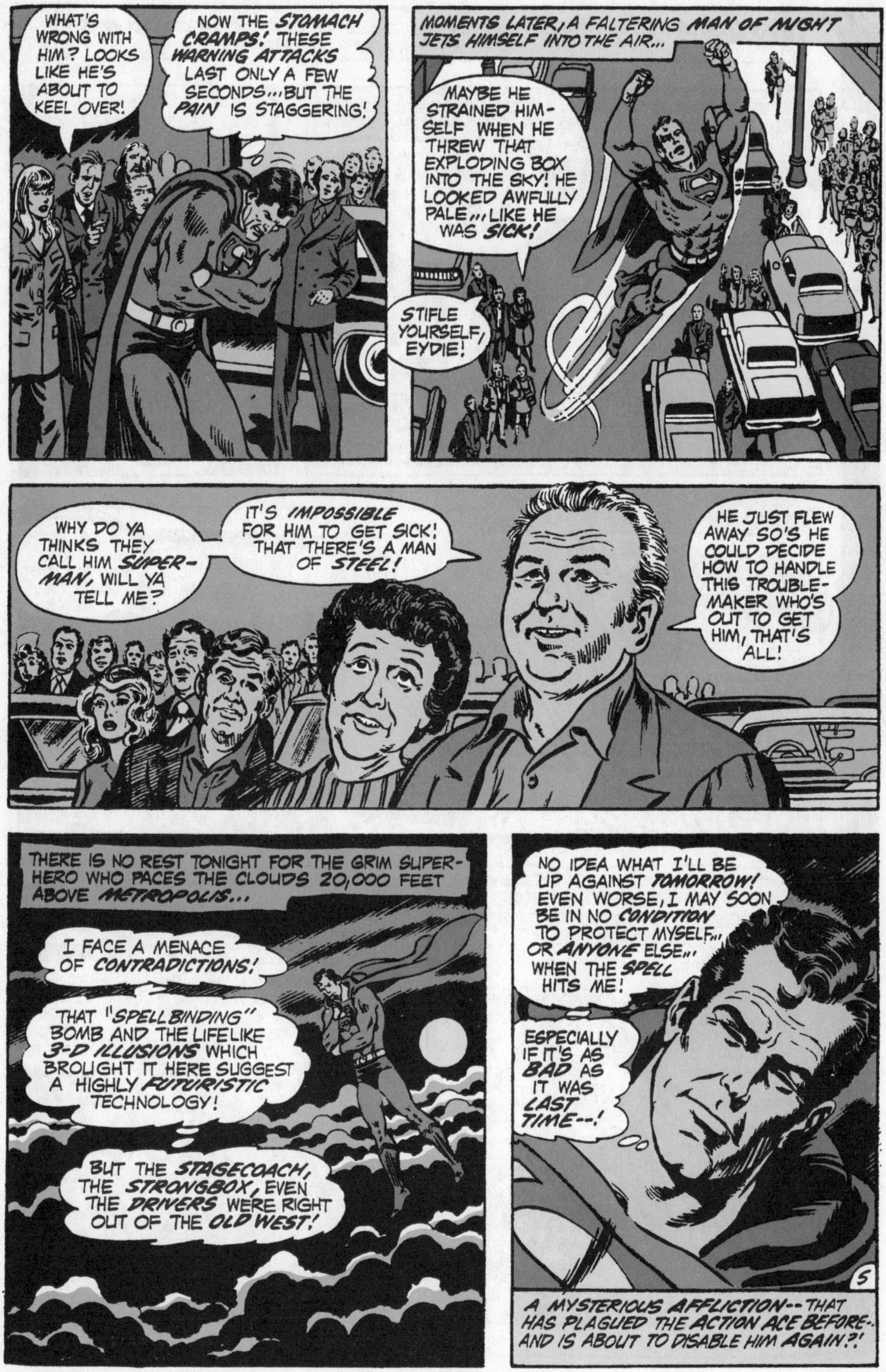
WHAT'S WRONG WITH HIM? LOOKS LIKE HE'S ABOUT TO KEEL OVER!
NOW THE STOMACH CRAMPS! THESE WARNING ATTACKS LAST ONLY A FEW SECONDS... BUT THE PAIN IS STAGGERING!
MOMENTS LATER, A FALTERING MAN OF MIGHT JETS HIMSELF INTO THE AIR...
MAYBE HE STRAINED HIMSELF WHEN HE THREW THAT EXPLODING BOX INTO THE SKY! HE LOOKED AWFULLY PALE... LIKE HE WAS SICK!
STIFLE YOURSELF, EYDIE!
WHY DO YA THINKS THEY CALL HIM SUPERMAN, WILL YA TELL ME?
IT'S IMPOSSIBLE FOR HIM TO GET SICK! THAT THERE'S A MAN OF STEEL!
HE JUST FLEW AWAY SO'S HE COULD DECIDE HOW TO HANDLE THIS TROUBLEMAKER WHO'S OUT TO GET HIM, THAT'S ALL!
THERE IS NO REST TONIGHT FOR THE GRIM SUPER-HERO WHO PACES THE CLOUDS 20,000 FEET ABOVE METROPOLIS...
I FACE A MENACE OF CONTRADICTIONS!
THAT "SPELLBINDING" BOMB AND THE LIFELIKE 3-D ILLUSIONS WHICH BROUGHT IT HERE SUGGEST A HIGHLY FUTURISTIC TECHNOLOGY!
BUT THE STAGECOACH, THE STRONGBOX, EVEN THE DRIVERS WERE RIGHT OUT OF THE OLD WEST!
NO IDEA WHAT I'LL BE UP AGAINST TOMORROW! EVEN WORSE, I MAY SOON BE IN NO CONDITION TO PROTECT MYSELF... OR ANYONE ELSE... WHEN THE SPELL HITS ME!
ESPECIALLY IF IT'S AS BAD AS IT WAS LAST TIME--!
5
A MYSTERIOUS AFFLICTION--THAT HAS PLAGUED THE ACTION ACE BEFORE-- AND IS ABOUT TO DISABLE HIM AGAIN?!

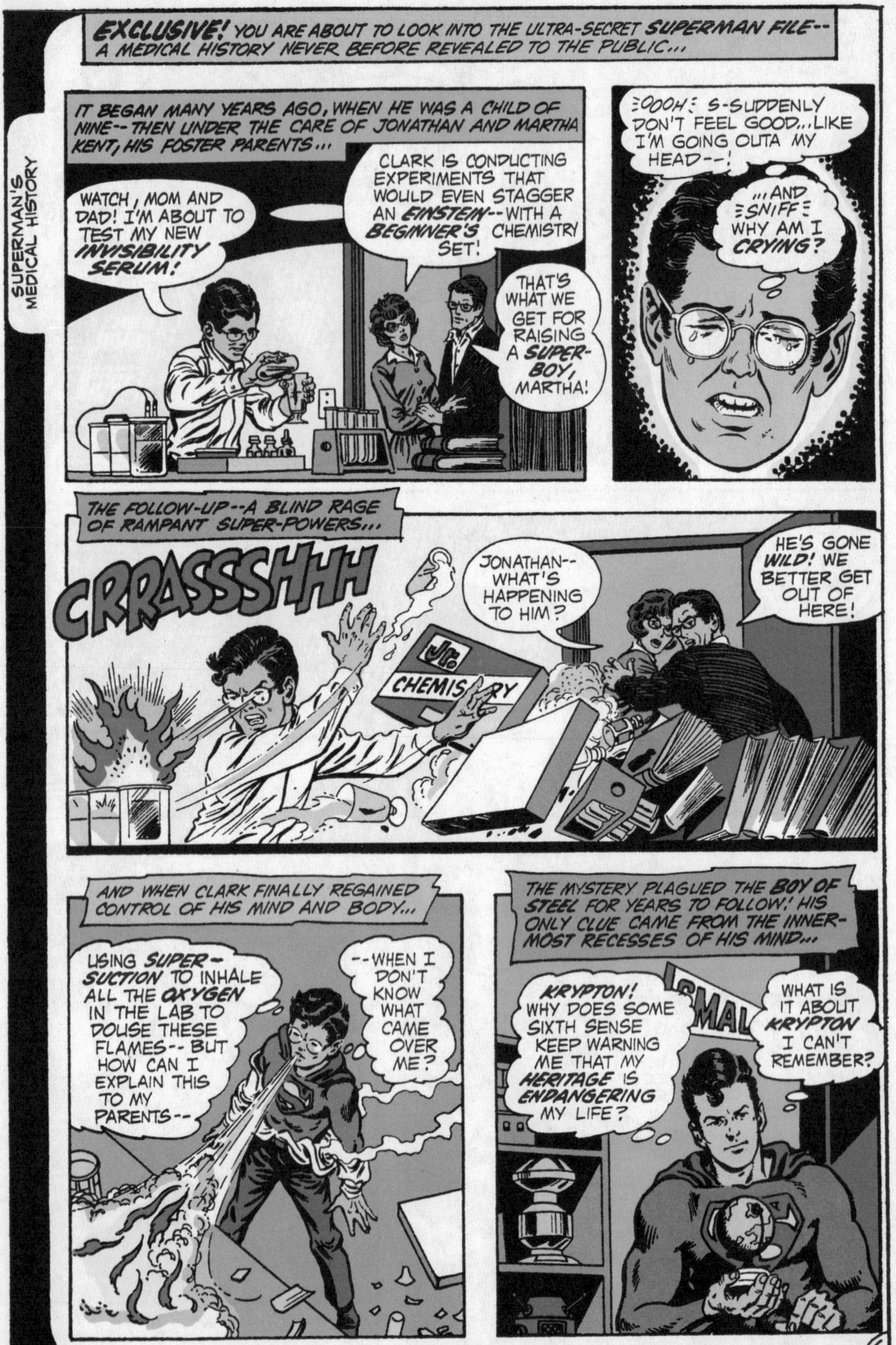
SUPERMAN'S MEDICAL HISTORY
EXCLUSIVE! YOU ARE ABOUT TO LOOK INTO THE ULTRA-SECRET SUPERMAN FILE-- A MEDICAL HISTORY NEVER BEFORE REVEALED TO THE PUBLIC...
IT BEGAN MANY YEARS AGO, WHEN HE WAS A CHILD OF NINE-- THEN UNDER THE CARE OF JONATHAN AND MARTHA KENT, HIS FOSTER PARENTS...
WATCH, MOM AND DAD! I'M ABOUT TO TEST MY NEW INVISIBILITY SERUM!
CLARK IS CONDUCTING EXPERIMENTS THAT WOULD EVEN STAGGER AN EINSTEIN--WITH A BEGINNER'S CHEMISTRY SET!
THAT'S WHAT WE GET FOR RAISING A SUPER-BOY, MARTHA!
OOOH! S-SUDDENLY DON'T FEEL GOOD...LIKE I'M GOING OUTA MY HEAD--!
...AND SNIFF WHY AM I CRYING?
THE FOLLOW-UP--A BLIND RAGE OF RAMPANT SUPER-POWERS...
CRRASSSHHH
JONATHAN-- WHAT'S HAPPENING TO HIM?
HE'S GONE WILD! WE BETTER GET OUT OF HERE!
CHEMIS RY
AND WHEN CLARK FINALLY REGAINED CONTROL OF HIS MIND AND BODY...
USING SUPER-SUCTION TO INHALE ALL THE OXYGEN IN THE LAB TO DOUSE THESE FLAMES-- BUT HOW CAN I EXPLAIN THIS TO MY PARENTS--
--WHEN I DON'T KNOW WHAT CAME OVER ME?
THE MYSTERY PLAGUED THE BOY OF STEEL FOR YEARS TO FOLLOW! HIS ONLY CLUE CAME FROM THE INNER-MOST RECESSES OF HIS MIND...
KRYPTON! WHY DOES SOME SIXTH SENSE KEEP WARNING ME THAT MY HERITAGE IS ENDANGERING MY LIFE?
WHAT IS IT ABOUT KRYPTON I CAN'T REMEMBER?
6

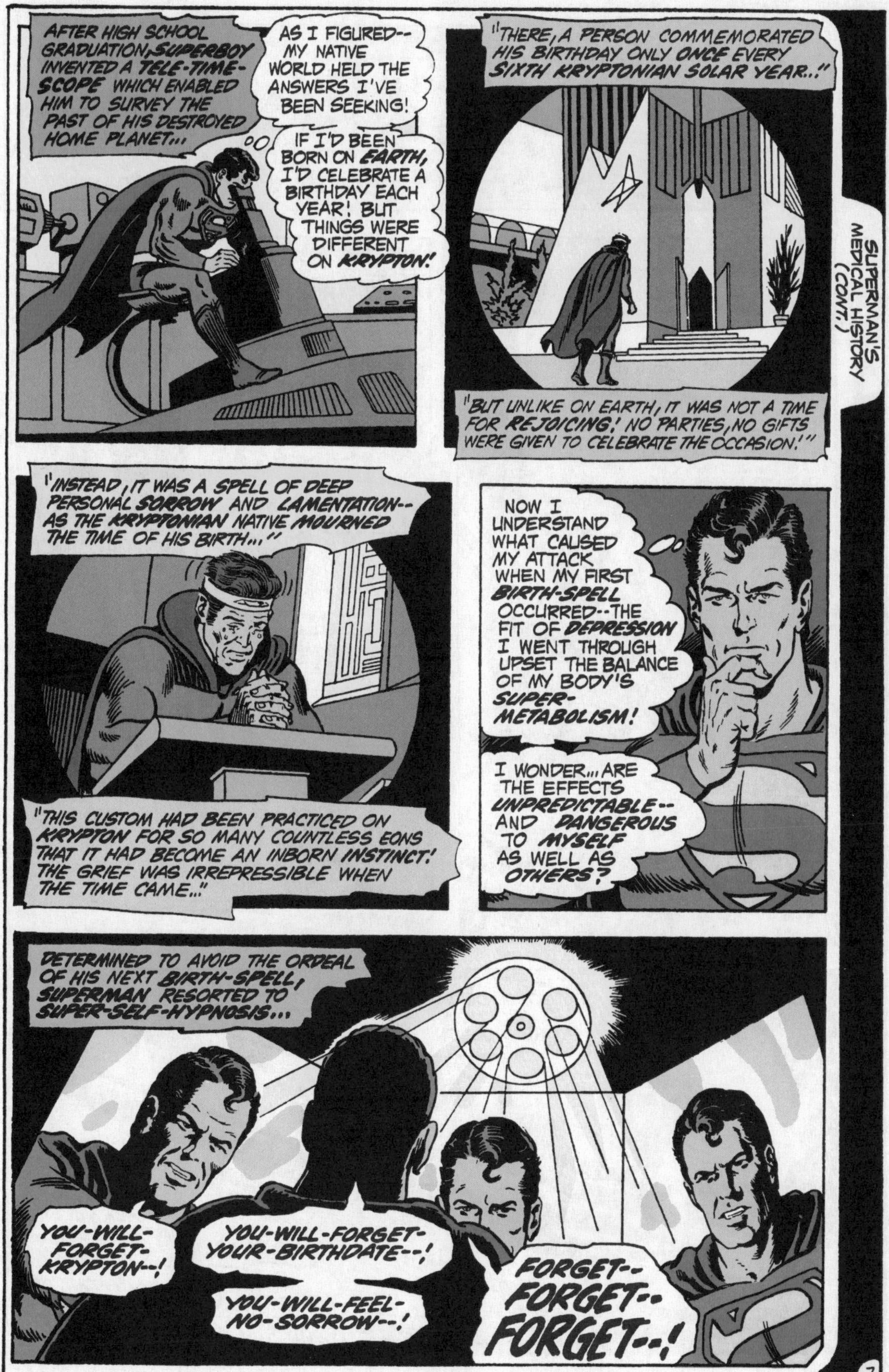
AFTER HIGH SCHOOL GRADUATION, SUPERBOY INVENTED A TELE-TIME-SCOPE WHICH ENABLED HIM TO SURVEY THE PAST OF HIS DESTROYED HOME PLANET...
AS I FIGURED-- MY NATIVE WORLD HELD THE ANSWERS I'VE BEEN SEEKING!
IF I'D BEEN BORN ON EARTH, I'D CELEBRATE A BIRTHDAY EACH YEAR! BUT THINGS WERE DIFFERENT ON KRYPTON!
"THERE, A PERSON COMMEMORATED HIS BIRTHDAY ONLY ONCE EVERY SIXTH KRYPTONIAN SOLAR YEAR..!"
"BUT UNLIKE ON EARTH, IT WAS NOT A TIME FOR REJOICING! NO PARTIES, NO GIFTS WERE GIVEN TO CELEBRATE THE OCCASION!"
SUPERMAN'S MEDICAL HISTORY (CONT.)
"INSTEAD, IT WAS A SPELL OF DEEP PERSONAL SORROW AND LAMENTATION-- AS THE KRYPTONIAN NATIVE MOURNED THE TIME OF HIS BIRTH..."
"THIS CUSTOM HAD BEEN PRACTICED ON KRYPTON FOR SO MANY COUNTLESS EONS THAT IT HAD BECOME AN INBORN INSTINCT! THE GRIEF WAS IRREPRESSIBLE WHEN THE TIME CAME..."
NOW I UNDERSTAND WHAT CAUSED MY ATTACK WHEN MY FIRST BIRTH-SPELL OCCURRED--THE FIT OF DEPRESSION I WENT THROUGH UPSET THE BALANCE OF MY BODY'S SUPER-METABOLISM!
I WONDER... ARE THE EFFECTS UNPREDICTABLE-- AND DANGEROUS TO MYSELF AS WELL AS OTHERS?
DETERMINED TO AVOID THE ORDEAL OF HIS NEXT BIRTH-SPELL, SUPERMAN RESORTED TO SUPER-SELF-HYPNOSIS...
YOU-WILL-FORGET-KRYPTON--!
YOU-WILL-FORGET-YOUR-BIRTHDATE--!
YOU-WILL-FEEL-NO-SORROW--!
FORGET-- FORGET-- FORGET--!
7

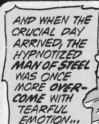

AND WHEN THE CRUCIAL DAY ARRIVED, THE HYPNOTIZED *MAN OF STEEL* WAS ONCE MORE *OVER-COME* WITH TEARFUL EMOTION...

WHAT MADE ME START *CRYING?* I GET THE FEELING I'VE *FORGOTTEN* SOMETHING--!

ALTHOUGH HE COULD BLOT OUT THE MEMORY OF HIS *BIRTH-SPELL--* SUPERMAN COULDN'T ERASE THE SUBCONSCIOUS *INSTINCTS* THAT MADE HIM A *KRYPTONIAN!*

SUPERMAN'S MEDICAL HISTORY (CONT.)

THE IMMENSE GRIEF WHICH FOLLOWED AGAIN DISRUPTED HIS SUPER-METABOLISM-- WITH *ALARMING* RESULTS...

CAN'T PULL OUT OF THE *CRASH-DIVE!* IN A FEW SECONDS WE'RE GONNA *HIT!*

LOOK-- *SUPERMAN* FLEW RIGHT PAST US WITHOUT STOPPING! WHY DIDN'T HE *HELP US?*

THE *BIRTH-SPELL'S* EFFECTS HAD MOMENTARILY BLANKED OUT HIS *SUPER-SIGHT* AND *HEARING...*

FLYING *BLIND* AND *DEAF--*

BUT MY SUPER-SENSE OF *SMELL* DETECTS THE ACRID ODOR OF *BURNING FUEL* HANGING IN THE AIR!

I'LL USE MY NOSE TO TRACE THE SOURCE!

GOOD OL' *SUPERMAN!* I SHOULD HAVE KNOWN HE WOULDN'T FAIL US!

LIKE I FIGURED-- WHAT I SMELLED WAS THE SMOKE OF A *PLANE* IN TROUBLE!

THIS *KRYPTONIAN AFFLICTION* ALMOST PREVENTED ME FROM SAVING INNOCENT LIVES!--*NEXT TIME* THE CONSEQUENCES MAY BE DISASTROUS!

8

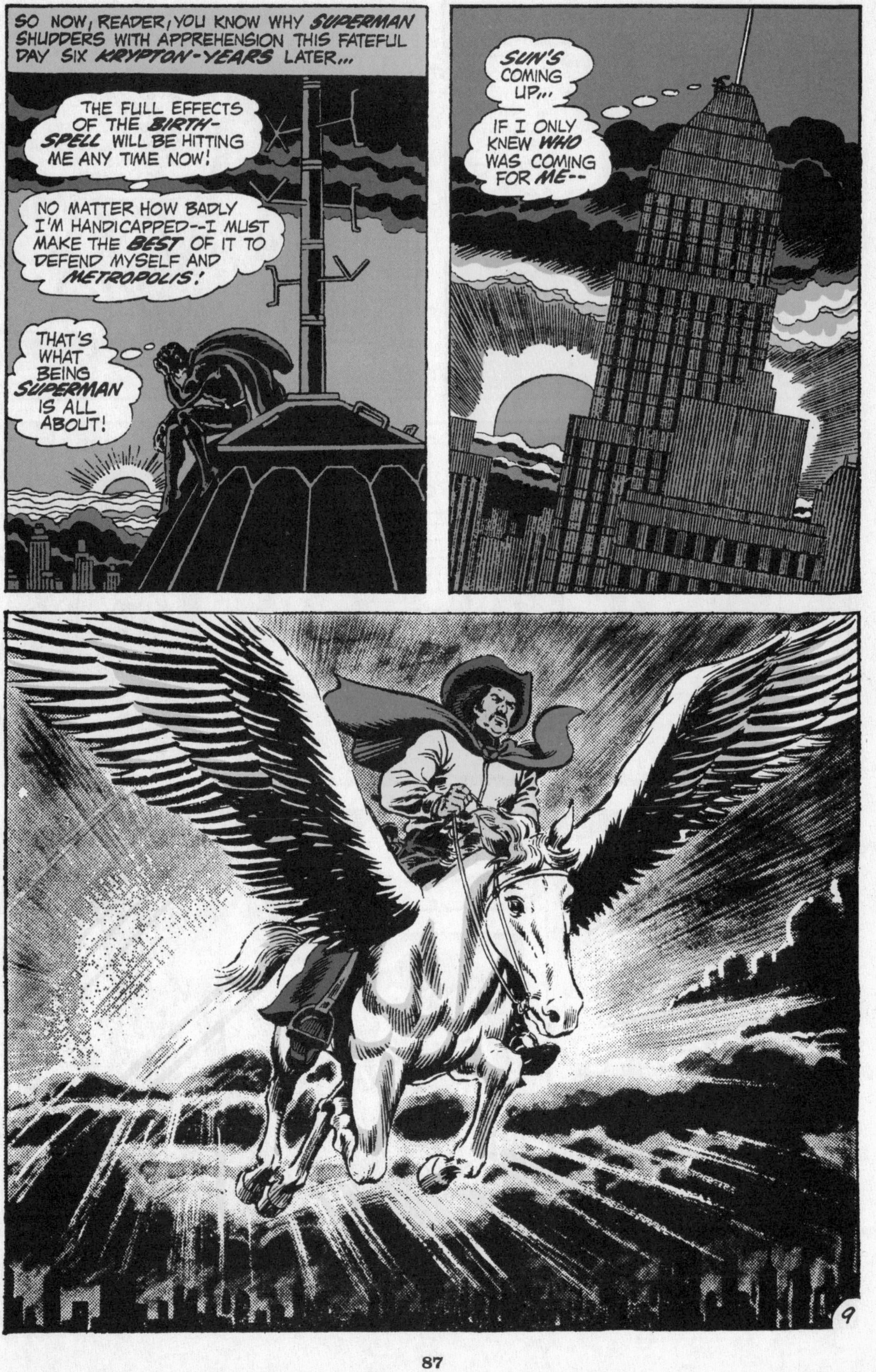
SO NOW, READER, YOU KNOW WHY SUPERMAN SHUDDERS WITH APPREHENSION THIS FATEFUL DAY SIX KRYPTON-YEARS LATER...
THE FULL EFFECTS OF THE BIRTH-SPELL WILL BE HITTING ME ANY TIME NOW!
NO MATTER HOW BADLY I'M HANDICAPPED--I MUST MAKE THE BEST OF IT TO DEFEND MYSELF AND METROPOLIS!
THAT'S WHAT BEING SUPERMAN IS ALL ABOUT!
SUN'S COMING UP...
IF I ONLY KNEW WHO WAS COMING FOR ME--
9

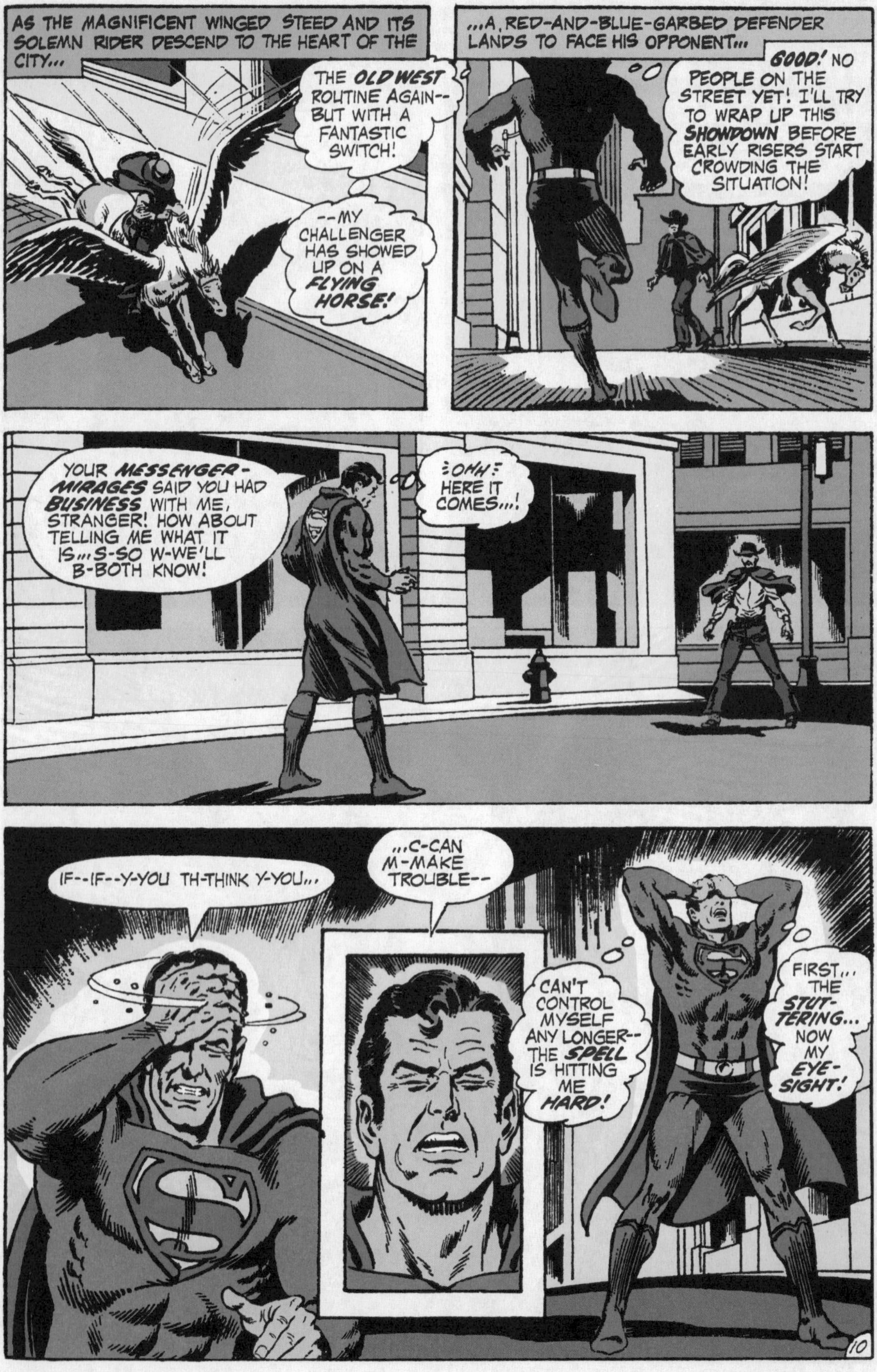
AS THE MAGNIFICENT WINGED STEED AND ITS SOLEMN RIDER DESCEND TO THE HEART OF THE CITY...
THE OLD WEST ROUTINE AGAIN-- BUT WITH A FANTASTIC SWITCH!
--MY CHALLENGER HAS SHOWED UP ON A FLYING HORSE!
...A RED-AND-BLUE-GARBED DEFENDER LANDS TO FACE HIS OPPONENT...
GOOD! NO PEOPLE ON THE STREET YET! I'LL TRY TO WRAP UP THIS SHOWDOWN BEFORE EARLY RISERS START CROWDING THE SITUATION!
YOUR MESSENGER-MIRAGES SAID YOU HAD BUSINESS WITH ME, STRANGER! HOW ABOUT TELLING ME WHAT IT IS... S-SO W-WE'LL B-BOTH KNOW!
OHH! HERE IT COMES...!
IF--IF--Y-YOU TH-THINK Y-YOU...
...C-CAN M-MAKE TROUBLE--
CAN'T CONTROL MYSELF ANY LONGER-- THE SPELL IS HITTING ME HARD!
FIRST... THE STUTTERING... NOW MY EYE-SIGHT!
10

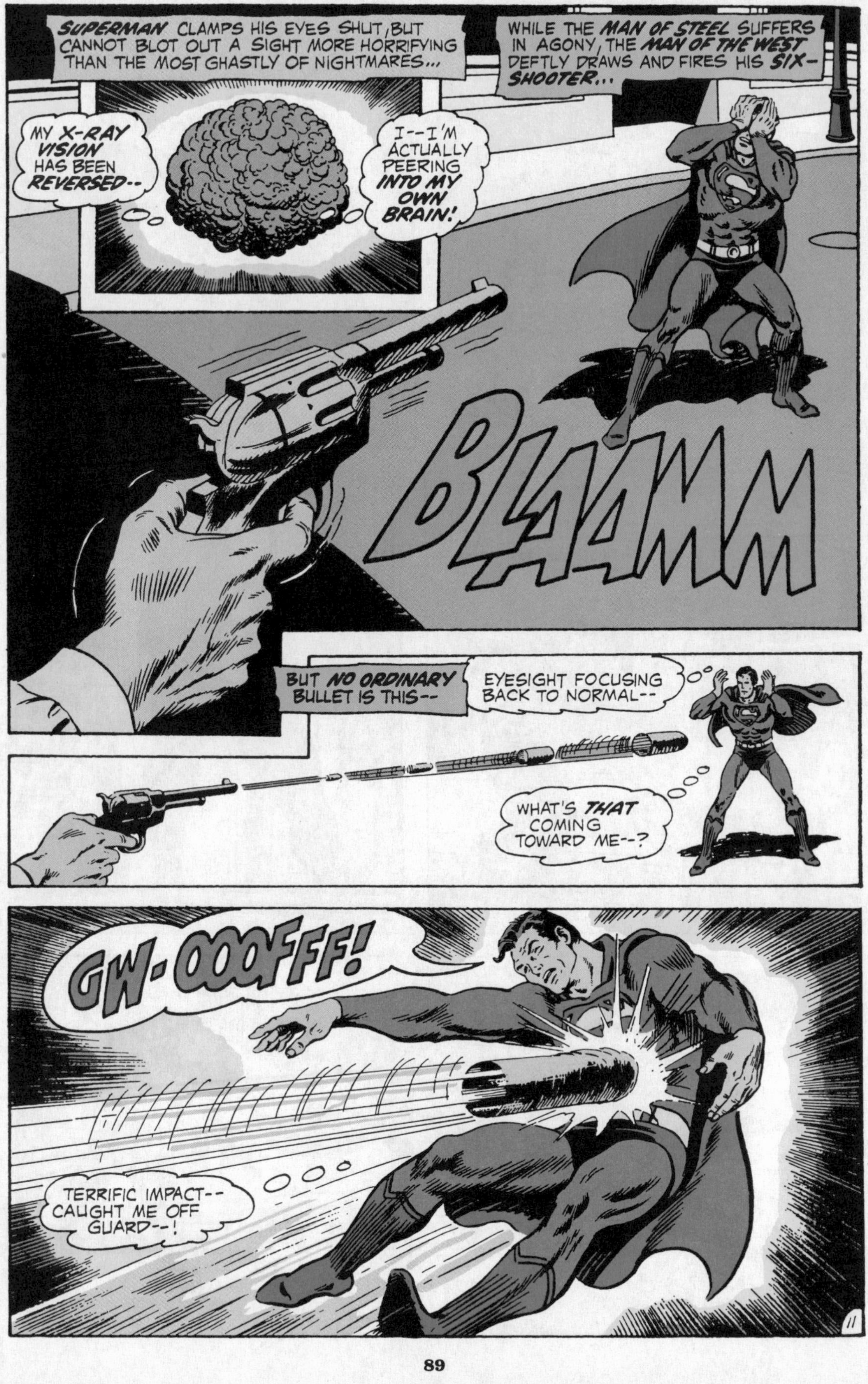
SUPERMAN CLAMPS HIS EYES SHUT, BUT CANNOT BLOT OUT A SIGHT MORE HORRIFYING THAN THE MOST GHASTLY OF NIGHTMARES...
MY X-RAY VISION HAS BEEN REVERSED--
I--I'M ACTUALLY PEERING INTO MY OWN BRAIN!
WHILE THE MAN OF STEEL SUFFERS IN AGONY, THE MAN OF THE WEST DEFTLY DRAWS AND FIRES HIS SIX-SHOOTER...
BLAMM
BUT NO ORDINARY BULLET IS THIS--
EYESIGHT FOCUSING BACK TO NORMAL--
WHAT'S THAT COMING TOWARD ME--?
GW-OOOFFF!
TERRIFIC IMPACT--CAUGHT ME OFF GUARD--!
11

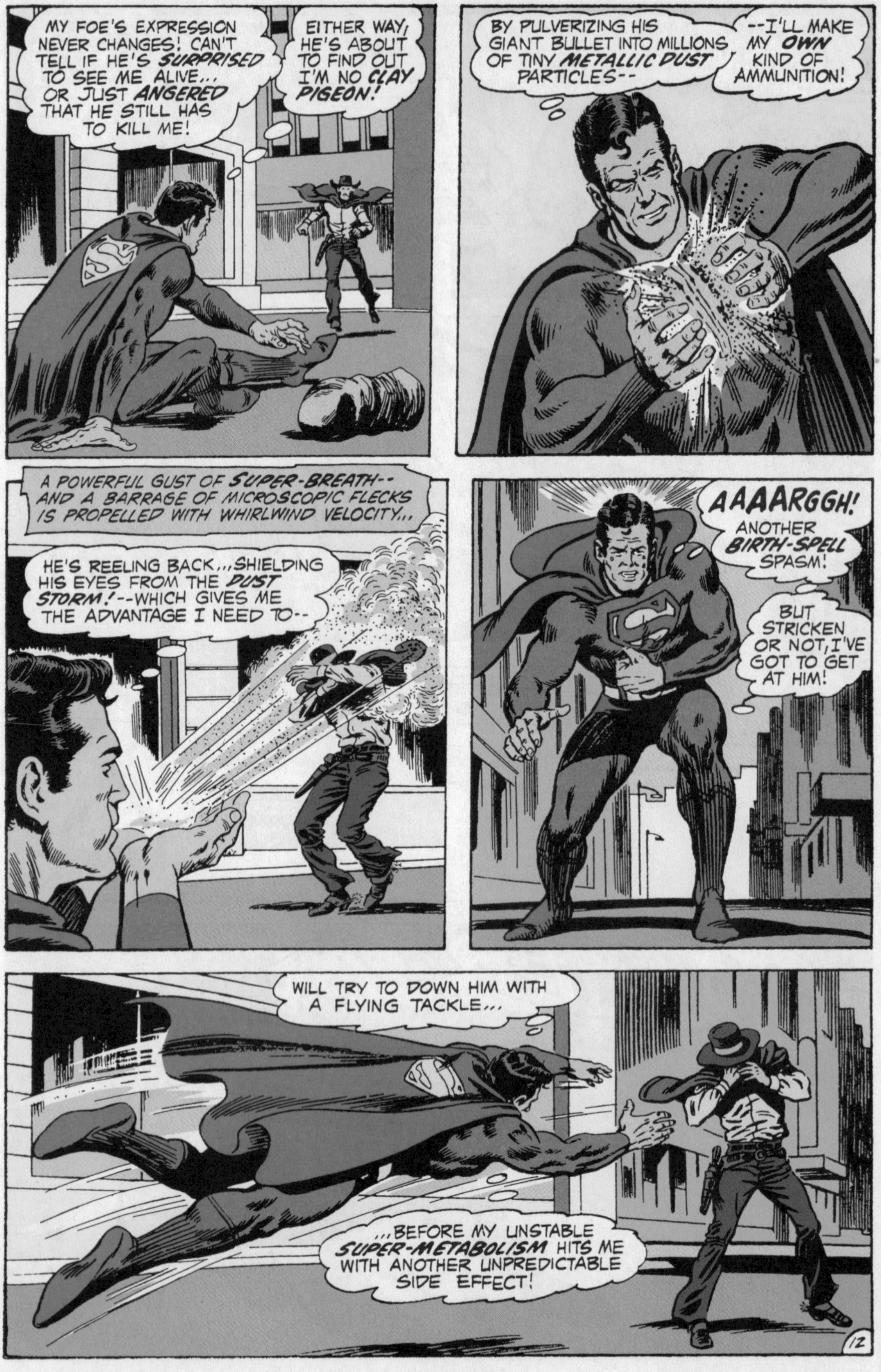
MY FOE'S EXPRESSION NEVER CHANGES! CAN'T TELL IF HE'S SURPRISED TO SEE ME ALIVE... OR JUST ANGERED THAT HE STILL HAS TO KILL ME!
EITHER WAY, HE'S ABOUT TO FIND OUT I'M NO CLAY PIGEON!
BY PULVERIZING HIS GIANT BULLET INTO MILLIONS OF TINY METALLIC DUST PARTICLES--
--I'LL MAKE MY OWN KIND OF AMMUNITION!
A POWERFUL GUST OF SUPER-BREATH-- AND A BARRAGE OF MICROSCOPIC FLECKS IS PROPELLED WITH WHIRLWIND VELOCITY...
HE'S REELING BACK... SHIELDING HIS EYES FROM THE DUST STORM! --WHICH GIVES ME THE ADVANTAGE I NEED TO--
AAAARGGH!
ANOTHER BIRTH-SPELL SPASM!
BUT STRICKEN OR NOT, I'VE GOT TO GET AT HIM!
WILL TRY TO DOWN HIM WITH A FLYING TACKLE...
...BEFORE MY UNSTABLE SUPER-METABOLISM HITS ME WITH ANOTHER UNPREDICTABLE SIDE EFFECT!
12

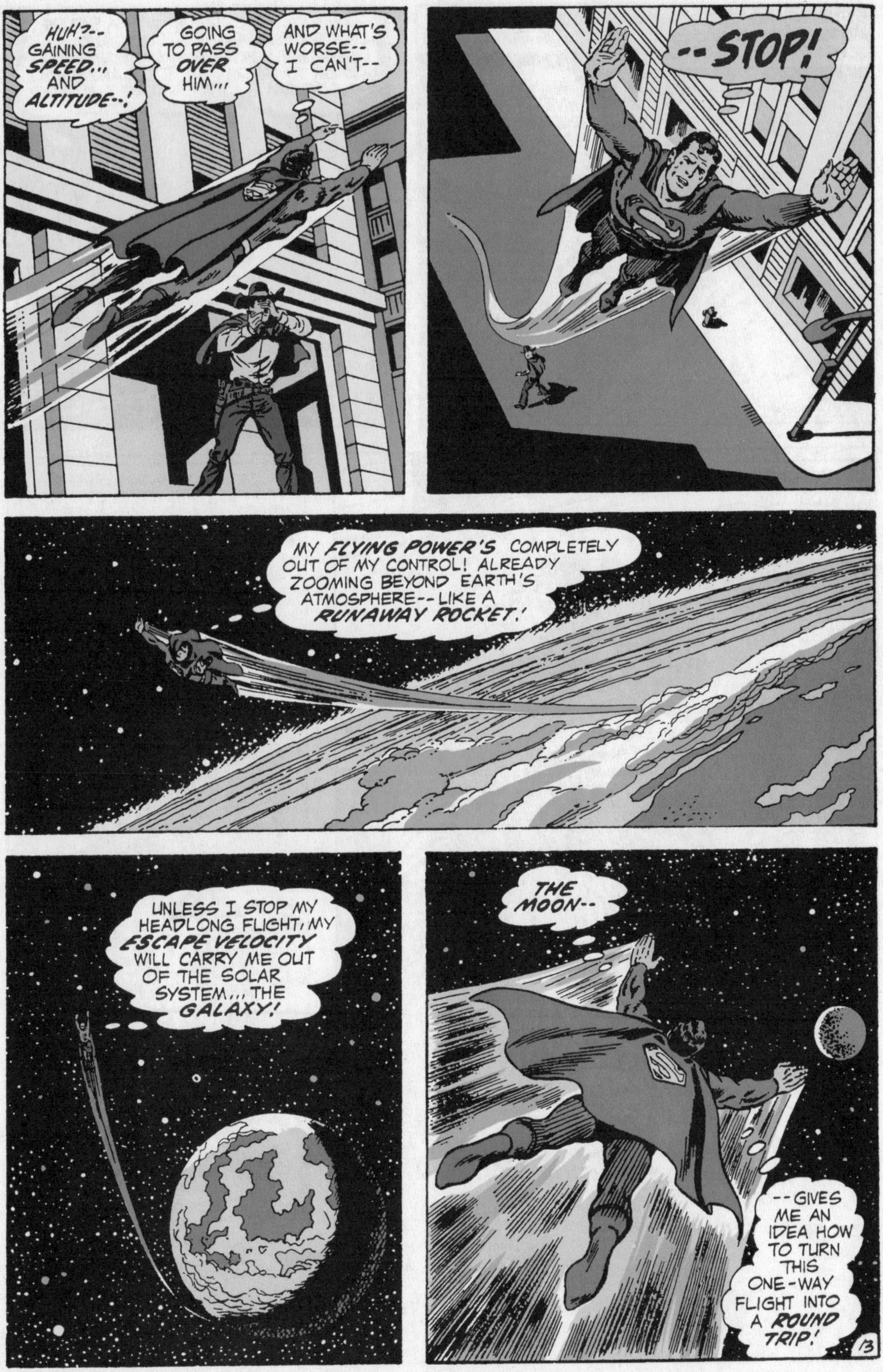
HUH?-- GAINING SPEED... AND ALTITUDE--!
GOING TO PASS OVER HIM...
AND WHAT'S WORSE-- I CAN'T--
--STOP!
MY FLYING POWER'S COMPLETELY OUT OF MY CONTROL! ALREADY ZOOMING BEYOND EARTH'S ATMOSPHERE--LIKE A RUNAWAY ROCKET!
UNLESS I STOP MY HEADLONG FLIGHT, MY ESCAPE VELOCITY WILL CARRY ME OUT OF THE SOLAR SYSTEM... THE GALAXY!
THE MOON--
--GIVES ME AN IDEA HOW TO TURN THIS ONE-WAY FLIGHT INTO A ROUND TRIP!
13

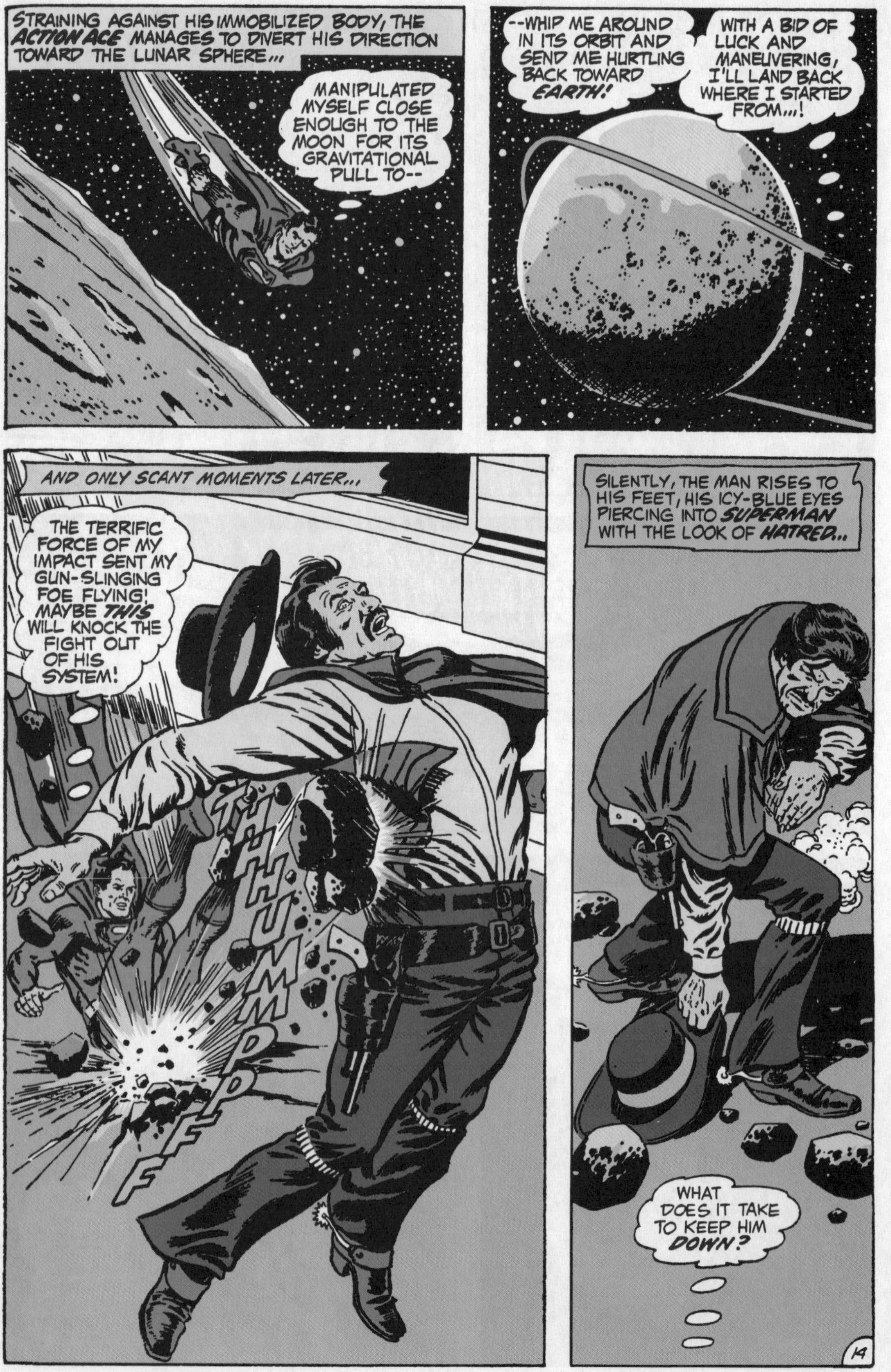
STRAINING AGAINST HIS IMMOBILIZED BODY, THE ACTION ACE MANAGES TO DIVERT HIS DIRECTION TOWARD THE LUNAR SPHERE...
MANIPULATED MYSELF CLOSE ENOUGH TO THE MOON FOR ITS GRAVITATIONAL PULL TO--
--WHIP ME AROUND IN ITS ORBIT AND SEND ME HURTLING BACK TOWARD EARTH!
WITH A BID OF LUCK AND MANEUVERING, I'LL LAND BACK WHERE I STARTED FROM...!
AND ONLY SCANT MOMENTS LATER...
THE TERRIFIC FORCE OF MY IMPACT SENT MY GUN-SLINGING FOE FLYING! MAYBE THIS WILL KNOCK THE FIGHT OUT OF HIS SYSTEM!
THHUMMPPFF
SILENTLY, THE MAN RISES TO HIS FEET, HIS ICY-BLUE EYES PIERCING INTO SUPERMAN WITH THE LOOK OF HATRED...
WHAT DOES IT TAKE TO KEEP HIM DOWN?
14

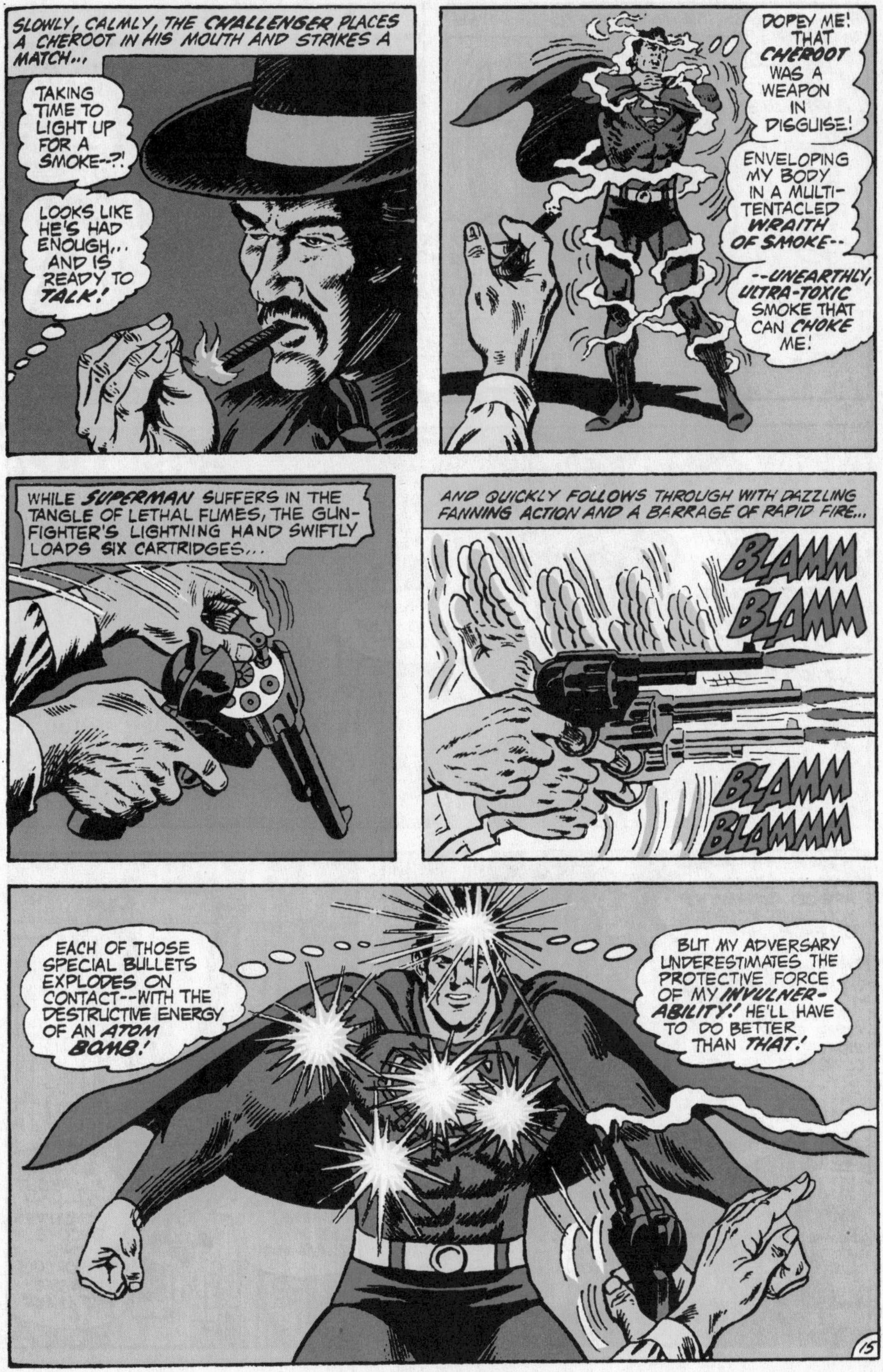
SLOWLY, CALMLY, THE CHALLENGER PLACES A CHEROOT IN HIS MOUTH AND STRIKES A MATCH...
TAKING TIME TO LIGHT UP FOR A SMOKE--?!
LOOKS LIKE HE'S HAD ENOUGH,.. AND IS READY TO TALK!
DOPEY ME! THAT CHEROOT WAS A WEAPON IN DISGUISE!
ENVELOPING MY BODY IN A MULTI-TENTACLED WRAITH OF SMOKE--
--UNEARTHLY, ULTRA-TOXIC SMOKE THAT CAN CHOKE ME!
WHILE SUPERMAN SUFFERS IN THE TANGLE OF LETHAL FUMES, THE GUN-FIGHTER'S LIGHTNING HAND SWIFTLY LOADS SIX CARTRIDGES...
AND QUICKLY FOLLOWS THROUGH WITH DAZZLING FANNING ACTION AND A BARRAGE OF RAPID FIRE...
BLAMM
BLAMM
BLAMM
BLAMMM
EACH OF THOSE SPECIAL BULLETS EXPLODES ON CONTACT--WITH THE DESTRUCTIVE ENERGY OF AN ATOM BOMB!
BUT MY ADVERSARY UNDERESTIMATES THE PROTECTIVE FORCE OF MY INVULNER-ABILITY! HE'LL HAVE TO DO BETTER THAN THAT!
15

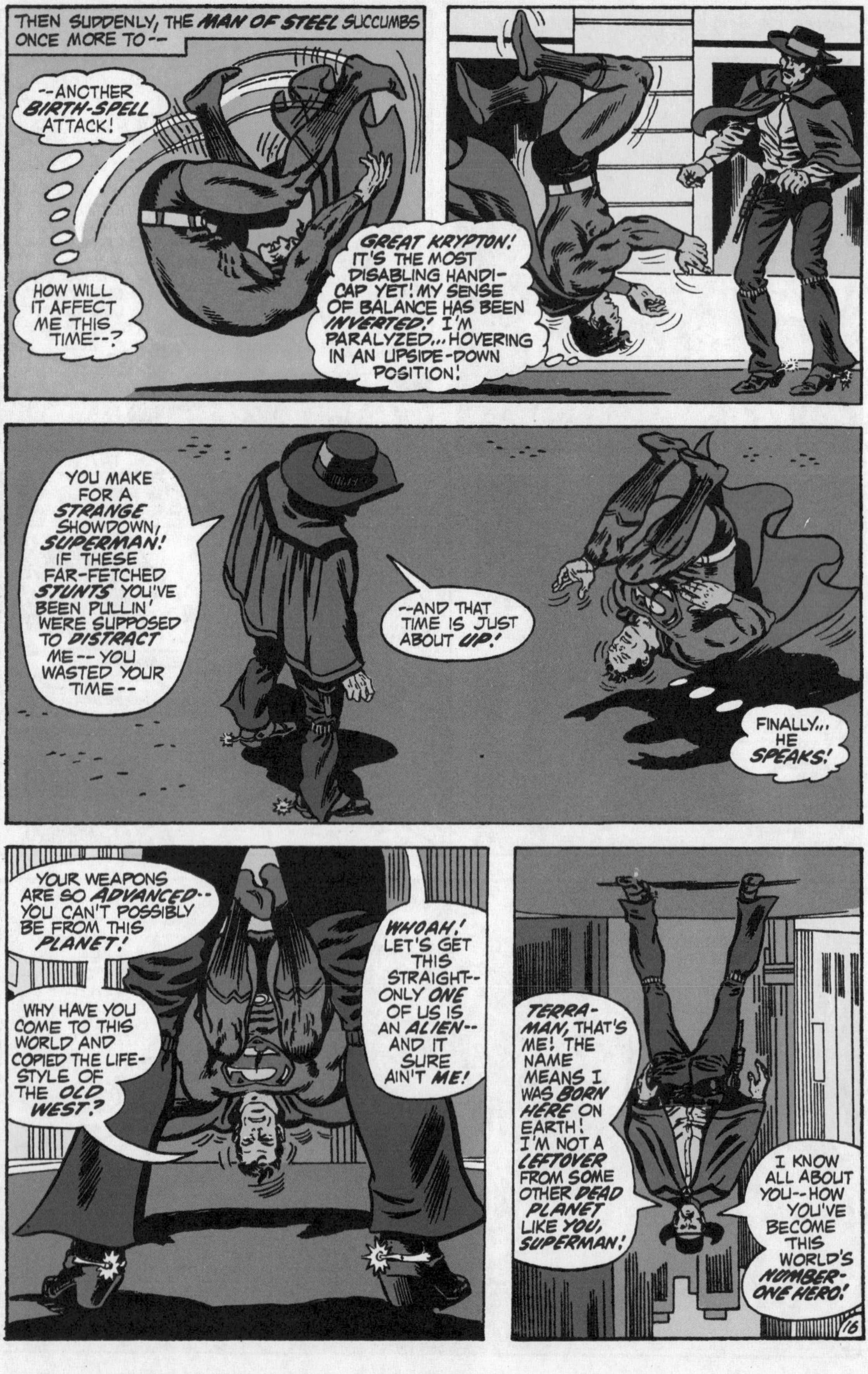
THEN SUDDENLY, THE MAN OF STEEL SUCCUMBS ONCE MORE TO--
--ANOTHER BIRTH-SPELL ATTACK!
HOW WILL IT AFFECT ME THIS TIME--?
GREAT KRYPTON! IT'S THE MOST DISABLING HANDI-CAP YET! MY SENSE OF BALANCE HAS BEEN INVERTED! I'M PARALYZED... HOVERING IN AN UPSIDE-DOWN POSITION!
YOU MAKE FOR A STRANGE SHOWDOWN, SUPERMAN! IF THESE FAR-FETCHED STUNTS YOU'VE BEEN PULLIN' WERE SUPPOSED TO DISTRACT ME -- YOU WASTED YOUR TIME --
--AND THAT TIME IS JUST ABOUT UP!
FINALLY... HE SPEAKS!
YOUR WEAPONS ARE SO ADVANCED-- YOU CAN'T POSSIBLY BE FROM THIS PLANET!
WHY HAVE YOU COME TO THIS WORLD AND COPIED THE LIFE-STYLE OF THE OLD WEST?
WHOAH! LET'S GET THIS STRAIGHT-- ONLY ONE OF US IS AN ALIEN-- AND IT SURE AIN'T ME!
TERRA-MAN, THAT'S ME! THE NAME MEANS I WAS BORN HERE ON EARTH! I'M NOT A LEFTOVER FROM SOME OTHER DEAD PLANET LIKE YOU, SUPERMAN!
I KNOW ALL ABOUT YOU--HOW YOU'VE BECOME THIS WORLD'S NUMBER-ONE HERO!
16

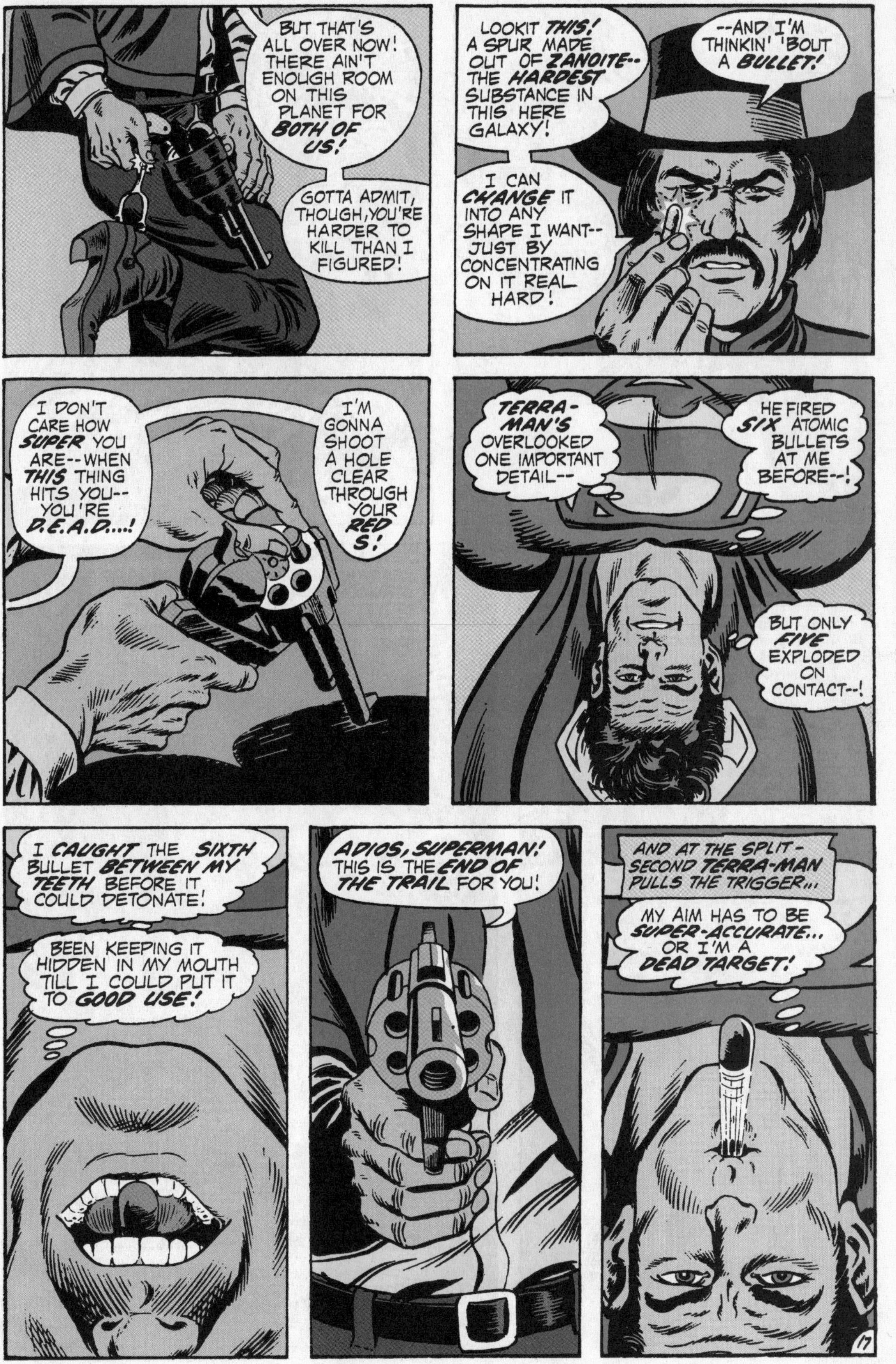
BUT THAT'S ALL OVER NOW! THERE AIN'T ENOUGH ROOM ON THIS PLANET FOR BOTH OF US!
GOTTA ADMIT, THOUGH, YOU'RE HARDER TO KILL THAN I FIGURED!
LOOKIT THIS! A SPUR MADE OUT OF ZANOITE-- THE HARDEST SUBSTANCE IN THIS HERE GALAXY!
I CAN CHANGE IT INTO ANY SHAPE I WANT-- JUST BY CONCENTRATING ON IT REAL HARD!
--AND I'M THINKIN' 'BOUT A BULLET!
I DON'T CARE HOW SUPER YOU ARE--WHEN THIS THING HITS YOU-- YOU'RE D.E.A.D....!
I'M GONNA SHOOT A HOLE CLEAR THROUGH YOUR RED S!
TERRA-MAN'S OVERLOOKED ONE IMPORTANT DETAIL--
HE FIRED SIX ATOMIC BULLETS AT ME BEFORE--!
BUT ONLY FIVE EXPLODED ON CONTACT--!
I CAUGHT THE SIXTH BULLET BETWEEN MY TEETH BEFORE IT COULD DETONATE!
BEEN KEEPING IT HIDDEN IN MY MOUTH TILL I COULD PUT IT TO GOOD USE!
ADIOS, SUPERMAN! THIS IS THE END OF THE TRAIL FOR YOU!
AND AT THE SPLIT-SECOND TERRA-MAN PULLS THE TRIGGER...
MY AIM HAS TO BE SUPER-ACCURATE... OR I'M A DEAD TARGET!
17

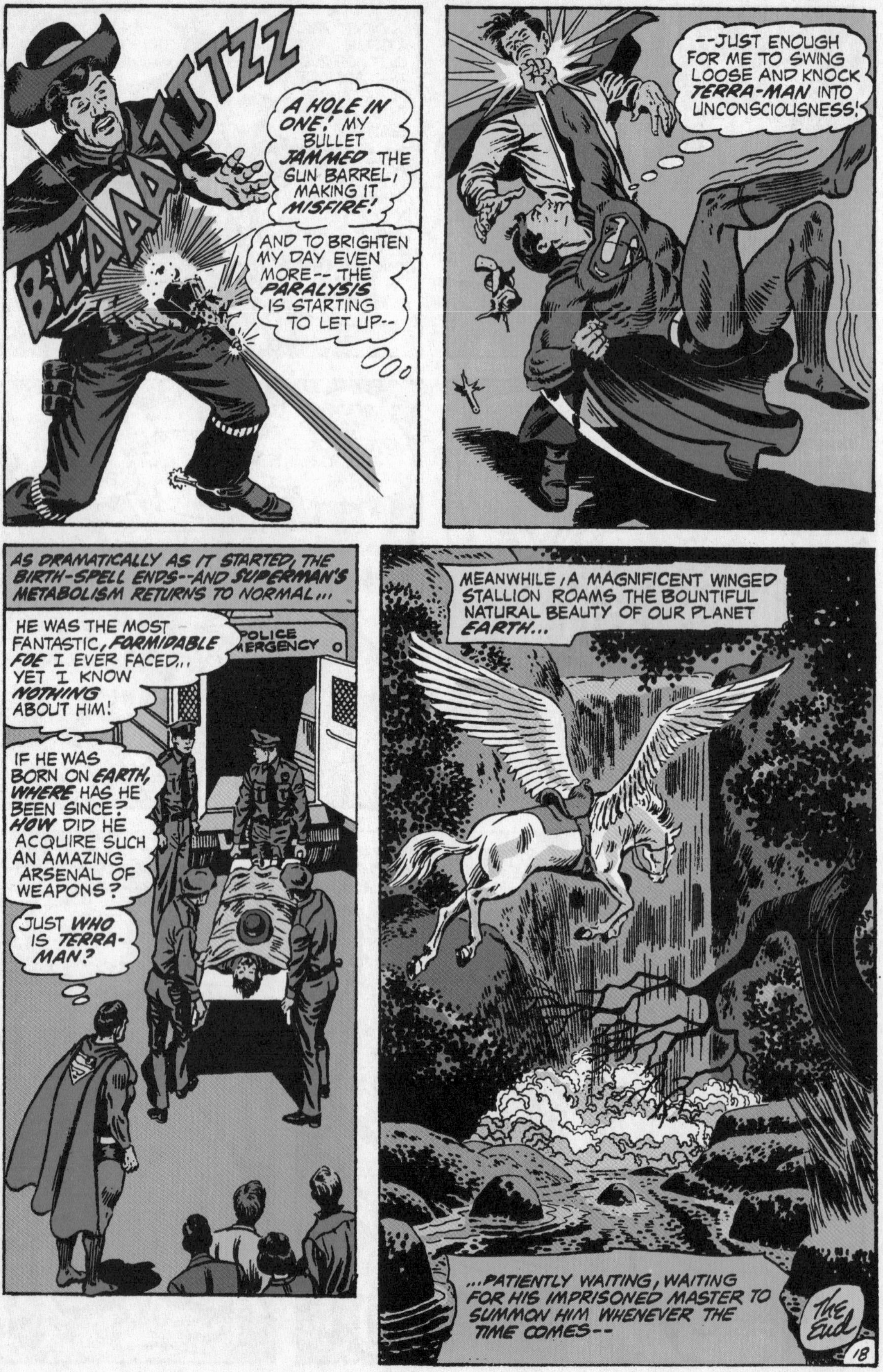
BLAAATTTZZ
A HOLE IN ONE! MY BULLET JAMMED THE GUN BARREL, MAKING IT MISFIRE!
AND TO BRIGHTEN MY DAY EVEN MORE-- THE PARALYSIS IS STARTING TO LET UP--
--JUST ENOUGH FOR ME TO SWING LOOSE AND KNOCK TERRA-MAN INTO UNCONSCIOUSNESS!
AS DRAMATICALLY AS IT STARTED, THE BIRTH-SPELL ENDS--AND SUPERMAN'S METABOLISM RETURNS TO NORMAL...
POLICE EMERGENCY
HE WAS THE MOST FANTASTIC, FORMIDABLE FOE I EVER FACED.. YET I KNOW NOTHING ABOUT HIM!
IF HE WAS BORN ON EARTH, WHERE HAS HE BEEN SINCE? HOW DID HE ACQUIRE SUCH AN AMAZING ARSENAL OF WEAPONS?
JUST WHO IS TERRA-MAN?
MEANWHILE, A MAGNIFICENT WINGED STALLION ROAMS THE BOUNTIFUL NATURAL BEAUTY OF OUR PLANET EARTH...
...PATIENTLY WAITING, WAITING FOR HIS IMPRISONED MASTER TO SUMMON HIM WHENEVER THE TIME COMES--
THE END
18

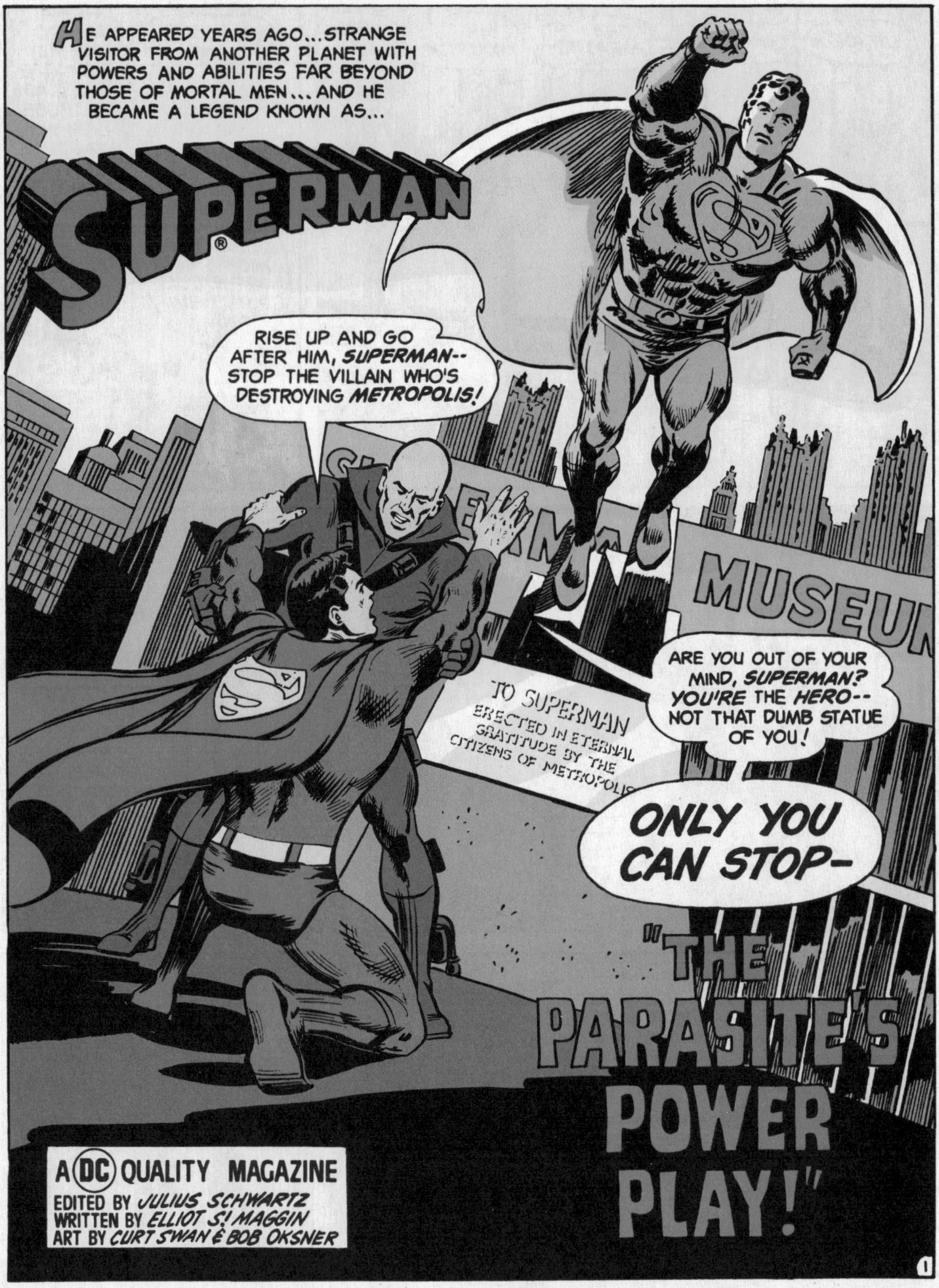
HE APPEARED YEARS AGO... STRANGE VISITOR FROM ANOTHER PLANET WITH POWERS AND ABILITIES FAR BEYOND THOSE OF MORTAL MEN... AND HE BECAME A LEGEND KNOWN AS...
SUPERMAN®
RISE UP AND GO AFTER HIM, SUPERMAN-- STOP THE VILLAIN WHO'S DESTROYING METROPOLIS!
MUSEUM
TO SUPERMAN ERECTED IN ETERNAL GRATITUDE BY THE CITIZENS OF METROPOLIS
ARE YOU OUT OF YOUR MIND, SUPERMAN? YOU'RE THE HERO-- NOT THAT DUMB STATUE OF YOU!
ONLY YOU CAN STOP-
"THE PARASITE'S POWER PLAY!"
A DC QUALITY MAGAZINE
EDITED BY JULIUS SCHWARTZ
WRITTEN BY ELLIOT S! MAGGIN
ART BY CURT SWAN & BOB OKSNER
1

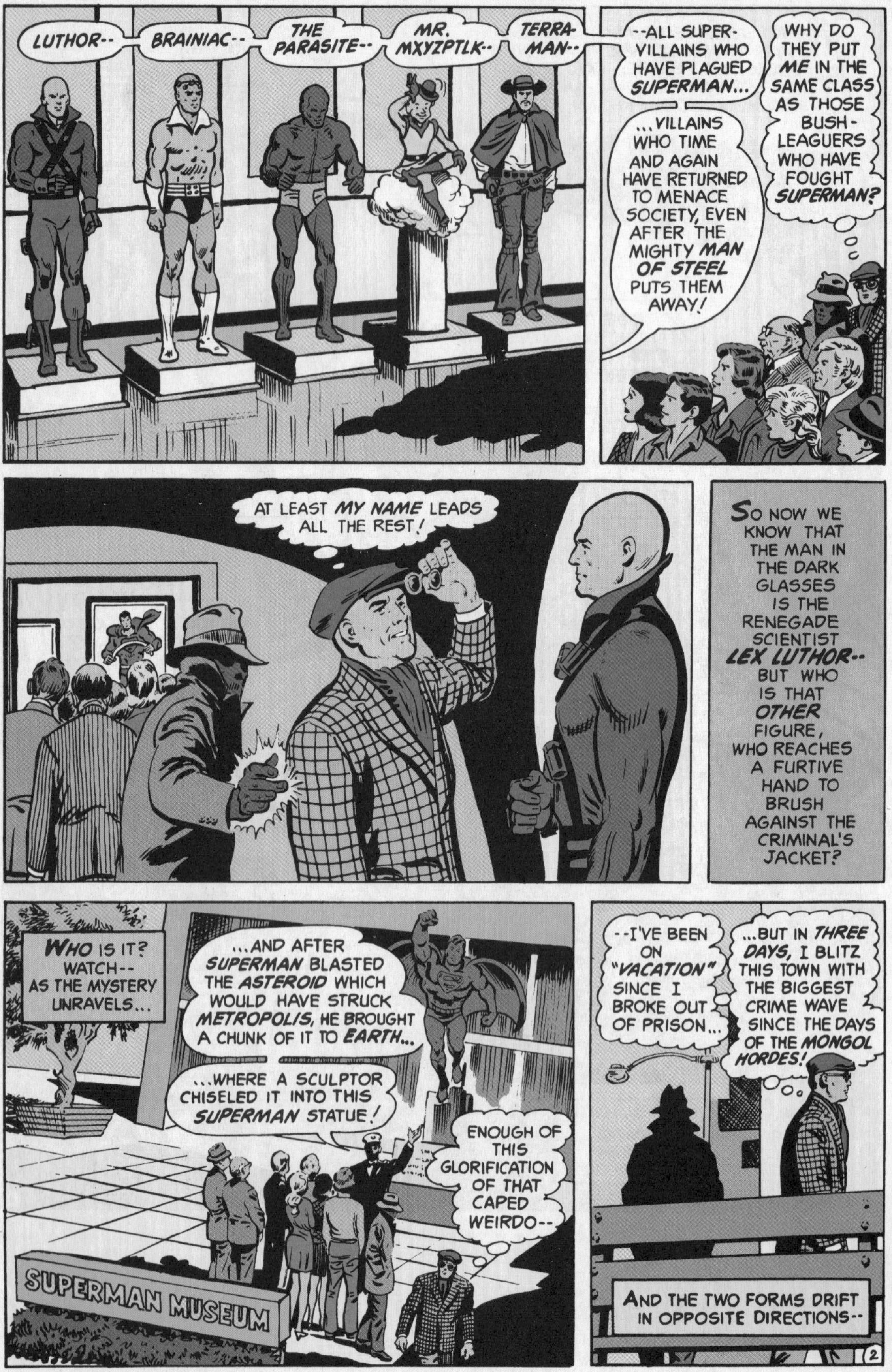
LUTHOR--
BRAINIAC--
THE PARASITE--
MR. MXYZPTLK--
TERRA-MAN--
--ALL SUPER-VILLAINS WHO HAVE PLAGUED SUPERMAN...
...VILLAINS WHO TIME AND AGAIN HAVE RETURNED TO MENACE SOCIETY, EVEN AFTER THE MIGHTY MAN OF STEEL PUTS THEM AWAY!
WHY DO THEY PUT ME IN THE SAME CLASS AS THOSE BUSH-LEAGUERS WHO HAVE FOUGHT SUPERMAN?
AT LEAST MY NAME LEADS ALL THE REST!
SO NOW WE KNOW THAT THE MAN IN THE DARK GLASSES IS THE RENEGADE SCIENTIST LEX LUTHOR-- BUT WHO IS THAT OTHER FIGURE, WHO REACHES A FURTIVE HAND TO BRUSH AGAINST THE CRIMINAL'S JACKET?
WHO IS IT? WATCH-- AS THE MYSTERY UNRAVELS...
...AND AFTER SUPERMAN BLASTED THE ASTEROID WHICH WOULD HAVE STRUCK METROPOLIS, HE BROUGHT A CHUNK OF IT TO EARTH...
...WHERE A SCULPTOR CHISELED IT INTO THIS SUPERMAN STATUE!
ENOUGH OF THIS GLORIFICATION OF THAT CAPED WEIRDO--
SUPERMAN MUSEUM
--I'VE BEEN ON "VACATION" SINCE I BROKE OUT OF PRISON...
...BUT IN THREE DAYS, I BLITZ THIS TOWN WITH THE BIGGEST CRIME WAVE SINCE THE DAYS OF THE MONGOL HORDES!
AND THE TWO FORMS DRIFT IN OPPOSITE DIRECTIONS--
2

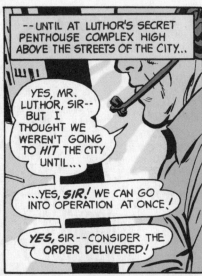

--UNTIL AT LUTHOR'S SECRET PENTHOUSE COMPLEX HIGH ABOVE THE STREETS OF THE CITY...

YES, MR. LUTHOR, SIR-- BUT I THOUGHT WE WEREN'T GOING TO *HIT* THE CITY UNTIL...

...YES, *SIR!* WE CAN GO INTO OPERATION AT ONCE!

YES, SIR--CONSIDER THE ORDER DELIVERED!

WITHIN MOMENTS, AT *STENGEL STADIUM*--AS THE *METROPOLIS METEORS* COME OUT OF A HUDDLE...

A *FLYING SAUCER!* POPPING UP LIKE A GIANT *GOPHER!*

I BELIEVE IN *UFO'S*-- BUT NOT FROM *INNER SPACE!*

AND AT THE *WGBS-TV* NEWSROOM, IN THE FABULOUS *GALAXY BUILDING*...

THAT WAS INSPECTOR HENDERSON ON THE LINE! GET OUT THE *FLYING NEWSROOM*...

--THERE'S BEEN A *DISTURBANCE* AT *STENGEL STADIUM!*

FROM THE TONE OF *JOSH COYLE'S* VOICE, THIS SOUNDS LIKE A JOB FOR...

...*SUPERMAN!*

WHAT IN BLAZES IS *THAT* UP THERE?

IT'S A *FLYING SAUCER*-- *MY* FLYING SAUCER!

THERE'S BEEN A *GOOF-UP!*

SOMEONE IN MY ORGANIZATION MADE THE MISTAKE OF LAUNCHING THAT CRAFT!

I SPENT MANY A NIGHT IN PRISON DESIGNING IT--

--AND I WON'T *STAND* FOR ITS MAKING AN APPEARANCE JUST SO *SUPERMAN* CAN HAVE *FUN* SPLATTERING IT ACROSS THE COUNTRYSIDE!

3

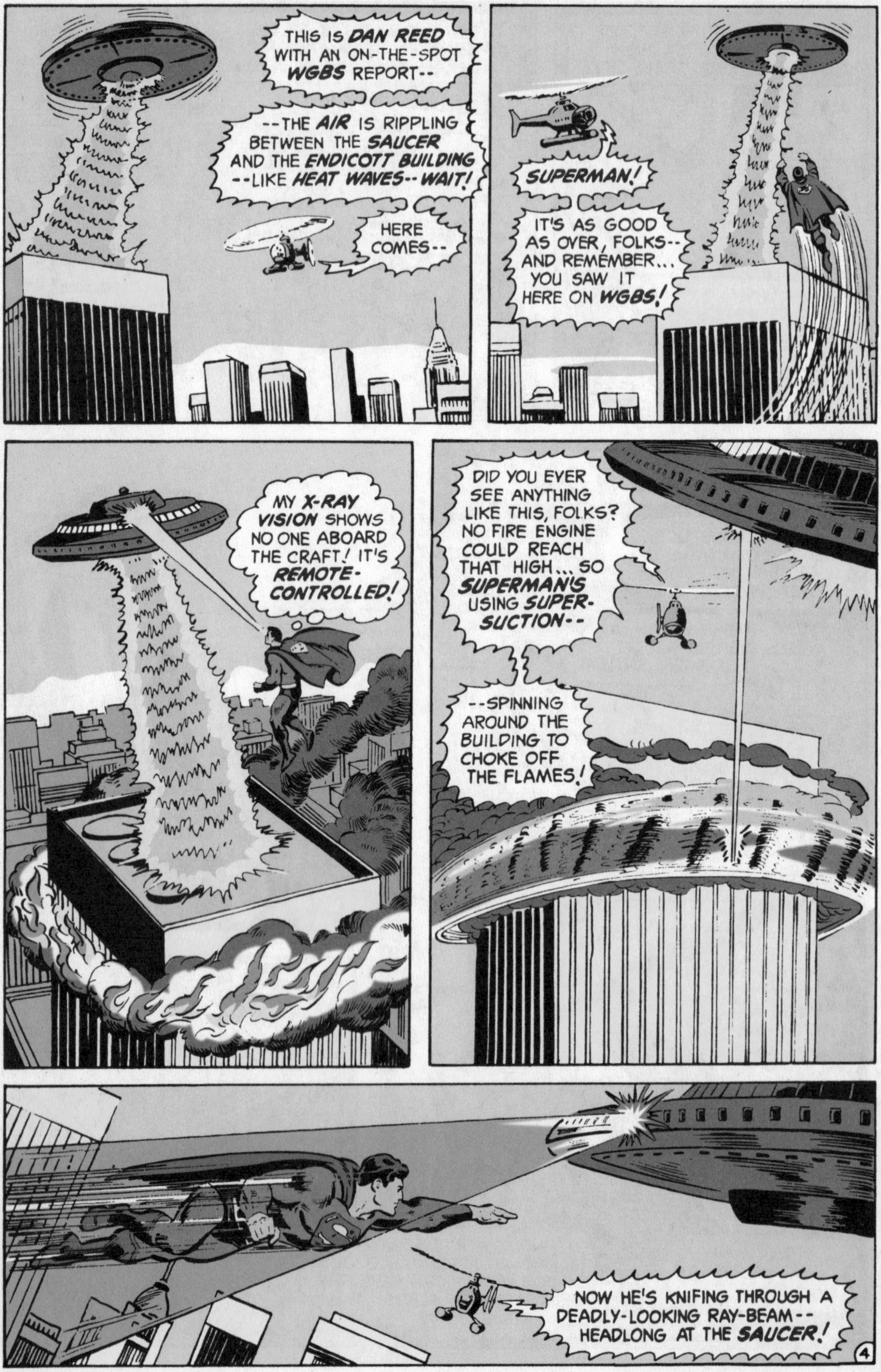
THIS IS DAN REED WITH AN ON-THE-SPOT WGBS REPORT--
--THE AIR IS RIPPLING BETWEEN THE SAUCER AND THE ENDICOTT BUILDING --LIKE HEAT WAVES-- WAIT!
HERE COMES--
SUPERMAN!
IT'S AS GOOD AS OVER, FOLKS-- AND REMEMBER... YOU SAW IT HERE ON WGBS!
MY X-RAY VISION SHOWS NO ONE ABOARD THE CRAFT! IT'S REMOTE-CONTROLLED!
DID YOU EVER SEE ANYTHING LIKE THIS, FOLKS? NO FIRE ENGINE COULD REACH THAT HIGH... SO SUPERMAN'S USING SUPER-SUCTION--
--SPINNING AROUND THE BUILDING TO CHOKE OFF THE FLAMES!
NOW HE'S KNIFING THROUGH A DEADLY-LOOKING RAY-BEAM-- HEADLONG AT THE SAUCER!
4

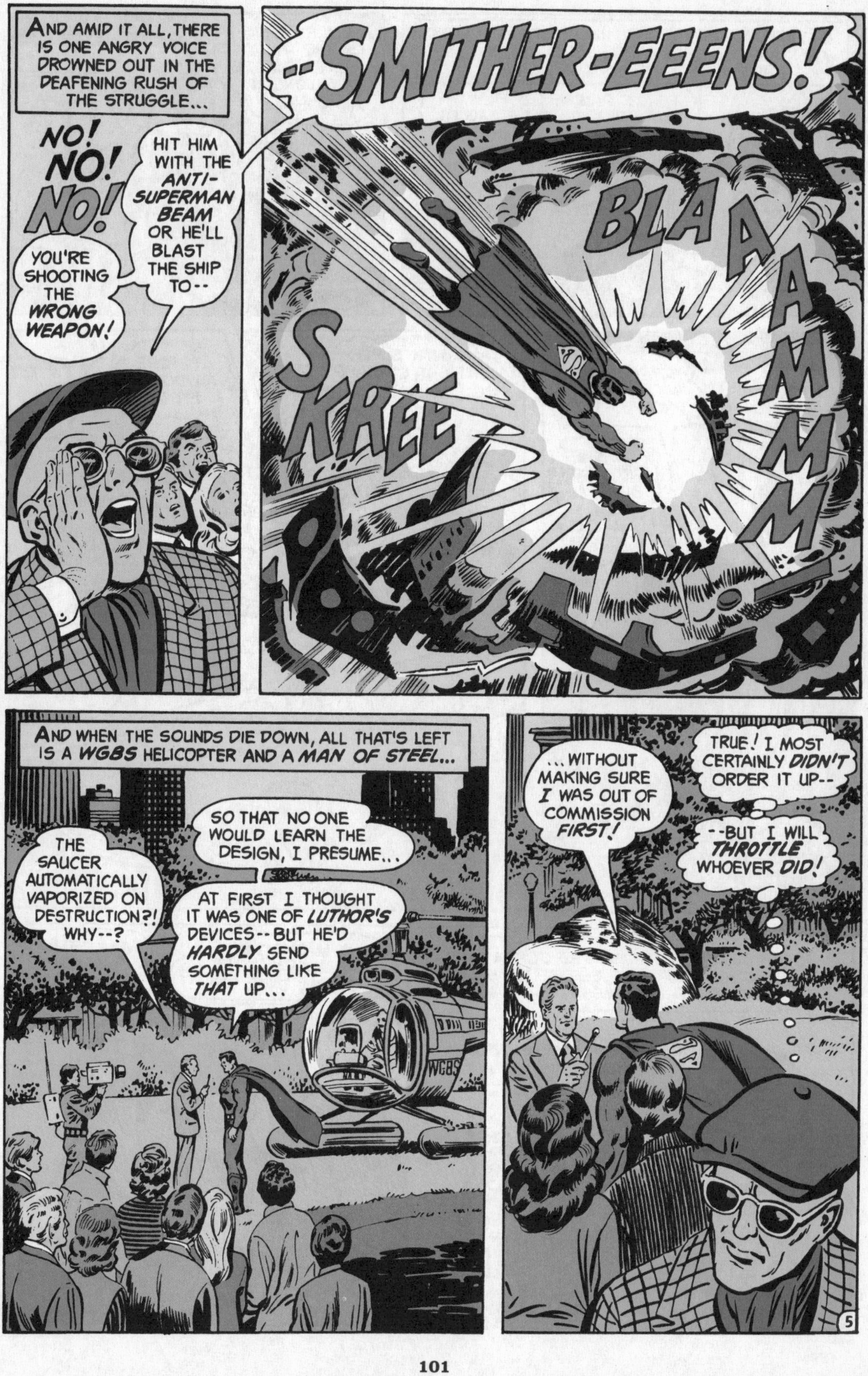
AND AMID IT ALL, THERE IS ONE ANGRY VOICE DROWNED OUT IN THE DEAFENING RUSH OF THE STRUGGLE...
NO! NO! NO!
YOU'RE SHOOTING THE WRONG WEAPON!
HIT HIM WITH THE ANTI-SUPERMAN BEAM OR HE'LL BLAST THE SHIP TO--
--SMITHER-EEENS!
SKREEE
BLAAAAMMM
AND WHEN THE SOUNDS DIE DOWN, ALL THAT'S LEFT IS A WGBS HELICOPTER AND A MAN OF STEEL...
THE SAUCER AUTOMATICALLY VAPORIZED ON DESTRUCTION?! WHY--?
SO THAT NO ONE WOULD LEARN THE DESIGN, I PRESUME...
AT FIRST I THOUGHT IT WAS ONE OF LUTHOR'S DEVICES--BUT HE'D HARDLY SEND SOMETHING LIKE THAT UP...
WGBS
...WITHOUT MAKING SURE I WAS OUT OF COMMISSION FIRST!
TRUE! I MOST CERTAINLY DIDN'T ORDER IT UP--
--BUT I WILL THROTTLE WHOEVER DID!
5

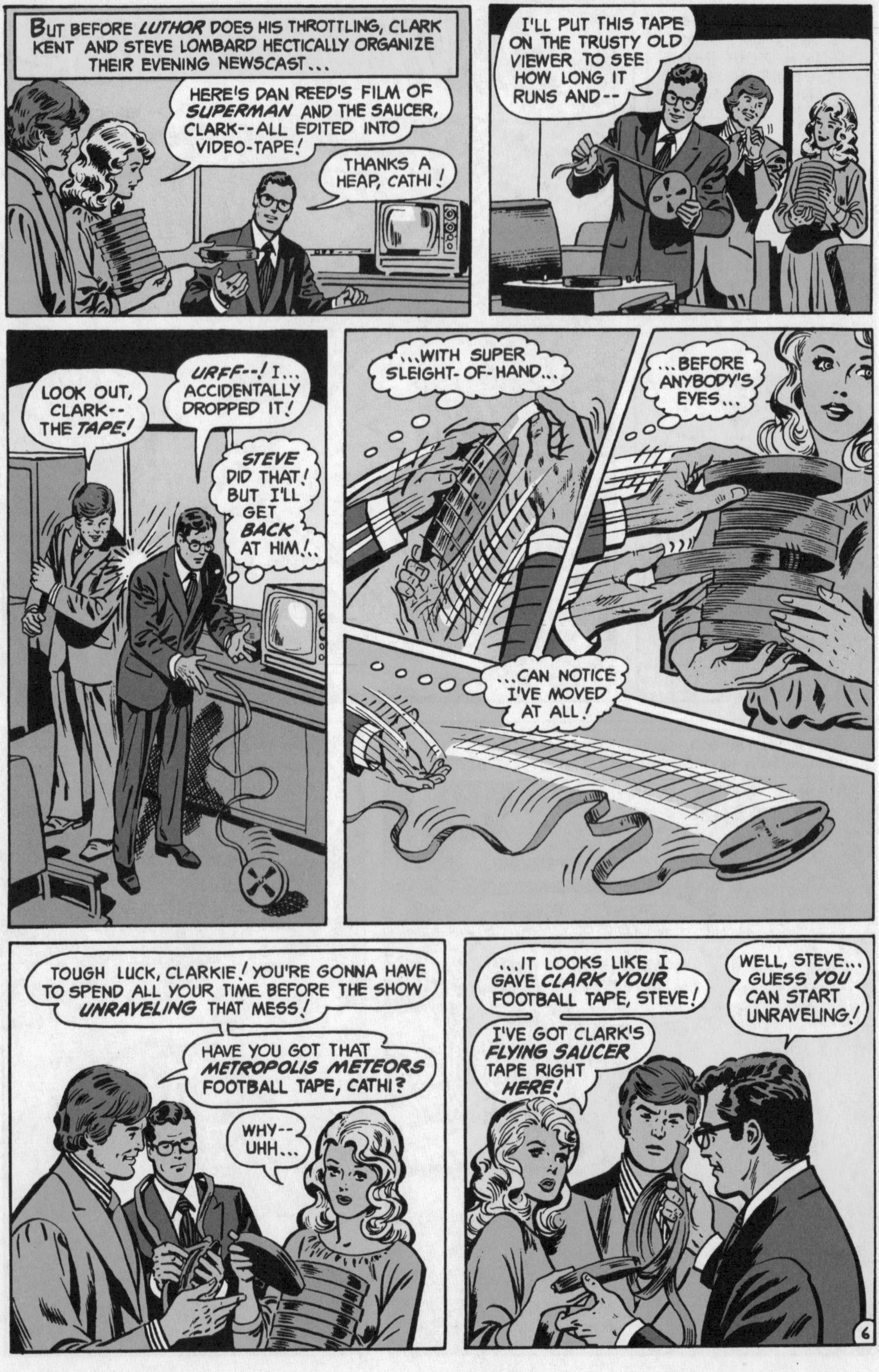

BUT BEFORE LUTHOR DOES HIS THROTTLING, CLARK KENT AND STEVE LOMBARD HECTICALLY ORGANIZE THEIR EVENING NEWSCAST...
HERE'S DAN REED'S FILM OF SUPERMAN AND THE SAUCER, CLARK--ALL EDITED INTO VIDEO-TAPE!
THANKS A HEAP, CATHI!
I'LL PUT THIS TAPE ON THE TRUSTY OLD VIEWER TO SEE HOW LONG IT RUNS AND--
LOOK OUT, CLARK-- THE TAPE!
URFF--! I... ACCIDENTALLY DROPPED IT!
STEVE DID THAT! BUT I'LL GET BACK AT HIM!..
...WITH SUPER SLEIGHT-OF-HAND...
...BEFORE ANYBODY'S EYES...
...CAN NOTICE I'VE MOVED AT ALL!
TOUGH LUCK, CLARKIE! YOU'RE GONNA HAVE TO SPEND ALL YOUR TIME BEFORE THE SHOW UNRAVELING THAT MESS!
HAVE YOU GOT THAT METROPOLIS METEORS FOOTBALL TAPE, CATHI?
WHY-- UHH...
...IT LOOKS LIKE I GAVE CLARK YOUR FOOTBALL TAPE, STEVE!
I'VE GOT CLARK'S FLYING SAUCER TAPE RIGHT HERE!
WELL, STEVE... GUESS YOU CAN START UNRAVELING!
6

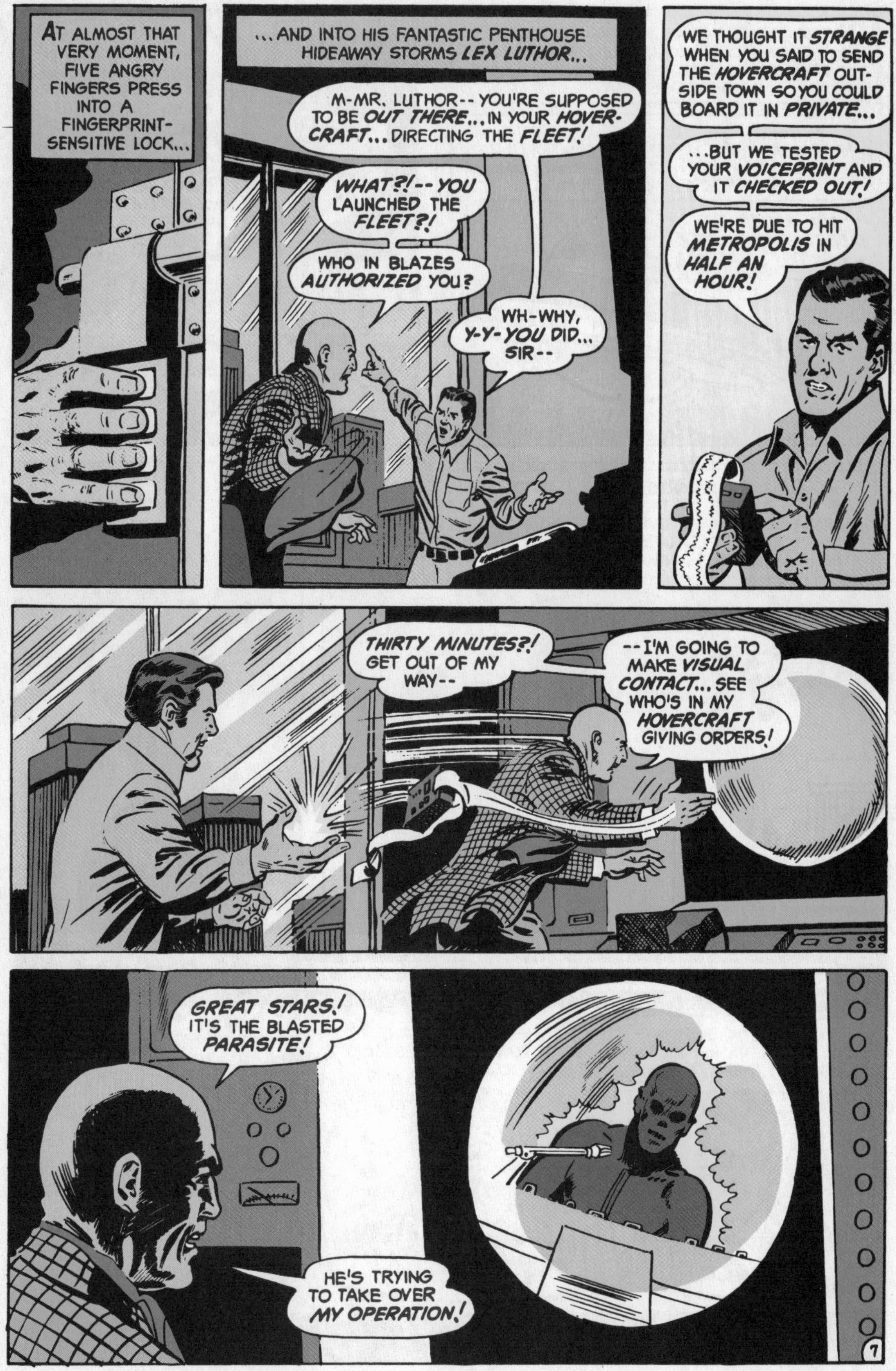
AT ALMOST THAT VERY MOMENT, FIVE ANGRY FINGERS PRESS INTO A FINGERPRINT-SENSITIVE LOCK...
...AND INTO HIS FANTASTIC PENTHOUSE HIDEAWAY STORMS LEX LUTHOR...
M-MR. LUTHOR-- YOU'RE SUPPOSED TO BE OUT THERE... IN YOUR HOVERCRAFT... DIRECTING THE FLEET!
WHAT?!--YOU LAUNCHED THE FLEET?!
WHO IN BLAZES AUTHORIZED YOU?
WH-WHY, Y-Y-YOU DID... SIR--
WE THOUGHT IT STRANGE WHEN YOU SAID TO SEND THE HOVERCRAFT OUTSIDE TOWN SO YOU COULD BOARD IT IN PRIVATE...
...BUT WE TESTED YOUR VOICEPRINT AND IT CHECKED OUT!
WE'RE DUE TO HIT METROPOLIS IN HALF AN HOUR!
THIRTY MINUTES?! GET OUT OF MY WAY--
--I'M GOING TO MAKE VISUAL CONTACT... SEE WHO'S IN MY HOVERCRAFT GIVING ORDERS!
GREAT STARS! IT'S THE BLASTED PARASITE!
HE'S TRYING TO TAKE OVER MY OPERATION!
7

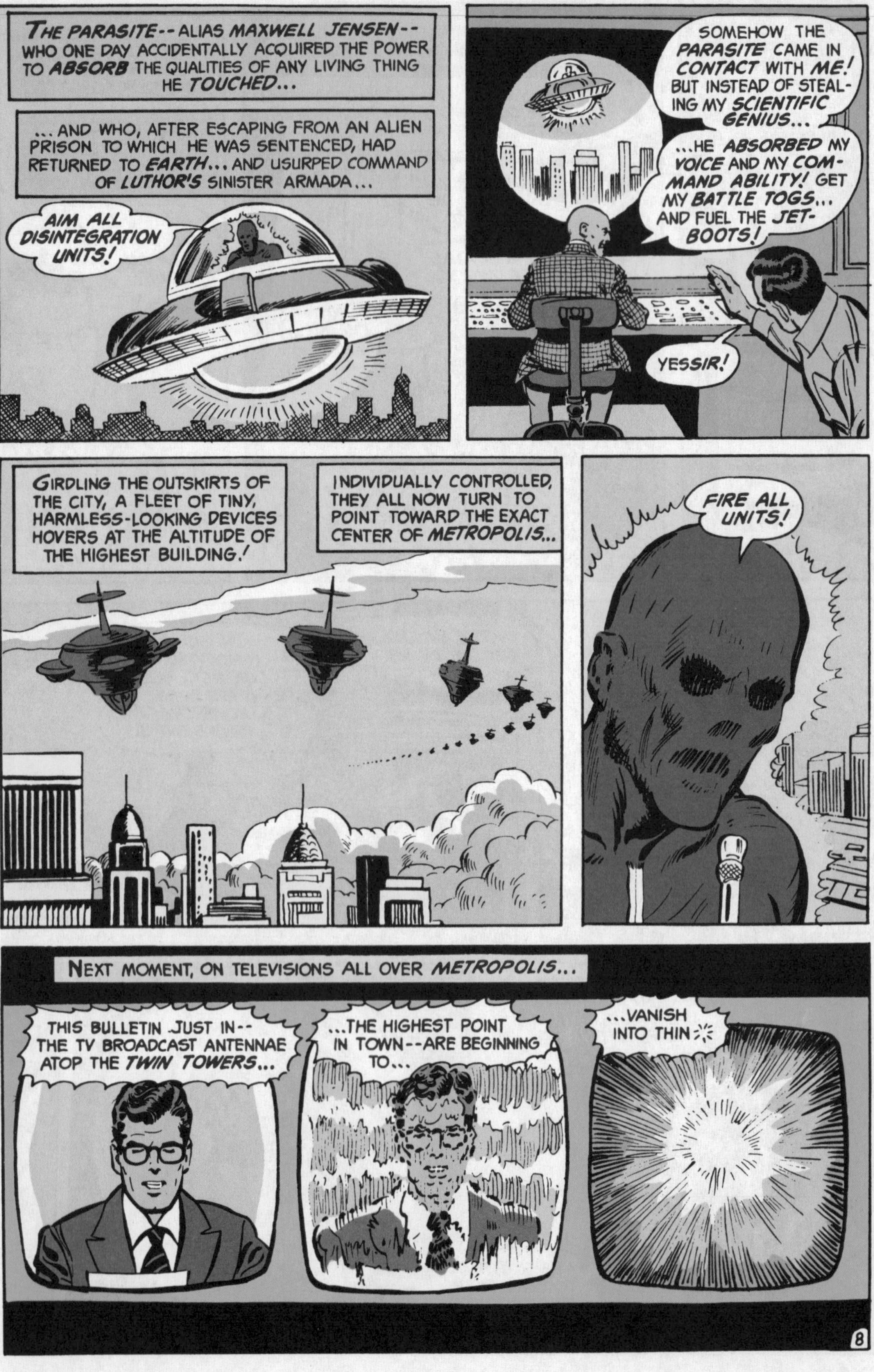
THE PARASITE--ALIAS MAXWELL JENSEN--WHO ONE DAY ACCIDENTALLY ACQUIRED THE POWER TO ABSORB THE QUALITIES OF ANY LIVING THING HE TOUCHED...
...AND WHO, AFTER ESCAPING FROM AN ALIEN PRISON TO WHICH HE WAS SENTENCED, HAD RETURNED TO EARTH... AND USURPED COMMAND OF LUTHOR'S SINISTER ARMADA...
AIM ALL DISINTEGRATION UNITS!
SOMEHOW THE PARASITE CAME IN CONTACT WITH ME! BUT INSTEAD OF STEALING MY SCIENTIFIC GENIUS...
...HE ABSORBED MY VOICE AND MY COMMAND ABILITY! GET MY BATTLE TOGS... AND FUEL THE JET-BOOTS!
YESSIR!
GIRDLING THE OUTSKIRTS OF THE CITY, A FLEET OF TINY, HARMLESS-LOOKING DEVICES HOVERS AT THE ALTITUDE OF THE HIGHEST BUILDING!
INDIVIDUALLY CONTROLLED, THEY ALL NOW TURN TO POINT TOWARD THE EXACT CENTER OF METROPOLIS...
FIRE ALL UNITS!
NEXT MOMENT, ON TELEVISIONS ALL OVER METROPOLIS...
THIS BULLETIN JUST IN--THE TV BROADCAST ANTENNAE ATOP THE TWIN TOWERS...
...THE HIGHEST POINT IN TOWN--ARE BEGINNING TO...
...VANISH INTO THIN
8

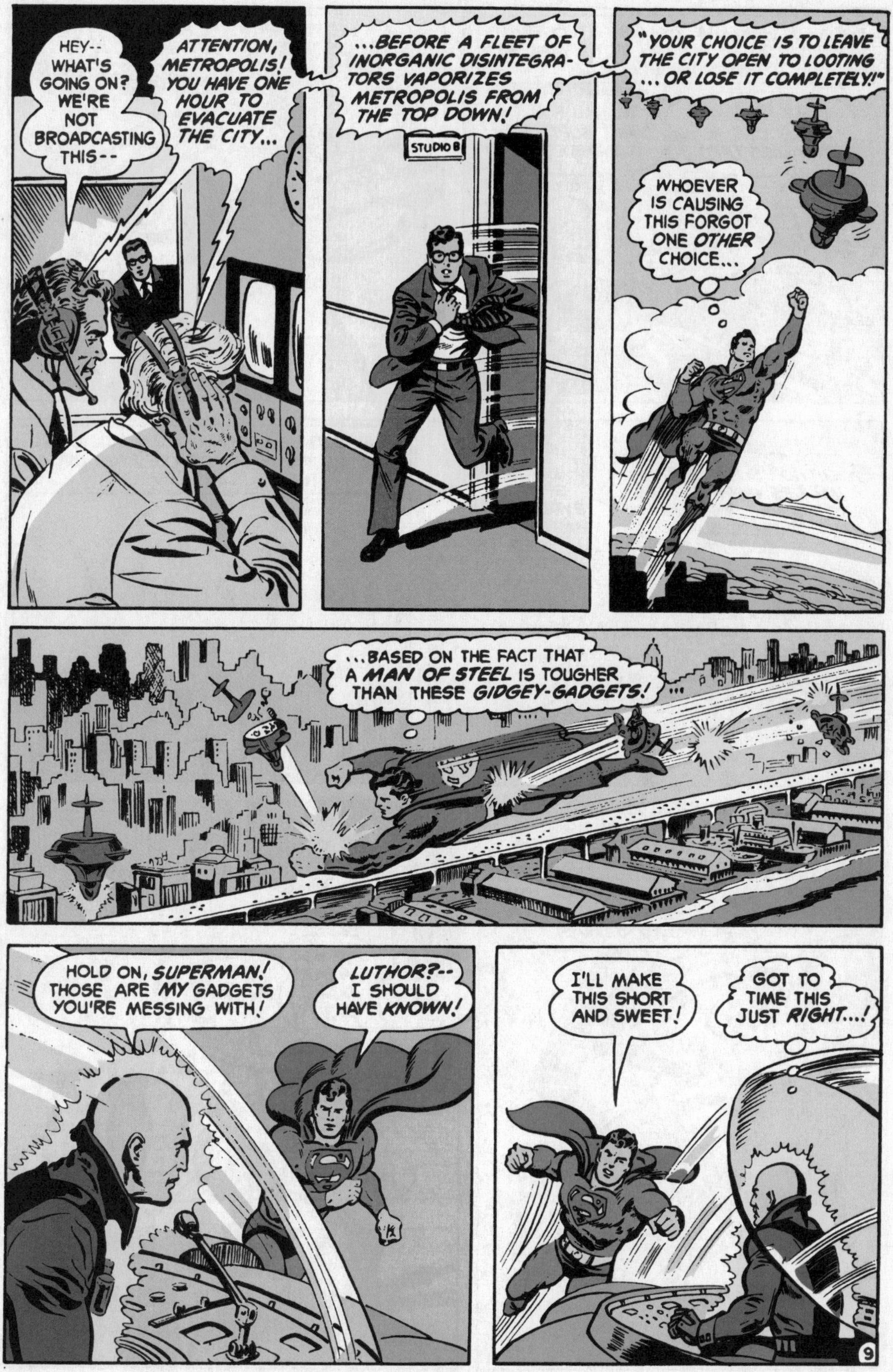
HEY-- WHAT'S GOING ON? WE'RE NOT BROADCASTING THIS--
ATTENTION, METROPOLIS! YOU HAVE ONE HOUR TO EVACUATE THE CITY...
...BEFORE A FLEET OF INORGANIC DISINTEGRATORS VAPORIZES METROPOLIS FROM THE TOP DOWN!
STUDIO B
"YOUR CHOICE IS TO LEAVE THE CITY OPEN TO LOOTING ...OR LOSE IT COMPLETELY!"
WHOEVER IS CAUSING THIS FORGOT ONE OTHER CHOICE...
...BASED ON THE FACT THAT A MAN OF STEEL IS TOUGHER THAN THESE GIDGEY-GADGETS!
HOLD ON, SUPERMAN! THOSE ARE MY GADGETS YOU'RE MESSING WITH!
LUTHOR?-- I SHOULD HAVE KNOWN!
I'LL MAKE THIS SHORT AND SWEET!
GOT TO TIME THIS JUST RIGHT...!
9

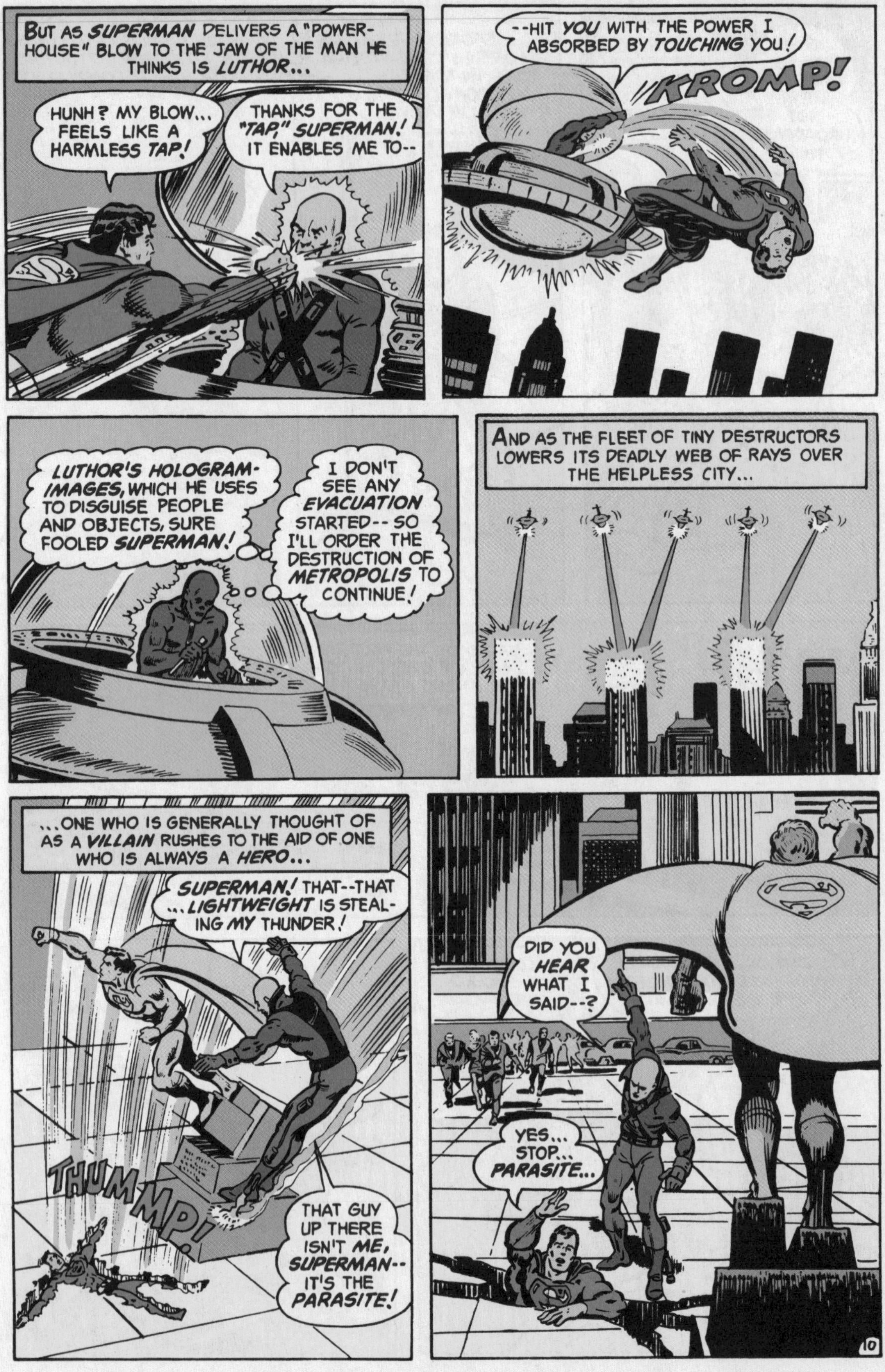
BUT AS SUPERMAN DELIVERS A "POWER-HOUSE" BLOW TO THE JAW OF THE MAN HE THINKS IS LUTHOR...
HUNH? MY BLOW... FEELS LIKE A HARMLESS TAP!
THANKS FOR THE "TAP," SUPERMAN! IT ENABLES ME TO--
--HIT YOU WITH THE POWER I ABSORBED BY TOUCHING YOU!
KROMP!
LUTHOR'S HOLOGRAM-IMAGES, WHICH HE USES TO DISGUISE PEOPLE AND OBJECTS, SURE FOOLED SUPERMAN!
I DON'T SEE ANY EVACUATION STARTED-- SO I'LL ORDER THE DESTRUCTION OF METROPOLIS TO CONTINUE!
AND AS THE FLEET OF TINY DESTRUCTORS LOWERS ITS DEADLY WEB OF RAYS OVER THE HELPLESS CITY...
...ONE WHO IS GENERALLY THOUGHT OF AS A VILLAIN RUSHES TO THE AID OF ONE WHO IS ALWAYS A HERO...
SUPERMAN! THAT--THAT ...LIGHTWEIGHT IS STEALING MY THUNDER!
THUMMP!
THAT GUY UP THERE ISN'T ME, SUPERMAN-- IT'S THE PARASITE!
DID YOU HEAR WHAT I SAID--?
YES... STOP... PARASITE...
10

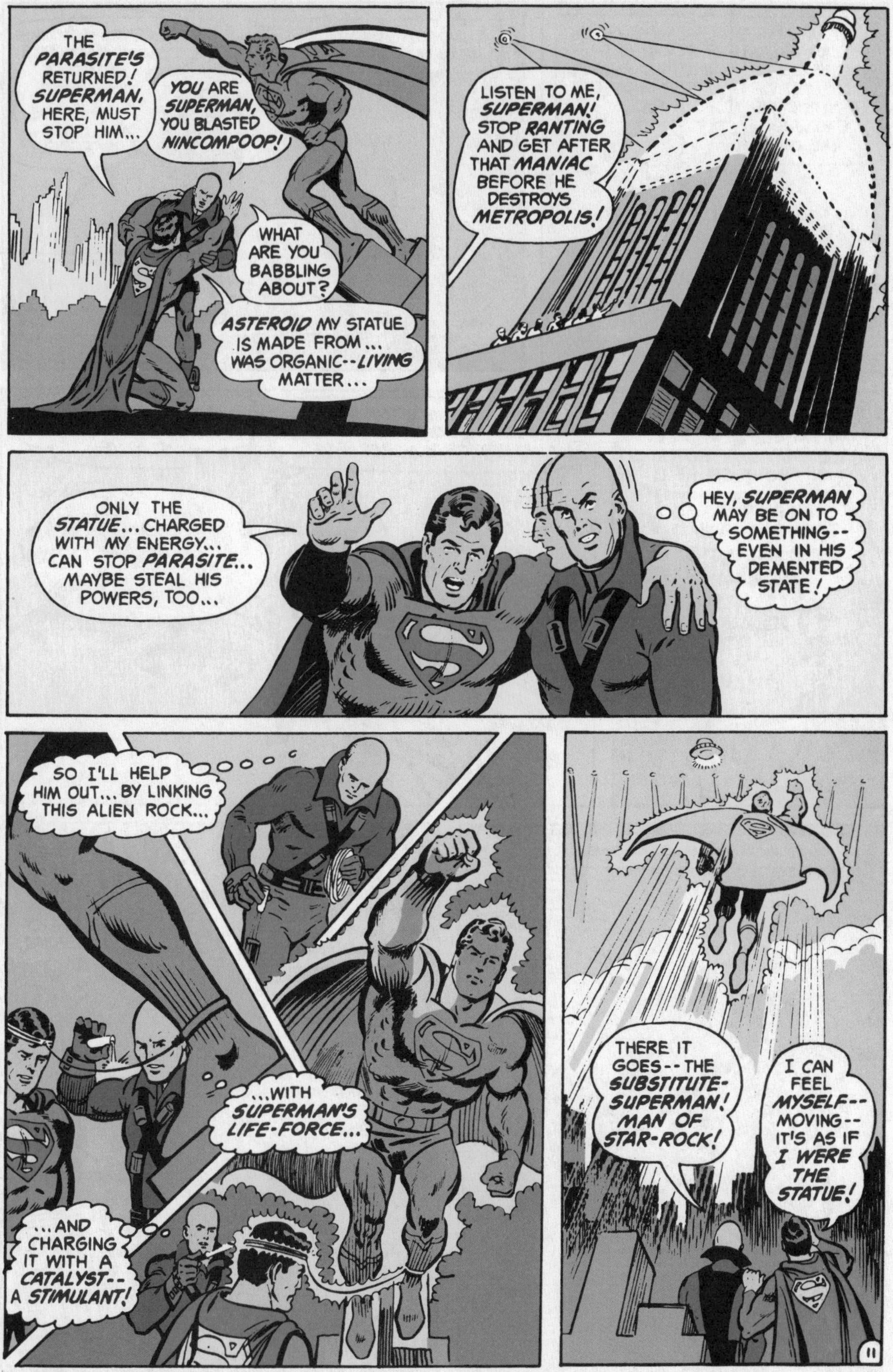
THE PARASITE'S RETURNED! SUPERMAN, HERE, MUST STOP HIM...
YOU ARE SUPERMAN, YOU BLASTED NINCOMPOOP!
WHAT ARE YOU BABBLING ABOUT?
ASTEROID MY STATUE IS MADE FROM... WAS ORGANIC--LIVING MATTER...
LISTEN TO ME, SUPERMAN! STOP RANTING AND GET AFTER THAT MANIAC BEFORE HE DESTROYS METROPOLIS!
ONLY THE STATUE... CHARGED WITH MY ENERGY... CAN STOP PARASITE... MAYBE STEAL HIS POWERS, TOO...
HEY, SUPERMAN MAY BE ON TO SOMETHING-- EVEN IN HIS DEMENTED STATE!
SO I'LL HELP HIM OUT... BY LINKING THIS ALIEN ROCK...
...WITH SUPERMAN'S LIFE-FORCE...
...AND CHARGING IT WITH A CATALYST-- A STIMULANT!
THERE IT GOES--THE SUBSTITUTE-SUPERMAN! MAN OF STAR-ROCK!
I CAN FEEL MYSELF--MOVING--IT'S AS IF I WERE THE STATUE!
11

UP, UP AND AWAY-- THROUGH THE NET OF DESTRUCTION GIRDLING THE CITY...

...FLIES THE CHUNK OF ROCK WITH THE MIND AND POWERS OF THE MAN OF STEEL...

AND HIGH ABOVE THE NEARLY RAVAGED CITY...

WHAT? SUPERMAN'S COMING BACK FOR MORE--?

UHHH...HE LOOKS... DIFFERENT!

THE WIND'S RUSHING BY MY FACE...I CAN SEE THE PARASITE HOVERING IN FRONT OF ME...

...HE'S TRYING TO TRICK ME AGAIN...

...BY USING HOLOGRAMS TO MAKE IT LOOK AS IF THERE IS A FLEET OF HOVERCRAFTS...

...BUT MY SUPER-VISION FOCUSED THROUGH THE STATUE...

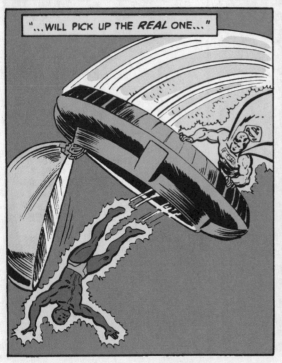

"...WILL PICK UP THE REAL ONE..."

GREAT GOING, SUPERMAN! THE MESH OF RAYS IS DISAPPEARING...

THE PARASITE IS TUMBLING THROUGH THE AIR--TRYING TO CATCH A BIRD AND ABSORB ITS POWER OF FLIGHT--IN VAIN!

SHOULD'VE TAKEN SUPERMAN'S FLYING ABILITY BEFORE...

108

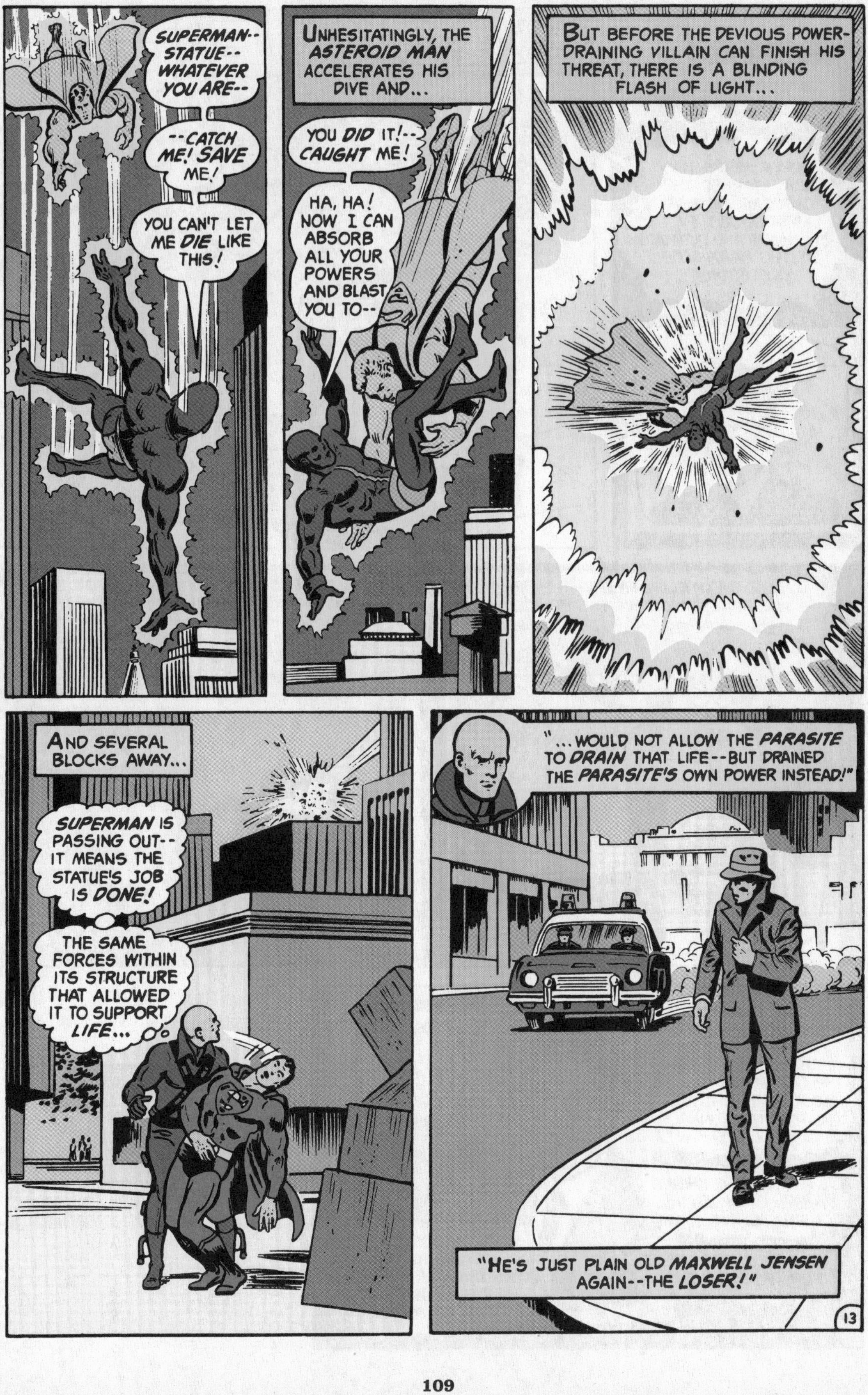
SUPERMAN--STATUE--WHATEVER YOU ARE--
--CATCH ME! SAVE ME!
YOU CAN'T LET ME DIE LIKE THIS!
UNHESITATINGLY, THE ASTEROID MAN ACCELERATES HIS DIVE AND...
YOU DID IT!--CAUGHT ME!
HA, HA! NOW I CAN ABSORB ALL YOUR POWERS AND BLAST YOU TO--
BUT BEFORE THE DEVIOUS POWER-DRAINING VILLAIN CAN FINISH HIS THREAT, THERE IS A BLINDING FLASH OF LIGHT...
AND SEVERAL BLOCKS AWAY...
SUPERMAN IS PASSING OUT--IT MEANS THE STATUE'S JOB IS DONE!
THE SAME FORCES WITHIN ITS STRUCTURE THAT ALLOWED IT TO SUPPORT LIFE...
"...WOULD NOT ALLOW THE PARASITE TO DRAIN THAT LIFE--BUT DRAINED THE PARASITE'S OWN POWER INSTEAD!"
"HE'S JUST PLAIN OLD MAXWELL JENSEN AGAIN--THE LOSER!"
13

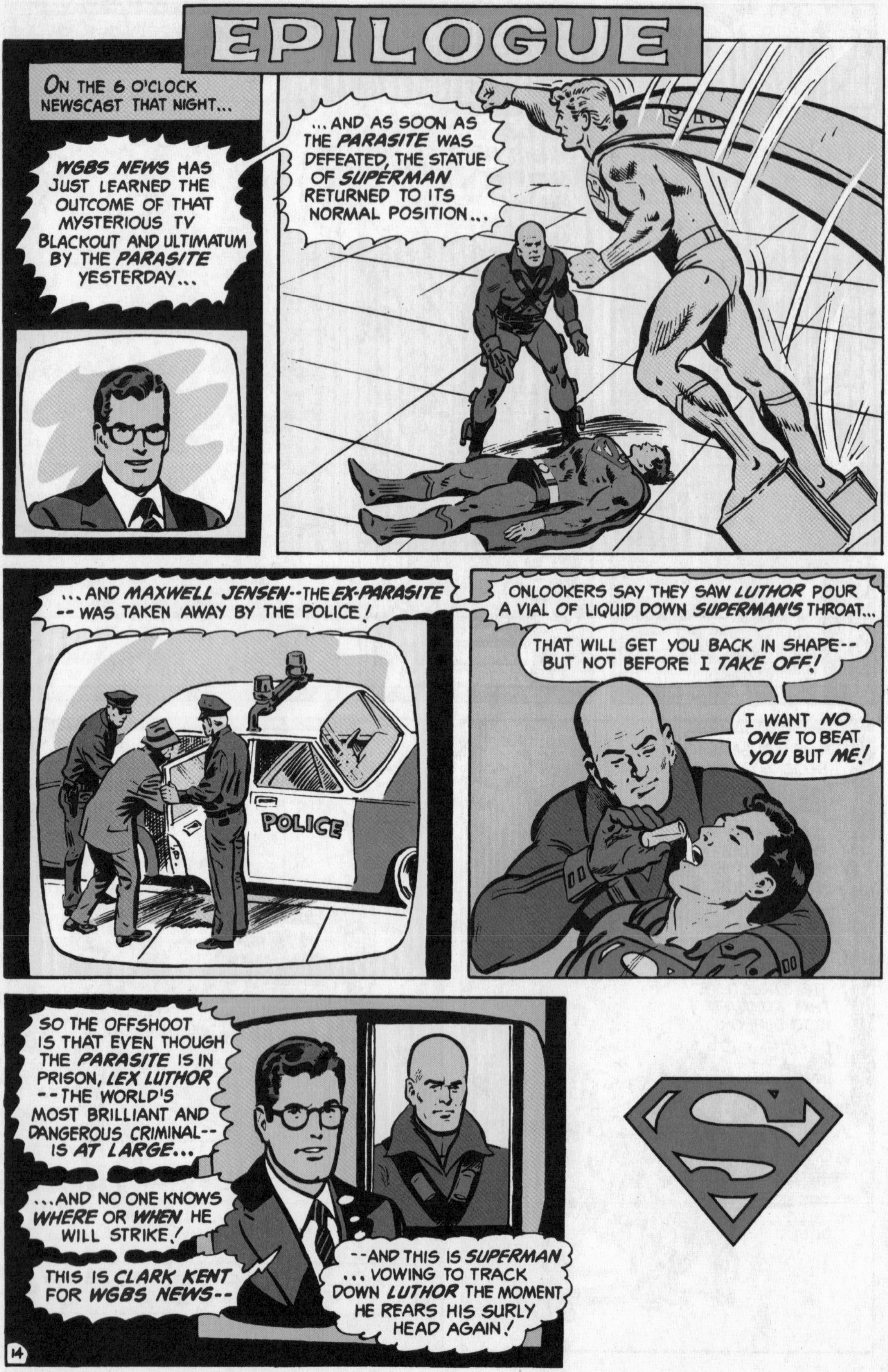
EPILOGUE
ON THE 6 O'CLOCK NEWSCAST THAT NIGHT...
WGBS NEWS HAS JUST LEARNED THE OUTCOME OF THAT MYSTERIOUS TV BLACKOUT AND ULTIMATUM BY THE PARASITE YESTERDAY...
...AND AS SOON AS THE PARASITE WAS DEFEATED, THE STATUE OF SUPERMAN RETURNED TO ITS NORMAL POSITION...
...AND MAXWELL JENSEN--THE EX-PARASITE --WAS TAKEN AWAY BY THE POLICE!
POLICE
ONLOOKERS SAY THEY SAW LUTHOR POUR A VIAL OF LIQUID DOWN SUPERMAN'S THROAT...
THAT WILL GET YOU BACK IN SHAPE--BUT NOT BEFORE I TAKE OFF!
I WANT NO ONE TO BEAT YOU BUT ME!
SO THE OFFSHOOT IS THAT EVEN THOUGH THE PARASITE IS IN PRISON, LEX LUTHOR --THE WORLD'S MOST BRILLIANT AND DANGEROUS CRIMINAL--IS AT LARGE...
...AND NO ONE KNOWS WHERE OR WHEN HE WILL STRIKE!
THIS IS CLARK KENT FOR WGBS NEWS--
--AND THIS IS SUPERMAN... VOWING TO TRACK DOWN LUTHOR THE MOMENT HE REARS HIS SURLY HEAD AGAIN!
14

SUPERMAN
THE MOVIE

**On December 15, 1978,
the world came to believe a man could fly.**

European producers Ilya and Alexander Salkind had been laboring for years to bring Superman to the silver screen — not as a simple children's cartoon or as camp fare, but rather as an epic and sophisticated film feature for all ages. No expense was spared as preproduction began: costly special effects technologies were invented; Mario Puzo (writer of *The Godfather*) was recruited to draft a screenplay; the world's largest sound-stage was specially constructed under the Salkinds' supervision; and in order to prove they were serious, the producers paid the legendary Marlon Brando the single highest actor's salary to date to play the role of Superman's Kryptonian father, Jor-El. Everything was moving steadily into place. There was only one problem: the filmmakers had no Superman.

Given the movie's stratospheric budget, conventional wisdom almost demanded a proven box-office draw wear the suit; among those under consideration were Robert Redford, Burt Reynolds, James Caan, and even Olympic athlete Bruce Jenner. In the end, the Salkinds decided the fame of a star might overshadow the role and instead went with an unknown, a rail-thin New York stage actor named Christopher Reeve. He didn't look anything like Superman.

But he looked exactly like Clark Kent.

Under a grueling body-building regimen, Reeve bulked up enough to fill the costume admirably and with style. More important, the innocent charm and charisma he brought to the role sold it completely. Clearly, Reeve believed in Superman — and thus so did we.

Superman the Movie went on to become one of the biggest film blockbusters of all time, spawning three sequels and reminding the world that the greatest super-hero of all was more vital and exciting than ever before.

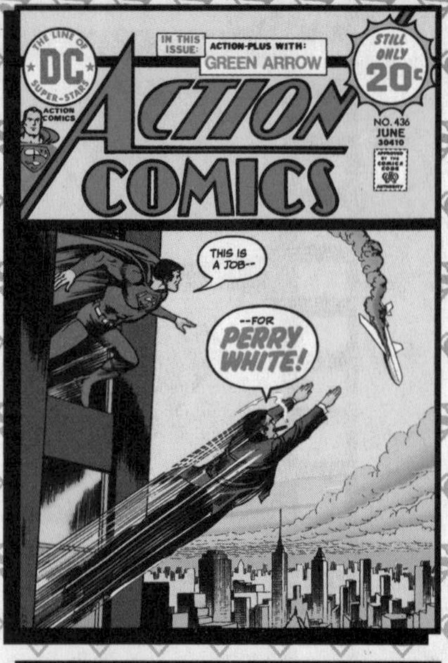
DC
IN THIS ISSUE
ACTION-PLUS WITH:
GREEN ARROW
STILL ONLY 20¢
ACTION COMICS
NO. 436
JUNE
THIS IS A JOB--
--FOR PERRY WHITE!

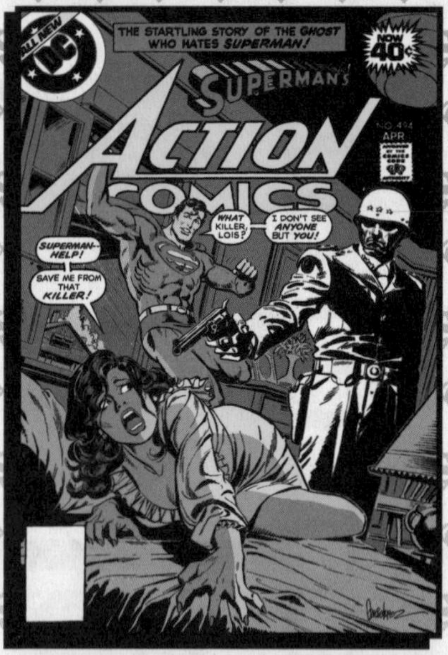
DC
THE STARTLING STORY OF THE GHOST WHO HATES SUPERMAN!
NOW 40¢
SUPERMAN'S
ACTION COMICS
APR
SUPERMAN--HELP!
WHAT KILLER, LOIS?
I DON'T SEE ANYONE BUT YOU!
SAVE ME FROM THAT KILLER!

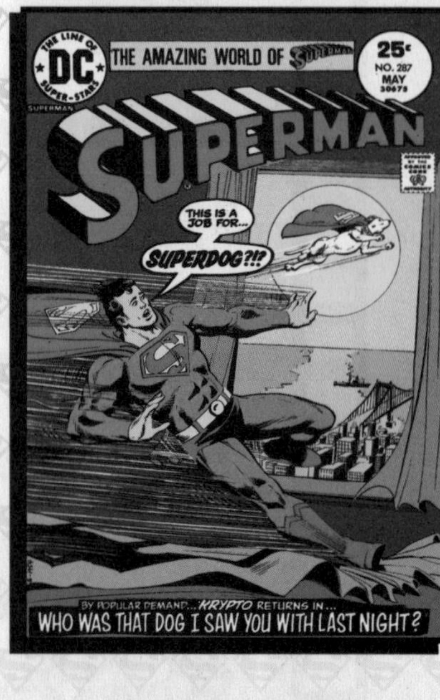
DC
THE AMAZING WORLD OF SUPERMAN
25¢
NO. 287
MAY
SUPERMAN
THIS IS A JOB FOR...
SUPERDOG?!?
BY POPULAR DEMAND... KRYPTO RETURNS IN...
WHO WAS THAT DOG I SAW YOU WITH LAST NIGHT?

THE CAST OF CHARACTERS

"KIRBY IS COMING!"

To diehard fans, the message was hardly cryptic. Jack Kirby, legendary artist and co-creator of the Marvel Universe, had been hired to lend his vision to the World of Superman. And while "King" Kirby's followers were undoubtedly puzzled to see him tackle not SUPERMAN or ACTION COMICS but SUPERMAN'S PAL, JIMMY OLSEN, the wonders he wrought there were staggering.

To say Kirby was ahead of his time is an understatement. The Golden Guardian and the D.N.Aliens introduced comics readers to the far-fetched concept of "cloning." "Mother Boxes" presaged handheld computers, and the sinister Darkseid — even more popular today than he was back then — launched a new era of cosmic villainy in the DC Universe. For the first time in years, Superman enjoyed adventures every bit as inventive and awe-inspiring as he himself had been in 1938.

By contrast, in the pages of SUPERMAN'S GIRL FRIEND, LOIS LANE, the Metropolis Marvel took a hard look at street-level issues. In an early attempt at social relevance, writer Robert Kanigher penned "I Am Curious (Black)," a play on the title of the 1967 Swedish movie *I Am Curious (Yellow)*. Here, like the heroine of *Yellow*, Lois Lane emerged from her middle-class cocoon to explore a harsh world new to her — transforming her in more ways than the obvious.

Through the seventies, the back pages of ACTION COMICS showcased other super-supporting characters: Superman's cousin, Supergirl, and super-dog, Krypto; Clark's boss, Perry White; and Clark's own "archfoe," the insufferably arrogant quarterback-turned-sportscaster Steve Lombard. Lombard delighted in tormenting Clark, but he never learned; no matter what horrible prank awaited "Clarkie-Boy," a quick and discreet burst of super-speed or heat vision always made it backfire — and messily. Yes, Superman is the paragon of kindness — but when it comes to bullies, even he has his limits.

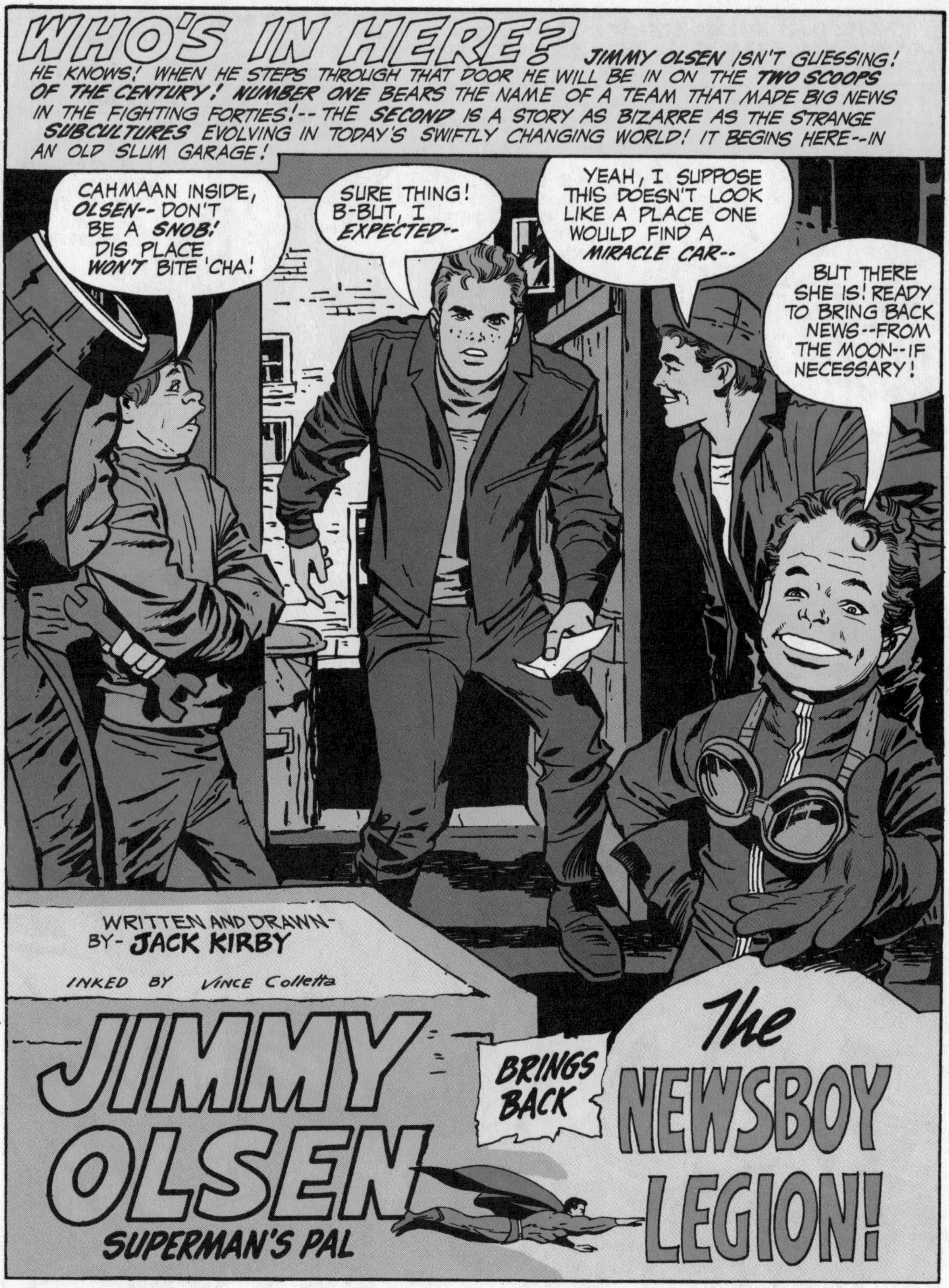
WHO'S IN HERE? JIMMY OLSEN ISN'T GUESSING! HE KNOWS! WHEN HE STEPS THROUGH THAT DOOR HE WILL BE IN ON THE TWO SCOOPS OF THE CENTURY! NUMBER ONE BEARS THE NAME OF A TEAM THAT MADE BIG NEWS IN THE FIGHTING FORTIES!-- THE SECOND IS A STORY AS BIZARRE AS THE STRANGE SUBCULTURES EVOLVING IN TODAY'S SWIFTLY CHANGING WORLD! IT BEGINS HERE--IN AN OLD SLUM GARAGE!
CAHMAAN INSIDE, OLSEN-- DON'T BE A SNOB! DIS PLACE WON'T BITE 'CHA!
SURE THING! B-BUT, I EXPECTED--
YEAH, I SUPPOSE THIS DOESN'T LOOK LIKE A PLACE ONE WOULD FIND A MIRACLE CAR--
BUT THERE SHE IS! READY TO BRING BACK NEWS--FROM THE MOON--IF NECESSARY!
WRITTEN AND DRAWN-BY- JACK KIRBY
INKED BY Vince Colletta
JIMMY OLSEN
SUPERMAN'S PAL
BRINGS BACK
The NEWSBOY LEGION!

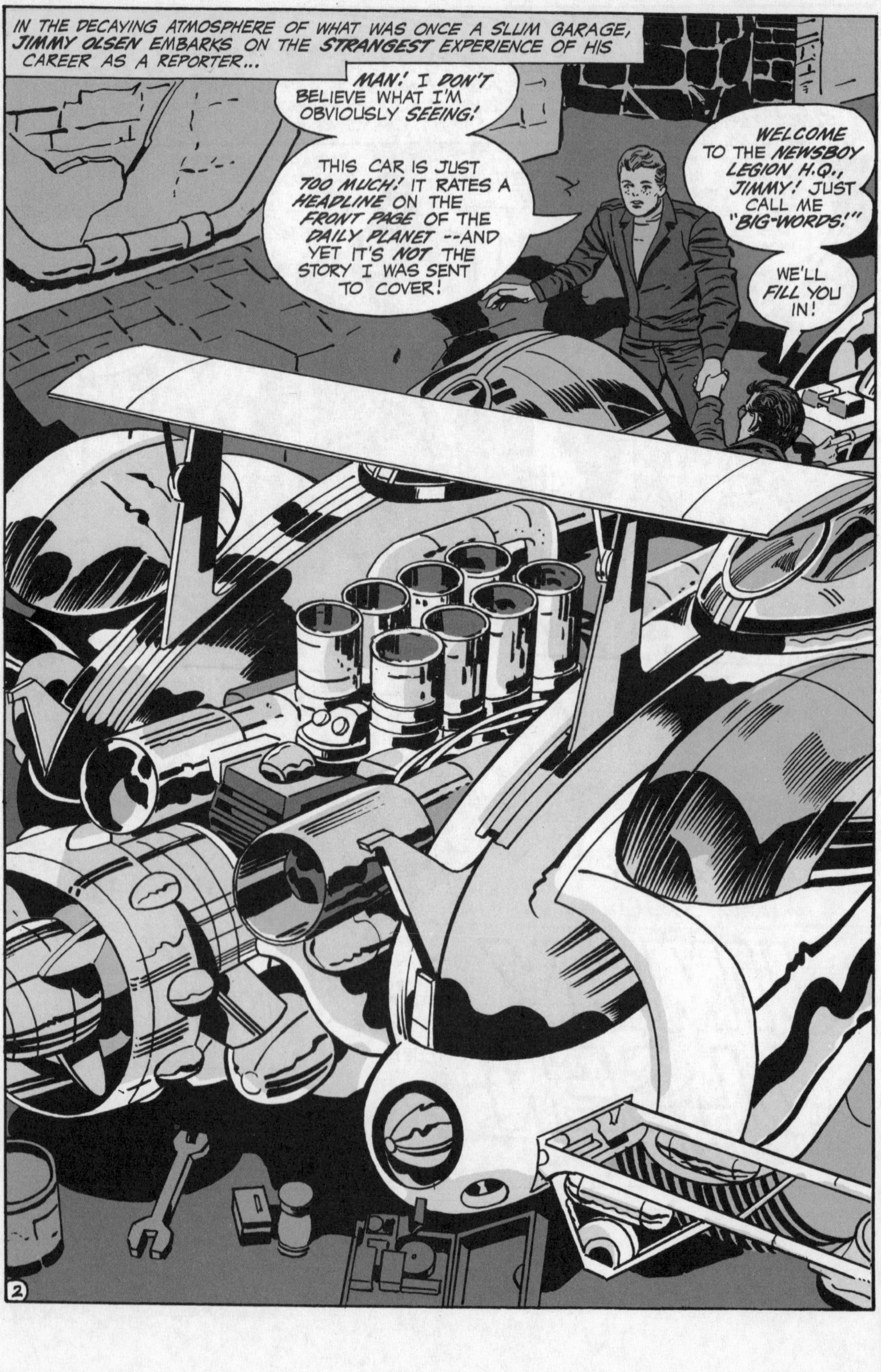
IN THE DECAYING ATMOSPHERE OF WHAT WAS ONCE A SLUM GARAGE, JIMMY OLSEN EMBARKS ON THE STRANGEST EXPERIENCE OF HIS CAREER AS A REPORTER...
MAN! I DON'T BELIEVE WHAT I'M OBVIOUSLY SEEING!
THIS CAR IS JUST TOO MUCH! IT RATES A HEADLINE ON THE FRONT PAGE OF THE DAILY PLANET --AND YET IT'S NOT THE STORY I WAS SENT TO COVER!
WELCOME TO THE NEWSBOY LEGION H.Q., JIMMY! JUST CALL ME "BIG-WORDS!"
WE'LL FILL YOU IN!
2

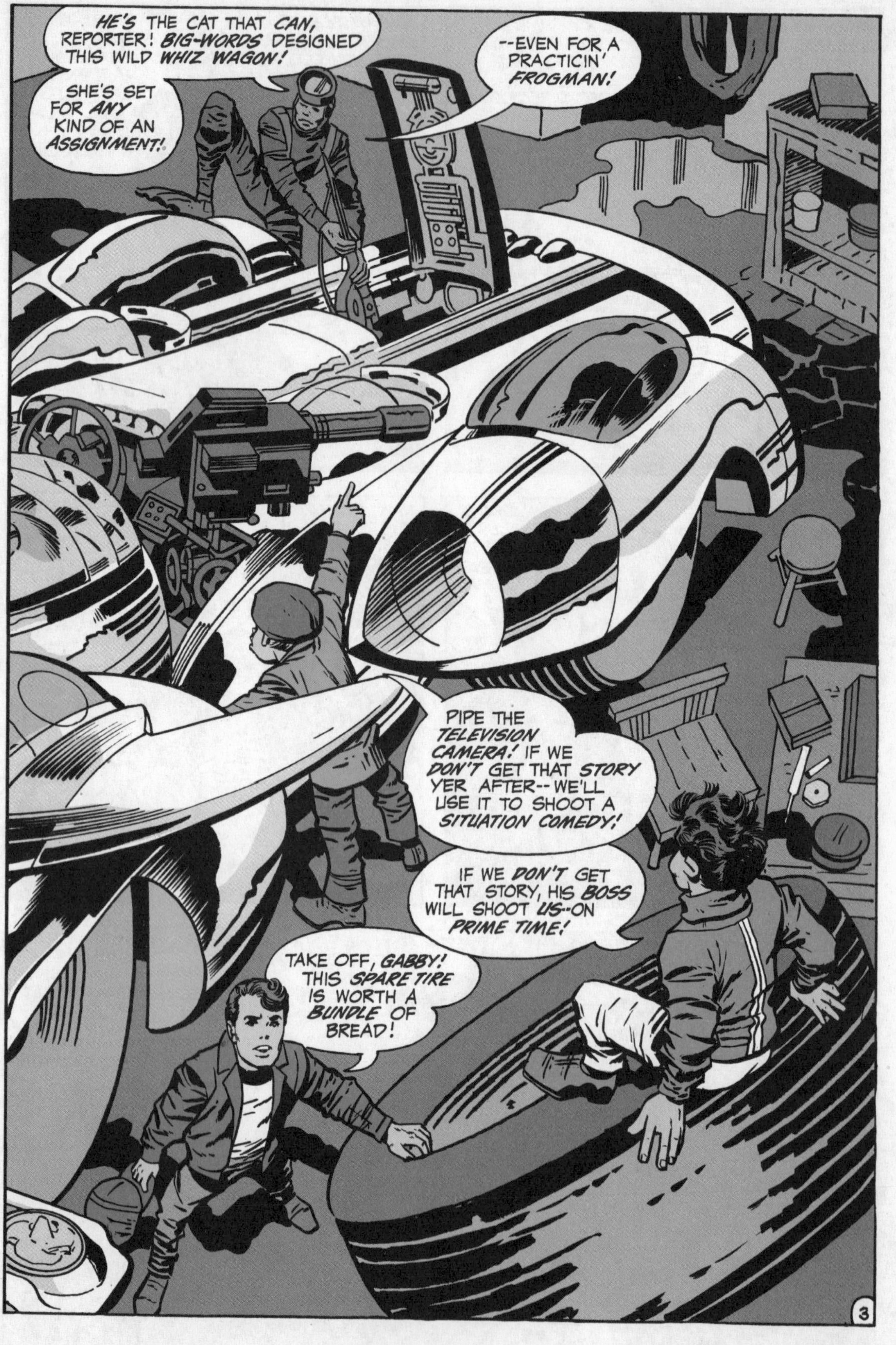
HE'S THE CAT THAT CAN, REPORTER! BIG-WORDS DESIGNED THIS WILD WHIZ WAGON!
SHE'S SET FOR ANY KIND OF AN ASSIGNMENT!
--EVEN FOR A PRACTICIN' FROGMAN!
PIPE THE TELEVISION CAMERA! IF WE DON'T GET THAT STORY YER AFTER--WE'LL USE IT TO SHOOT A SITUATION COMEDY!
IF WE DON'T GET THAT STORY, HIS BOSS WILL SHOOT US--ON PRIME TIME!
TAKE OFF, GABBY! THIS SPARE TIRE IS WORTH A BUNDLE OF BREAD!
3

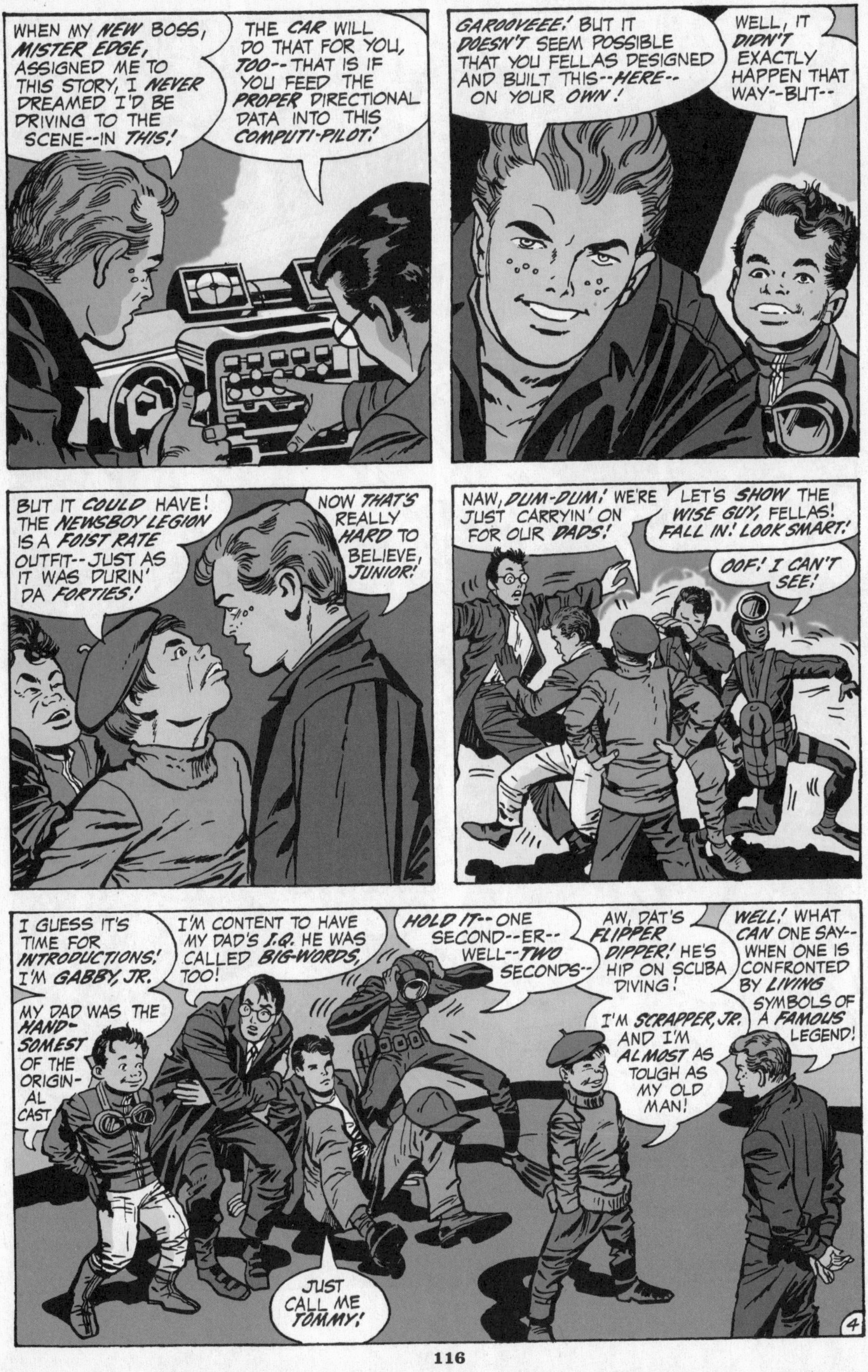

WHEN MY NEW BOSS, MISTER EDGE, ASSIGNED ME TO THIS STORY, I NEVER DREAMED I'D BE DRIVING TO THE SCENE--IN THIS!
THE CAR WILL DO THAT FOR YOU, TOO--THAT IS IF YOU FEED THE PROPER DIRECTIONAL DATA INTO THIS COMPUTI-PILOT!
GAROOVEEE! BUT IT DOESN'T SEEM POSSIBLE THAT YOU FELLAS DESIGNED AND BUILT THIS--HERE--ON YOUR OWN!
WELL, IT DIDN'T EXACTLY HAPPEN THAT WAY--BUT--
BUT IT COULD HAVE! THE NEWSBOY LEGION IS A FOIST RATE OUTFIT--JUST AS IT WAS DURIN' DA FORTIES!
NOW THAT'S REALLY HARD TO BELIEVE, JUNIOR!
NAW, DUM-DUM! WE'RE JUST CARRYIN' ON FOR OUR DADS!
LET'S SHOW THE WISE GUY, FELLAS! FALL IN! LOOK SMART!
OOF! I CAN'T SEE!
I GUESS IT'S TIME FOR INTRODUCTIONS! I'M GABBY, JR.
MY DAD WAS THE HAND-SOMEST OF THE ORIGIN-AL CAST
I'M CONTENT TO HAVE MY DAD'S I.Q. HE WAS CALLED BIG-WORDS, TOO!
HOLD IT--ONE SECOND--ER--WELL--TWO SECONDS--
JUST CALL ME TOMMY!
AW, DAT'S FLIPPER DIPPER! HE'S HIP ON SCUBA DIVING!
I'M SCRAPPER, JR. AND I'M ALMOST AS TOUGH AS MY OLD MAN!
WELL! WHAT CAN ONE SAY--WHEN ONE IS CONFRONTED BY LIVING SYMBOLS OF A FAMOUS LEGEND!
4

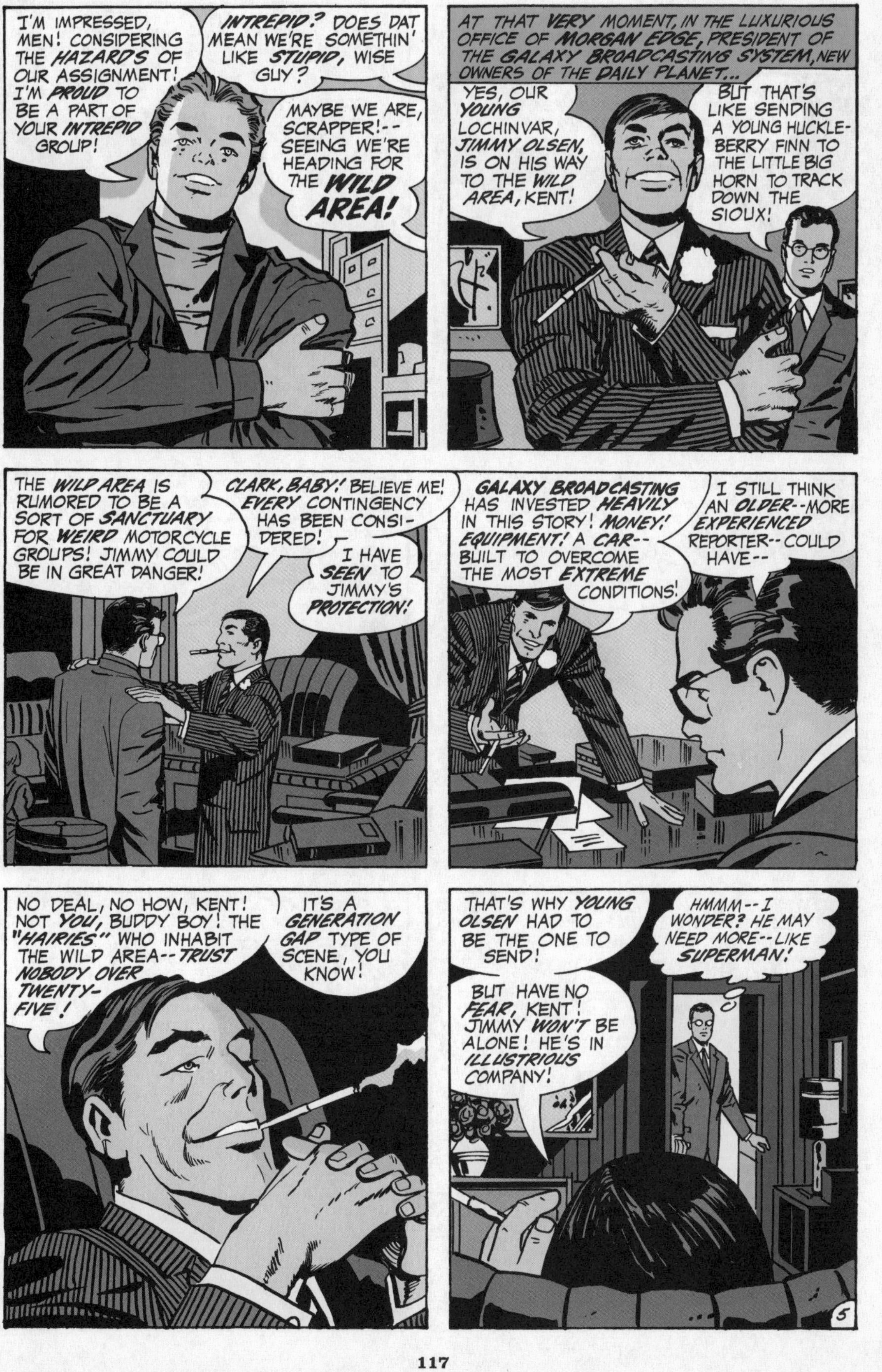
I'M IMPRESSED, MEN! CONSIDERING THE HAZARDS OF OUR ASSIGNMENT! I'M PROUD TO BE A PART OF YOUR INTREPID GROUP!
INTREPID? DOES DAT MEAN WE'RE SOMETHIN' LIKE STUPID, WISE GUY?
MAYBE WE ARE, SCRAPPER!-- SEEING WE'RE HEADING FOR THE WILD AREA!
AT THAT VERY MOMENT, IN THE LUXURIOUS OFFICE OF MORGAN EDGE, PRESIDENT OF THE GALAXY BROADCASTING SYSTEM, NEW OWNERS OF THE DAILY PLANET...
YES, OUR YOUNG LOCHINVAR, JIMMY OLSEN, IS ON HIS WAY TO THE WILD AREA, KENT!
BUT THAT'S LIKE SENDING A YOUNG HUCKLEBERRY FINN TO THE LITTLE BIG HORN TO TRACK DOWN THE SIOUX!
THE WILD AREA IS RUMORED TO BE A SORT OF SANCTUARY FOR WEIRD MOTORCYCLE GROUPS! JIMMY COULD BE IN GREAT DANGER!
CLARK, BABY! BELIEVE ME! EVERY CONTINGENCY HAS BEEN CONSIDERED!
I HAVE SEEN TO JIMMY'S PROTECTION!
GALAXY BROADCASTING HAS INVESTED HEAVILY IN THIS STORY! MONEY! EQUIPMENT! A CAR-- BUILT TO OVERCOME THE MOST EXTREME CONDITIONS!
I STILL THINK AN OLDER--MORE EXPERIENCED REPORTER--COULD HAVE--
NO DEAL, NO HOW, KENT! NOT YOU, BUDDY BOY! THE "HAIRIES" WHO INHABIT THE WILD AREA--TRUST NOBODY OVER TWENTY-FIVE!
IT'S A GENERATION GAP TYPE OF SCENE, YOU KNOW!
THAT'S WHY YOUNG OLSEN HAD TO BE THE ONE TO SEND!
HMMM--I WONDER? HE MAY NEED MORE--LIKE SUPERMAN!
BUT HAVE NO FEAR, KENT! JIMMY WON'T BE ALONE! HE'S IN ILLUSTRIOUS COMPANY!
5

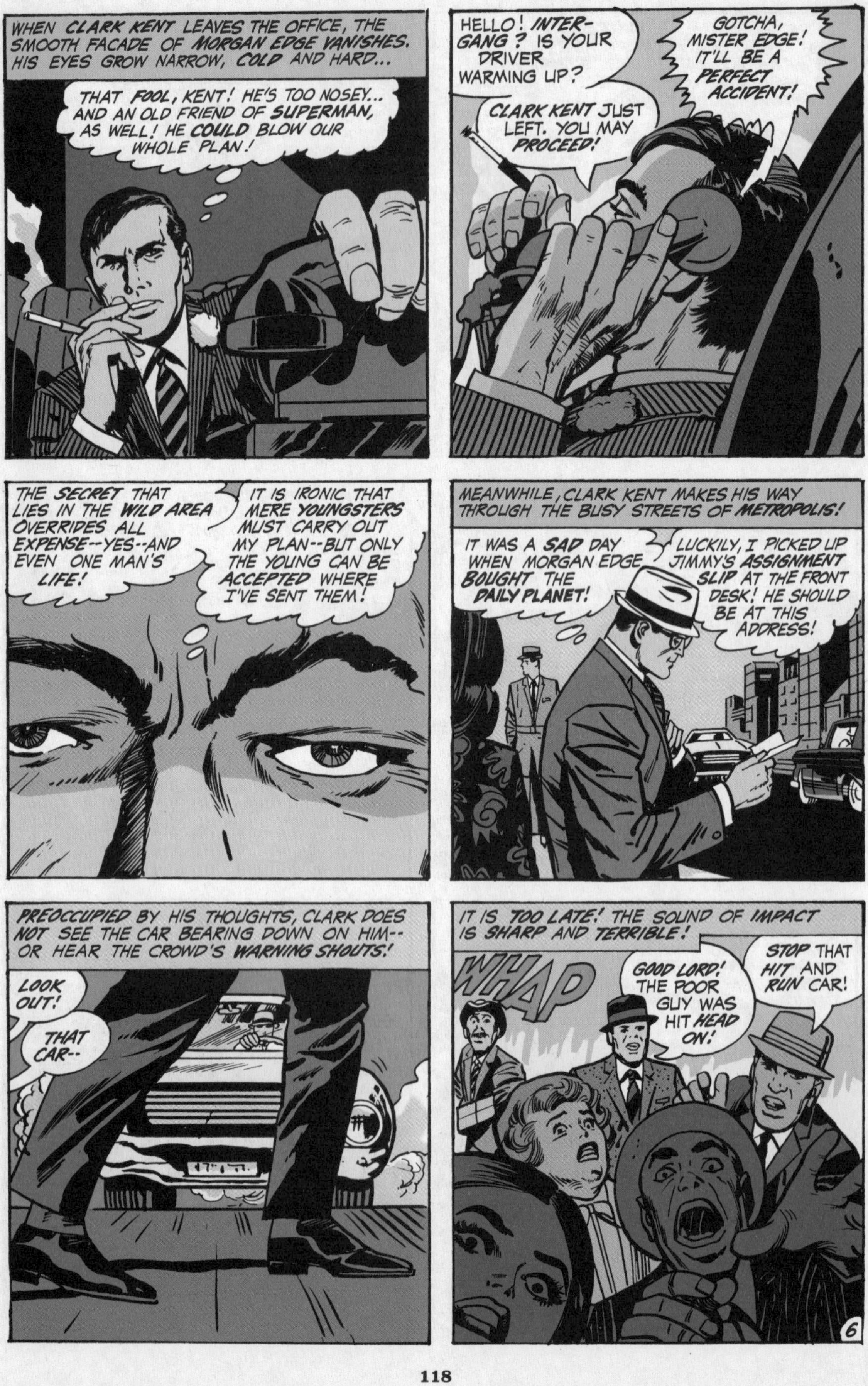
WHEN CLARK KENT LEAVES THE OFFICE, THE SMOOTH FACADE OF MORGAN EDGE VANISHES. HIS EYES GROW NARROW, COLD AND HARD...
THAT FOOL, KENT! HE'S TOO NOSEY... AND AN OLD FRIEND OF SUPERMAN, AS WELL! HE COULD BLOW OUR WHOLE PLAN!
HELLO! INTER-GANG? IS YOUR DRIVER WARMING UP?
CLARK KENT JUST LEFT. YOU MAY PROCEED!
GOTCHA, MISTER EDGE! IT'LL BE A PERFECT ACCIDENT!
THE SECRET THAT LIES IN THE WILD AREA OVERRIDES ALL EXPENSE--YES--AND EVEN ONE MAN'S LIFE!
IT IS IRONIC THAT MERE YOUNGSTERS MUST CARRY OUT MY PLAN--BUT ONLY THE YOUNG CAN BE ACCEPTED WHERE I'VE SENT THEM!
MEANWHILE, CLARK KENT MAKES HIS WAY THROUGH THE BUSY STREETS OF METROPOLIS!
IT WAS A SAD DAY WHEN MORGAN EDGE BOUGHT THE DAILY PLANET!
LUCKILY, I PICKED UP JIMMY'S ASSIGNMENT SLIP AT THE FRONT DESK! HE SHOULD BE AT THIS ADDRESS!
PREOCCUPIED BY HIS THOUGHTS, CLARK DOES NOT SEE THE CAR BEARING DOWN ON HIM-- OR HEAR THE CROWD'S WARNING SHOUTS!
LOOK OUT!
THAT CAR--
IT IS TOO LATE! THE SOUND OF IMPACT IS SHARP AND TERRIBLE!
WHAP
GOOD LORD! THE POOR GUY WAS HIT HEAD ON!
STOP THAT HIT AND RUN CAR!
6

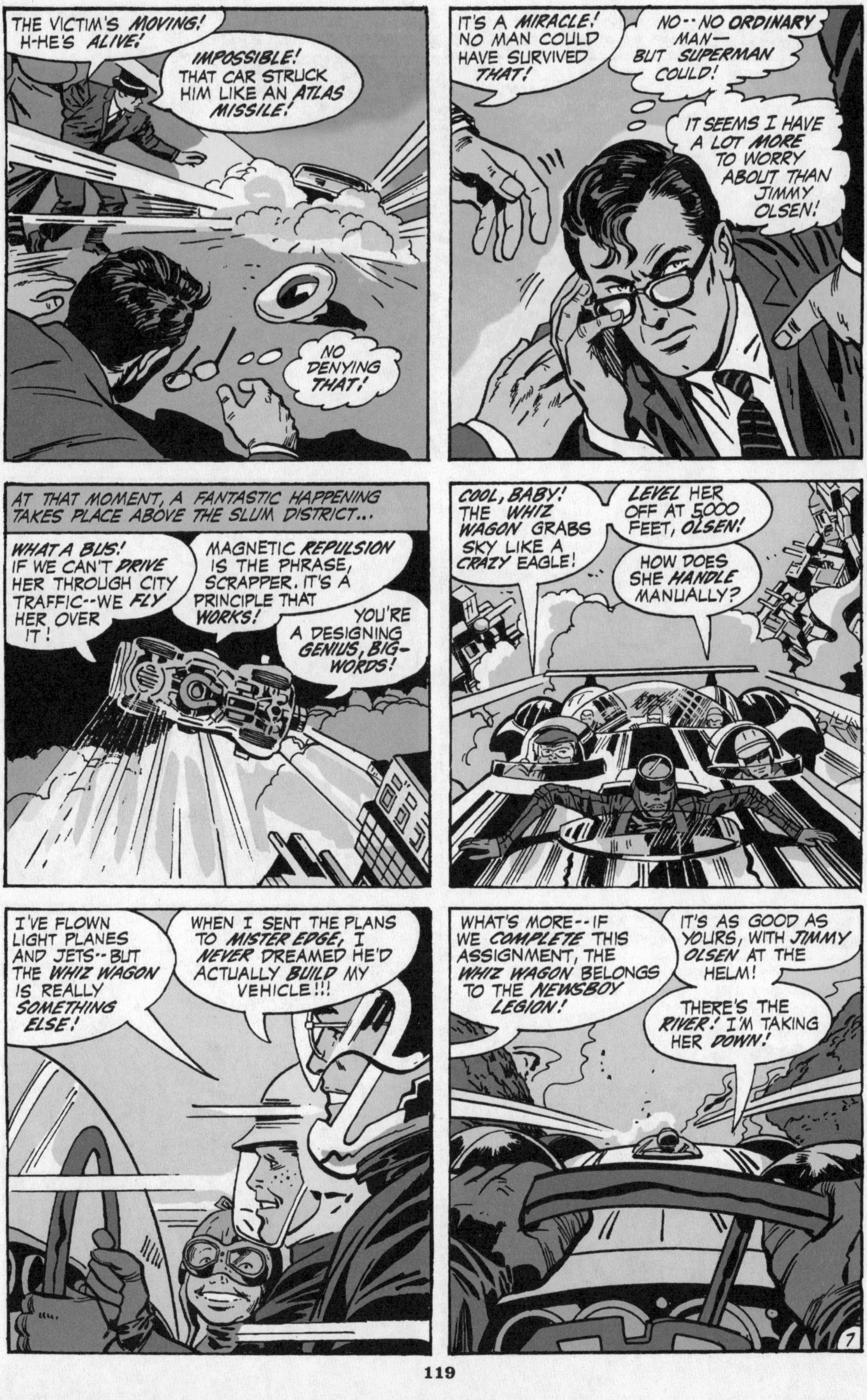
THE VICTIM'S MOVING! H-HE'S ALIVE!
IMPOSSIBLE! THAT CAR STRUCK HIM LIKE AN ATLAS MISSILE!
NO DENYING THAT!
IT'S A MIRACLE! NO MAN COULD HAVE SURVIVED THAT!
NO-- NO ORDINARY MAN— BUT SUPERMAN COULD!
IT SEEMS I HAVE A LOT MORE TO WORRY ABOUT THAN JIMMY OLSEN!
AT THAT MOMENT, A FANTASTIC HAPPENING TAKES PLACE ABOVE THE SLUM DISTRICT...
WHAT A BUS! IF WE CAN'T DRIVE HER THROUGH CITY TRAFFIC--WE FLY HER OVER IT!
MAGNETIC REPULSION IS THE PHRASE, SCRAPPER. IT'S A PRINCIPLE THAT WORKS!
YOU'RE A DESIGNING GENIUS, BIG-WORDS!
COOL, BABY! THE WHIZ WAGON GRABS SKY LIKE A CRAZY EAGLE!
LEVEL HER OFF AT 5000 FEET, OLSEN!
HOW DOES SHE HANDLE MANUALLY?
I'VE FLOWN LIGHT PLANES AND JETS-- BUT THE WHIZ WAGON IS REALLY SOMETHING ELSE!
WHEN I SENT THE PLANS TO MISTER EDGE, I NEVER DREAMED HE'D ACTUALLY BUILD MY VEHICLE!!!
WHAT'S MORE--IF WE COMPLETE THIS ASSIGNMENT, THE WHIZ WAGON BELONGS TO THE NEWSBOY LEGION!
IT'S AS GOOD AS YOURS, WITH JIMMY OLSEN AT THE HELM!
THERE'S THE RIVER! I'M TAKING HER DOWN!
7

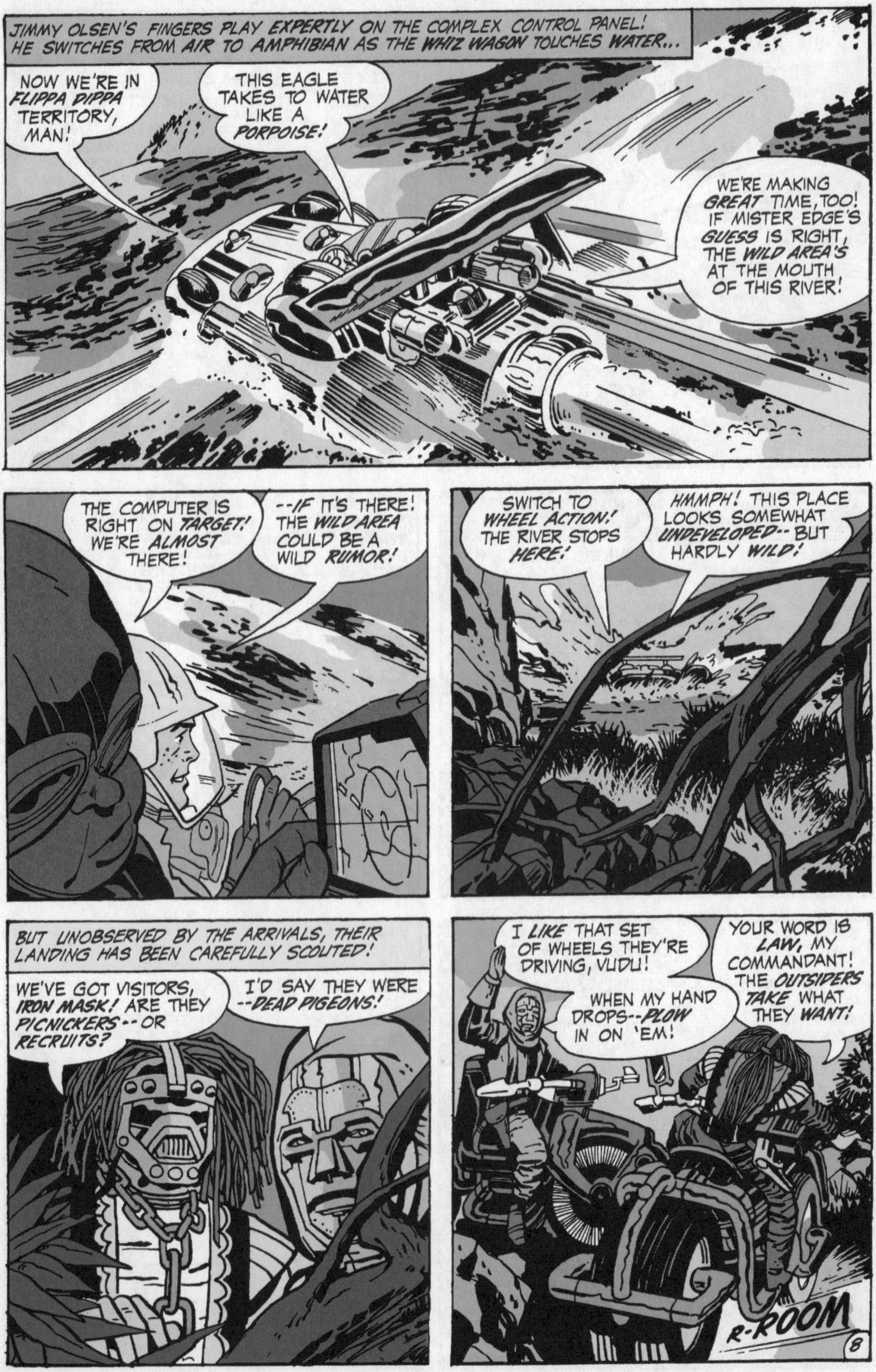

JIMMY OLSEN'S FINGERS PLAY EXPERTLY ON THE COMPLEX CONTROL PANEL! HE SWITCHES FROM AIR TO AMPHIBIAN AS THE WHIZ WAGON TOUCHES WATER...
NOW WE'RE IN FLIPPA DIPPA TERRITORY, MAN!
THIS EAGLE TAKES TO WATER LIKE A PORPOISE!
WE'RE MAKING GREAT TIME, TOO! IF MISTER EDGE'S GUESS IS RIGHT, THE WILD AREA'S AT THE MOUTH OF THIS RIVER!
THE COMPUTER IS RIGHT ON TARGET! WE'RE ALMOST THERE!
--IF IT'S THERE! THE WILD AREA COULD BE A WILD RUMOR!
SWITCH TO WHEEL ACTION! THE RIVER STOPS HERE!
HMMPH! THIS PLACE LOOKS SOMEWHAT UNDEVELOPED-- BUT HARDLY WILD!
BUT UNOBSERVED BY THE ARRIVALS, THEIR LANDING HAS BEEN CAREFULLY SCOUTED!
WE'VE GOT VISITORS, IRON MASK! ARE THEY PICNICKERS -- OR RECRUITS?
I'D SAY THEY WERE --DEAD PIGEONS!
I LIKE THAT SET OF WHEELS THEY'RE DRIVING, VUDU!
WHEN MY HAND DROPS--PLOW IN ON 'EM!
YOUR WORD IS LAW, MY COMMANDANT! THE OUTSIDERS TAKE WHAT THEY WANT!
R-ROOM
8

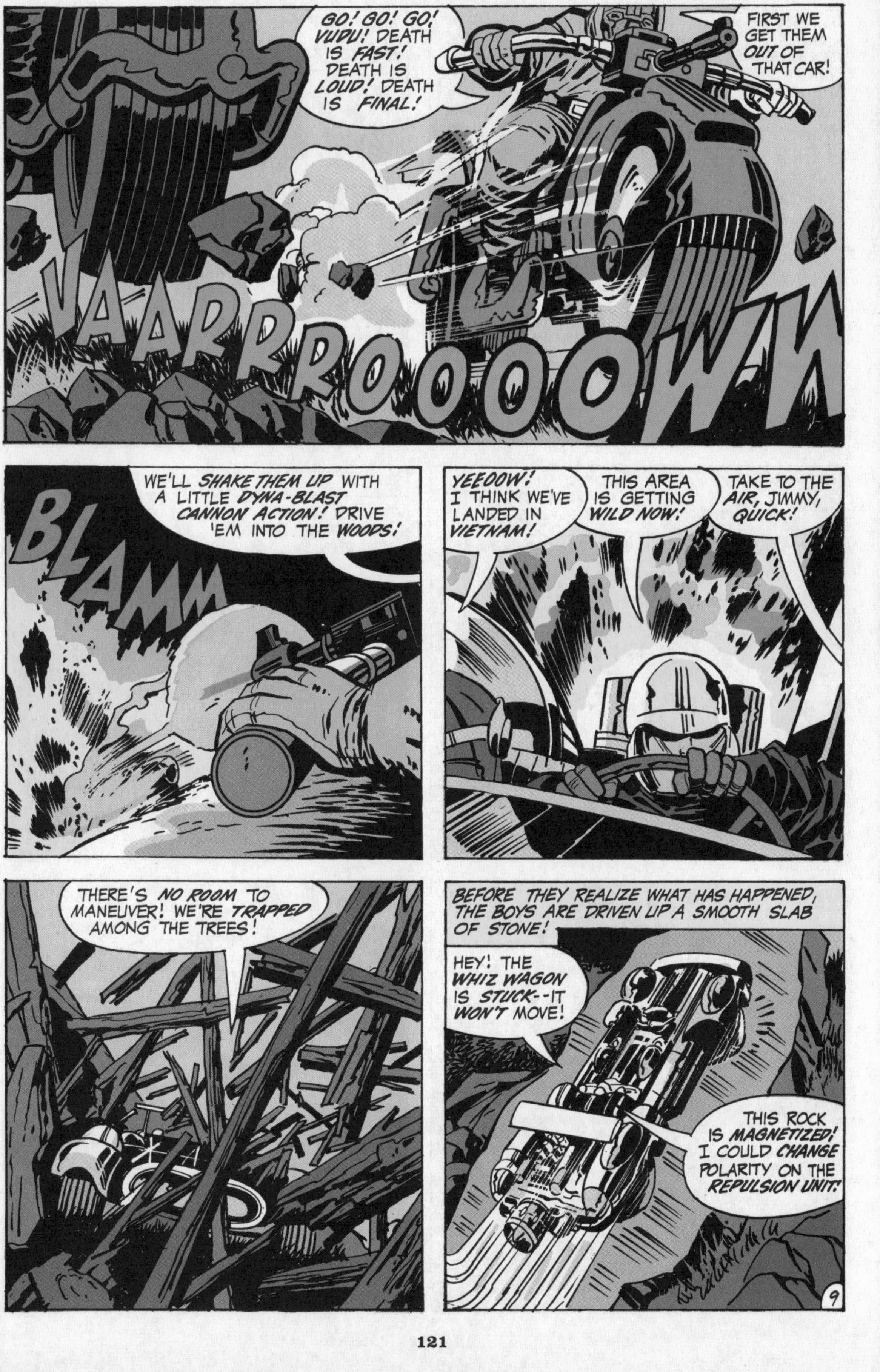
GO! GO! GO! VUDU! DEATH IS FAST! DEATH IS LOUD! DEATH IS FINAL!
FIRST WE GET THEM OUT OF THAT CAR!
VAARRROOOOOWW
WE'LL SHAKE THEM UP WITH A LITTLE DYNA-BLAST CANNON ACTION! DRIVE 'EM INTO THE WOODS!
BLAMM
YEEOOW! I THINK WE'VE LANDED IN VIETNAM!
THIS AREA IS GETTING WILD NOW!
TAKE TO THE AIR, JIMMY, QUICK!
THERE'S NO ROOM TO MANEUVER! WE'RE TRAPPED AMONG THE TREES!
BEFORE THEY REALIZE WHAT HAS HAPPENED, THE BOYS ARE DRIVEN UP A SMOOTH SLAB OF STONE!
HEY! THE WHIZ WAGON IS STUCK--IT WON'T MOVE!
THIS ROCK IS MAGNETIZED! I COULD CHANGE POLARITY ON THE REPULSION UNIT!
9

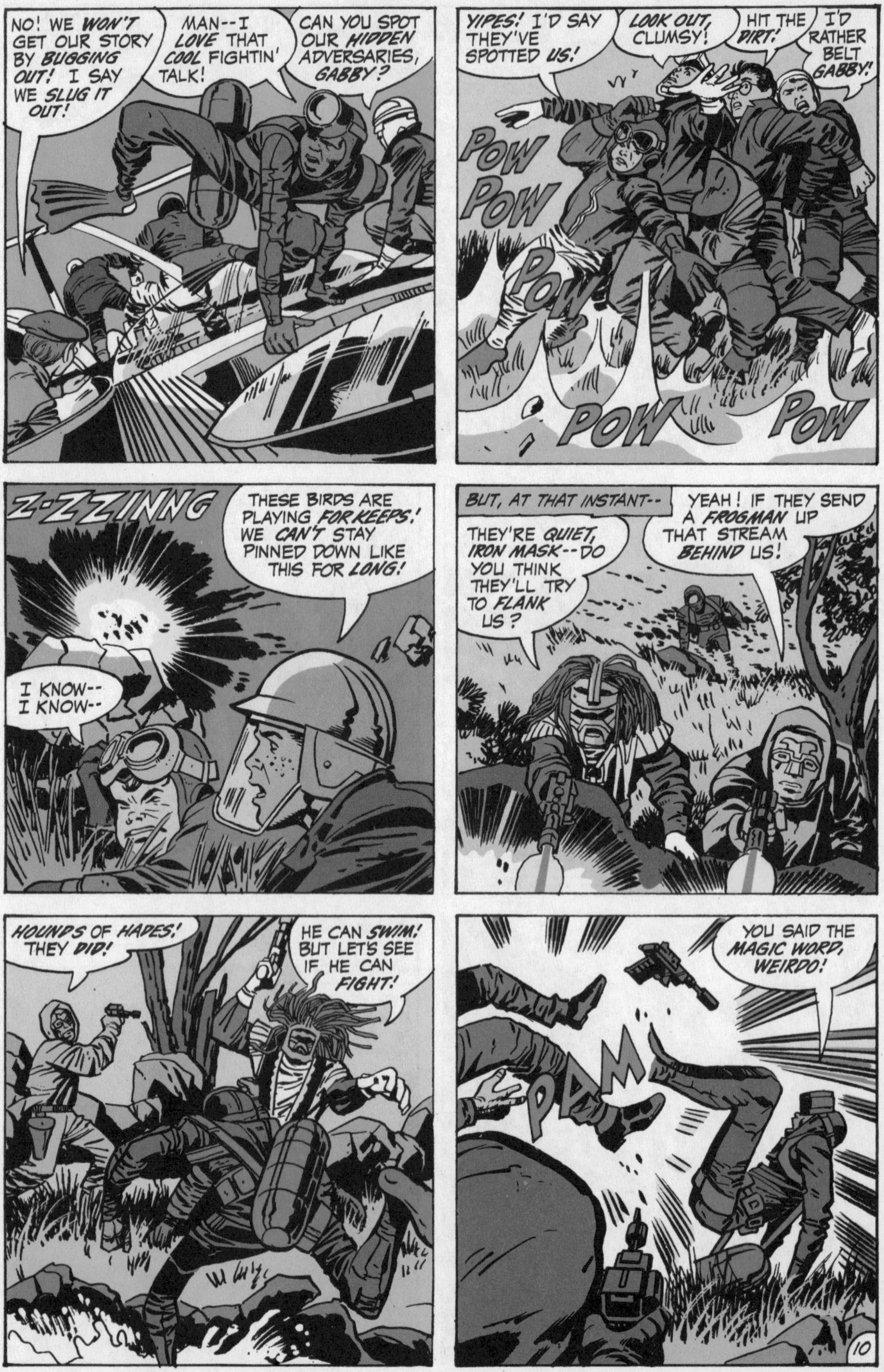
NO! WE WON'T GET OUR STORY BY BUGGING OUT! I SAY WE SLUG IT OUT!
MAN--I LOVE THAT COOL FIGHTIN' TALK!
CAN YOU SPOT OUR HIDDEN ADVERSARIES, GABBY?
YIPES! I'D SAY THEY'VE SPOTTED US!
LOOK OUT, CLUMSY!
HIT THE DIRT!
I'D RATHER BELT GABBY!
POW
POW
POW
POW
POW
Z-ZZZINNG
THESE BIRDS ARE PLAYING FOR KEEPS! WE CAN'T STAY PINNED DOWN LIKE THIS FOR LONG!
I KNOW-- I KNOW--
BUT, AT THAT INSTANT--
THEY'RE QUIET, IRON MASK--DO YOU THINK THEY'LL TRY TO FLANK US?
YEAH! IF THEY SEND A FROGMAN UP THAT STREAM BEHIND US!
HOUNDS OF HADES! THEY DID!
HE CAN SWIM! BUT LET'S SEE IF HE CAN FIGHT!
YOU SAID THE MAGIC WORD, WEIRDO!
PAM
10

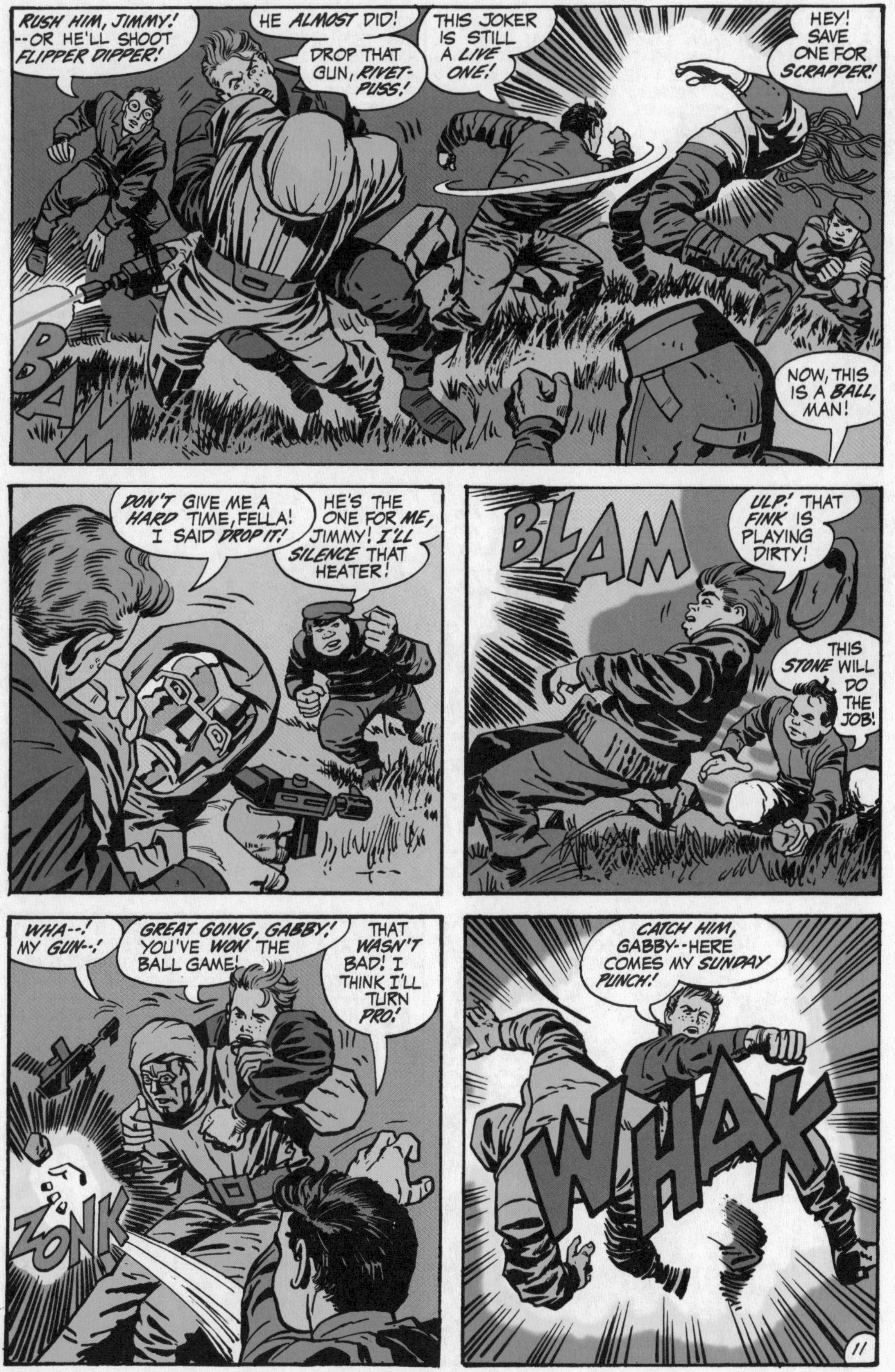
RUSH HIM, JIMMY! --OR HE'LL SHOOT FLIPPER DIPPER!
HE ALMOST DID!
DROP THAT GUN, RIVET-PUSS!
THIS JOKER IS STILL A LIVE ONE!
HEY! SAVE ONE FOR SCRAPPER!
BAM
NOW, THIS IS A BALL, MAN!
DON'T GIVE ME A HARD TIME, FELLA! I SAID DROP IT!
HE'S THE ONE FOR ME, JIMMY! I'LL SILENCE THAT HEATER!
BLAM
ULP! THAT FINK IS PLAYING DIRTY!
THIS STONE WILL DO THE JOB!
WHA--! MY GUN--!
GREAT GOING, GABBY! YOU'VE WON THE BALL GAME!
THAT WASN'T BAD! I THINK I'LL TURN PRO!
ZONK
CATCH HIM, GABBY--HERE COMES MY SUNDAY PUNCH!
WHAK
11

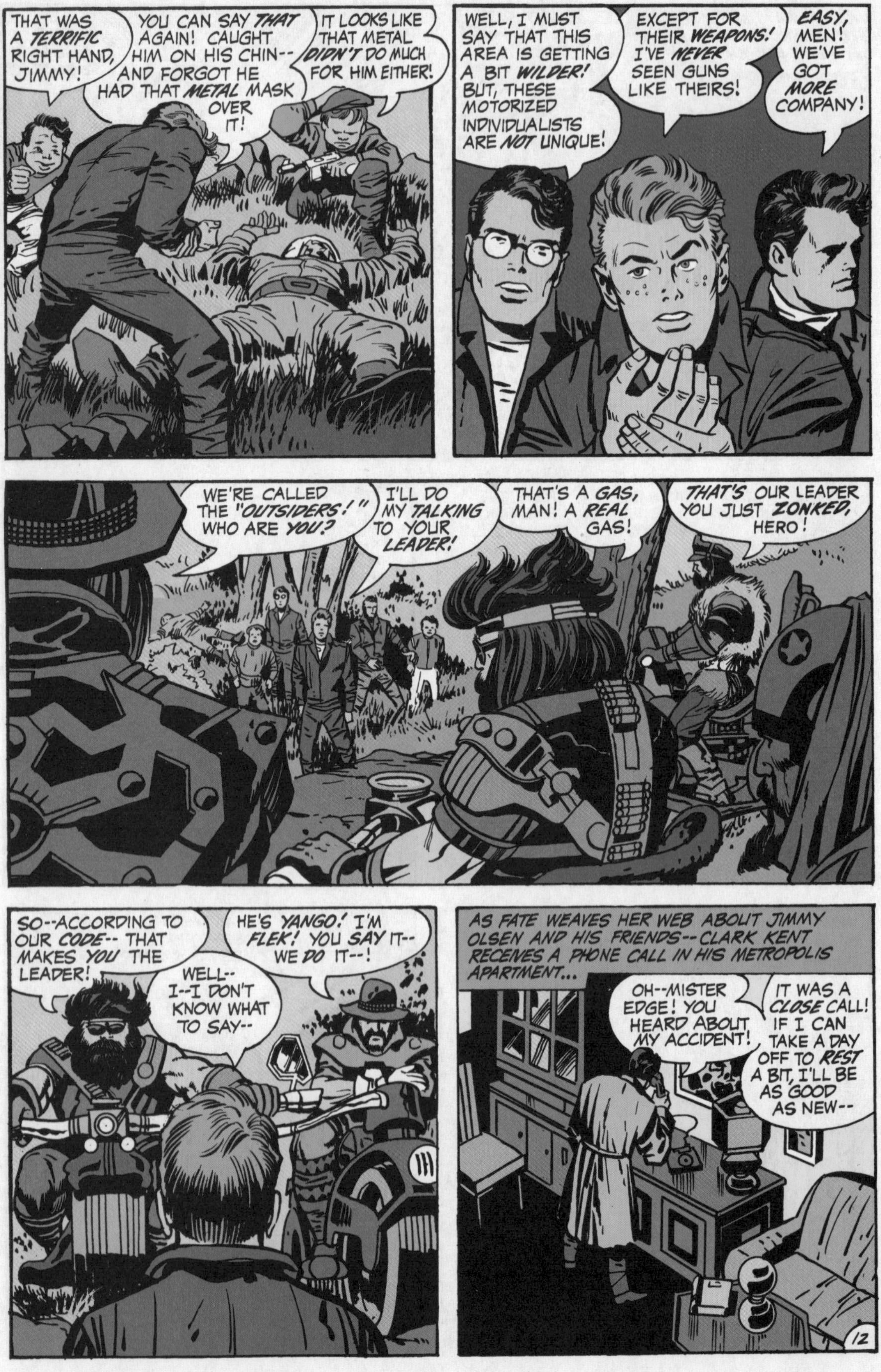
THAT WAS A TERRIFIC RIGHT HAND, JIMMY!
YOU CAN SAY THAT AGAIN! CAUGHT HIM ON HIS CHIN--AND FORGOT HE HAD THAT METAL MASK OVER IT!
IT LOOKS LIKE THAT METAL DIDN'T DO MUCH FOR HIM EITHER!
WELL, I MUST SAY THAT THIS AREA IS GETTING A BIT WILDER! BUT, THESE MOTORIZED INDIVIDUALISTS ARE NOT UNIQUE!
EXCEPT FOR THEIR WEAPONS! I'VE NEVER SEEN GUNS LIKE THEIRS!
EASY, MEN! WE'VE GOT MORE COMPANY!
WE'RE CALLED THE "OUTSIDERS!" WHO ARE YOU?
I'LL DO MY TALKING TO YOUR LEADER!
THAT'S A GAS, MAN! A REAL GAS!
THAT'S OUR LEADER YOU JUST ZONKED, HERO!
SO--ACCORDING TO OUR CODE-- THAT MAKES YOU THE LEADER!
HE'S YANGO! I'M FLEK! YOU SAY IT--WE DO IT--!
WELL--I--I DON'T KNOW WHAT TO SAY--
AS FATE WEAVES HER WEB ABOUT JIMMY OLSEN AND HIS FRIENDS--CLARK KENT RECEIVES A PHONE CALL IN HIS METROPOLIS APARTMENT...
OH--MISTER EDGE! YOU HEARD ABOUT MY ACCIDENT!
IT WAS A CLOSE CALL! IF I CAN TAKE A DAY OFF TO REST A BIT, I'LL BE AS GOOD AS NEW--
12

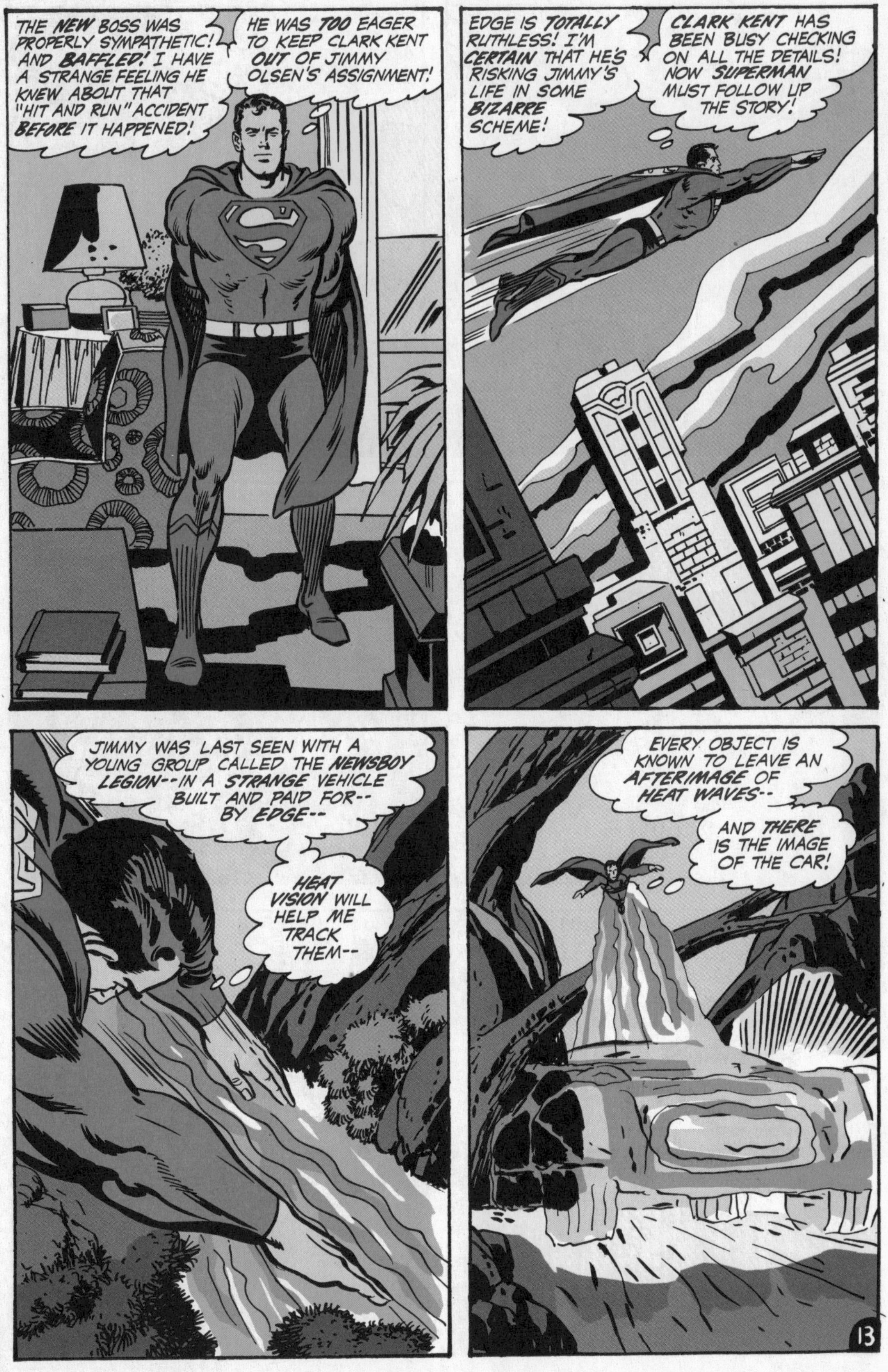
THE NEW BOSS WAS PROPERLY SYMPATHETIC! AND BAFFLED! I HAVE A STRANGE FEELING HE KNEW ABOUT THAT "HIT AND RUN" ACCIDENT BEFORE IT HAPPENED!
HE WAS TOO EAGER TO KEEP CLARK KENT OUT OF JIMMY OLSEN'S ASSIGNMENT!
EDGE IS TOTALLY RUTHLESS! I'M CERTAIN THAT HE'S RISKING JIMMY'S LIFE IN SOME BIZARRE SCHEME!
CLARK KENT HAS BEEN BUSY CHECKING ON ALL THE DETAILS! NOW SUPERMAN MUST FOLLOW UP THE STORY!
JIMMY WAS LAST SEEN WITH A YOUNG GROUP CALLED THE NEWSBOY LEGION--IN A STRANGE VEHICLE BUILT AND PAID FOR-- BY EDGE--
HEAT VISION WILL HELP ME TRACK THEM--
EVERY OBJECT IS KNOWN TO LEAVE AN AFTERIMAGE OF HEAT WAVES--
AND THERE IS THE IMAGE OF THE CAR!
13

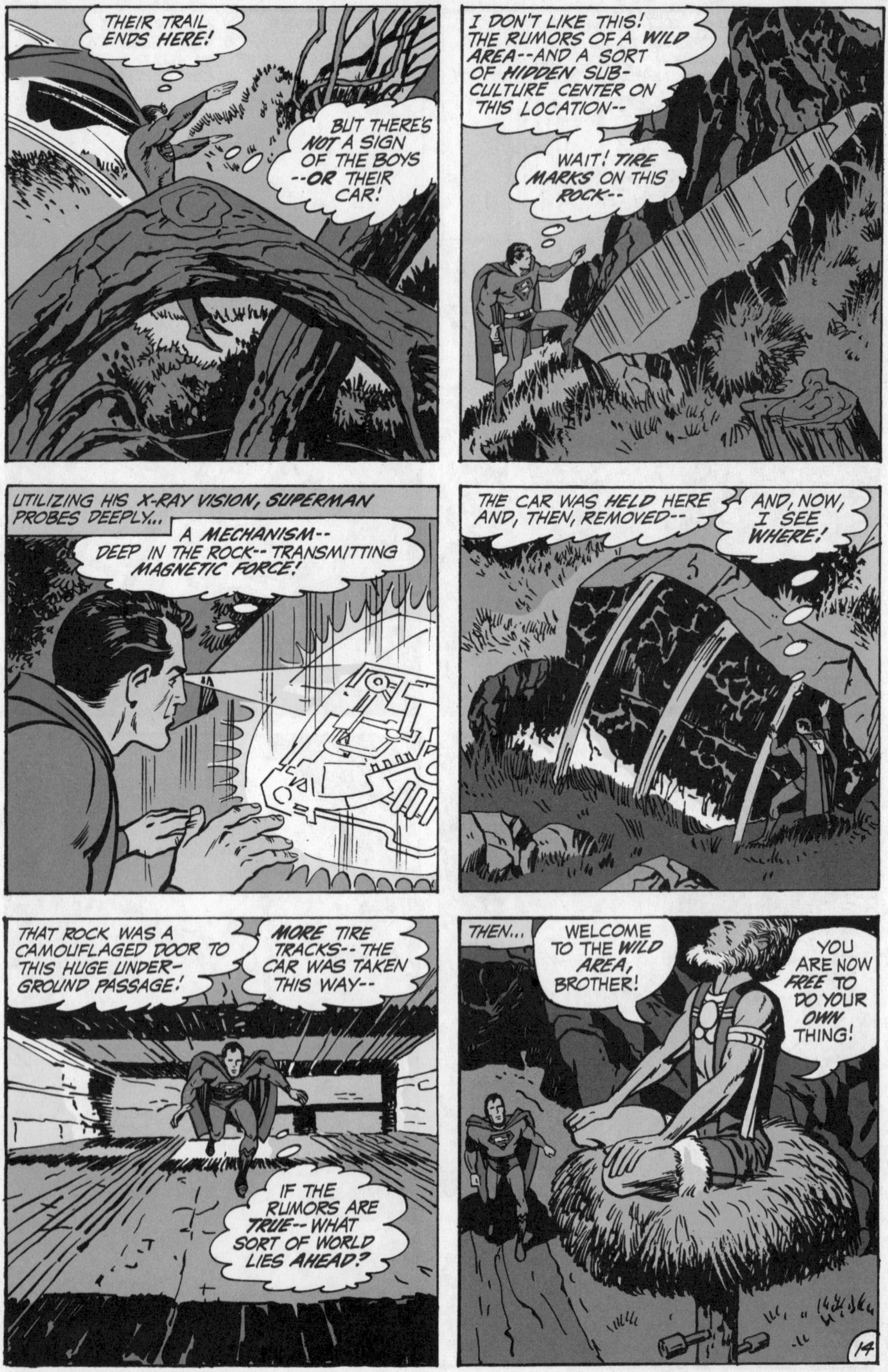
THEIR TRAIL ENDS HERE!
BUT THERE'S NOT A SIGN OF THE BOYS --OR THEIR CAR!
I DON'T LIKE THIS! THE RUMORS OF A WILD AREA--AND A SORT OF HIDDEN SUB-CULTURE CENTER ON THIS LOCATION--
WAIT! TIRE MARKS ON THIS ROCK--
UTILIZING HIS X-RAY VISION, SUPERMAN PROBES DEEPLY...
A MECHANISM-- DEEP IN THE ROCK-- TRANSMITTING MAGNETIC FORCE!
THE CAR WAS HELD HERE AND, THEN, REMOVED--
AND, NOW, I SEE WHERE!
THAT ROCK WAS A CAMOUFLAGED DOOR TO THIS HUGE UNDER-GROUND PASSAGE!
MORE TIRE TRACKS-- THE CAR WAS TAKEN THIS WAY--
IF THE RUMORS ARE TRUE-- WHAT SORT OF WORLD LIES AHEAD?
THEN...
WELCOME TO THE WILD AREA, BROTHER!
YOU ARE NOW FREE TO DO YOUR OWN THING!
14

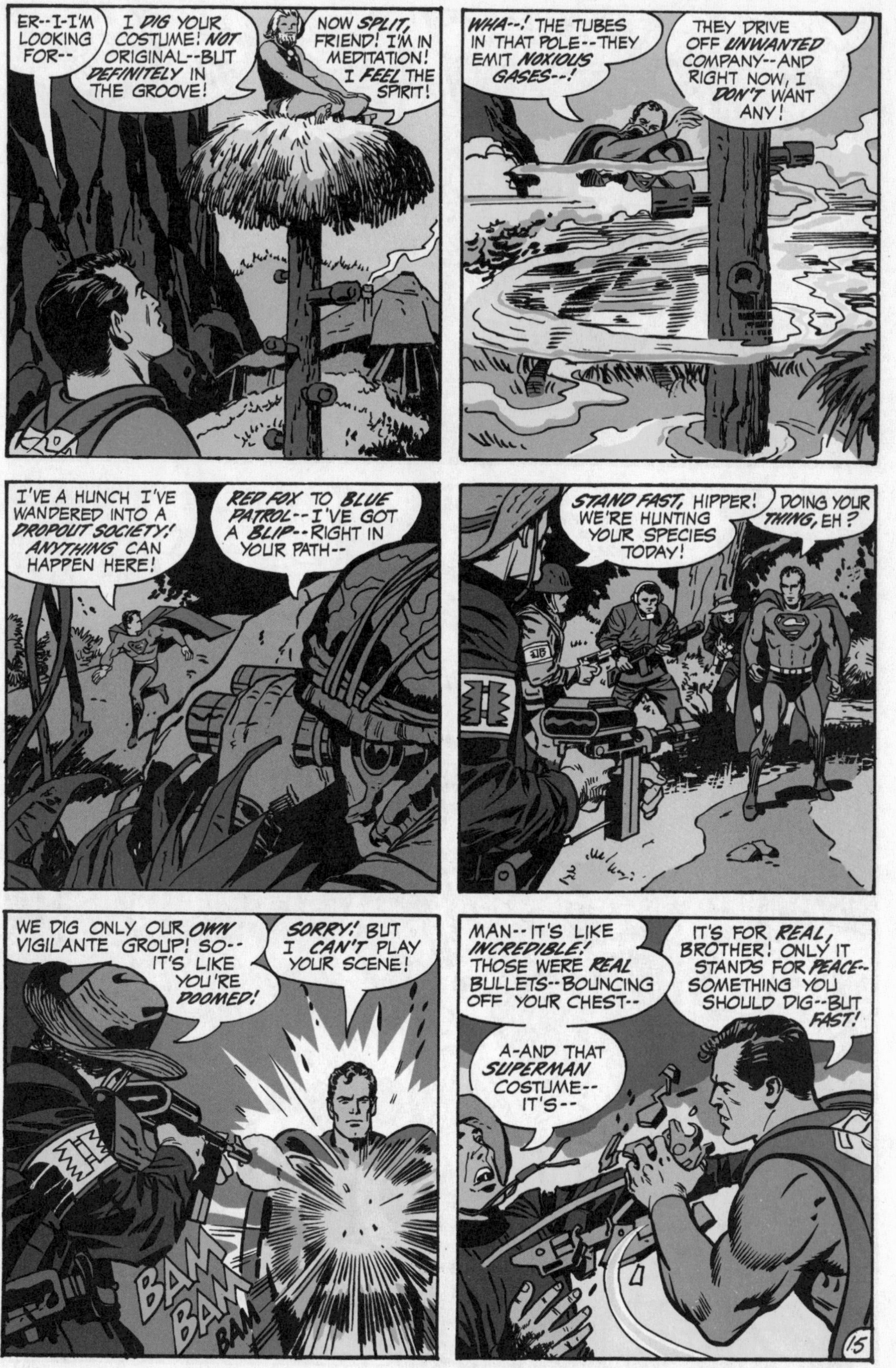
ER--I-I'M LOOKING FOR--
I DIG YOUR COSTUME! NOT ORIGINAL--BUT DEFINITELY IN THE GROOVE!
NOW SPLIT, FRIEND! I'M IN MEDITATION! I FEEL THE SPIRIT!
WHA--! THE TUBES IN THAT POLE--THEY EMIT NOXIOUS GASES--!
THEY DRIVE OFF UNWANTED COMPANY--AND RIGHT NOW, I DON'T WANT ANY!
I'VE A HUNCH I'VE WANDERED INTO A DROPOUT SOCIETY! ANYTHING CAN HAPPEN HERE!
RED FOX TO BLUE PATROL--I'VE GOT A BLIP--RIGHT IN YOUR PATH--
STAND FAST, HIPPER! WE'RE HUNTING YOUR SPECIES TODAY!
DOING YOUR THING, EH?
WE DIG ONLY OUR OWN VIGILANTE GROUP! SO--IT'S LIKE YOU'RE DOOMED!
SORRY! BUT I CAN'T PLAY YOUR SCENE!
BAM
BAM
BAM
MAN--IT'S LIKE INCREDIBLE! THOSE WERE REAL BULLETS--BOUNCING OFF YOUR CHEST--
IT'S FOR REAL, BROTHER! ONLY IT STANDS FOR PEACE--SOMETHING YOU SHOULD DIG--BUT FAST!
A-AND THAT SUPERMAN COSTUME--IT'S--
15

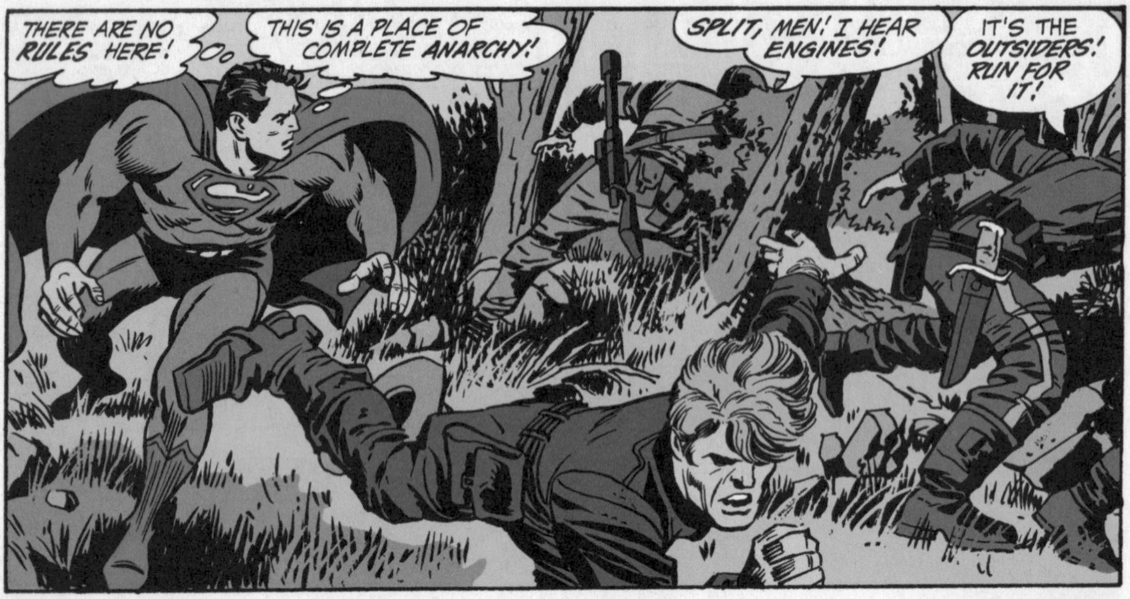
THERE ARE NO RULES HERE!
THIS IS A PLACE OF COMPLETE ANARCHY!
SPLIT, MEN! I HEAR ENGINES!
IT'S THE OUTSIDERS! RUN FOR IT!

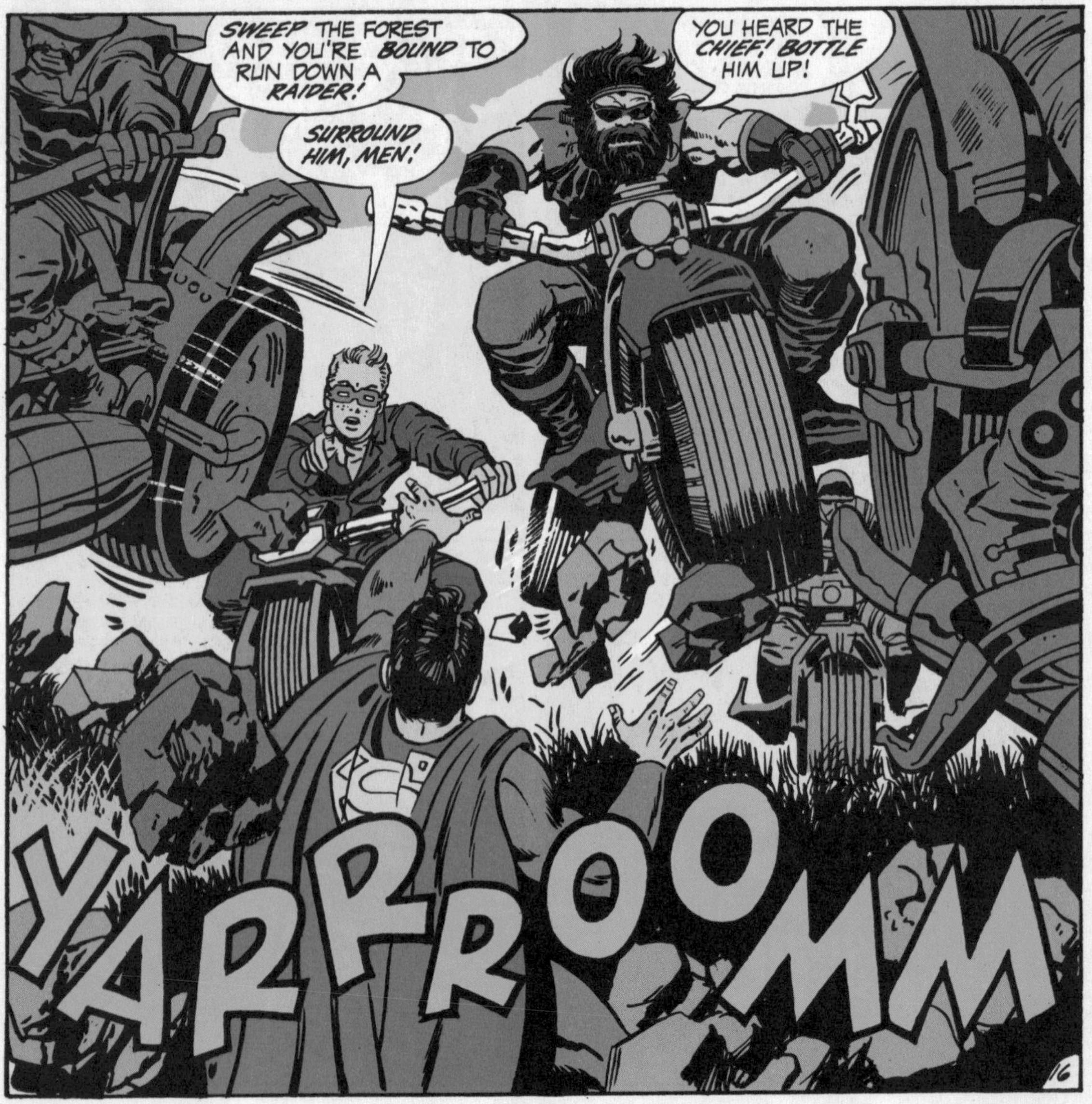
SWEEP THE FOREST AND YOU'RE BOUND TO RUN DOWN A RAIDER!
SURROUND HIM, MEN!
YOU HEARD THE CHIEF! BOTTLE HIM UP!
YARRROOMM
16

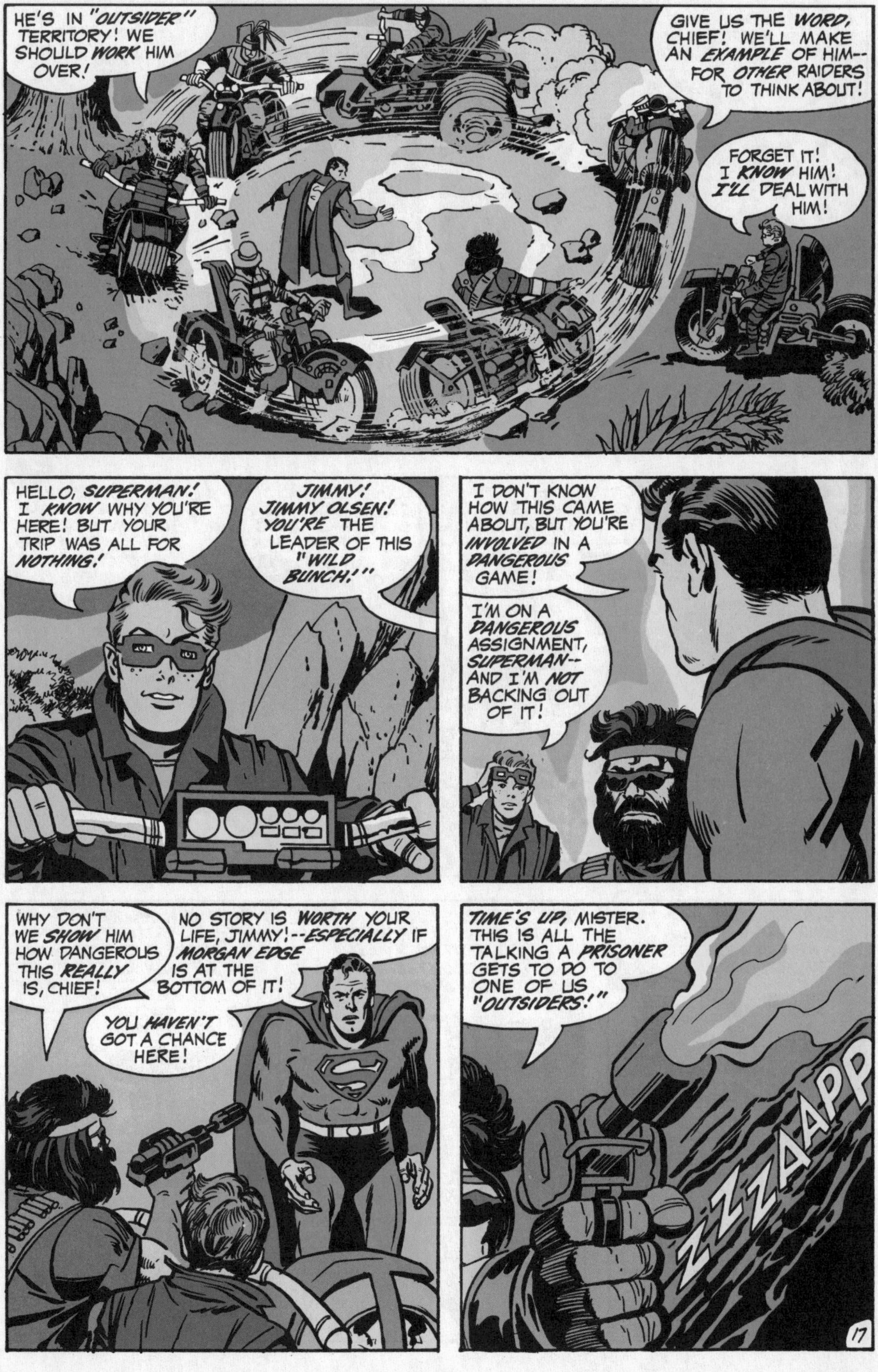
HE'S IN "OUTSIDER" TERRITORY! WE SHOULD WORK HIM OVER!
GIVE US THE WORD, CHIEF! WE'LL MAKE AN EXAMPLE OF HIM-- FOR OTHER RAIDERS TO THINK ABOUT!
FORGET IT! I KNOW HIM! I'LL DEAL WITH HIM!
HELLO, SUPERMAN! I KNOW WHY YOU'RE HERE! BUT YOUR TRIP WAS ALL FOR NOTHING!
JIMMY! JIMMY OLSEN! YOU'RE THE LEADER OF THIS "WILD BUNCH!"
I DON'T KNOW HOW THIS CAME ABOUT, BUT YOU'RE INVOLVED IN A DANGEROUS GAME!
I'M ON A DANGEROUS ASSIGNMENT, SUPERMAN-- AND I'M NOT BACKING OUT OF IT!
WHY DON'T WE SHOW HIM HOW DANGEROUS THIS REALLY IS, CHIEF!
NO STORY IS WORTH YOUR LIFE, JIMMY!--ESPECIALLY IF MORGAN EDGE IS AT THE BOTTOM OF IT!
YOU HAVEN'T GOT A CHANCE HERE!
TIME'S UP, MISTER. THIS IS ALL THE TALKING A PRISONER GETS TO DO TO ONE OF US "OUTSIDERS!"
ZZZAAPP
17

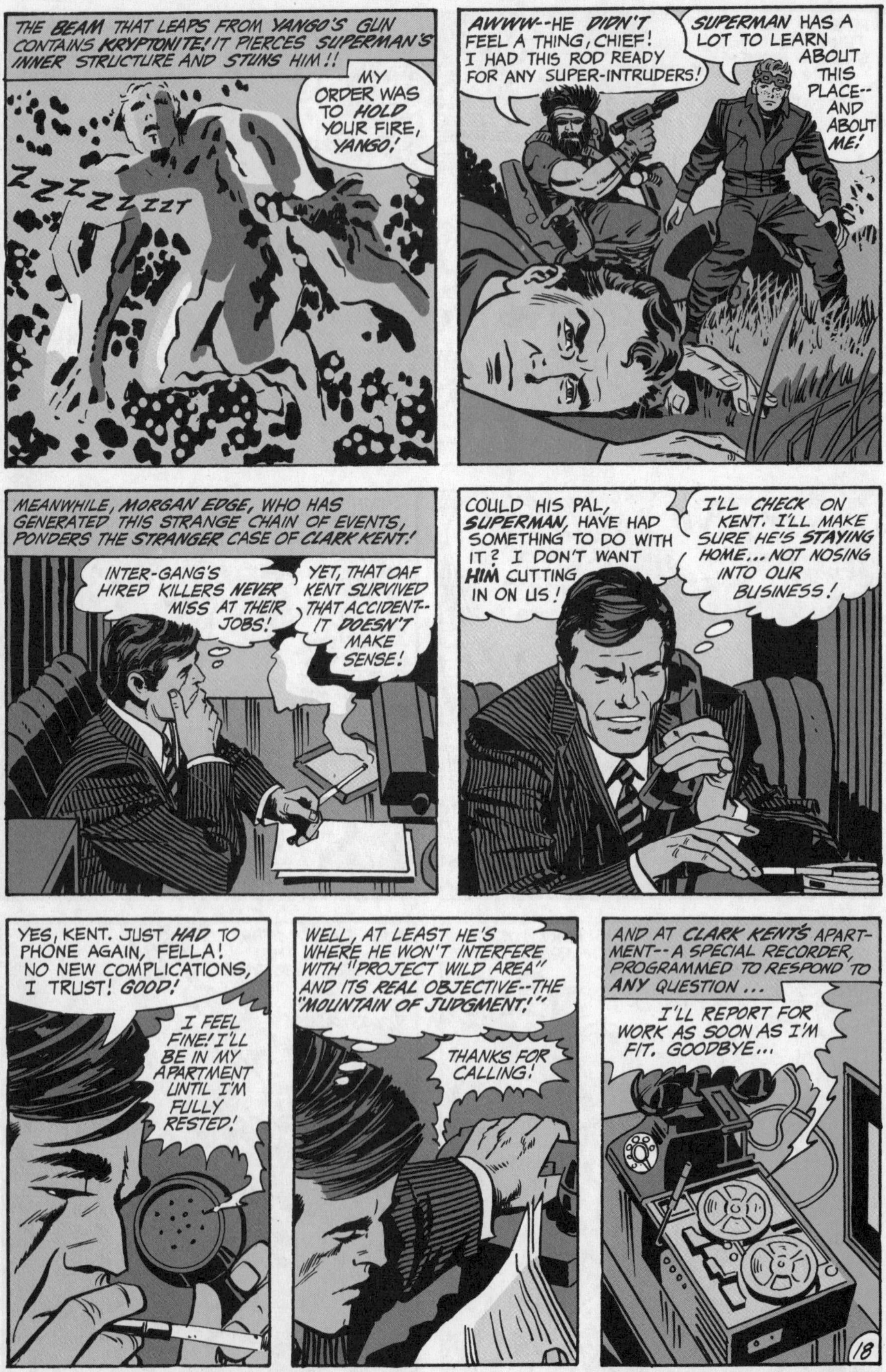
THE BEAM THAT LEAPS FROM YANGO'S GUN CONTAINS KRYPTONITE! IT PIERCES SUPERMAN'S INNER STRUCTURE AND STUNS HIM!!
MY ORDER WAS TO HOLD YOUR FIRE, YANGO!
ZZZZZZZZT
AWWW--HE DIDN'T FEEL A THING, CHIEF! I HAD THIS ROD READY FOR ANY SUPER-INTRUDERS!
SUPERMAN HAS A LOT TO LEARN ABOUT THIS PLACE-- AND ABOUT ME!
MEANWHILE, MORGAN EDGE, WHO HAS GENERATED THIS STRANGE CHAIN OF EVENTS, PONDERS THE STRANGER CASE OF CLARK KENT!
INTER-GANG'S HIRED KILLERS NEVER MISS AT THEIR JOBS!
YET, THAT OAF KENT SURVIVED THAT ACCIDENT-- IT DOESN'T MAKE SENSE!
COULD HIS PAL, SUPERMAN, HAVE HAD SOMETHING TO DO WITH IT? I DON'T WANT HIM CUTTING IN ON US!
I'LL CHECK ON KENT. I'LL MAKE SURE HE'S STAYING HOME... NOT NOSING INTO OUR BUSINESS!
YES, KENT. JUST HAD TO PHONE AGAIN, FELLA! NO NEW COMPLICATIONS, I TRUST! GOOD!
I FEEL FINE! I'LL BE IN MY APARTMENT UNTIL I'M FULLY RESTED!
WELL, AT LEAST HE'S WHERE HE WON'T INTERFERE WITH "PROJECT WILD AREA" AND ITS REAL OBJECTIVE--THE "MOUNTAIN OF JUDGMENT!"
THANKS FOR CALLING!
AND AT CLARK KENT'S APARTMENT--A SPECIAL RECORDER, PROGRAMMED TO RESPOND TO ANY QUESTION...
I'LL REPORT FOR WORK AS SOON AS I'M FIT. GOODBYE...
18

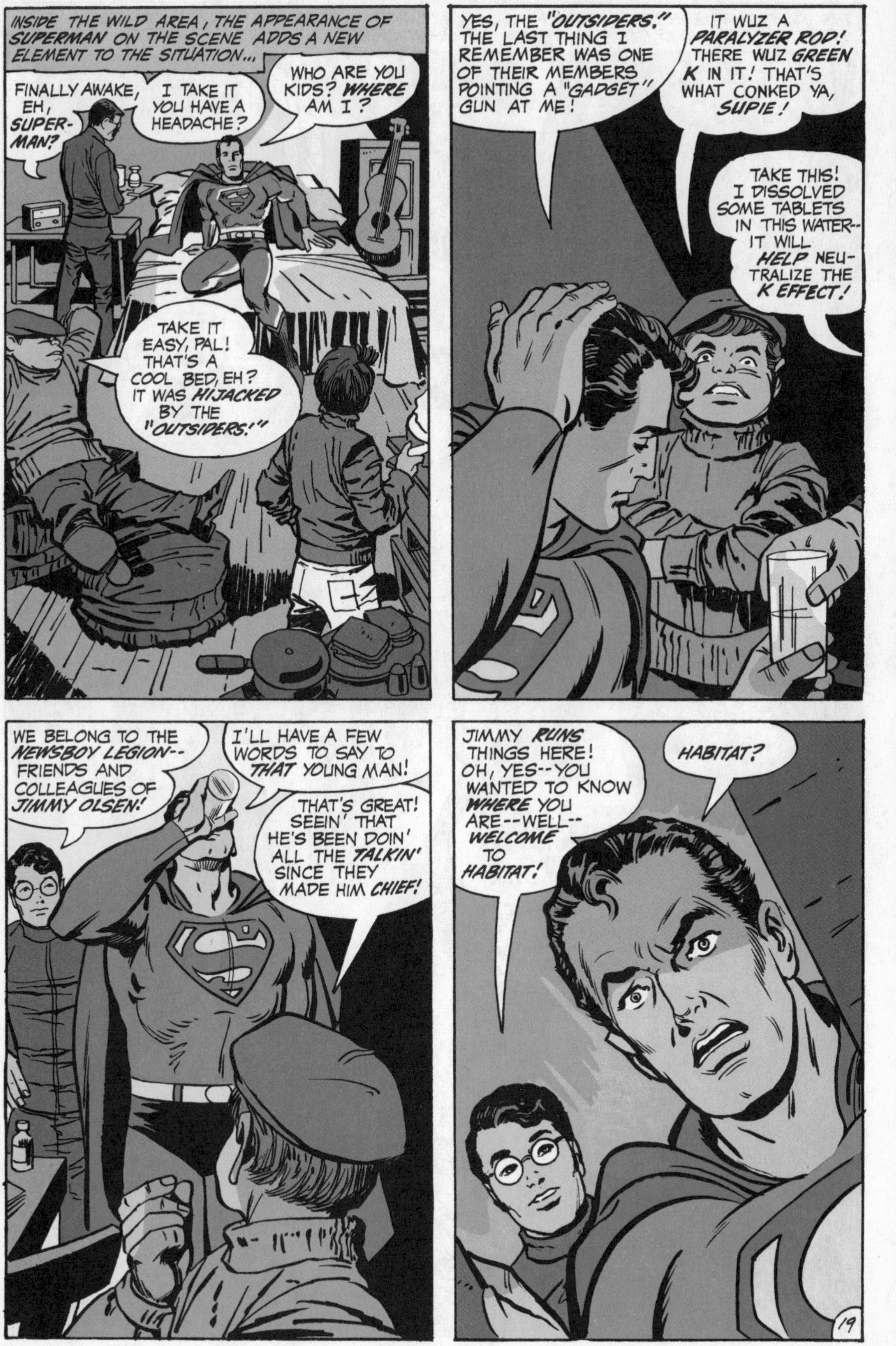
INSIDE THE WILD AREA, THE APPEARANCE OF SUPERMAN ON THE SCENE ADDS A NEW ELEMENT TO THE SITUATION...
FINALLY AWAKE, EH, SUPER-MAN?
I TAKE IT YOU HAVE A HEADACHE?
WHO ARE YOU KIDS? WHERE AM I?
TAKE IT EASY, PAL! THAT'S A COOL BED, EH? IT WAS HIJACKED BY THE "OUTSIDERS!"
YES, THE "OUTSIDERS." THE LAST THING I REMEMBER WAS ONE OF THEIR MEMBERS POINTING A "GADGET" GUN AT ME!
IT WUZ A PARALYZER ROD! THERE WUZ GREEN K IN IT! THAT'S WHAT CONKED YA, SUPIE!
TAKE THIS! I DISSOLVED SOME TABLETS IN THIS WATER-- IT WILL HELP NEU-TRALIZE THE K EFFECT!
WE BELONG TO THE NEWSBOY LEGION-- FRIENDS AND COLLEAGUES OF JIMMY OLSEN!
I'LL HAVE A FEW WORDS TO SAY TO THAT YOUNG MAN!
THAT'S GREAT! SEEIN' THAT HE'S BEEN DOIN' ALL THE TALKIN' SINCE THEY MADE HIM CHIEF!
JIMMY RUNS THINGS HERE! OH, YES--YOU WANTED TO KNOW WHERE YOU ARE--WELL-- WELCOME TO HABITAT!
HABITAT?
19

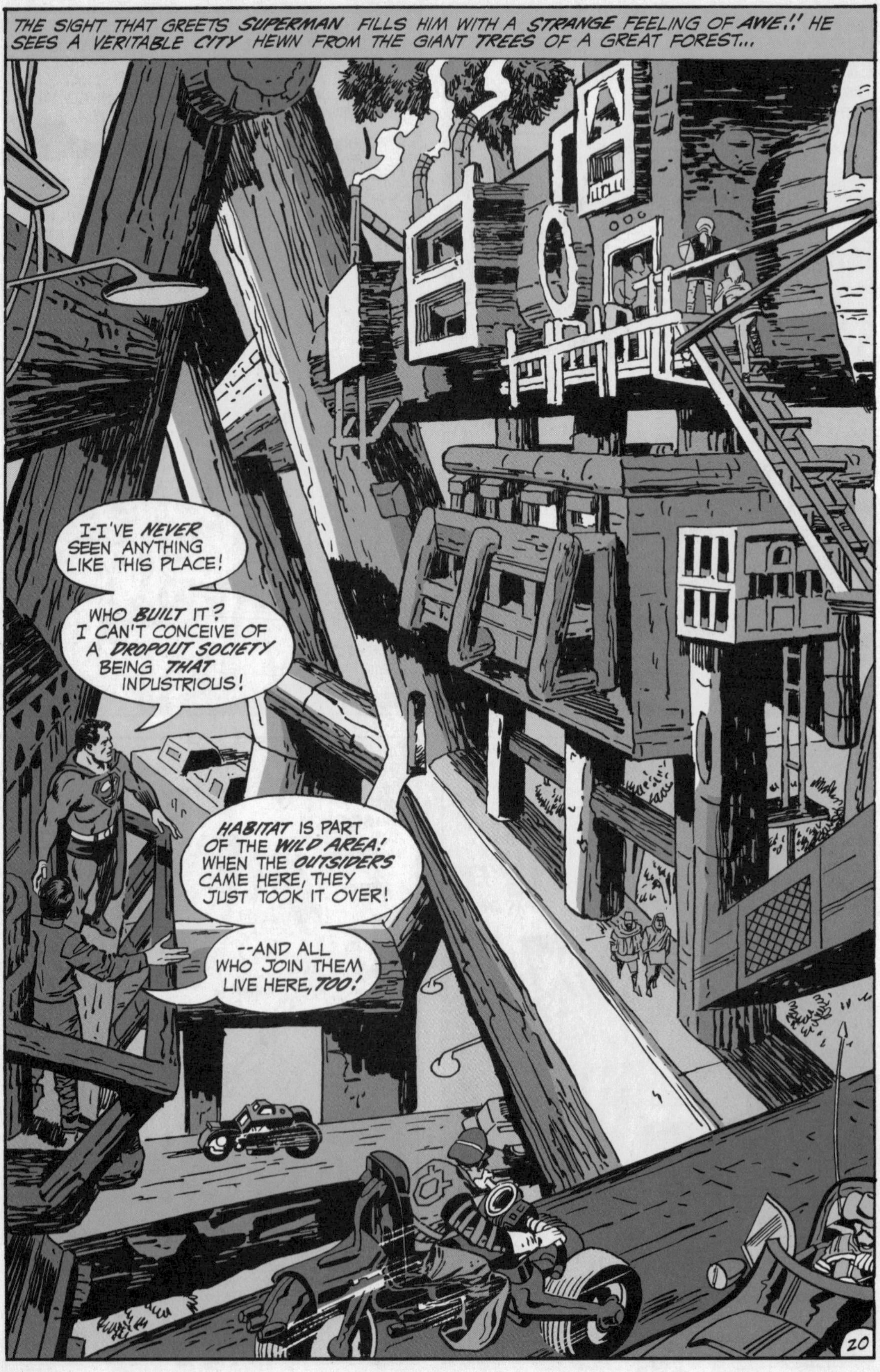
THE SIGHT THAT GREETS SUPERMAN FILLS HIM WITH A STRANGE FEELING OF AWE.'.' HE SEES A VERITABLE CITY HEWN FROM THE GIANT TREES OF A GREAT FOREST...
I-I'VE NEVER SEEN ANYTHING LIKE THIS PLACE!
WHO BUILT IT? I CAN'T CONCEIVE OF A DROPOUT SOCIETY BEING THAT INDUSTRIOUS!
HABITAT IS PART OF THE WILD AREA! WHEN THE OUTSIDERS CAME HERE, THEY JUST TOOK IT OVER!
--AND ALL WHO JOIN THEM LIVE HERE, TOO!
20

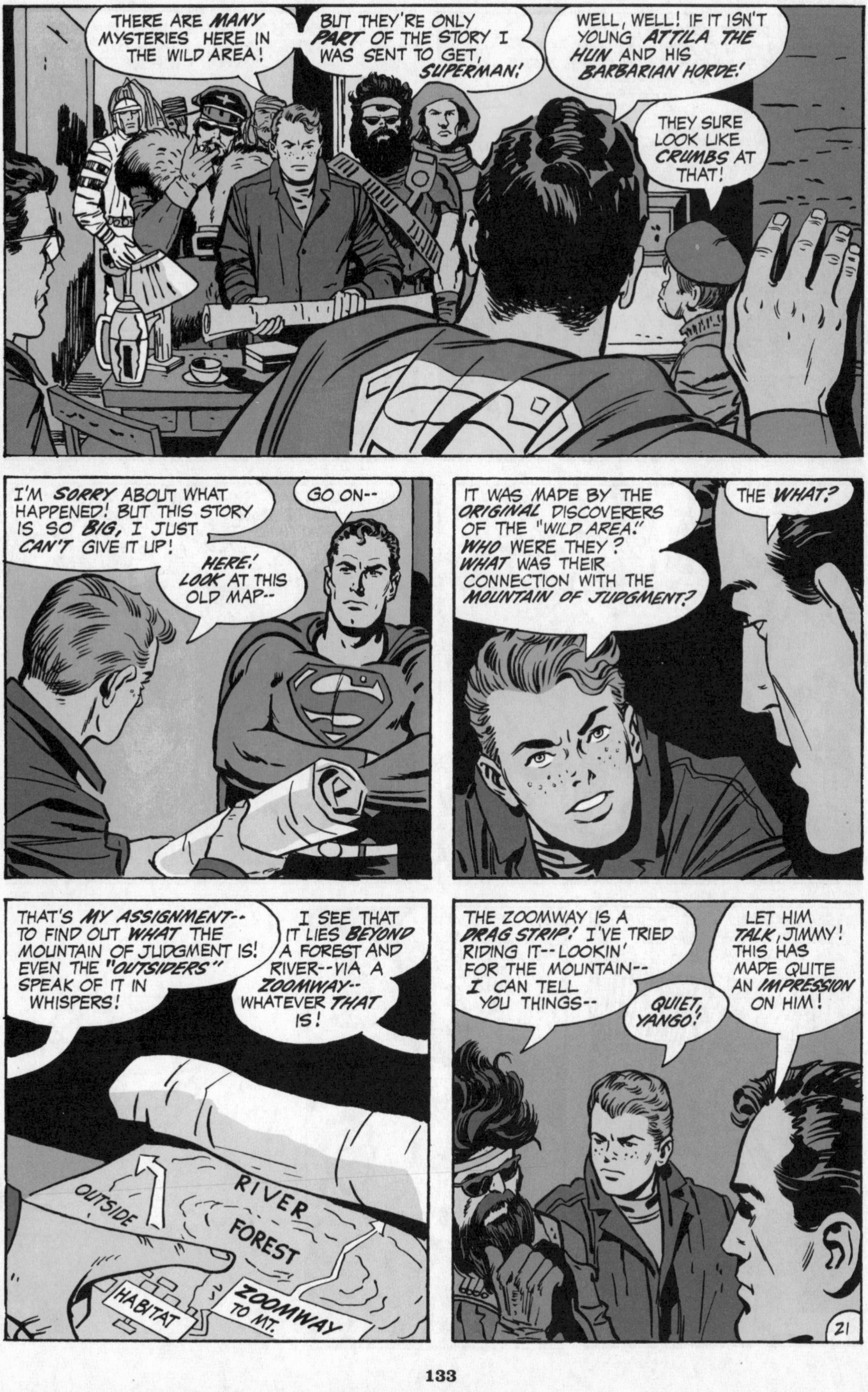
THERE ARE MANY MYSTERIES HERE IN THE WILD AREA!
BUT THEY'RE ONLY PART OF THE STORY I WAS SENT TO GET, SUPERMAN!
WELL, WELL! IF IT ISN'T YOUNG ATTILA THE HUN AND HIS BARBARIAN HORDE!
THEY SURE LOOK LIKE CRUMBS AT THAT!
I'M SORRY ABOUT WHAT HAPPENED! BUT THIS STORY IS SO BIG, I JUST CAN'T GIVE IT UP!
GO ON--
HERE! LOOK AT THIS OLD MAP--
IT WAS MADE BY THE ORIGINAL DISCOVERERS OF THE "WILD AREA!" WHO WERE THEY? WHAT WAS THEIR CONNECTION WITH THE MOUNTAIN OF JUDGMENT?
THE WHAT?
THAT'S MY ASSIGNMENT-- TO FIND OUT WHAT THE MOUNTAIN OF JUDGMENT IS! EVEN THE "OUTSIDERS" SPEAK OF IT IN WHISPERS!
I SEE THAT IT LIES BEYOND A FOREST AND RIVER--VIA A ZOOMWAY-- WHATEVER THAT IS!
RIVER
OUTSIDE
FOREST
HABITAT
ZOOMWAY TO MT.
THE ZOOMWAY IS A DRAG STRIP! I'VE TRIED RIDING IT--LOOKIN' FOR THE MOUNTAIN-- I CAN TELL YOU THINGS--
QUIET, YANGO!
LET HIM TALK, JIMMY! THIS HAS MADE QUITE AN IMPRESSION ON HIM!
21

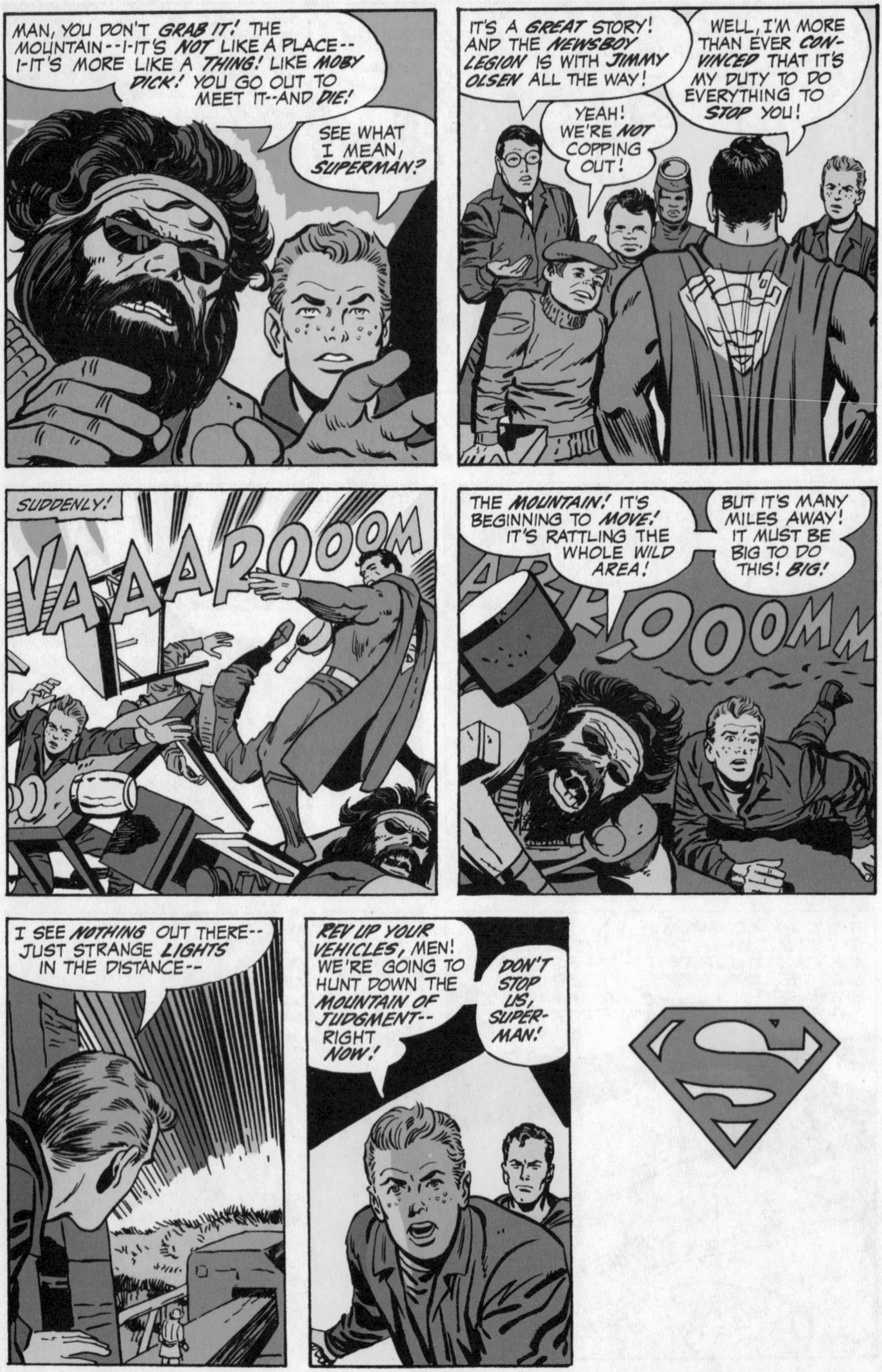

MAN, YOU DON'T GRAB IT! THE MOUNTAIN--I-IT'S NOT LIKE A PLACE--I-IT'S MORE LIKE A THING! LIKE MOBY DICK! YOU GO OUT TO MEET IT--AND DIE!
SEE WHAT I MEAN, SUPERMAN?
IT'S A GREAT STORY! AND THE NEWSBOY LEGION IS WITH JIMMY OLSEN ALL THE WAY!
YEAH! WE'RE NOT COPPING OUT!
WELL, I'M MORE THAN EVER CONVINCED THAT IT'S MY DUTY TO DO EVERYTHING TO STOP YOU!
SUDDENLY!
VAAAROOOOM
THE MOUNTAIN! IT'S BEGINNING TO MOVE! IT'S RATTLING THE WHOLE WILD AREA!
BUT IT'S MANY MILES AWAY! IT MUST BE BIG TO DO THIS! BIG!
-OOOMM
I SEE NOTHING OUT THERE--JUST STRANGE LIGHTS IN THE DISTANCE--
REV UP YOUR VEHICLES, MEN! WE'RE GOING TO HUNT DOWN THE MOUNTAIN OF JUDGMENT--RIGHT NOW!
DON'T STOP US, SUPERMAN!

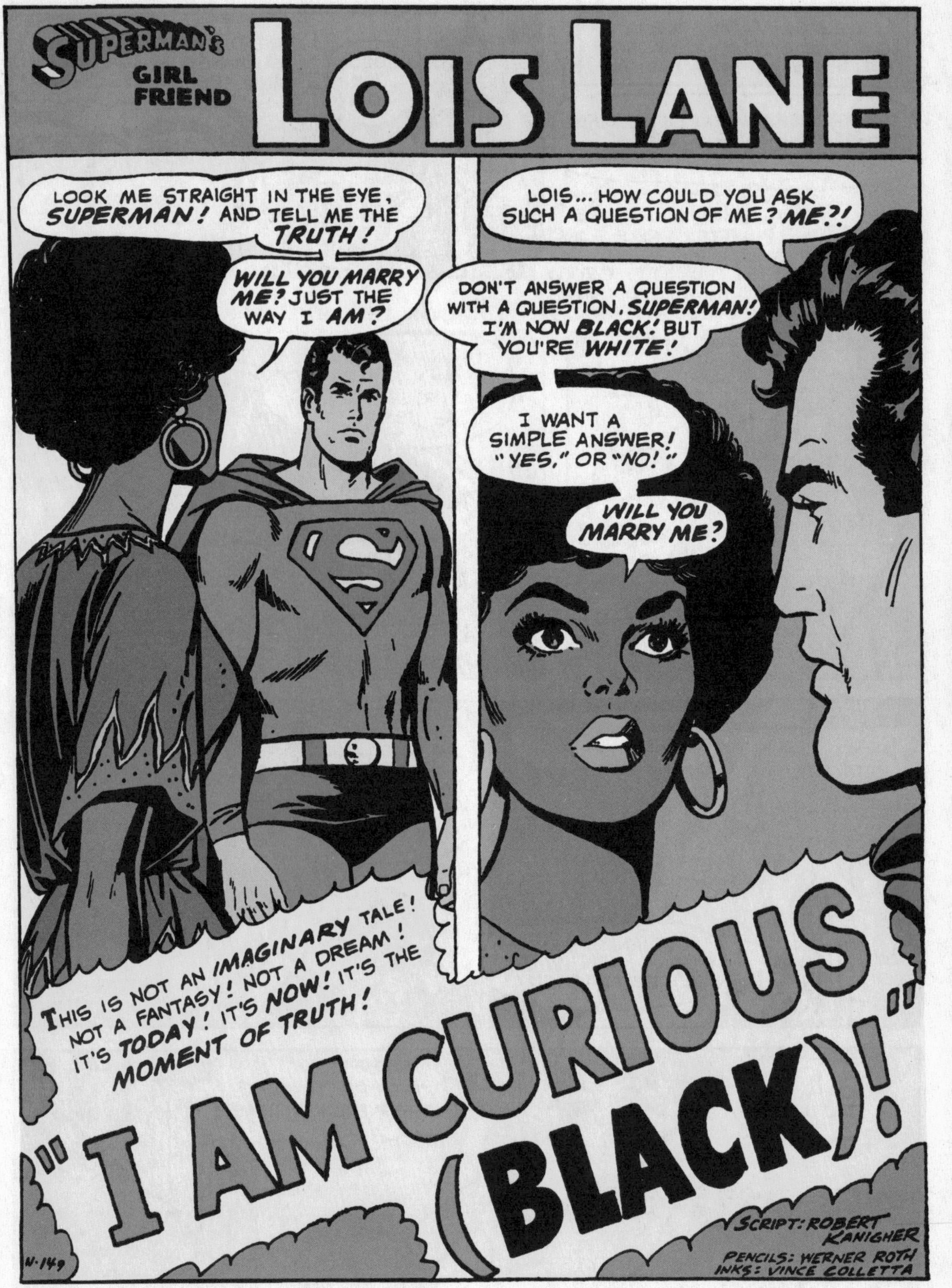
SUPERMAN'S GIRL FRIEND LOIS LANE
LOOK ME STRAIGHT IN THE EYE, SUPERMAN! AND TELL ME THE TRUTH!
WILL YOU MARRY ME? JUST THE WAY I AM?
LOIS... HOW COULD YOU ASK SUCH A QUESTION OF ME? ME?!
DON'T ANSWER A QUESTION WITH A QUESTION, SUPERMAN! I'M NOW BLACK! BUT YOU'RE WHITE!
I WANT A SIMPLE ANSWER! "YES," OR "NO!"
WILL YOU MARRY ME?
THIS IS NOT AN IMAGINARY TALE! NOT A FANTASY! NOT A DREAM! IT'S TODAY! IT'S NOW! IT'S THE MOMENT OF TRUTH!
"I AM CURIOUS (BLACK)!"
SCRIPT: ROBERT KANIGHER
PENCILS: WERNER ROTH
INKS: VINCE COLLETTA
N-149

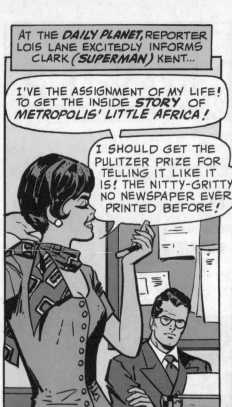

At the *Daily Planet*, reporter Lois Lane excitedly informs Clark (*Superman*) Kent...

I'VE THE ASSIGNMENT OF MY LIFE! TO GET THE INSIDE *STORY* OF *METROPOLIS' LITTLE AFRICA!*

I SHOULD GET THE PULITZER PRIZE FOR TELLING IT LIKE IT IS! THE NITTY-GRITTY NO NEWSPAPER EVER PRINTED BEFORE!

GOOD LUCK, LOIS!

JUST THE SAME... I'M GOING TO CHANGE TO *SUPERMAN* AND KEEP AN EYE ON HER!

Outside the newspaper building...

TAXI, MISS LANE? *BENNY THE BERET* AT YOUR SERVICE... AS USUAL!

TAKE ME TO *LITTLE AFRICA,* BENNY!

Shortly, in *Metropolis'* black community...

WANT ME TO WAIT, MISS LANE?

NO, THANKS, BENNY! I DON'T KNOW *WHEN* I'LL BE FINISHED!

HI, KIDS! I'M LOIS LANE, REPORTER FOR THE *DAILY PLANET!*

I WANT TO ASK YOU ABOUT SCHOOL! WHA...?

NO...WAIT! I JUST...

THEY'RE TURNING THEIR BACKS ON ME!

2

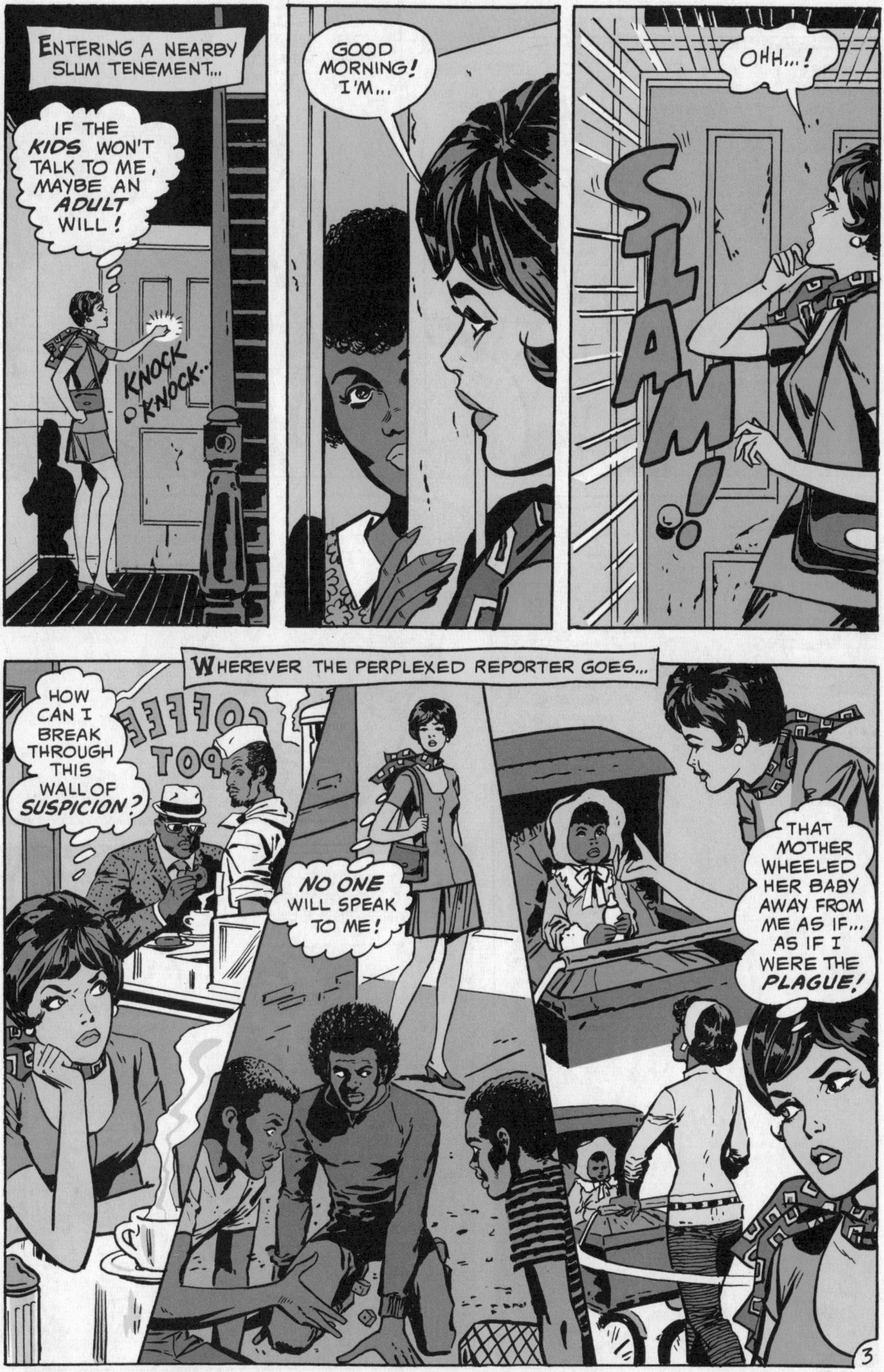
ENTERING A NEARBY SLUM TENEMENT...
IF THE KIDS WON'T TALK TO ME, MAYBE AN ADULT WILL!
KNOCK KNOCK...
GOOD MORNING! I'M...
OHH...!
SLAM!
WHEREVER THE PERPLEXED REPORTER GOES...
HOW CAN I BREAK THROUGH THIS WALL OF SUSPICION?
COFFEE POT
NO ONE WILL SPEAK TO ME!
THAT MOTHER WHEELED HER BABY AWAY FROM ME AS IF... AS IF I WERE THE PLAGUE!
3

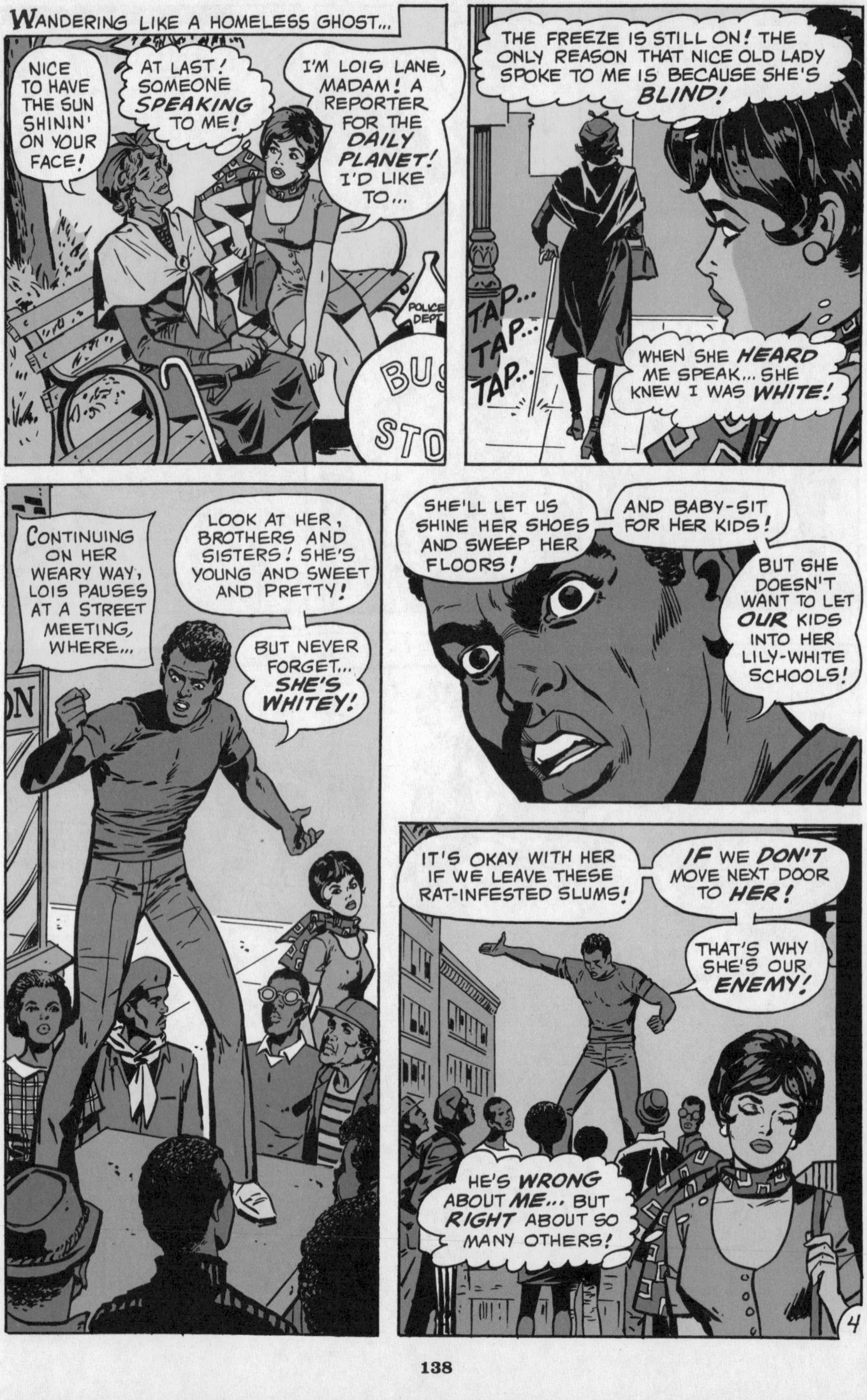

WANDERING LIKE A HOMELESS GHOST...
NICE TO HAVE THE SUN SHININ' ON YOUR FACE!
AT LAST! SOMEONE SPEAKING TO ME!
I'M LOIS LANE, MADAM! A REPORTER FOR THE DAILY PLANET! I'D LIKE TO...
POLICE DEPT
BUS STO
THE FREEZE IS STILL ON! THE ONLY REASON THAT NICE OLD LADY SPOKE TO ME IS BECAUSE SHE'S BLIND!
TAP... TAP... TAP...
WHEN SHE HEARD ME SPEAK... SHE KNEW I WAS WHITE!
CONTINUING ON HER WEARY WAY, LOIS PAUSES AT A STREET MEETING, WHERE...
LOOK AT HER, BROTHERS AND SISTERS! SHE'S YOUNG AND SWEET AND PRETTY!
BUT NEVER FORGET... SHE'S WHITEY!
SHE'LL LET US SHINE HER SHOES AND SWEEP HER FLOORS!
AND BABY-SIT FOR HER KIDS!
BUT SHE DOESN'T WANT TO LET OUR KIDS INTO HER LILY-WHITE SCHOOLS!
IT'S OKAY WITH HER IF WE LEAVE THESE RAT-INFESTED SLUMS!
IF WE DON'T MOVE NEXT DOOR TO HER!
THAT'S WHY SHE'S OUR ENEMY!
HE'S WRONG ABOUT ME... BUT RIGHT ABOUT SO MANY OTHERS!
4

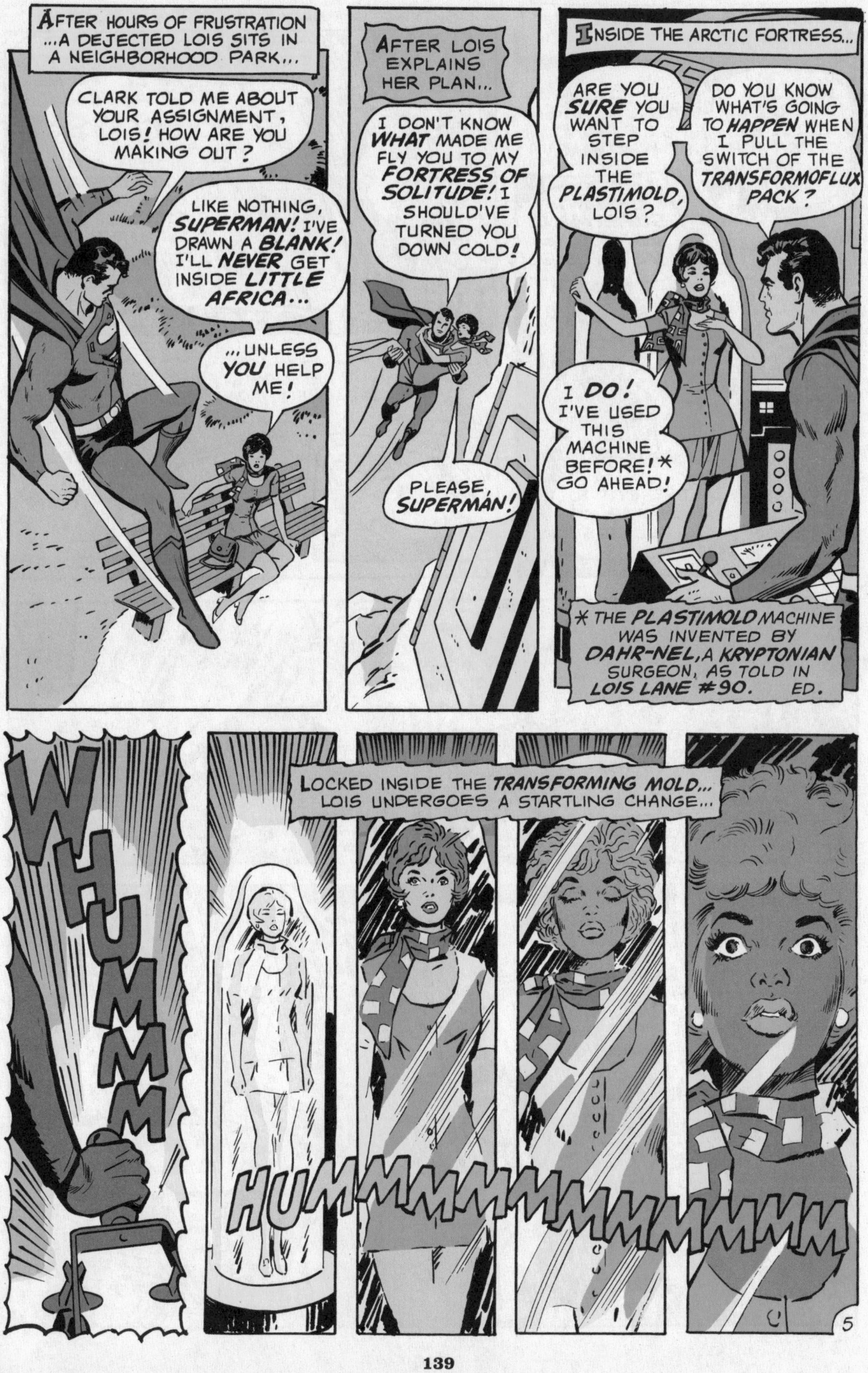
AFTER HOURS OF FRUSTRATION ...A DEJECTED LOIS SITS IN A NEIGHBORHOOD PARK...
CLARK TOLD ME ABOUT YOUR ASSIGNMENT, LOIS! HOW ARE YOU MAKING OUT?
LIKE NOTHING, SUPERMAN! I'VE DRAWN A BLANK! I'LL NEVER GET INSIDE LITTLE AFRICA...
...UNLESS YOU HELP ME!
AFTER LOIS EXPLAINS HER PLAN...
I DON'T KNOW WHAT MADE ME FLY YOU TO MY FORTRESS OF SOLITUDE! I SHOULD'VE TURNED YOU DOWN COLD!
PLEASE, SUPERMAN!
INSIDE THE ARCTIC FORTRESS...
ARE YOU SURE YOU WANT TO STEP INSIDE THE PLASTIMOLD, LOIS?
DO YOU KNOW WHAT'S GOING TO HAPPEN WHEN I PULL THE SWITCH OF THE TRANSFORMOFLUX PACK?
I DO! I'VE USED THIS MACHINE BEFORE!* GO AHEAD!
* THE PLASTIMOLD MACHINE WAS INVENTED BY DAHR-NEL, A KRYPTONIAN SURGEON, AS TOLD IN LOIS LANE #90. ED.
WHUMMMM
LOCKED INSIDE THE TRANSFORMING MOLD... LOIS UNDERGOES A STARTLING CHANGE...
HUMMMMMMMMMMMMMMMMM
5

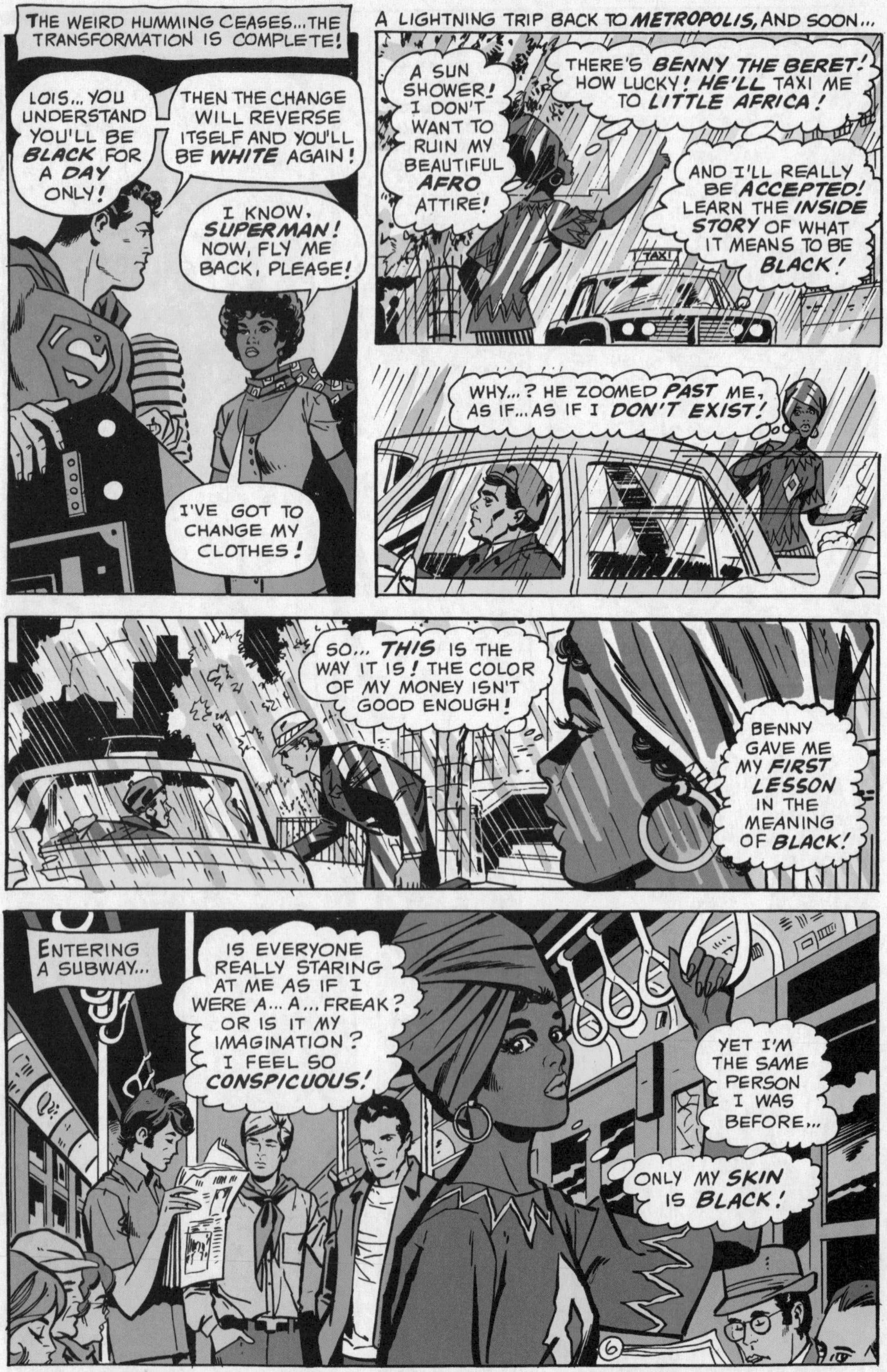
THE WEIRD HUMMING CEASES... THE TRANSFORMATION IS COMPLETE!
LOIS... YOU UNDERSTAND YOU'LL BE BLACK FOR A DAY ONLY!
THEN THE CHANGE WILL REVERSE ITSELF AND YOU'LL BE WHITE AGAIN!
I KNOW, SUPERMAN! NOW, FLY ME BACK, PLEASE!
I'VE GOT TO CHANGE MY CLOTHES!
A LIGHTNING TRIP BACK TO METROPOLIS, AND SOON...
A SUN SHOWER! I DON'T WANT TO RUIN MY BEAUTIFUL AFRO ATTIRE!
THERE'S BENNY THE BERET! HOW LUCKY! HE'LL TAXI ME TO LITTLE AFRICA!
AND I'LL REALLY BE ACCEPTED! LEARN THE INSIDE STORY OF WHAT IT MEANS TO BE BLACK!
TAXI
WHY...? HE ZOOMED PAST ME, AS IF... AS IF I DON'T EXIST!
SO... THIS IS THE WAY IT IS! THE COLOR OF MY MONEY ISN'T GOOD ENOUGH!
BENNY GAVE ME MY FIRST LESSON IN THE MEANING OF BLACK!
ENTERING A SUBWAY...
IS EVERYONE REALLY STARING AT ME AS IF I WERE A... A... FREAK? OR IS IT MY IMAGINATION? I FEEL SO CONSPICUOUS!
YET I'M THE SAME PERSON I WAS BEFORE...
ONLY MY SKIN IS BLACK!
6

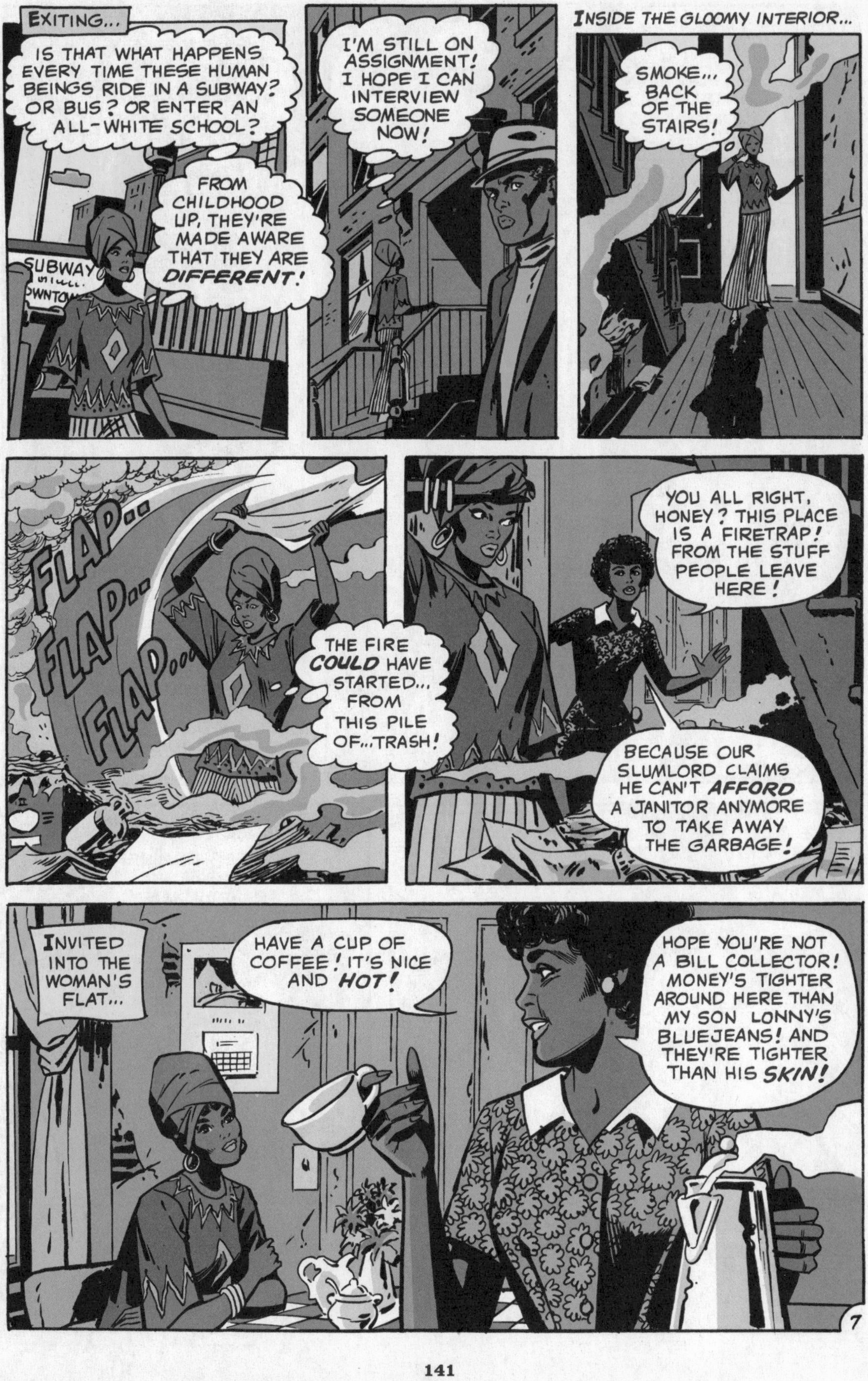
EXITING...
IS THAT WHAT HAPPENS EVERY TIME THESE HUMAN BEINGS RIDE IN A SUBWAY? OR BUS? OR ENTER AN ALL-WHITE SCHOOL?
FROM CHILDHOOD UP, THEY'RE MADE AWARE THAT THEY ARE DIFFERENT!
SUBWAY
I'M STILL ON ASSIGNMENT! I HOPE I CAN INTERVIEW SOMEONE NOW!
INSIDE THE GLOOMY INTERIOR...
SMOKE... BACK OF THE STAIRS!
FLAP.. FLAP.. FLAP...
THE FIRE COULD HAVE STARTED... FROM THIS PILE OF...TRASH!
YOU ALL RIGHT, HONEY? THIS PLACE IS A FIRETRAP! FROM THE STUFF PEOPLE LEAVE HERE!
BECAUSE OUR SLUMLORD CLAIMS HE CAN'T AFFORD A JANITOR ANYMORE TO TAKE AWAY THE GARBAGE!
INVITED INTO THE WOMAN'S FLAT...
HAVE A CUP OF COFFEE! IT'S NICE AND HOT!
HOPE YOU'RE NOT A BILL COLLECTOR! MONEY'S TIGHTER AROUND HERE THAN MY SON LONNY'S BLUEJEANS! AND THEY'RE TIGHTER THAN HIS SKIN!
7

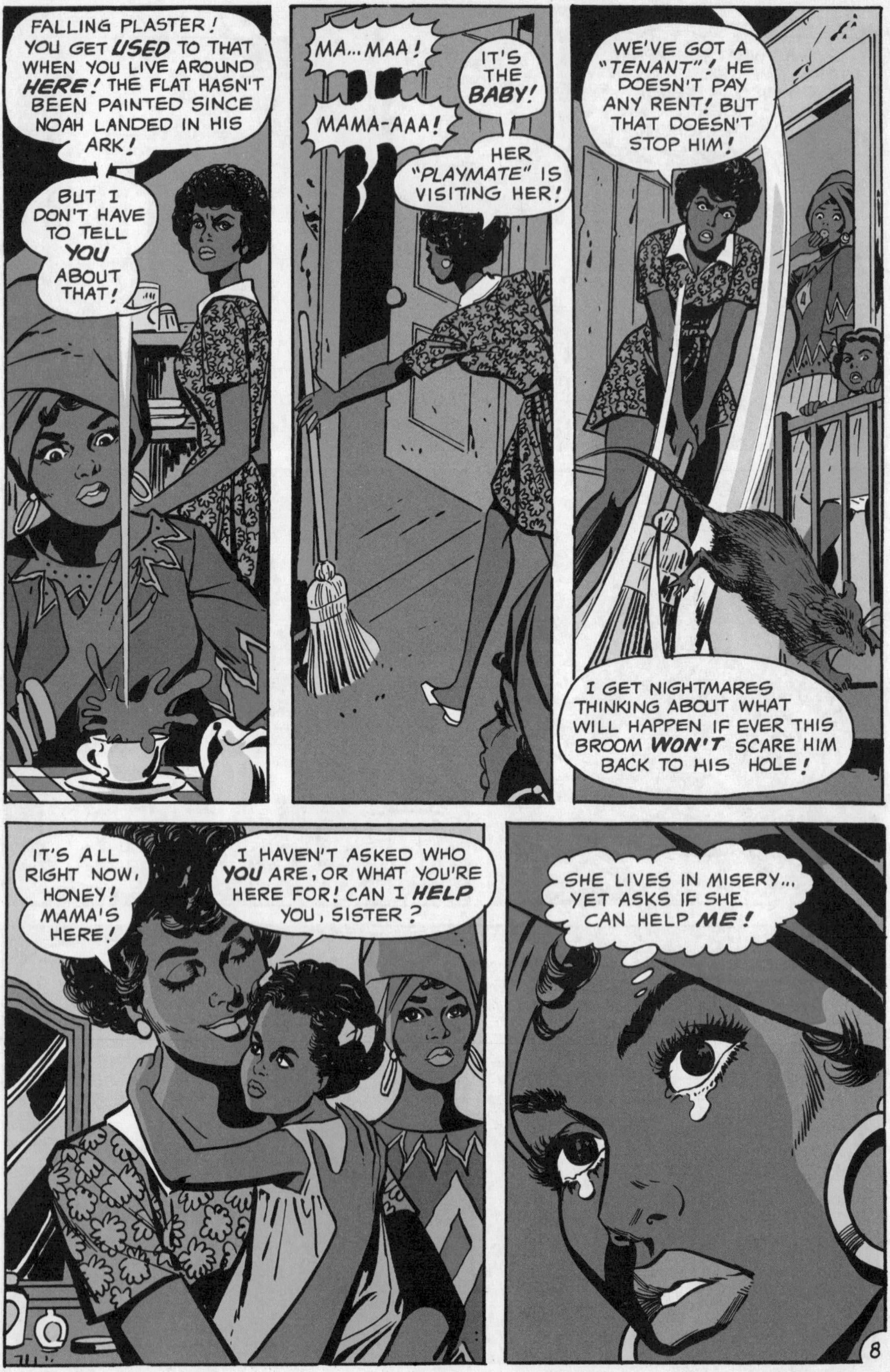
FALLING PLASTER! YOU GET USED TO THAT WHEN YOU LIVE AROUND HERE! THE FLAT HASN'T BEEN PAINTED SINCE NOAH LANDED IN HIS ARK!
BUT I DON'T HAVE TO TELL YOU ABOUT THAT!
MA...MAA!
MAMA-AAA!
IT'S THE BABY!
HER "PLAYMATE" IS VISITING HER!
WE'VE GOT A "TENANT"! HE DOESN'T PAY ANY RENT! BUT THAT DOESN'T STOP HIM!
I GET NIGHTMARES THINKING ABOUT WHAT WILL HAPPEN IF EVER THIS BROOM WON'T SCARE HIM BACK TO HIS HOLE!
IT'S ALL RIGHT NOW, HONEY! MAMA'S HERE!
I HAVEN'T ASKED WHO YOU ARE, OR WHAT YOU'RE HERE FOR! CAN I HELP YOU, SISTER?
SHE LIVES IN MISERY... YET ASKS IF SHE CAN HELP ME!
8

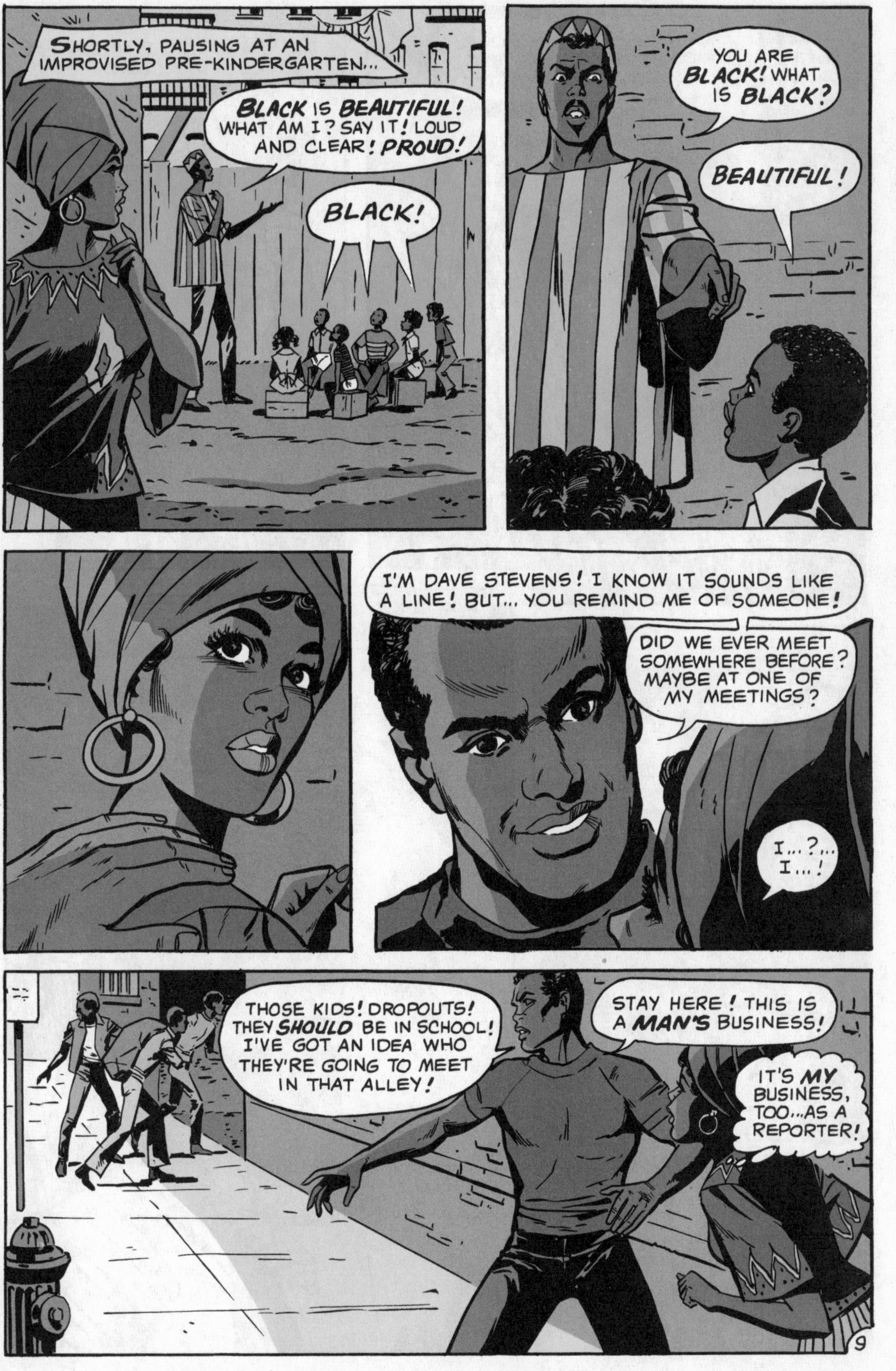

SHORTLY, PAUSING AT AN IMPROVISED PRE-KINDERGARTEN...
BLACK IS BEAUTIFUL! WHAT AM I? SAY IT! LOUD AND CLEAR! PROUD!
BLACK!
YOU ARE BLACK! WHAT IS BLACK?
BEAUTIFUL!
I'M DAVE STEVENS! I KNOW IT SOUNDS LIKE A LINE! BUT... YOU REMIND ME OF SOMEONE!
DID WE EVER MEET SOMEWHERE BEFORE? MAYBE AT ONE OF MY MEETINGS?
I... ?... I...!
THOSE KIDS! DROPOUTS! THEY SHOULD BE IN SCHOOL! I'VE GOT AN IDEA WHO THEY'RE GOING TO MEET IN THAT ALLEY!
STAY HERE! THIS IS A MAN'S BUSINESS!
IT'S MY BUSINESS, TOO...AS A REPORTER!
9

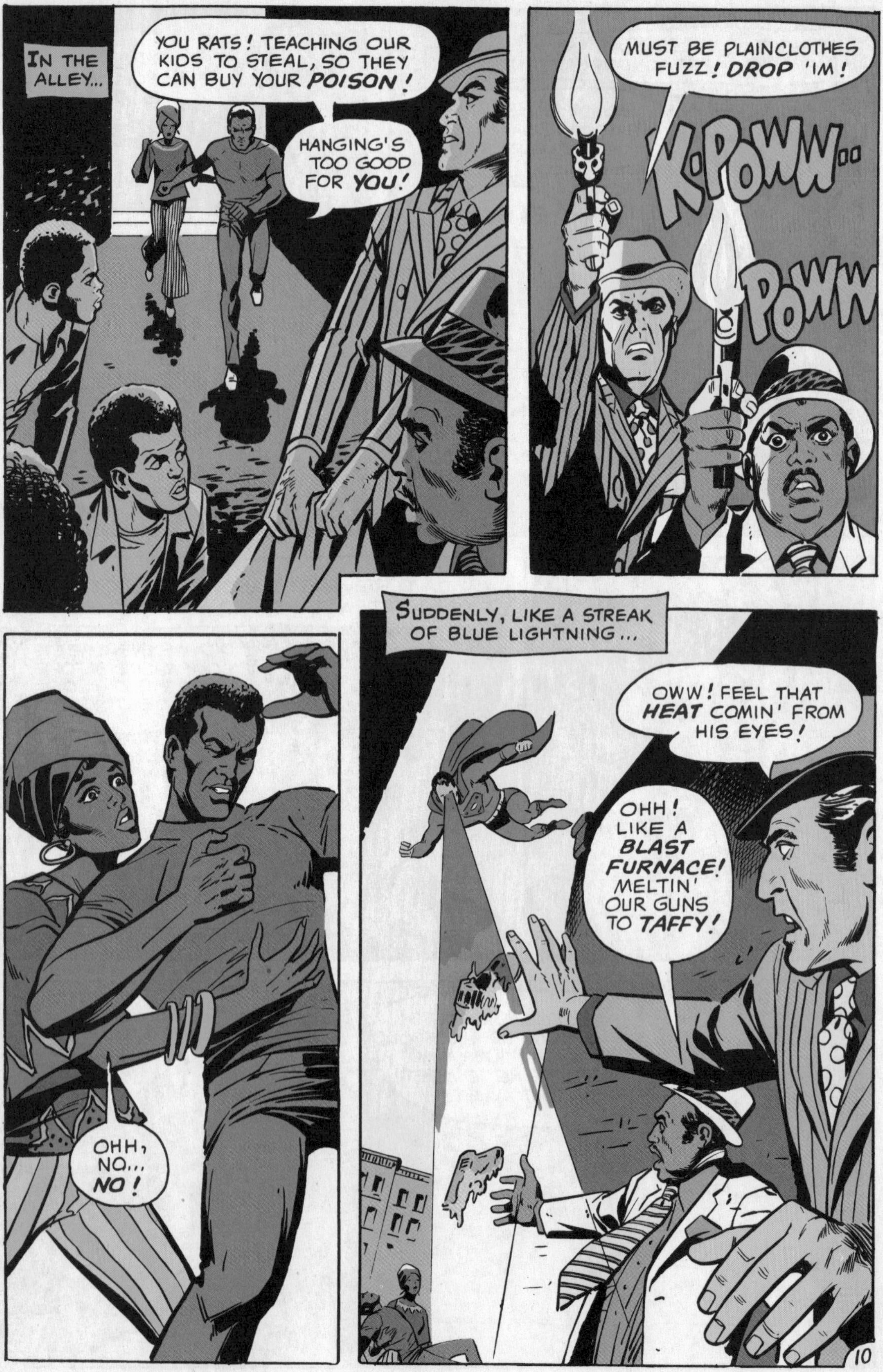
IN THE ALLEY...
YOU RATS! TEACHING OUR KIDS TO STEAL, SO THEY CAN BUY YOUR POISON!
HANGING'S TOO GOOD FOR YOU!
MUST BE PLAINCLOTHES FUZZ! DROP 'IM!
K-POWW..
POWW
SUDDENLY, LIKE A STREAK OF BLUE LIGHTNING...
OHH, NO... NO!
OWW! FEEL THAT HEAT COMIN' FROM HIS EYES!
OHH! LIKE A BLAST FURNACE! MELTIN' OUR GUNS TO TAFFY!
10

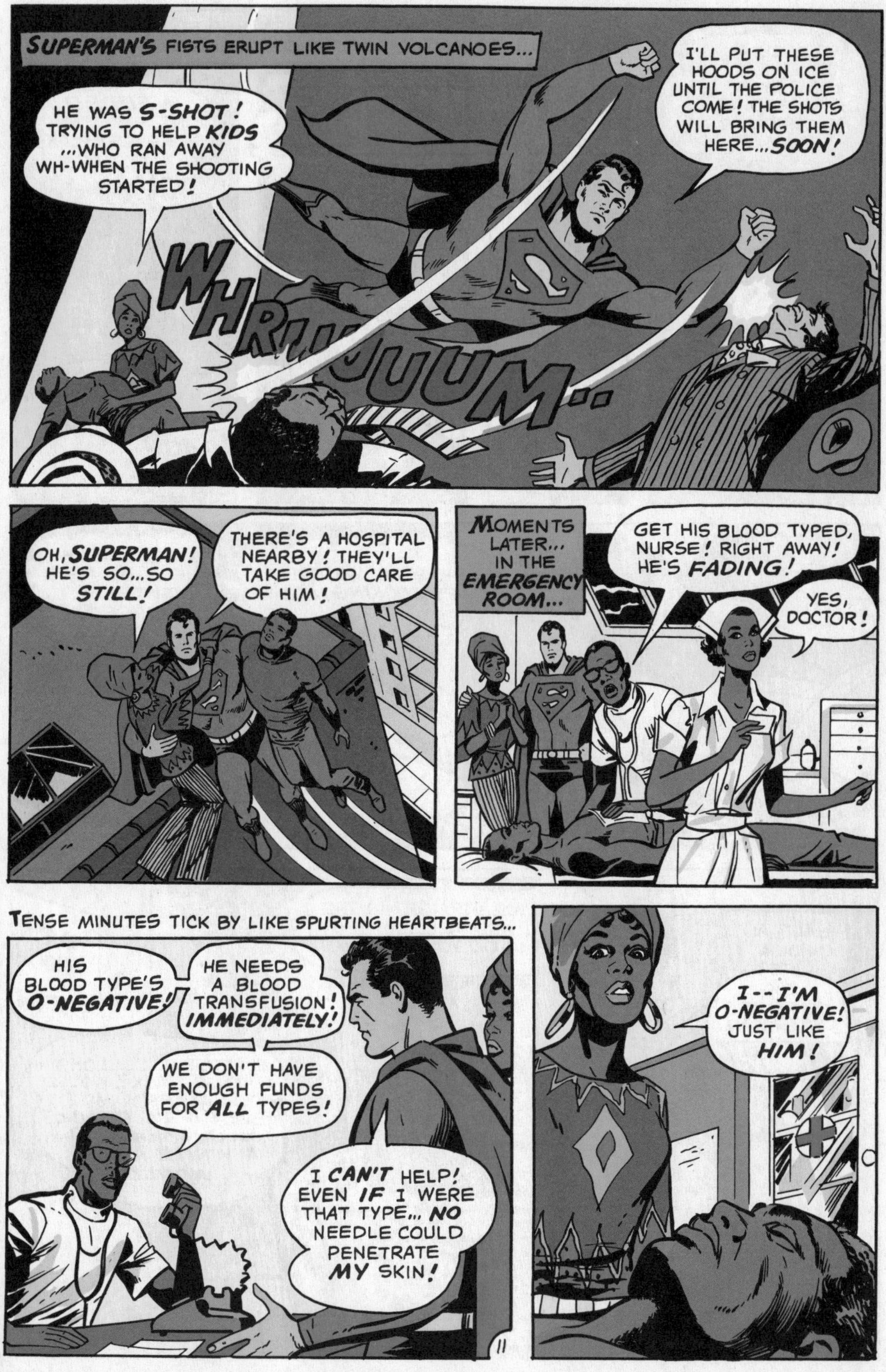
SUPERMAN'S FISTS ERUPT LIKE TWIN VOLCANOES...
HE WAS S-SHOT! TRYING TO HELP KIDS ...WHO RAN AWAY WH-WHEN THE SHOOTING STARTED!
I'LL PUT THESE HOODS ON ICE UNTIL THE POLICE COME! THE SHOTS WILL BRING THEM HERE...SOON!
WHRUUUUUM..
OH, SUPERMAN! HE'S SO...SO STILL!
THERE'S A HOSPITAL NEARBY! THEY'LL TAKE GOOD CARE OF HIM!
MOMENTS LATER... IN THE EMERGENCY ROOM...
GET HIS BLOOD TYPED, NURSE! RIGHT AWAY! HE'S FADING!
YES, DOCTOR!
TENSE MINUTES TICK BY LIKE SPURTING HEARTBEATS...
HIS BLOOD TYPE'S O-NEGATIVE!
HE NEEDS A BLOOD TRANSFUSION! IMMEDIATELY!
WE DON'T HAVE ENOUGH FUNDS FOR ALL TYPES!
I CAN'T HELP! EVEN IF I WERE THAT TYPE... NO NEEDLE COULD PENETRATE MY SKIN!
11
I--I'M O-NEGATIVE! JUST LIKE HIM!

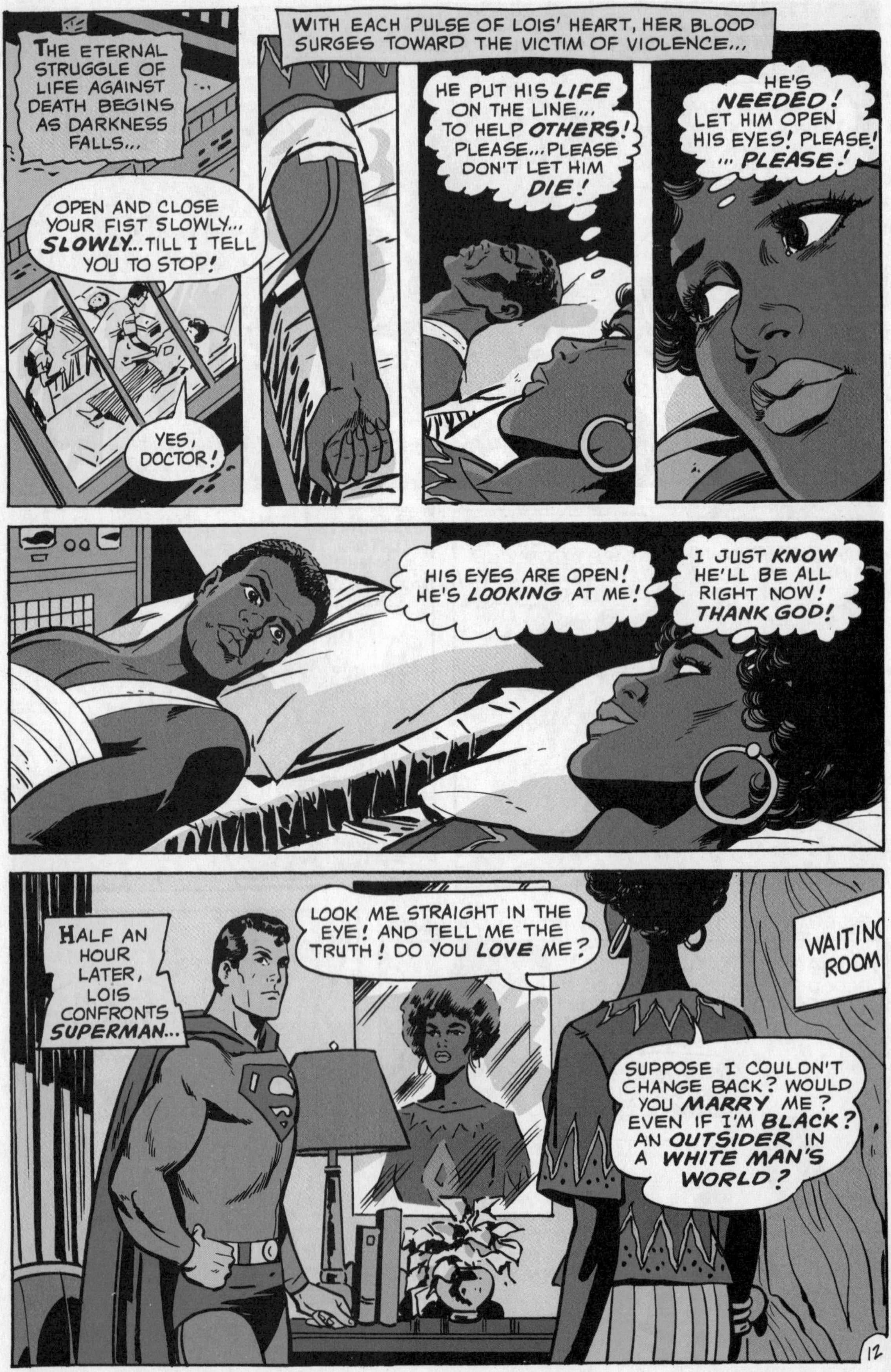

THE ETERNAL STRUGGLE OF LIFE AGAINST DEATH BEGINS AS DARKNESS FALLS...
OPEN AND CLOSE YOUR FIST SLOWLY... SLOWLY...TILL I TELL YOU TO STOP!
YES, DOCTOR!
WITH EACH PULSE OF LOIS' HEART, HER BLOOD SURGES TOWARD THE VICTIM OF VIOLENCE...
HE PUT HIS LIFE ON THE LINE... TO HELP OTHERS! PLEASE...PLEASE DON'T LET HIM DIE!
HE'S NEEDED! LET HIM OPEN HIS EYES! PLEASE! ... PLEASE!
HIS EYES ARE OPEN! HE'S LOOKING AT ME!
I JUST KNOW HE'LL BE ALL RIGHT NOW! THANK GOD!
HALF AN HOUR LATER, LOIS CONFRONTS SUPERMAN...
LOOK ME STRAIGHT IN THE EYE! AND TELL ME THE TRUTH! DO YOU LOVE ME?
WAITING ROOM
SUPPOSE I COULDN'T CHANGE BACK? WOULD YOU MARRY ME? EVEN IF I'M BLACK? AN OUTSIDER IN A WHITE MAN'S WORLD?
12

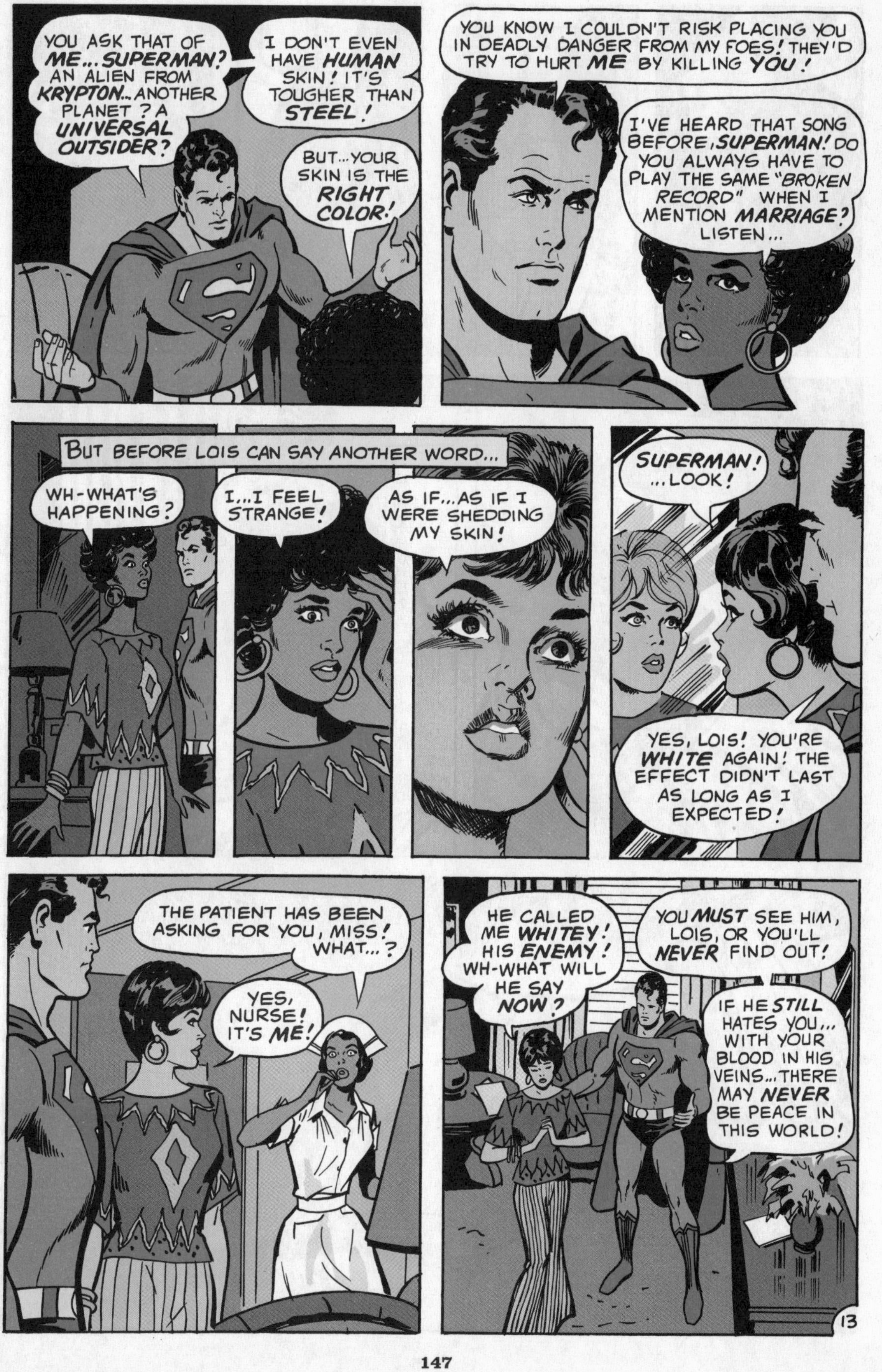
YOU ASK THAT OF ME... SUPERMAN? AN ALIEN FROM KRYPTON... ANOTHER PLANET? A UNIVERSAL OUTSIDER?
I DON'T EVEN HAVE HUMAN SKIN! IT'S TOUGHER THAN STEEL!
BUT... YOUR SKIN IS THE RIGHT COLOR!
YOU KNOW I COULDN'T RISK PLACING YOU IN DEADLY DANGER FROM MY FOES! THEY'D TRY TO HURT ME BY KILLING YOU!
I'VE HEARD THAT SONG BEFORE, SUPERMAN! DO YOU ALWAYS HAVE TO PLAY THE SAME "BROKEN RECORD" WHEN I MENTION MARRIAGE? LISTEN...
BUT BEFORE LOIS CAN SAY ANOTHER WORD...
WH-WHAT'S HAPPENING?
I... I FEEL STRANGE!
AS IF... AS IF I WERE SHEDDING MY SKIN!
SUPERMAN! ...LOOK!
YES, LOIS! YOU'RE WHITE AGAIN! THE EFFECT DIDN'T LAST AS LONG AS I EXPECTED!
THE PATIENT HAS BEEN ASKING FOR YOU, MISS! WHAT...?
YES, NURSE! IT'S ME!
HE CALLED ME WHITEY! HIS ENEMY! WH-WHAT WILL HE SAY NOW?
YOU MUST SEE HIM, LOIS, OR YOU'LL NEVER FIND OUT!
IF HE STILL HATES YOU... WITH YOUR BLOOD IN HIS VEINS... THERE MAY NEVER BE PEACE IN THIS WORLD!
13

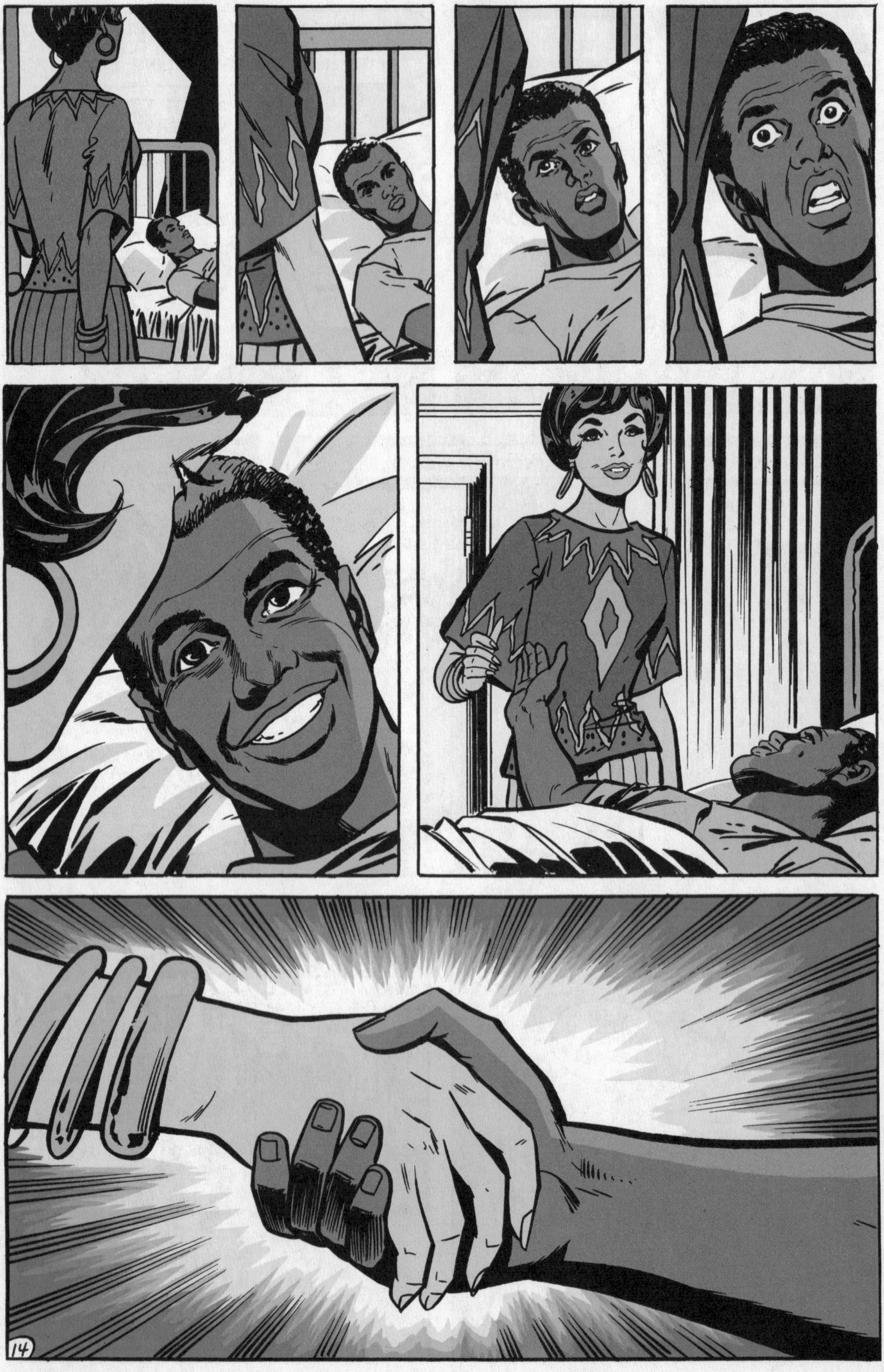
14

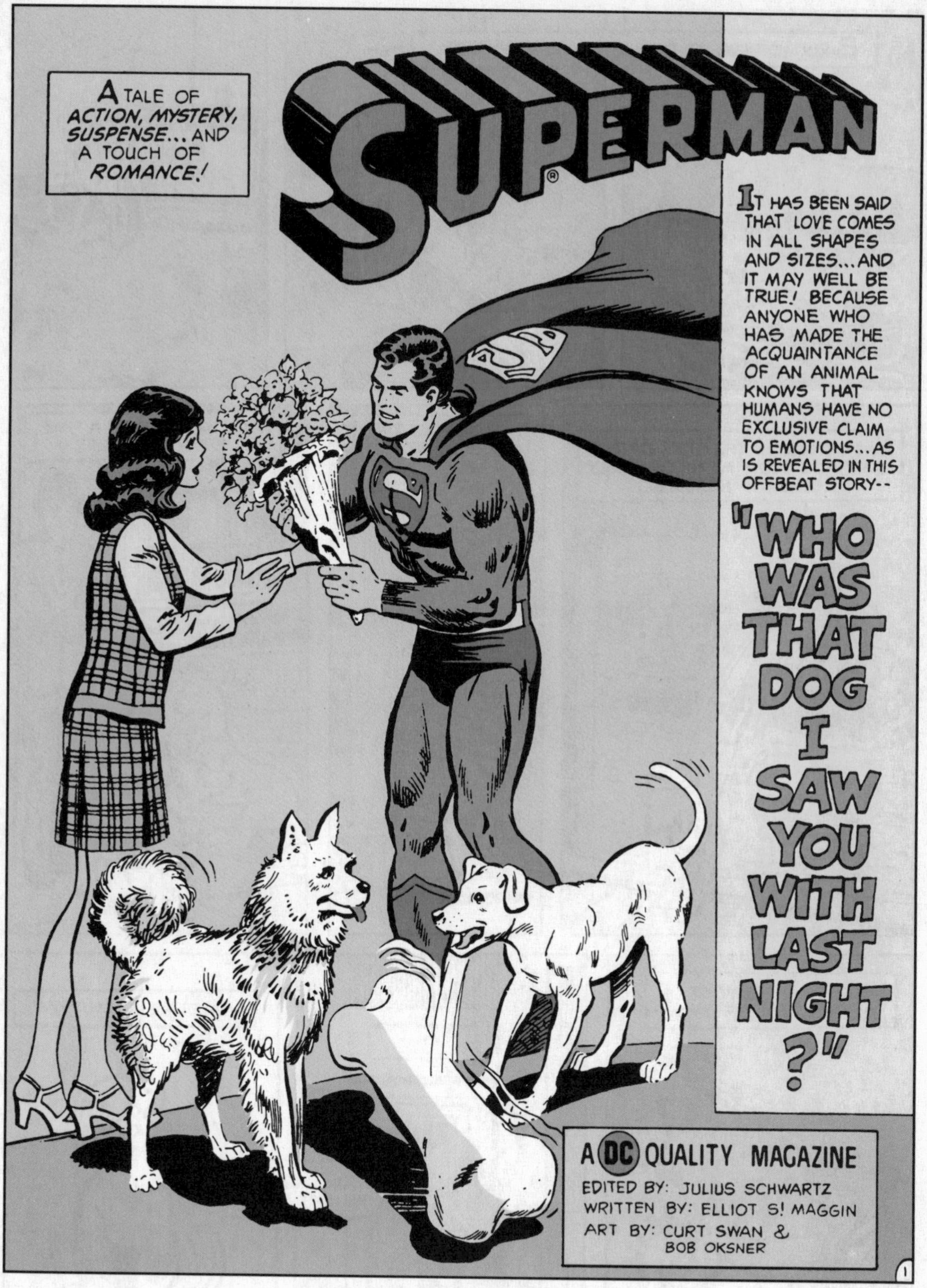

A TALE OF ACTION, MYSTERY, SUSPENSE... AND A TOUCH OF ROMANCE!
SUPERMAN®
IT HAS BEEN SAID THAT LOVE COMES IN ALL SHAPES AND SIZES... AND IT MAY WELL BE TRUE! BECAUSE ANYONE WHO HAS MADE THE ACQUAINTANCE OF AN ANIMAL KNOWS THAT HUMANS HAVE NO EXCLUSIVE CLAIM TO EMOTIONS... AS IS REVEALED IN THIS OFFBEAT STORY--
"WHO WAS THAT DOG I SAW YOU WITH LAST NIGHT?"
A DC QUALITY MAGAZINE
EDITED BY: JULIUS SCHWARTZ
WRITTEN BY: ELLIOT S! MAGGIN
ART BY: CURT SWAN & BOB OKSNER
1

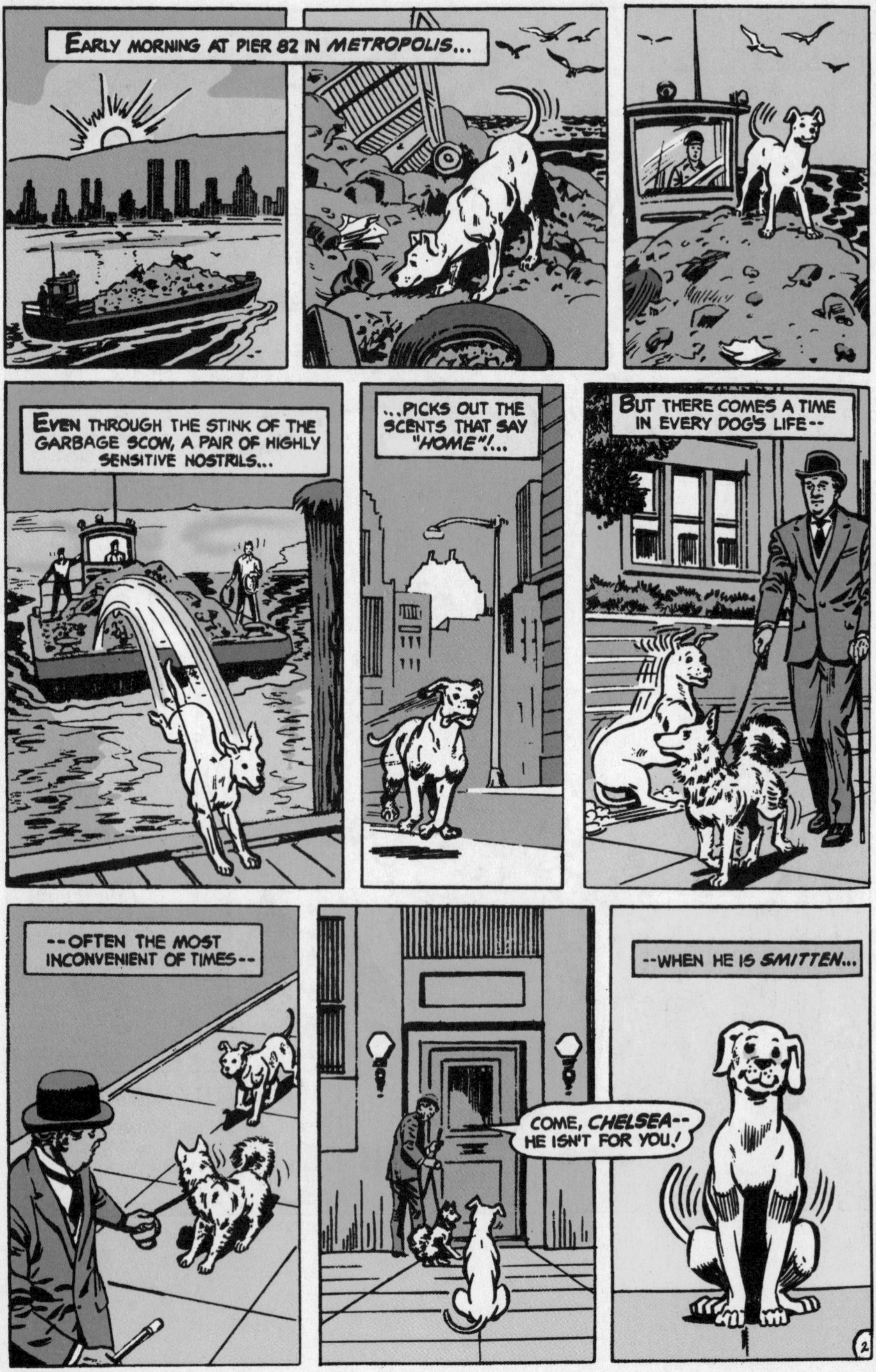
EARLY MORNING AT PIER 82 IN METROPOLIS...
EVEN THROUGH THE STINK OF THE GARBAGE SCOW, A PAIR OF HIGHLY SENSITIVE NOSTRILS...
...PICKS OUT THE SCENTS THAT SAY "HOME"!...
BUT THERE COMES A TIME IN EVERY DOG'S LIFE--
--OFTEN THE MOST INCONVENIENT OF TIMES--
COME, CHELSEA-- HE ISN'T FOR YOU!
--WHEN HE IS SMITTEN...
2

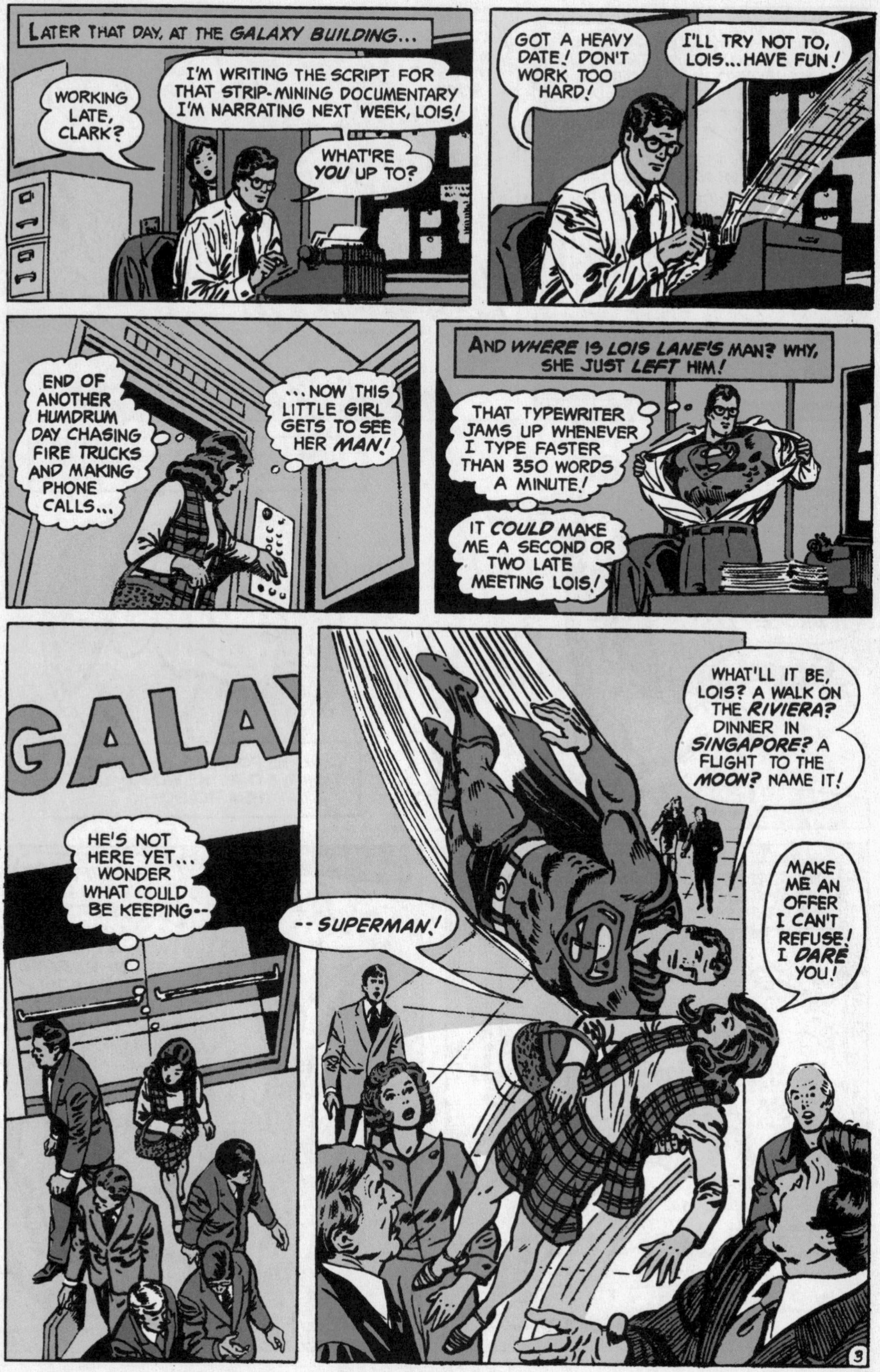
LATER THAT DAY, AT THE GALAXY BUILDING...
WORKING LATE, CLARK?
I'M WRITING THE SCRIPT FOR THAT STRIP-MINING DOCUMENTARY I'M NARRATING NEXT WEEK, LOIS!
WHAT'RE YOU UP TO?
GOT A HEAVY DATE! DON'T WORK TOO HARD!
I'LL TRY NOT TO, LOIS...HAVE FUN!
END OF ANOTHER HUMDRUM DAY CHASING FIRE TRUCKS AND MAKING PHONE CALLS...
...NOW THIS LITTLE GIRL GETS TO SEE HER MAN!
AND WHERE IS LOIS LANE'S MAN? WHY, SHE JUST LEFT HIM!
THAT TYPEWRITER JAMS UP WHENEVER I TYPE FASTER THAN 350 WORDS A MINUTE!
IT COULD MAKE ME A SECOND OR TWO LATE MEETING LOIS!
GALA
HE'S NOT HERE YET... WONDER WHAT COULD BE KEEPING--
--SUPERMAN!
WHAT'LL IT BE, LOIS? A WALK ON THE RIVIERA? DINNER IN SINGAPORE? A FLIGHT TO THE MOON? NAME IT!
MAKE ME AN OFFER I CAN'T REFUSE! I DARE YOU!
3

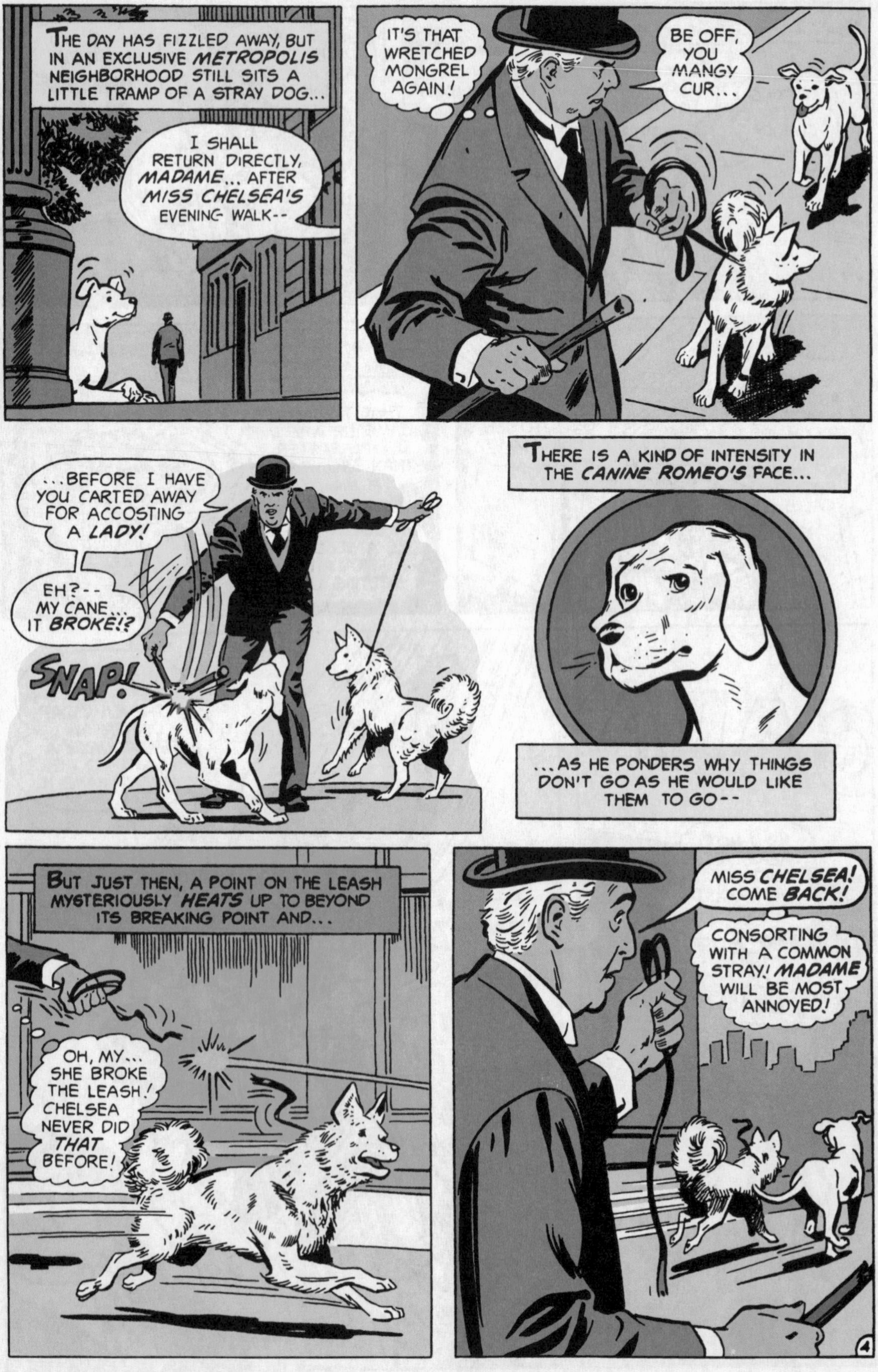
THE DAY HAS FIZZLED AWAY, BUT IN AN EXCLUSIVE METROPOLIS NEIGHBORHOOD STILL SITS A LITTLE TRAMP OF A STRAY DOG...
I SHALL RETURN DIRECTLY, MADAME... AFTER MISS CHELSEA'S EVENING WALK--
IT'S THAT WRETCHED MONGREL AGAIN!
BE OFF, YOU MANGY CUR...
...BEFORE I HAVE YOU CARTED AWAY FOR ACCOSTING A LADY!
EH?-- MY CANE... IT BROKE!?
SNAP!
THERE IS A KIND OF INTENSITY IN THE CANINE ROMEO'S FACE...
...AS HE PONDERS WHY THINGS DON'T GO AS HE WOULD LIKE THEM TO GO--
BUT JUST THEN, A POINT ON THE LEASH MYSTERIOUSLY HEATS UP TO BEYOND ITS BREAKING POINT AND...
OH, MY... SHE BROKE THE LEASH! CHELSEA NEVER DID THAT BEFORE!
MISS CHELSEA! COME BACK!
CONSORTING WITH A COMMON STRAY! MADAME WILL BE MOST ANNOYED!
4

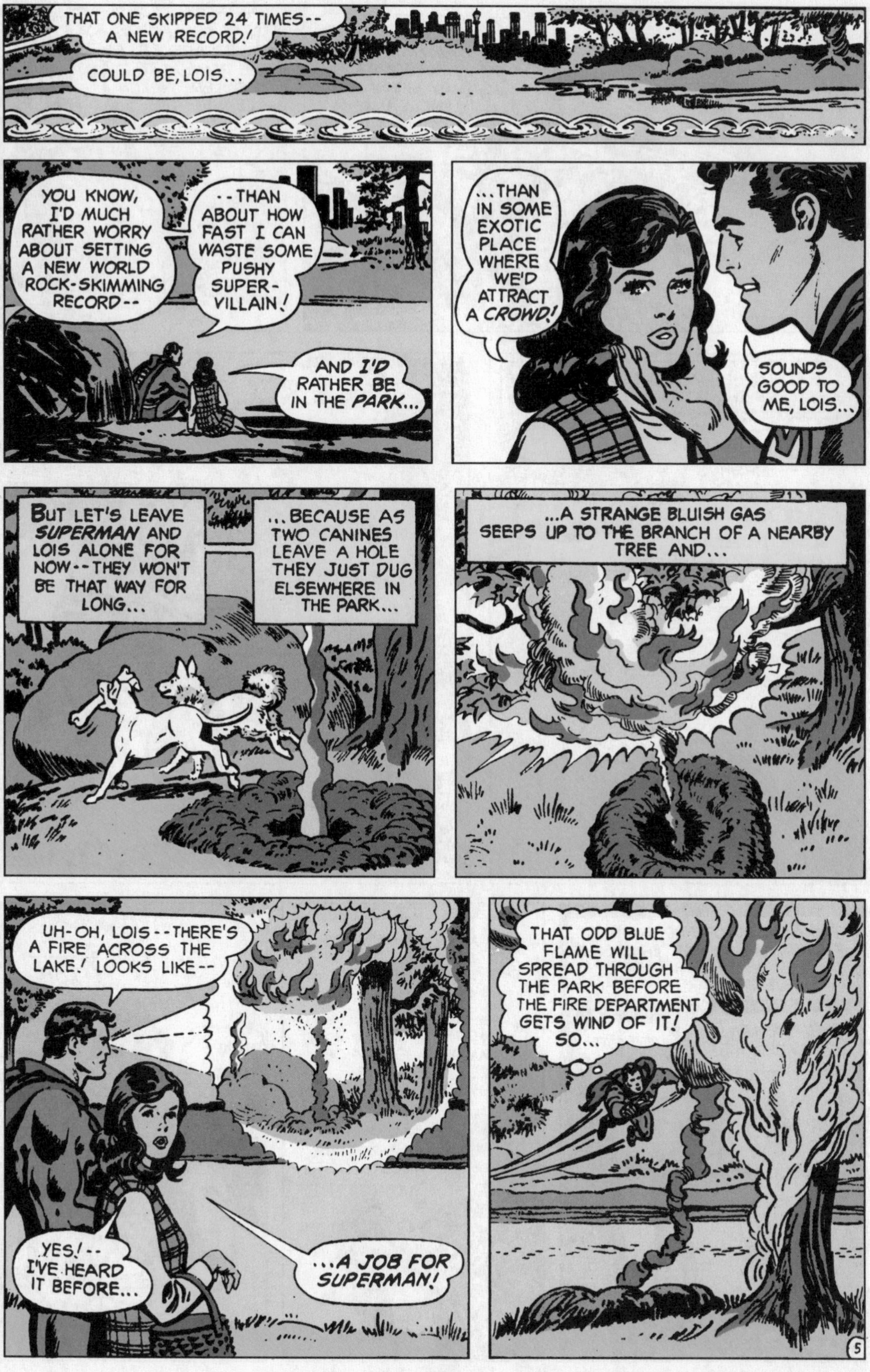
THAT ONE SKIPPED 24 TIMES-- A NEW RECORD!
COULD BE, LOIS...
YOU KNOW, I'D MUCH RATHER WORRY ABOUT SETTING A NEW WORLD ROCK-SKIMMING RECORD--
--THAN ABOUT HOW FAST I CAN WASTE SOME PUSHY SUPER-VILLAIN!
AND I'D RATHER BE IN THE PARK...
...THAN IN SOME EXOTIC PLACE WHERE WE'D ATTRACT A CROWD!
SOUNDS GOOD TO ME, LOIS...
BUT LET'S LEAVE SUPERMAN AND LOIS ALONE FOR NOW--THEY WON'T BE THAT WAY FOR LONG...
...BECAUSE AS TWO CANINES LEAVE A HOLE THEY JUST DUG ELSEWHERE IN THE PARK...
...A STRANGE BLUISH GAS SEEPS UP TO THE BRANCH OF A NEARBY TREE AND...
UH-OH, LOIS--THERE'S A FIRE ACROSS THE LAKE! LOOKS LIKE--
YES!-- I'VE HEARD IT BEFORE...
...A JOB FOR SUPERMAN!
THAT ODD BLUE FLAME WILL SPREAD THROUGH THE PARK BEFORE THE FIRE DEPARTMENT GETS WIND OF IT! SO...
5

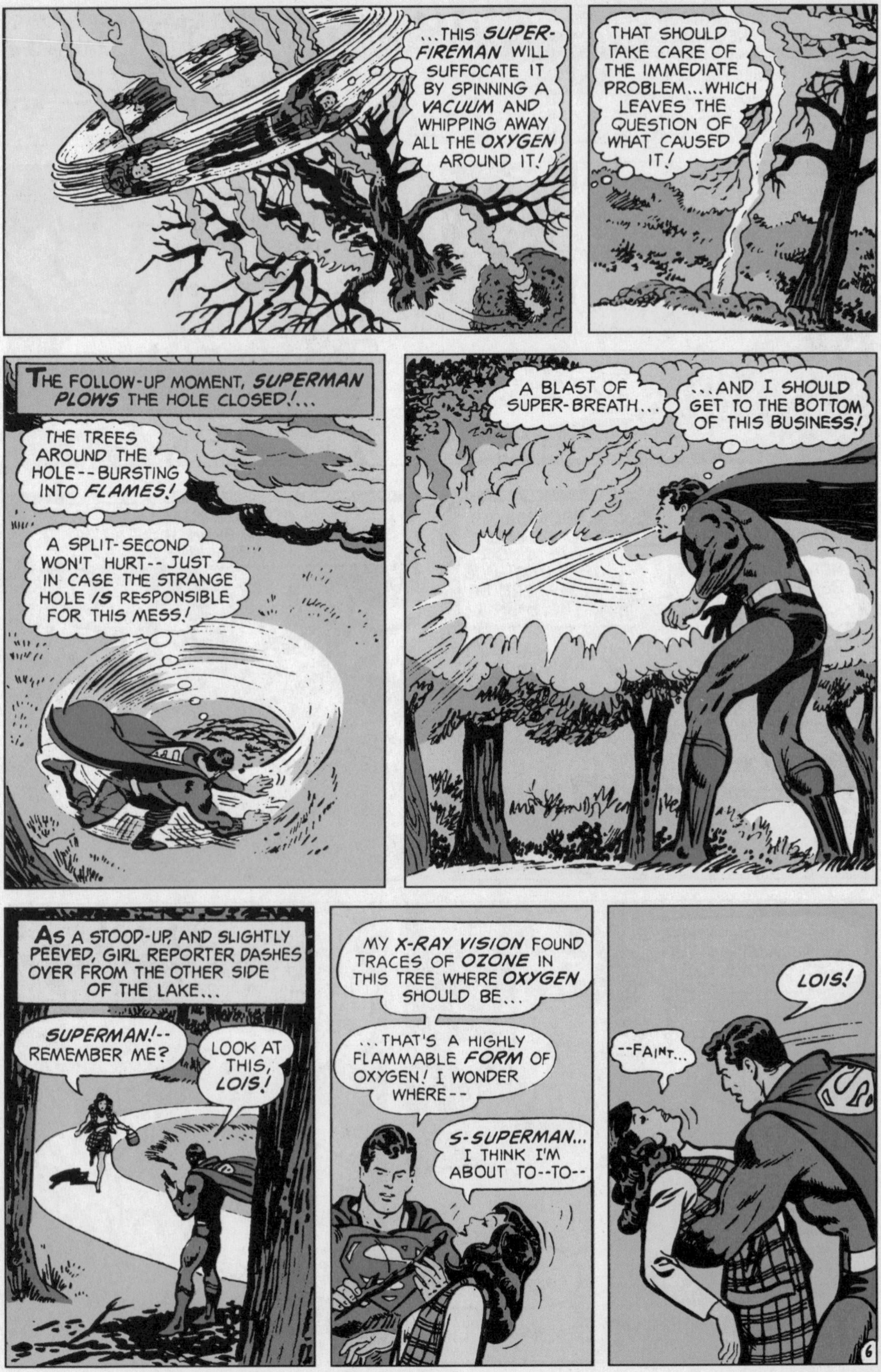

...THIS SUPER-FIREMAN WILL SUFFOCATE IT BY SPINNING A VACUUM AND WHIPPING AWAY ALL THE OXYGEN AROUND IT!
THAT SHOULD TAKE CARE OF THE IMMEDIATE PROBLEM...WHICH LEAVES THE QUESTION OF WHAT CAUSED IT!
THE FOLLOW-UP MOMENT, SUPERMAN PLOWS THE HOLE CLOSED!...
THE TREES AROUND THE HOLE--BURSTING INTO FLAMES!
A SPLIT-SECOND WON'T HURT--JUST IN CASE THE STRANGE HOLE IS RESPONSIBLE FOR THIS MESS!
A BLAST OF SUPER-BREATH...
...AND I SHOULD GET TO THE BOTTOM OF THIS BUSINESS!
AS A STOOD-UP, AND SLIGHTLY PEEVED, GIRL REPORTER DASHES OVER FROM THE OTHER SIDE OF THE LAKE...
SUPERMAN!--REMEMBER ME?
LOOK AT THIS, LOIS!
MY X-RAY VISION FOUND TRACES OF OZONE IN THIS TREE WHERE OXYGEN SHOULD BE...
...THAT'S A HIGHLY FLAMMABLE FORM OF OXYGEN! I WONDER WHERE--
S-SUPERMAN... I THINK I'M ABOUT TO--TO--
LOIS!
--FAINT...
6

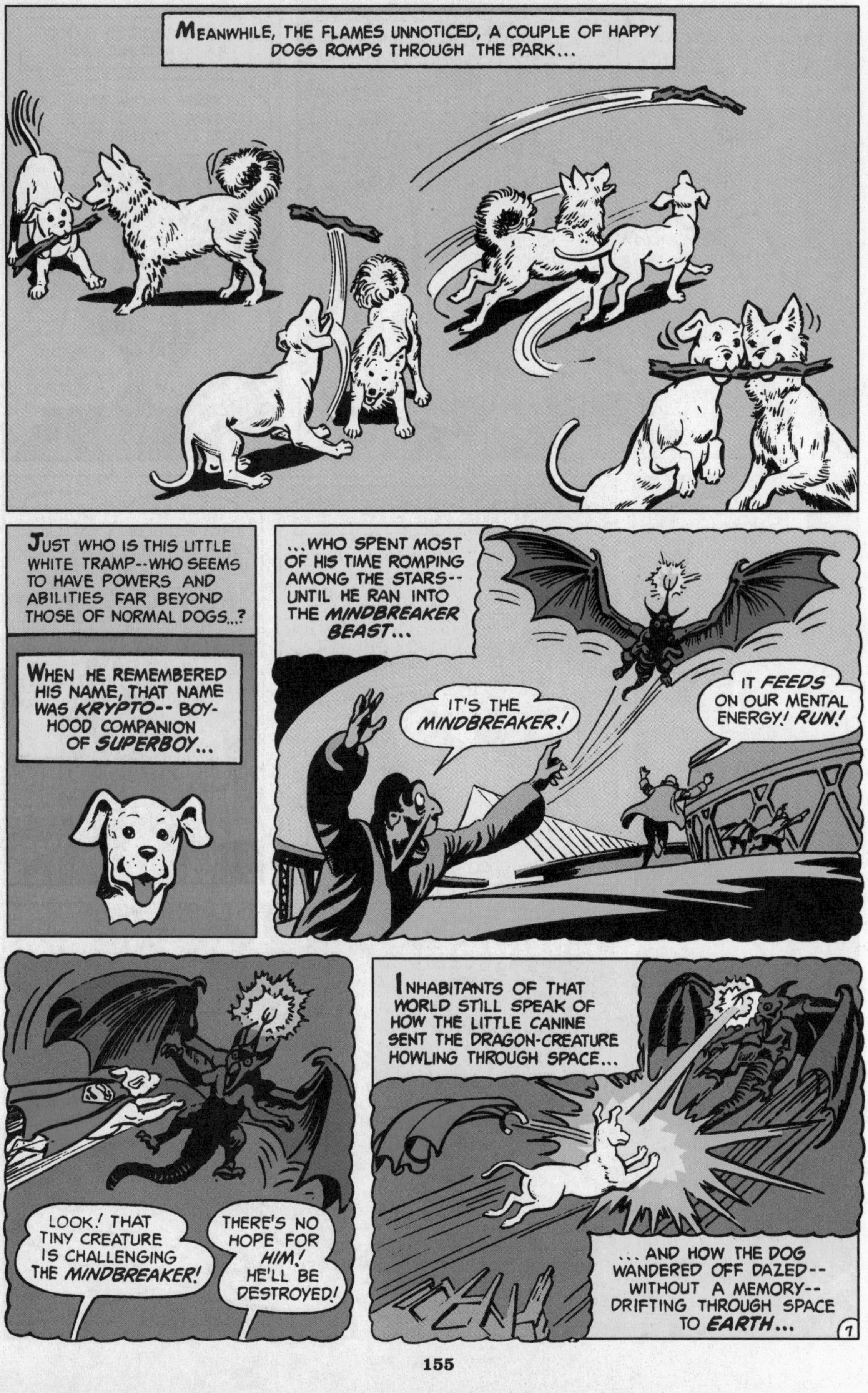
MEANWHILE, THE FLAMES UNNOTICED, A COUPLE OF HAPPY DOGS ROMPS THROUGH THE PARK...
JUST WHO IS THIS LITTLE WHITE TRAMP--WHO SEEMS TO HAVE POWERS AND ABILITIES FAR BEYOND THOSE OF NORMAL DOGS...?
WHEN HE REMEMBERED HIS NAME, THAT NAME WAS KRYPTO-- BOYHOOD COMPANION OF SUPERBOY...
...WHO SPENT MOST OF HIS TIME ROMPING AMONG THE STARS-- UNTIL HE RAN INTO THE MINDBREAKER BEAST...
IT'S THE MINDBREAKER!
IT FEEDS ON OUR MENTAL ENERGY! RUN!
LOOK! THAT TINY CREATURE IS CHALLENGING THE MINDBREAKER!
THERE'S NO HOPE FOR HIM! HE'LL BE DESTROYED!
INHABITANTS OF THAT WORLD STILL SPEAK OF HOW THE LITTLE CANINE SENT THE DRAGON-CREATURE HOWLING THROUGH SPACE...
...AND HOW THE DOG WANDERED OFF DAZED-- WITHOUT A MEMORY-- DRIFTING THROUGH SPACE TO EARTH...
7

BUT NOW A NEW SURPRISE GREETS THIS DOG FROM THE STARS AS HE HAPPENS TO LOOK UPWARD AND SEE...

...SCREAMING ACROSS THE SKY...

...AND MEMORIES FLOOD BACK INTO HIS MIND...

I DON'T KNOW WHAT DID THIS TO YOU, LOIS... BUT I'M GOING TO--

YIP! YIP!

GREAT GALAXIES! KRYPTO!

FOLLOW ME, KRYPTO! LOIS IS IN TROUBLE!

AS A LITTLE DOG LOOKS UP INTO THE AIR, CONFUSED... BEGINNING TO BE SCARED...

AND SOON, AT METRO GENERAL HOSPITAL...

HER PULSE IS GETTING STRONGER!

YES, MISS LANE'S REGAINING CONSCIOUSNESS, SUPERMAN! IT'S A LUCKY THING YOU BROUGHT HER RIGHT HERE...

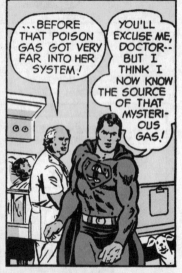

...BEFORE THAT POISON GAS GOT VERY FAR INTO HER SYSTEM!

YOU'LL EXCUSE ME, DOCTOR-- BUT I THINK I NOW KNOW THE SOURCE OF THAT MYSTERIOUS GAS!

UHH, DOCTOR-- WAS THAT A FLYING DOG I JUST SAW?

AFRAID SO, MISS LANE...

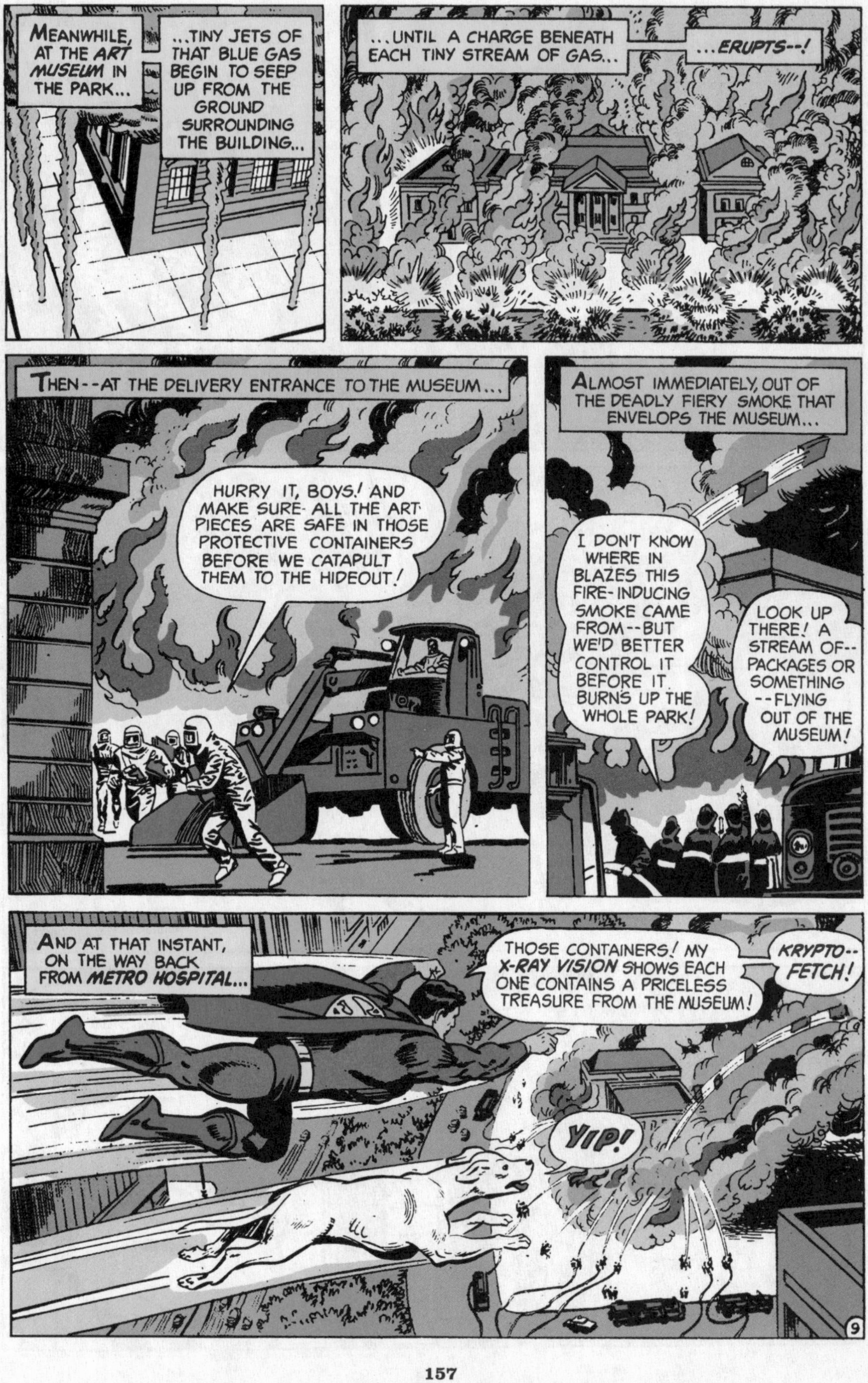
MEANWHILE, AT THE ART MUSEUM IN THE PARK...
...TINY JETS OF THAT BLUE GAS BEGIN TO SEEP UP FROM THE GROUND SURROUNDING THE BUILDING...
...UNTIL A CHARGE BENEATH EACH TINY STREAM OF GAS...
...ERUPTS--!
THEN--AT THE DELIVERY ENTRANCE TO THE MUSEUM...
HURRY IT, BOYS! AND MAKE SURE ALL THE ART PIECES ARE SAFE IN THOSE PROTECTIVE CONTAINERS BEFORE WE CATAPULT THEM TO THE HIDEOUT!
ALMOST IMMEDIATELY, OUT OF THE DEADLY FIERY SMOKE THAT ENVELOPS THE MUSEUM...
I DON'T KNOW WHERE IN BLAZES THIS FIRE-INDUCING SMOKE CAME FROM--BUT WE'D BETTER CONTROL IT BEFORE IT BURNS UP THE WHOLE PARK!
LOOK UP THERE! A STREAM OF--PACKAGES OR SOMETHING--FLYING OUT OF THE MUSEUM!
AND AT THAT INSTANT, ON THE WAY BACK FROM METRO HOSPITAL...
THOSE CONTAINERS! MY X-RAY VISION SHOWS EACH ONE CONTAINS A PRICELESS TREASURE FROM THE MUSEUM!
KRYPTO--FETCH!
YIP!
9

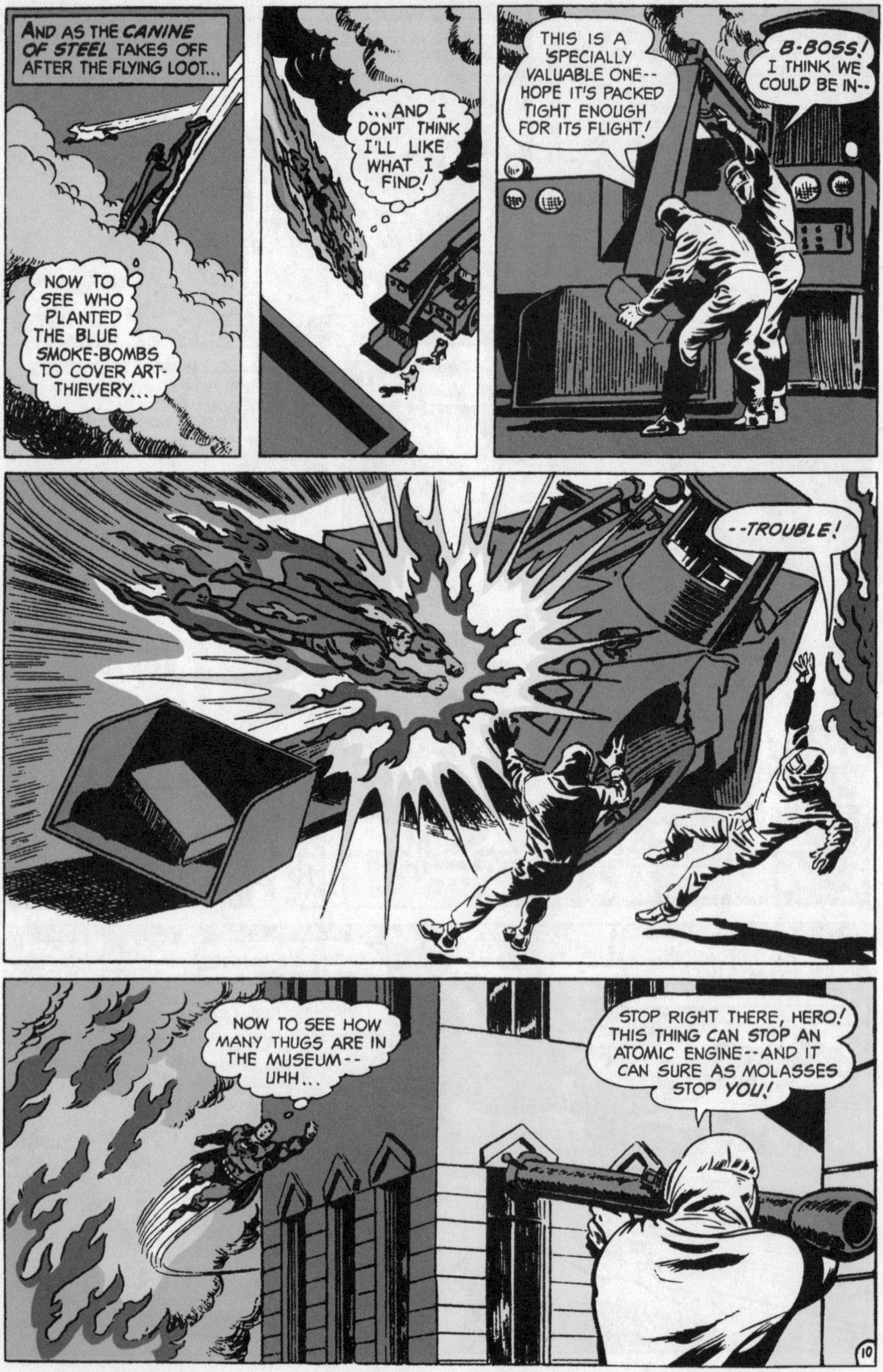
AND AS THE CANINE OF STEEL TAKES OFF AFTER THE FLYING LOOT...
NOW TO SEE WHO PLANTED THE BLUE SMOKE-BOMBS TO COVER ART-THIEVERY...
...AND I DON'T THINK I'LL LIKE WHAT I FIND!
THIS IS A 'SPECIALLY VALUABLE ONE--HOPE IT'S PACKED TIGHT ENOUGH FOR ITS FLIGHT!
B-BOSS! I THINK WE COULD BE IN--
--TROUBLE!
NOW TO SEE HOW MANY THUGS ARE IN THE MUSEUM--UHH...
STOP RIGHT THERE, HERO! THIS THING CAN STOP AN ATOMIC ENGINE--AND IT CAN SURE AS MOLASSES STOP YOU!
10

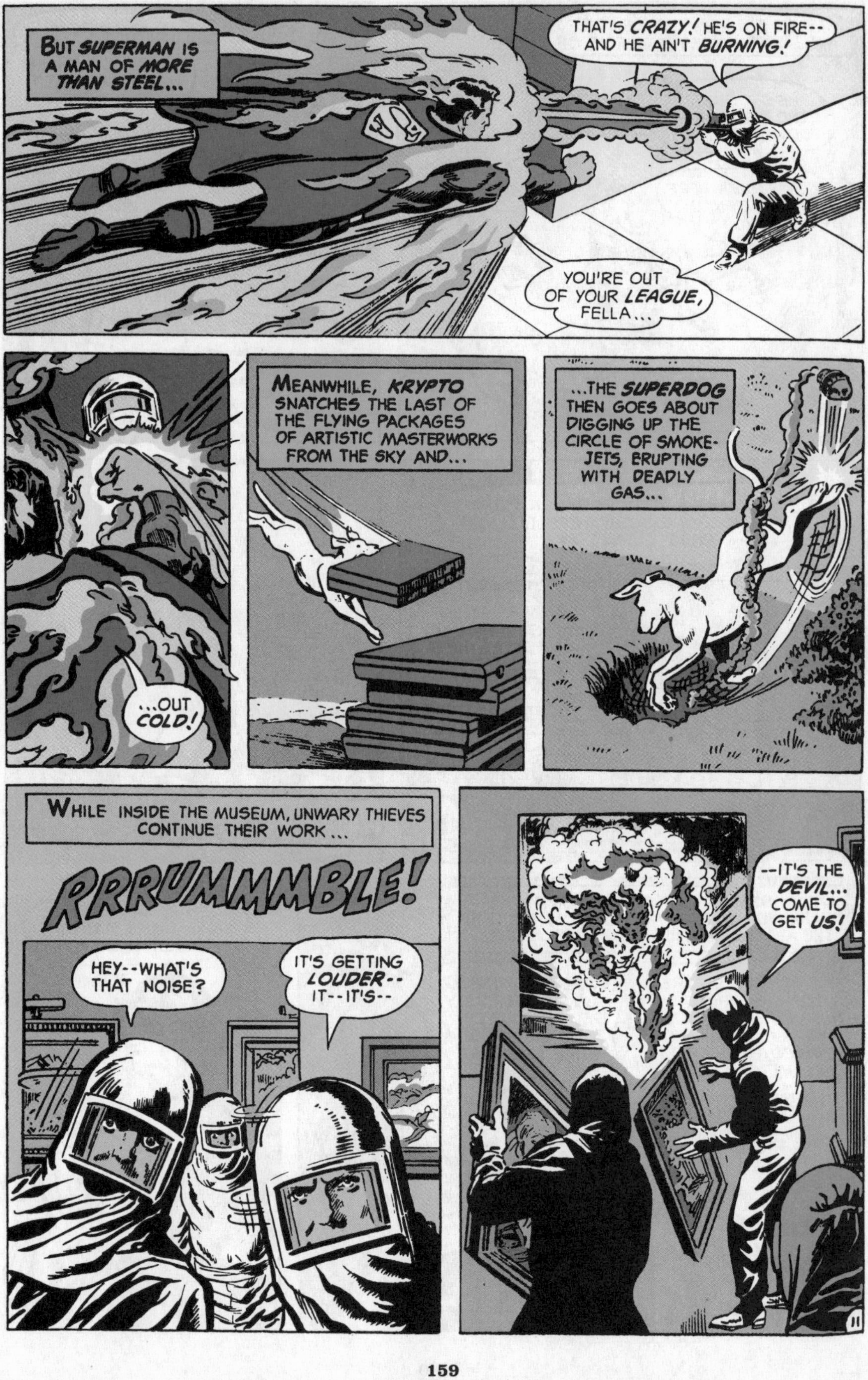
But SUPERMAN is a man of MORE THAN STEEL...
THAT'S CRAZY! HE'S ON FIRE-- AND HE AIN'T BURNING!
YOU'RE OUT OF YOUR LEAGUE, FELLA...
...OUT COLD!
MEANWHILE, KRYPTO SNATCHES THE LAST OF THE FLYING PACKAGES OF ARTISTIC MASTERWORKS FROM THE SKY AND...
...THE SUPERDOG THEN GOES ABOUT DIGGING UP THE CIRCLE OF SMOKE-JETS, ERUPTING WITH DEADLY GAS...
WHILE INSIDE THE MUSEUM, UNWARY THIEVES CONTINUE THEIR WORK...
RRRUMMMMBLE!
HEY--WHAT'S THAT NOISE?
IT'S GETTING LOUDER-- IT--IT'S--
--IT'S THE DEVIL... COME TO GET US!
11

BEFORE THE PETRIFIED CROOKS CAN MOVE, THEY ARE SURROUNDED BY A RING OF FLAME...

HE'S GONNA SEND US STRAIGHT DOWN TO HELL!

C'MON OUTA HERE WITH ME, YOU GUYS!

NOT ME! I AIN'T MOVING!

THAT DEVIL'S THROWING FIRE-BALLS AT THOSE GUYS TRYING TO RUN OFF!

I'M STASHING YOU CROOKS IN YOUR FIREPROOF SUITS OUT HERE TILL THIS MESS CLEARS UP!

HEY--THIS GUY AIN'T NO DEVIL...HE'S SOMETHING FAR WORSE--

--HE'S SUPERMAN!

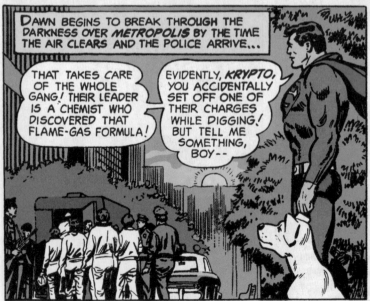

DAWN BEGINS TO BREAK THROUGH THE DARKNESS OVER METROPOLIS BY THE TIME THE AIR CLEARS AND THE POLICE ARRIVE...

THAT TAKES CARE OF THE WHOLE GANG! THEIR LEADER IS A CHEMIST WHO DISCOVERED THAT FLAME-GAS FORMULA!

EVIDENTLY, KRYPTO, YOU ACCIDENTALLY SET OFF ONE OF THEIR CHARGES WHILE DIGGING! BUT TELL ME SOMETHING, BOY--

--WHO WAS THAT DOG I SAW YOU WITH LAST NIGHT?

12

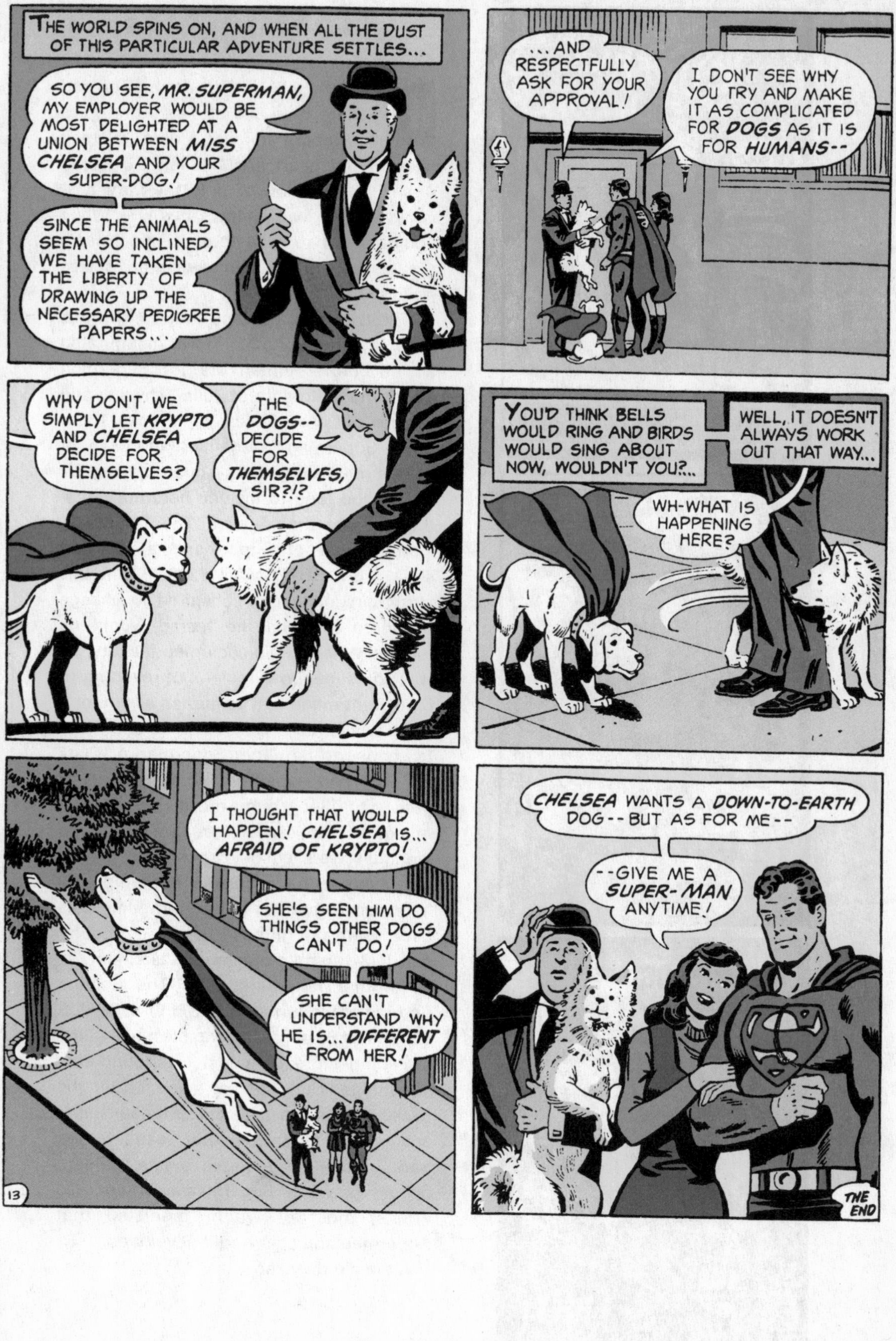
THE WORLD SPINS ON, AND WHEN ALL THE DUST OF THIS PARTICULAR ADVENTURE SETTLES...
SO YOU SEE, MR. SUPERMAN, MY EMPLOYER WOULD BE MOST DELIGHTED AT A UNION BETWEEN MISS CHELSEA AND YOUR SUPER-DOG!
SINCE THE ANIMALS SEEM SO INCLINED, WE HAVE TAKEN THE LIBERTY OF DRAWING UP THE NECESSARY PEDIGREE PAPERS...
...AND RESPECTFULLY ASK FOR YOUR APPROVAL!
I DON'T SEE WHY YOU TRY AND MAKE IT AS COMPLICATED FOR DOGS AS IT IS FOR HUMANS--
WHY DON'T WE SIMPLY LET KRYPTO AND CHELSEA DECIDE FOR THEMSELVES?
THE DOGS-- DECIDE FOR THEMSELVES, SIR?!?
YOU'D THINK BELLS WOULD RING AND BIRDS WOULD SING ABOUT NOW, WOULDN'T YOU?...
WELL, IT DOESN'T ALWAYS WORK OUT THAT WAY...
WH-WHAT IS HAPPENING HERE?
I THOUGHT THAT WOULD HAPPEN! CHELSEA IS... AFRAID OF KRYPTO!
SHE'S SEEN HIM DO THINGS OTHER DOGS CAN'T DO!
SHE CAN'T UNDERSTAND WHY HE IS... DIFFERENT FROM HER!
13
CHELSEA WANTS A DOWN-TO-EARTH DOG -- BUT AS FOR ME --
--GIVE ME A SUPER-MAN ANYTIME!
THE END

THE AMAZING NEW ADVENTURES OF
DC SUPERMAN
15¢
SUPERMAN
JUNE
NO!
PLEASE--
I AM NOT HUMAN! I CARE NOTHING FOR YOU AND YOUR WORLD!
YOU'RE THE ONLY ONE ON EARTH WHO CAN HELP--
EXTRA! A NEW STORY ABOUT THE FABULOUS WORLD of KRYPTON!

SUPERMAN
THE LINE OF DC SUPER-STARS
A NERVE-TINGLING NOVEL: "CLARK KENT-- GET OUT OF MY LIFE!"
30¢
NO. 298
APR.
SUPERMAN
CLARK KENT--
--I'M SO GLAD YOU FINALLY REALIZED THE WORLD CAN GET ALONG WITHOUT SUPERMAN!

SUPERMAN
THE LINE OF DC SUPER-STARS
SUPERMAN'S 300th-- AND GREATEST-- ISSUE!
30¢
NO. 300
JUNE
SUPERMAN
2001
JUST IMAGINE THE MAN OF STEEL COMING TO EARTH AS A BABY TODAY--
--AND GROWING UP IN THE WORLD OF TOMORROW!

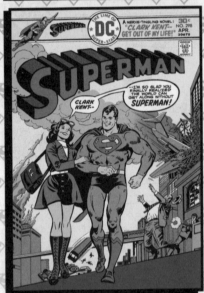

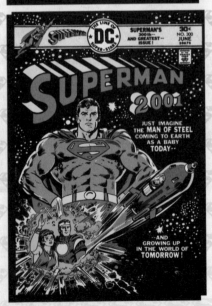

CLASSIC TALES

During the 1970s, Superman appeared in more than 800 stories, from epics like "Superman Takes A Wife" to small tales of the heart like "I Can't Go Home Again." A selection of only the very best could still fill five volumes this size. While you're about to read four of Superman's greatest adventures, winnowing the list was no easy feat.

The two most obvious choices lead this chapter. "Kryptonite No More" inaugurated a new, more human era for Superman under the editorship of Julie Schwartz and the pen of Denny O'Neil, while "Must There Be A Superman?" redefined the Man of Steel's role as humanity's guardian angel.

Far too long to include here but nonetheless memorable was "The Double-or-Nothing Life of Superman," a four-part serial from SUPERMAN #296-299. In this story, circumstances conspired to change our hero for what he feared would be forever. When in his costumed identity, he was still super-powered — but reverting to Clark Kent made him as human as you or I. For a while, Kal-El believed he would have to choose to be either Superman or Clark full-time and experimented to see which guise fulfilled him more. Eventually, of course, he came to realize that both identities were equally as much a part of him even as he overcame his temporary handicap — but not before intriguing Lois Lane with a glimpse of a confident, decidedly un-mild-mannered Clark Kent.

Another landmark tale, "The Second Coming of Superman" (DC SPECIAL SERIES #5) was, at 63 pages, a veritable novel — the sweeping story of a lost civilization that worshipped Superman as a god formed the backdrop for the decade's ultimate battle against the Brainiac-Luthor team. In the back of that issue raged a letter-column debate between Superman's writers and artists, most of whom predicted that Superman and Lois would never wed.

Little did they know...

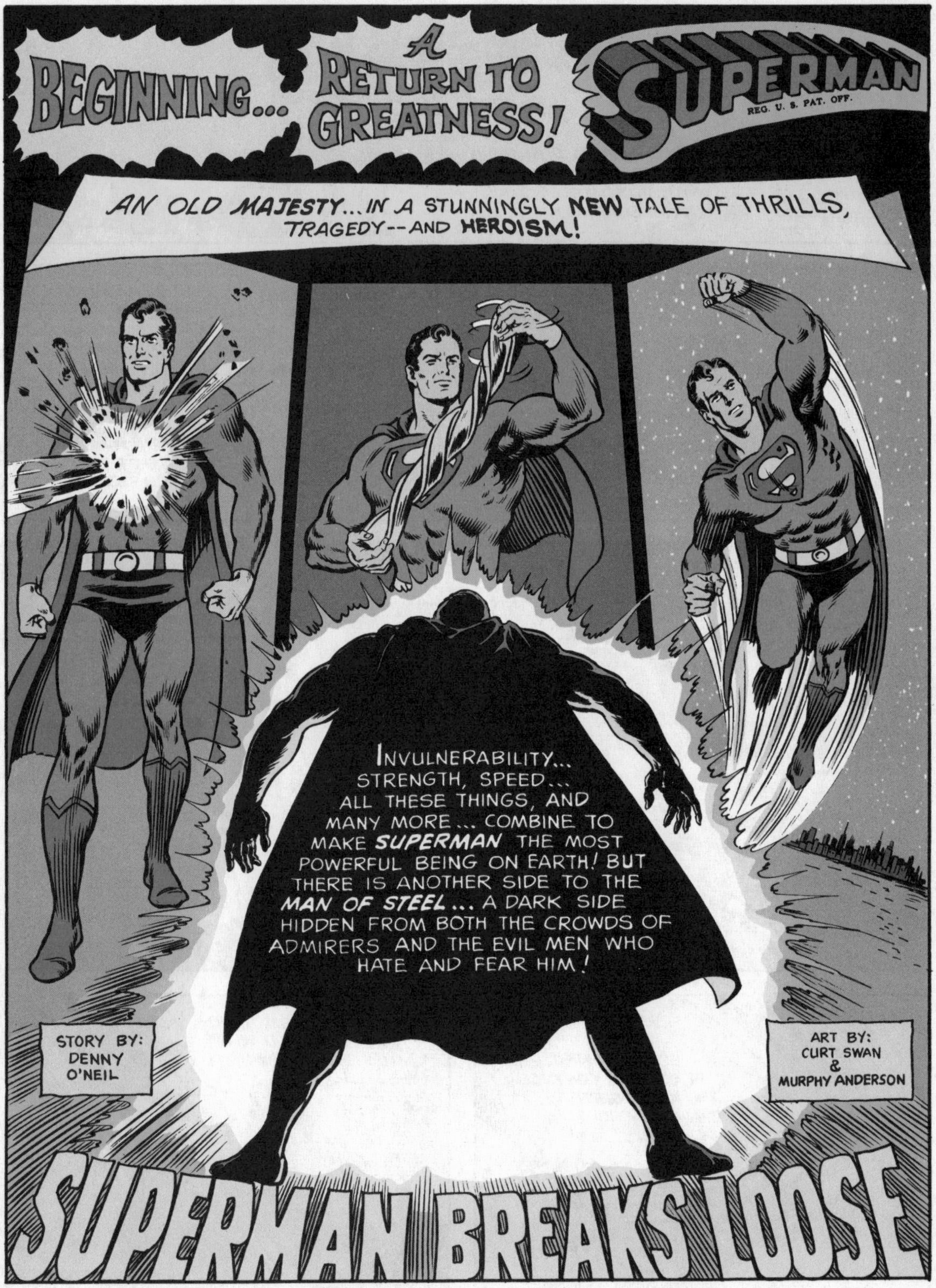
BEGINNING... A RETURN TO GREATNESS!
SUPERMAN
REG. U. S. PAT. OFF.
AN OLD MAJESTY... IN A STUNNINGLY NEW TALE OF THRILLS, TRAGEDY--AND HEROISM!
INVULNERABILITY... STRENGTH, SPEED... ALL THESE THINGS, AND MANY MORE... COMBINE TO MAKE SUPERMAN THE MOST POWERFUL BEING ON EARTH! BUT THERE IS ANOTHER SIDE TO THE MAN OF STEEL... A DARK SIDE HIDDEN FROM BOTH THE CROWDS OF ADMIRERS AND THE EVIL MEN WHO HATE AND FEAR HIM!
STORY BY: DENNY O'NEIL
ART BY: CURT SWAN & MURPHY ANDERSON
SUPERMAN BREAKS LOOSE

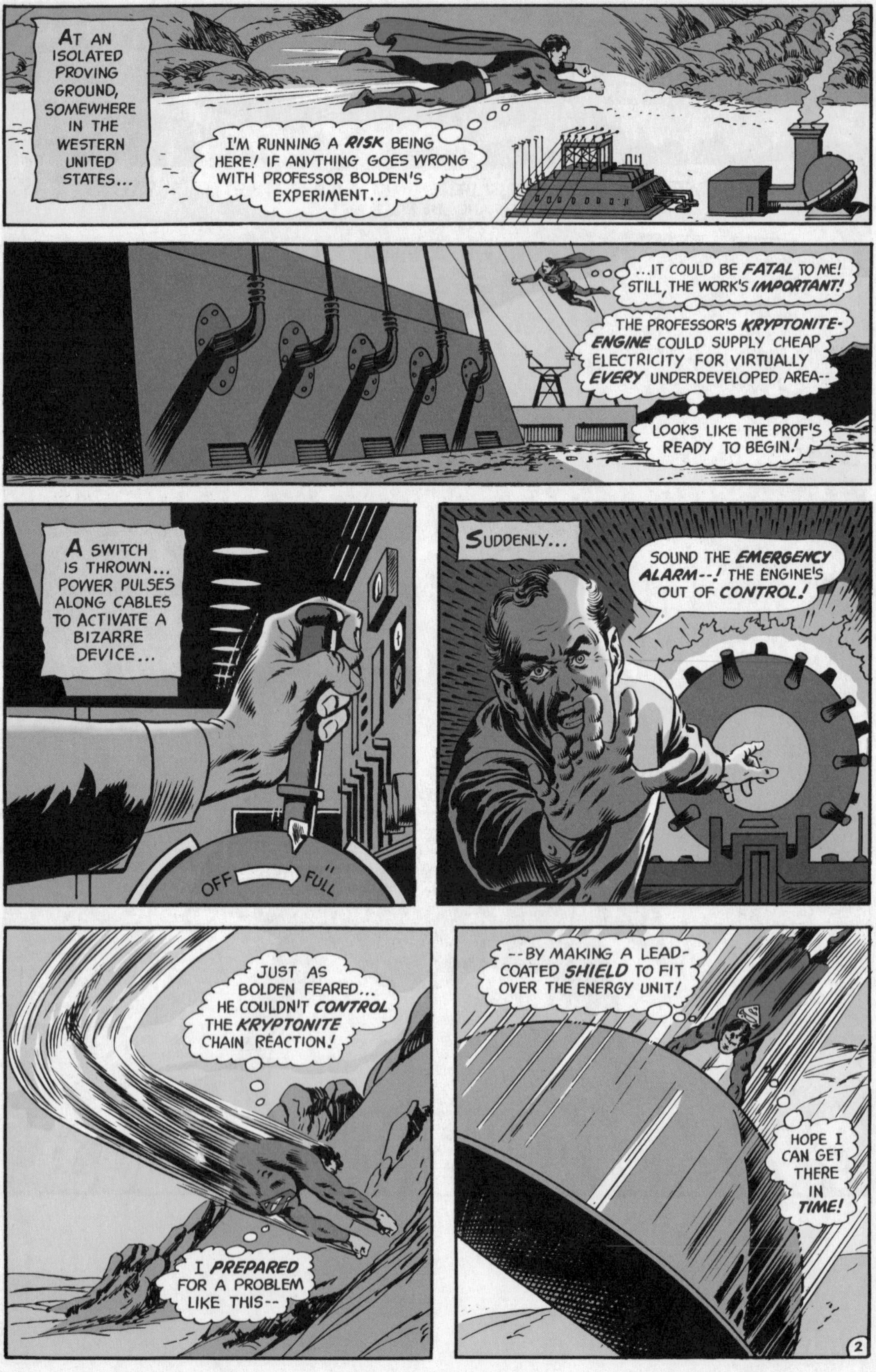
AT AN ISOLATED PROVING GROUND, SOMEWHERE IN THE WESTERN UNITED STATES...
I'M RUNNING A RISK BEING HERE! IF ANYTHING GOES WRONG WITH PROFESSOR BOLDEN'S EXPERIMENT...
...IT COULD BE FATAL TO ME! STILL, THE WORK'S IMPORTANT!
THE PROFESSOR'S KRYPTONITE-ENGINE COULD SUPPLY CHEAP ELECTRICITY FOR VIRTUALLY EVERY UNDERDEVELOPED AREA--
LOOKS LIKE THE PROF'S READY TO BEGIN!
A SWITCH IS THROWN... POWER PULSES ALONG CABLES TO ACTIVATE A BIZARRE DEVICE...
OFF FULL
SUDDENLY...
SOUND THE EMERGENCY ALARM--! THE ENGINE'S OUT OF CONTROL!
JUST AS BOLDEN FEARED... HE COULDN'T CONTROL THE KRYPTONITE CHAIN REACTION!
I PREPARED FOR A PROBLEM LIKE THIS--
--BY MAKING A LEAD-COATED SHIELD TO FIT OVER THE ENERGY UNIT!
HOPE I CAN GET THERE IN TIME!
2

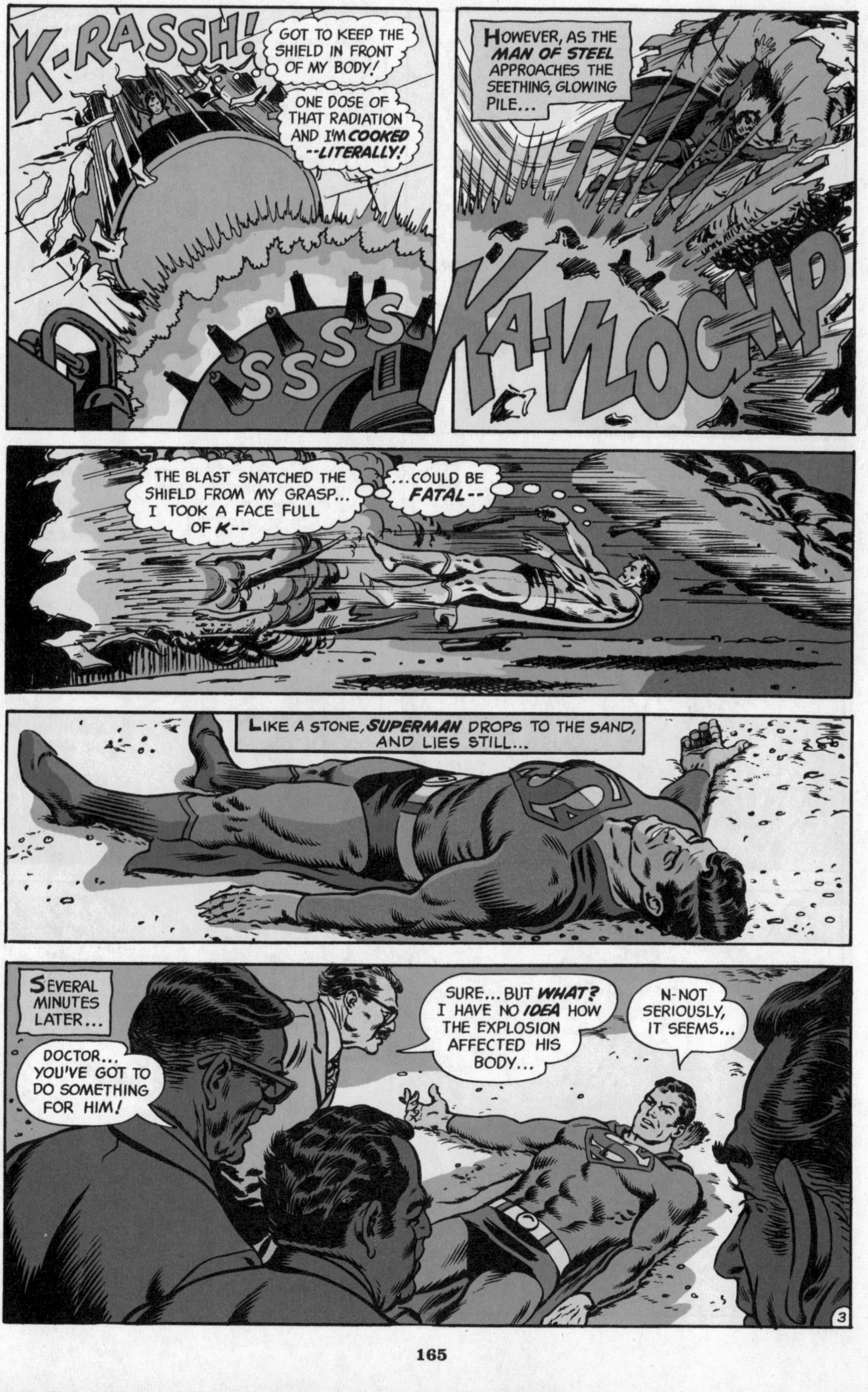
K-RASSH!
GOT TO KEEP THE SHIELD IN FRONT OF MY BODY!
ONE DOSE OF THAT RADIATION AND I'M COOKED --LITERALLY!
SSSSS!
HOWEVER, AS THE MAN OF STEEL APPROACHES THE SEETHING, GLOWING PILE...
KA-VLOOMP
THE BLAST SNATCHED THE SHIELD FROM MY GRASP... I TOOK A FACE FULL OF K--
...COULD BE FATAL--
LIKE A STONE, SUPERMAN DROPS TO THE SAND, AND LIES STILL...
SEVERAL MINUTES LATER...
DOCTOR... YOU'VE GOT TO DO SOMETHING FOR HIM!
SURE... BUT WHAT? I HAVE NO IDEA HOW THE EXPLOSION AFFECTED HIS BODY...
N-NOT SERIOUSLY, IT SEEMS...
3

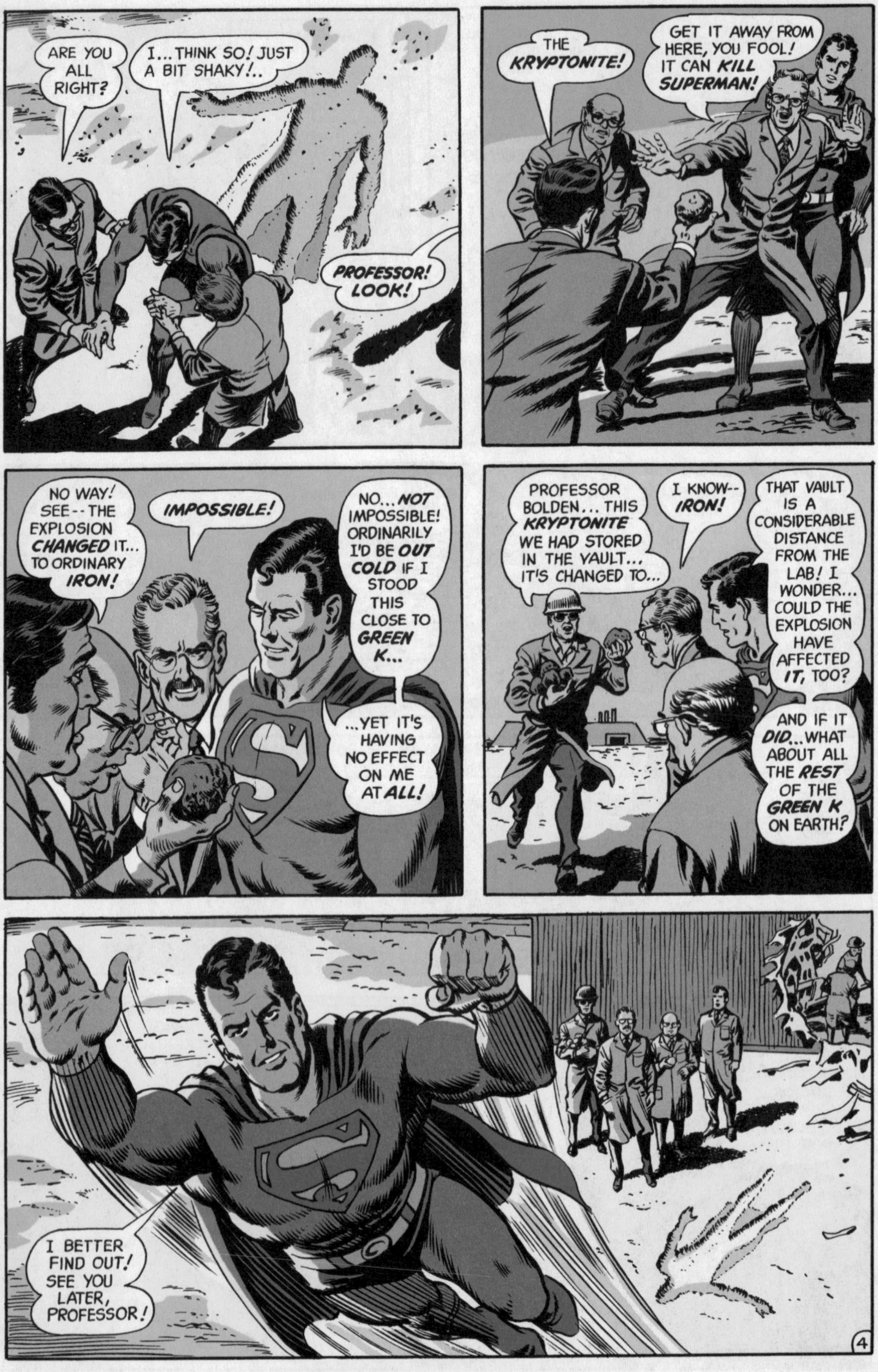
ARE YOU ALL RIGHT?
I... THINK SO! JUST A BIT SHAKY!..
PROFESSOR! LOOK!
THE KRYPTONITE!
GET IT AWAY FROM HERE, YOU FOOL! IT CAN KILL SUPERMAN!
NO WAY! SEE--THE EXPLOSION CHANGED IT... TO ORDINARY IRON!
IMPOSSIBLE!
NO... NOT IMPOSSIBLE! ORDINARILY I'D BE OUT COLD IF I STOOD THIS CLOSE TO GREEN K...
...YET IT'S HAVING NO EFFECT ON ME AT ALL!
PROFESSOR BOLDEN... THIS KRYPTONITE WE HAD STORED IN THE VAULT... IT'S CHANGED TO...
I KNOW-- IRON!
THAT VAULT IS A CONSIDERABLE DISTANCE FROM THE LAB! I WONDER... COULD THE EXPLOSION HAVE AFFECTED IT, TOO?
AND IF IT DID... WHAT ABOUT ALL THE REST OF THE GREEN K ON EARTH?
I BETTER FIND OUT! SEE YOU LATER, PROFESSOR!
4

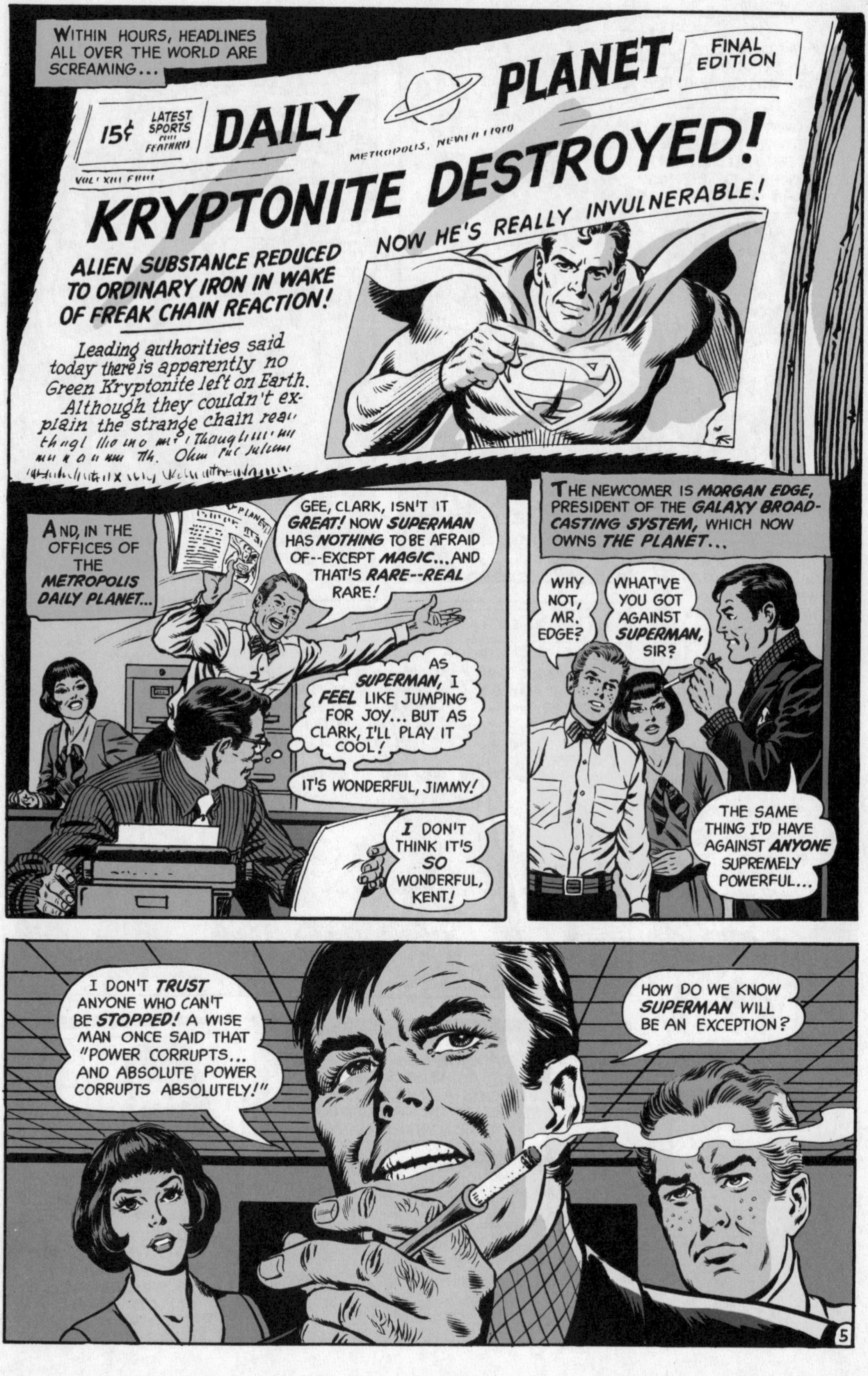
WITHIN HOURS, HEADLINES ALL OVER THE WORLD ARE SCREAMING...
DAILY PLANET
FINAL EDITION
15¢
LATEST SPORTS
KRYPTONITE DESTROYED!
NOW HE'S REALLY INVULNERABLE!
ALIEN SUBSTANCE REDUCED TO ORDINARY IRON IN WAKE OF FREAK CHAIN REACTION!
Leading authorities said today there is apparently no Green Kryptonite left on Earth. Although they couldn't explain the strange chain rea
AND, IN THE OFFICES OF THE METROPOLIS DAILY PLANET...
GEE, CLARK, ISN'T IT GREAT! NOW SUPERMAN HAS NOTHING TO BE AFRAID OF--EXCEPT MAGIC...AND THAT'S RARE--REAL RARE!
AS SUPERMAN, I FEEL LIKE JUMPING FOR JOY... BUT AS CLARK, I'LL PLAY IT COOL!
IT'S WONDERFUL, JIMMY!
I DON'T THINK IT'S SO WONDERFUL, KENT!
THE NEWCOMER IS MORGAN EDGE, PRESIDENT OF THE GALAXY BROADCASTING SYSTEM, WHICH NOW OWNS THE PLANET...
WHY NOT, MR. EDGE?
WHAT'VE YOU GOT AGAINST SUPERMAN, SIR?
THE SAME THING I'D HAVE AGAINST ANYONE SUPREMELY POWERFUL...
I DON'T TRUST ANYONE WHO CAN'T BE STOPPED! A WISE MAN ONCE SAID THAT "POWER CORRUPTS... AND ABSOLUTE POWER CORRUPTS ABSOLUTELY!"
HOW DO WE KNOW SUPERMAN WILL BE AN EXCEPTION?
5

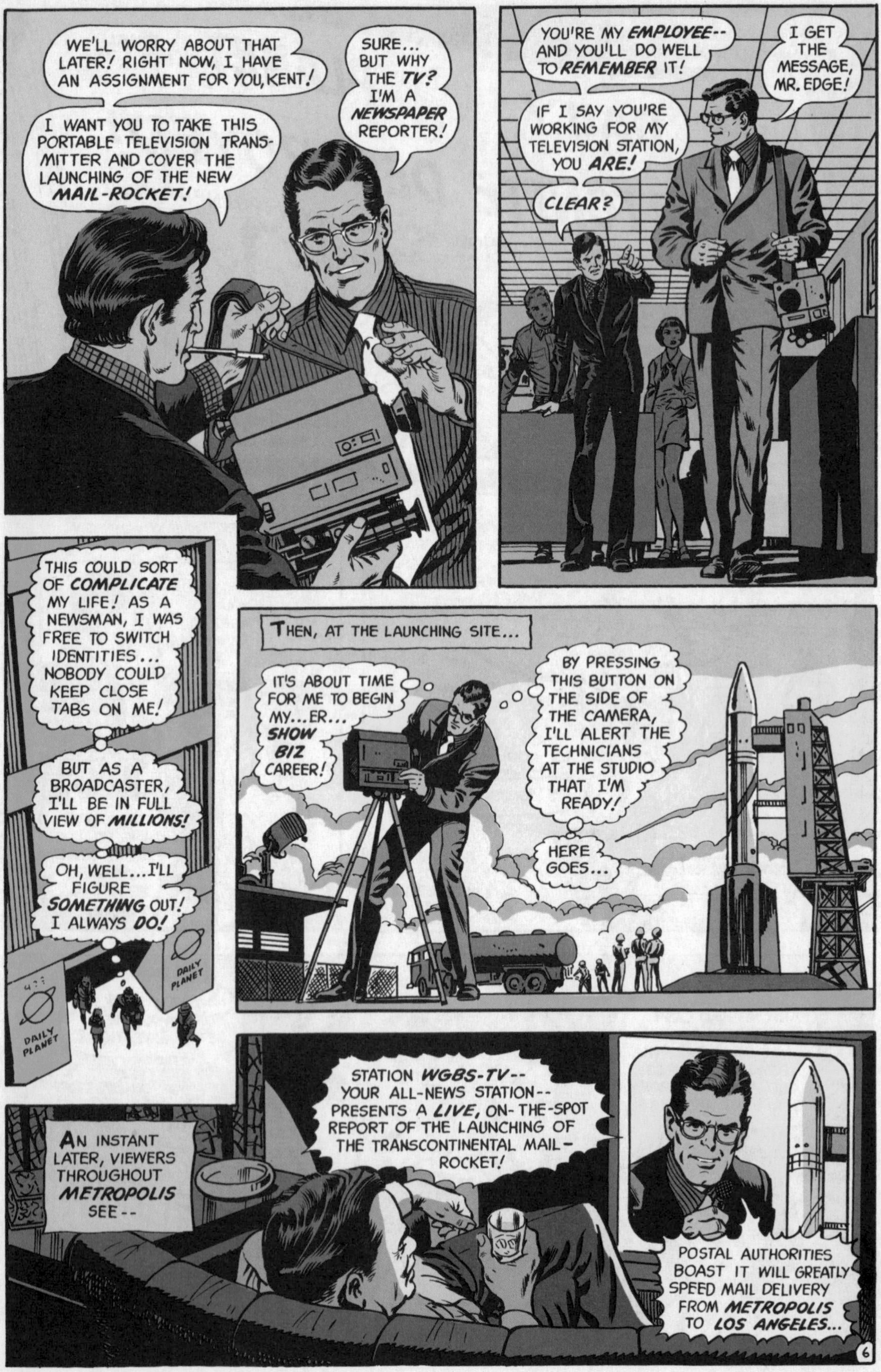

WE'LL WORRY ABOUT THAT LATER! RIGHT NOW, I HAVE AN ASSIGNMENT FOR YOU, KENT!
I WANT YOU TO TAKE THIS PORTABLE TELEVISION TRANSMITTER AND COVER THE LAUNCHING OF THE NEW MAIL-ROCKET!
SURE... BUT WHY THE TV? I'M A NEWSPAPER REPORTER!
YOU'RE MY EMPLOYEE-- AND YOU'LL DO WELL TO REMEMBER IT!
IF I SAY YOU'RE WORKING FOR MY TELEVISION STATION, YOU ARE!
CLEAR?
I GET THE MESSAGE, MR. EDGE!
THIS COULD SORT OF COMPLICATE MY LIFE! AS A NEWSMAN, I WAS FREE TO SWITCH IDENTITIES... NOBODY COULD KEEP CLOSE TABS ON ME!
BUT AS A BROADCASTER, I'LL BE IN FULL VIEW OF MILLIONS!
OH, WELL...I'LL FIGURE SOMETHING OUT! I ALWAYS DO!
DAILY PLANET
DAILY PLANET
THEN, AT THE LAUNCHING SITE...
IT'S ABOUT TIME FOR ME TO BEGIN MY...ER... SHOW BIZ CAREER!
BY PRESSING THIS BUTTON ON THE SIDE OF THE CAMERA, I'LL ALERT THE TECHNICIANS AT THE STUDIO THAT I'M READY!
HERE GOES...
AN INSTANT LATER, VIEWERS THROUGHOUT METROPOLIS SEE--
STATION WGBS-TV-- YOUR ALL-NEWS STATION-- PRESENTS A LIVE, ON-THE-SPOT REPORT OF THE LAUNCHING OF THE TRANSCONTINENTAL MAIL-ROCKET!
POSTAL AUTHORITIES BOAST IT WILL GREATLY SPEED MAIL DELIVERY FROM METROPOLIS TO LOS ANGELES...
6

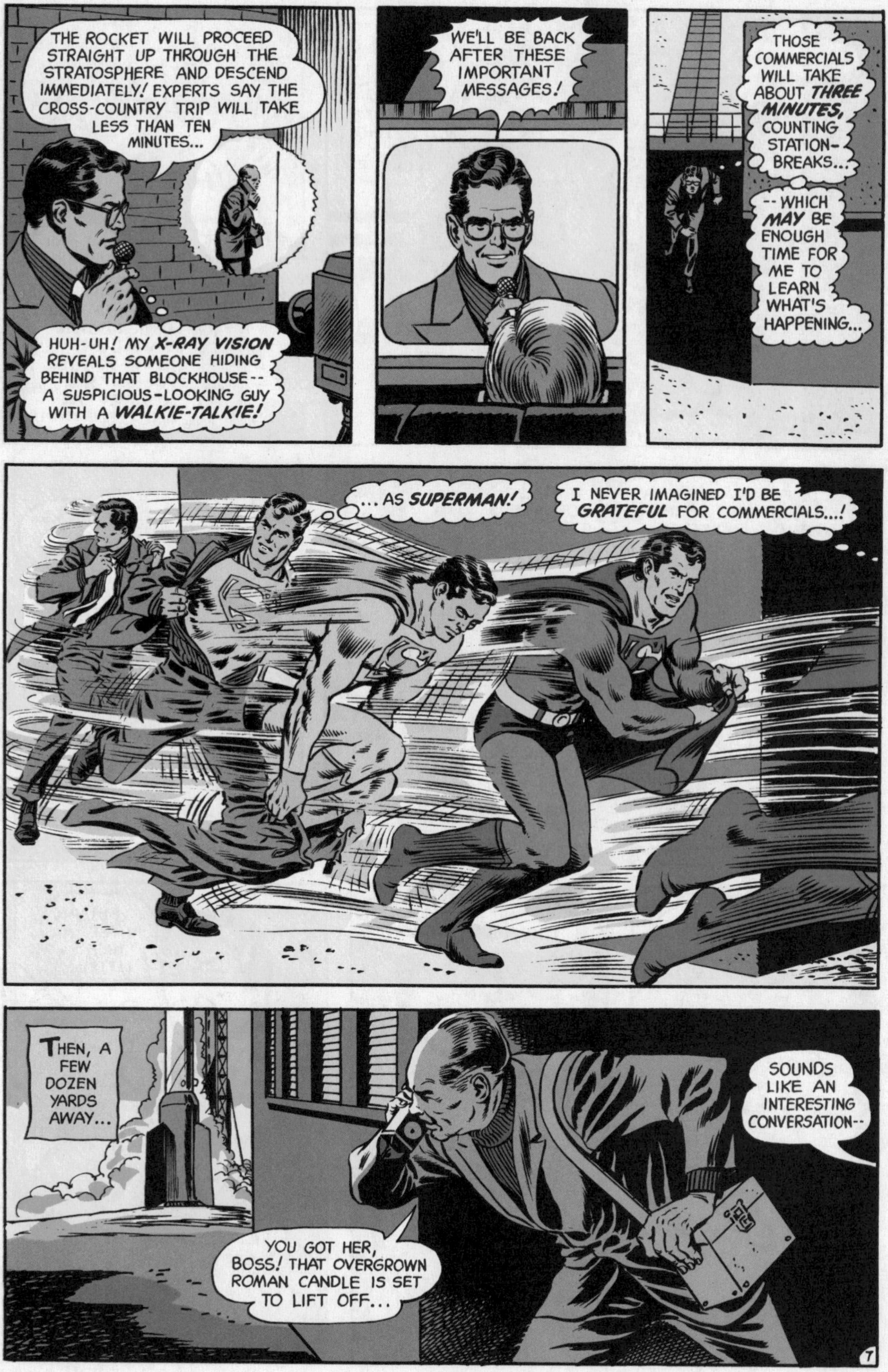
THE ROCKET WILL PROCEED STRAIGHT UP THROUGH THE STRATOSPHERE AND DESCEND IMMEDIATELY! EXPERTS SAY THE CROSS-COUNTRY TRIP WILL TAKE LESS THAN TEN MINUTES...
HUH-UH! MY X-RAY VISION REVEALS SOMEONE HIDING BEHIND THAT BLOCKHOUSE-- A SUSPICIOUS-LOOKING GUY WITH A WALKIE-TALKIE!
WE'LL BE BACK AFTER THESE IMPORTANT MESSAGES!
THOSE COMMERCIALS WILL TAKE ABOUT THREE MINUTES, COUNTING STATION-BREAKS...
--WHICH MAY BE ENOUGH TIME FOR ME TO LEARN WHAT'S HAPPENING...
...AS SUPERMAN!
I NEVER IMAGINED I'D BE GRATEFUL FOR COMMERCIALS...!
THEN, A FEW DOZEN YARDS AWAY...
YOU GOT HER, BOSS! THAT OVERGROWN ROMAN CANDLE IS SET TO LIFT OFF...
SOUNDS LIKE AN INTERESTING CONVERSATION--
7

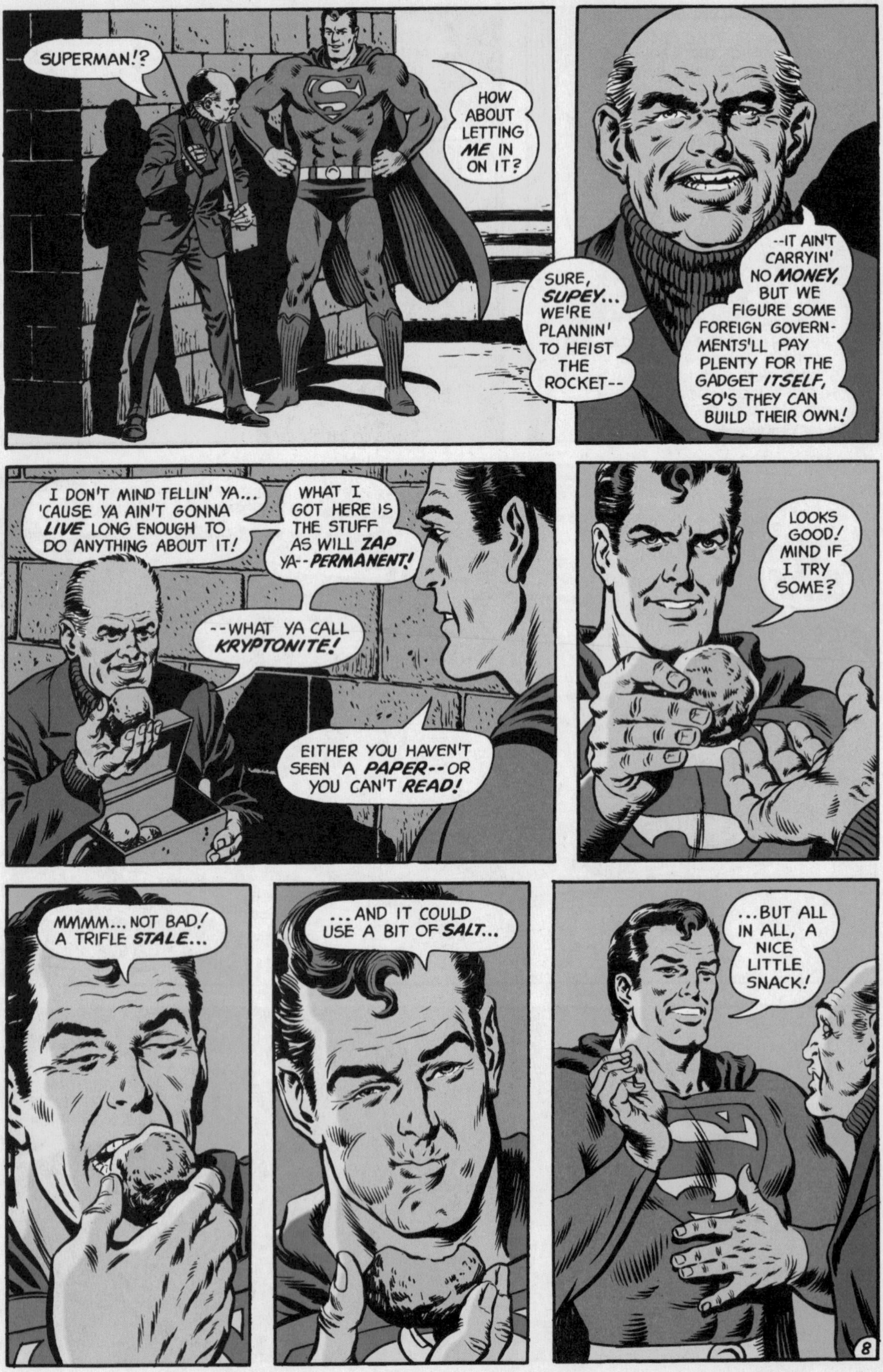
SUPERMAN!?
HOW ABOUT LETTING ME IN ON IT?
SURE, SUPEY... WE'RE PLANNIN' TO HEIST THE ROCKET--
--IT AIN'T CARRYIN' NO MONEY, BUT WE FIGURE SOME FOREIGN GOVERN-MENTS'LL PAY PLENTY FOR THE GADGET ITSELF, SO'S THEY CAN BUILD THEIR OWN!
I DON'T MIND TELLIN' YA... 'CAUSE YA AIN'T GONNA LIVE LONG ENOUGH TO DO ANYTHING ABOUT IT!
WHAT I GOT HERE IS THE STUFF AS WILL ZAP YA--PERMANENT!
--WHAT YA CALL KRYPTONITE!
EITHER YOU HAVEN'T SEEN A PAPER--OR YOU CAN'T READ!
LOOKS GOOD! MIND IF I TRY SOME?
MMMM... NOT BAD! A TRIFLE STALE...
...AND IT COULD USE A BIT OF SALT...
...BUT ALL IN ALL, A NICE LITTLE SNACK!
8

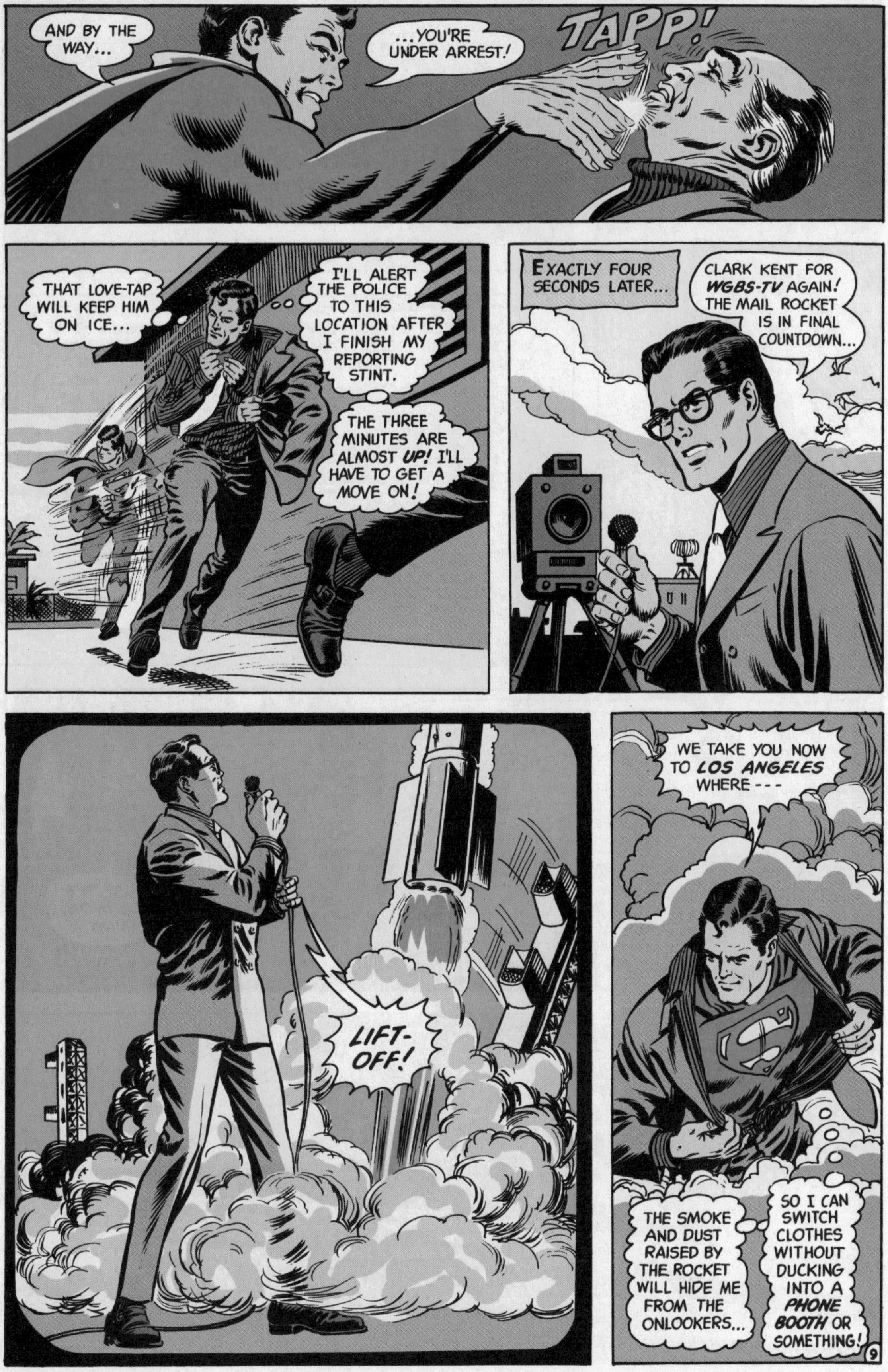

AND BY THE WAY...
...YOU'RE UNDER ARREST!
TAPP!
THAT LOVE-TAP WILL KEEP HIM ON ICE...
I'LL ALERT THE POLICE TO THIS LOCATION AFTER I FINISH MY REPORTING STINT.
THE THREE MINUTES ARE ALMOST UP! I'LL HAVE TO GET A MOVE ON!
EXACTLY FOUR SECONDS LATER...
CLARK KENT FOR WGBS-TV AGAIN! THE MAIL ROCKET IS IN FINAL COUNTDOWN...
LIFT-OFF!
WE TAKE YOU NOW TO LOS ANGELES WHERE ---
THE SMOKE AND DUST RAISED BY THE ROCKET WILL HIDE ME FROM THE ONLOOKERS...
SO I CAN SWITCH CLOTHES WITHOUT DUCKING INTO A PHONE BOOTH OR SOMETHING!
9

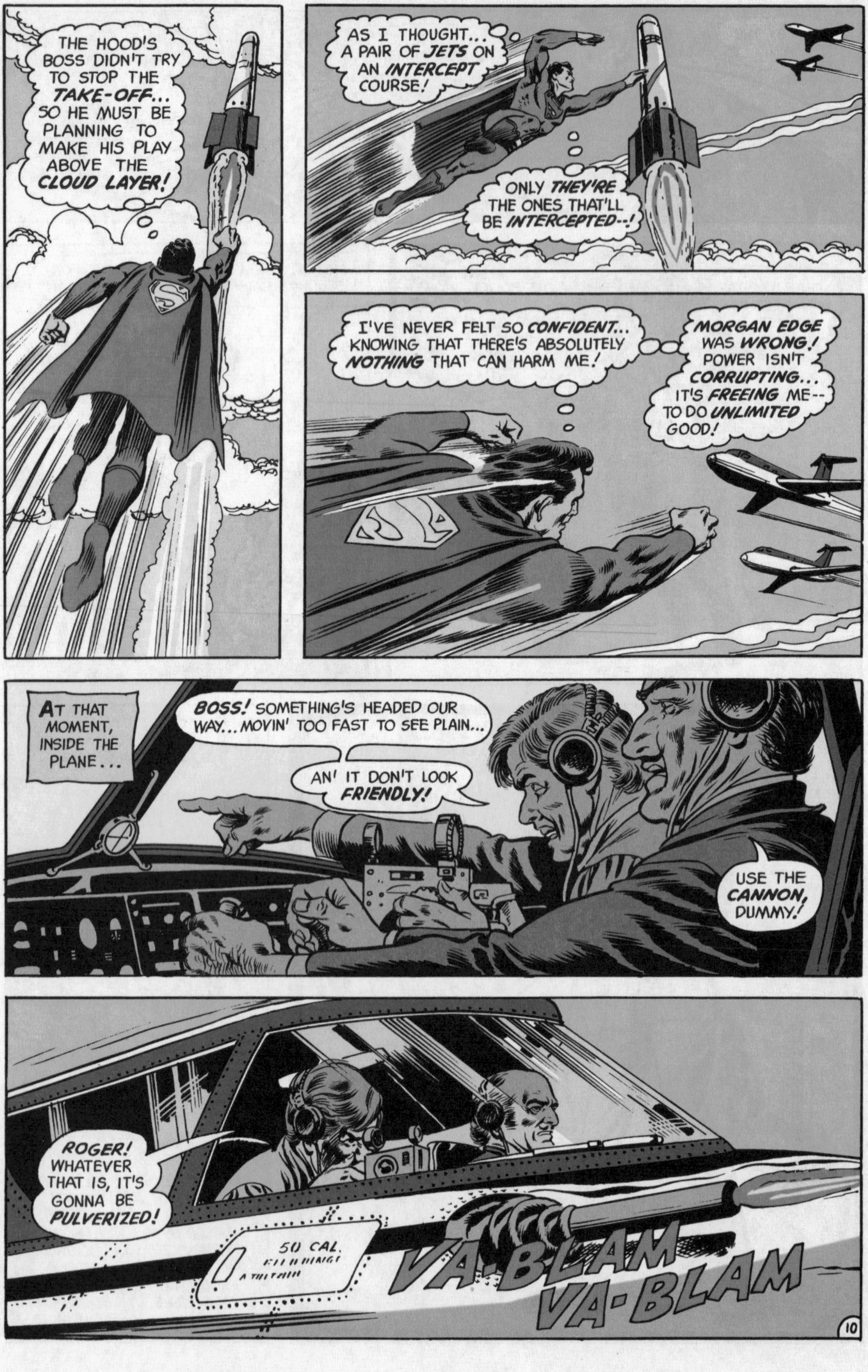
THE HOOD'S BOSS DIDN'T TRY TO STOP THE TAKE-OFF... SO HE MUST BE PLANNING TO MAKE HIS PLAY ABOVE THE CLOUD LAYER!
AS I THOUGHT... A PAIR OF JETS ON AN INTERCEPT COURSE!
ONLY THEY'RE THE ONES THAT'LL BE INTERCEPTED--!
I'VE NEVER FELT SO CONFIDENT... KNOWING THAT THERE'S ABSOLUTELY NOTHING THAT CAN HARM ME!
MORGAN EDGE WAS WRONG! POWER ISN'T CORRUPTING... IT'S FREEING ME-- TO DO UNLIMITED GOOD!
AT THAT MOMENT, INSIDE THE PLANE...
BOSS! SOMETHING'S HEADED OUR WAY... MOVIN' TOO FAST TO SEE PLAIN...
AN' IT DON'T LOOK FRIENDLY!
USE THE CANNON, DUMMY!
ROGER! WHATEVER THAT IS, IT'S GONNA BE PULVERIZED!
50 CAL.
VA-BLAM
VA-BLAM
10

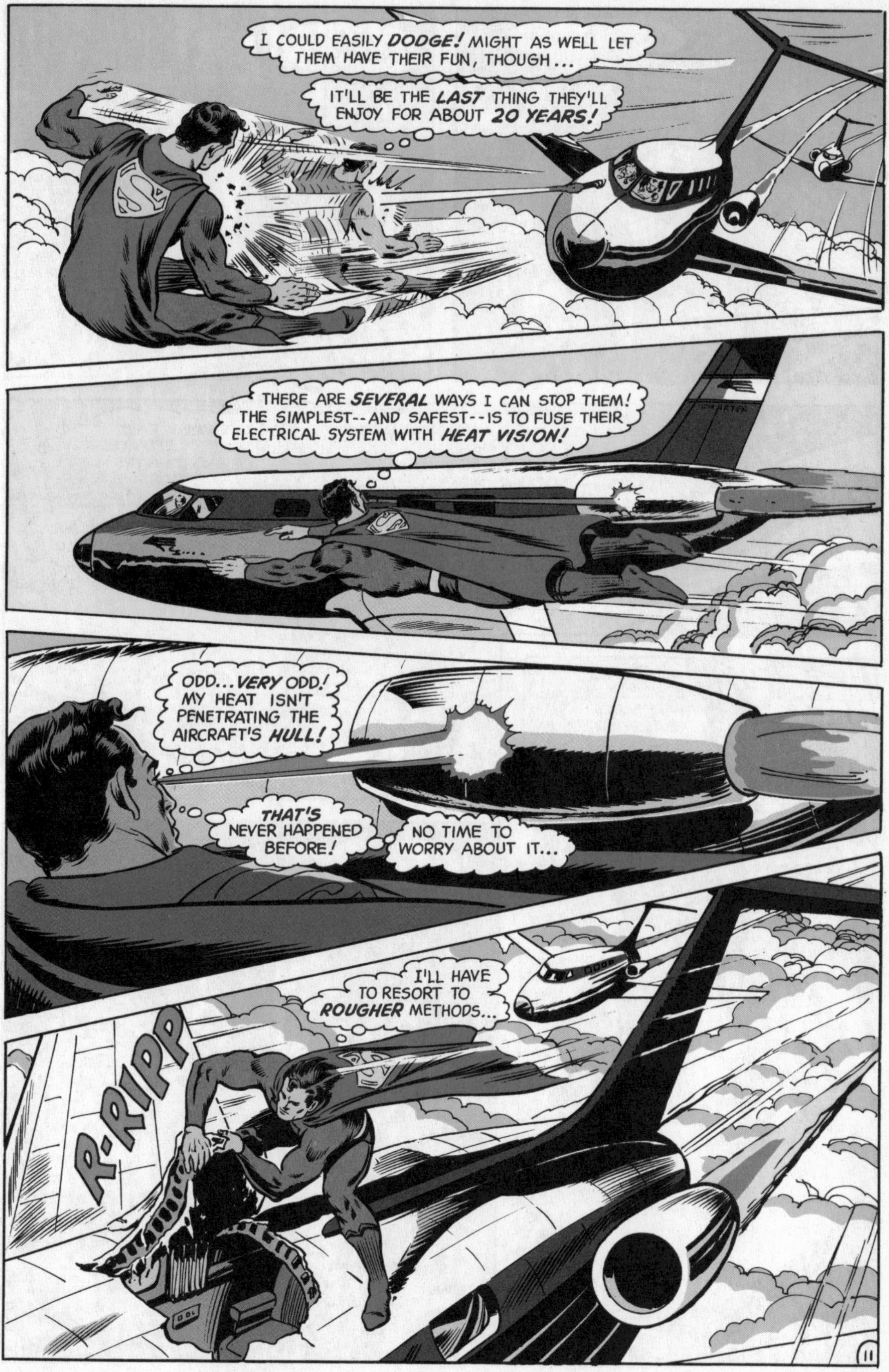
I COULD EASILY DODGE! MIGHT AS WELL LET THEM HAVE THEIR FUN, THOUGH...
IT'LL BE THE LAST THING THEY'LL ENJOY FOR ABOUT 20 YEARS!
THERE ARE SEVERAL WAYS I CAN STOP THEM! THE SIMPLEST--AND SAFEST--IS TO FUSE THEIR ELECTRICAL SYSTEM WITH HEAT VISION!
ODD...VERY ODD! MY HEAT ISN'T PENETRATING THE AIRCRAFT'S HULL!
THAT'S NEVER HAPPENED BEFORE!
NO TIME TO WORRY ABOUT IT...
I'LL HAVE TO RESORT TO ROUGHER METHODS...
R-RIPP
11

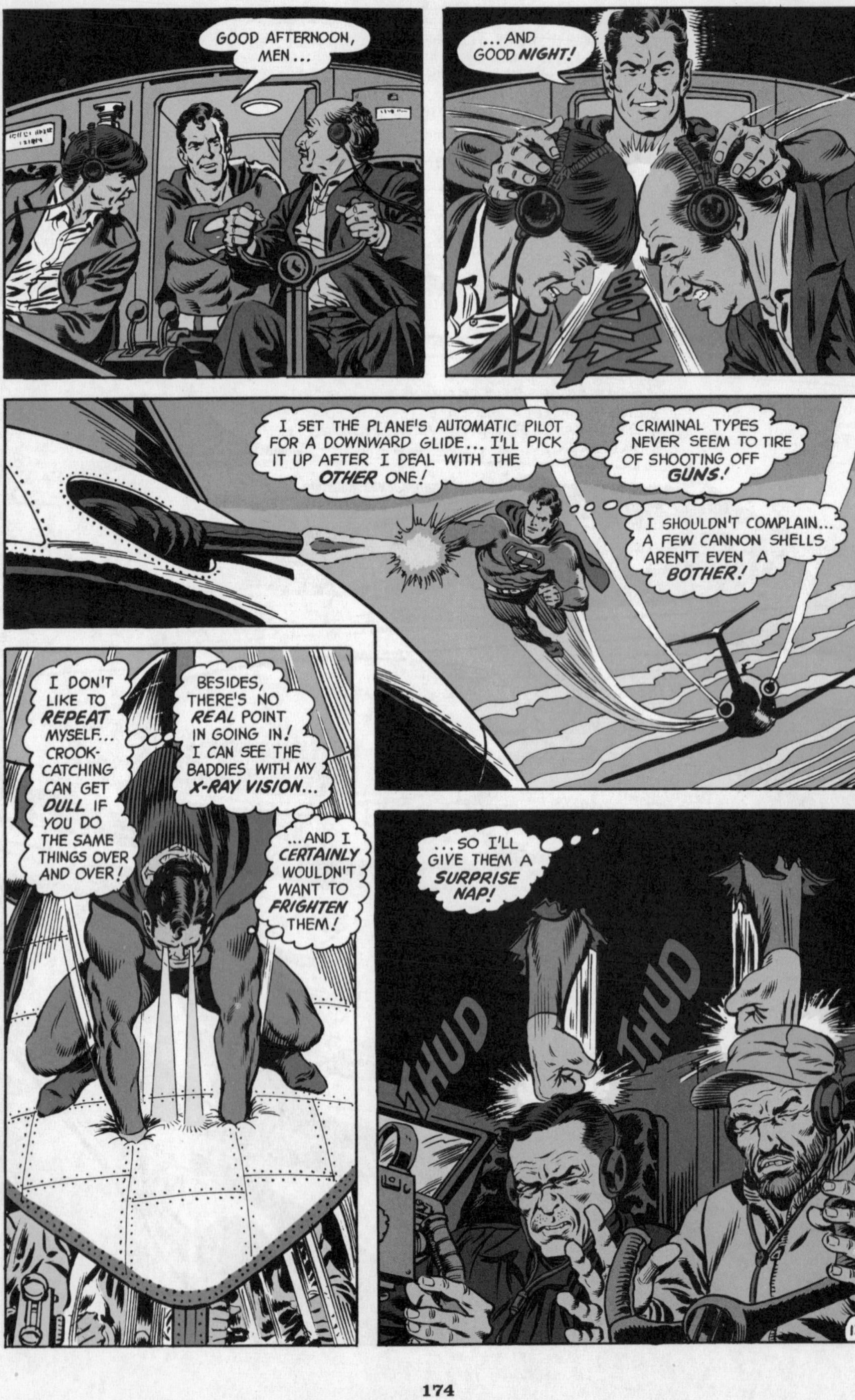
GOOD AFTERNOON, MEN...
...AND GOOD NIGHT!
I SET THE PLANE'S AUTOMATIC PILOT FOR A DOWNWARD GLIDE... I'LL PICK IT UP AFTER I DEAL WITH THE OTHER ONE!
CRIMINAL TYPES NEVER SEEM TO TIRE OF SHOOTING OFF GUNS!
I SHOULDN'T COMPLAIN... A FEW CANNON SHELLS AREN'T EVEN A BOTHER!
I DON'T LIKE TO REPEAT MYSELF... CROOK-CATCHING CAN GET DULL IF YOU DO THE SAME THINGS OVER AND OVER!
BESIDES, THERE'S NO REAL POINT IN GOING IN! I CAN SEE THE BADDIES WITH MY X-RAY VISION...
...AND I CERTAINLY WOULDN'T WANT TO FRIGHTEN THEM!
...SO I'LL GIVE THEM A SURPRISE NAP!
THUD
THUD
12

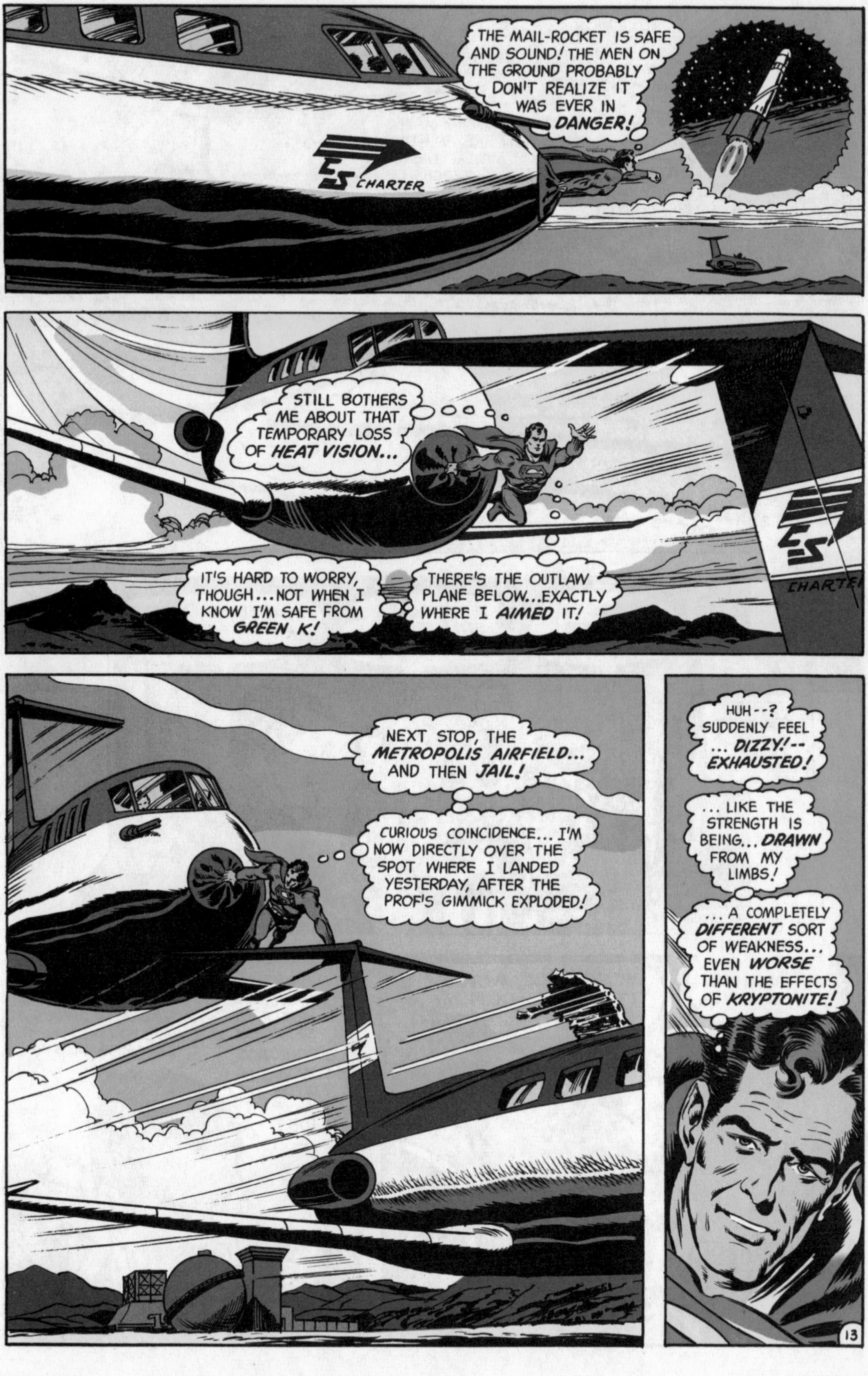
THE MAIL-ROCKET IS SAFE AND SOUND! THE MEN ON THE GROUND PROBABLY DON'T REALIZE IT WAS EVER IN DANGER!
CHARTER
STILL BOTHERS ME ABOUT THAT TEMPORARY LOSS OF HEAT VISION...
IT'S HARD TO WORRY, THOUGH...NOT WHEN I KNOW I'M SAFE FROM GREEN K!
THERE'S THE OUTLAW PLANE BELOW...EXACTLY WHERE I AIMED IT!
NEXT STOP, THE METROPOLIS AIRFIELD... AND THEN JAIL!
CURIOUS COINCIDENCE... I'M NOW DIRECTLY OVER THE SPOT WHERE I LANDED YESTERDAY, AFTER THE PROF'S GIMMICK EXPLODED!
HUH--? SUDDENLY FEEL ... DIZZY!-- EXHAUSTED!
... LIKE THE STRENGTH IS BEING... DRAWN FROM MY LIMBS!
... A COMPLETELY DIFFERENT SORT OF WEAKNESS... EVEN WORSE THAN THE EFFECTS OF KRYPTONITE!
13

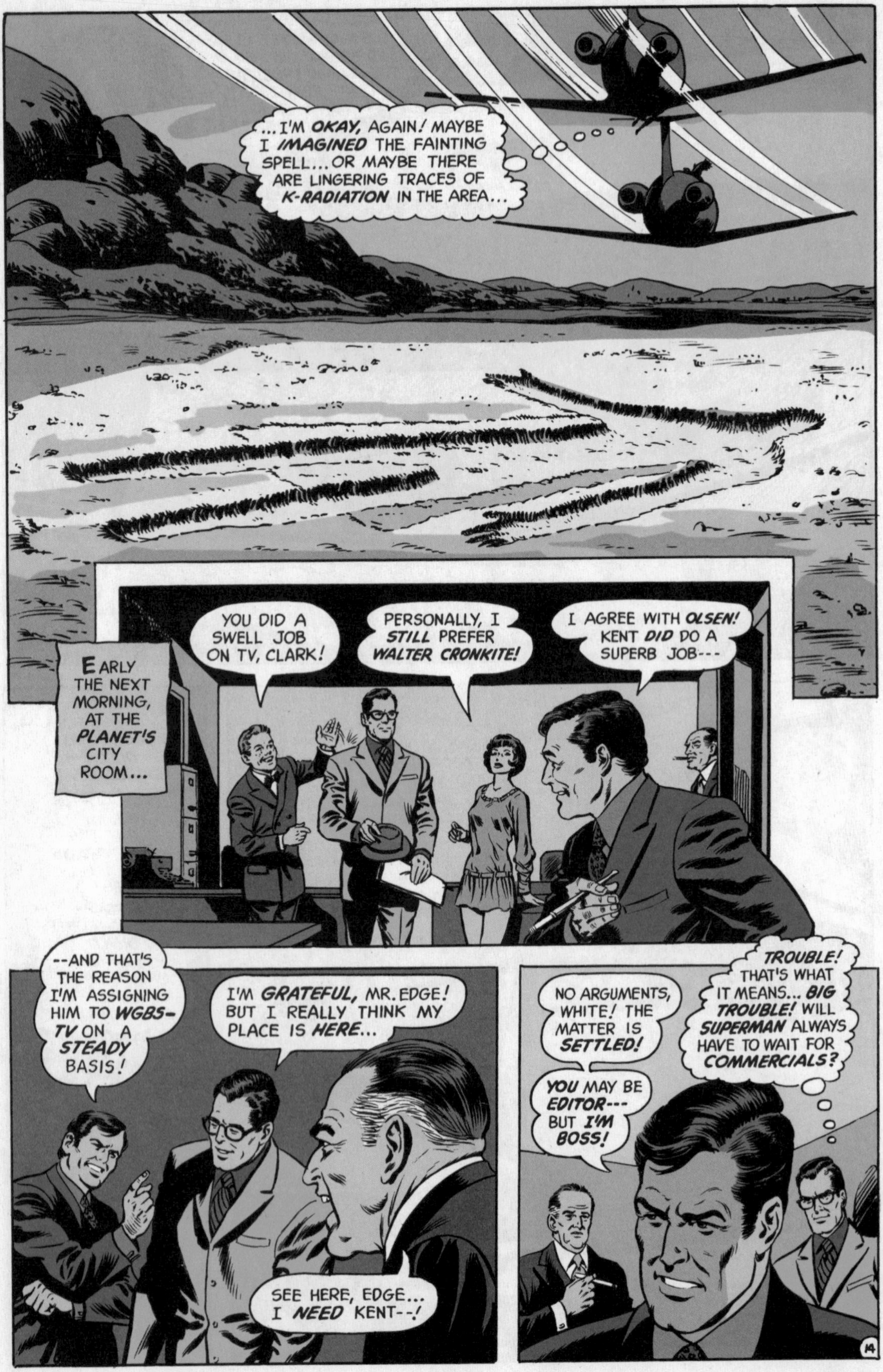
...I'M OKAY, AGAIN! MAYBE I IMAGINED THE FAINTING SPELL...OR MAYBE THERE ARE LINGERING TRACES OF K-RADIATION IN THE AREA...
EARLY THE NEXT MORNING, AT THE PLANET'S CITY ROOM...
YOU DID A SWELL JOB ON TV, CLARK!
PERSONALLY, I STILL PREFER WALTER CRONKITE!
I AGREE WITH OLSEN! KENT DID DO A SUPERB JOB---
--AND THAT'S THE REASON I'M ASSIGNING HIM TO WGBS-TV ON A STEADY BASIS!
I'M GRATEFUL, MR. EDGE! BUT I REALLY THINK MY PLACE IS HERE...
SEE HERE, EDGE... I NEED KENT--!
NO ARGUMENTS, WHITE! THE MATTER IS SETTLED!
YOU MAY BE EDITOR--- BUT I'M BOSS!
TROUBLE! THAT'S WHAT IT MEANS... BIG TROUBLE! WILL SUPERMAN ALWAYS HAVE TO WAIT FOR COMMERCIALS?
14

EPILOGUE

EVEN AS CLARK PONDERS NEW COMPLICATIONS, A BLAZING SUN BEATS UPON THE DESERT...UPON A FIGURE IN THE SAND...

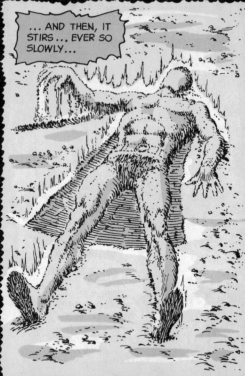

... AND THEN, IT STIRS... EVER SO SLOWLY...

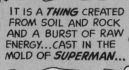

IT IS A *THING* CREATED FROM SOIL AND ROCK AND A BURST OF RAW ENERGY...CAST IN THE MOLD OF *SUPERMAN*...

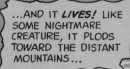

...AND IT *LIVES!* LIKE SOME NIGHTMARE CREATURE, IT PLODS TOWARD THE DISTANT MOUNTAINS...

...AND TOWARD THE VILLAGES AND TOWNS AND CITIES BEYOND...

...MOVING SLOWLY, RELENTLESSLY TO A TERRIBLE DESTINY...

END

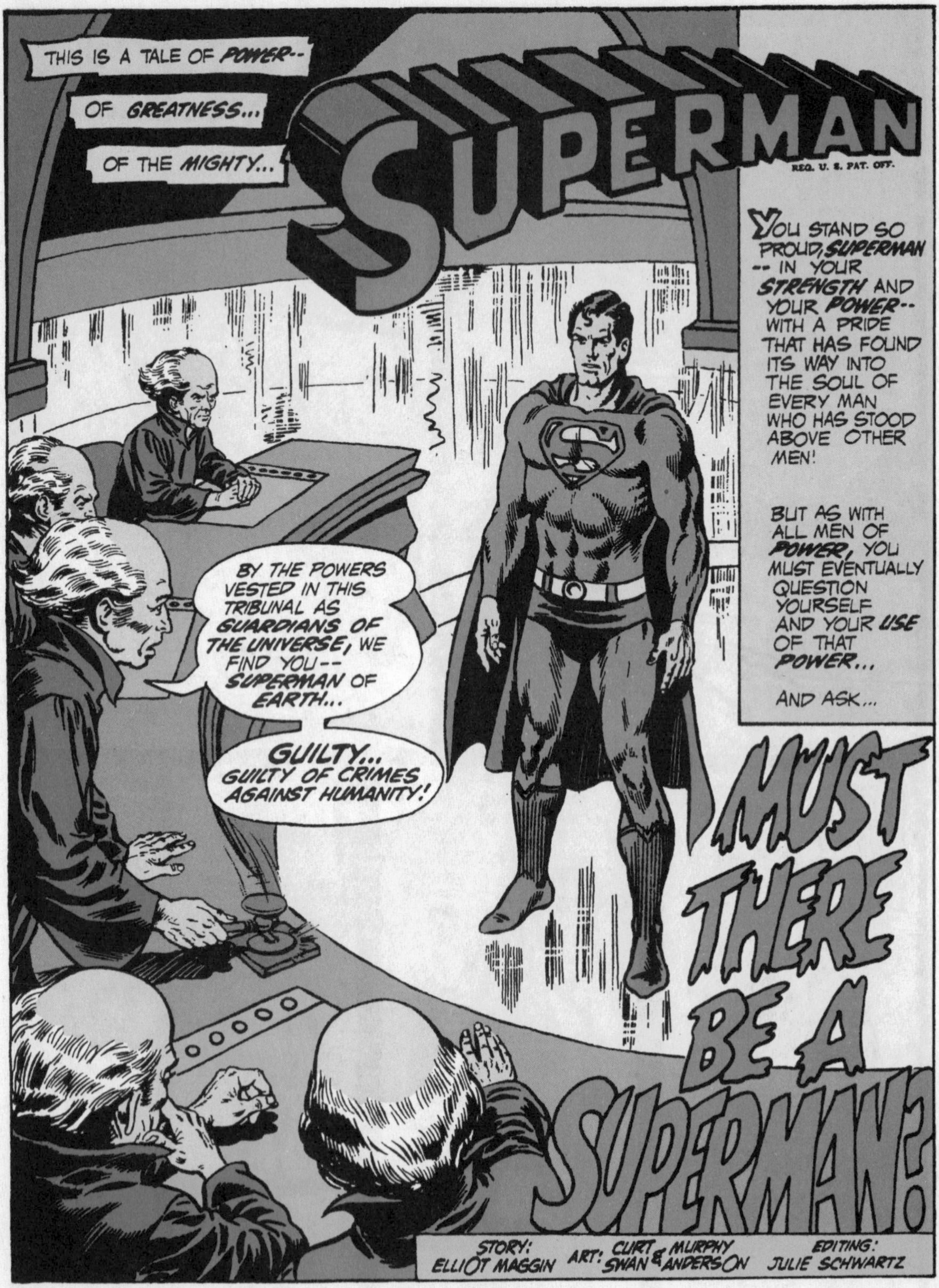
THIS IS A TALE OF POWER--
OF GREATNESS...
OF THE MIGHTY...
SUPERMAN
REG. U. S. PAT. OFF.
YOU STAND SO PROUD, SUPERMAN -- IN YOUR STRENGTH AND YOUR POWER-- WITH A PRIDE THAT HAS FOUND ITS WAY INTO THE SOUL OF EVERY MAN WHO HAS STOOD ABOVE OTHER MEN!
BUT AS WITH ALL MEN OF POWER, YOU MUST EVENTUALLY QUESTION YOURSELF AND YOUR USE OF THAT POWER...
AND ASK...
BY THE POWERS VESTED IN THIS TRIBUNAL AS GUARDIANS OF THE UNIVERSE, WE FIND YOU-- SUPERMAN OF EARTH...
GUILTY... GUILTY OF CRIMES AGAINST HUMANITY!
MUST THERE BE A SUPERMAN?
STORY: ELLIOT MAGGIN
ART: CURT SWAN & MURPHY ANDERSON
EDITING: JULIE SCHWARTZ

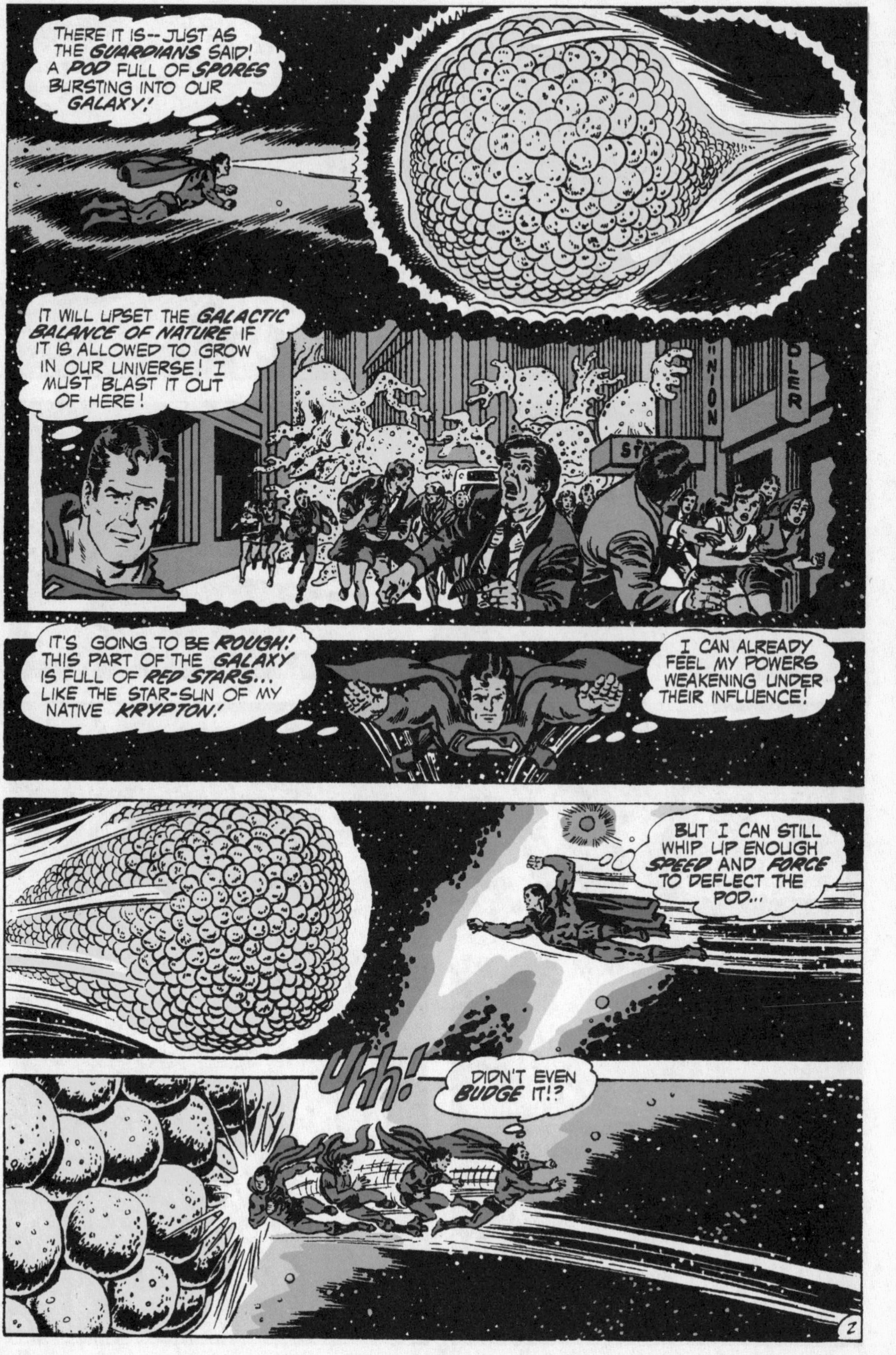
THERE IT IS-- JUST AS THE GUARDIANS SAID! A POD FULL OF SPORES BURSTING INTO OUR GALAXY!
IT WILL UPSET THE GALACTIC BALANCE OF NATURE IF IT IS ALLOWED TO GROW IN OUR UNIVERSE! I MUST BLAST IT OUT OF HERE!
UNION
DLER
IT'S GOING TO BE ROUGH! THIS PART OF THE GALAXY IS FULL OF RED STARS... LIKE THE STAR-SUN OF MY NATIVE KRYPTON!
I CAN ALREADY FEEL MY POWERS WEAKENING UNDER THEIR INFLUENCE!
BUT I CAN STILL WHIP UP ENOUGH SPEED AND FORCE TO DEFLECT THE POD...
UHH!
DIDN'T EVEN BUDGE IT!?
2

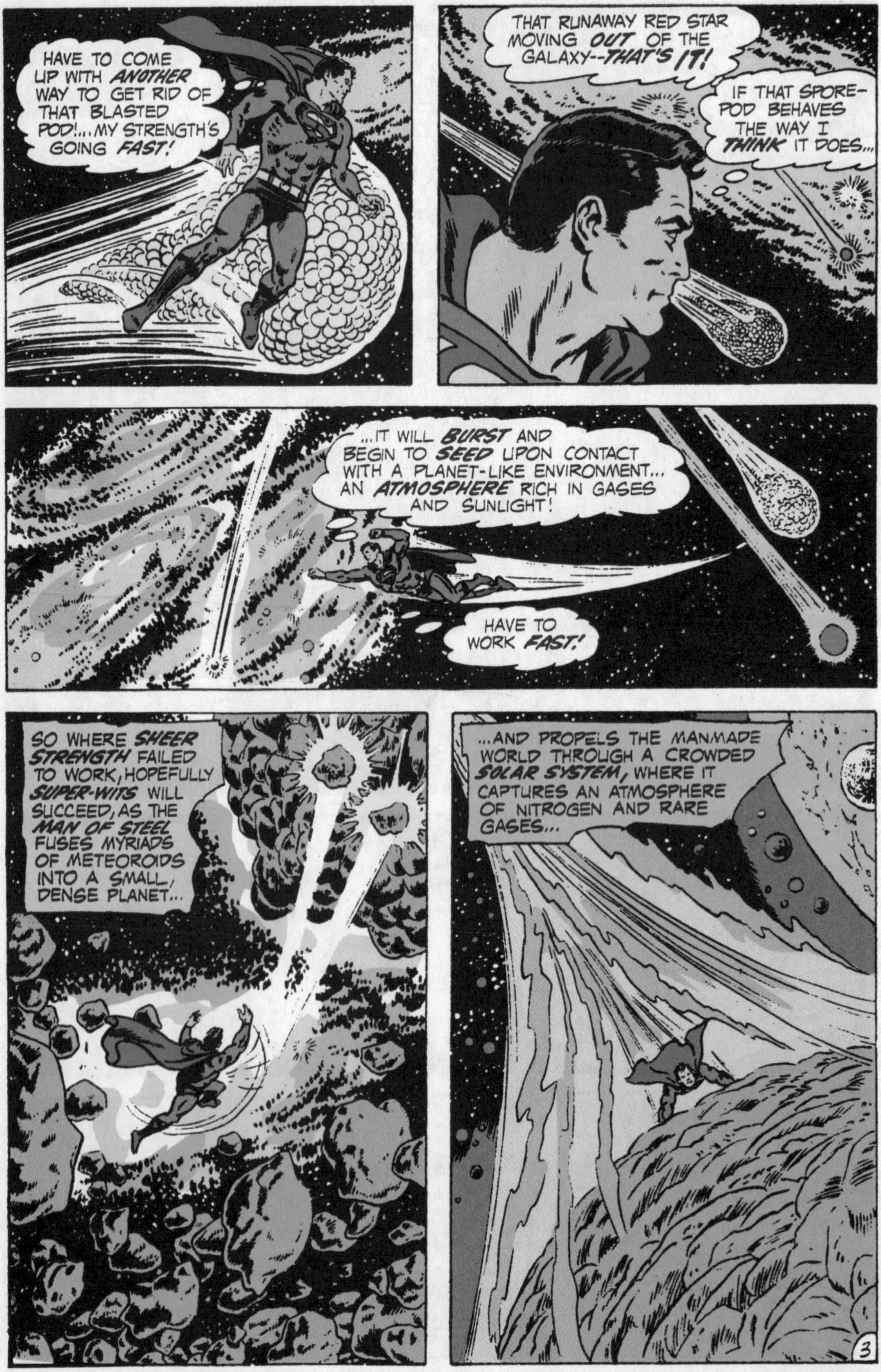
HAVE TO COME UP WITH ANOTHER WAY TO GET RID OF THAT BLASTED POD!... MY STRENGTH'S GOING FAST!
THAT RUNAWAY RED STAR MOVING OUT OF THE GALAXY--THAT'S IT!
IF THAT SPORE-POD BEHAVES THE WAY I THINK IT DOES...
...IT WILL BURST AND BEGIN TO SEED UPON CONTACT WITH A PLANET-LIKE ENVIRONMENT... AN ATMOSPHERE RICH IN GASES AND SUNLIGHT!
HAVE TO WORK FAST!
SO WHERE SHEER STRENGTH FAILED TO WORK, HOPEFULLY SUPER-WITS WILL SUCCEED, AS THE MAN OF STEEL FUSES MYRIADS OF METEOROIDS INTO A SMALL, DENSE PLANET...
...AND PROPELS THE MANMADE WORLD THROUGH A CROWDED SOLAR SYSTEM, WHERE IT CAPTURES AN ATMOSPHERE OF NITROGEN AND RARE GASES...
3

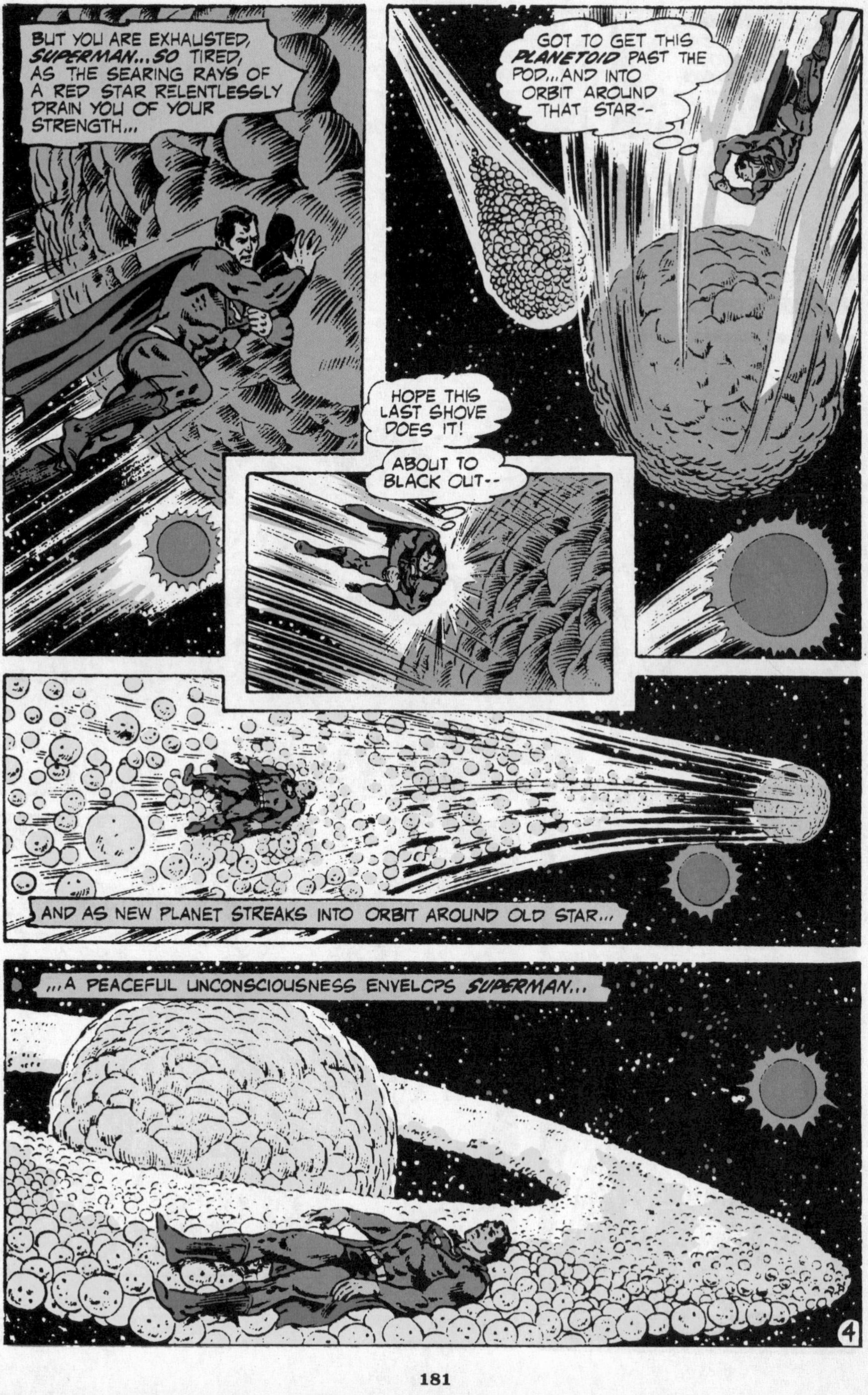
BUT YOU ARE EXHAUSTED, SUPERMAN... SO TIRED, AS THE SEARING RAYS OF A RED STAR RELENTLESSLY DRAIN YOU OF YOUR STRENGTH...
GOT TO GET THIS PLANETOID PAST THE POD... AND INTO ORBIT AROUND THAT STAR--
HOPE THIS LAST SHOVE DOES IT!
ABOUT TO BLACK OUT--
AND AS NEW PLANET STREAKS INTO ORBIT AROUND OLD STAR...
...A PEACEFUL UNCONSCIOUSNESS ENVELOPS SUPERMAN...
4

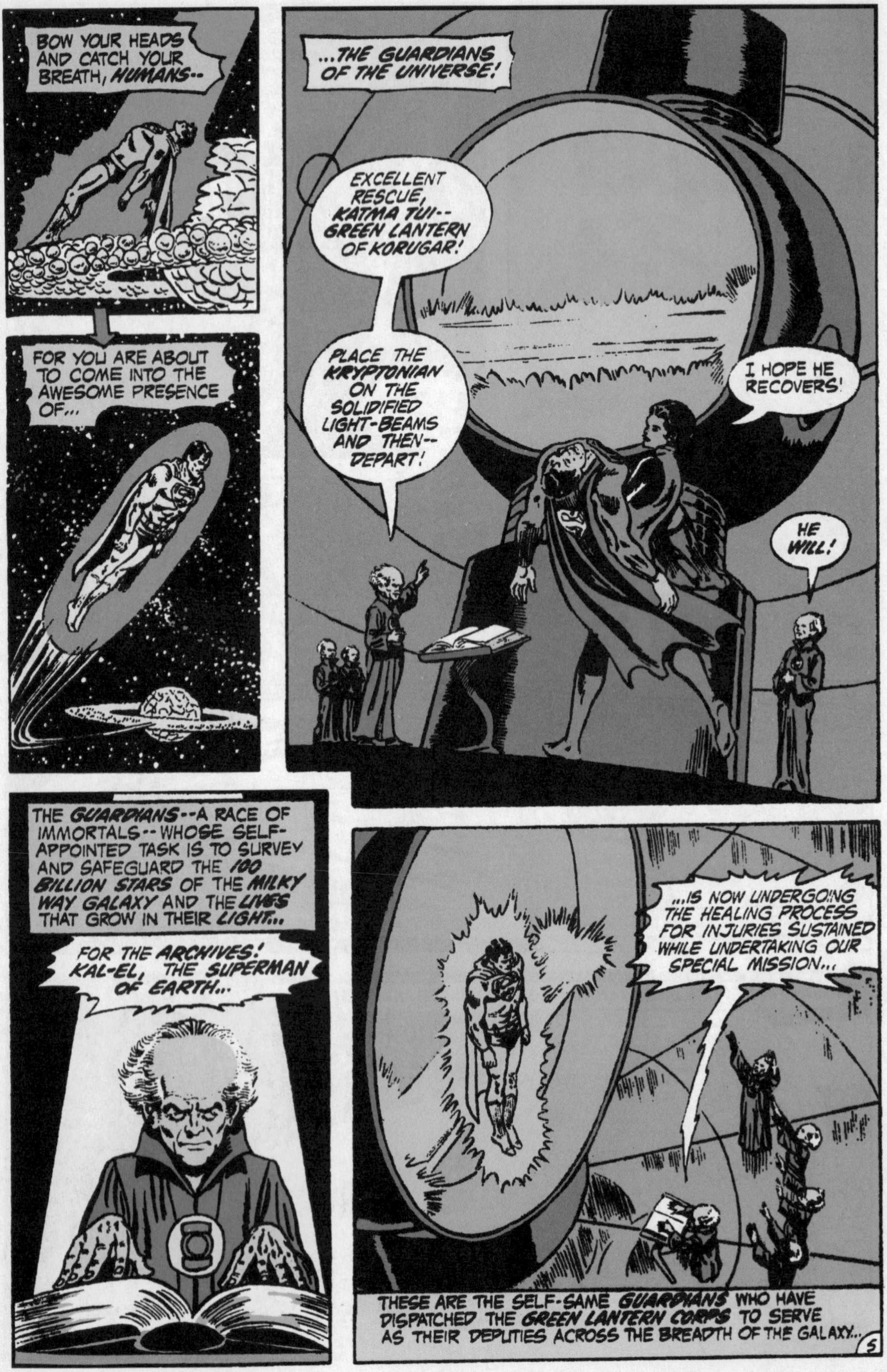
BOW YOUR HEADS AND CATCH YOUR BREATH, HUMANS--
FOR YOU ARE ABOUT TO COME INTO THE AWESOME PRESENCE OF...
...THE GUARDIANS OF THE UNIVERSE!
EXCELLENT RESCUE, KATMA TUI-- GREEN LANTERN OF KORUGAR!
PLACE THE KRYPTONIAN ON THE SOLIDIFIED LIGHT-BEAMS AND THEN-- DEPART!
I HOPE HE RECOVERS!
HE WILL!
THE GUARDIANS--A RACE OF IMMORTALS--WHOSE SELF-APPOINTED TASK IS TO SURVEY AND SAFEGUARD THE 100 BILLION STARS OF THE MILKY WAY GALAXY AND THE LIVES THAT GROW IN THEIR LIGHT...
FOR THE ARCHIVES! KAL-EL, THE SUPERMAN OF EARTH...
...IS NOW UNDERGOING THE HEALING PROCESS FOR INJURIES SUSTAINED WHILE UNDERTAKING OUR SPECIAL MISSION...
THESE ARE THE SELF-SAME GUARDIANS WHO HAVE DISPATCHED THE GREEN LANTERN CORPS TO SERVE AS THEIR DEPUTIES ACROSS THE BREADTH OF THE GALAXY...
5

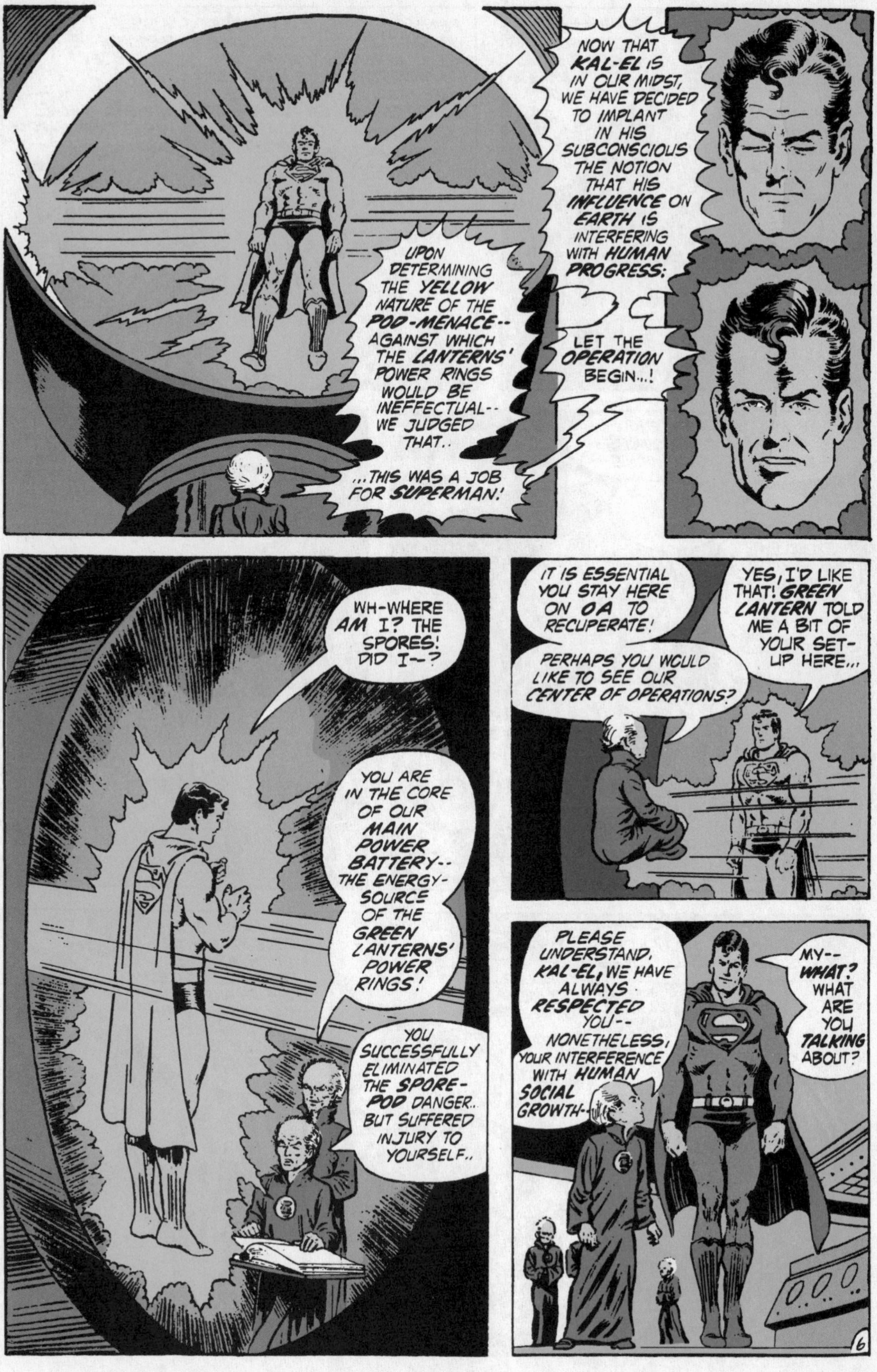
UPON DETERMINING THE YELLOW NATURE OF THE POD-MENACE-- AGAINST WHICH THE LANTERNS' POWER RINGS WOULD BE INEFFECTUAL-- WE JUDGED THAT..
...THIS WAS A JOB FOR SUPERMAN!
NOW THAT KAL-EL IS IN OUR MIDST, WE HAVE DECIDED TO IMPLANT IN HIS SUBCONSCIOUS THE NOTION THAT HIS INFLUENCE ON EARTH IS INTERFERING WITH HUMAN PROGRESS:
LET THE OPERATION BEGIN...!
WH-WHERE AM I? THE SPORES! DID I--?
YOU ARE IN THE CORE OF OUR MAIN POWER BATTERY-- THE ENERGY-SOURCE OF THE GREEN LANTERNS' POWER RINGS!
YOU SUCCESSFULLY ELIMINATED THE SPORE-POD DANGER.. BUT SUFFERED INJURY TO YOURSELF..
IT IS ESSENTIAL YOU STAY HERE ON OA TO RECUPERATE!
PERHAPS YOU WOULD LIKE TO SEE OUR CENTER OF OPERATIONS?
YES, I'D LIKE THAT! GREEN LANTERN TOLD ME A BIT OF YOUR SET-UP HERE...
PLEASE UNDERSTAND, KAL-EL, WE HAVE ALWAYS RESPECTED YOU-- NONETHELESS, YOUR INTERFERENCE WITH HUMAN SOCIAL GROWTH--
MY-- WHAT? WHAT ARE YOU TALKING ABOUT?
6

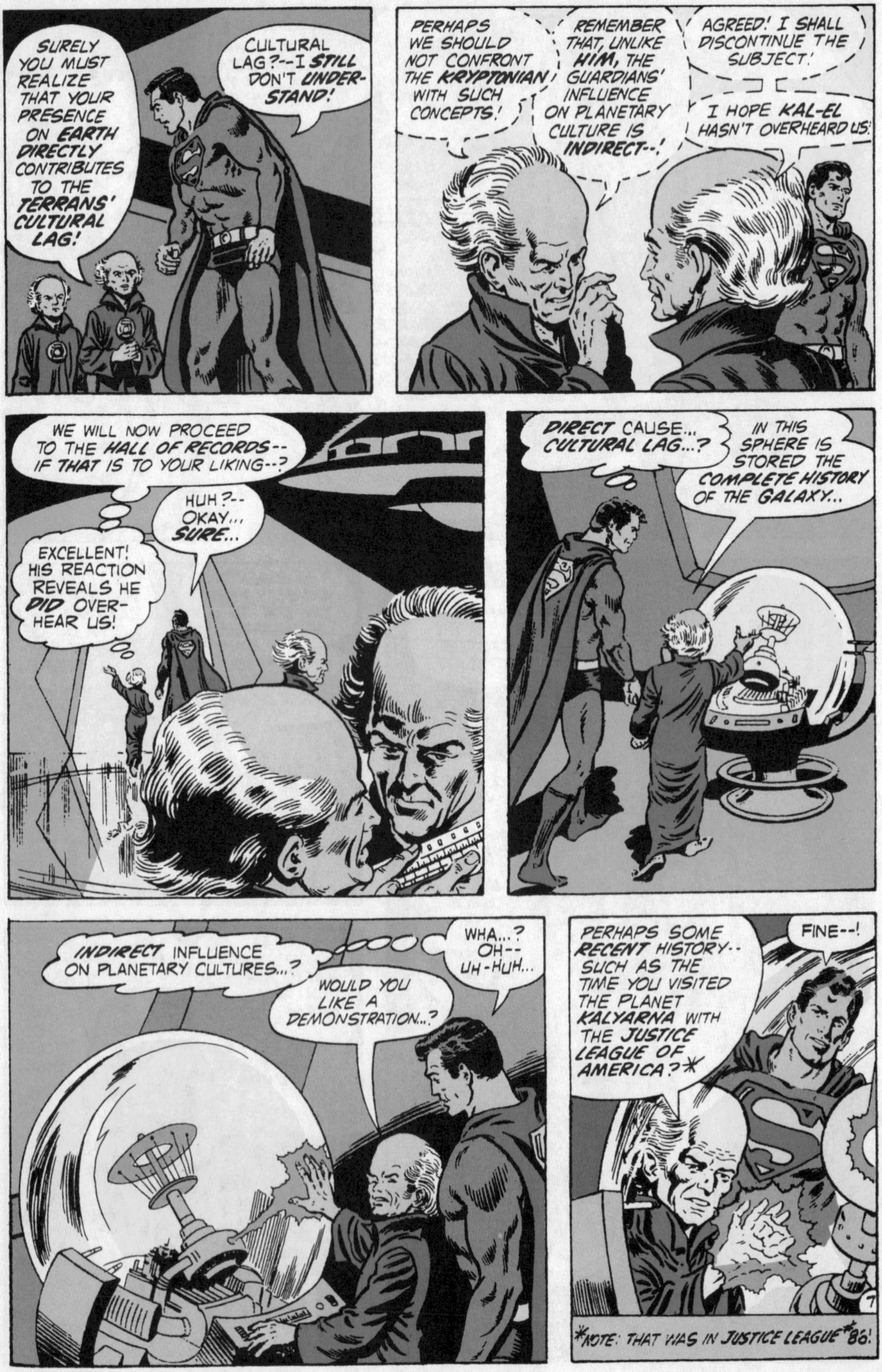
SURELY YOU MUST REALIZE THAT YOUR PRESENCE ON EARTH DIRECTLY CONTRIBUTES TO THE TERRANS' CULTURAL LAG!
CULTURAL LAG?--I STILL DON'T UNDERSTAND!
PERHAPS WE SHOULD NOT CONFRONT THE KRYPTONIAN WITH SUCH CONCEPTS!
REMEMBER THAT, UNLIKE HIM, THE GUARDIANS' INFLUENCE ON PLANETARY CULTURE IS INDIRECT--!
AGREED! I SHALL DISCONTINUE THE SUBJECT!
I HOPE KAL-EL HASN'T OVERHEARD US!
WE WILL NOW PROCEED TO THE HALL OF RECORDS--IF THAT IS TO YOUR LIKING--?
HUH?--OKAY... SURE...
EXCELLENT! HIS REACTION REVEALS HE DID OVERHEAR US!
DIRECT CAUSE... CULTURAL LAG...?
IN THIS SPHERE IS STORED THE COMPLETE HISTORY OF THE GALAXY...
INDIRECT INFLUENCE ON PLANETARY CULTURES...?
WHA...? OH--UH-HUH...
WOULD YOU LIKE A DEMONSTRATION...?
PERHAPS SOME RECENT HISTORY--SUCH AS THE TIME YOU VISITED THE PLANET KALYARNA WITH THE JUSTICE LEAGUE OF AMERICA?*
FINE--!
7
*NOTE: THAT WAS IN JUSTICE LEAGUE #86!

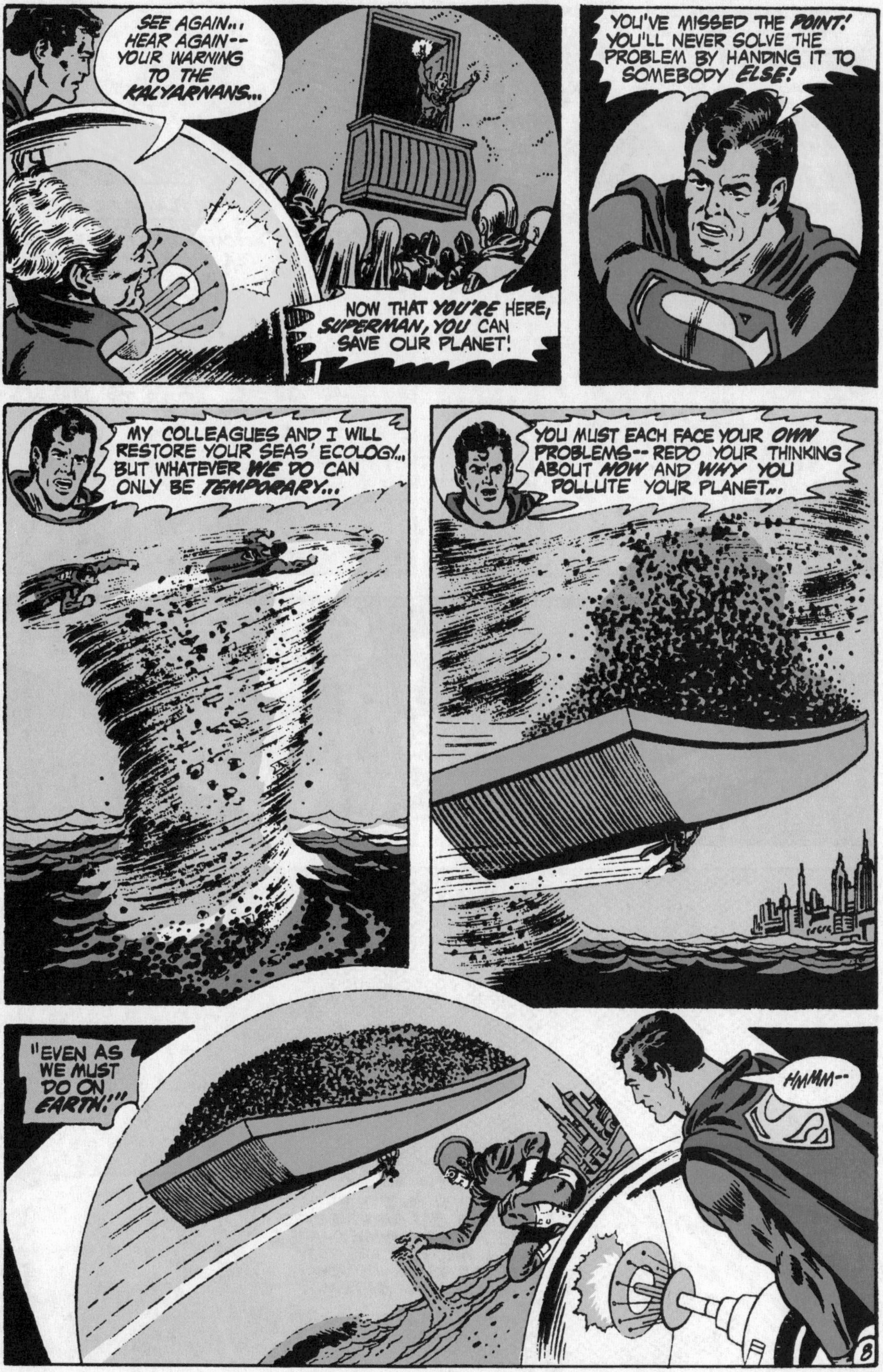

SEE AGAIN... HEAR AGAIN-- YOUR WARNING TO THE KALYARNANS...
NOW THAT YOU'RE HERE, SUPERMAN, YOU CAN SAVE OUR PLANET!
YOU'VE MISSED THE POINT! YOU'LL NEVER SOLVE THE PROBLEM BY HANDING IT TO SOMEBODY ELSE!
MY COLLEAGUES AND I WILL RESTORE YOUR SEAS' ECOLOGY... BUT WHATEVER WE DO CAN ONLY BE TEMPORARY...
YOU MUST EACH FACE YOUR OWN PROBLEMS-- REDO YOUR THINKING ABOUT HOW AND WHY YOU POLLUTE YOUR PLANET...
"EVEN AS WE MUST DO ON EARTH!"
HMMM--
8

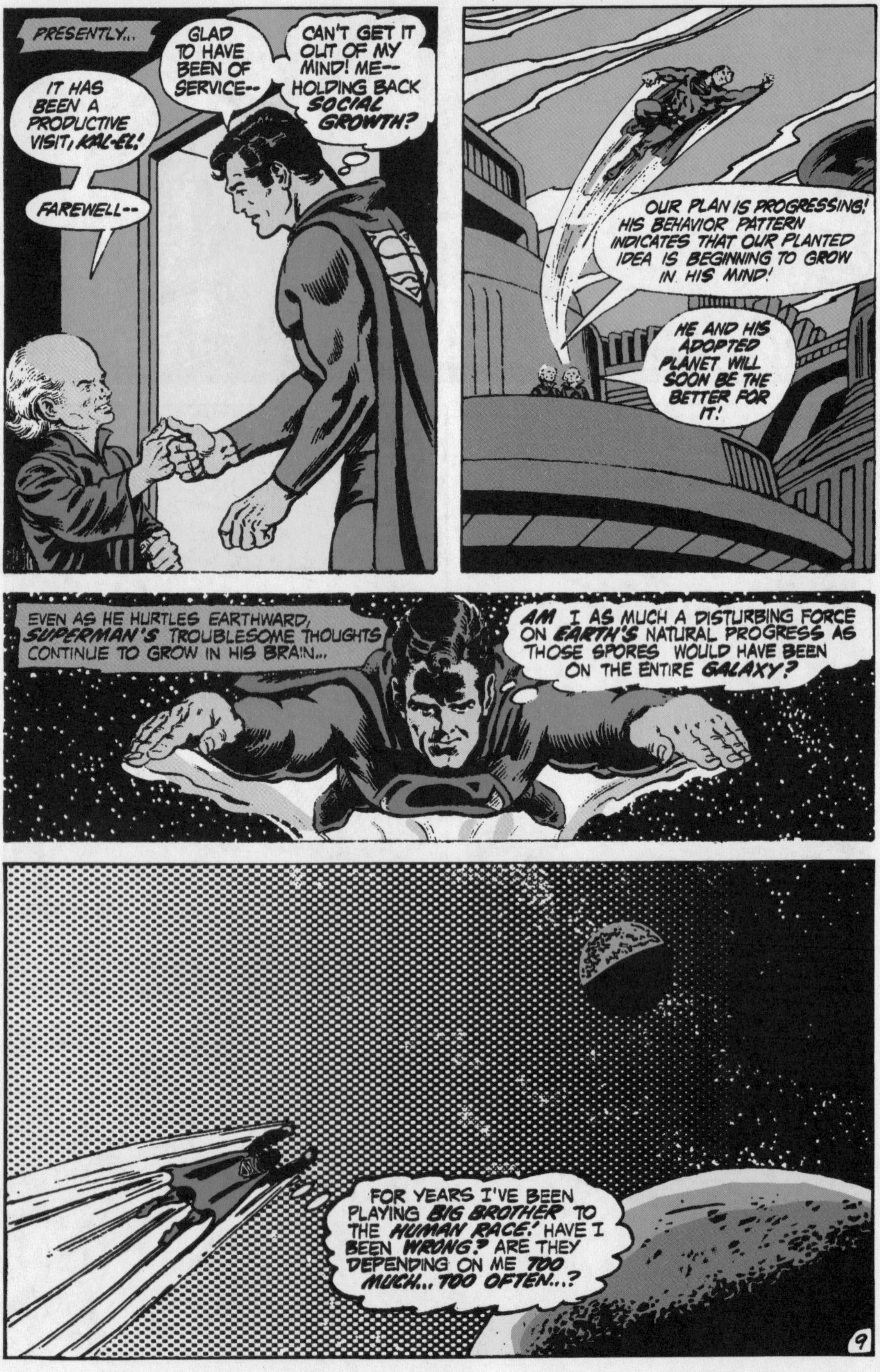
PRESENTLY...
IT HAS BEEN A PRODUCTIVE VISIT, KAL-EL!
GLAD TO HAVE BEEN OF SERVICE--
FAREWELL--
CAN'T GET IT OUT OF MY MIND! ME--HOLDING BACK SOCIAL GROWTH?
OUR PLAN IS PROGRESSING! HIS BEHAVIOR PATTERN INDICATES THAT OUR PLANTED IDEA IS BEGINNING TO GROW IN HIS MIND!
HE AND HIS ADOPTED PLANET WILL SOON BE THE BETTER FOR IT!
EVEN AS HE HURTLES EARTHWARD, SUPERMAN'S TROUBLESOME THOUGHTS CONTINUE TO GROW IN HIS BRAIN...
AM I AS MUCH A DISTURBING FORCE ON EARTH'S NATURAL PROGRESS AS THOSE SPORES WOULD HAVE BEEN ON THE ENTIRE GALAXY?
FOR YEARS I'VE BEEN PLAYING BIG BROTHER TO THE HUMAN RACE! HAVE I BEEN WRONG? ARE THEY DEPENDING ON ME TOO MUCH... TOO OFTEN...?
9

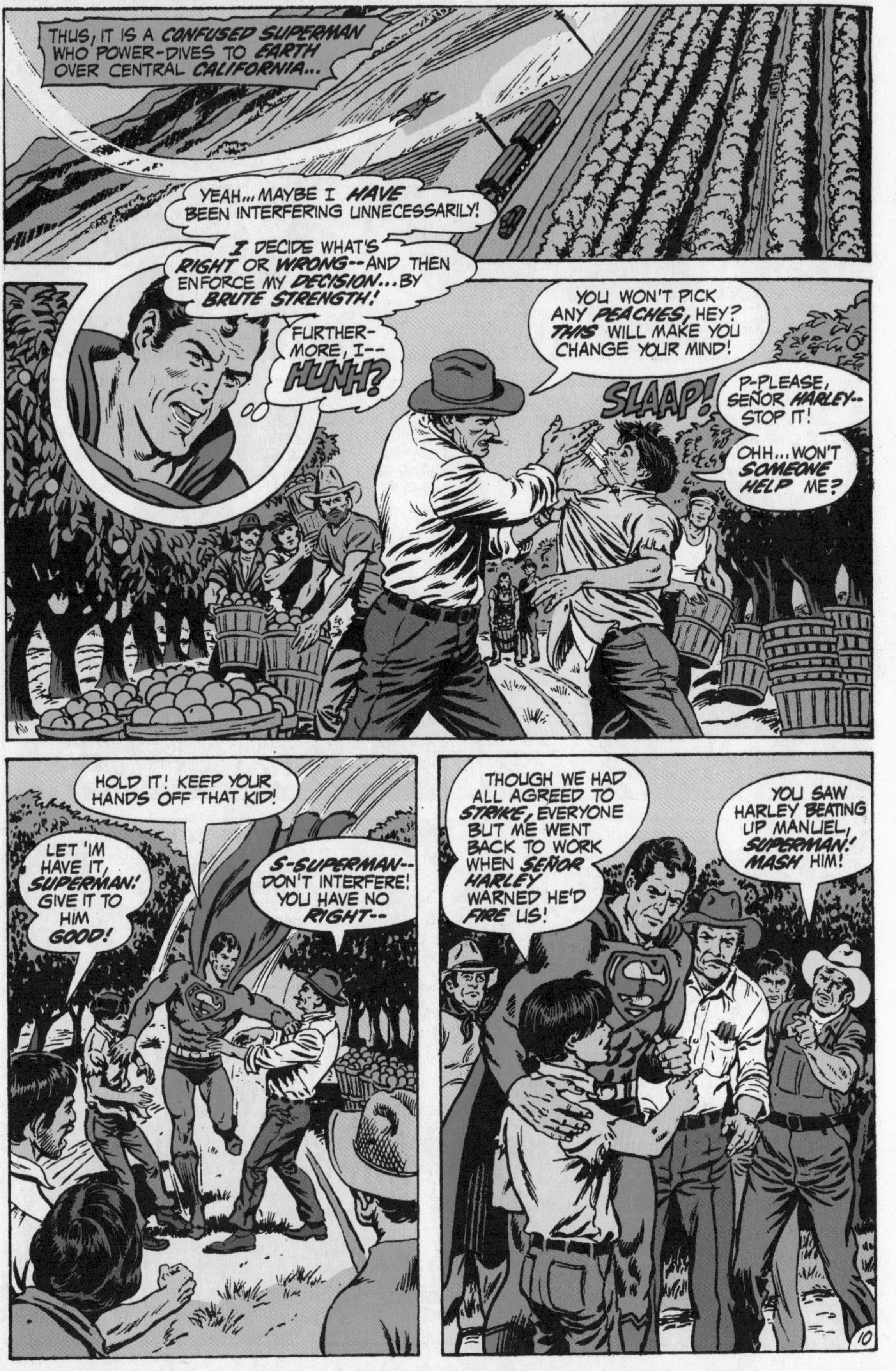
THUS, IT IS A CONFUSED SUPERMAN WHO POWER-DIVES TO EARTH OVER CENTRAL CALIFORNIA...
YEAH... MAYBE I HAVE BEEN INTERFERING UNNECESSARILY!
I DECIDE WHAT'S RIGHT OR WRONG--AND THEN ENFORCE MY DECISION... BY BRUTE STRENGTH!
FURTHER-MORE, I-- HUNH?
YOU WON'T PICK ANY PEACHES, HEY? THIS WILL MAKE YOU CHANGE YOUR MIND!
SLAAP!
P-PLEASE, SEÑOR HARLEY-- STOP IT!
OHH... WON'T SOMEONE HELP ME?
HOLD IT! KEEP YOUR HANDS OFF THAT KID!
LET 'IM HAVE IT, SUPERMAN! GIVE IT TO HIM GOOD!
S-SUPERMAN-- DON'T INTERFERE! YOU HAVE NO RIGHT--
THOUGH WE HAD ALL AGREED TO STRIKE, EVERYONE BUT ME WENT BACK TO WORK WHEN SEÑOR HARLEY WARNED HE'D FIRE US!
YOU SAW HARLEY BEATING UP MANUEL, SUPERMAN! MASH HIM!
10

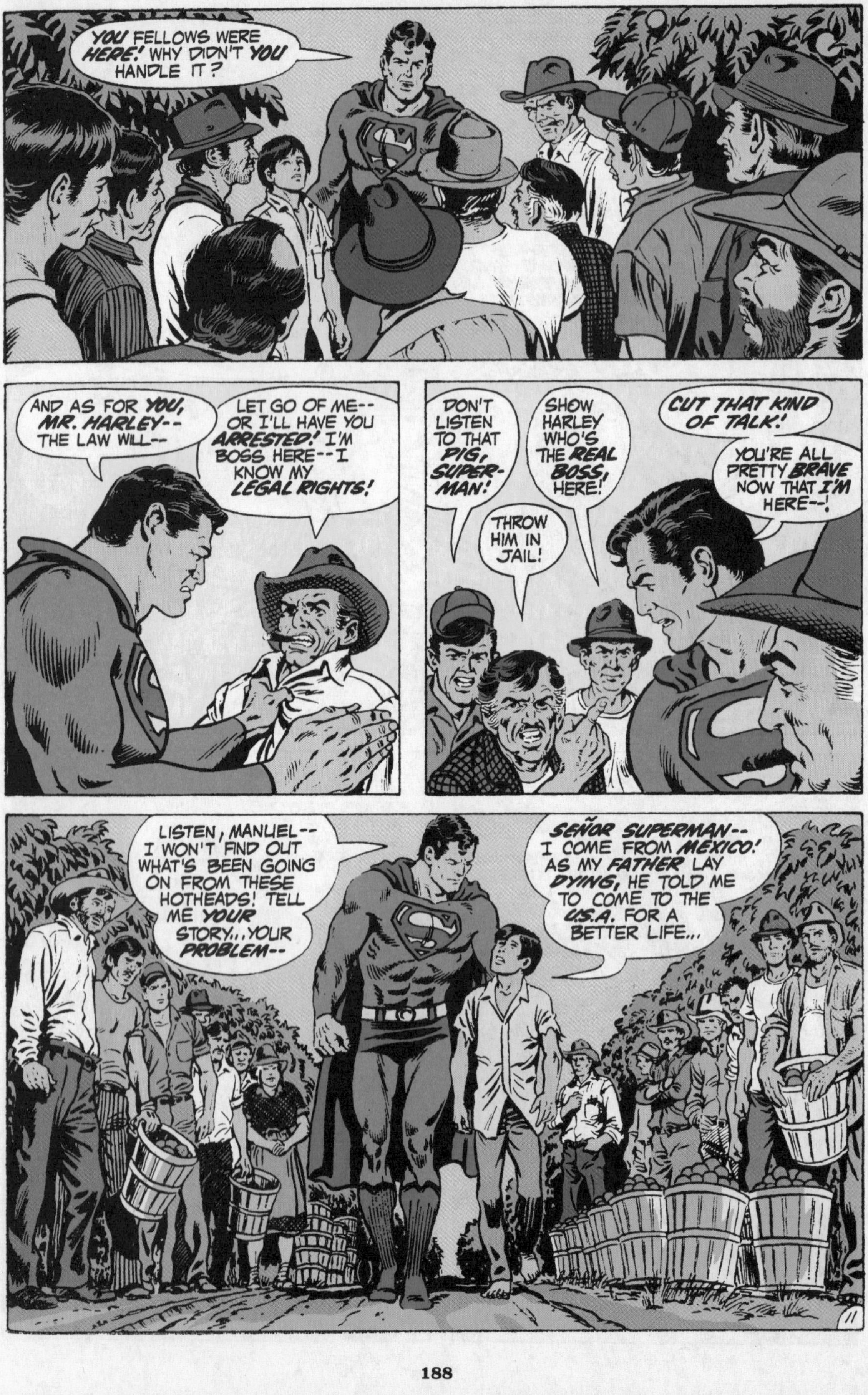
YOU FELLOWS WERE HERE! WHY DIDN'T YOU HANDLE IT?
AND AS FOR YOU, MR. HARLEY-- THE LAW WILL--
LET GO OF ME-- OR I'LL HAVE YOU ARRESTED! I'M BOSS HERE--I KNOW MY LEGAL RIGHTS!
DON'T LISTEN TO THAT PIG, SUPER-MAN!
SHOW HARLEY WHO'S THE REAL BOSS, HERE!
THROW HIM IN JAIL!
CUT THAT KIND OF TALK!
YOU'RE ALL PRETTY BRAVE NOW THAT I'M HERE--!
LISTEN, MANUEL-- I WON'T FIND OUT WHAT'S BEEN GOING ON FROM THESE HOTHEADS! TELL ME YOUR STORY... YOUR PROBLEM--
SEÑOR SUPERMAN-- I COME FROM MEXICO! AS MY FATHER LAY DYING, HE TOLD ME TO COME TO THE U.S.A. FOR A BETTER LIFE...
11

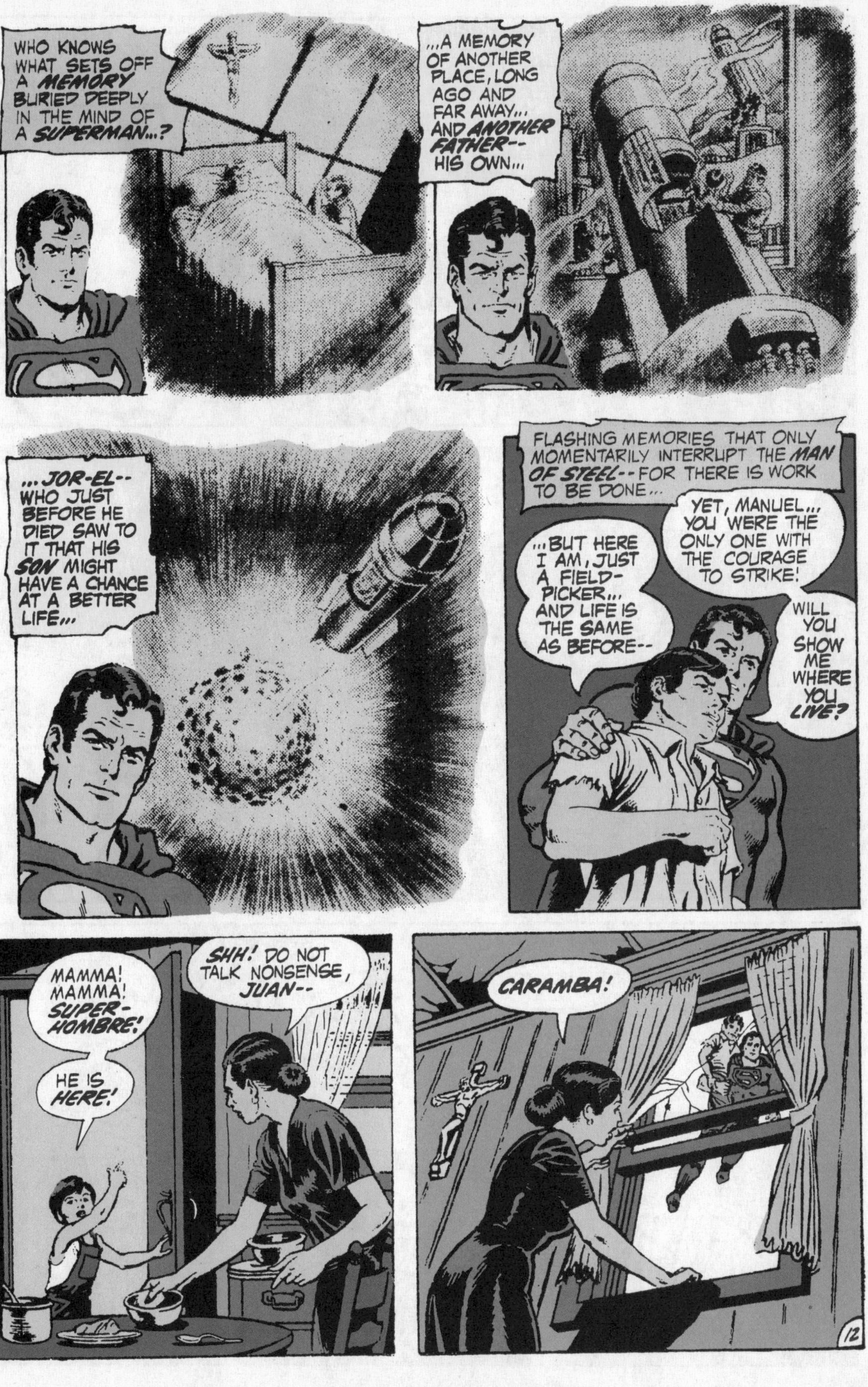
WHO KNOWS WHAT SETS OFF A MEMORY BURIED DEEPLY IN THE MIND OF A SUPERMAN...?
...A MEMORY OF ANOTHER PLACE, LONG AGO AND FAR AWAY... AND ANOTHER FATHER-- HIS OWN...
...JOR-EL-- WHO JUST BEFORE HE DIED SAW TO IT THAT HIS SON MIGHT HAVE A CHANCE AT A BETTER LIFE...
FLASHING MEMORIES THAT ONLY MOMENTARILY INTERRUPT THE MAN OF STEEL-- FOR THERE IS WORK TO BE DONE...
...BUT HERE I AM, JUST A FIELD-PICKER... AND LIFE IS THE SAME AS BEFORE--
YET, MANUEL... YOU WERE THE ONLY ONE WITH THE COURAGE TO STRIKE!
WILL YOU SHOW ME WHERE YOU LIVE?
MAMMA! MAMMA! SUPER-HOMBRE!
HE IS HERE!
SHH! DO NOT TALK NONSENSE, JUAN--
CARAMBA!
12

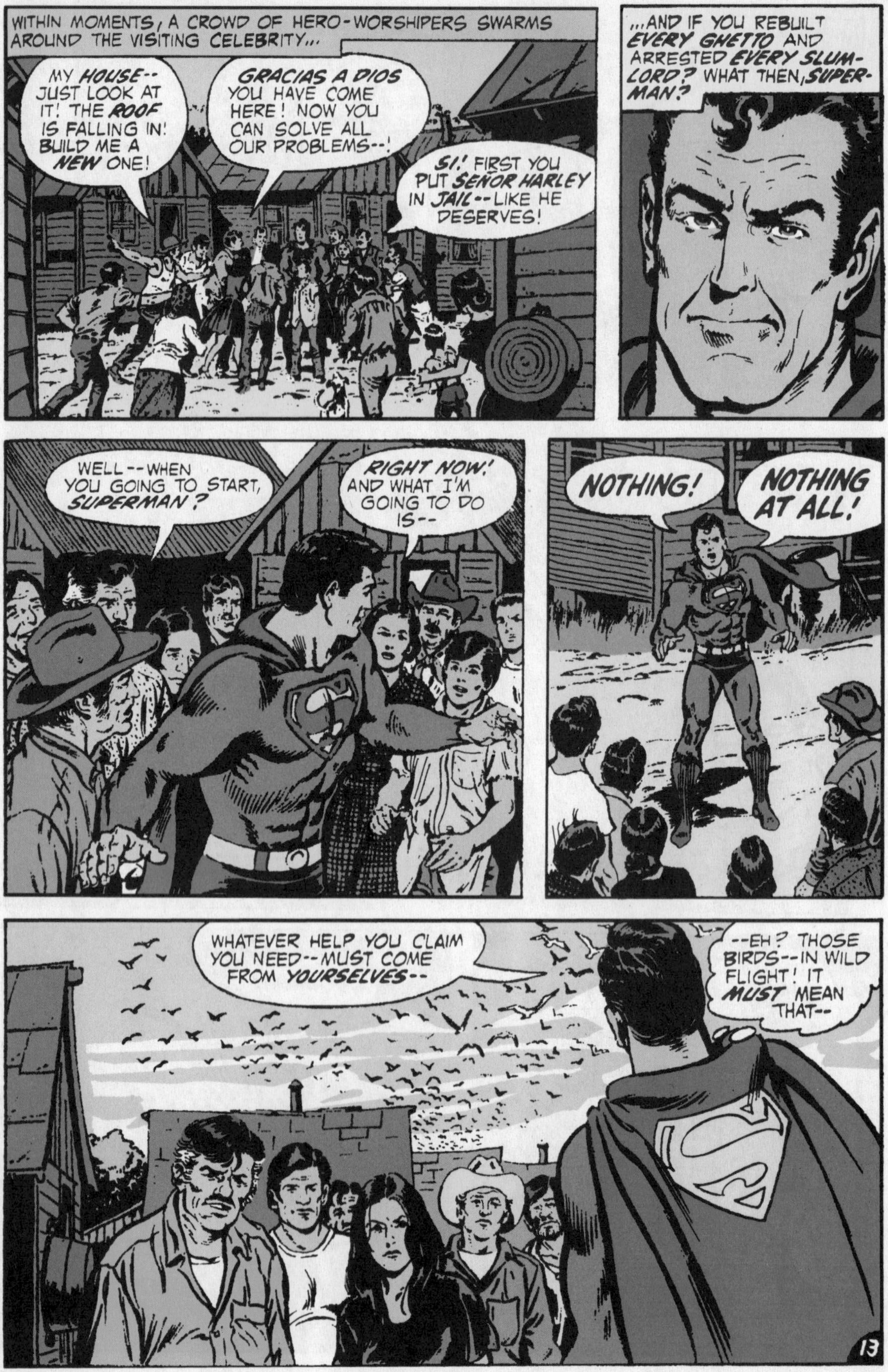
WITHIN MOMENTS, A CROWD OF HERO-WORSHIPERS SWARMS AROUND THE VISITING CELEBRITY...
MY HOUSE-- JUST LOOK AT IT! THE ROOF IS FALLING IN! BUILD ME A NEW ONE!
GRACIAS A DIOS YOU HAVE COME HERE! NOW YOU CAN SOLVE ALL OUR PROBLEMS--!
SI! FIRST YOU PUT SEÑOR HARLEY IN JAIL--LIKE HE DESERVES!
...AND IF YOU REBUILT EVERY GHETTO AND ARRESTED EVERY SLUMLORD? WHAT THEN, SUPERMAN?
WELL--WHEN YOU GOING TO START, SUPERMAN?
RIGHT NOW! AND WHAT I'M GOING TO DO IS--
NOTHING!
NOTHING AT ALL!
WHATEVER HELP YOU CLAIM YOU NEED--MUST COME FROM YOURSELVES--
--EH? THOSE BIRDS--IN WILD FLIGHT! IT MUST MEAN THAT--
13

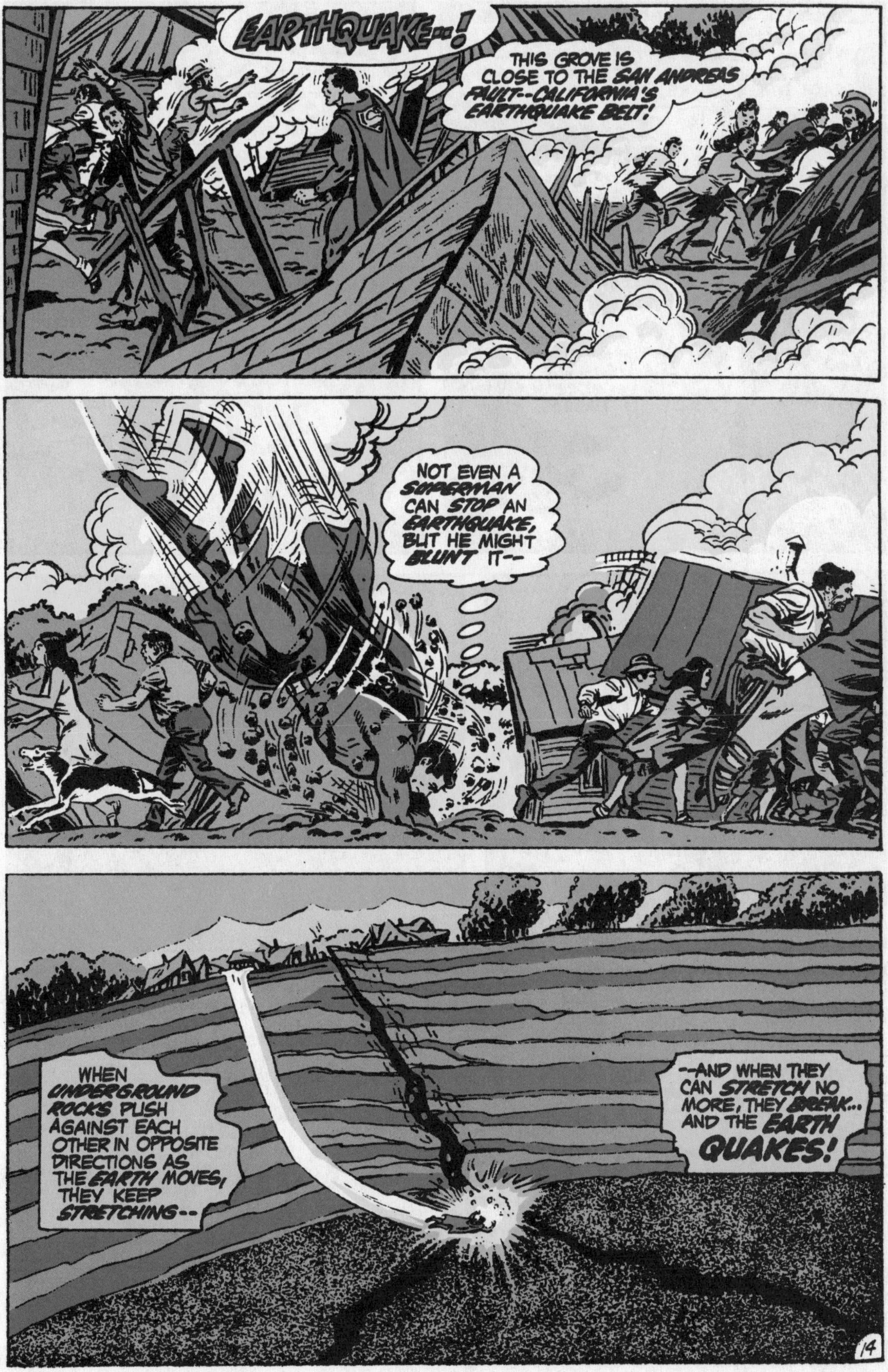
EARTHQUAKE--!
THIS GROVE IS CLOSE TO THE SAN ANDREAS FAULT--CALIFORNIA'S EARTHQUAKE BELT!
NOT EVEN A SUPERMAN CAN STOP AN EARTHQUAKE, BUT HE MIGHT BLUNT IT--
WHEN UNDERGROUND ROCKS PUSH AGAINST EACH OTHER IN OPPOSITE DIRECTIONS AS THE EARTH MOVES, THEY KEEP STRETCHING--
--AND WHEN THEY CAN STRETCH NO MORE, THEY BREAK... AND THE EARTH QUAKES!
14

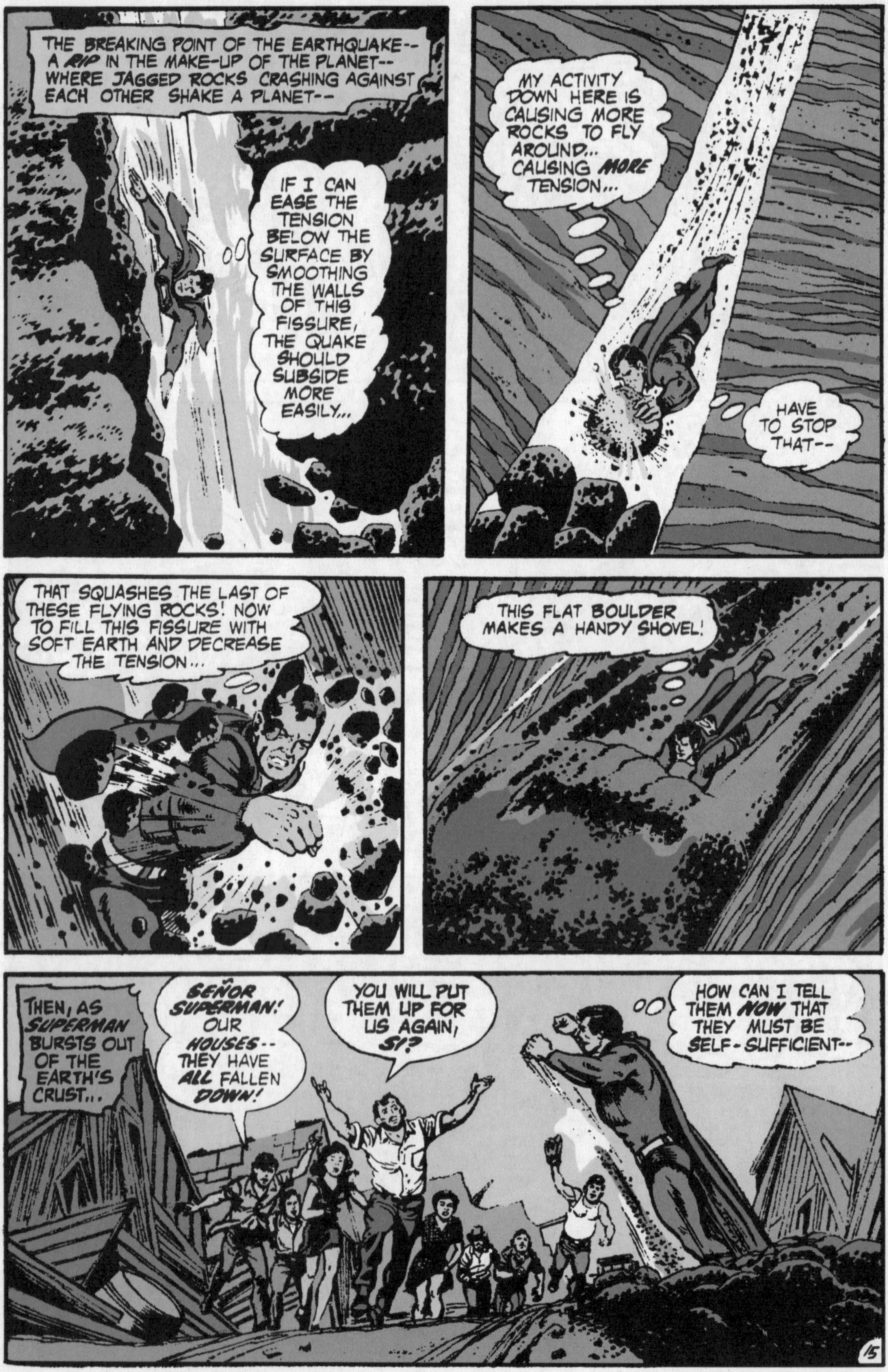

THE BREAKING POINT OF THE EARTHQUAKE-- A RIP IN THE MAKE-UP OF THE PLANET-- WHERE JAGGED ROCKS CRASHING AGAINST EACH OTHER SHAKE A PLANET--
IF I CAN EASE THE TENSION BELOW THE SURFACE BY SMOOTHING THE WALLS OF THIS FISSURE, THE QUAKE SHOULD SUBSIDE MORE EASILY...
MY ACTIVITY DOWN HERE IS CAUSING MORE ROCKS TO FLY AROUND... CAUSING MORE TENSION...
HAVE TO STOP THAT--
THAT SQUASHES THE LAST OF THESE FLYING ROCKS! NOW TO FILL THIS FISSURE WITH SOFT EARTH AND DECREASE THE TENSION...
THIS FLAT BOULDER MAKES A HANDY SHOVEL!
THEN, AS SUPERMAN BURSTS OUT OF THE EARTH'S CRUST...
SEÑOR SUPERMAN! OUR HOUSES-- THEY HAVE ALL FALLEN DOWN!
YOU WILL PUT THEM UP FOR US AGAIN, SI?
HOW CAN I TELL THEM NOW THAT THEY MUST BE SELF-SUFFICIENT--
15

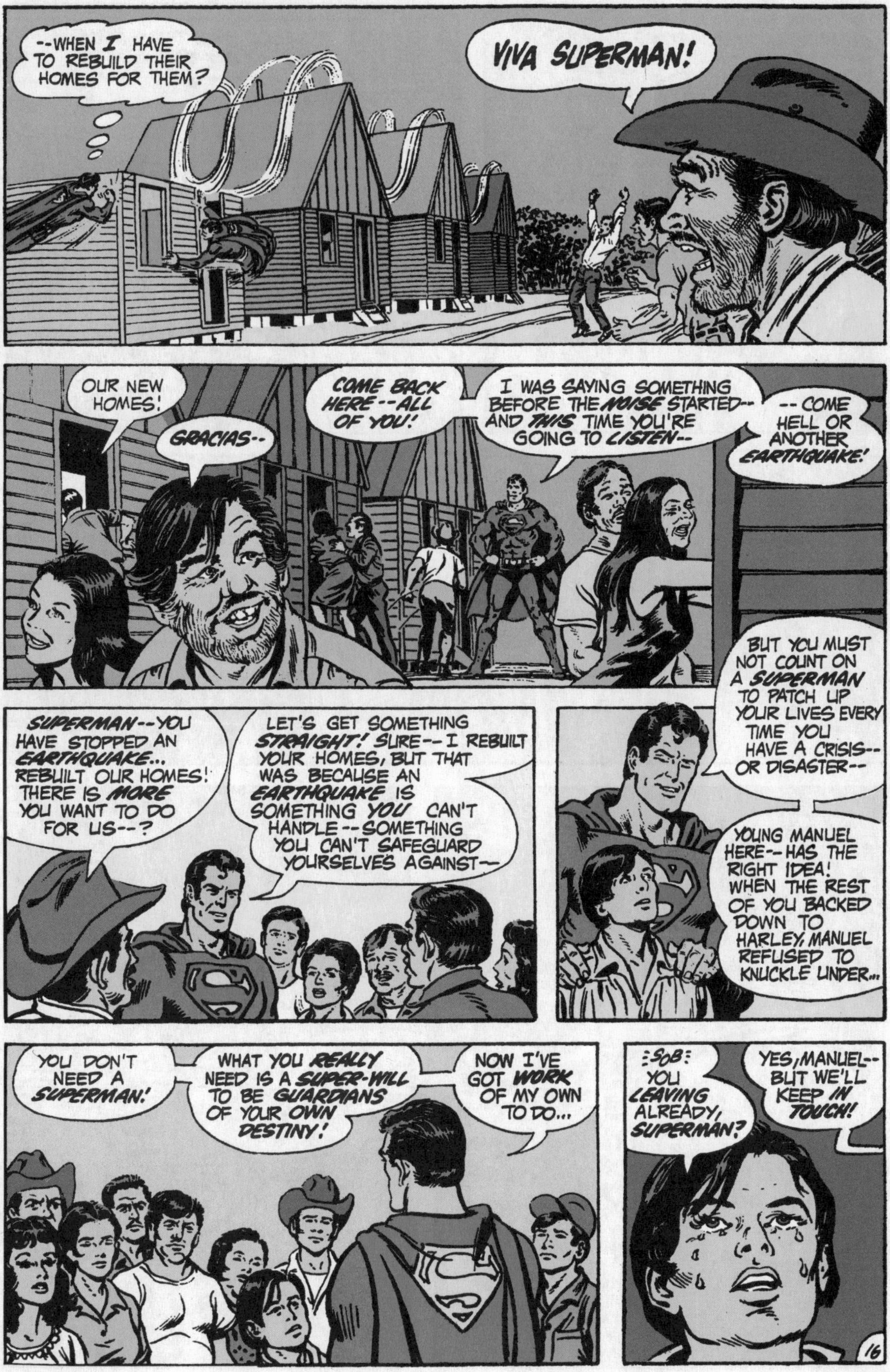
--WHEN I HAVE TO REBUILD THEIR HOMES FOR THEM?
VIVA SUPERMAN!
OUR NEW HOMES!
GRACIAS--
COME BACK HERE--ALL OF YOU!
I WAS SAYING SOMETHING BEFORE THE NOISE STARTED-- AND THIS TIME YOU'RE GOING TO LISTEN--
--COME HELL OR ANOTHER EARTHQUAKE!
SUPERMAN--YOU HAVE STOPPED AN EARTHQUAKE... REBUILT OUR HOMES! THERE IS MORE YOU WANT TO DO FOR US--?
LET'S GET SOMETHING STRAIGHT! SURE--I REBUILT YOUR HOMES, BUT THAT WAS BECAUSE AN EARTHQUAKE IS SOMETHING YOU CAN'T HANDLE--SOMETHING YOU CAN'T SAFEGUARD YOURSELVES AGAINST--
BUT YOU MUST NOT COUNT ON A SUPERMAN TO PATCH UP YOUR LIVES EVERY TIME YOU HAVE A CRISIS--OR DISASTER--
YOUNG MANUEL HERE--HAS THE RIGHT IDEA! WHEN THE REST OF YOU BACKED DOWN TO HARLEY, MANUEL REFUSED TO KNUCKLE UNDER...
YOU DON'T NEED A SUPERMAN!
WHAT YOU REALLY NEED IS A SUPER-WILL TO BE GUARDIANS OF YOUR OWN DESTINY!
NOW I'VE GOT WORK OF MY OWN TO DO...
:SOB: YOU LEAVING ALREADY, SUPERMAN?
YES, MANUEL-- BUT WE'LL KEEP IN TOUCH!
16

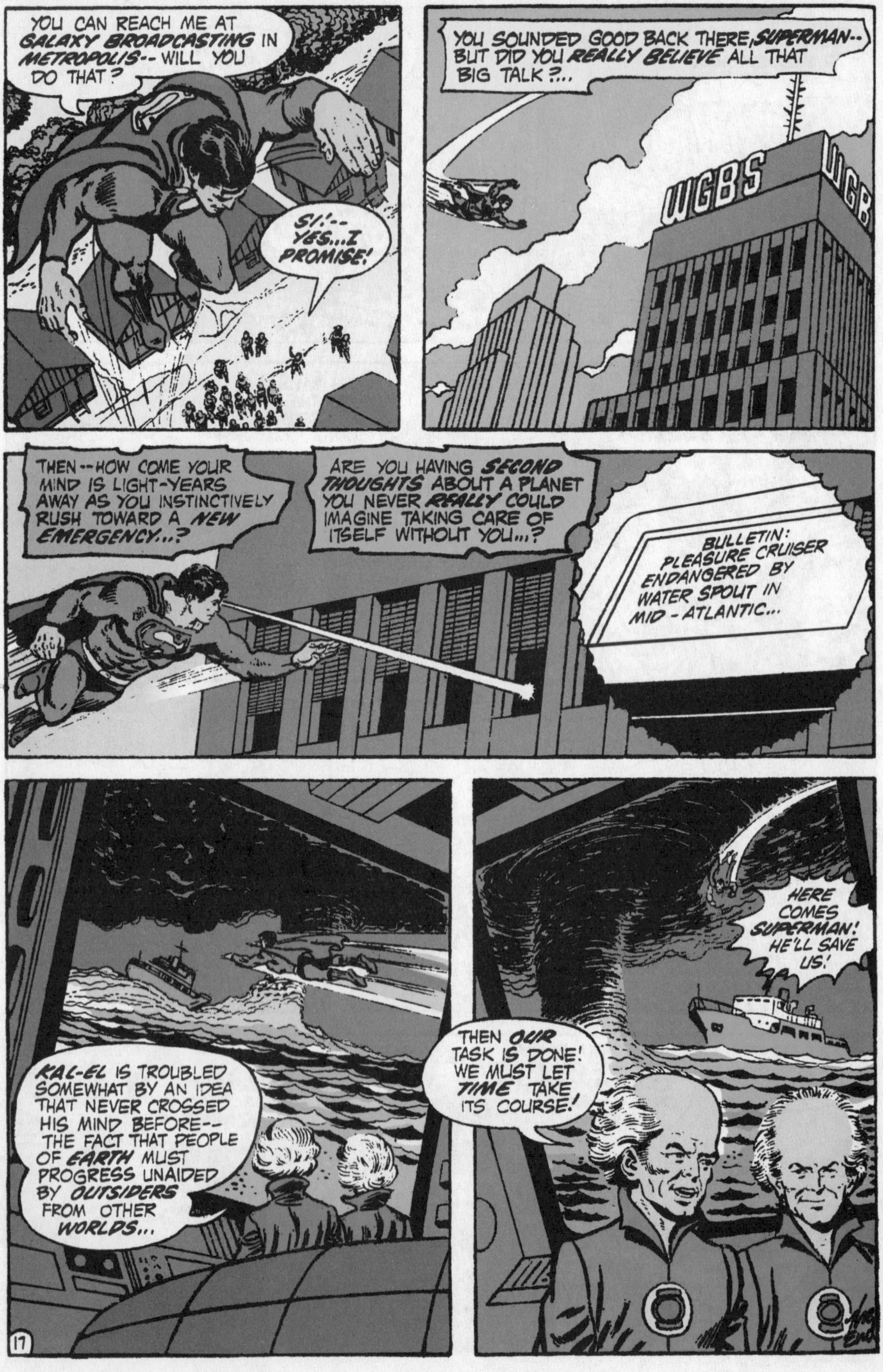
YOU CAN REACH ME AT GALAXY BROADCASTING IN METROPOLIS-- WILL YOU DO THAT?
SI!-- YES...I PROMISE!
YOU SOUNDED GOOD BACK THERE, SUPERMAN-- BUT DID YOU REALLY BELIEVE ALL THAT BIG TALK?...
WGBS
THEN--HOW COME YOUR MIND IS LIGHT-YEARS AWAY AS YOU INSTINCTIVELY RUSH TOWARD A NEW EMERGENCY...?
ARE YOU HAVING SECOND THOUGHTS ABOUT A PLANET YOU NEVER REALLY COULD IMAGINE TAKING CARE OF ITSELF WITHOUT YOU...?
BULLETIN: PLEASURE CRUISER ENDANGERED BY WATER SPOUT IN MID-ATLANTIC...
KAL-EL IS TROUBLED SOMEWHAT BY AN IDEA THAT NEVER CROSSED HIS MIND BEFORE-- THE FACT THAT PEOPLE OF EARTH MUST PROGRESS UNAIDED BY OUTSIDERS FROM OTHER WORLDS...
17
HERE COMES SUPERMAN! HE'LL SAVE US!
THEN OUR TASK IS DONE! WE MUST LET TIME TAKE ITS COURSE!

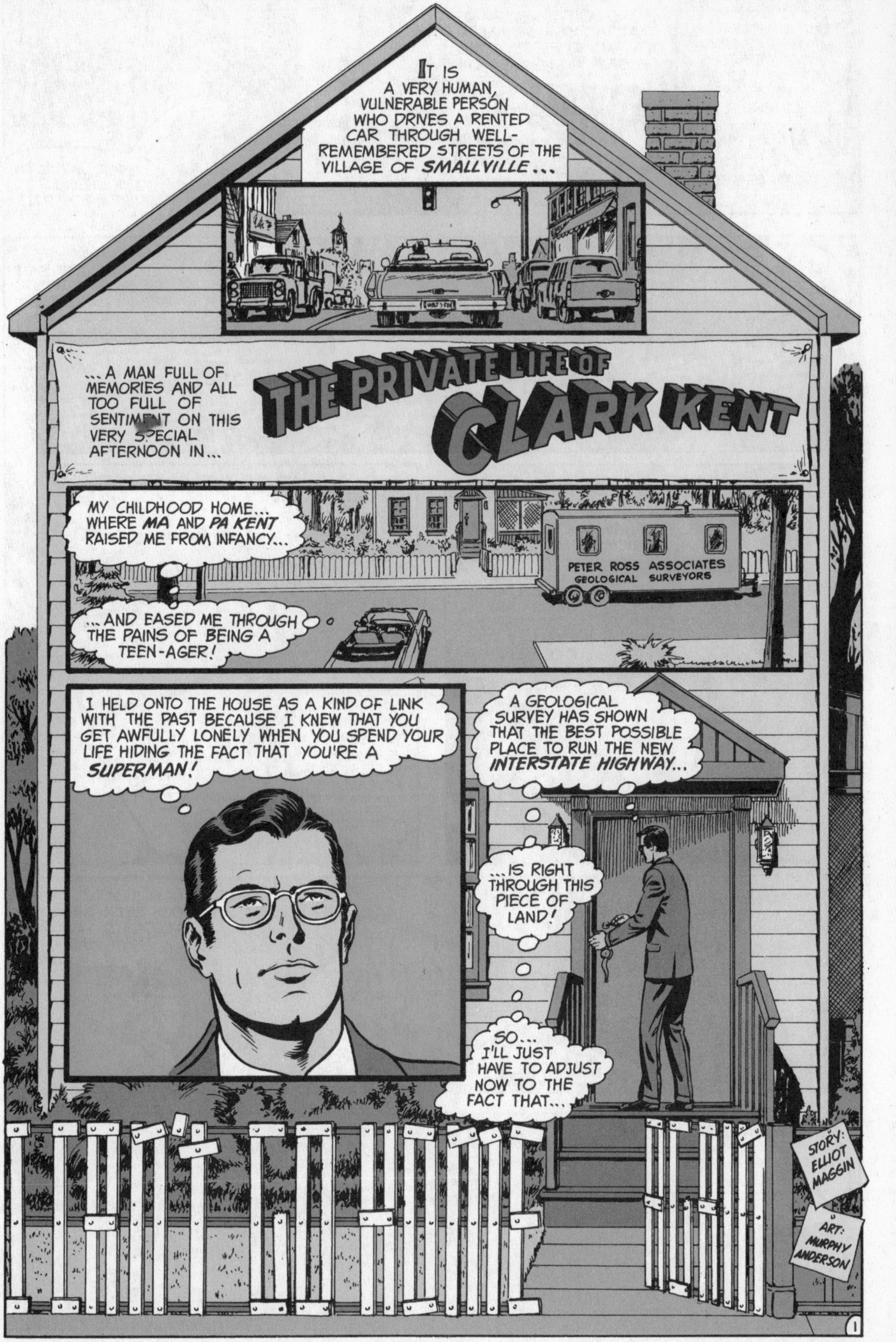

IT IS A VERY HUMAN, VULNERABLE PERSON WHO DRIVES A RENTED CAR THROUGH WELL-REMEMBERED STREETS OF THE VILLAGE OF SMALLVILLE...
...A MAN FULL OF MEMORIES AND ALL TOO FULL OF SENTIMENT ON THIS VERY SPECIAL AFTERNOON IN...
THE PRIVATE LIFE OF CLARK KENT
MY CHILDHOOD HOME... WHERE MA AND PA KENT RAISED ME FROM INFANCY...
PETER ROSS ASSOCIATES GEOLOGICAL SURVEYORS
...AND EASED ME THROUGH THE PAINS OF BEING A TEEN-AGER!
I HELD ONTO THE HOUSE AS A KIND OF LINK WITH THE PAST BECAUSE I KNEW THAT YOU GET AWFULLY LONELY WHEN YOU SPEND YOUR LIFE HIDING THE FACT THAT YOU'RE A SUPERMAN!
A GEOLOGICAL SURVEY HAS SHOWN THAT THE BEST POSSIBLE PLACE TO RUN THE NEW INTERSTATE HIGHWAY...
...IS RIGHT THROUGH THIS PIECE OF LAND!
SO... I'LL JUST HAVE TO ADJUST NOW TO THE FACT THAT...
STORY: ELLIOT MAGGIN
ART: MURPHY ANDERSON
1

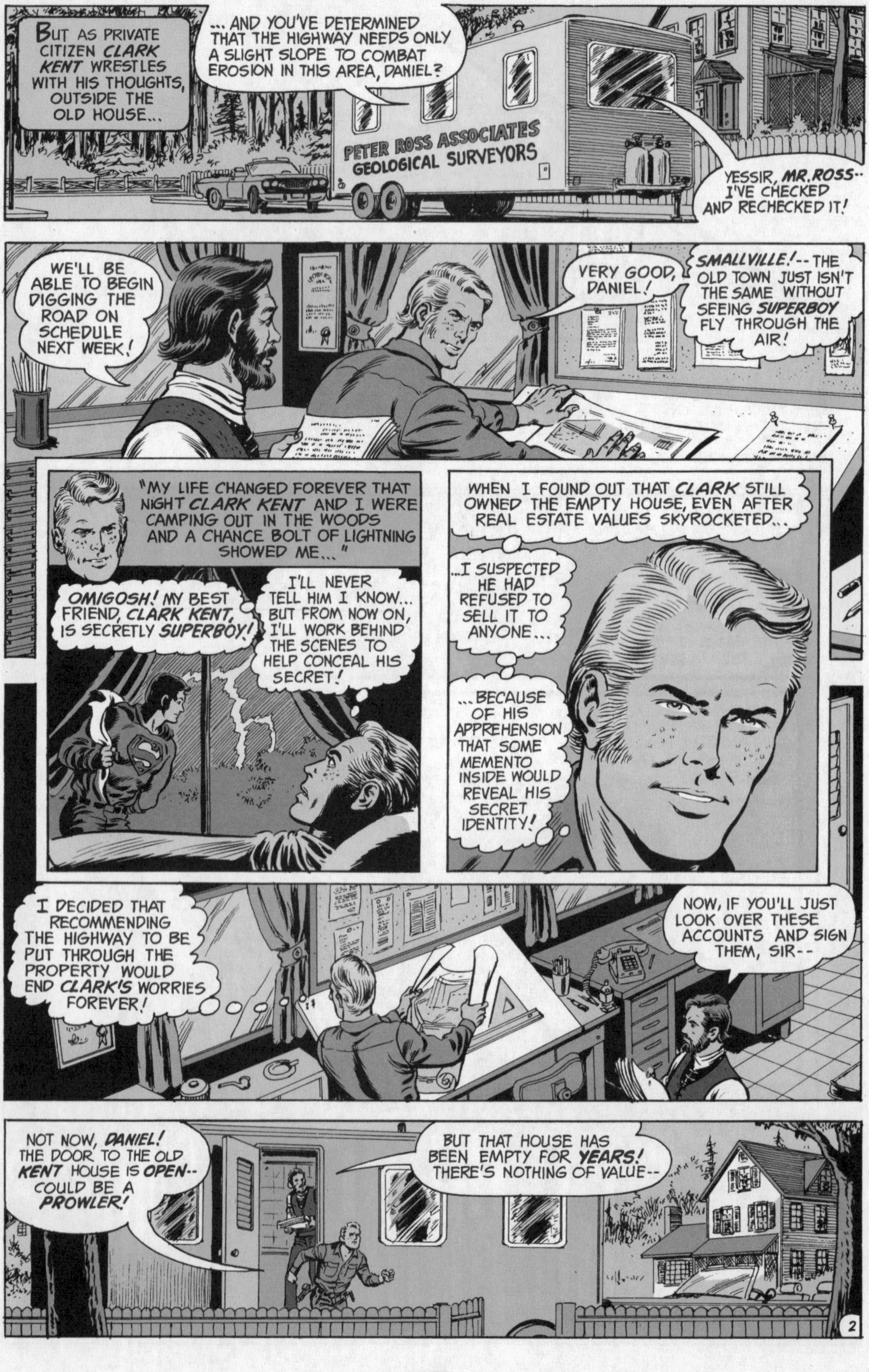
BUT AS PRIVATE CITIZEN CLARK KENT WRESTLES WITH HIS THOUGHTS, OUTSIDE THE OLD HOUSE...
...AND YOU'VE DETERMINED THAT THE HIGHWAY NEEDS ONLY A SLIGHT SLOPE TO COMBAT EROSION IN THIS AREA, DANIEL?
PETER ROSS ASSOCIATES GEOLOGICAL SURVEYORS
YESSIR, MR. ROSS-- I'VE CHECKED AND RECHECKED IT!
WE'LL BE ABLE TO BEGIN DIGGING THE ROAD ON SCHEDULE NEXT WEEK!
VERY GOOD, DANIEL!
SMALLVILLE!--THE OLD TOWN JUST ISN'T THE SAME WITHOUT SEEING SUPERBOY FLY THROUGH THE AIR!
"MY LIFE CHANGED FOREVER THAT NIGHT CLARK KENT AND I WERE CAMPING OUT IN THE WOODS AND A CHANCE BOLT OF LIGHTNING SHOWED ME..."
OMIGOSH! MY BEST FRIEND, CLARK KENT, IS SECRETLY SUPERBOY!
I'LL NEVER TELL HIM I KNOW... BUT FROM NOW ON, I'LL WORK BEHIND THE SCENES TO HELP CONCEAL HIS SECRET!
WHEN I FOUND OUT THAT CLARK STILL OWNED THE EMPTY HOUSE, EVEN AFTER REAL ESTATE VALUES SKYROCKETED...
...I SUSPECTED HE HAD REFUSED TO SELL IT TO ANYONE...
...BECAUSE OF HIS APPREHENSION THAT SOME MEMENTO INSIDE WOULD REVEAL HIS SECRET IDENTITY!
I DECIDED THAT RECOMMENDING THE HIGHWAY TO BE PUT THROUGH THE PROPERTY WOULD END CLARK'S WORRIES FOREVER!
NOW, IF YOU'LL JUST LOOK OVER THESE ACCOUNTS AND SIGN THEM, SIR--
NOT NOW, DANIEL! THE DOOR TO THE OLD KENT HOUSE IS OPEN-- COULD BE A PROWLER!
BUT THAT HOUSE HAS BEEN EMPTY FOR YEARS! THERE'S NOTHING OF VALUE--
2

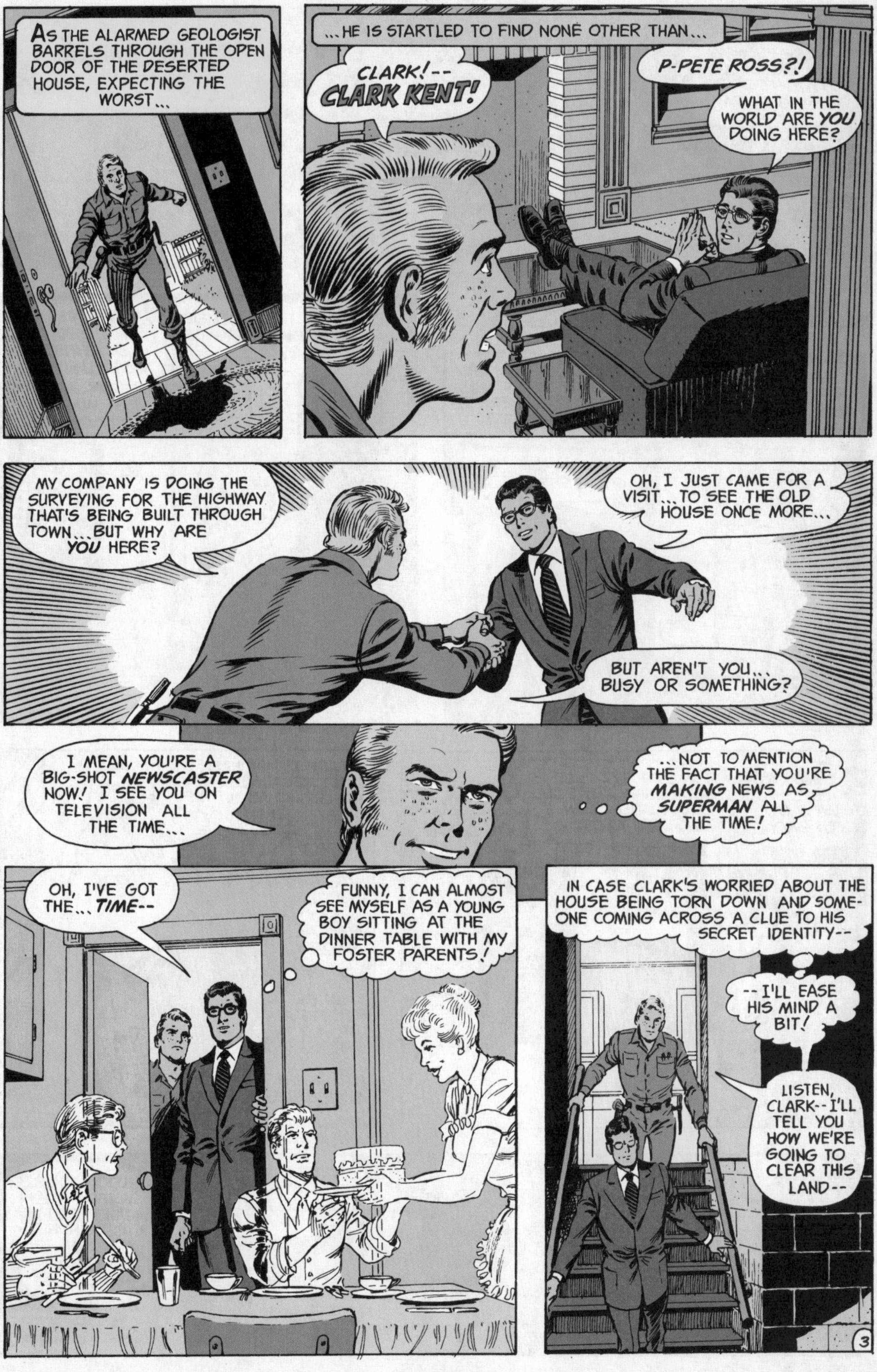
AS THE ALARMED GEOLOGIST BARRELS THROUGH THE OPEN DOOR OF THE DESERTED HOUSE, EXPECTING THE WORST...
...HE IS STARTLED TO FIND NONE OTHER THAN...
CLARK!-- CLARK KENT!
P-PETE ROSS?!
WHAT IN THE WORLD ARE YOU DOING HERE?
MY COMPANY IS DOING THE SURVEYING FOR THE HIGHWAY THAT'S BEING BUILT THROUGH TOWN...BUT WHY ARE YOU HERE?
OH, I JUST CAME FOR A VISIT...TO SEE THE OLD HOUSE ONCE MORE...
BUT AREN'T YOU... BUSY OR SOMETHING?
I MEAN, YOU'RE A BIG-SHOT NEWSCASTER NOW! I SEE YOU ON TELEVISION ALL THE TIME...
...NOT TO MENTION THE FACT THAT YOU'RE MAKING NEWS AS SUPERMAN ALL THE TIME!
OH, I'VE GOT THE...TIME--
FUNNY, I CAN ALMOST SEE MYSELF AS A YOUNG BOY SITTING AT THE DINNER TABLE WITH MY FOSTER PARENTS!
IN CASE CLARK'S WORRIED ABOUT THE HOUSE BEING TORN DOWN AND SOME-ONE COMING ACROSS A CLUE TO HIS SECRET IDENTITY--
--I'LL EASE HIS MIND A BIT!
LISTEN, CLARK--I'LL TELL YOU HOW WE'RE GOING TO CLEAR THIS LAND--
3

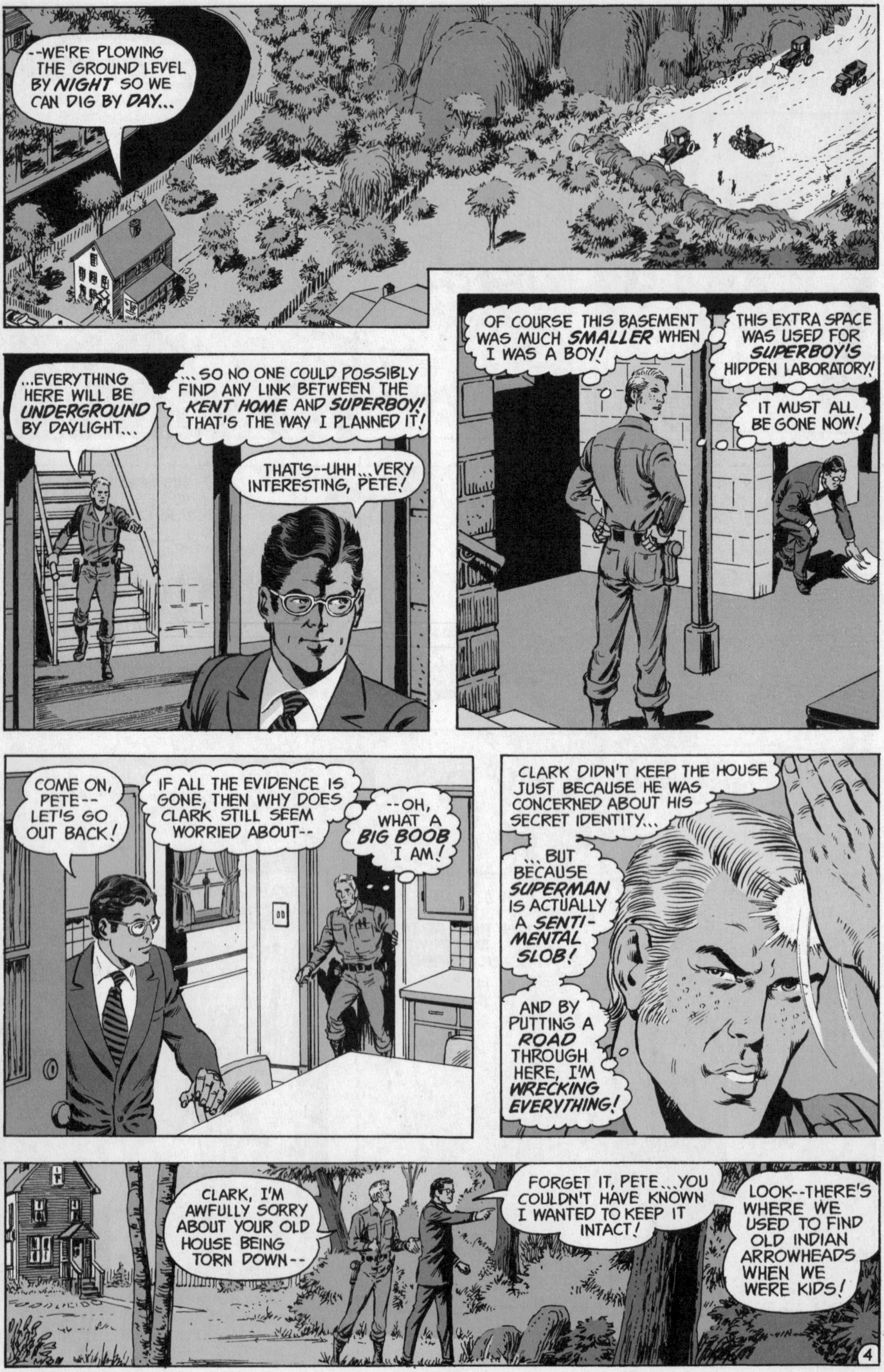
--WE'RE PLOWING THE GROUND LEVEL BY NIGHT SO WE CAN DIG BY DAY...
...EVERYTHING HERE WILL BE UNDERGROUND BY DAYLIGHT...
...SO NO ONE COULD POSSIBLY FIND ANY LINK BETWEEN THE KENT HOME AND SUPERBOY! THAT'S THE WAY I PLANNED IT!
THAT'S--UHH...VERY INTERESTING, PETE!
OF COURSE THIS BASEMENT WAS MUCH SMALLER WHEN I WAS A BOY!
THIS EXTRA SPACE WAS USED FOR SUPERBOY'S HIDDEN LABORATORY!
IT MUST ALL BE GONE NOW!
COME ON, PETE--LET'S GO OUT BACK!
IF ALL THE EVIDENCE IS GONE, THEN WHY DOES CLARK STILL SEEM WORRIED ABOUT--
--OH, WHAT A BIG BOOB I AM!
CLARK DIDN'T KEEP THE HOUSE JUST BECAUSE HE WAS CONCERNED ABOUT HIS SECRET IDENTITY...
...BUT BECAUSE SUPERMAN IS ACTUALLY A SENTI-MENTAL SLOB!
AND BY PUTTING A ROAD THROUGH HERE, I'M WRECKING EVERYTHING!
CLARK, I'M AWFULLY SORRY ABOUT YOUR OLD HOUSE BEING TORN DOWN--
FORGET IT, PETE...YOU COULDN'T HAVE KNOWN I WANTED TO KEEP IT INTACT!
LOOK--THERE'S WHERE WE USED TO FIND OLD INDIAN ARROWHEADS WHEN WE WERE KIDS!
4

As the two old friends approach an old cave they explored as teen-agers...

THERE'S THE CAVE WE THOUGHT WAS HAUNTED BY AN OLD MEDICINE MAN!

THAT *CAVE!--* OF *COURSE...* THAT'S THE WAY TO DIVERT THE NEW ROAD *AROUND* THE HOUSE!

HEY, GIVE ME YOUR FLASHLIGHT, PETE!

I'D LIKE TO SHOW YOU SOME OLD *INDIAN MARKINGS* YOU'LL BE INTERESTED IN!

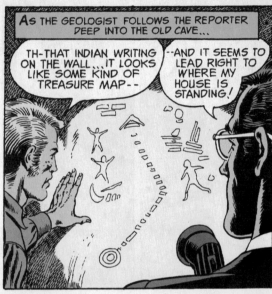

As the geologist follows the reporter deep into the old cave...

TH-THAT INDIAN WRITING ON THE WALL... IT LOOKS LIKE SOME KIND OF TREASURE MAP--

--AND IT SEEMS TO LEAD RIGHT TO WHERE MY HOUSE IS STANDING!

I FOUND THAT MAP WHEN I WAS A BOY!

TRANSLATED, IT REVEALS THAT THE PRECIOUS REMAINS OF AN INDIAN CIVILIZATION ARE BURIED BENEATH MY HOUSE!

...BUT CAN I HELP IT IF I HAPPEN TO KNOW ALL EARTH LANGUAGES--PAST AND PRESENT?

I'M NOT REALLY USING MY *SUPER-POWERS* TO DIVERT THE ROAD...

As Pete and Clark excitedly rush back to the house...

LISTEN, CLARK-- I'M GOING TO DELAY THE ROAD UNTIL I CAN FIND AN INDIAN PICTURE-WRITING EXPERT TO DECODE THAT MAP!

I HAVE A HUNCH WE CAN SAVE YOUR HOUSE AFTER ALL!

REALLY?-- WHAT A *SURPRISE!*

5

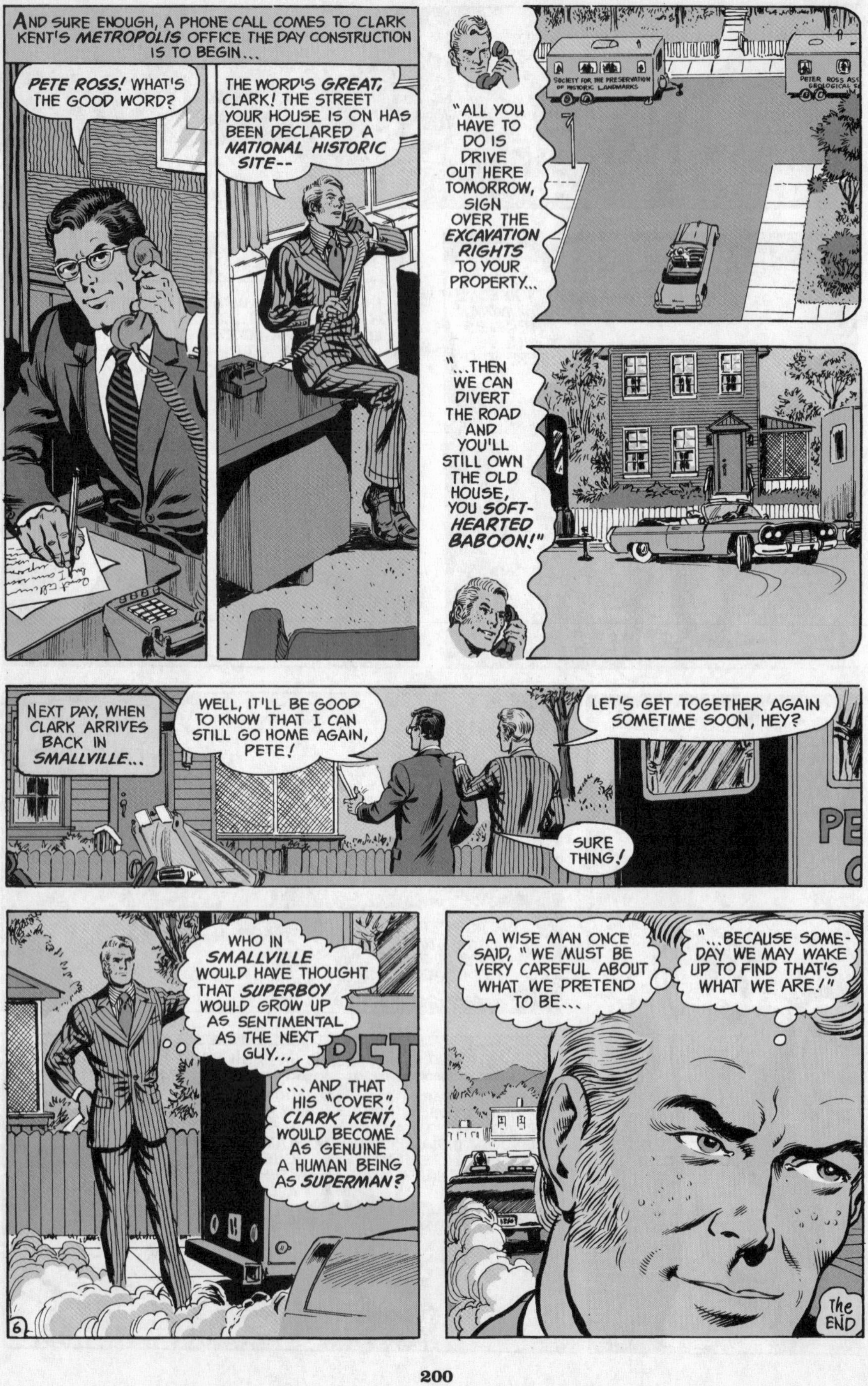
AND SURE ENOUGH, A PHONE CALL COMES TO CLARK KENT'S METROPOLIS OFFICE THE DAY CONSTRUCTION IS TO BEGIN...
PETE ROSS! WHAT'S THE GOOD WORD?
THE WORD'S GREAT, CLARK! THE STREET YOUR HOUSE IS ON HAS BEEN DECLARED A NATIONAL HISTORIC SITE--
"ALL YOU HAVE TO DO IS DRIVE OUT HERE TOMORROW, SIGN OVER THE EXCAVATION RIGHTS TO YOUR PROPERTY...
SOCIETY FOR THE PRESERVATION OF HISTORIC LANDMARKS
"...THEN WE CAN DIVERT THE ROAD AND YOU'LL STILL OWN THE OLD HOUSE, YOU SOFT-HEARTED BABOON!"
NEXT DAY, WHEN CLARK ARRIVES BACK IN SMALLVILLE...
WELL, IT'LL BE GOOD TO KNOW THAT I CAN STILL GO HOME AGAIN, PETE!
LET'S GET TOGETHER AGAIN SOMETIME SOON, HEY?
SURE THING!
WHO IN SMALLVILLE WOULD HAVE THOUGHT THAT SUPERBOY WOULD GROW UP AS SENTIMENTAL AS THE NEXT GUY...
...AND THAT HIS "COVER", CLARK KENT, WOULD BECOME AS GENUINE A HUMAN BEING AS SUPERMAN?
6
A WISE MAN ONCE SAID, "WE MUST BE VERY CAREFUL ABOUT WHAT WE PRETEND TO BE...
"...BECAUSE SOME-DAY WE MAY WAKE UP TO FIND THAT'S WHAT WE ARE!"
The END

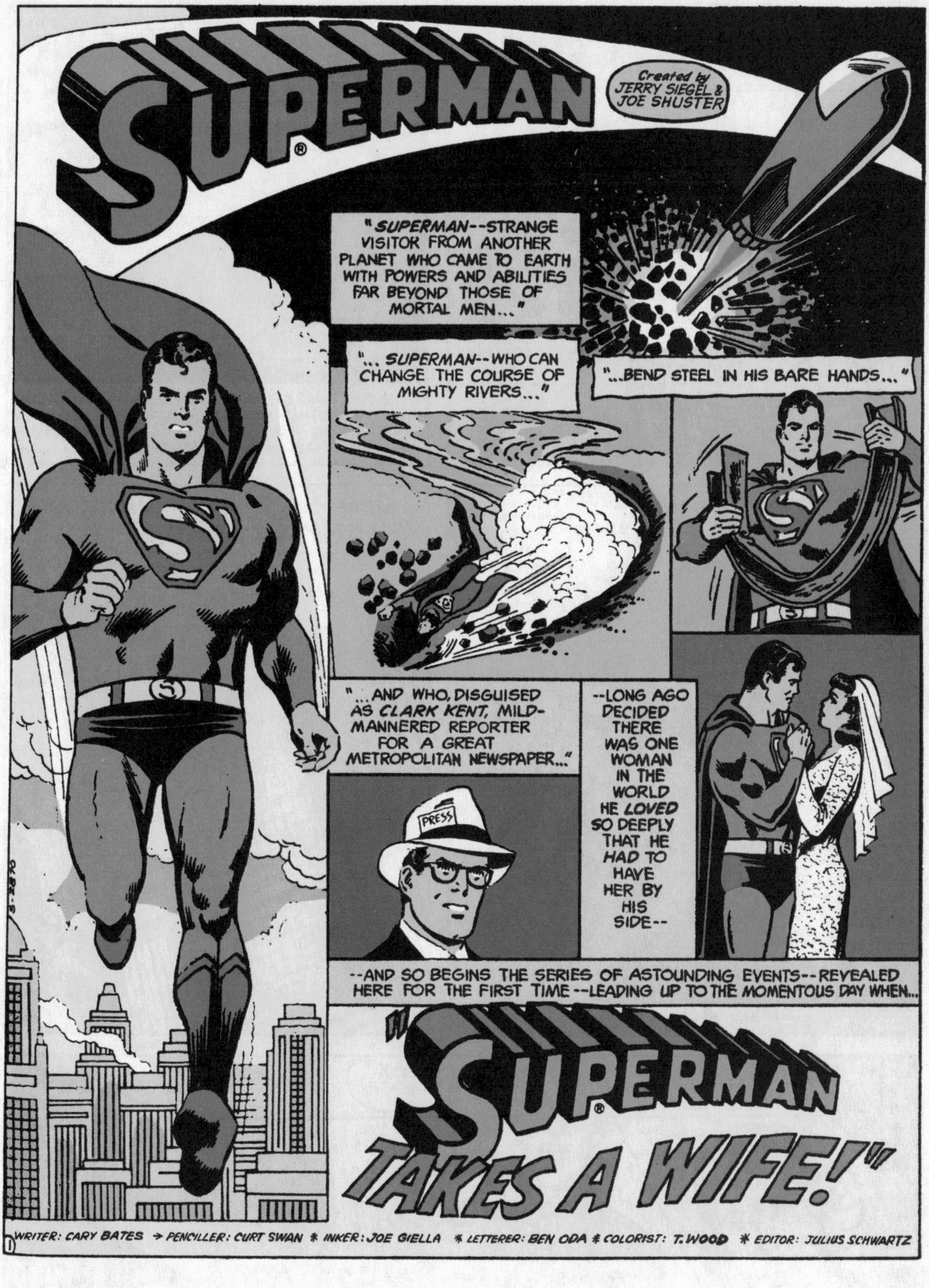
SUPERMAN®
Created by JERRY SIEGEL & JOE SHUSTER
"SUPERMAN--STRANGE VISITOR FROM ANOTHER PLANET WHO CAME TO EARTH WITH POWERS AND ABILITIES FAR BEYOND THOSE OF MORTAL MEN..."
"... SUPERMAN--WHO CAN CHANGE THE COURSE OF MIGHTY RIVERS..."
"...BEND STEEL IN HIS BARE HANDS..."
"...AND WHO, DISGUISED AS CLARK KENT, MILD-MANNERED REPORTER FOR A GREAT METROPOLITAN NEWSPAPER..."
PRESS
--LONG AGO DECIDED THERE WAS ONE WOMAN IN THE WORLD HE LOVED SO DEEPLY THAT HE HAD TO HAVE HER BY HIS SIDE--
--AND SO BEGINS THE SERIES OF ASTOUNDING EVENTS--REVEALED HERE FOR THE FIRST TIME--LEADING UP TO THE MOMENTOUS DAY WHEN...
"SUPERMAN® TAKES A WIFE!"
1 WRITER: CARY BATES → PENCILLER: CURT SWAN * INKER: JOE GIELLA * LETTERER: BEN ODA * COLORIST: T. WOOD * EDITOR: JULIUS SCHWARTZ

ONE DAY, IN THE MASSIVE *GALAXY BUILDING* THAT MAJESTICALLY TOWERS OVER MIDTOWN *METROPOLIS...*

OOPS!

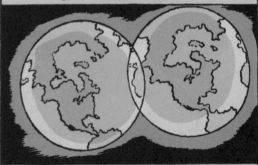

SORRY-- *WRONG EARTH!* THE EVENTS YOU ARE ABOUT TO WITNESS *NEVER HAPPENED* TO THE *SUPERMAN* WHO IS SECRETLY *CLARK KENT,* ANCHORMAN FOR *WGBS-TV* AND THE *GALAXY BROADCASTING SYSTEM*--FOR HE LIVES ON *EARTH-ONE* IN *1978!*

THE *SETTING* OF *THIS* STORY IS *EARTH-TWO*-- A CO-EXISTING WORLD IN A *PARALLEL DIMENSION* -- NOT *IDENTICAL,* BUT *SIMILAR* TO ITS TWIN IN MANY RESPECTS!

IT'S NO SURPRISE, THEN, THAT *EARTH-TWO* HAS HAD A *MAN OF STEEL* ALL ITS OWN FOR MANY YEARS-- BUT WHAT *WILL* SURPRISE YOU ARE THE SPECTACULAR EVENTS REVOLVING AROUND THE *SUPERMAN* OF THIS STORY...

...A STORY THAT *ACTUALLY* OCCURRED...

...Once upon a time... in Metropolis... long ago and far away...

DAILY STAR

LOOK! UP IN THE *SKY!*

IS IT A *BIRD*--?

--A *PLANE*--?

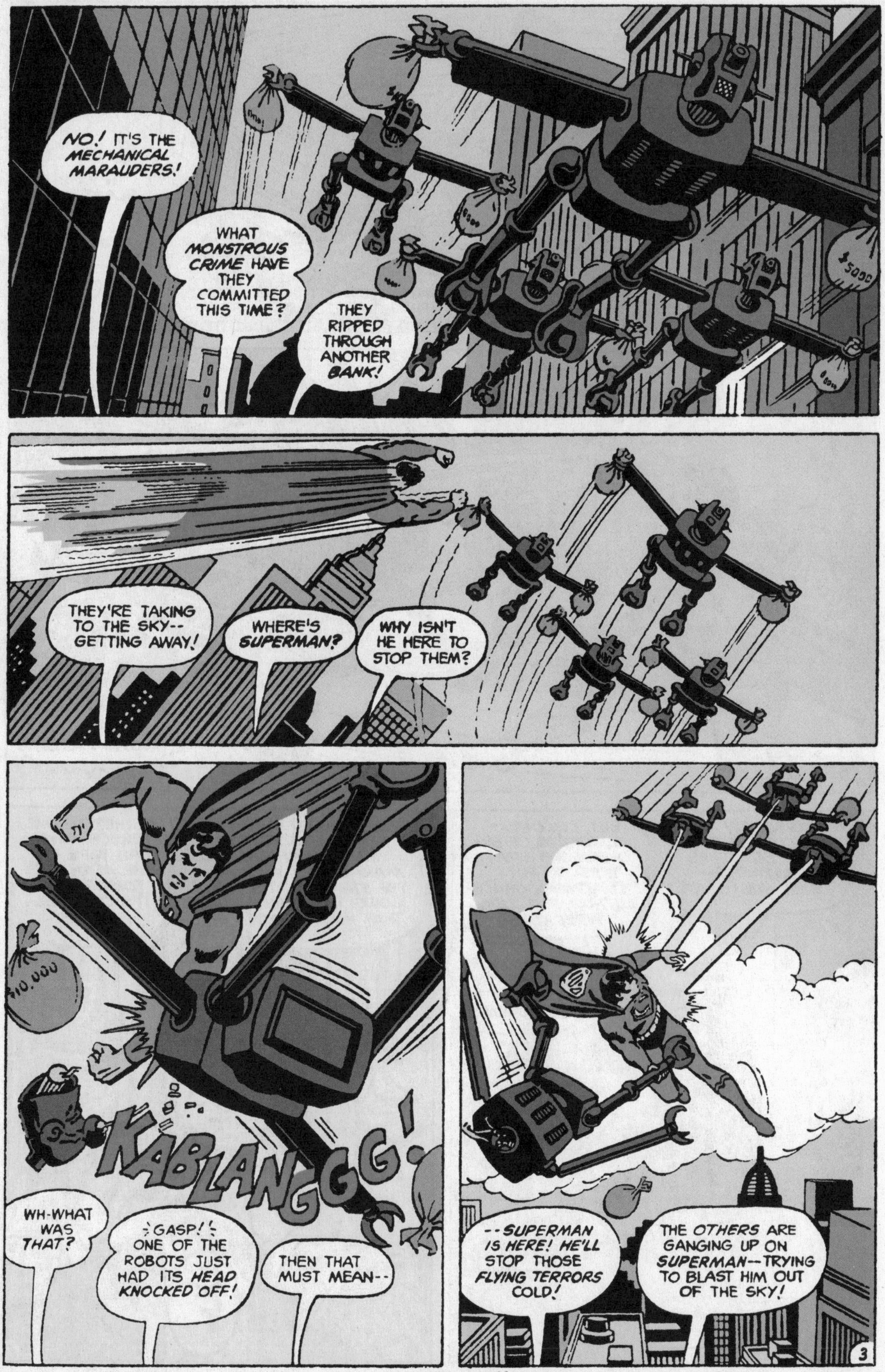
NO! IT'S THE MECHANICAL MARAUDERS!
WHAT MONSTROUS CRIME HAVE THEY COMMITTED THIS TIME?
THEY RIPPED THROUGH ANOTHER BANK!
$5000
THEY'RE TAKING TO THE SKY-- GETTING AWAY!
WHERE'S SUPERMAN?
WHY ISN'T HE HERE TO STOP THEM?
$10,000
KABLANGGG!
WH-WHAT WAS THAT?
GASP! ONE OF THE ROBOTS JUST HAD ITS HEAD KNOCKED OFF!
THEN THAT MUST MEAN--
--SUPERMAN IS HERE! HE'LL STOP THOSE FLYING TERRORS COLD!
THE OTHERS ARE GANGING UP ON SUPERMAN--TRYING TO BLAST HIM OUT OF THE SKY!
3

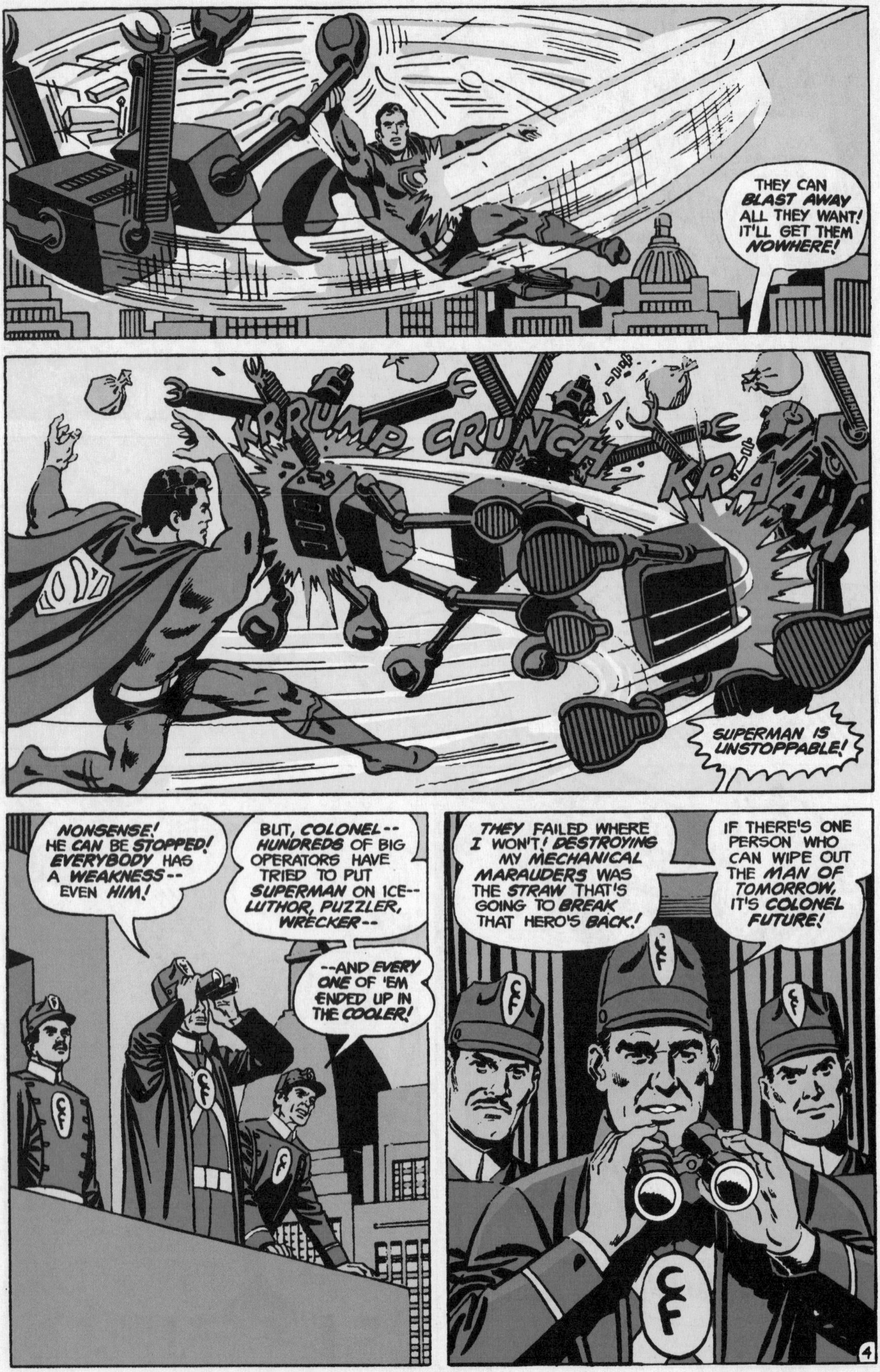

THEY CAN BLAST AWAY ALL THEY WANT! IT'LL GET THEM NOWHERE!
KRRUMP
CRUNCH
KRAAM
SUPERMAN IS UNSTOPPABLE!
NONSENSE! HE CAN BE STOPPED! EVERYBODY HAS A WEAKNESS-- EVEN HIM!
BUT, COLONEL-- HUNDREDS OF BIG OPERATORS HAVE TRIED TO PUT SUPERMAN ON ICE-- LUTHOR, PUZZLER, WRECKER--
--AND EVERY ONE OF 'EM ENDED UP IN THE COOLER!
THEY FAILED WHERE I WON'T! DESTROYING MY MECHANICAL MARAUDERS WAS THE STRAW THAT'S GOING TO BREAK THAT HERO'S BACK!
IF THERE'S ONE PERSON WHO CAN WIPE OUT THE MAN OF TOMORROW, IT'S COLONEL FUTURE!
4

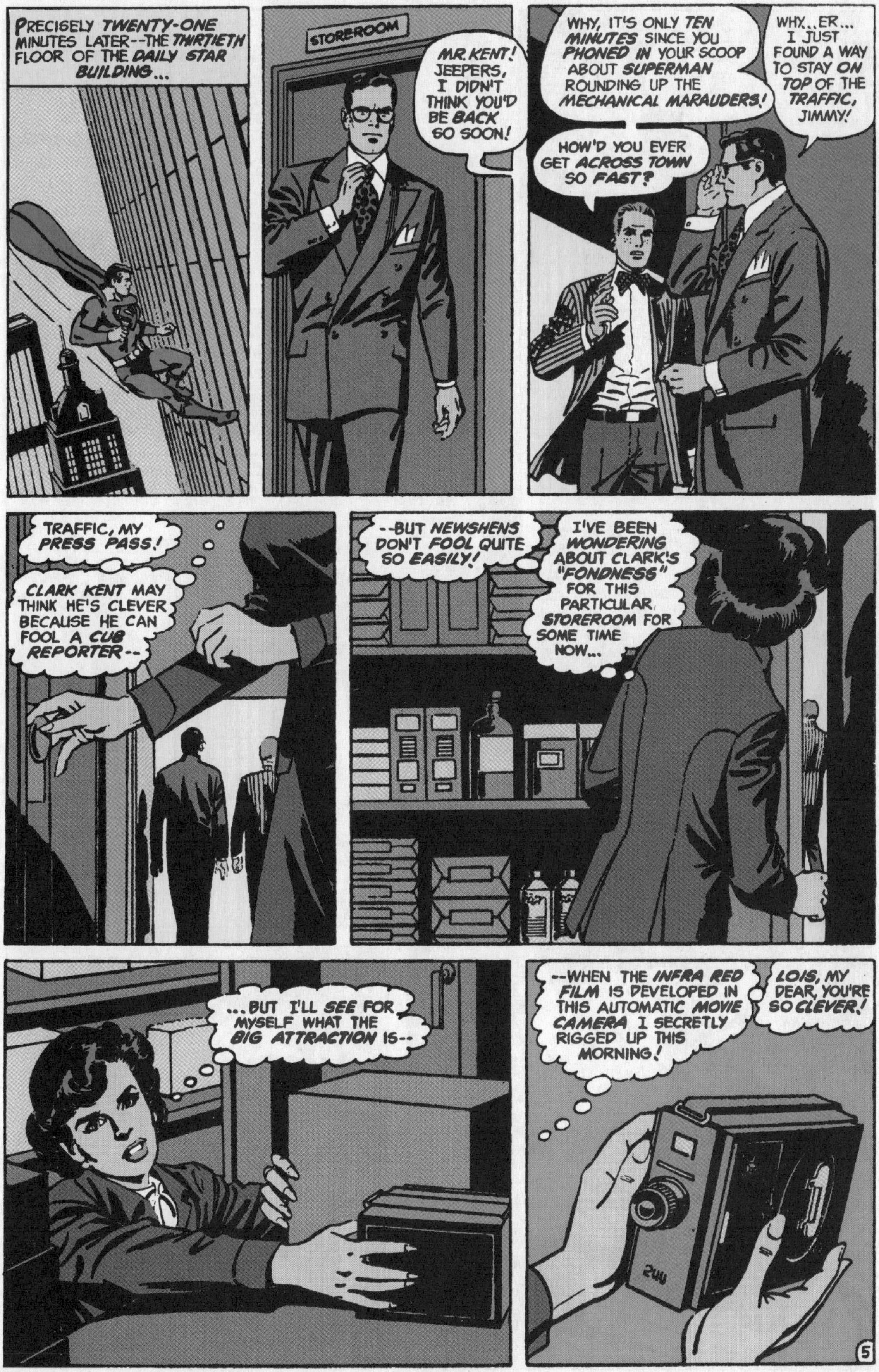
PRECISELY TWENTY-ONE MINUTES LATER--THE THIRTIETH FLOOR OF THE DAILY STAR BUILDING...
STOREROOM
MR. KENT! JEEPERS, I DIDN'T THINK YOU'D BE BACK SO SOON!
WHY, IT'S ONLY TEN MINUTES SINCE YOU PHONED IN YOUR SCOOP ABOUT SUPERMAN ROUNDING UP THE MECHANICAL MARAUDERS!
HOW'D YOU EVER GET ACROSS TOWN SO FAST?
WHY...ER... I JUST FOUND A WAY TO STAY ON TOP OF THE TRAFFIC, JIMMY!
TRAFFIC, MY PRESS PASS!
CLARK KENT MAY THINK HE'S CLEVER BECAUSE HE CAN FOOL A CUB REPORTER--
--BUT NEWSHENS DON'T FOOL QUITE SO EASILY!
I'VE BEEN WONDERING ABOUT CLARK'S "FONDNESS" FOR THIS PARTICULAR STOREROOM FOR SOME TIME NOW...
...BUT I'LL SEE FOR MYSELF WHAT THE BIG ATTRACTION IS--
--WHEN THE INFRA RED FILM IS DEVELOPED IN THIS AUTOMATIC MOVIE CAMERA I SECRETLY RIGGED UP THIS MORNING!
LOIS, MY DEAR, YOU'RE SO CLEVER!
5

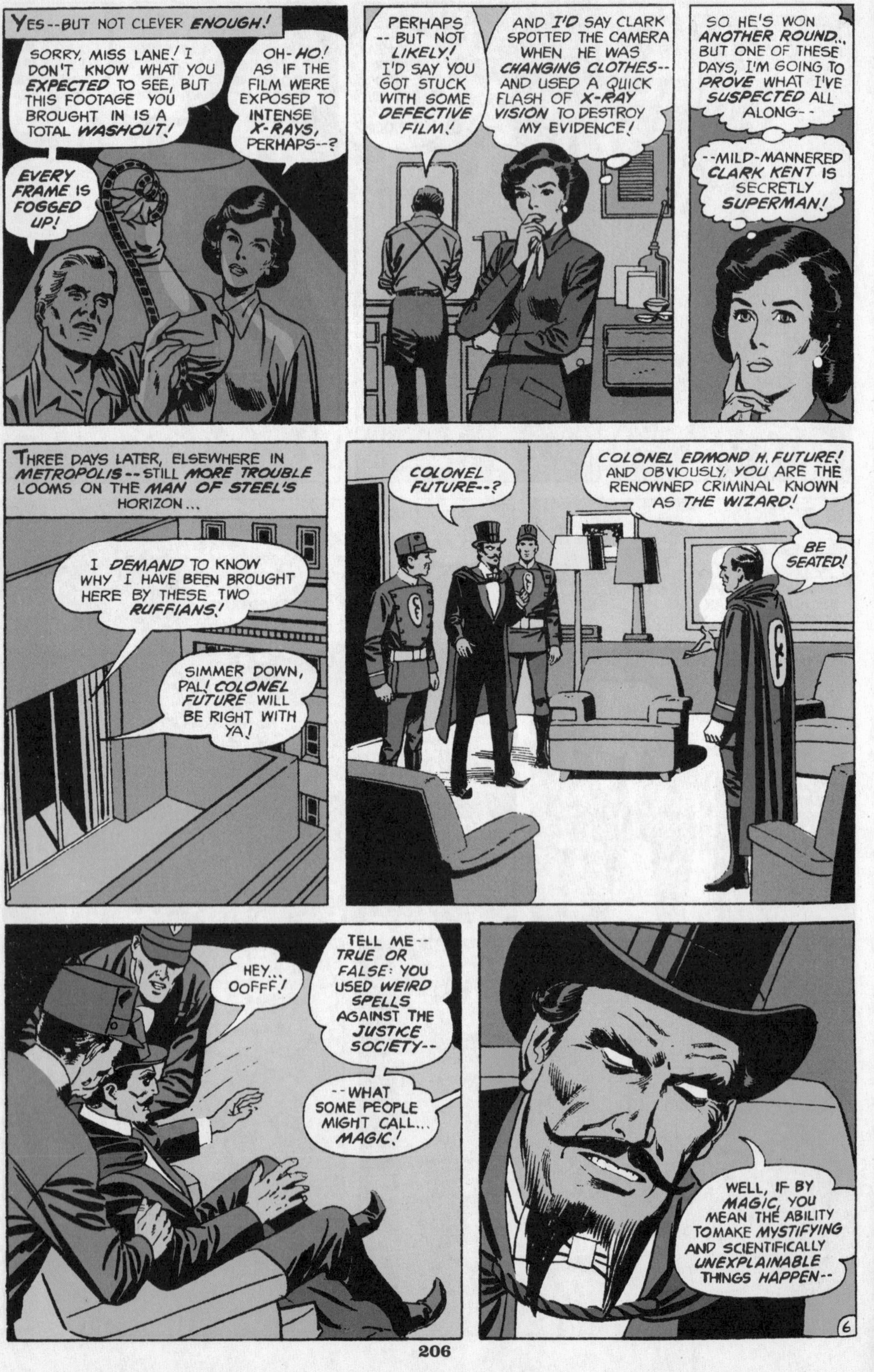
YES--BUT NOT CLEVER ENOUGH!
SORRY, MISS LANE! I DON'T KNOW WHAT YOU EXPECTED TO SEE, BUT THIS FOOTAGE YOU BROUGHT IN IS A TOTAL WASHOUT!
EVERY FRAME IS FOGGED UP!
OH-HO! AS IF THE FILM WERE EXPOSED TO INTENSE X-RAYS, PERHAPS--?
PERHAPS --BUT NOT LIKELY! I'D SAY YOU GOT STUCK WITH SOME DEFECTIVE FILM!
AND I'D SAY CLARK SPOTTED THE CAMERA WHEN HE WAS CHANGING CLOTHES--AND USED A QUICK FLASH OF X-RAY VISION TO DESTROY MY EVIDENCE!
SO HE'S WON ANOTHER ROUND.. BUT ONE OF THESE DAYS, I'M GOING TO PROVE WHAT I'VE SUSPECTED ALL ALONG--
--MILD-MANNERED CLARK KENT IS SECRETLY SUPERMAN!
THREE DAYS LATER, ELSEWHERE IN METROPOLIS--STILL MORE TROUBLE LOOMS ON THE MAN OF STEEL'S HORIZON...
I DEMAND TO KNOW WHY I HAVE BEEN BROUGHT HERE BY THESE TWO RUFFIANS!
SIMMER DOWN, PAL! COLONEL FUTURE WILL BE RIGHT WITH YA!
COLONEL FUTURE--?
COLONEL EDMOND H. FUTURE! AND OBVIOUSLY, YOU ARE THE RENOWNED CRIMINAL KNOWN AS THE WIZARD!
BE SEATED!
HEY... OOFFF!
TELL ME--TRUE OR FALSE: YOU USED WEIRD SPELLS AGAINST THE JUSTICE SOCIETY--
--WHAT SOME PEOPLE MIGHT CALL... MAGIC!
WELL, IF BY MAGIC, YOU MEAN THE ABILITY TO MAKE MYSTIFYING AND SCIENTIFICALLY UNEXPLAINABLE THINGS HAPPEN--
6

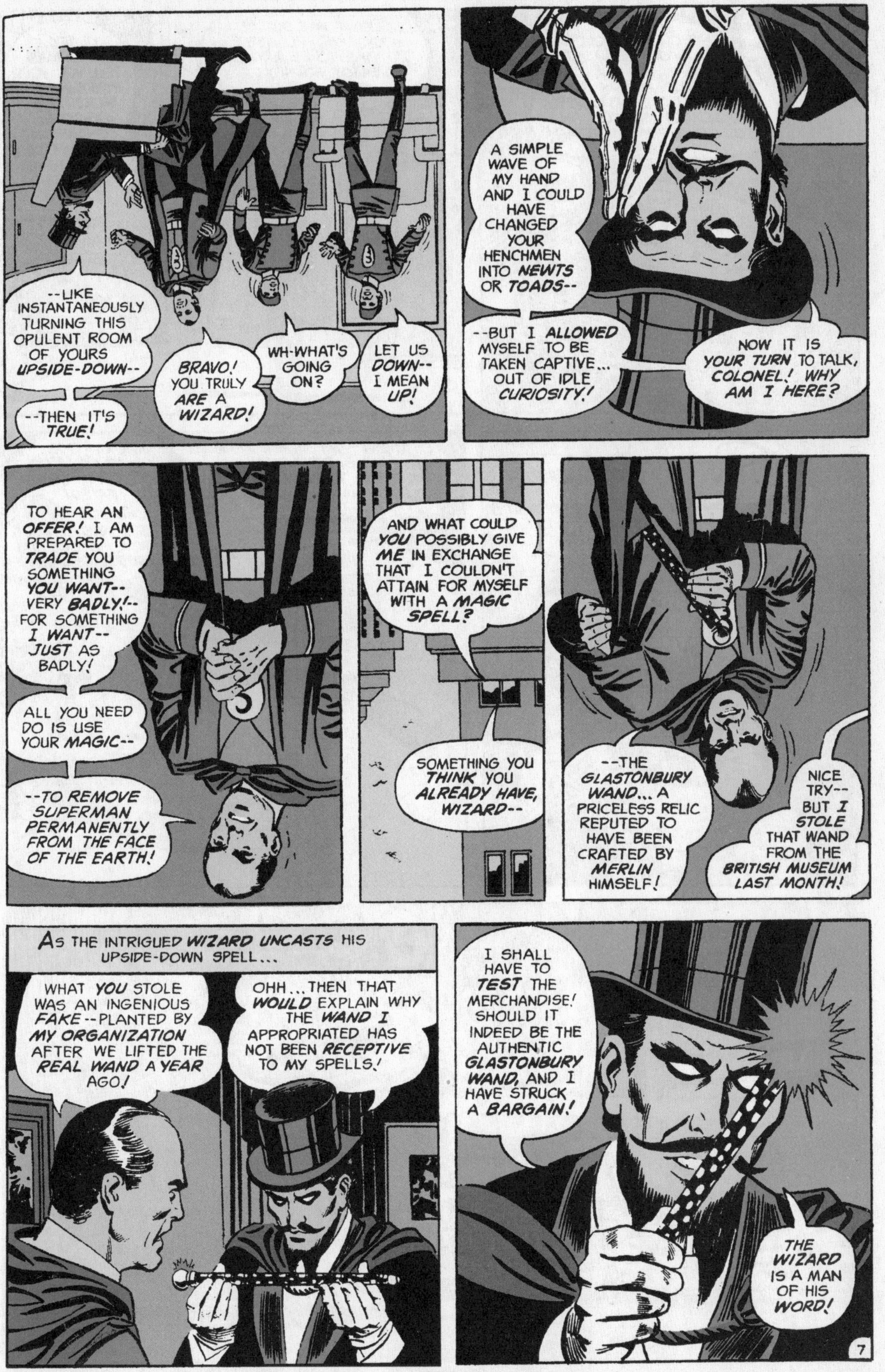
--LIKE INSTANTANEOUSLY TURNING THIS OPULENT ROOM OF YOURS UPSIDE-DOWN--
--THEN IT'S TRUE!
BRAVO! YOU TRULY ARE A WIZARD!
WH-WHAT'S GOING ON?
LET US DOWN-- I MEAN UP!
A SIMPLE WAVE OF MY HAND AND I COULD HAVE CHANGED YOUR HENCHMEN INTO NEWTS OR TOADS--
--BUT I ALLOWED MYSELF TO BE TAKEN CAPTIVE... OUT OF IDLE CURIOSITY!
NOW IT IS YOUR TURN TO TALK, COLONEL! WHY AM I HERE?
TO HEAR AN OFFER! I AM PREPARED TO TRADE YOU SOMETHING YOU WANT-- VERY BADLY!-- FOR SOMETHING I WANT-- JUST AS BADLY!
ALL YOU NEED DO IS USE YOUR MAGIC--
--TO REMOVE SUPERMAN PERMANENTLY FROM THE FACE OF THE EARTH!
AND WHAT COULD YOU POSSIBLY GIVE ME IN EXCHANGE THAT I COULDN'T ATTAIN FOR MYSELF WITH A MAGIC SPELL?
SOMETHING YOU THINK YOU ALREADY HAVE, WIZARD--
--THE GLASTONBURY WAND... A PRICELESS RELIC REPUTED TO HAVE BEEN CRAFTED BY MERLIN HIMSELF!
NICE TRY-- BUT I STOLE THAT WAND FROM THE BRITISH MUSEUM LAST MONTH!
AS THE INTRIGUED WIZARD UNCASTS HIS UPSIDE-DOWN SPELL...
WHAT YOU STOLE WAS AN INGENIOUS FAKE--PLANTED BY MY ORGANIZATION AFTER WE LIFTED THE REAL WAND A YEAR AGO!
OHH...THEN THAT WOULD EXPLAIN WHY THE WAND I APPROPRIATED HAS NOT BEEN RECEPTIVE TO MY SPELLS!
I SHALL HAVE TO TEST THE MERCHANDISE! SHOULD IT INDEED BE THE AUTHENTIC GLASTONBURY WAND, AND I HAVE STRUCK A BARGAIN!
THE WIZARD IS A MAN OF HIS WORD!
7

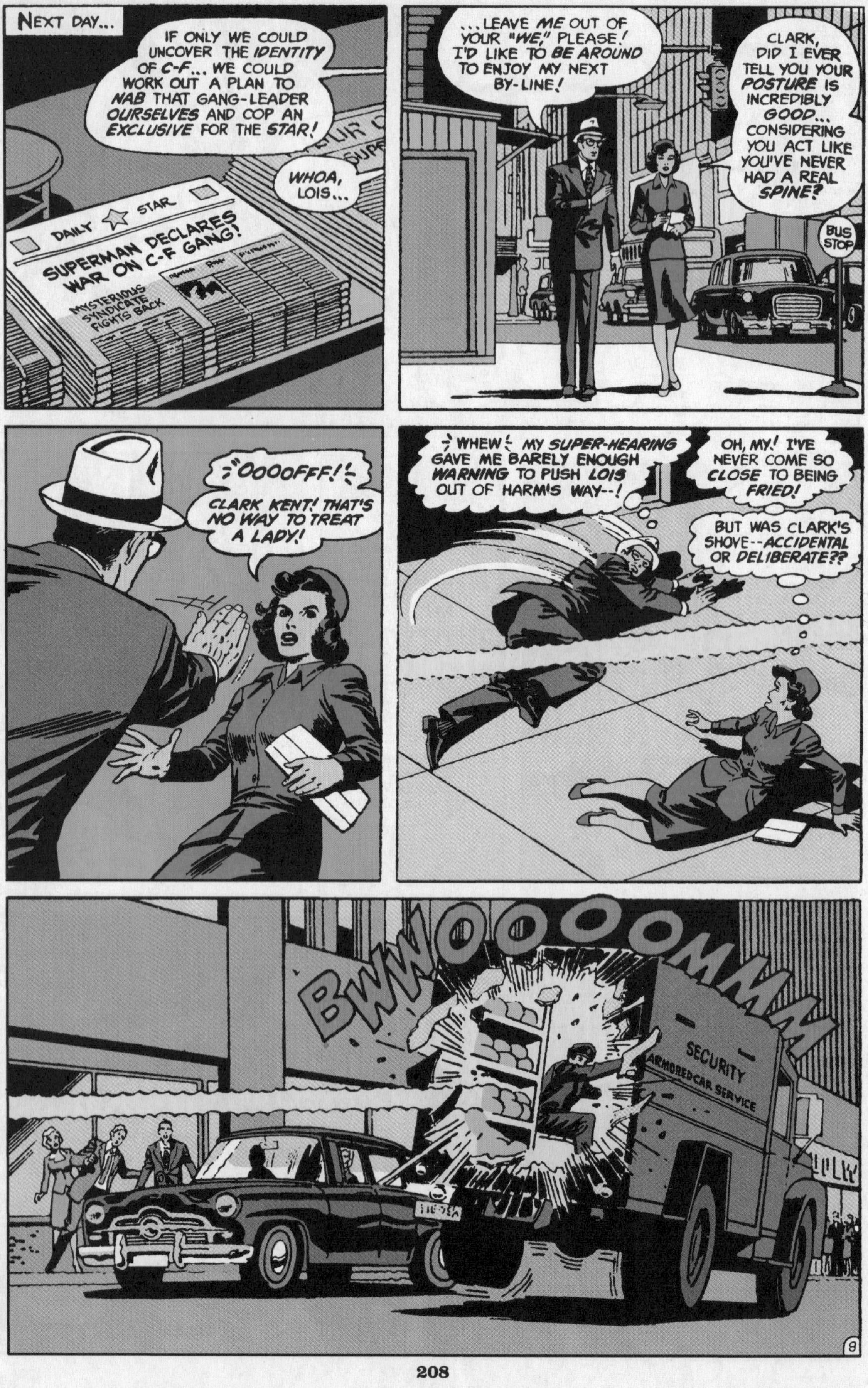
NEXT DAY...
IF ONLY WE COULD UNCOVER THE IDENTITY OF C-F... WE COULD WORK OUT A PLAN TO NAB THAT GANG-LEADER OURSELVES AND COP AN EXCLUSIVE FOR THE STAR!
WHOA, LOIS...
DAILY STAR
SUPERMAN DECLARES WAR ON C-F GANG!
MYSTERIOUS SYNDICATE FIGHTS BACK
...LEAVE ME OUT OF YOUR "WE," PLEASE! I'D LIKE TO BE AROUND TO ENJOY MY NEXT BY-LINE!
CLARK, DID I EVER TELL YOU YOUR POSTURE IS INCREDIBLY GOOD... CONSIDERING YOU ACT LIKE YOU'VE NEVER HAD A REAL SPINE?
BUS STOP
"OOOOFFF!"
CLARK KENT! THAT'S NO WAY TO TREAT A LADY!
WHEW! MY SUPER-HEARING GAVE ME BARELY ENOUGH WARNING TO PUSH LOIS OUT OF HARM'S WAY--!
OH, MY! I'VE NEVER COME SO CLOSE TO BEING FRIED!
BUT WAS CLARK'S SHOVE--ACCIDENTAL OR DELIBERATE??
BWWOOOOOMMMM
SECURITY
ARMOREDCAR SERVICE
8

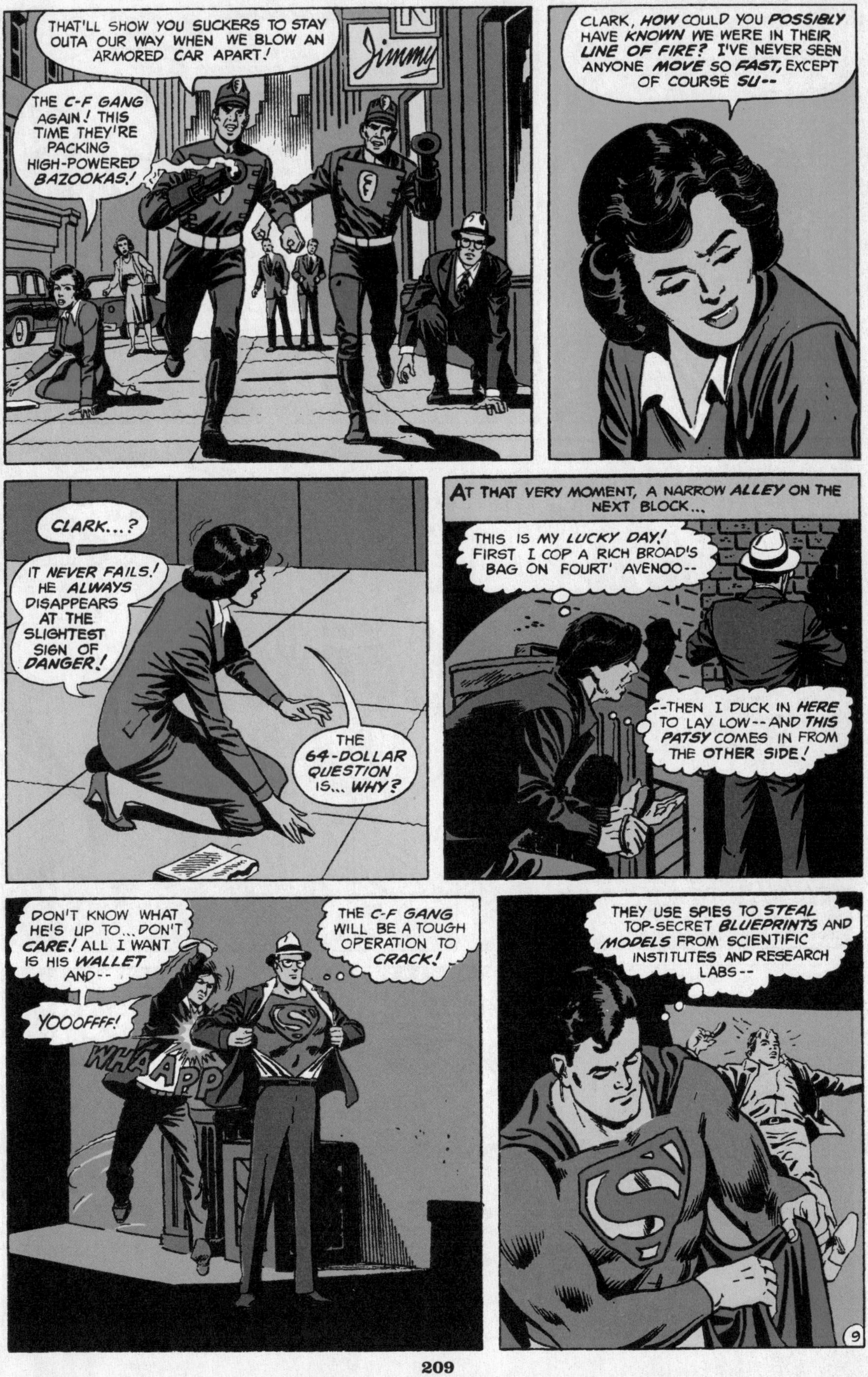
THAT'LL SHOW YOU SUCKERS TO STAY OUTA OUR WAY WHEN WE BLOW AN ARMORED CAR APART!
THE C-F GANG AGAIN! THIS TIME THEY'RE PACKING HIGH-POWERED BAZOOKAS!
Jimmy
CLARK, HOW COULD YOU POSSIBLY HAVE KNOWN WE WERE IN THEIR LINE OF FIRE? I'VE NEVER SEEN ANYONE MOVE SO FAST, EXCEPT OF COURSE SU--
CLARK...?
IT NEVER FAILS! HE ALWAYS DISAPPEARS AT THE SLIGHTEST SIGN OF DANGER!
THE 64-DOLLAR QUESTION IS... WHY?
AT THAT VERY MOMENT, A NARROW ALLEY ON THE NEXT BLOCK...
THIS IS MY LUCKY DAY! FIRST I COP A RICH BROAD'S BAG ON FOURT' AVENOO--
--THEN I DUCK IN HERE TO LAY LOW--AND THIS PATSY COMES IN FROM THE OTHER SIDE!
DON'T KNOW WHAT HE'S UP TO... DON'T CARE! ALL I WANT IS HIS WALLET AND--
YOOOFFFF!
WHAAPP
THE C-F GANG WILL BE A TOUGH OPERATION TO CRACK!
THEY USE SPIES TO STEAL TOP-SECRET BLUEPRINTS AND MODELS FROM SCIENTIFIC INSTITUTES AND RESEARCH LABS--
9

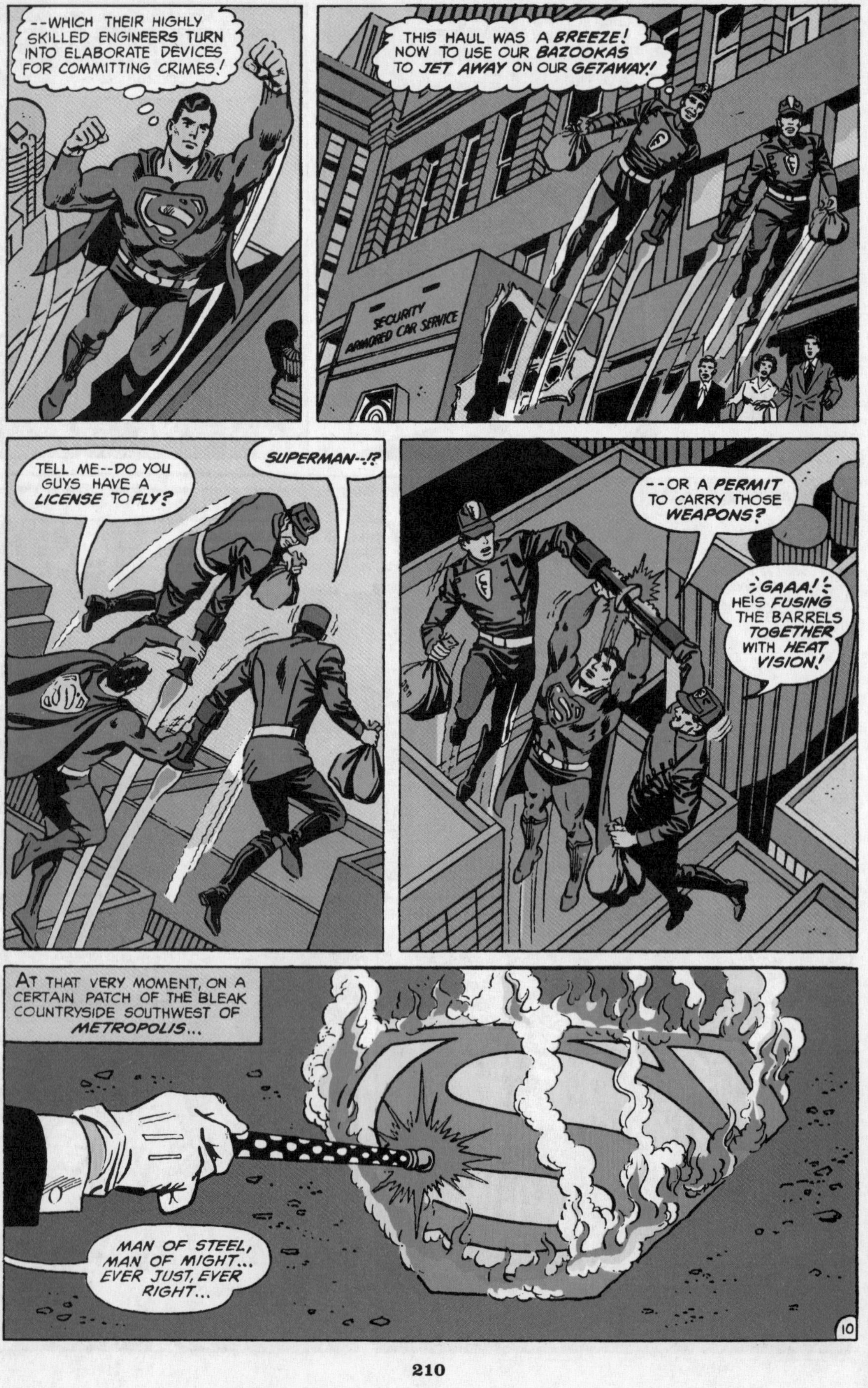
--WHICH THEIR HIGHLY SKILLED ENGINEERS TURN INTO ELABORATE DEVICES FOR COMMITTING CRIMES!
THIS HAUL WAS A BREEZE! NOW TO USE OUR BAZOOKAS TO JET AWAY ON OUR GETAWAY!
SECURITY ARMORED CAR SERVICE
TELL ME--DO YOU GUYS HAVE A LICENSE TO FLY?
SUPERMAN--!?
--OR A PERMIT TO CARRY THOSE WEAPONS?
GAAA! HE'S FUSING THE BARRELS TOGETHER WITH HEAT VISION!
AT THAT VERY MOMENT, ON A CERTAIN PATCH OF THE BLEAK COUNTRYSIDE SOUTHWEST OF METROPOLIS...
MAN OF STEEL, MAN OF MIGHT... EVER JUST, EVER RIGHT...
10

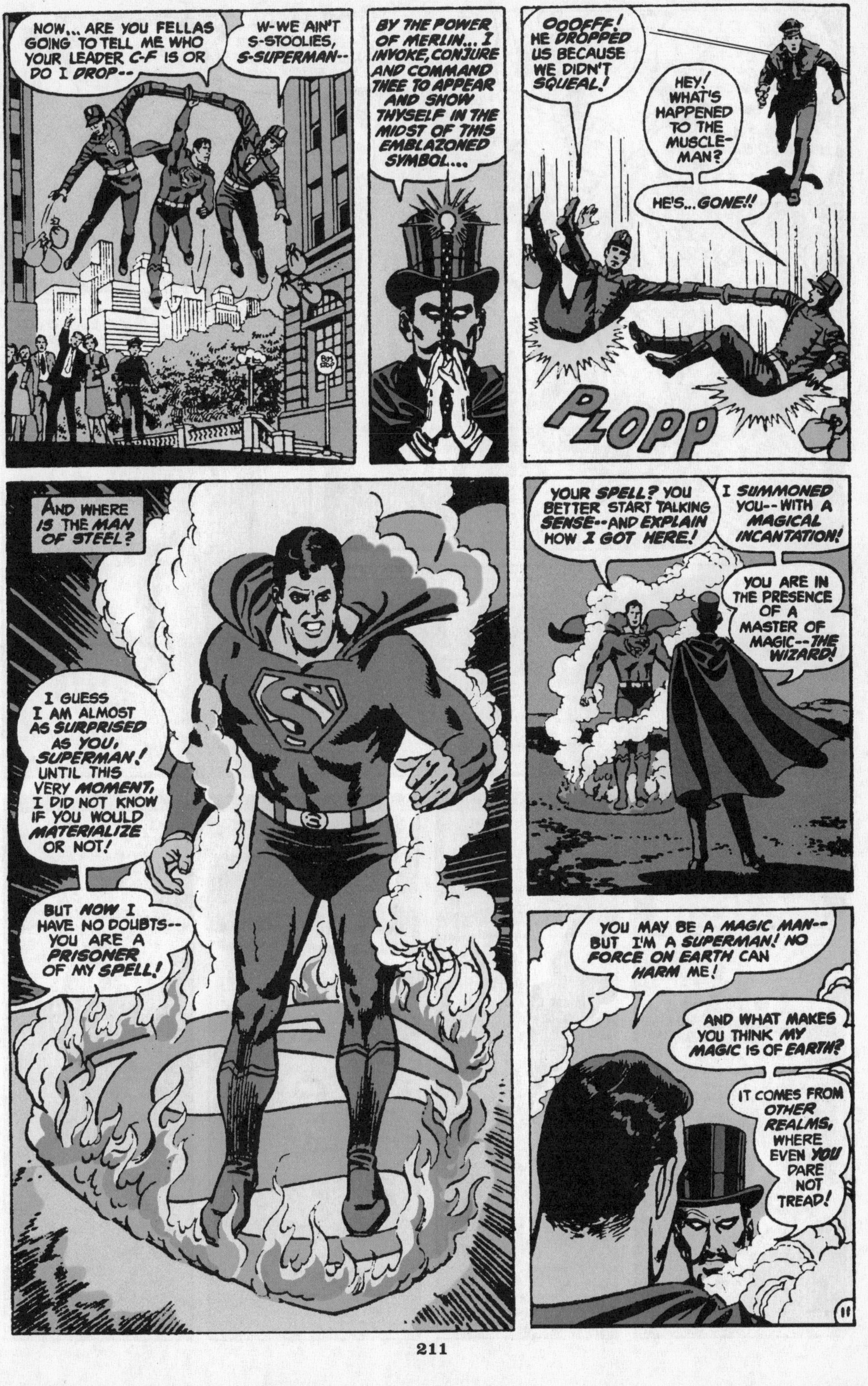
NOW... ARE YOU FELLAS GOING TO TELL ME WHO YOUR LEADER C-F IS OR DO I DROP--
W-WE AIN'T S-STOOLIES, S-SUPERMAN--
BY THE POWER OF MERLIN... I INVOKE, CONJURE AND COMMAND THEE TO APPEAR AND SHOW THYSELF IN THE MIDST OF THIS EMBLAZONED SYMBOL...
OOOFFF! HE DROPPED US BECAUSE WE DIDN'T SQUEAL!
HEY! WHAT'S HAPPENED TO THE MUSCLE-MAN?
HE'S...GONE!!
PLOPP
AND WHERE IS THE MAN OF STEEL?
I GUESS I AM ALMOST AS SURPRISED AS YOU, SUPERMAN! UNTIL THIS VERY MOMENT, I DID NOT KNOW IF YOU WOULD MATERIALIZE OR NOT!
BUT NOW I HAVE NO DOUBTS-- YOU ARE A PRISONER OF MY SPELL!
YOUR SPELL? YOU BETTER START TALKING SENSE--AND EXPLAIN HOW I GOT HERE!
I SUMMONED YOU--WITH A MAGICAL INCANTATION!
YOU ARE IN THE PRESENCE OF A MASTER OF MAGIC--THE WIZARD!
YOU MAY BE A MAGIC MAN-- BUT I'M A SUPERMAN! NO FORCE ON EARTH CAN HARM ME!
AND WHAT MAKES YOU THINK MY MAGIC IS OF EARTH?
IT COMES FROM OTHER REALMS, WHERE EVEN YOU DARE NOT TREAD!
11

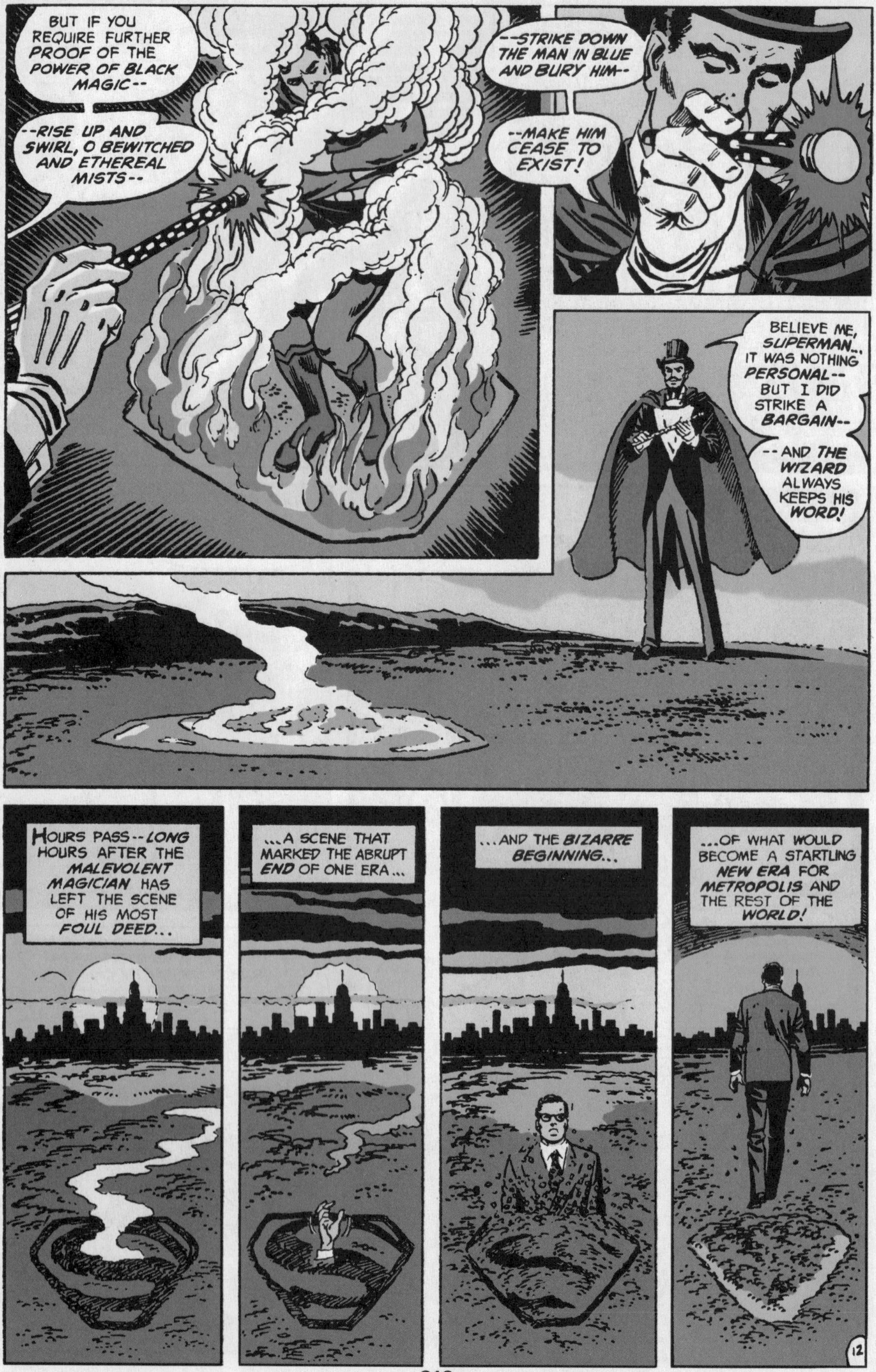
BUT IF YOU REQUIRE FURTHER PROOF OF THE POWER OF BLACK MAGIC--
--RISE UP AND SWIRL, O BEWITCHED AND ETHEREAL MISTS--
--STRIKE DOWN THE MAN IN BLUE AND BURY HIM--
--MAKE HIM CEASE TO EXIST!
BELIEVE ME, SUPERMAN... IT WAS NOTHING PERSONAL-- BUT I DID STRIKE A BARGAIN--
--AND THE WIZARD ALWAYS KEEPS HIS WORD!
HOURS PASS--LONG HOURS AFTER THE MALEVOLENT MAGICIAN HAS LEFT THE SCENE OF HIS MOST FOUL DEED...
...A SCENE THAT MARKED THE ABRUPT END OF ONE ERA...
...AND THE BIZARRE BEGINNING...
...OF WHAT WOULD BECOME A STARTLING NEW ERA FOR METROPOLIS AND THE REST OF THE WORLD!
12

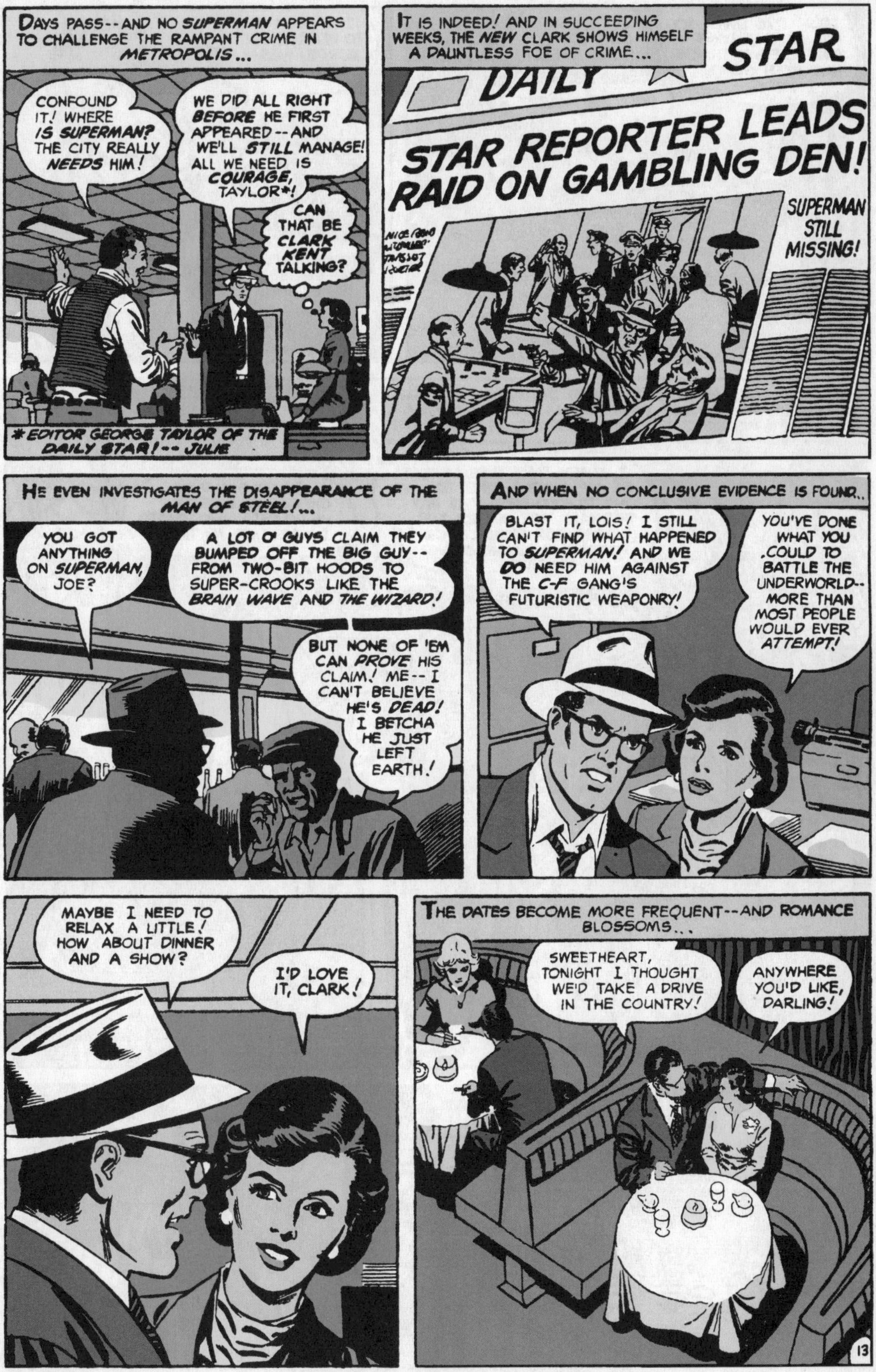
DAYS PASS--AND NO SUPERMAN APPEARS TO CHALLENGE THE RAMPANT CRIME IN METROPOLIS...
CONFOUND IT! WHERE IS SUPERMAN? THE CITY REALLY NEEDS HIM!
WE DID ALL RIGHT BEFORE HE FIRST APPEARED--AND WE'LL STILL MANAGE! ALL WE NEED IS COURAGE, TAYLOR*!
CAN THAT BE CLARK KENT TALKING?
* EDITOR GEORGE TAYLOR OF THE DAILY STAR!--JULIE
IT IS INDEED! AND IN SUCCEEDING WEEKS, THE NEW CLARK SHOWS HIMSELF A DAUNTLESS FOE OF CRIME...
DAILY STAR
STAR REPORTER LEADS RAID ON GAMBLING DEN!
SUPERMAN STILL MISSING!
HE EVEN INVESTIGATES THE DISAPPEARANCE OF THE MAN OF STEEL!...
YOU GOT ANYTHING ON SUPERMAN, JOE?
A LOT O' GUYS CLAIM THEY BUMPED OFF THE BIG GUY--FROM TWO-BIT HOODS TO SUPER-CROOKS LIKE THE BRAIN WAVE AND THE WIZARD!
BUT NONE OF 'EM CAN PROVE HIS CLAIM! ME--I CAN'T BELIEVE HE'S DEAD! I BETCHA HE JUST LEFT EARTH!
AND WHEN NO CONCLUSIVE EVIDENCE IS FOUND..
BLAST IT, LOIS! I STILL CAN'T FIND WHAT HAPPENED TO SUPERMAN! AND WE DO NEED HIM AGAINST THE C-F GANG'S FUTURISTIC WEAPONRY!
YOU'VE DONE WHAT YOU COULD TO BATTLE THE UNDERWORLD--MORE THAN MOST PEOPLE WOULD EVER ATTEMPT!
MAYBE I NEED TO RELAX A LITTLE! HOW ABOUT DINNER AND A SHOW?
I'D LOVE IT, CLARK!
THE DATES BECOME MORE FREQUENT--AND ROMANCE BLOSSOMS...
SWEETHEART, TONIGHT I THOUGHT WE'D TAKE A DRIVE IN THE COUNTRY!
ANYWHERE YOU'D LIKE, DARLING!
13

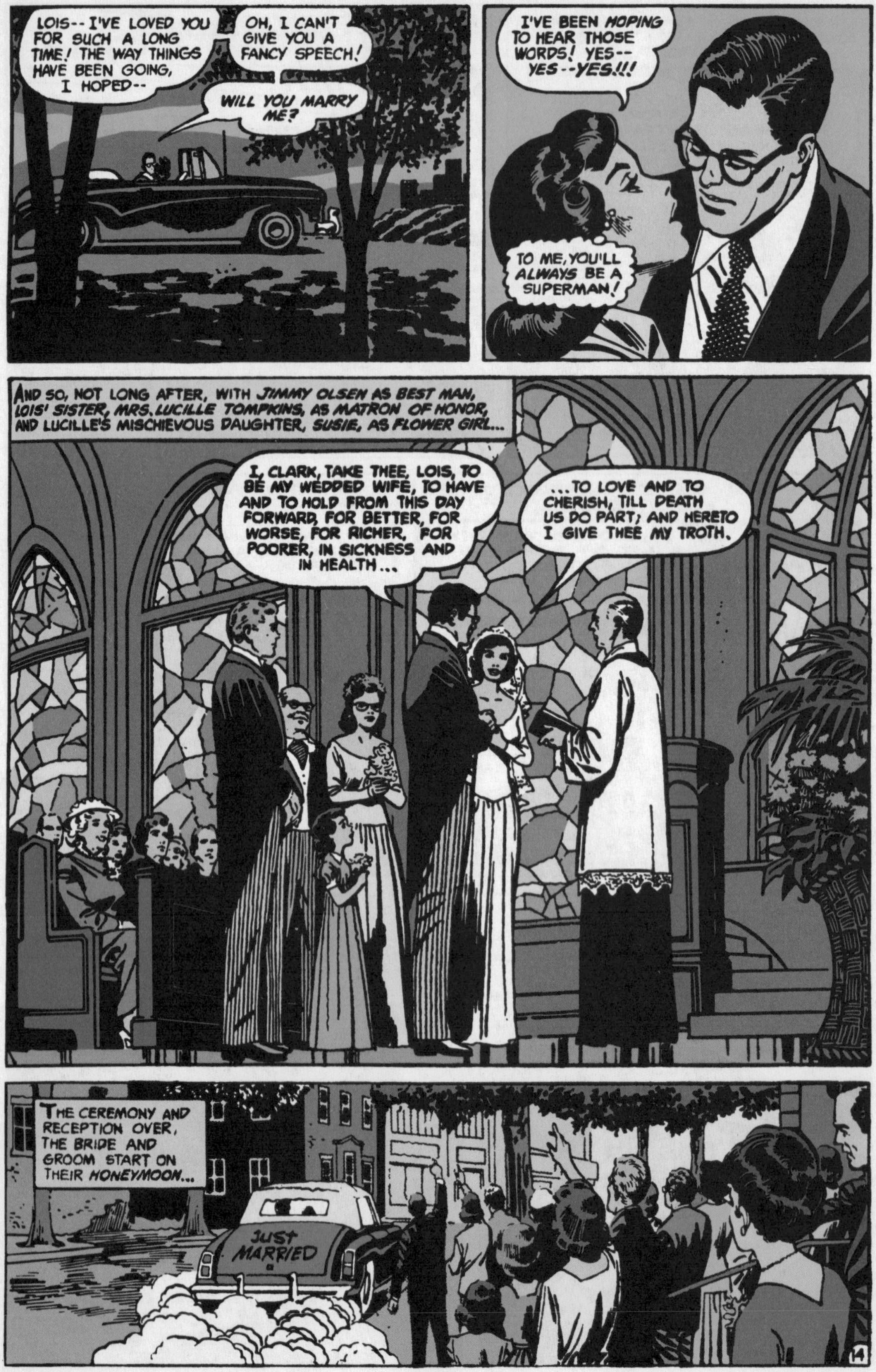
LOIS-- I'VE LOVED YOU FOR SUCH A LONG TIME! THE WAY THINGS HAVE BEEN GOING, I HOPED--
OH, I CAN'T GIVE YOU A FANCY SPEECH!
WILL YOU MARRY ME?
I'VE BEEN HOPING TO HEAR THOSE WORDS! YES-- YES --YES!!!
TO ME, YOU'LL ALWAYS BE A SUPERMAN!
AND SO, NOT LONG AFTER, WITH JIMMY OLSEN AS BEST MAN, LOIS' SISTER, MRS. LUCILLE TOMPKINS, AS MATRON OF HONOR, AND LUCILLE'S MISCHIEVOUS DAUGHTER, SUSIE, AS FLOWER GIRL...
I, CLARK, TAKE THEE, LOIS, TO BE MY WEDDED WIFE, TO HAVE AND TO HOLD FROM THIS DAY FORWARD, FOR BETTER, FOR WORSE, FOR RICHER, FOR POORER, IN SICKNESS AND IN HEALTH...
...TO LOVE AND TO CHERISH, TILL DEATH US DO PART; AND HERETO I GIVE THEE MY TROTH.
THE CEREMONY AND RECEPTION OVER, THE BRIDE AND GROOM START ON THEIR HONEYMOON...
JUST MARRIED
14

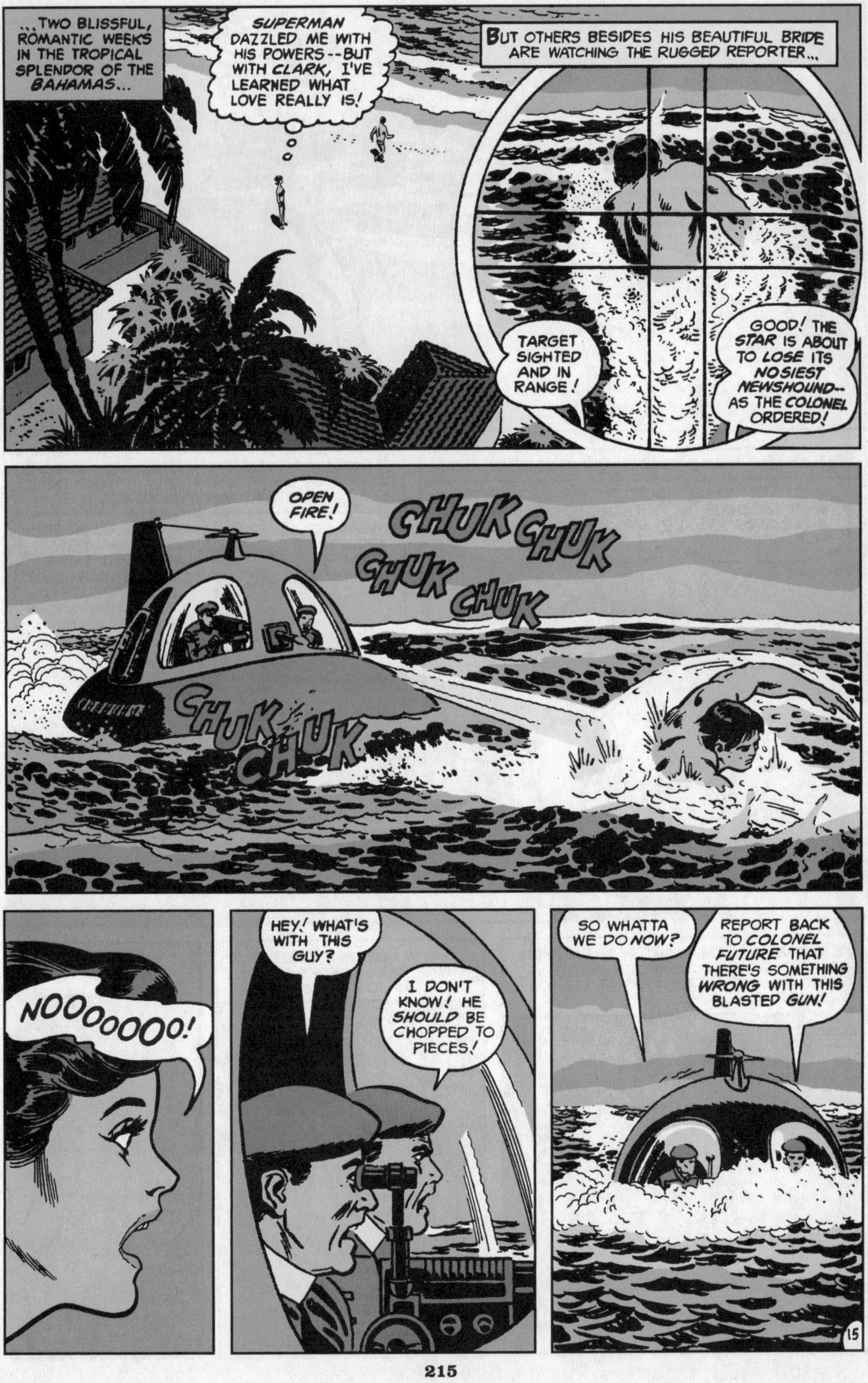
...TWO BLISSFUL, ROMANTIC WEEKS IN THE TROPICAL SPLENDOR OF THE BAHAMAS...
SUPERMAN DAZZLED ME WITH HIS POWERS--BUT WITH CLARK, I'VE LEARNED WHAT LOVE REALLY IS!
BUT OTHERS BESIDES HIS BEAUTIFUL BRIDE ARE WATCHING THE RUGGED REPORTER...
TARGET SIGHTED AND IN RANGE!
GOOD! THE STAR IS ABOUT TO LOSE ITS NOSIEST NEWSHOUND-- AS THE COLONEL ORDERED!
OPEN FIRE!
CHUK CHUK
CHUK CHUK
CHUK CHUK
NOOOOOOO!
HEY! WHAT'S WITH THIS GUY?
I DON'T KNOW! HE SHOULD BE CHOPPED TO PIECES!
SO WHATTA WE DO NOW?
REPORT BACK TO COLONEL FUTURE THAT THERE'S SOMETHING WRONG WITH THIS BLASTED GUN!
15

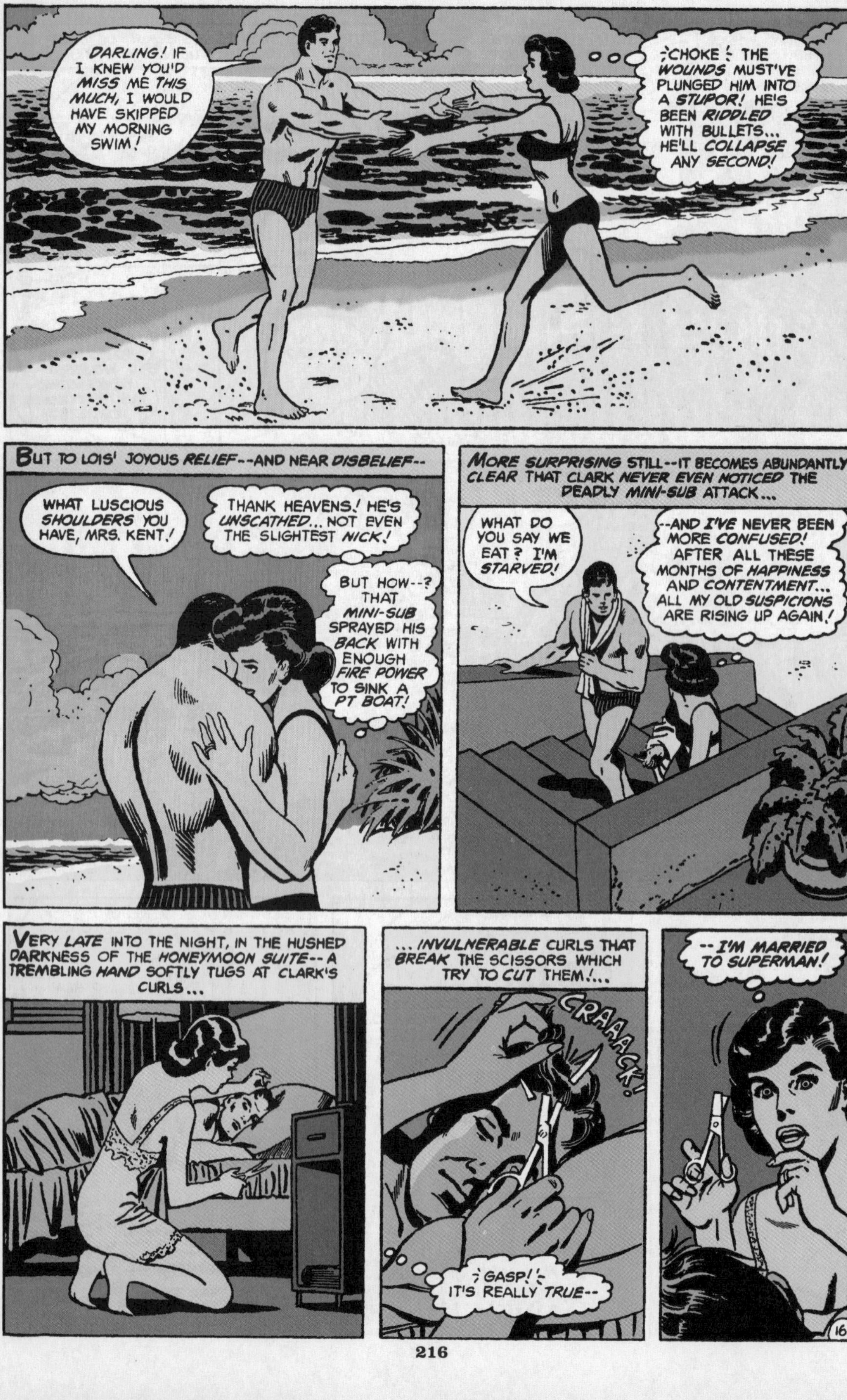
DARLING! IF I KNEW YOU'D MISS ME THIS MUCH, I WOULD HAVE SKIPPED MY MORNING SWIM!
CHOKE THE WOUNDS MUST'VE PLUNGED HIM INTO A STUPOR! HE'S BEEN RIDDLED WITH BULLETS... HE'LL COLLAPSE ANY SECOND!
BUT TO LOIS' JOYOUS RELIEF--AND NEAR DISBELIEF--
WHAT LUSCIOUS SHOULDERS YOU HAVE, MRS. KENT!
THANK HEAVENS! HE'S UNSCATHED... NOT EVEN THE SLIGHTEST NICK!
BUT HOW--? THAT MINI-SUB SPRAYED HIS BACK WITH ENOUGH FIRE POWER TO SINK A PT BOAT!
MORE SURPRISING STILL--IT BECOMES ABUNDANTLY CLEAR THAT CLARK NEVER EVEN NOTICED THE DEADLY MINI-SUB ATTACK...
WHAT DO YOU SAY WE EAT? I'M STARVED!
--AND I'VE NEVER BEEN MORE CONFUSED! AFTER ALL THESE MONTHS OF HAPPINESS AND CONTENTMENT... ALL MY OLD SUSPICIONS ARE RISING UP AGAIN!
VERY LATE INTO THE NIGHT, IN THE HUSHED DARKNESS OF THE HONEYMOON SUITE--A TREMBLING HAND SOFTLY TUGS AT CLARK'S CURLS...
...INVULNERABLE CURLS THAT BREAK THE SCISSORS WHICH TRY TO CUT THEM!...
CRAAACK!
GASP! IT'S REALLY TRUE--
--I'M MARRIED TO SUPERMAN!
16

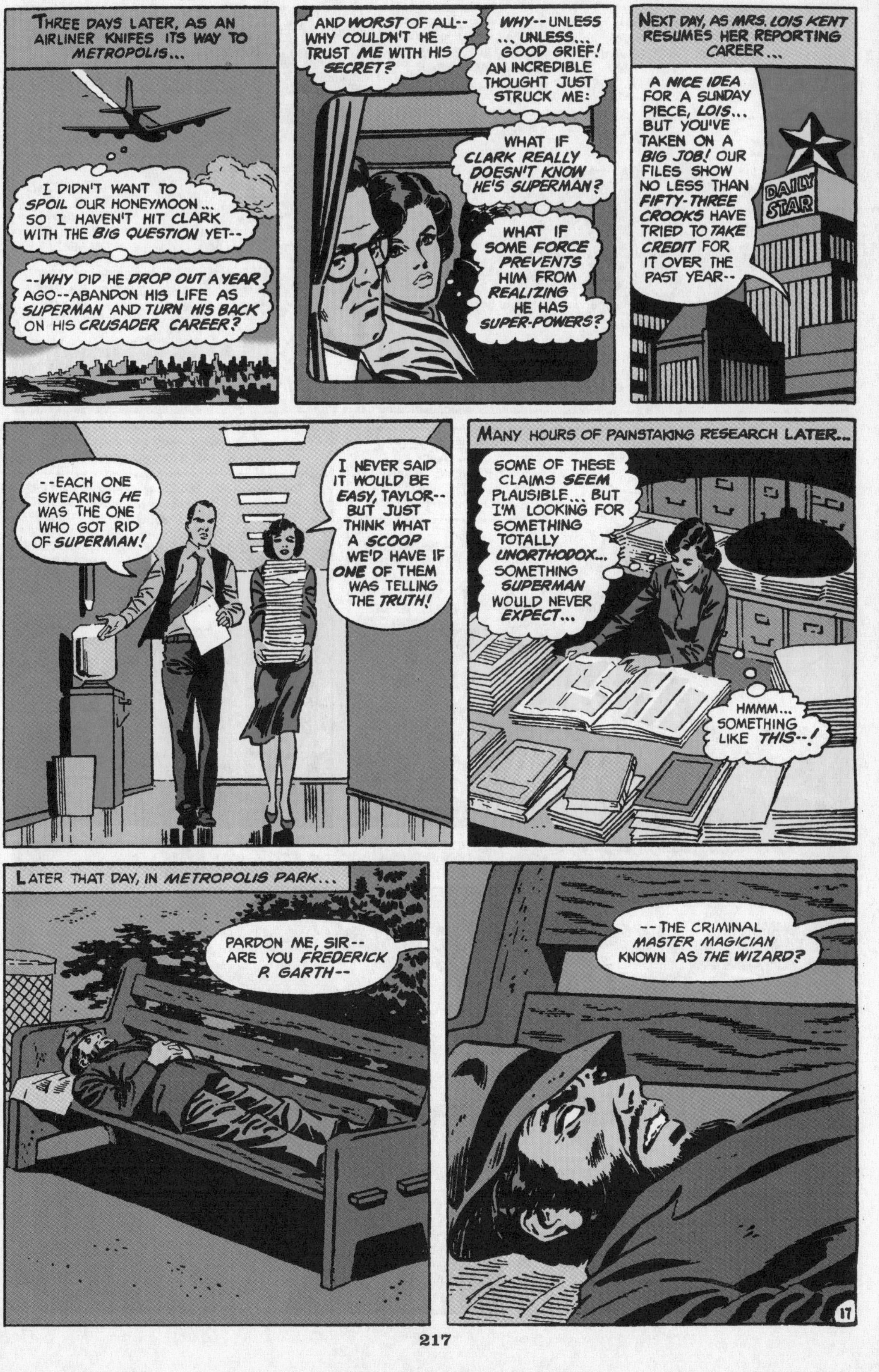
THREE DAYS LATER, AS AN AIRLINER KNIFES ITS WAY TO METROPOLIS...
I DIDN'T WANT TO SPOIL OUR HONEYMOON... SO I HAVEN'T HIT CLARK WITH THE BIG QUESTION YET--
--WHY DID HE DROP OUT A YEAR AGO--ABANDON HIS LIFE AS SUPERMAN AND TURN HIS BACK ON HIS CRUSADER CAREER?
AND WORST OF ALL-- WHY COULDN'T HE TRUST ME WITH HIS SECRET?
WHY--UNLESS ... UNLESS... GOOD GRIEF! AN INCREDIBLE THOUGHT JUST STRUCK ME:
WHAT IF CLARK REALLY DOESN'T KNOW HE'S SUPERMAN?
WHAT IF SOME FORCE PREVENTS HIM FROM REALIZING HE HAS SUPER-POWERS?
NEXT DAY, AS MRS. LOIS KENT RESUMES HER REPORTING CAREER...
A NICE IDEA FOR A SUNDAY PIECE, LOIS... BUT YOU'VE TAKEN ON A BIG JOB! OUR FILES SHOW NO LESS THAN FIFTY-THREE CROOKS HAVE TRIED TO TAKE CREDIT FOR IT OVER THE PAST YEAR--
DAILY STAR
--EACH ONE SWEARING HE WAS THE ONE WHO GOT RID OF SUPERMAN!
I NEVER SAID IT WOULD BE EASY, TAYLOR-- BUT JUST THINK WHAT A SCOOP WE'D HAVE IF ONE OF THEM WAS TELLING THE TRUTH!
MANY HOURS OF PAINSTAKING RESEARCH LATER...
SOME OF THESE CLAIMS SEEM PLAUSIBLE... BUT I'M LOOKING FOR SOMETHING TOTALLY UNORTHODOX... SOMETHING SUPERMAN WOULD NEVER EXPECT...
HMMM... SOMETHING LIKE THIS--!
LATER THAT DAY, IN METROPOLIS PARK...
PARDON ME, SIR-- ARE YOU FREDERICK P. GARTH--
--THE CRIMINAL MASTER MAGICIAN KNOWN AS THE WIZARD?
17

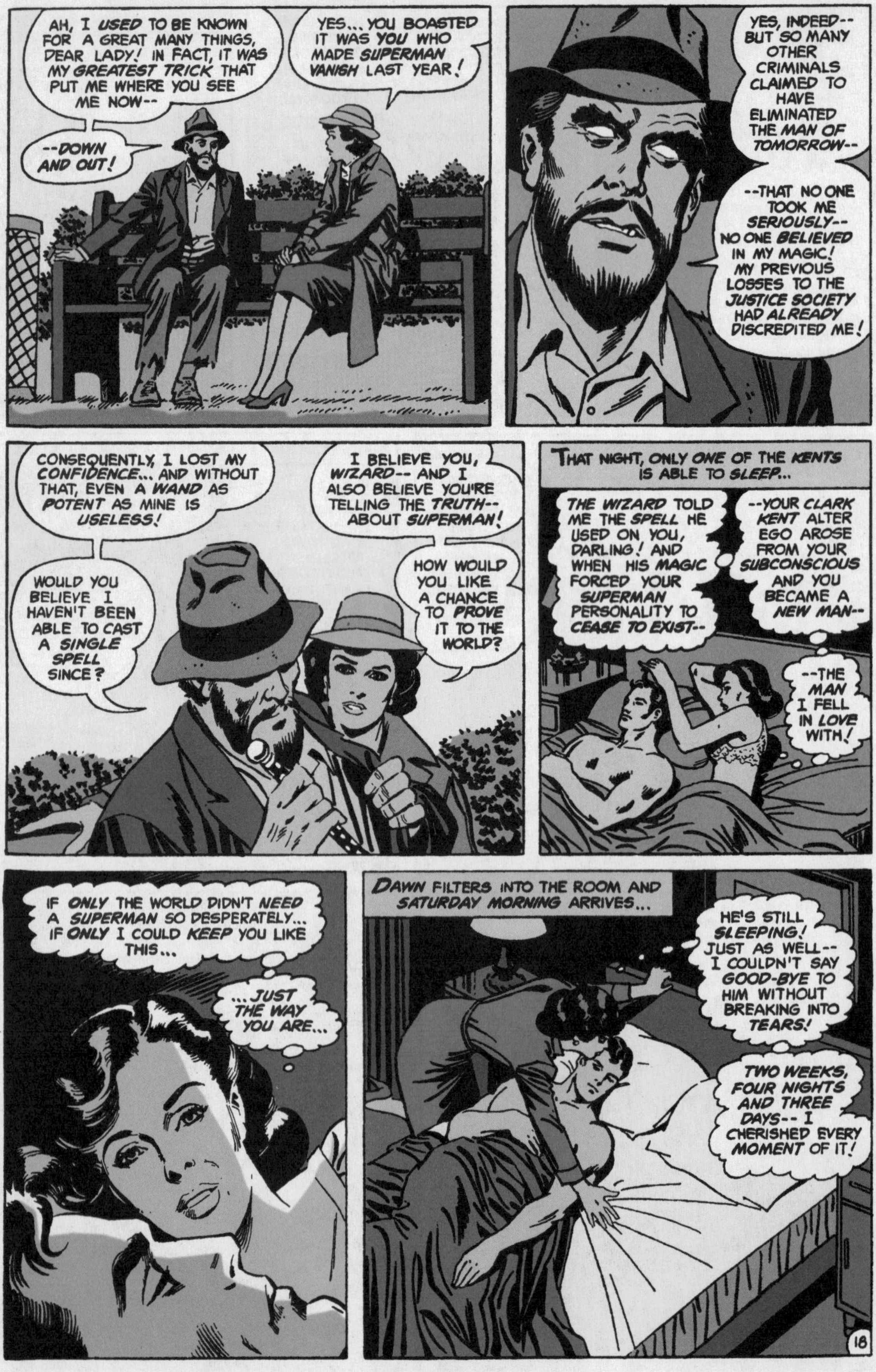
AH, I USED TO BE KNOWN FOR A GREAT MANY THINGS, DEAR LADY! IN FACT, IT WAS MY GREATEST TRICK THAT PUT ME WHERE YOU SEE ME NOW--
--DOWN AND OUT!
YES... YOU BOASTED IT WAS YOU WHO MADE SUPERMAN VANISH LAST YEAR!
YES, INDEED-- BUT SO MANY OTHER CRIMINALS CLAIMED TO HAVE ELIMINATED THE MAN OF TOMORROW--
--THAT NO ONE TOOK ME SERIOUSLY-- NO ONE BELIEVED IN MY MAGIC! MY PREVIOUS LOSSES TO THE JUSTICE SOCIETY HAD ALREADY DISCREDITED ME!
CONSEQUENTLY, I LOST MY CONFIDENCE... AND WITHOUT THAT, EVEN A WAND AS POTENT AS MINE IS USELESS!
WOULD YOU BELIEVE I HAVEN'T BEEN ABLE TO CAST A SINGLE SPELL SINCE?
I BELIEVE YOU, WIZARD-- AND I ALSO BELIEVE YOU'RE TELLING THE TRUTH-- ABOUT SUPERMAN!
HOW WOULD YOU LIKE A CHANCE TO PROVE IT TO THE WORLD?
THAT NIGHT, ONLY ONE OF THE KENTS IS ABLE TO SLEEP...
THE WIZARD TOLD ME THE SPELL HE USED ON YOU, DARLING! AND WHEN HIS MAGIC FORCED YOUR SUPERMAN PERSONALITY TO CEASE TO EXIST--
--YOUR CLARK KENT ALTER EGO AROSE FROM YOUR SUBCONSCIOUS AND YOU BECAME A NEW MAN--
--THE MAN I FELL IN LOVE WITH!
IF ONLY THE WORLD DIDN'T NEED A SUPERMAN SO DESPERATELY... IF ONLY I COULD KEEP YOU LIKE THIS...
...JUST THE WAY YOU ARE...
DAWN FILTERS INTO THE ROOM AND SATURDAY MORNING ARRIVES...
HE'S STILL SLEEPING! JUST AS WELL-- I COULDN'T SAY GOOD-BYE TO HIM WITHOUT BREAKING INTO TEARS!
TWO WEEKS, FOUR NIGHTS AND THREE DAYS-- I CHERISHED EVERY MOMENT OF IT!
18

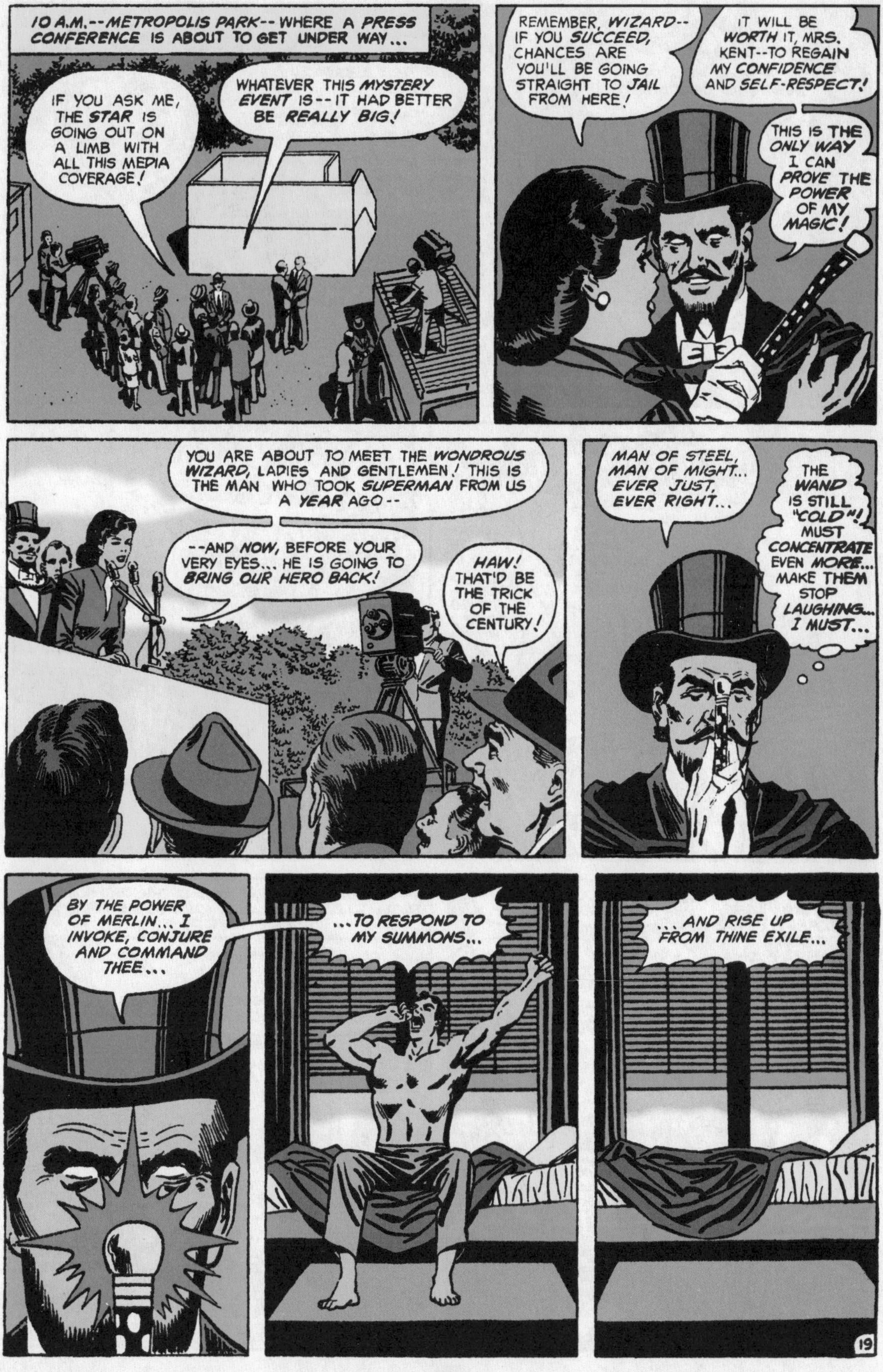
10 A.M.--METROPOLIS PARK--WHERE A PRESS CONFERENCE IS ABOUT TO GET UNDER WAY...
IF YOU ASK ME, THE STAR IS GOING OUT ON A LIMB WITH ALL THIS MEDIA COVERAGE!
WHATEVER THIS MYSTERY EVENT IS--IT HAD BETTER BE REALLY BIG!
REMEMBER, WIZARD--IF YOU SUCCEED, CHANCES ARE YOU'LL BE GOING STRAIGHT TO JAIL FROM HERE!
IT WILL BE WORTH IT, MRS. KENT--TO REGAIN MY CONFIDENCE AND SELF-RESPECT!
THIS IS THE ONLY WAY I CAN PROVE THE POWER OF MY MAGIC!
YOU ARE ABOUT TO MEET THE WONDROUS WIZARD, LADIES AND GENTLEMEN! THIS IS THE MAN WHO TOOK SUPERMAN FROM US A YEAR AGO--
--AND NOW, BEFORE YOUR VERY EYES... HE IS GOING TO BRING OUR HERO BACK!
HAW! THAT'D BE THE TRICK OF THE CENTURY!
MAN OF STEEL, MAN OF MIGHT... EVER JUST, EVER RIGHT...
THE WAND IS STILL "COLD"! MUST CONCENTRATE EVEN MORE... MAKE THEM STOP LAUGHING... I MUST...
BY THE POWER OF MERLIN... I INVOKE, CONJURE AND COMMAND THEE...
...TO RESPOND TO MY SUMMONS...
...AND RISE UP FROM THINE EXILE...
19

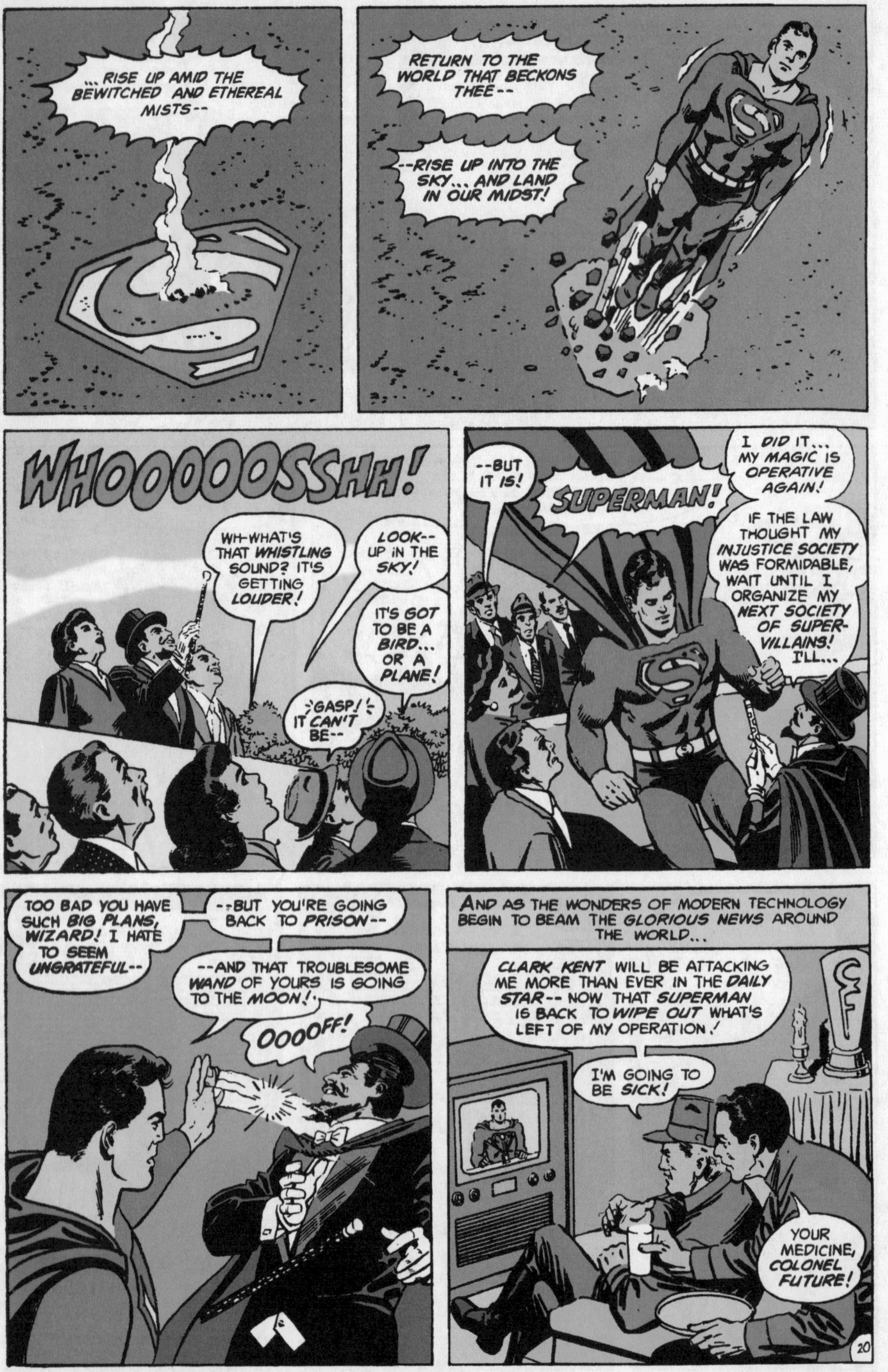
...RISE UP AMID THE BEWITCHED AND ETHEREAL MISTS--
RETURN TO THE WORLD THAT BECKONS THEE--
--RISE UP INTO THE SKY... AND LAND IN OUR MIDST!
WHOOOOOOSSHH!
WH-WHAT'S THAT WHISTLING SOUND? IT'S GETTING LOUDER!
LOOK-- UP IN THE SKY!
IT'S GOT TO BE A BIRD... OR A PLANE!
GASP! IT CAN'T BE--
--BUT IT IS!
SUPERMAN!
I DID IT... MY MAGIC IS OPERATIVE AGAIN!
IF THE LAW THOUGHT MY INJUSTICE SOCIETY WAS FORMIDABLE, WAIT UNTIL I ORGANIZE MY NEXT SOCIETY OF SUPER-VILLAINS! I'LL...
TOO BAD YOU HAVE SUCH BIG PLANS, WIZARD! I HATE TO SEEM UNGRATEFUL--
--BUT YOU'RE GOING BACK TO PRISON--
--AND THAT TROUBLESOME WAND OF YOURS IS GOING TO THE MOON!
OOOOFF!
AND AS THE WONDERS OF MODERN TECHNOLOGY BEGIN TO BEAM THE GLORIOUS NEWS AROUND THE WORLD...
CLARK KENT WILL BE ATTACKING ME MORE THAN EVER IN THE DAILY STAR-- NOW THAT SUPERMAN IS BACK TO WIPE OUT WHAT'S LEFT OF MY OPERATION!
I'M GOING TO BE SICK!
YOUR MEDICINE, COLONEL FUTURE!
20

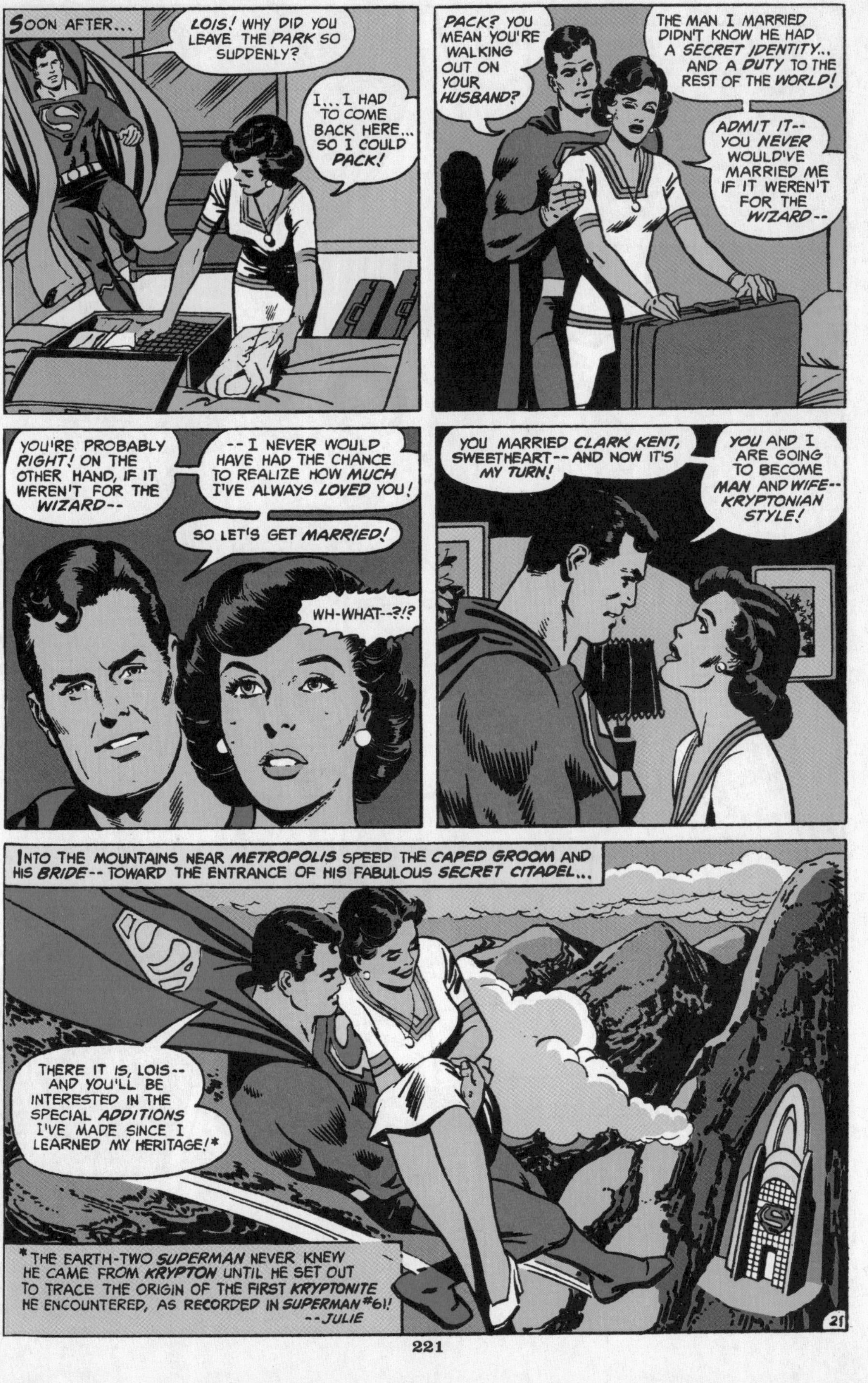
SOON AFTER...
LOIS! WHY DID YOU LEAVE THE PARK SO SUDDENLY?
I...I HAD TO COME BACK HERE... SO I COULD PACK!
PACK? YOU MEAN YOU'RE WALKING OUT ON YOUR HUSBAND?
THE MAN I MARRIED DIDN'T KNOW HE HAD A SECRET IDENTITY... AND A DUTY TO THE REST OF THE WORLD!
ADMIT IT-- YOU NEVER WOULD'VE MARRIED ME IF IT WEREN'T FOR THE WIZARD--
YOU'RE PROBABLY RIGHT! ON THE OTHER HAND, IF IT WEREN'T FOR THE WIZARD--
--I NEVER WOULD HAVE HAD THE CHANCE TO REALIZE HOW MUCH I'VE ALWAYS LOVED YOU!
SO LET'S GET MARRIED!
WH-WHAT--?!?
YOU MARRIED CLARK KENT, SWEETHEART-- AND NOW IT'S MY TURN!
YOU AND I ARE GOING TO BECOME MAN AND WIFE-- KRYPTONIAN STYLE!
INTO THE MOUNTAINS NEAR METROPOLIS SPEED THE CAPED GROOM AND HIS BRIDE-- TOWARD THE ENTRANCE OF HIS FABULOUS SECRET CITADEL...
THERE IT IS, LOIS-- AND YOU'LL BE INTERESTED IN THE SPECIAL ADDITIONS I'VE MADE SINCE I LEARNED MY HERITAGE!*
* THE EARTH-TWO SUPERMAN NEVER KNEW HE CAME FROM KRYPTON UNTIL HE SET OUT TO TRACE THE ORIGIN OF THE FIRST KRYPTONITE HE ENCOUNTERED, AS RECORDED IN SUPERMAN #61! --JULIE
21

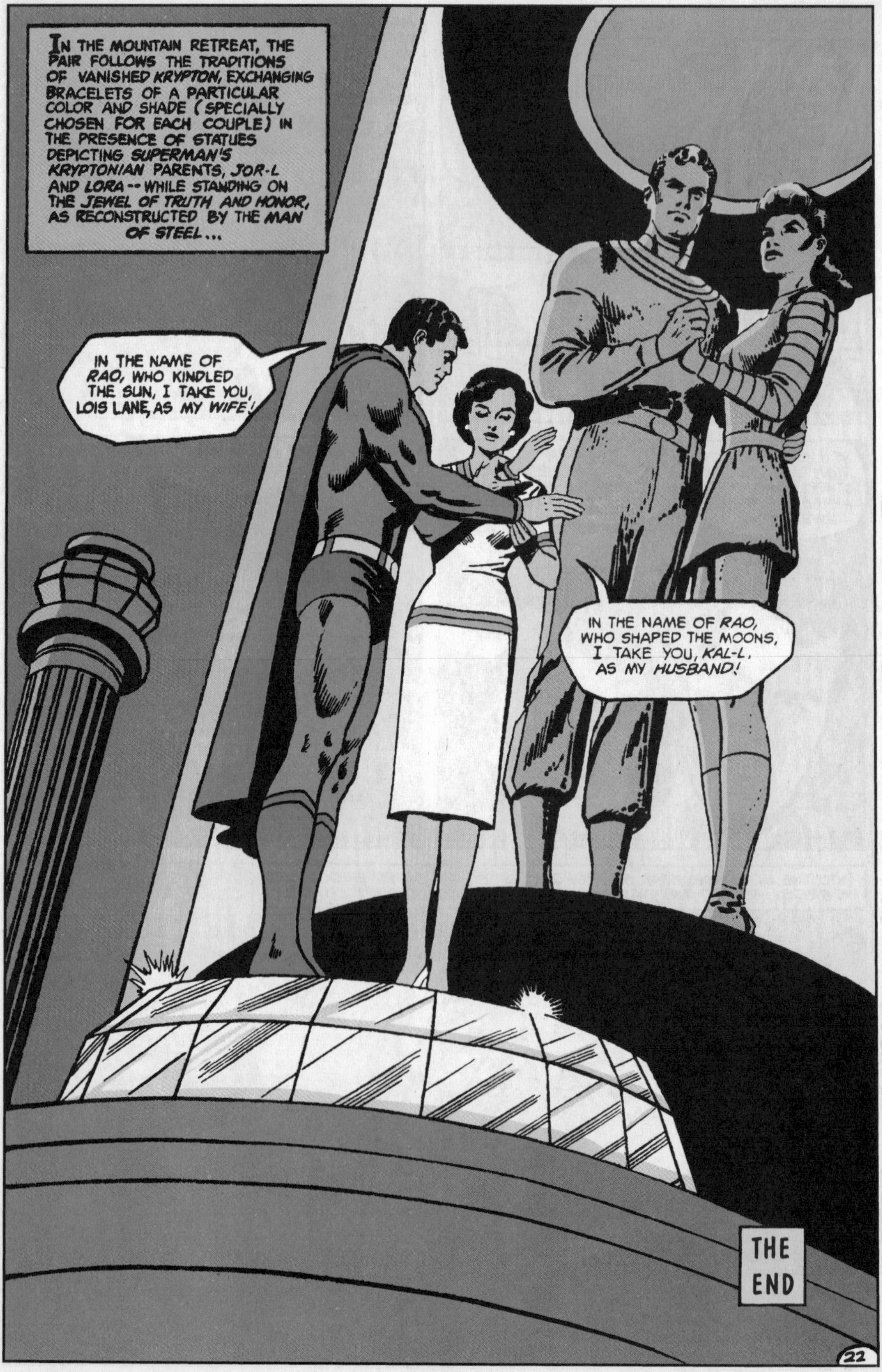
In the mountain retreat, the pair follows the traditions of vanished Krypton, exchanging bracelets of a particular color and shade (specially chosen for each couple) in the presence of statues depicting Superman's Kryptonian parents, Jor-L and Lora -- while standing on the Jewel of Truth and Honor, as reconstructed by the Man of Steel...
IN THE NAME OF RAO, WHO KINDLED THE SUN, I TAKE YOU, LOIS LANE, AS MY WIFE!
IN THE NAME OF RAO, WHO SHAPED THE MOONS, I TAKE YOU, KAL-L, AS MY HUSBAND!
THE END
22

CONTRIBUTORS

MURPHY ANDERSON

Murphy Anderson entered comics in 1944 drawing features for Fiction House and, after a tour with the Navy, worked for a variety of publishers. In 1947, he took over drawing the *Buck Rogers* syndicated newspaper strip. Anderson began his long association with DC in 1950, drawing countless super-hero and science-fiction stories, including Captain Comet, the Atomic Knights, Hawkman, and the Spectre. In addition to pencilling, Anderson was one of comics' best and most versatile inkers, with numerous credits on such strips as Adam Strange, the Atom, Batman and, of course, Superman. Anderson has also produced instructional comic books for the U.S. Army and headed a publisher's support service company that provided color separations and typesetting for the comics industry.

CARY BATES

Cary Bates was one of the early members of the new wave of talent that entered the comic-book field in the late 1960s. Beginning in 1967, Cary scripted stories for virtually all of DC's major characters, including a long run as one of the mainstay writers on SUPERMAN for editor Julie Schwartz. His other credits include the entire Superman family of characters, the Elongated Man, the Legion of Super-Heroes, El Diablo, Rose and Thorn, and a long and fondly remembered stint on THE FLASH. Cary left the comics field in 1988 and has since devoted his creative energies to screenwriting, which included a credit on 1992's *1492*.

VINCE COLLETTA

Vince Colletta began his comic-book career in 1954 for Marvel (then Atlas) Comics, working primarily as an inker on features in mystery, war, and Western comics. His work also appeared in anthology titles published by Charlton and Dell Comics. During the 1960s, Vinnie divided his freelance inking efforts between DC and Marvel for THE FLASH, LOIS LANE, DC's romance comics line, CHALLENGERS OF THE UNKNOWN, *Thor*, *Daredevil*, *Iron Man*, *The Avengers* and many others. Vinnie served as DC's art director in the mid-1970s. He continued working in the field for a variety of publishers until his death in 1991.

DICK DILLIN

Dick Dillin was a mainstay DC Comics artist from 1956 through the 1970s. He began his career in 1951 at Fiction House, but soon moved over to Quality Comics. When DC acquired the Quality Comics line in 1956, Dick came along and continued his run on BLACKHAWK. His distinctive style also began showing up in DC's science-fiction anthology titles as well as on such strips as Green Lantern, Challengers of the Unknown, Hawkman, Batman, Kid Flash, and others. When Mike Sekowsky gave up his long-running pencilling assignment on JUSTICE LEAGUE OF AMERICA, editor Julie Schwartz tapped Dick as his replacement. Dillin was also a portraitist and storyboard artist for television animation. He died in 1980.

JOE GIELLA

Inker Joe Giella began his career in the 1940s as an inker for Hillman Publications and Timely Comics, the company that would later become Marvel. Giella first worked for DC Comics in 1951. In the 1960s, his style of embellishment became associated with some of the company's greatest heroes, including Batman (over the work of penciller Sheldon Moldoff), the Flash (with artist Carmine Infantino), and the Atom (with penciller Gil Kane). Giella, who also pencilled and inked a run of the Batman syndicated newspaper strip during the 1960s, retired from comics in the early 1980s.

DICK GIORDANO

Dick Giordano began his career as an artist for Charlton Comics in 1952 and became the company's editor-in-chief in 1965. In that capacity, he revamped their line by adding an emphasis on such action heroes as the Question, Captain Atom, and the Blue Beetle. In 1967, Dick came over to DC for a three-year stint as editor, bringing with him many of the talents who would help shape the industry of the day. Winner of numerous industry awards, Giordano later returned to DC, rising to the position of Vice President-Executive Editor before "retiring" in 1993 to once again pursue a full-time career as penciller and inker.

ROBERT KANIGHER

Robert Kanigher has long been recognized as one of the most prolific and innovative writers and editors in the comic-book field. Since the 1940s, Kanigher has written and/or created more characters than nearly anyone, including Batman, Blue Beetle, Steel Sterling, Black Canary, Captain Marvel, Flash, Sgt. Rock, the Haunted Tank, Wonder Woman, Lois Lane, and innumerable war, horror, and romance scripts.

JACK KIRBY

Jack "King" Kirby's comics career began in 1937 and continued for nearly six decades. With partner Joe Simon, Kirby went on to draw and/or create numerous features, including Captain America, the Young Allies, Sandman, the Newsboy Legion, and Manhunter. During the 1940s and 1950s, Simon and Kirby were responsible for a slew of titles and concepts, including THE FIGHTING AMERICAN, BOYS' RANCH, and the creation of the romance comics genre. In 1961, the first issue of Marvel's FANTASTIC FOUR cemented Jack's reputation as comics' preeminent creator. Jack returned to DC in 1971 with his classic "Fourth World Trilogy," which was followed by THE DEMON, OMAC and KAMANDI. Jack Kirby continued working and innovating in comics until his death in 1994.

PAUL LEVITZ

Best known today as the publisher of DC Comics, Paul Levitz hasn't always sat behind a corporate desk. His long run as the writer of LEGION OF SUPER-HEROES turned that title into a fan-favorite and best-seller in the 1970s and 1980s. Longtime readers also remember fondly his turns at AQUAMAN and ALL STAR COMICS.

ELLIOT S. MAGGIN

Elliot Maggin broke into comics in 1972 with a legendary Green Arrow story originally written as a college treatise. So impressed with Maggin's style was editor Julius Schwartz that Maggin quickly became a key writer in Schwartz's creative stable, penning years of Superman stories as well as the occasional Batman — or, more often, Robin — tale. Now living in California, Maggin continues to write comics as circumstances allow while enjoying a teaching career.

BOB OKSNER

Bob Oksner began his career in the 1950s as the artist on a wide variety of DC's licensed humor comics. He remained one of the mainstays of DC's humor line throughout the 1960s. Known for his ability to draw beautiful women, one of his most fondly remembered strips was ANGEL AND THE APE. Oksner also contributed a great deal of work to DC's super-hero line as both penciller and inker on the Superman family of titles, most notably on SUPERGIRL. Bob was the artist on the 1950s *I Love Lucy* syndicated newspaper strip and was a longtime writer of *Dondi*.

DENNIS O'NEIL

Dennis O'Neil began his career as a comic-book writer in 1965 at Charlton, where then-editor Dick Giordano assigned him to several features, later bringing him to DC. At DC, O'Neil scripted several series for Giordano and Julius Schwartz, quickly becoming one of the most respected writers in comics. O'Neil earned a reputation for being able to "revamp" such characters as Superman, Green Lantern, Captain Marvel — and the Batman, whom O'Neil (with the help of Neal Adams and Giordano) brought back to his roots as a dark, mysterious, gothic avenger. Besides being the most important Batman writer of the 1970s, O'Neil served as an editor at both Marvel and DC. Fittingly, he is the current group editor of the Batman line of comics.

WERNER ROTH

Werner Roth began his comics career in 1951 with art for such DC titles as HOUSE OF SECRETS, HEART THROBS and YOUNG LOVE. In the 1960s, Werner went on to pencil *The X-Men*, *Sub-Mariner*, *Rawhide Kid* and other western tales for Marvel (under the pen name Jay Gavin), while continuing his contributions to DC's romance titles and, later, as penciller of SUPERMAN'S GIRL FRIEND, LOIS LANE. He also drew *Mandrake the Magician* for King Features

and served as an assistant on the syndicated newspaper strip *On Stage*. Roth died in 1973.

CURT SWAN

While serving during World War Two illustrating the Army newspaper *Stars and Stripes*, Swan worked with DC writer France E. ("Eddie") Herron. On Herron's suggestion, Swan found work at DC after the war. Swan's versatile pencils, which he remembers applying first to BOY COMMANDOS, soon appeared on various DC features, including Superman, Batman, Newsboy Legion, Big Town, Mr. District Attorney, Tommy Tomorrow, and Superboy. Swan served various stints on almost all the Superman titles of the 1950s and 1960s, and remained the near-exclusive Superman penciller throughout the 1970s and much of the 1980s. Although he "retired" in 1986, Swan continued to work for DC until his death in 1996. To generations of professionals and fans, Curt Swan's Superman will always be the definitive version.

LEN WEIN

Len Wein began writing for comics in 1969 with stories for DC's anthology titles HOUSE OF MYSTERY and HOUSE OF SECRETS. It was in the pages of HOUSE OF SECRETS that Len co-created, with artist Berni Wrightson, his most famous creation, Swamp Thing. Len has also scripted stories for a wide range of titles at DC and Marvel, including SUPERMAN, BATMAN, THE FLASH, JUSTICE LEAGUE, THE PHANTOM STRANGER, *Spider-Man*, *The Fantastic Four* and many others. Among Len's other creations are the Human Target (with Carmine Infantino), the New X-Men (with Dave Cockrum), and Wolverine (with Herb Trimpe).

Biographies researched and written by Jerry Bails, Paul Kupperberg, Richard Morrissey and Mark Waid.

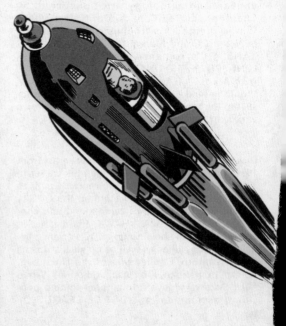